Faith and Reason

Paul Helm is Professor of the History and Philosophy of Religion at King's College, London. Among his books are *Eternal God* (1988), *The Providence of God* (1993), *Belief Policies* (1994), *Faith and Understanding* (1997) and *Faith With Reason* (1999).

'Paul Helm's *Faith and Reason* distinguishes itself from other anthologies in the philosophy of religion in two ways. First, it attempts to locate the debates over the proper roles of faith and reason in the context of the history of western philosophy as a whole. Second, it focuses its material by concentrating on two types of selection—explicit discussions of the nature and proper places of reason and faith, and arguments for and against the claim the the world is created *ex nihilo* that illustrate those discussions. *Faith and Reason*'s well-chosen selections have a coherence that is lacking in most anthologies in the philosophy of religion.'

William Wainright
University of Wisconsin at Milwaukee

'*Faith and Reason* offers a wide selection including items rarely anthologised in such collections … This is ideal for courses in philosophy of religion and theology and is a very useful work of reference.'

John Haldane
University of St Andrews

'Paul Helm has done a masterful job in his introductory essays of structuring his smorgasbord of goodies by showing the underlying issues within each of its seven historical epochs concerning what was meant by faith and reason. The manner in which the earlier epochs influenced the later ones is brilliantly explored as well.'

Richard Gale
University of Pittsburg

'Paul Helm … has included not only standardly anthologized philosophers such as Anselm and Aquinas, but also authors who deserve much more attention than they generally receive, such as Saadia and Jeremy Taylor. Furthermore, Helm makes some effort to include material from medieval Judaism and Islam as well as Christianity, and his collection manages to span all of Western philosophy, from Plato to the present.'

Eleonore Stump
St Louis University

OXFORD **READERS**

The Oxford Readers series represents a unique interdisciplinary resource, offering authoritative collections of primary and secondary sources on the core issues which have shaped history and continue to affect current events.

Available

Aesthetics
Edited by Patrick Maynard and Susan Feagin

Class
Edited by Patrick Joyce

Classical Thought
Edited by Terence Irwin

Ethics
Edited by Peter Singer

Ethnicity
Edited by John Hutchinson and Anthony D. Smith

Evolution
Edited by Mark Ridley

Faith and Reason
Edited by Paul Helm

Fascism
Edited by Roger Griffin

Feminisms
Edited by Sandra Kemp and Judith Squires

The Mind
Edited by Daniel Robinson

Nationalism
Edited by John Hutchinson and Anthony D. Smith

Racism
Edited by Martin Bulmer and John Solomos

War
Edited by Lawrence Freedman

Forthcoming

Antisemitism
Edited by Paul Lawrence Rose

The British Empire
Edited by Jane Samson

Consciousness
Edited by Geoffrey Underwood

Nazism
Edited by Neil Gregor

Political Thought
Edited by Jonathan Wolff and Michael Rosen

Revolution
Edited by Jack Goldstone

Sexuality
Edited by Robert Nye

Slavery
Edited by Stanley Engerman, Seymour Drescher, and Robert Paquette

OXFORD **READERS**

Faith and Reason

Edited by Paul Helm

Oxford · New York
OXFORD UNIVERSITY PRESS
1999

Oxford University Press, Great Clarendon Street, Oxford OX2 6DP
www.oup.co.uk

Oxford New York
Athens Auckland Bangkok Bogota Bombay Buenos Aires
Calcutta Cape Town Dar es Salaam Delhi Florence Hong Kong Istanbul
Karachi Kuala Lumpur Madras Madrid Melbourne Mexico City
Nairobi Paris Singapore Taipei Tokyo Toronto Warsaw

and associated companies in
Berlin Ibadan

Oxford is a registered trade mark of Oxford University Press

Introduction, selection, and editorial material
© Paul Helm 1999

British Library Cataloguing in Publication Data
Data available

Library of Congress Cataloging in Publication Data
Data available

ISBN 0-19-289290-8

1 3 5 7 9 10 8 6 4 2

Typeset by Cambrian Typesetters, Frimley, Surrey
Printed in Great Britain
on acid-free paper by
Biddles Ltd,
Guildford and King's Lynn

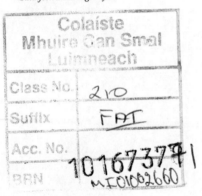

FOR PAUL AND JACKIE

Preface

Faith and Reason is an attempt to display in historical perspective some of the rich dialogue and dialectic between faith and reason, and to show that this is part of the warp and woof of Western philosophy. Readers will find a wider range of material than is usual in anthologies in 'the philosophy of religion'. However, it is an implication of the form of this particular collection that the philosophy of religion does not denote a discrete discipline, but it refers simply to the philosophical discussion of those theological and religious issues that philosophers have argued about, and still argue about. While it may be an exaggeration to say that there is nothing new under the sun, what is new in philosophy usually has more than a family resemblance to what went before. The Reader aims to reinforce this conservative conviction.

The range of extracts is wider than usual but the selections themselves are fairly short: tasters rather than main meals; bite-size pieces with something to chew on. To help digestion I have tried wherever possible to use accessible editions of the chosen material, and I have not encumbered the text with the footnotes and endnotes of the originals. Full references to each extract make access to the original sources straightforward. The hope is that the readers' taste buds will be sufficiently enlivened for them to make their own way down the menu.

This material could not have been assembled without the help of many people. I wish to acknowledge advice given (and usually acted on) from Peter Byrne, William Lane Craig, Stephen Davis, Stephen Evans, Jerry Gellman, Graham Gould, John Haldane, Douglas Hedley, Joe Houston, Mark Nelson, Katherin Rogers, Richard Sorabji, Eleonore Stump, Rene Van Woudenberg, William Wainwright, Tom Weinandy, and Stephen Williams. They have persuaded me not only to include certain items, but also to keep some out, but no doubt my own idiosyncrasies and preferences are revealed in what has finally appeared.

My colleague at King's College, Martin Stone, has read drafts of the Introduction, provided bibliographical advice, and kindly made fresh translations of some of the material from the medieval period. Julian Willard, one of my postgraduate students, has been an indispensable research assistant and has, in addition, provided the bulk of the biographical notes on twentieth-century contributors. Most of the remainder of these notes were prepared by Angela Helm, who has also acted as a modernizer of English, and kept a watchful eye on my own prose. My secretary Lavinia Harvey has provided assistance whenever this was needed. The help given by the Libraries at King's College, by Dr Williams's Library, and by the Library of the Faculty of Divinity at New College, Edinburgh, has been invaluable. Oxford University Press, and particularly George Miller, have advised and supported in many different ways. My thanks to them all.

Contents

III. The Medieval Period

IV. Renaissance and Reformation

V. The Seventeenth and Eighteenth Centuries

VI. The Nineteenth Century

VII. The Twentieth Century: I. Faith and Hard Science

VIII. The Twentieth Century: II. Faith, Realism, and Pluralism

IX. The Twentieth Century: III. Reason and Belief in God

Faith and Reason

Introduction

The relations between faith and reason have a long and nuanced history, and it is almost impossible to understand the contemporary alliances and conflicts between the two without going back to the beginning. For these conflicts and alliances are primarily philosophical in nature, and contemporary philosophical debates about such issues, in effect if not always in intention, carry forward earlier debates. Philosophical controversy rarely if ever appears unannounced, but builds upon previous debates. Furthermore, the controversy between faith and reason represents a very important strand in the history of Western philosophy.

This is why this Reader is historically sequenced. Section I introduces some of the main philosophical concepts and arguments that were applied to Greek and Roman religion but then, more significantly, were applied to Judaeo-Christianity when it began to interact with classical culture. In the case of Christianity, this happened soon after it began to spread from Palestine; and in the case of Judaism, about the same time, though one must not forget the Hellenistic influence on Judaism before the Christian era began, as well as its later influence on Islam.

It is crude, but not wholly inaccurate, to say that the classical period provided the tools of reason which were applied to faith, and have been ever since. Crude because it ignores the intellectual structure and argumentative force of parts of the New Testament, notably the Apostle Paul's letter to the Romans, and his dialogue with the philosophers on Mars' Hill, recorded in Acts 17, as well as the Hellenic influences on the Gospel according to St John. Nevertheless the Judaeo-Christian revelation, just like the Greek myths, did not by and large provide any tools of reason, though it did provide, or at least countenance, what one might call philosophical strategies, of which more below. This is because the writings which formed the revelation for Jews, together with those writings which, added to the Old Testament, formed the revelation for Christians, are not argumentative in the philosophical sense. The genres of the writings through which, it is claimed, God reveals himself are very different—historical, prophetic, epigrammatic, visionary, apocalyptic—disclosing facts, plans, and purposes not otherwise accessible, and doing so in the language of the people. Classical philosophy knew nothing of the keenness of conflict between faith and reason as it later emerged, quite simply because in that culture the idea of a divine revelation was nothing like as sharp as it later became.

As Plato, Aristotle, the Stoics, and the Epicureans sought to sift and systematize in philosophical fashion the language and thought of the Greek myths as expressed in cultic and civic religion, so this tradition of thinking came to be applied to the characteristic claims of Judaeo-Christianity, thus initiating a tradition of debate that has continued until the present day, and to which almost every noteworthy European philosopher has contributed.

The classical tradition of thinking was applied in two ways: in attacks upon the alleged barbarism and superstition of Christian claims by those philosophers who did not share allegiance to them; and by defences of Christianity from such attacks by apologists who had to appropriate (and sometimes adapt) the terminology of their opponents in the hope of mounting a convincing response. The classical tradition may also be said to be repudiated, or at least held at arm's length, by those who held that any appeal to 'human reason' was an encroachment upon the primacy and self-sufficiency of revelation.

So the Reader may be said to deal with one tradition, in the broadest sense, a tradition with recurring and developing themes. The use of reason in the critical reflection on the nature and claims of religious faith is not an invention of the Enlightenment. This tradition of debate has become more complex, not less so, as the years have gone on. One of the aims of this Reader is to introduce ideas as they first become formulated in each succeeding epoch of the tradition, and so to initiate the reader into this tradition. I shall attempt to illustrate this growing complexity first by saying something about reason, and then about faith, and then about their various relationships.

The senses of 'reason'

One must distinguish talking about reason from using it. Here I am concerned with our talk of reason, acknowledging that those who use reason in some particular way might not recognize that they are doing so, and might not talk about it in these terms.

The narrowest sense of reason equates it with the rules of logical inference, both inductive and deductive. These rules record and tabulate and to some extent explain, extend, and defend intellectual procedures which are purely formal in character, and which can be explained in formal terms, in abstraction from their employment to reason about some particular subject-matter. Reasoning in this sense starts from a premiss or premisses, and derives, either deductively, or inductively, one or more conclusions. If the deduction is valid, if it is in accord with the rules of logic, then the conclusion is true if the premisses are true; if the induction is valid, the premisses render the conclusion probable. If Gertrude is a giraffe then Gertrude must be an animal, if all giraffes are animals; she cannot fail to be. If most giraffes live in zoos, and Gertrude is a giraffe, then it is likely that Gertrude lives in a zoo; but she may fail to, for she may be among those who live in the wild.

The key to the use and power of such procedures (assuming that they are appropriately valid, either deductively or inductively) lies in the premisses. For clearly, once a particular premiss (or premisses) is accepted, then the logic inexorably gets to work upon them. So the crucial questions to be asked in assessing the relation between faith and reason, used in this sense, become: what sorts of premises are admissible as far as logical argument about matters of faith are concerned? And, more controversially, is there a reason derived from faith which limits the employment of deductive or inductive reason in matters of faith? To such questions there have been, broadly, three types of answer, though they are not all exclusive of each other. We shall look at these answers below.

Secondly, reason may be used in a more substantive sense, referring to the accumulated wisdom of a tradition, particularly (in our case) the accumulated wisdom of the classical tradition. This is a more substantive sense of reason than that which confines it to inductive and deductive logical procedures because, unlike the appeal to deductive or inductive logic, the wisdom of the tradition expressed itself in certain core beliefs or attitudes, and certain ethical and intellectual virtues. When the alleged barbarism of the early Christians was challenged on intellectual grounds, it was generally with such substantive questions in mind, and particularly with the charge that the claims of Judaeo-Christianity flouted the received wisdom of the culture; alternatively, when Christians sought to commend their religion to pagans, one strategy that they endeavoured to use was to show that Christianity was in accord with the wisdom of the ages, and even that the Christian revelation was the climax or culmination of that wisdom, the true philosophy. Hence the (to us) fanciful claims that Plato must have sat at the feet of Moses.

Whereas the first sense of 'reason' is primarily logical and formal in character, this sense is primarily epistemological. That is, the received wisdom embodies claims to know certain things about the world, for example, that it is designed by a designer, and certain claims about moral rightness and wrongness. Since a claim is made to know certain truths, the truths of reason, of the true philosophy, questions are inevitably raised about how such truths are known. Revelation, and hence a faith based upon it, may augment or re-publish such truths, but it cannot overturn or substantially amend them. Or, alternatively, it is held that human epistemic powers are adversely affected by sin so that the mind is blind to evidence, or interprets it perversely; the mind needs renewing by divine grace before it begins to function as it ought to.

So reason, in this epistemological sense, can also be used in a more destructive and negative way. It can be argued, in sceptical fashion, that we can know nothing, or very little, and so reason, as a source of truth about the world, proves to be rather threadbare, and such scepticism was another important philosophical legacy of the ancient world. By a strange twist, sceptical claims of this sort have not always been destructive of religious faith, but it has sometimes been argued that scepticism creates a gap which only the claims of faith can fill. The influence of scepticism is not so much characteristic of the early debates between Christians and pagans as one strand in the more complex dialectic bequeathed by the Renaissance and the Reformation.

Philosophical wisdom of the sort handed down by the ancient world can be understood as a merely *de facto* matter, as what the tradition in fact has come up with. But a third possible appeal to 'reason' is as an appeal to certain rational principles which all men recognize and which must be or ought to be employed in the responsible prosecution of any intellectual enquiry. Such principles may be exemplified in the ancient wisdom, but are, so to speak, detachable from it, capable of new applications in new fields. Appeal to such principles can be used to critique existing theologies or popular religion and to attempt to establish a religion of reason, a set of beliefs which allegedly are derived from self-evident principles of reason. It is as if human reason forces us to make certain moves. Such a position is characteristic of the rationalist strand in the Enlightenment, and of deism.

In the twentieth century in particular (but with deep historical roots) 'reason' has often been equated to 'the scientific consensus' or 'the latest scientific findings'. The appeal to reason has thus been to a set of empirical facts, or empirical claims, and more particularly to the naturalistic methods that have led to the discovery of these facts. This is a weaker and more untidy sort of appeal to reason, because the facts may be disputed, and findings may be overturned by later findings. There may also be legitimate disputes over what are the appropriate methods for discovering the facts. And questions may arise over what exactly the success of these methods implies. The appeal to scientific findings characteristic of our culture can be part of a more general and vaguer appeal to common sense, to what it is 'reasonable' at any one time to believe.

And so, finally, 'reason' is frequently used as a shorthand for what is reasonable. This usage is loose and rather culturally conditioned. For what is reasonable might be thought of as what is in accordance with common sense, but what is in accordance with common sense varies from time to time; for example, it varies with the popularity and influence of certain scientific, religious, or metaphysical ideas. Thus it may be reasonable to burn witches, or to take it for granted that the earth is flat, or that the design evidenced in nature requires a designer.

Running as a thread through these main senses as well as other possible senses of 'reason' is the possibility of taking such claims, the claims of reason, in a weaker or a stronger sense. One may take the claim that the matters of faith are in accordance with reason as involving the positive *demonstration* of their reasonableness by the production of appropriate, generally convincing arguments: the tradition of natural theology. Or one might rest content with the sustainable claim that the propositions of faith have not been shown to be unreasonable. Or that they no more need the support of reason than do other sorts of claim to which, it may be argued, they bear a strong analogy. It may be claimed that the question of the existence of God is more like the question of the existence of other minds, or of the past, than the existence of the Abominable Snowman. This type of claim is weaker than the first, because it is obviously harder to prove something than to fail to disprove it, since to prove something one has to be in the position of anticipating every possible objection; not so in the case of the weaker claim.

It must not be forgotten that 'reason' has a practical as well as a theoretical sense, a distinction going back as far as Aristotle, and influentially renewed by Immanuel Kant in the eighteenth century. All the uses of 'reason' that we have glanced at so far, even those which are more loose and informal, may be called theoretical uses; they are concerned with understanding the universe, and its divine origin, if it has one, and with assessing rival claims to truth about such matters. Practical reason concerns what it is reasonable to do. One of the great watersheds in the tradition of debate between faith and reason occurred when Immanuel Kant argued that the theoretical reason was unable to acquire truths about God, but that nevertheless his existence was necessary for the fulfilment of practical reason, the requirements of morality. Carrying out this programme required reconceptualizings of many fundamental terms of the Christian faith—'faith', 'prayer', 'the church', and so on—for all had to be understood in ways that did not imply any theoretical knowledge of God. This programme was brilliantly essayed in Kant's *Religion within the Limits of Reason Alone*, which has ever since become both the touchstone and the fountainhead of liberal Protestant thinking about the relation between faith and reason. The theological application of such an approach sees theology as *sapientia* (practical wisdom) rather than *scientia* (demonstrable truth).

The senses of 'faith'

We have looked at some of the main ways in which 'reason' is used in the debate between faith and reason. Faith is no less diverse. The most obvious distinction (one that we have already noted in passing) is between faith as an act of trust or reliance, and *the* faith, the proposition or set of propositions believed. Obviously it is possible to have faith in, to trust, anything which is regarded as a fit object of trust—the ladders, the postal service, one's neighbour. Trust in the religious sense is usually taken to involve belief in some proposition or propositions which are included in *the* faith. Propositions such as: *The universe was created by God*; *Jesus will come again to judge the world*. The faith of a Christian, understood as the body of his beliefs, those which form and call forth his religious trust, is typically a very varied, complex body of propositions, covering matters of metaphysics (for example, What is God, and what is his relation to the universe? What is a human person?), epistemology (the claim that God has made himself known), history and geography (Jesus Christ was crucified under Pontius Pilate), and ethics ('Thou shalt do no murder'). Where these claims are empirical claims, or involve empirical claims, the task of reason simply becomes the careful, objective empirical investigation of these claims by appropriate methods. Such empirical enquiry falls outside the scope of this volume, which is concerned with the philosophical issues arising in the debate between faith and reason. The various and sometimes conflicting metaphysical and episte-mological claims made by religion and theology are central.

Faith, as was said, covers also the personal attitude of trust, and here again there are important distinctions that it is necessary to be aware of. There is, to begin with, the distinction between *evidence-sensitive* and *evidence-insensitive* views of faith. In much of the mainstream of the tradition we are concerned with, personal faith involves belief, and for faith to be reasonable it must be well grounded. So faith is sensitive to evidence, and to the status of that evidence. If evidence is called into question, then faith will, other things being equal, be weakened, unless a rebuttal can be found.

This well-groundedness has in turn been thought to involve two main types of appeal: to reason (as we have already been seeing) and to revelation, under-stood as the testimony of God to us. From the point of view of the tradition of classical thought the claim of the Judaeo-Christian tradition that God has revealed himself was a novel, and a potentially disturbing claim, though some-times strategies were sought for containing the disturbance. So that one of the ways in which the reason–faith debate has expressed itself has been in the reason–revelation debate. Granted the possibility of revelation, what has to be present for us to believe that a particular source of information, a book, or a prophet, say, is God's revelation? Has the revelation itself to be seen to be reason-able, both the fact of revelation and what it contains, or the fact of revelation only, or neither? If neither, is there then some other general test of the authen-ticity of a revelation? And these questions are particularly acute when the reve-lation allegedly contains claims that appear to run counter to human reason, say, the claim that God has become man, or to run counter to received philosophical wisdom, as when it is claimed (by appeal to revelation) that the universe is created *ex nihilo*, and so is contingent and not necessary. Issues involving the authentication of revelation, and the place of reason in this process, came to a head at the period of Reformation when the mainstream Reformers and their followers appealed to the principle of 'Scripture alone' against the claims of the Church of Rome to be the only authentic interpreter of Scripture, and against the more enthusiastic and rationalistic strands in the Reformation upheaval.

But, again by a strange reversal, revelation has not always been understood as the disclosure of truths that would not otherwise be understood. According to one influential strand of thinking revelation is simply a re-publication, in vivid, pictorial, user-friendly ways, of truths of reason, particularly moral truths which the masses do not have the wit or the leisure to work out for them-selves. The interplay between faith, reason, and language surfaces here, as well as the more familiar philosophical contrast between appearance and reality.

In sharp contrast to evidence-sensitive views of faith are accounts in which the question of its well-groundedness or otherwise is regarded as irrelevant. Indeed, it has been held by some that the beliefs of faith are not well grounded, and that they appear to be unreasonable and even incoherent may be regarded as a virtue. Faith is an act of reliance upon God, but its well-groundedness is not open to investigation, either because it does not claim to be well grounded but a gamble, or a risk, or a leap into the unknown; or because it is believed to be well grounded, but its grounds are not susceptible to human investigation, being epistemologically inscrutable; or because it is held that the evidential grounds of faith are not important, or even that attention to them obscures the religious authenticity of faith. Such views are characteristic of those who follow in the tradition of Kant. On such views faith is immune to evidential refutation, but faith that is detached from the normal conditions of responsible belief looks to be heading for vacuousness.

One might put the contrast between these two types of faith as a contrast between the intellect and the will. The first view stresses faith, or at least the belief that underlies faith, as an act of the intellect; hence it is reasonable to open up the propositions believed to scrutiny. The other view thinks of faith as primarily an act of the will, as a gambling against the odds, or as an act of which the likelihood of success cannot be calculated. Since on this view faith is an unreasonable act, or an act which cannot be assessed in terms of its unreason-ableness or otherwise, it cannot be attacked by the use of reason.

But even within evidence-sensitive views of faith, faith which involves belief, greater or lesser roles have been found for the will. There have been a number of reasons for this. There is a tension between belief, which it is not plausible to think is a matter of the will (one cannot believe that God exists by an act of pure will), and trust, which is a matter of the will, of faithful reliance upon what is believed. And wider theological interests may intrude. Those—let us call them Catholics—who think of faith as meritorious have a good reason to think of the will as important in faith. While those—let us call them Protestants—who do not regard faith as meritorious (since it is utterly a matter of God's grace) may nevertheless stress the importance of the will because they wish to emphasize the fiducial aspect of faith.

A second important distinction is between cognitive and non-cognitive accounts of faith. If faith normally implies belief, what if the proposition that forms the belief appears to be meaningless (because, say, it is unverifiable by sense-experience), or that there are no grounds for believing that it is true (because all the reasons offered for such beliefs are found to be unconvincing)? The usual reaction to such situations would be to abandon the belief, and so abandon the faith. But some people, faced with these circumstances, retain the language, while acknowledging that there is nothing to which, in their judge-ment, such language refers. Why do they keep it? Why say 'God is our Father' when it is held that all talk of God is either meaningless or unjustifiable? The answer is that for such people the language of religion or theology can have *instrumental* value. Just as we can benefit from reading fiction—by finding solace, or gaining inspiration or insight, say—while knowing full well that it *is* fiction, so it is held that the language of religion can elevate and inspire even though it is not about anything. So faith is detached from belief, but remains integral to the practice of religion.

The relations between faith and reason

So far we have sketched some of the main views of reason and of faith as they have interacted together in the Western philosophical tradition. The views that we have noted are not exhaustive, but it is obvious, more obvious than may have at first appeared, that the relations between faith and reason are complex. It may be helpful to sketch some of the main ones.

One of the chief and most noteworthy debates has been over whether it is possible to establish the existence of God, or render his existence more probable than not, by using arguments, and particularly the premises of the arguments, that any rational person would accept as true. Such a programme carries over from Aristotle's appeal to an unmoved mover, and to design arguments for the existence of God as reported by Cicero in *The Nature of the Gods*, and includes one outstanding post-classical development, the ontological argument of Anselm, though there is reason to think that some of the key ideas of the argument were formulated earlier, and controversy remains over whether the ontological argument is intended by Anselm as a piece of natural theology, or as a meditative reflection by the believer.

So one prominent type of relation between faith and reason is where it is held that the faith, or crucial parts of the faith, may be established by reason. (Whether they *have* to be established by reason before it is reasonable for anyone to believe them is another, further area of controversy.) So on this view it is possible (or may be possible, or must be possible) to start from premises which are not theological, or which any rational person of whatever persuasion would agree about, and attempt to derive conclusions about God by logical arguments of either a deductive or an inductive kind (using reason in its narrowest and purest sense), and in particular the conclusion that he exists. To start from non-theology and to conclude with theology is the great ambition of the tradition of natural theology; it began with the Greeks, and continues to be one of the central logical and epistemological debates in philosophy.

If natural theology has any success, then some of the beliefs of faith will have been shown to be reasonable beliefs in the narrowest and purest sense. And such success has obvious attractions in apologetics, the task of defending and vindicating the faith against objections. There is reason to think that the project of natural theology was at first undertaken for its own sake, but later on, particularly in the Enlightenment period and subsequently, the development of effective apologetic tools was undoubtedly one important motive for engaging in natural theology.

A second possible relation of faith to reason is to say that whether or not it is possible to derive conclusions about God from premises that do not refer to him, one other, central way of using logic is on some proposition (or set of propositions) of the faith. Logic is thus, typically, used to draw out implications of some theological proposition, or to show that a set of propositions is consistent with some other, non-theological proposition, and that there is no incoherence or logical fallacy in the faith at this point. This is the great tradition of faith seeking understanding, generally thought to have been initiated, at least as a self-conscious programme in religious thought, by Augustine of Hippo. According to it, logic is the handmaid of the propositions of faith, endeavouring to draw out their implications and even to establish their independent rationale; to show that such propositions, though known only through revelation, are nevertheless in accordance with reason.

As I suggested, these first two ways are themselves not obviously inconsistent, and as a matter of history have often gone together, as they did, for example, in Anselm, who was both a notable natural theologian and a brilliant exponent of the faith seeking understanding programme. Like Anselm, one may both take a positive line on natural theology and also use logic to explore the implications of some aspect or other of one's faith. But it is also possible to do the second without doing the first, though less plausible to do the first without attempting the second, since it is attractive to carry the use of reason which a successful natural theology exemplifies into a consideration of the ideas and propositions of revealed theology.

As was noted earlier, a third relation between faith and reason is more negative, one of basic incompatibility or at least of deep suspicion. It is to claim that reason is unfitted to explore some, or all, of the propositions of faith. At the most basic, this is a frank and unreflective fideism. But the fideism may take a more reflective form, offering reasons why reason has no place in religion.

Two types of argument have been offered for this, though these two ways may amount to two ways of expressing the same overall objection. The first is that the propositions of the faith, or at least some of the crucial ones, are 'above reason'. We mentioned earlier that the admissibility of premisses, and particularly the reasons for admitting them, or not, is crucial to this use of reason. When it is said that the propositions of faith are above reason one thing that has sometimes been meant is that their meaning cannot be given in any human language. And if not, then of course logic cannot be employed in discussing them, since logic can only operate on language if that language has a meaning. Consideration of mystical and other ineffable states or claims fall outside the scope of this Reader, since we are concerned only with those claims of faith that can possibly be the object of critical reflection.

Another type of argument asserts that the language in which the propositions of faith are expressed is stretched language; it employs metaphor, or analogy, or other instances of non-literalness. The consequence of this is not that no inferences are possible but that enquirers must be guarded in the sort of inferences they think follow from the premisses.

Recently a position that falls somewhere between the tradition of natural theology and that of critical or reflective fideism has been developed. It has been argued that a believer has no intellectual obligation to develop a natural theology because no philosophically convincing reason has been given, nor can be given, for why such a responsibility should be shouldered. The objection is not from the side of faith, that there is something special about the faith that inoculates it against the ravages of reason, but from the side of reason, the claim that natural theology, at least in its strong foundationalist forms, is self-referentially incoherent. Though a late twentieth-century development, 'Reformed' epistemology appeals to some claims of the Reformer John Calvin who in turn appealed to Cicero's *The Nature of the Gods*.

But there may be objections from the side of faith to the need for the faith to gain the support of reason. For another thing that might be meant by saying that the propositions of faith are above reason is not that while there is no absolute bar on the use of logic, it is none the less inappropriate to use it. It is rather like making jokes during a funeral service: possible, but out of place. This is sometimes expressed by the view that logic is a human construction and that our thought and language about God should not be subjected to it. Another way of making a similar point is to allege that logic is worldly thinking. An even more extreme claim is that God is the author of logic and so cannot himself be subject to it.

The nature of the selected material

It should be clear from all this, then, that the relations between faith and reason are complex, and the selections have been chosen to reflect this complexity without, it is hoped, confusing the reader. They are of four main types of extract.

First, there are representative statements and arguments, from each of the eras, about the relation between faith and reason. In making these selections I have tried to give extracts which are original to and characteristic of the particular era from which they are drawn; I have not provided extracts of commentary and scholarly discussion on these, as this would have made the Reader impossibly long; nor have I given extracts from later eras expressing precisely these same ideas, even when the ideas in question remained influential. For this would have made the Reader boringly repetitive.

Secondly, some of the main findings that, it is claimed, reason provides are represented: proofs of the existence of God, which are illustrated rather than given comprehensive coverage; sceptical counter-examples; and illustrations of the more nuanced relations between faith and reason outlined above.

Thirdly, throughout the selections, there is a focus upon one particular test case of the relations between faith and reason, namely the issue of the necessity or contingency of the universe. In the classical period it was widely held that the universe was necessary. Plato's account of creation in the *Timaeus* is of the Demiurge fashioning matter that was pre-existing, not bringing it into being out of nothing. To claim, as Judaeo-Christianity does, that the universe is created *ex nihilo* is thus to go against this established philosophical tradition. It is also to raise the question of whether the universe was created in time, or was eternal. But the typical reaction, though not the sole reaction, is not to claim that the arguments of the Greeks were faulty, but that, though reason alone shows that the universe was necessary, the knowledge that the universe is contingent is derived from revelation's account of the creation. So the issue of the nature of the universe becomes embroiled in debates about the status of the Christian revelation. Does revelation, sometimes at least, carry the day *against* the dictates of reason?

In the modern era, since the development of cosmology as a branch of physics, and the theory of the evolution of species by natural selection, some of these old arguments have re-emerged in speculations on the beginning of the universe, and its metaphysical status, as well as providing strong sceptical arguments against the idea of a designer-God. Do claims that the Big Bang is the moment of creation, or that the universe carries its own explanation and therefore disqualifies God as Creator, or that naturalistic accounts of the origin of species are incompatible with divine design, themselves embody confusions between science and metaphysics, and misunderstandings about the nature of God?

A third thread running throughout the selections concerns the relation between language and thought about God. As we noted earlier, what one can infer from a proposition depends upon what that proposition means. The extent to which one can reason about matters of faith, and particularly reason about God himself, depends upon what one takes the status of our language about God to be. If we can only say what God is not, this limits us more than if we can say what God is; and if we can only say what God is in some oblique, non-literal way, this limits us more than if we can say what God is literally. Though religious language is not a major theme of this Reader, we shall note these and other views about language about God, particularly in their medieval and their modern forms.

In focusing the material in this way I have had to ignore whole topics which might legitimately shelter under the umbrella of 'faith and reason'. There is nothing directly on the problem of evil as an issue in rationality; nothing on aspects of faith other than the cognitive and fiduciary. There is little, for example, on faith as a virtue, and there is nothing on ethics, where the dialectic between appeals to natural law and to special revelation-based ethics mirrors to a large extent the controversies over the powers and limitations of human reason in matters of faith. There is nothing, either, on the question of the nature of the human person and its mortality or otherwise. And although in this Introduction we have noted the importance of the faith seeking understanding tradition in the development of the relation between faith and reason, selections exemplifying this tradition are few, because they mainly concern specific matters of Christian doctrine such as the Trinity, the Incarnation, and the relation between grace and free will. To have included philosophical discussion of these topics would have changed the character of the Reader.

In selecting material some hard choices have had to be made. I have tried to find pieces that have not been anthologized before. And although the Reader is not an exercise in comparative religion or inter-faith dialogue, I have included some Jewish as well as one or two Islamic sources. The hardest choices of all have been in making selections from the voluminous and ever growing literature of the twentieth century, even though about a third of the entire Reader is devoted to our own century. I have tried to provide material from different phases of the intellectual life of the twentieth century, but I have tried even harder to include material that provides argument and counter-argument on fairly specific issues of faith and reason rather than isolated, representative but rather general statements. For this Reader is above all intended to provide not so much a history of the ideas of faith and reason as a sampling of historically important and enduring arguments, and to introduce the reader to this fascinating and enduring tradition of philosophical engagement.

Section I

The Classical Background

INTRODUCTION

Natural theology, the use of unaided human reason to draw theological conclusions, began with the Greeks. But they knew little or nothing of faith as a personal attitude of reliance upon God, or even of religious belief of the sort that we are familiar with. And so there are no expressions, in this section, of the attempt to support faith by reason, or to show that there is a principled conflict between faith and reason, or whatever. There is no developed idea of a divine revelation, either, and so no attempt to show that the conclusions of natural theology support, or fail to support, the deliverances of such a revelation. This section is nevertheless an indispensable preliminary to the sections that follow.

Where we pick up the story, with Plato (remembering, however, that the Presocratics may also be said to theologize), the philosophically significant contrast is between the gods of popular religion on the one hand and the metaphysical reality to which recognition of the activity of the gods may be said to point, in faltering fashion. And the project is to achieve some overarching explanation of the ever-changing universe, including the changing activities of the gods of civic religion, in terms of something (or someone?) which (or who) is the unchanging ground of change. Not a genetic explanation, but one in terms of reasons.

The sort of principle that was sought, by Plato and then by Aristotle, was a principle of intellectual organization which provides the stopping place of a regress of explanation. This project is an intrinsic part of the search for wisdom which is for the Greeks constitutive of philosophy.

In Plato this explanation is intrinsically tied up with his doctrine of the forms. The forms are meant by him to provide an explanatory account of the fact that our experience of the world is both the experience of sameness and of difference. Two different things may both be red; and they are red, the same red, because they each participate in the form of redness, the forms being abstract though real universals. These individual forms are then in some obscure way interconnected in the Form of the Good which is the ultimate principle of explanation.

It is not altogether easy to see the consistency of the Form of the Good and the activity of the Demiurge in the *Timaeus*. For what is the Demiurge's relation to the Forms? And is Plato being serious in the *Timaeus*, or offering a tongue-in-cheek piece of speculation? It would seem that in the *Timaeus* the beauty and organization of the natural world is explained, by what he calls 'a likely myth', in terms of the activity of the Demiurge who is the form of the universe, its principle of intelligibility and rationality, or, more strongly, who forms the universe from eternal matter. (This reminds us of another sharp contrast between Greek thought and what came later, that between a Demiurge who is a fashioner of pre-existing stuff, and a God who creates the universe *ex nihilo*.) Why is this principle of intelligibility said by Plato to be God? Because it must have, if it is to play the explanatory role required of it, simplicity and necessity and (more boldly and contentiously) goodness and intelligence.

The extract from Plato's *The Laws* which forms the third extract can be thought of as the first piece of recorded religious apologetics. For here Plato seems to be offering an argument against those who are inclined to atheism. How 'the gods' whose existence Plato here attempts to prove relate to the Demiurge of the *Timaeus*, and to the Form of the Good, is by no means clear. Perhaps Plato is arguing *ad hominem*, and being content if he can persuade others of the existence of the gods.

For the Greeks such theological matters were not detached or merely of theoretical interest, as they might at first glance seem, but were concerned with the pursuit of personal virtue arising out of the primary virtue of relentlessly pursuing the truth.

Aristotle follows Plato in his metaphysical interests, seeing in theology the study of being itself, but he is even less inclined than Plato to invoke mythical elements such as the idea of the craftsman, and of course he is resolutely opposed to Plato's doctrine of the Forms. For Aristotle theology is concerned with the study of unchangeable entities. God is the impassible unmoved mover, that around which the whole changing universe hinges. In another much-discussed passage, this primary substance has intelligence, he is 'thought thinking itself', plausibly rendered as having in his mind those elements which form the blueprint of what constitutes the universe, the programme of which the ordered universe is the printout. But there is some tension between the idea of the unmoved mover as simple, and the idea that he thinks. One finds in Plato's invocation of the Demiurge and Aristotle's proofs of an unmoved mover the main elements in many later arguments for God's existence.

Hellenistic philosophy, arising shortly after the death of Aristotle, gave rise to two schools, Stoicism and Epicureanism, as well as to Scepticism. But as no complete writings of major Stoics or Sceptics are extant our views on their theology come from various sources, notably Cicero's *The Nature of the Gods*, which is a valuable source for many views of Hellenistic philosophy, though it no doubt simplifies what is a very complex intellectual picture. *The*

Nature of the Gods has been very important in the development of ideas about religion and philosophy. The Dialogue has three characters besides Cicero himself: Velleius, an Epicurean, Cotta, a not uncritical defender of traditional religion, and Balbus, a Stoic. The view expressed by Velleius that the idea of God (or of the gods) is innately imprinted on the human mind is influential later, as we shall see. The God of Stoicism is immortal, a provident God, not metaphysically distinct from the physical universe but immanent within it. Theology, for the Stoics, was not a branch of metaphysics, but of physics, so that God is a kind of physical explanation of the order and harmony of the universe. But in their rejection of the teleology of Plato and Aristotle in favour of a more mechanistic account the Stoics denied that God has created the universe with a purpose; he is simply what accounts for the universe.

Epicureanism has a much more sceptical temper; its anti-dogmatic, relaxed attitude is well brought out in the latter from Epicurus to Menoeceus. It is argued by some that Epicureanism was basically atheistic, the gods being projections based upon fear. On the other hand Epicurus does refer to God as immortal. Such scepticism, applied to theological claims, is further seen in Sextus Empiricus, whose main charge is that Stoic theology is dogmatic.

Plotinus, who wrote extensively on theological themes, more extensively than all the philosophers who had preceded him, takes Platonic elements further, though his originality as a philosopher is unfairly diminished by thinking of him as merely 'Neoplatonic'. For him God is the One, existing beyond our comprehension; not *nous* (as Aristotle held), for *nous* implies a distinction between thinking and what is thought, whereas the One is simple. The extract from Plotinus criticizes Stoic materialism, his proof of the existence of the One, and his discussion of the nature of the One. The One is infinite being, not a being, and the cause of beings. So Plotinus presents a deeper idea of creation than that of Plato's craftsman, a view that was to be taken up by Christian writers in their own distinctive ways. Because of the transcendence of the One, there are also the beginnings of negative theology in Plotinus; we can say what the One is not better than we can say what he is. For to say what he is like diminishes his utter transcendence. The human soul is the immanent aspect of deity. The appeal of this to Christian theologians is obvious.

The line between Plato, Aristotle, and Plotinus is a line of argument offering further refinements of this idea of ultimate causal explanation and what it entails. The conflict in classical thought between this theological strain and the more sceptical, materialist approach, a debate within classical philosophy, is one that the thinkers of the Christian era inevitably take sides in, as we shall see.

1 The Form of the Good

Yes, I said, but I must first come to an understanding with you, and remind you of what I have mentioned in the course of this discussion, and at many other times.

What?

The old story, that there is a many beautiful and a many good, and so of other things which we describe and define; to all of them 'many' is applied.

True, he said.

And there is an absolute beauty and an absolute good, and of other things to which the term 'many' is applied there is an absolute; for they may be brought under a single idea, which is called the essence of each.

Very true.

The many, as we say, are seen but not known, and the ideas are known but not seen.

Exactly.

And what is the organ with which we see the visible things?

The sight, he said.

And with the hearing, I said, we hear, and with the other senses perceive the other objects of sense?

True.

But have you remarked that sight is by far the most costly and complex piece of workmanship which the artificer of the senses ever contrived?

No, I never have, he said.

Then reflect: has the ear or voice need of any third or additional nature in order that the one may be able to hear and the other to be heard?

Nothing of the sort.

No, indeed, I replied; and the same is true of most, if not all, the other senses—you would not say that any of them requires such an addition?

Certainly not.

But you see that without the addition of some other nature there is no seeing or being seen?

How do you mean?

Sight being, as I conceive, in the eyes, and he who has eyes wanting to see; colour being also present in them, still unless there be a third nature specially adapted to the purpose, the owner of the eyes will see nothing and the colours will be invisible.

Of what nature are you speaking?

Of that which you term light, I replied.

True, he said.

Noble, then, is the bond which links together sight and visibility, and great beyond other bonds by no small difference of nature; for light is their bond, and light is no ignoble thing?

Nay, he said, the reverse of ignoble.

And which, I said, of the gods in heaven would you say was the lord of this element? Whose is that light which makes the eye to see perfectly and the visible to appear?

You mean the sun, as you and all mankind say.

May not the relation of sight to this deity be described as follows?

How?

Neither sight nor the eye in which sight resides is the sun?

No.

Yet of all the organs of sense the eye is the most like the sun?

By far the most like.

And the power which the eye possesses is a sort of effluence which is dispensed from the sun?

Exactly.

Then the sun is not sight, but the author of sight who is recognized by sight.

True, he said.

And this is he whom I call the child of the good, whom the good begat in his own likeness, to be in the visible world, in relation to sight and the things of sight, what the good is in the intellectual world in relation to mind and the things of mind.

Will you be a little more explicit? he said.

Why, you know, I said, that the eyes, when a person directs them towards objects on which the light of day is no longer shining, but the moon and stars only, see dimly, and are nearly blind; they seem to have no clearness of vision in them?

Very true.

But when they are directed towards objects on which the sun shines, they see clearly and there is sight in them?

Certainly.

And the soul is like the eye: when resting upon that on which truth and being shine, the soul perceives and understands and is radiant with intelligence; but when turned towards the twilight of becoming and perishing, then she has opinion only, and goes blinking about, and is first of one opinion and then of another, and seems to have no intelligence?

Just so.

Now, that which imparts truth to the known and the power of knowing to the knower is what I would have you term the idea of good, and this you will deem to be the cause of science, and of truth in so far as the latter becomes the subject of knowledge; beautiful too, as are both truth and knowledge, you will be right in esteeming this other nature as more beautiful than either; and, as in the previous instance, light and sight may be truly said to be like the sun, and yet not to be the sun, so in this other sphere, science and truth may be deemed to be like the good, but not the good; the good has a place of honour yet higher.

What a wonder of beauty that must be, he said, which is the author of science and truth, and yet surpasses them in beauty; for you surely cannot mean to say that pleasure is the good?

God forbid, I replied; but may I ask you to consider the image in another point of view?

In what point of view?

You would say, would you not, that the sun is not only the author of visibility in all visible things, but of generation and nourishment and growth, though he himself is not generation?

Certainly.

In like manner the good may be said to be not only the author of knowledge to all things known, but of their being and essence, and yet the good is not essence, but far exceeds essence in dignity and power.

[*The Republic* vi (*The Dialogues of Plato*, trans. B. Jowett, New York: Random House, 1892, i. 768–70).]

PLATO

2   Creation

Timaeus. First, if I am not mistaken, we must determine, What is that which always is and has no becoming; and what is that which is always becoming and never is. That which is apprehended by intelligence and reason always is, and is the same; but that which is conceived by opinion with the help of sensation and without reason, is always in a process of becoming and perishing and never really is. Now everything that becomes or is created must of necessity be created by some cause, for nothing can be created without a cause. The work of the artificer who looks always to the abiding and the unchangeable, and who designs and fashions his work after an unchangeable pattern, must of necessity be made fair and perfect; but that of an artificer who looks to the created only, and fashions his work after a created pattern, is not fair or perfect. Was the heaven then or the world, whether called by this or any other more acceptable name—assuming the name, I am asking a question which has to be asked at the beginning of every enquiry—was the world, I say, always in existence and without beginning? or created and having a beginning? Created, I reply, being visible and tangible and having a body, and therefore sensible; and all sensible things which are apprehended by opinion and sense are in a process of creation and created. Now that which is created must of necessity be created by a cause. But how can we find out the father and maker of all this universe? And when we have found him, to speak of his nature to all men is impossible. Yet one more question has to be asked about him, Which of the patterns had the artificer in view when he made the world, the pattern which is unchangeable, or that which is created? If the world be indeed fair and the artificer good, then, as is plain, he must have looked to that which is eternal. But if what cannot be said without blasphemy is true, then he looked to the created pattern. Every one will see that he must have looked to the eternal, for the world is the fairest of creations and He is the best of causes. And having been created in this way the world has been framed with a view to that which is apprehended by reason and mind and is unchangeable, and must if this be admitted of necessity be the copy of something. Now that the beginning of everything should be according to nature is a great matter. And in speaking of the copy and original we may assume that words are akin to the matter which they describe; when they relate to the lasting and permanent and intelligible, they ought to be lasting and unfailing, and as far as in their nature is irrefutable and immovable—nothing less. But when they express only the copy or image and not the eternal things themselves, they need only be probable and analogous to the real words. As being is to becoming, so is truth to belief. If then, Socrates, amid the many opinions about the gods and the generation of the universe, we are not able to give notions which are in every way exact and consistent with one another, do not be surprised. Enough, if we adduce probabilities as likely as any others, for we must remember that I who am the speaker, and you who are the judges, are only mortal men, and we ought to accept the tale which is probable and not enquire further.

Socrates. Excellent, Timaeus; and you may be assured that we will. The prelude is charming, and is already accepted—may we beg of you to proceed to the strain?

Tim. Let me tell you then why the creator created and made the universe. He was good, and no goodness can ever have any jealousy of anything. And being free from jealousy, he desired that all things should be as like himself as possible. This is the true beginning of creation and of the world, as we shall do well in believing on the testimony of wise men: God desired that all things should be good and nothing bad in so far as this could be accomplished. Wherefore also finding the whole visible sphere not at rest, moving in an irregular and disorderly manner, out of disorder he brought order, considering that this was far better than the other. Now the deeds of him who is the best can never be or have been other than the fairest; and the creator reflecting upon the visible work of nature, found that no unintelligent creature taken as a whole was fairer than the intelligent taken as a whole; and that intelligence could not exist in anything which was devoid of soul. For these reasons he put intelligence in soul, and soul in body, and framed the universe to be the best and fairest work in the order of nature. And therefore using the language of probability, we may say that the world became a living soul and truly rational through the providence of God.

[*Timaeus* 27d5–30c1 (*The Dialogues of Plato*, trans. B. Jowett, New York: Random House, 1892, ii. 612–14).]

3 The Existence of the Gods

Athenian. Come, then, and if ever we are to call upon the Gods, let us call upon them now in all seriousness to come to the demonstration of their own existence. And so holding fast to the rope we will venture upon the depths of the argument. When questions of this sort are asked of me, my safest answer would appear to be as follows:—Someone says to me, 'O Stranger, are all things at rest and nothing in motion, or is the exact opposite of this true, or are some things in motion and others at rest?'—To this I shall reply that some things are in motion and others at rest. 'And do not things which move move in a place, and are not the things which are at rest at rest in a place?' Certainly. 'And some move or rest in one place and some in more places than one?' You mean to say, we shall rejoin, that those things which rest at the centre move in one place, just as the circumference goes round of globes which are said to be at rest? 'Yes.' And we observe that, in the revolution, the motion which carries round the larger and the lesser circle at the same time is proportionally distributed to greater and smaller, and is greater and smaller in a certain proportion. Here is a wonder which might be thought an impossibility, that the same motion should impart swiftness and slowness in due proportion to larger and lesser circles. 'Very true.' And when you speak of bodies moving in many places, you seem to me to mean those which move from one place to another, and sometimes have one centre of motion and sometimes more than one because they turn upon their axis; and whenever they meet anything, if it be stationary, they are divided by it; but if they get in the midst between bodies which are approaching and moving towards the same spot from opposite directions, they unite with them. 'I admit the truth of what you are saying.' Also when they unite they grow, and when they are divided they waste away,—that is, supposing the constitution of each to remain, or if that fails, then there is a second reason of their dissolution. 'And when are all things created and how?' Clearly, they are created when the first principle receives increase and attains to the second dimension, and from this arrives at the one which is neighbour to this, and after reaching the third becomes perceptible to sense. Everything which is thus changing and moving is in process of generation; only when at rest has it real existence, but when passing into another state it is destroyed utterly. Have we not mentioned all motions that there are, and comprehended them under their kinds and numbered them with the exception, my friends, of two?

Cleinias. Which are they?

Ath. Just the two, with which our present enquiry is concerned.

Cle. Speak plainer.

Ath. I suppose that our enquiry has reference to the soul?

Cle. Very true.

Ath. Let us assume that there is a motion able to move other things, but not to move itself;—that is one kind; and there is another kind which can move itself as well as other things, working in composition and decomposition, by increase and diminution and generation and destruction,—that is also one of the many kinds of motion.

Cle. Granted.

Ath. And we will assume that which moves other, and changed by other, to be the ninth, and that which changes itself and others, and is co-incident with every action and every passion, and is the true principle of change and motion in all that is,—that we shall be inclined to call the tenth.

Cle. Certainly.

Ath. And which of these ten motions ought we to prefer as being the mightiest and most efficient?

Cle. I must say that the motion which is able to move itself is ten thousand times superior to all the others.

Ath. Very good; but may I make one or two corrections in what I have been saying?

Cle. What are they?

Ath. When I spoke of the tenth sort of motion, that was not quite correct.

Cle. What was the error?

Ath. According to the true order, the tenth was really the first in generation and power; then follows the second, which was strangely enough termed the ninth by us.

Cle. What do you mean?

Ath. I mean this: when one thing changes another, and that another, of such will there be any primary changing element? How can a thing which is moved by another ever be the beginning of change? Impossible. But when the self-moved changes other, and that again other, and thus thousands upon tens of thousands of bodies are set in motion, must not the beginning of all this motion be the change of the self-moving principle?

Cle. Very true, and I quite agree.

Ath. Or, to put the question in another way, making answer to ourselves:—If, as most of these philosophers have the audacity to affirm, all things were at rest in one mass, which of the above-mentioned principles of motion would first spring up among them?

Cle. Clearly the self-moving; for there could be no change in them arising out of any external cause; the change must first take place in themselves.

Ath. Then we must say that self-motion being the origin of all motions, and the first which arises among things at rest as well as among things in motion, is the eldest and mightiest principle of change, and that which is changed by another and yet moves other is second.

[*Laws* x (*The Dialogues of Plato*, trans. B. Jowett, New York: Random House, 1892, ii. 278–80).]

4 The Everlastingness of Motion

It remains to consider the following question. Was there ever a becoming of motion before which it had no being, and is it perishing again so as to leave nothing in motion? Or are we to say that it never had any becoming and is not perishing, but always was and always will be? Is it in fact an immortal never-failing property of things that are, a sort of life as it were to all naturally constituted things?

Now the *existence* of motion is asserted by all who have anything to say about nature, because they all concern themselves with the construction of the world and study the question of becoming and perishing, which processes could not come about without the existence of motion. But those who say that there is an infinite number of worlds, some of which are in process of becoming while others are in process of perishing, assert that there is always motion (for these processes of becoming and perishing of the worlds necessarily involve motion), whereas those who hold that there is only one world, whether everlasting or not, make corresponding assumptions in regard to motion. If then it is possible that at any time nothing should be in motion, this must come about in one of two ways: either in the manner described by Anaxagoras, who says that all things were together and at rest for an infinite period of time, and that then Mind introduced motion and separated them; or in the manner described by Empedocles, according to whom the universe is alternately in motion and at rest—in motion, when Love is making the one out of many, or Strife is making many out of one, and at rest in the intermediate periods of time—his account being as follows:

> 'Since One hath learned to spring from Manifold,
> And One disjoined makes Manifold arise,
> Thus they Become, nor stable is their life:
> But since their motion must alternate be,
> Thus have they ever Rest upon their round':

for we must suppose that he means by this that they alternate from the one motion to the other. We must consider, then, how this matter stands, for the discovery of the truth about it is of importance, not only for the study of nature, but also for the investigation of the First Principle.

Let us take our start from what we have already laid down in our course on Physics. Motion, we say, is the fulfilment of the movable in so far as it is movable. Each kind of motion, therefore, necessarily involves the presence of the things that are capable of that motion. In fact, even apart from the definition of motion, everyone would admit that in each kind of motion it is that which is capable of that motion that is in motion: thus it is that which is capable of alteration that is altered, and that which is capable of local change that is in locomotion: and so there must be something capable of being burned before there can be a process of being burned, and something capable of burning before there can be a process of burning. Moreover, these things also must either have a beginning before which they had no being, or they must be eternal. Now if there was a becoming of every movable thing, it follows that before the motion in question another change or motion must have taken place in which that which was capable of being moved or of causing motion had its becoming. To suppose, on the other hand, that these things were in being throughout all previous time without there being any motion appears unreasonable on a moment's thought, and still more unreasonable, we shall find, on further consideration. For if we are to say that, while there are on the one hand things that are movable, and on the other hand things that are motive, there is a time when there is a first movent and a first moved, and another time when there is no such thing but only something that is at rest, then this thing that is at rest must previously have been in process of change: for there must have been some cause of its rest, rest being the privation of motion. Therefore, before this first change there will be a previous change. For some things cause motion in only one way, while others can produce either of two contrary motions: thus fire causes heating but not cooling, whereas it would seem that knowledge may be directed to two contrary ends while remaining one and the same. Even in the former class, however, there seems to be something similar, for a cold thing in a sense causes heating by turning away and retiring, just as one possessed of knowledge voluntarily makes an error when he uses his knowledge in the reverse way. But at any rate all things that are capable respectively of affecting and being affected, or of causing motion and being moved, are capable of it not under all conditions, but only when they are in a particular condition and approach one another: so it is on the approach of one thing to another that the one causes motion and the other is moved, and when they are present under such conditions as rendered the one motive and the other movable. So if the motion was not always in process, it is clear that they must have been in a condition not such as to render them capable respectively of being moved and of causing motion, and one or other of them must have been in process of change: for in what is relative this is a necessary consequence: e.g. if one thing is double another when before it was not so, one or other of them, if not both, must have been in process of change. It follows, then, that there will be a process of change previous to the first.

(Further, how can there be any 'before' and 'after' without the existence of time? Or how can there be any time without the existence of motion? If, then, time is the number of motion or itself a kind of motion, it follows that, if there is always time, motion must also be eternal. But so far as time is concerned we see that all with one exception are in agreement in saying that it is uncreated: in fact, it is just this that enables Democritus to show that all things cannot have

had a becoming: for time, he says, is uncreated. Plato alone asserts the creation of time, saying that it had a becoming together with the universe, the universe according to him having had a becoming. Now since time cannot exist and is unthinkable apart from the moment, and the moment is a kind of middle-point, uniting as it does in itself both a beginning and an end, a beginning of future time and an end of past time, it follows that there must always be time: for the extremity of the last period of time that we take must be found in some moment, since time contains no point of contact for us except the moment. Therefore, since the moment is both a beginning and an end, there must always be time on both sides of it. But if this is true of time, it is evident that it must also be true of motion, time being a kind of affection of motion.)

The same reasoning will also serve to show the imperishability of motion: just as a becoming of motion would involve, as we saw, the existence of a process of change previous to the first, in the same way a perishing of motion would involve the existence of a process of change subsequent to the last: for when a thing ceases to be moved, it does not therefore at the same time cease to be movable—e.g. the cessation of the process of being burned does not involve the cessation of the capacity of being burned, since a thing may be capable of being burned without being in process of being burned—nor, when a thing ceases to be movent, does it therefore at the same time cease to be motive. Again, the destructive agent will have to be destroyed, after what it destroys has been destroyed, and then that which has the capacity of destroying it will have to be destroyed afterwards, (so that there will be a process of change subsequent to the last,) for being destroyed also is a kind of change. If, then, the view which we are criticizing involves these impossible consequences, it is clear that motion is eternal and cannot have existed at one time and not at another: in fact, such a view can hardly be described as anything else than fantastic. [. . .]

[. . .] And if we consider the matter in yet a third way we shall get this same result as follows: If everything that is in motion is moved by something that is in motion, either this being in motion is an accidental attribute of the movements in question, so that each of them moves something while being itself in motion, but not always because it is itself in motion, or it is not an accidental but an essential attribute. Let us consider the former alternative. If then it is an accidental attribute, it is not necessary that that which is in motion should be in motion: and if this is so it is clear that there may be a time when nothing that exists is in motion, since the accidental is not necessary but contingent. Now if we assume the existence of a possibility, any conclusion that we thereby reach will not be an impossibility, though it may be contrary to fact. But the non-existence of motion is an impossibility: for we have shown above that there must always be motion.

Moreover, the conclusion to which we have been led is a reasonable one. For there must be three things—the moved, the movent, and the instrument of motion. Now the moved must be in motion, but it need not move anything else:

the instrument of motion must both move something else and be itself in motion (for it changes together with the moved, with which it is in contact and continuous, as is clear in the case of things that move other things locally, in which case the two things must up to a certain point be in contact): and the movent—that is to say, that which causes motion in such a manner that it is not merely the instrument of motion—must be unmoved. Now we have visual experience of the last term in this series, namely that which has the capacity of being in motion, but does not contain a motive principle, and also of that which is in motion but is moved by itself and not by anything else: it is reasonable, therefore, not to say necessary, to suppose the existence of the third term also, that which causes motion but is itself unmoved. So, too, Anaxagoras is right when he says that Mind is impassive and unmixed, since he makes it the principle of motion: for it could cause motion in this sense only by being itself unmoved, and have supreme control only by being unmixed.

[*Physics* viii. 1, 5 (*The Basic Works of Aristotle*, ed. Richard McKeon, New York: Random House, 1941, 354–7, 368–9).]

ARISTOTLE

5 The Unmoved Mover

Since there were three kinds of substance, two of them physical and one unmovable, regarding the latter we must assert that it is necessary that there should be an eternal unmovable substance. For substances are the first of existing things, and if they are all destructible, all things are destructible. But it is impossible that movement should either have come into being or cease to be (for it must always have existed), or that time should. For there could not be a before and an after if time did not exist. Movement also is continuous, then, in the sense in which time is; for time is either the same thing as movement or an attribute of movement. And there is no continuous movement except movement in place, and of this only that which is circular is continuous.

But if there is something which is capable of moving things or acting on them, but is not actually doing so, there will not necessarily be movement; for that which has a potency need not exercise it. Nothing, then, is gained even if we suppose eternal substances, as the believers in the Forms do, unless there is to be in them some principle which can cause change; nay, even this is not enough, nor is another substance besides the Forms enough; for if it is not to *act*, there will be no movement. Further, even if it acts, this will not be enough, if its essence is potency; for there will not be *eternal* movement, since that which is potentially may possibly not be. There must, then, be such a principle, whose very essence is actuality. Further, then, these substances must be without matter; for they must be eternal, if *anything* is eternal. Therefore they must be actuality.

Yet there is a difficulty; for it is thought that everything that acts is able to act, but that not everything that is able to act acts, so that the potency is prior. But if this is so, nothing that is need be; for it is possible for all things to be capable of existing but not yet to exist.

Yet if we follow the theologians who generate the world from night, or the natural philosophers who say that 'all things were together', the same impossible result ensues. For how will there be movement, if there is no actually existing cause? Wood will surely not move itself—the carpenter's art must act on it; nor will the menstrual blood nor the earth set themselves in motion, but the seeds must act on the earth and the *semen* on the menstrual blood.

This is why some suppose eternal actuality—e.g. Leucippus and Plato; for they say there is always movement. But why and what this movement is they do not say, nor, if the world moves in this way or that, do they tell us the cause of its doing so. Now nothing is moved at random, but there must always be something present to move it; e.g. as a matter of fact a thing moves in one way by nature, and in another by force or through the influence of reason or something else. (Further, what sort of movement is primary? This makes a vast difference.) But again for Plato, at least, it is not permissible to name here that which he sometimes supposes to be the source of movement—that which moves itself; for the soul is later, and coeval with the heavens, according to his account. To suppose potency prior to actuality, then, is in a sense right, and in a sense not; and we have specified these senses. That actuality is prior is testified by Anaxagoras (for his 'reason' is actuality) and by Empedocles in his doctrine of love and strife, and by those who say that there is always movement, e.g. Leucippus. Therefore chaos or night did not exist for an infinite time, but the same things have always existed (either passing through a cycle of changes or obeying some other law), since actuality is prior to potency. If, then, there is a constant cycle, something must always remain, acting in the same way. And if there is to be generation and destruction, there must be something else which is always acting in different ways. This must, then, act in one way in virtue of itself, and in another in virtue of something else—either of a third agent, therefore, or of the first. Now it must be in virtue of the first. For otherwise this again causes the motion both of the second agent and of the third. Therefore it is better to say 'the first'. For it was the cause of eternal uniformity; and something else is the cause of variety, and evidently both together are the cause of eternal variety. This, accordingly, is the character which the motions actually exhibit. What need then is there to seek for other principles?

Since (1) this is a possible account of the matter, and (2) if it were not true, the world would have proceeded out of night and 'all things together' and out of non-being, these difficulties may be taken as solved. There is, then, something which is always moved with an unceasing motion, which is motion in a circle;

and this is plain not in theory only but in fact. Therefore the first heaven must be eternal. There is therefore also something which moves it. And since that which is moved and moves is intermediate, there is something which moves without being moved, being eternal, substance, and actuality. And the object of desire and the object of thought move in this way; they move without being moved. The primary objects of desire and of thought are the same. For the apparent good is the object of appetite, and the real good is the primary object of rational wish. But desire is consequent on opinion rather than opinion on desire; for the thinking is the starting-point. And thought is moved by the object of thought, and one of the two columns of opposites is in itself the object of thought; and in this, substance is first, and in substance, that which is simple and exists actually. (The one and the simple are not the same; for 'one' means a measure, but 'simple' means that the thing itself has a certain nature.) But the beautiful, also, and that which is in itself desirable are in the same column; and the first in any class is always best, or analogous to the best.

That a final cause may exist among unchangeable entities is shown by the distinction of its meanings. For the final cause is (*a*) some being for whose good an action is done, and (*b*) something at which the action aims; and of these the latter exists among unchangeable entities though the former does not. The final cause, then, produces motion as being loved, but all other things move by being moved.

Now if something is moved it is capable of being otherwise than as it is. Therefore if its actuality is the primary form of spatial motion, then in so far as it is subject to change, in this respect it is capable of being otherwise—in place, even if not in substance. But since there is something which moves while itself unmoved, existing actually, this can in no way be otherwise than as it is. For motion in space is the first of the kinds of change, and motion in a circle the first kind of spatial motion; and this the first mover *produces*. The first mover, then, exists of necessity; and in so far as it exists by necessity, its mode of being is good, and it is in this sense a first principle. For the necessary has all these senses—that which is necessary perforce because it is contrary to the natural impulse, that without which the good is impossible, and that which cannot be otherwise but can exist only in a single way.

On such a principle, then, depend the heavens and the world of nature. And it is a life such as the best which we enjoy, and enjoy for but a short time (for it is ever in this state, which we cannot be), since its actuality is also pleasure. (And for this reason are waking, perception, and thinking most pleasant, and hopes and memories are so on account of these.) And thinking in itself deals with that which is best in itself, and that which is thinking in the fullest sense with that which is best in the fullest sense. And thought thinks on itself because it shares the nature of the object of thought; for it becomes an object of thought in coming into contact with and thinking its objects, so that thought and object of thought are the same. For that which is *capable* of receiving the object of thought, i.e. the essence, is thought. But it is *active* when it *possesses* this object. Therefore the possession rather than the receptivity is the divine element which thought seems to contain, and the act of contemplation is what is most pleasant and best. If, then, God is always in that good state in which we sometimes are, this compels our wonder; and if in a better this compels it yet more. And God *is* in a better state. And life also belongs to God; for the actuality of thought is life, and God is that actuality; and God's self-dependent actuality is life most good and eternal. We say therefore that God is a living being, eternal, most good, so that life and duration continuous and eternal belong to God; for this *is* God.

Those who suppose, as the Pythagoreans and Speusippus do, that supreme beauty and goodness are not present in the beginning, because the beginnings both of plants and of animals are *causes*, but beauty and completeness are in the *effects* of these, are wrong in their opinion. For the seed comes from other individuals which are prior and complete, and the first thing is not seed but the complete being; e.g. we must say that before the seed there is a man—not the man produced from the seed, but another from whom the seed comes.

It is clear then from what has been said that there is a substance which is eternal and unmovable and separate from sensible things. It has been shown also that this substance cannot have any magnitude, but is without parts and indivisible (for it produces movement through infinite time, but nothing finite has infinite power; and, while every magnitude is either infinite or finite, it cannot, for the above reason, have finite magnitude, and it cannot have infinite magnitude because there is no infinite magnitude at all). But it has also been shown that it is impassive and unalterable; for all the other changes are posterior to change of place.

[*Metaphysics* xii. 6, 7 (*The Basic Works of Aristotle*, ed. Richard McKeon, New York: Random House, 1941, 877–81).]

ARISTOTLE

6 Divine Thought

The nature of the divine thought involves certain problems; for while thought is held to be the most divine of things observed by us, the question how it must be situated in order to have that character involves difficulties. For if it thinks of nothing, what is there here of dignity? It is just like one who sleeps. And if it thinks, but this depends on something else, then (since that which is its substance is not the act of thinking, but a potency) it cannot be the best substance; for it is through thinking that its value belongs to it. Further, whether its substance is the faculty of thought or the act of thinking, what does it think of? Either of itself or of something else; and if of something else, either of the same thing always or of something different. Does it matter, then, or not, whether it thinks of the good or of any chance thing? Are there not some things about which it is incredible that it should think? Evidently, then, it thinks of that which is most divine and precious, and it does not change; for change would be change for the worse, and this would be already a movement. First, then, if 'thought' is not the act of thinking but a potency, it would be reasonable to suppose that the continuity of its thinking is wearisome to it. Secondly, there would evidently be something else more precious than thought, viz. that which is thought of. For both thinking and the act of thought will belong even to one who thinks of the worst thing in the world, so that if this ought to be avoided (and it ought, for there are even some things which it is better not to see than to see), the act of thinking cannot be the best of things. Therefore it must be of itself that the divine thought thinks (since it is the most excellent of things), and its thinking is a thinking on thinking.

But evidently knowledge and perception and opinion and understanding have always something else as their object, and themselves only by the way. Further, if thinking and being thought of are different, in respect of which does goodness belong to thought? For to *be* an act of thinking and to *be* an object of thought are not the same thing. We answer that in some cases the knowledge is the object. In the productive sciences it is the substance or essence of the object, matter omitted, and in the theoretical sciences the definition or the act of thinking is the object. Since, then, thought and the object of thought are not different in the case of things that have not matter, the divine thought and its object will be the same, i.e. the thinking will be one with the object of its thought.

A further question is left—whether the object of the divine thought is composite; for if it were, thought would change in passing from part to part of the whole. We answer that everything which has not matter is indivisible—as human thought, or rather the thought of composite beings, is in a certain period of time (for it does not possess the good at this moment or at that, but its best, being something *different* from it, is attained only in a whole period of time), so throughout eternity is the thought which has *itself* for its object.

[*Metaphysics* xii. 9 (*The Basic Works of Aristotle*, ed. Richard McKeon, New York: Random House, 1941, 884–5).]

CICERO
....

7   Creation and Providence

Then up spoke Velleius, with all the confidence of men of his school (whose only anxiety is lest they may seem to be in doubt on any point), as if he had himself just returned to earth from some council of the gods held in one of those abodes of theirs 'between the worlds' which Epicurus talks about. 'Listen,' said he. 'From me you will get no mere figments of the imagination, such as the god whom Plato describes in his *Timaeus* as the creator and artificer of the world, or the fortune-telling old witch whom the Stoics call Providence, or some theory of the universe being itself endowed with mind and senses, a sort of spherical, incandescent and revolving god. All such marvels and monstrosities as these are not philosophy but merely dreams.

'How could your friend Plato in his mind's eye comprehend so vast a piece of architecture as the building of a universe, and how God laboured to create it? How did he think God went about it? What tools did he use? What levers? What machines? Who assisted him in so vast an enterprise? And how came air and fire and earth and water to serve and obey the will of this creator? And whence sprang those five archetypal shapes of his, from which everything else was derived, so neatly devised to influence the mind and stimulate the senses? It would be tedious to say more, for it is all the stuff of dreams rather than the search for truth.

'Most ridiculous of all, Plato first presents us with a world which has not only had a beginning but is actually a sort of manufactured article, and then asserts that it will endure for ever! A man must have the merest smattering of natural science who can imagine that anything which has had a beginning will not also have an end. For what composite substance is there which cannot be dissolved? What is there which can have a beginning but no end? And as for your "Providence", Lucilius, if she is like Plato's god, then I ask again what agents and machines she used, what was the whole scope and method of the work? But if she is not the same, then I ask why she made a world subject to time, and not, as did Plato's god, a world to last for ever.

'I ask you both, why did these creators of the world suddenly wake up, after apparently having been asleep from time immemorial? Even if there was then no world, time must still have been passing. Time, I say, and not those periods of time which are measured by the number of nights and days in the course of a year. I admit that these depend upon the circular movement of the world. But from all eternity there has been an infinite time, unmeasurable by any periodical divisions. This we can understand from the analogy of space. But we cannot even conceive that once upon a time there was no time at all.

'So I ask you, Balbus, why that "Providence" of yours remained quiescent through that mighty lapse of time? Was she work-shy? But work has no terrors for God, since all the natural elements, sky and fire and earth and sea, obey his divine power. Why should God in any case wish to decorate the universe with lights and signs, like some Minister of Public Works? Was it so that he could live in it himself? If so I suppose he had previously always lived in darkness, like a pauper in a hovel? Or are we to suppose that he only later acquired a taste for variety, and so embellished heaven and earth just as they now appear? But what pleasure would God find in this? And if it did please him, then why did he so long forgo the pleasure? Or was it for the benefit of mankind, as you tend to say, that God created all these things? For the benefit of the wise perhaps? In that case never was so much undertaken for the sake of so few. Then for the benefit of fools? But why should God put himself out for people who do not deserve it? And in any case what would be the point? All foolish people are bound to be unhappy: their own folly will usually see to that. There is nothing like folly to beget misery. But also because there is much unpleasantness in life, which wise men are able to alleviate by the compensation of the good things which they can enjoy. But a fool can neither escape the future nor endure the present.

'As for those who say that the world itself is a conscious intelligence, they have not grasped the nature of consciousness, or understood in what shape it can be manifest. I shall say something about this a little latter. At present I would only express my astonishment at the stupidity of those who say that the universe itself is a conscious and immortal being, divinely blest, and then say that it is a sphere, because Plato thought this to be the most beautiful of all shapes. I for one find more beauty in the shape of a cylinder, a square, a cone or a pyramid.

'What sort of consciousness do they attribute to this spherical god of theirs? They say that the sphere revolves with a speed which to us is inconceivable. In which case I do not see how it can be the abode of a constant mind and a life of divine beatitude. Any spinning movement affecting any smallest part of our own bodies is unpleasant: so why would it not be unpleasant to a god?'

[*The Nature of the Gods* i. 17–24 (trans. Horace C. P. McGregor, Harmondsworth: Penguin, 1972, 77–9).]

8   The Innate Idea of the Gods

'Anyone who considers how rash and foolish are all these beliefs ought to admire Epicurus and to include him in the list of those divine beings whose nature we are discussing. He alone saw that gods must exist because nature herself has imprinted an idea of them in the minds of all mankind. What race of men or nation is there which does not have some untaught apprehension of the gods? Such an innate idea Epicurus calls "prolepsis", that is to say, a certain form of knowledge which is inborn in the mind, and without which there can be no other knowledge, no rational thought or argument. The force and value of this doctrine we can see from his own inspired work on *The Standard of Judgement*.

'So you see that the foundation-stone of our inquiry has been well laid. This is not a belief which has been prescribed to us by some authority, or law, or custom: it rests rather upon a firm and continuing consensus of opinion that we must admit the existence of the gods because this knowledge is implanted in our minds from birth. And an idea that by its nature commands universal agreement must be true. We must therefore admit that there are gods. Indeed the truth of this is almost universally admitted not only by philosophers but by the common man also, so let us take it as agreed that we have a preconception or "an innate idea" (as I have called it) or a prior knowledge of the divine. New concepts demand new terms, just as Epicurus called this innate idea "prolepsis", a term which had never been used in this sense before. This innate idea is such as to cause us also to think of the gods as happy and immortal. The same nature which has given us knowledge of the existence of the gods has also imprinted in our minds a belief in their blessedness and immortality. If this is so, the famous maxim of Epicurus is true, that "whatever is blessed and eternal must itself be free from care, and cause no care to others, and so must be untouched by anger or by affection. For all such things are signs of weakness."

'If we were seeking only in piety to reverence the gods and to free ourselves from superstition, then I should have said enough. The gods in their grandeur will be revered and worshipped by mankind, if they are recognized as blessed and immortal, for every excellence inspires a proper reverence. We would also have banished all fear of the power and anger of the gods, once we had understood that a blessed and immortal being knows nothing of anger or of affection. And when these are gone, what is left for us to fear from the powers above?

'But further to confirm these beliefs, the mind seeks to know the shape and form of the gods, their way of life, and the thought and movement of their minds.

'As to the form and shape of the gods, we have both the prompting of nature and our reason to guide us. By the prompting of nature all of us of every race can conceive the gods only in human form. In what other form have they ever appeared to anyone, either awake or in his dreams? But we need not rely entirely on such instinctive ideas: reason herself leads us to the same conclusion. It seems fitting that beings of the highest excellence, happy and eternal, should also be most beautiful: and what disposition of the limbs, what harmony of features, what shape and form could be more beautiful than the human? You Stoics, Lucilius, are accustomed—unlike our friend Cotta, who oscillates from one opinion to another—you Stoics are accustomed to illustrate the skill of the divine artificer by explaining how everything about the human form is apt both for our use and pleasure. But if the human form excels the shape of all other living beings, as the gods too are living beings, their shape and form must be the most beautiful of all. As we all agree that the gods are happy, and no happiness is possible without virtue: and there is no virtue without reason: and reason is associated only with the human form: then it must follow that the gods themselves have human shape. This shape is not a body, but analogous to a body. It has no blood, but something analogous to blood.'

[*The Nature of the Gods* i. 43–9 (trans. Horace C. P. McGregor, Harmondsworth: Penguin, 1972, 87–9).]

9 | The Existence of the Gods

'It has also been well said by Aristotle that everything which moves is moved either by nature, by external force or by its own will. The sun and moon and stars are all in movement. But things which are moved by nature are carried either downward by their weight or upwards by their lightness. But in neither case is this true of the stars, whose motion is in a circular orbit. Neither can we say that the stars are moved contrary to their own nature by some greater external force. For what could this greater force be? It therefore follows that the stars move of their own volition.

'Once we have understood this, we should be not only stupid but also impious if we deny the existence of the gods. It does not make much difference either, whether we deny it or merely deprive the gods of all activity and purpose. For it seems to me that anything which is entirely inactive might as well not exist. But it is so clear that the gods exist that I am inclined to doubt the sanity of anybody who denies it.

'It remains for us to consider the nature of these gods. Here we are faced with the great difficulty of opening the eyes of the mind in place of the eyes of the body. It is because of this difficulty that the man in the street and the philosophers of common sense are unable to imagine the immortal gods except in human form. Cotta has already exposed the folly of this notion, so I need say no more about it. But as we have an innate idea in our minds that God must be a living God and supreme above all else in the world, there seems to me nothing more consonant with this idea than to recognize the whole universe, than which there can be nothing more sublime, as being itself the living God.

'Epicurus may make a joke of this if he likes, although humour was never his strong point—an Athenian without the "Attic salt"! He may say that he can make no sense of a "spherical and revolving god". But he will never move me from the one view which even he himself accepts. He agrees that gods exist, because there must be some supreme being which is superior to all else. But there cannot be anything greater than the whole universe. And it is clear that a being which is alive with sense and reason is better than one without them. It follows that the universe must be a living being, endowed with sense and mind and reason: and so by this argument too we may infer that the universe is God.

'But this I shall shortly prove more clearly from the works of the universe itself. In the meantime I beseech you, Velleius, not to expose further your complete ignorance of science. You say that a cone or a cylinder or a pyramid seems to you more beautiful than a sphere. In this you show some novelty in your aesthetic judgement! But let us suppose these other shapes are more beautiful, in appearance at least, although I do not think so. For what can be more beautiful than the shape which alone contains and includes all others? A shape which has in it no irregularity, nothing to offend, no sharp angles, no bends, no protrusions, no concavity or deficiency of any kind? There are in fact two pre-eminent shapes: among solids the solid globe, or "sphere" (*sphaera*) as it is called in Greek, and among plane figures the round or orb, or "circle" (*kyklos*) as the Greeks would say. These are the only two shapes in which all the parts are similar one to another and the centre is at an equal distance from every point on the circumference, the model of perfect symmetry. But if you cannot see this, because you have never stooped to learn from the dust, then perhaps you have at least a sufficient smattering of physics to understand that no other shape could preserve such uniformity of motion and regularity in orbit? So that nothing could be more unscientific than the theory which you proclaim when you say that it is not certain that the world is round and it may have some other shape, and there are innumerable worlds, all variously formed: a proposition which Epicurus could never have propounded, if he had ever learned that twice two is four. But he was too busy filling his own mouth ever to look up (as Ennius says) into "the mouth of the sky".

'Now there are two kinds of stars. One kind moves in constant courses from their rising to their setting, never wavering from their path. The other kind moves in two ways at once while preserving the same courses and orbits. Both of them reveal the rotation of the universe and the circular motion of the stars, which implies that the universe is spherical in form.

'First of them all the sun, the emperor of the stars, moves in such a way that when he sheds his light far and wide on the earth first one part and then another is left in darkness. It is the interposition of the earth's own shadow which veils the sunlight and brings on the night. And so we have the uniform procession of the days and nights. In the same way the slight approach to or recession of the sun from our earth controls the degree of heat or cold which we experience. The yearly cycle is made up of three hundred and sixty-five daily revolutions of the sun's orbit, with six hours added. But the sun in its orbit swings now to the north and now to the south, bringing summer and winter in their turn, and spring and autumn. And from these four changing seasons derives the cause and origin of everything to which the earth or sea gives birth.

'The annual course of the sun is overtaken by the monthly courses of the moon. The light of the moon is least when it is nearest to the sun and greatest when at its furthest distance from it. And not only does its apparent shape and form change, now waxing, and now gradually waning back again to its starting-point: but its position also, now to the north and now to the south. In the course of the moon there occurs also something analogous to the winter and summer solstices. And the moon gives out many emanations which influence the growth and nourishment of animals as well as the growth and ripening of all the plants which grow on earth.

'Most wonderful of all are the movements of those five stars which are wrongly called "the planets" or wandering stars. For there is no "wandering" in a star which through all eternity preserves its constant progress and recession and all its other regular and measured movements. And it is even more wonderful in these stars which are now hidden, and then appear again: now approach and then recede: now precede, and then follow: move now faster and now slower: and on occasion do not move at all but remain stationary for a time. From the diverse movements of these stars the mathematicians have calculated what they call "the Great Year". This is fulfilled when the sun and moon and these five stars complete their courses and return to the same relative positions which they had at the beginning. There is much disagreement about the length of this "Great Year": but it is certain that it must comprise a fixed and definite period. For the star which we call Saturn, and the Greeks 'The Shining One', and which is the furthest from the earth, completes its orbit in about thirty years. And in the course of this orbit it goes through a number of remarkable motions, now going forward and then hanging back again, now vanishing in the evening and appearing again at dawn: and through all the course of the ages there is no change in all these motions or the times in which they are completed. Below this star and nearer to the earth is Jupiter, which the Greeks call "The Blazing One". Jupiter makes the same journey through the twelve signs of the zodiac in a period of twelve years, and its orbit shows diversities similar to those of Saturn. Next below this star is the nearer orbit of "The Fiery One", which we call Mars. This completes a similar orbit, as I believe, in twenty-four months less six days. Below this is the star Mercury, which the Greeks call "The Gleaming One". This completes its course through the signs of the zodiac in about a year and is never distant from the sun by more than a single sign, being sometimes ahead of it and sometimes behind it. The lowest of the five planets and the nearest to the earth is Venus, called "The Light Bearer" by the Greeks—Lucifer in Latin—when it appears in front of the sun: and when it follows the sun, Hesperus. Venus completes its orbit in a year, traversing the zodiac in a zig-zag movement as do the other four. It is never distant more than two signs of the zodiac from the sun, sometimes ahead of it, sometimes behind it.

'I cannot understand this regularity in the stars, this harmony of time and motion in their various orbits through all eternity, except as the expression of reason, mind and purpose in the planets themselves, which we must therefore reckon in the number of the gods.

'Those which we call the fixed stars show the same evidence of mind and purpose. They too in their daily revolution keep a constant regularity. They are not carried along by the aether, or as a part of the general movement of the sky, as is taught by many who are ignorant of physics. The nature of the aether is not such as to enable it to hold the stars in its embrace and to cause them to revolve through the power of its own motion. The aether is too subtle and translucent and too equable in its temperature to be the material setting of the stars. The fixed stars have their own sphere, remote and free from any influence of the aether. Their constant and eternal motion, wonderful and mysterious in its regularity, declares the indwelling power of a divine intelligence. If any man cannot feel the power of God when he looks upon the stars, then I doubt whether he is capable of any feeling at all.

'In the heavens there is nothing accidental, nothing arbitrary, nothing out of order, nothing erratic. Everywhere is order, truth, reason, constancy. Those things which lack these qualities—all that is false and delusive and full of error— such things either circle the earth below the orbit of the moon (the lowest of the heavenly bodies) or have their being upon the earth itself. But from the mysterious order and enduring wonder of the heavens flows all saving power and grace. If anyone thinks it mindless then he himself must be out of his mind.

'I therefore believe I shall not go wrong in taking my lead from Zeno, who was the first to seek out the truth of this matter. Zeno defines nature as "a creative fire which goes its own way, as an artist does, to bring its works to birth". In his opinion the essence of all art is creation. Our artists construct their works by the skill of their hands. Nature does the same but in a fashion far more subtle. Nature is a creative fire and the teacher of all the other arts. She is herself a creative artist. In each of her creations she follows her own path and her own principles. But Nature in the universe as a whole, which holds and encompasses everything in its embrace, is not an artist only but the master-artist, from whose plan and providence springs all the harvest of the times and seasons. Finite natures are born of their own seeds and grow each within the limits of their own form, but the infinite Nature of the universe as a whole is the original source of all freedom and all movement and acts in accordance with its own strivings and desires (which the Greeks call "hormae"), just as we are moved to action by our own minds and senses. Such is the nature of the moving spirit of the universe, so that it may properly be called the divine wisdom or providence ("pronoia" in the Greek), which has formed the world to endure and lack for nothing and to abound in all grace and beauty.'

[*The Nature of the Gods* ii. 42 (trans. Horace C. P. McGregor, Harmondsworth: Penguin, 1972, 140–6).]

SEXTUS EMPIRICUS

10   Concerning God

Since, then, the majority have declared that God is a most efficient Cause, let us begin by inquiring about God, first premising that although, following the ordinary view, we affirm undogmatically that Gods exist and reverence Gods and ascribe to them foreknowledge, yet as against the rashness of the Dogmatists we argue as follows.

When we conceive objects we ought to form conceptions of their substances as well, as, for instance, whether they are corporeal or incorporeal. And also of their forms; for no one could conceive 'Horse' unless he had first learnt the horse's form. And of course the object conceived must be conceived <as existing> somewhere. Since, then, some of the Dogmatists assert that God is corporeal, others that he is incorporeal, and some that he has human form, others not, and some that he exists in space, others not; and of those who assert that he is in space some put him inside the world, others outside; how shall we be able to reach a conception of God when we have no agreement about his substance or his form or his place of abode? Let them first agree and consent together that God is of such and such a nature, and then, when they have sketched out for us that nature, let them require that we should form a conception of God. But so long as they disagree interminably, we cannot say what agreed notion we are to derive from them.

But, say they, when you have conceived of a Being imperishable and blessed, regard this as God. But this is foolish; for just as one who does not know Dion is unable also to conceive the properties which belong to him as Dion, so also when we do not know the substance of God we shall also be unable to learn and conceive his properties. And apart from this, let them tell us what a 'blessed' thing is—whether it is that which energizes according to virtue and foreknows what is subject to itself, or that which is void of energy and neither performs any work itself nor provides work for another. For indeed about this also they disagree interminably and thus render 'the blessed' something we cannot conceive, and therefore God also.

Further, in order to form a conception of God one must necessarily—so far as depends on the Dogmatists—suspend judgement as to his existence or non-existence. For the existence of God is not pre-evident. For if God impressed us automatically, the Dogmatists would have agreed together regarding his essence, his character, and his place; whereas their interminable disagreement has made him seem to us non-evident and needing demonstration. Now he that demonstrates the existence of God does so by means of what is either pre-evident or non-evident. Certainly not, then, by means of the pre-evident; for if what demonstrates God's existence were pre-evident, then—since the thing proved is conceived together with that which proves it, and therefore is appre-hended along with it as well, as we have established—God's existence also will be pre-evident, it being apprehended along with the pre-evident fact which proves it. But, as we have shown, it is not pre-evident; therefore it is not proved, either, by a pre-evident fact. Nor yet by what is non-evident. For if the non-evident fact which is capable of proving God's existence, needing proof as it does, shall be said to be proved by means of a pre-evident fact, it will no longer be non-evident but pre-evident. Therefore the non-evident fact which proves his existence is not proved by what is pre-evident. Nor yet by what is non-evident; for he who asserts this will be driven into circular reasoning when we keep demanding proof every time for the non-evident fact which he produces as proof of the one last propounded. Consequently, the existence of God cannot be proved from any other fact. But if God's existence is neither automatically pre-evident nor proved from another fact, it will be inapprehensible.

There is this also to be said. He who affirms that God exists either declares that he has, or that he has not, forethought for the things in the universe, and in the former case that such forethought is for all things or for some things. But if he had forethought for all, there would have been nothing bad and no badness in the world; yet all things, they say, are full of badness; hence it shall not be said that God forethinks all things. If, again, he forethinks some, why does he forethink these things and not those? For either he has both the will and the power to forethink all things, or else he has the will but not the power, or the power but not the will, or neither the will nor the power. But if he had had both the will and the power he would have had forethought for all things; but for the reasons stated above he does not forethink all; therefore he has not both the will and the power to forethink all. And if he has the will but not the power, he is less strong than the cause which renders him unable to forethink what he does not forethink: but it is contrary to our notion of God that he should be weaker than anything. And if, again, he has the power but not the will to have forethought for all, he will be held to be malignant; while if he has neither the will nor the power, he is both malignant and weak—an impious thing to say about God. Therefore God has no forethought for the things in the universe.

But if he exercises no forethought for anything, and there exists no work nor product of his, no one will be able to name the source of the apprehension of God's existence, inasmuch as he neither appears of himself nor is apprehended by means of any of his products. So for these reasons we cannot apprehend whether God exists. And from this we further conclude that those who positively affirm God's existence are probably compelled to be guilty of impiety; for if they say that he forethinks all things they will be declaring that God is the cause of what is evil, while if they say that he forethinks some things or nothing they will be forced to say that God is either malignant or weak, and obviously this is to use impious language.

[Outlines of Pyrrhonism iii. 3 (trans. R. G. Bury, Loeb Classical Library, London: Heinemann, 1933, 325–33).]

EPICURUS

11 Death is Nothing to Us

Epicurus to Menoeceus, greetings:

Let no one delay the study of philosophy while young nor weary of it when old. For no one is either too young or too old for the health of the soul. He who says either that the time for philosophy has not yet come or that it has passed is like someone who says that the time for happiness has not yet come or that it has passed. Therefore, both young and old must philosophize, the latter so that although old he may stay young in good things owing to gratitude for what has occurred, the former so that although young he too may be like an old man owing to his lack of fear of what is to come. Therefore, one must practise the things which produce happiness, since if that is present we have everything and if it is absent we do everything in order to have it.

Do and practise what I constantly told you to do, believing these to be the elements of living well. First, believe that god is an indestructible and blessed animal, in accordance with the general conception of god commonly held, and do not ascribe to god anything foreign to his indestructibility or repugnant to his blessedness. Believe of him everything which is able to preserve his blessedness and indestructibility. For gods do exist, since we have clear knowledge of them. But they are not such as the many believe them to be. For they do not adhere to their own views about the gods. The man who denies the gods of the many is not impious, but rather he who ascribes to the gods the opinions of the many. For the pronouncements of the many about the gods are not basic grasps but false suppositions. Hence come the greatest harm from the gods to bad men and the greatest benefits [to the good]. For the gods always welcome men who are like themselves, being congenial to their own virtues and considering that whatever is not such is uncongenial.

Get used to believing that death is nothing to us. For all good and bad consists in sense-experience, and death is the privation of sense-experience. Hence, a correct knowledge of the fact that death is nothing to us makes the mortality of life a matter for contentment, not by adding a limitless time [to life] but by removing the longing for immortality. For there is nothing fearful in life for one who has grasped that there is nothing fearful in the absence of life. Thus, he is a fool who says that he fears death not because it will be painful when present but because it is painful when it is still to come. For that which while present causes no distress causes unnecessary pain when merely anticipated. So death, the most frightening of bad things, is nothing to us; since when we exist, death is not yet present, and when death is present, then we do not exist. Therefore, it is relevant neither to the living nor to the dead, since it does not affect the former, and the latter do not exist. But the many sometimes flee death as the greatest of bad things and sometimes choose it as a relief from the bad things in life. But the wise man neither rejects life nor fears death. For living does not offend him, nor does he believe not living to be something bad. And just as he does not unconditionally choose the largest amount of food but the most pleasant food, so he savours not the longest time but the most pleasant. He who advises the young man to live well and the old man to die well is simple-minded, not just because of the pleasing aspects of life but because the same kind of practice produces a good life and a good death. Much worse is he who says that it is good not to be born, 'but when born to pass through the gates of Hades as quickly as possible.' For if he really believes what he says, why doesn't he leave life? For it is easy for him to do, if he has firmly decided on it. But if he is joking, he is wasting his time among men who don't welcome it. We must remember that what will happen is neither unconditionally within our power nor unconditionally outside our power, so that we will not unconditionally expect that it will occur nor despair of it as unconditionally not going to occur.

One must reckon that of desires some are natural, some groundless; and of the natural desires some are necessary and some merely natural; and of the necessary, some are necessary for happiness and some for freeing the body from troubles and some for life itself. The unwavering contemplation of these enables one to refer every choice and avoidance to the health of the body and the freedom of the soul from disturbance, since this is the goal of a blessed life. For we do everything for the sake of being neither in pain nor in terror. As soon as we achieve this state every storm in the soul is dispelled, since the animal is not in a position to go after some need nor to seek something else to complete the good of the body and the soul. For we are in need of pleasure only when we are in pain because of the absence of pleasure, and when we are not in pain, then we no longer need pleasure.

And this is why we say that pleasure is the starting-point and goal of living blessedly. For we recognized this as our first innate good, and this is our starting point for every choice and avoidance and we come to this by judging every good by the criterion of feeling. And it is just because this is the first innate good, that we do not choose every pleasure; but sometimes we pass up many pleasures when we get a larger amount of what is uncongenial from them. And we believe many pains to be better than pleasures when a greater pleasure follows for a long while if we endure the pains. So every pleasure is a good thing, since it has a nature congenial [to us], but not every one is to be chosen. Just as every pain too is a bad thing, but not every one is such as to be always avoided. It is, however, appropriate to make all these decisions by comparative measurement and an examination of the advantages and disadvantages. For at some times we treat the good thing as bad and, conversely, the bad thing as good.

And we believe that self-sufficiency is a great good, not in order that we might make do with few things under all circumstances, but so that if we do not have a lot we can make do with few, being genuinely convinced that those who least need extravagance enjoy it most; and that everything natural is easy to obtain and whatever is groundless is hard to obtain; and that simple flavours provide a pleasure equal to that of an extravagant life-style when all pain from want is removed, and barley cakes and water provide the highest pleasure when someone in want takes them. Therefore, becoming accustomed to simple, not extravagant, ways of life makes one completely healthy, makes man unhesitant in the face of life's necessary duties, puts us in a better condition for the times of extravagance which occasionally come along, and makes us fearless in the face of chance. So when we say that pleasure is the goal we do not mean the pleasures of the profligate or the pleasures of consumption, as some believe, either from ignorance and disagreement or from deliberate misinterpretation, but rather the lack of pain in the body and disturbance in the soul. For it is not drinking bouts and continuous partying and enjoying boys and women, or consuming fish and the other dainties of an extravagant table, which produce the pleasant life, but sober calculation which searches out the reasons for every choice and avoidance and drives out the opinions which are the source of the greatest turmoil for men's souls.

[*Letter to Menoeceus* (in Brad Inwood and L. P. Gerson (eds. and trans.), *The Epicurean Reader*, Indianapolis: Hackett, 1994, 28–31).]

PLOTINUS

12   The One

Those who believe that the world of being is governed by luck or by chance and that it depends upon material causes are far removed from the divine and from the notion of The One. It is not such men as these that we address but such as admit the existence of a world other than the corporeal and at least acknowledge the existence of soul. These men should apply themselves to the study of soul, learning among other things that it proceeds from The Intelligence and attains virtue by participating in the reason that proceeds from The Intelligence. Next, they must realize that The Intelligence is different from our faculty of reasoning (the so-called rational principle), that reasoning implies, as it were, separate steps and movements. They must see that knowledge consists in the manifestation of the rational forms that exist in The Soul and come to The Soul from The Intelligence, the source of knowledge. After one has see The Intelligence, which like a thing of sense is immediately perceived (but which, although it transcends the soul, is its begetter and the author of the intelligible world), one must think of it as quiet, unwavering movement; embracing all things and being all things, in its multiplicity it is both indivisible and divisible. It is not divisible as are the ingredients of discursive reason, conceived item by item. Still its content is not confused either: each element is distinct from the other, just as in science the theories form an indivisible whole and yet each theory has its own separate status. This multitude of coexisting beings, the intelligible realm, is near The One. (Its existence is necessary, as reason demonstrates, if one admits The Soul exists, to which it is superior.) It is nevertheless not the supreme because it is neither one nor simple.

The One, the source of all things, is simple. It is above even the highest in the world of being because it is above The Intelligence, which itself, not The One but like The One, would become The One. Not sundered from The One, close to The One, but to itself present, it has to a degree dared secession.

The awesome existent above, The One, is not a being for then its unity would repose in another than itself. There is no name that suits it, really. But, since name it we must, it may appropriately be called 'one,' on the understanding, however, that it is not a substance that possesses unity only as an attribute. So, the strictly nameless, it is difficult to know. The best approach is through its offspring, Being: we know it brings The Intelligence into existence, that it is the source of all that is best, the self-sufficing and unflagging begetter of every being, to be numbered among none of them since it is their prior.

We are necessarily led to call this 'The One' in our discussions the better to designate 'partlessness' while we strive to bring our minds to 'oneness.' But when we say that it is one and partless, it is not in the same sense that we speak of geometrical point or numerical unit, where 'one' is the quantitative principle which would not exist unless substance, and that which precedes substance and being, were there first. It is not of this kind of unity that we are to think, but simply use such things here below—in their simplicity and the absence of multiplicity and division—as symbols of the higher.

In what sense, then, do we call the supreme The One? How can we conceive of it?

We shall have to insist that its unity is much more perfect than that of the numerical unit or the geometrical point. For with regard to these, the soul, abstracting from magnitude and numerical plurality, stops indeed at that which is smallest and comes to rest in something indivisible. This kind of unity is found in something that is divisible and exists in a subject other than itself. But 'what is not in another than itself' is not in the divisible. Nor is it indivisible in the same sense in which the smallest is indivisible. On the contrary, The One is the greatest, not physically but dynamically. Hence it is indivisible, not physically but dynamically. So also the beings that proceed from it; they are, not in mass but in might, indivisible and partless. Also, The One is infinite not as extension or a numerical series is infinite, but in its limitless power. Conceive it as intelligence or divinity; it is more than that. Compress unity within your mind, it is still more than that. Here is unity superior to any your thought lays hold of, unity that exists by itself and in itself and is without attributes.

Something of its unity can be understood from its self-sufficiency. It is necessarily the most powerful, the most self-sufficient, the most independent of all. Whatever is not one, but multiple, needs something else. Its being needs unification. But The One is already one. It does not even need itself. A being that is multiple, in order to be what it is, needs the multiplicity of things it contains. And each of the things contained is what it is by its union with the others and not by itself, and so it needs the others. Accordingly, such a being is deficient both with regard to its parts and as a whole. There must be something that is fully self-sufficient. That is The One; it alone, within and without, is without need. It needs nothing outside itself either to exist, to achieve well-being, or to be sustained in existence. As it is the cause of the other things, how could it owe its existence to them? And how could it derive its well-being from outside itself since its well-being is not something contingent but is its very nature? And, since it does not occupy space, how can it need support or foundation? What needs foundation is the material mass which, unfounded, falls. The One is the foundation of all other things and gives them, at one and the same time, existence and location; what needs locating is not self-sufficing.

Again, no principle needs others after it. The principle of all has no need of anything at all. Deficient being is deficient because it aspires to its principle. But if The One were to aspire to anything, it would evidently seek not to be The One, that is, it would aspire to that which destroys it. Everything in need needs well-being and preservation. Hence The One cannot aim at any good or desire anything: it is superior to the Good; it is the Good, not for itself, but for other things to the extent to which they can share in it.

The One is not an intellective existence. If it were, it would constitute a duality. It is motionless because it is prior to motion quite as it is prior to thinking. Anyhow, what would it think? Would it think itself? If it did, it would be in a state of ignorance before thinking, and the self-sufficient would be in need of thought. Neither should one suppose it to be in a state of ignorance on the ground that it does not know itself and does not think itself. Ignorance presupposes a dual relationship: one does not know another. But The One, in its aloneness, can neither know nor be ignorant of anything. Being with itself, it does not need to know itself. Still, we should not even attribute to it this presence with itself if we are to preserve its unity.

Excluded from it are both thinking of itself and thinking of others. It is not like that which thinks but, rather, like the activity of thinking. The activity of thinking does not itself think; it is the cause that has some other being think and cause cannot be identical with effect. This cause, therefore, of all existing things cannot be any one of them. Because it is the cause of good it cannot, then, be called the Good; yet in another sense it is the Good above all.

If the mind reels at this, The One being none of the things we mentioned, a start yet can be made from them to contemplate it.

Do not let yourself be distracted by anything exterior, for The One is not in some one place, depriving all the rest of its presence. It is present to all those who can touch it and absent only to those who cannot. No man can concentrate on one thing by thinking of some other thing; so he should not connect something else with the object he is thinking of if he wishes really to grasp it. Similarly, it is impossible for a soul, impressed with something else, to conceive of The One so long as such an impression occupies its attention, just as it is impossible that a soul, at the moment when it is attentive to other things, should receive the form of what is their contrary. It is said that matter must be void of all qualities in order to be capable of receiving all forms. So must the soul, and for a stronger reason, be stripped of all forms if it would be filled and fired by the supreme without any hindrance from within itself.

Having thus freed itself of all externals, the soul must turn totally inward; not allowing itself to be wrested back towards the outer, it must forget everything, the subjective first and, finally, the objective. It must not even know that it is itself that is applying itself to contemplation of The One.

After having dwelled with it sufficiently, the soul should, if it can, reveal to others this transcendent communion. (Doubtless it was enjoyment of this communion that was the basis of calling Minos 'the confidant of Zeus'; remembering, he made laws that are the image of The One, inspired to legislate by his contact with the divine.) If a man looks down on the life of the city as unworthy of him, he should, if he so wishes, remain in this world above. This does indeed happen to those who have contemplated much.

This divinity, it is said, is not outside any being but, on the contrary, is present to all beings though they may not know it. They are fugitives from the divine, or rather from themselves. What they turn from they cannot reach. Themselves lost, they can find no other. A son distraught and beside himself is not likely to recognize his father. But the man who has learned to know himself will at the same time discover whence he comes.

[*Ennead* vi. 9 (*The Essential Plotinus*, trans. Elmer O'Brien SJ, Indianapolis: Hackett, 1964, 79–83).]

Section II

The Interaction of Judaeo-Christianity and the Classical World

INTRODUCTION

The philosophical and theological writing of the early years of the Christian era discloses the impact of classical Greek ideas and arguments (sampled in Section I) on both Jewish and Christian thinkers. As Christians focused on God's supreme revelation of himself in Christ, the climax of his revelation in the Old Testament, so revelation, and faith in the God who has spoken, came to play a role unknown to the classical Greeks. For Christian thinkers of this period, and for many centuries subsequently, faith was or contained a cognitive element; belief in what God had revealed, and especially in Christ, God's supreme revelation. Various scriptural claims came to have philosophical significance; God as the creator of the universe out of nothing, and Christ as the creative word of God; the idea of faith as reliance upon the word of God. The precedent set by the Apostle Paul was of great significance; his address to the Athenians recorded in Acts 17, with its citing of the poet Aratus, became one model of the relation between faith and reason, though his affirmation to the Corinthian Christians that Christ is the wisdom of God and is foolishness to the Greeks was somewhat less easy to assimilate, and took some Christian thinkers in a direction that proved less hospitable to the legacy of Greek philosophy.

Recognition of Scriptural authority meant that potential conflicts existed between the propositions of the faith, Christian beliefs, and philosophical wisdom, for Jews as well as Christians. One such area was in the idea of creation, with Jewish thinkers such as Philo, as well as Christians, taking their cue from Genesis 1, stressing the contingency of the universe and its creation *ex nihilo*.

Three broad patterns of reaction may be discerned. According to the first type of reaction, Christian thinkers thought of the Christian revelation, and the good news that it contained, as taking the place of ancient philosophy. The one supplants the other. Christ is the true wisdom, and true happiness is to be found in the knowledge and service of God.

A number of separate reasons are given for this, the supplanting strategy, as we might call it. For example, those who think of Christianity primarily as an ethical and spiritual discipline, a practical way of coping with the demands and uncertainties of life, see it as taking over the claim of some ancient philosophies to provide the intellectual framework for living well. This is seen in the extract from Justin Martyr. The supplanting strategy can also be seen rather differently in the idea that Christianity completes and fulfils the ancient wisdom (as with Justin, and as is also seen from the extracts from Augustine of Hippo and Scotus Eriugena). However, a second strategy is discernible, the confrontational strategy, in which, though Christianity takes over the role of the ancient wisdom, it does so by opposing it. The stress is on discontinuity. In a fiery writer such as Tertullian the philosophical virtue of Christianity is said to be its offensiveness to natural reason as exemplified in the Greeks. Jerusalem has nothing to do with Athens.

A third, more positive relationship between faith and reason that begins to develop during this period is the harnessing of Greek philosophical ideas and arguments for the elucidation and propagation of Jewish and Christian theological ideas. No doubt the original motivation for such a move is apologetic, and much of the argument is *ad hominem* in character. In order to engage the secular opponents of the Christian faith effectively, a Christian thinker had to take over their ways of thinking, in so far as this was possible within the limits of orthodoxy. An early form of this can be found in the extract from Clement of Alexandria. As Clement puts it, faith is 'a compendious knowledge of the essentials, but knowledge is sure and firm demonstration of the things received through faith'. Such a view is characteristic of the early creeds of Christianity, with their use of 'substance', 'being', 'person', in order to draw subtle distinctions to combat various kinds of unorthodoxy, and to place the central tenets of the faith on a firmer intellectual foundation by affirming their inner coherence and rationality. Sometimes, as with Origen, the influence of classical ideas is much more dominant, and a distinction is drawn between the popular faith of the multitude and the philosophical working out of that faith by those who are capable of philosophical discussion. Some, such as Philoponus, argued acutely against the idea of the eternity of matter, giving philosophical expression to the revealed truth that the universe was created by God *ex nihilo*, while others, such as the Jewish thinker Saadia, are content to contrast the idea of creation with pagan thought. But it is in the writings of Augustine that the faith seeks understanding approach gained its greatest expression, and an enduring influence.

Thought, reason, and language are clearly closely connected. What we think about we can express in words, and what we cannot express in words we cannot reason about. Faith can only seek understanding if God, the object of faith, is open to the human mind. There are places in both the Old and New Testaments in which the utter transcendence of God is stressed, and this theme is taken up and codified in the very influential writings of Pseudo-Dionysius, who in the sixth century wrote *The Divine Names*. Heavily influenced by Neoplatonism, this stressed that our language about God does not convey information about him but serves to protect his otherness. We cannot know what God is, only what he is not. There is a close connection at points between this pure agnosticism about the nature of God and a mystical, intuitive, non-discursive apprehension of God. Such a view clearly also has important consequences for both faith and reason, and was later to be given expression in the distinction between those matters of faith which are in accordance with reason, those which are against reason, and those which are above reason.

In the beginning when God created the heavens and the earth, the earth was a formless void and darkness covered the face of the deep, while a wind from God swept over the face of the waters. Then God said, 'Let there be light'; and there was light. And God saw that the light was good; and God separated the light from the darkness. God called the light Day, and the darkness he called Night. And there was evening and there was morning, the first day. [. . .]

In the beginning was the Word, and the Word was with God, and the Word was God. He was in the beginning with God. All things came into being through him, and without him not one thing came into being. What has come into being in him was life, and the life was the light of all people. The light shines in the darkness, and the darkness did not overcome it.

There was a man sent from God, whose name was John. He came as a witness to testify to the light, so that all might believe through him. He himself was not the light, but he came to testify to the light. The true light, which enlightens everyone, was coming into the world.

He was in the world, and the world came into being through him; yet the world did not know him. He came to what was his own, and his own people did not accept him. But to all who received him, who believed in his name, he gave power to become children of God, who were born, not of blood or of the will of the flesh or of the will of man, but of God. [. . .]

While Paul was waiting for them in Athens, he was deeply distressed to see that the city was full of idols. So he argued in the synagogue with the Jews and the devout persons, and also in the market-place every day with those who happened to be there. Also some Epicurean and Stoic philosophers debated with him. Some said, 'What does this babbler want to say?' Others said, 'He seems to be a proclaimer of foreign divinities.' (This was because he was telling the good news about Jesus and the resurrection.) So they took him and brought him to the Areopagus and asked him, 'May we know what this new teaching is that you are presenting? It sounds rather strange to us, so we would like to know what it means.' Now all the Athenians and the foreigners living there would spend their time in nothing but telling or hearing something new.

Then Paul stood in front of the Areopagus and said, 'Athenians, I see how extremely religious you are in every way. For as I went through the city and looked carefully at the objects of your worship, I found among them an altar with the inscription, "To an unknown god." What therefore you worship as unknown, this I proclaim to you. The God who made the world and everything in it, he who is Lord of heaven and earth, does not live in shrines made by human hands, nor is he served by human hands, as though he needed anything, since he himself gives to all mortals life and breath and all things. From one ancestor he made all nations to inhabit the whole earth, and he allotted the times of their existence and the boundaries of the places where they would live, so that they would search for God and perhaps grope for him and find him— though indeed he is not far from each one of us. For "In him we live and move and have our being"; as even some of your own poets have said,

"For we too are his offspring."

'Since we are God's offspring, we ought not to think that the deity is like gold, or silver, or stone, an image formed by the art and imagination of mortals. While God has overlooked the times of human ignorance, now he commands all people everywhere to repent, because he has fixed a day on which he will have the world judged in righteousness by a man whom he has appointed, and of this he has given assurance to all by raising him from the dead.'

When they heard of the resurrection of the dead, some scoffed; but others said 'We will hear you again about this.' At that point Paul left them. But some of them joined him and became believers including Dionysius the Areopagite and a woman named Damaris, and others with them. [. . .]

For the message about the cross is foolishness to those who are perishing, but to us who are being saved it is the power of God. For it is written,

'I will destroy the wisdom of the wise,
and the discernment of the discerning I will thwart.'

Where is the one who is wise? Where is the scribe? Where is the debater of this age? Has not God made foolish the wisdom of the world? For since, in the wisdom of God, the world did not know God through wisdom, God decided, through the foolishness of our proclamation, to save those who believe. For Jews demand signs and Greeks desire wisdom, but we proclaim Christ crucified, a stumbling-block to Jews and foolishness to Gentiles, but to those who are the called, both Jews and Greeks, Christ the power of God and the wisdom of God. For God's foolishness is wiser than human wisdom, and God's weakness is stronger than human strength.

Consider your own call, brothers and sisters: not many of you were wise by human standards, not many were powerful, not many were of noble birth. But God chose what is foolish in the world to shame the wise; God chose what is weak in the world to shame the strong; God chose what is low and despised in the world, things that are not, to reduce to nothing things that are, so that no one might boast in the presence of God. [. . .]

Now faith is the assurance of things hoped for, the conviction of things not seen. Indeed, by faith our ancestors received approval. By faith we understand that the worlds were prepared by the word of God, so that what is seen was made from things that are not visible.

[Genesis 1: 1–5; John 1: 1–13; Acts 17: 16–34; 1 Corinthians 1: 18–29; Hebrews 11: 1–3 (The New Revised Standard Version of the Bible, Oxford: Oxford University Press 1995).]

PHILO

14 On the Creation

For some men, admiring the world itself rather than the Creator of the world, have represented it as existing without any maker, and eternal; and as impiously as falsely have represented God as existing in a state of complete inactivity, while it would have been right on the other hand to marvel at the might of God as the creator and father of all, and to admire the world in a degree not exceeding the bounds of moderation.

But Moses, who had early reached the very summits of philosophy, and who had learnt from the oracles of God the most numerous and important of the principles of nature, was well aware that it is indispensable that in all existing things there must be an active cause, and a passive subject; and that the active cause is the intellect of the universe, thoroughly unadulterated and thoroughly unmixed, superior to virtue and superior to science, superior even to abstract good or abstract beauty; while the passive subject is something inanimate and incapable of motion by any intrinsic power of its own, but having been set in motion, and fashioned, and endowed with life by the intellect, became transformed into that most perfect work, this world. And those who describe it as being uncreated, do, without being aware of it, cut off the most useful and necessary of all the qualities which tend to produce piety, namely, providence: for reason proves that the father and creator has a care for that which has been created; for a father is anxious for the life of his children, and a workman aims at the duration of his works, and employs every device imaginable to ward off everything that is pernicious or injurious, and is desirous by every means in his power to provide everything which is useful or profitable for them. But with regard to that which has not been created, there is no feeling of interest as if it were his own in the breast of him who has not created it.

It is then a pernicious doctrine, and one for which no one should contend, to establish a system in this world, such as anarchy is in a city, so that it should have no superintendent, or regulator, or judge, by whom everything must be managed and governed.

But the great Moses, thinking that a thing which has not been uncreated is as alien as possible from that which is visible before our eyes (for everything which is the subject of our senses exists in birth and in changes, and is not always in the same condition), has attributed eternity to that which is invisible and discerned only by our intellect as a kinsman and a brother, while of that which is the object of our external senses he had predicated generation as an appropriate description. Since, then, this world is visible and the object of our external senses, it follows of necessity that it must have been created; on which account it was not without a wise purpose that he recorded its creation, giving a very venerable account of God.

And he says that the world was made in six days, not because the Creator stood in need of a length of time (for it is natural that God should do everything at once, not merely by uttering a command, but by even thinking of it); but because the things created required arrangement; and number is akin to arrangement; and, of all numbers, six is, by the laws of nature, the most productive: for of all the numbers, from the unit upwards, it is the first perfect one, being made equal to its parts, and being made complete by them; the number three being half of it, and the number two a third of it, and the unit a sixth of it, and, so to say, it is formed so as to be both male and female, and is made up of the power of both natures; for in existing things the odd number is the male, and the even number is the female; accordingly, of odd numbers the first is the number three, and of even numbers the first is two, and the two numbers multiplied together make six. It was fitting therefore, that the world, being the most perfect of created things, should be made according to the perfect number, namely, six: and, as it was to have in it the causes of both, which arise from combination, that it should be formed according to a mixed number, the first combination of odd and even numbers, since it was to embrace the character both of the male who sows the seed, and of the female who receives it. And he allotted each of the six days to one of the portions of the whole, taking out the first day, which he does not even call the first day, that it may not be numbered with the others, but entitling it one, he names it rightly, perceiving in it, and ascribing to it the nature and appellation of the limit.

We must mention as much as we can of the matters contained in his account, since to enumerate them all is impossible; for he embraces that beautiful world which is perceptible only by the intellect, as the account of the first day will show: for God, as apprehending beforehand, as a God must do, that there could not exist a good imitation without a good model, and that of the things perceptible to the external senses nothing could be faultless which was not fashioned with reference to some archetypal idea conceived by the intellect, when he had determined to create this visible world, previously formed that one which is perceptible only by the intellect, in order that so using an incorporeal model formed as far as possible on the image of God, he might then make this corporeal world, a younger likeness of the elder creation, which should embrace as many different genera perceptible to the external senses, as the other world contains of those which are visible only to the intellect.

[*On the Creation* ii. 4 (*The Works of Philo*, trans. C. D. Yonge, Peabody, Mass.: Hendrickson Publishers, 1993, 3–4).]

15   True Philosophy

1. 'Those philosophers then know nothing about these things, for they cannot even tell us what sort of thing the soul is.'

'It does not seem so.'

'And assuredly one may not speak of it as immortal. Because if it is immortal it plainly is also unbegotten.'

'It is both unbegotten and immortal according to some Platonists, as they are called.'

'Do you then speak of the world as unbegotten?'

'There are some who say so, yet I myself do not agree with them.'

2. 'Rightly so. For what reason has one to suppose that a body so hard, and resisting, and compound, and altering, and perishing, and coming into being every day has not had its being from a beginning of some sort? But if the world is begotten, it follows necessarily that souls have come into being, and perhaps may cease to be; for they come into being for the sake of men and the other living creatures, if you will admit without reserve that they have come into being by themselves, and not with the bodies that they each possess.'

'This appears to be right.'

'They are not then immortal.'

'No, since even the world, as we saw, was begotten.'

3. 'But, certainly, I personally do not say that all the souls die. For that would in truth be a piece of luck for the bad. What do I say? That the souls of the pious dwell in some better place, but the unrighteous and wicked in a worse, awaiting then the time of judgement. Thus the one sort, as plainly worthy of God, die not any more; but the others are punished, as long as God wills them both to exist and to be punished.'

4. 'Is then your meaning much as Plato intimates about the world in his *Timaeus*, when he says that it is corruptible inasmuch as it has come into being, but, because of the will of God, will not be dissolved nor meet with that fate, death? Does this precise doctrine seem to you to be taught also about the soul, and, in short, about all things? For he means that what things soever are after God, or ever will be, have a corruptible nature, and can disappear and be no more. For God alone is unbegotten and incorrupt, and is for this reason God, but all else after Him is begotten and corruptible. 5. For this reason the souls both die and are punished, since, if they were unbegotten, they would neither sin at all nor be filled full of folly, nor be cowardly and then again courageous, nor would they of their own accord ever go off into swine and serpents and dogs. Neither assuredly would it be even right to compel them to do so, if, that is to say, they are unbegotten. For the unbegotten is like the Unbegotten, and equal, and the same, and one may not be preferred to the other in power or

dignity. 6. Hence the things that are unbegotten are not many. For if there were any difference in them, you could not by examination find any cause for this difference, but, if you send back your thought for ever to infinity you will sooner or later stay exhausted upon one thing that was unbegotten, and this you will say was the cause of all. Did all this, I say, escape the notice of such sages as Plato and Pythagoras, who became for us a very wall and bulwark of philosophy?'

1. 'I care nothing,' he said, 'about Plato or Pythagoras, nor, in fact, about any one at all who holds such opinions. For the truth is in this wise, and you may learn from it. The soul either is life or has life. If then it is life, it would make something else live, which is not itself, as motion also would make something else move rather than itself. And that the soul lives, none would gainsay. But, if it lives, it does not live as being life but as sharing in life, and anything which partakes is other than that of which it partakes. But a soul partakes of life when God wills it to live. 2. In the same way then it will also not partake (of life) at the moment, whenever that is, that He wishes it not to live. For living is not proper to it as it is to God. But a man does not exist for ever, and as the body is not always connected with the soul, but, when it is necessary for this concord to be broken, the soul forsakes the body and the man is no more, so also, in the same way, when it is necessary for the soul to be no more, the spirit of life departs from it, and the soul is no more, but (spontaneously) goes back again thither whence it was taken.'

1. 'Whom else then, I reply, could one take as teacher, or from what quarter might one derive advantage, if the truth is not even in these philosophers?'
'There were a long time ago men of greater antiquity than all these reputed philosophers, men blessed and righteous and beloved of God who spake by the Divine Spirit, and foretold those things of the future, which indeed have come to pass. Prophets do men call them. They, and they only, saw the truth and declared it to mankind, without fear or shame of any, not dominated by ambition, but saying only what they had heard and seen, filled as they were with the Holy Spirit. 2. Now their writings still remain with us even to the present time, and it is open to anyone to consult these, and to gain most valuable knowledge both about the origin of things and their end, and all else that a philosopher ought to know, if he believes what they say. For they have not made their discourses, when they wrote, with logical proof, inasmuch as being trustworthy witnesses of the truth they are superior to all such proof, but the things that did take place and are taking place now compel agreement with what they have spoken. 3. And yet even on account of the miracles which they wrought they were entitled to belief, for they both glorified the Maker of all things as God and Father, and proclaimed the Christ sent from Him, as His Son, a thing which the false prophets who are filled with the seducing and unclean spirit never did nor ever do, but dare to work miracles of a sort to amaze men, and

give glory to the spirits of error and demons. But pray that before all else the gates of light may be opened to thee. For things are not seen nor comprehended of all, save of him to whom God, and His Christ, shall have given under-standing.'

[*The Dialogue with Trypho* iii. 5–7 (trans. A. Lukyn Williams, London: SPCK, 1930, 11–16).]

CLEMENT OF ALEXANDRIA

16 Philosophy and the Comprehension of Divine Truth

As many men drawing down the ship, cannot be called many causes, but one cause consisting of many;—for each individual by himself is not the cause of the ship being drawn, but along with the rest;—so also philosophy, being the search for truth, contributes to the comprehension of truth; not as being the cause of comprehension, but a cause along with other things, and cooperator; perhaps also a joint cause. And as the several virtues are causes of the happiness of one individual; and as both the sun, and the fire, and the bath, and clothing are of one getting warm: so while truth is one, many things contribute to its investigation. But its discovery is by the Son. If then we consider, virtue is, in power, one. But it is the case, that when exhibited in some things, it is called prudence, in others temperance, and in others manliness or righteousness. By the same analogy, while truth is one, in geometry there is the truth of geometry; in music, that of music; and in the right philosophy, there will be Hellenic truth. But that is the only authentic truth, unassailable, in which we are instructed by the Son of God. In the same way we say, that the drachma being one and the same, when given to the shipmaster, is called the fare; to the tax-gatherer, tax; to the landlord, rent; to the teacher, fees; to the seller, an earnest. And each, whether it be virtue or truth, called by the same name, is the cause of its own peculiar effect alone; and from the blending of them arises a happy life. For we are not made happy by names alone, when we say that a good life is happiness, and that the man who is adorned in his soul with virtue is happy. But if philosophy contributes remotely to the discovery of truth, by reaching, by diverse essays, after the knowledge which touches close on the truth, the knowledge possessed by us, it aids him who aims at grasping it, in accordance with the Word, to apprehend knowledge. But the Hellenic truth is distinct from that held by us (although it has got the same name), both in respect of extent of knowledge, certainly of demonstration, divine power, and the like. For we are taught of God, being instructed in the truly 'sacred letters' by the Son of God. Whence those, to whom we refer, influence souls not in the way we do, but by different teaching. And if, for the sake of those who are fond of fault-finding, we must draw a distinction, by saying that philosophy is a concurrent and cooperating cause of true apprehension, being the search for truth, then we shall avow it to be a preparatory training for the enlightened man (τοῦ γνωστικοῦ); not assigning as the cause that which is but the joint-cause; nor as the upholding cause, what is merely cooperative; nor giving to philosophy the place of a *sine quâ non*. Since almost all of us, without training in arts and sciences, and the Hellenic philosophy, and some even without learning at all, through the influence of a philosophy divine and barbarous, and by power, have through faith received the word concerning God, trained by self-operating wisdom. But that which acts in conjunction with something else, being of itself incapable of operating by itself, we describe as co-operating and concausing, and say that it becomes a cause only in virtue of its being a joint-cause, and receives the name of cause only in respect of its concurring with something else, but that it cannot by itself produce the right effect.

Although at one time philosophy justified the Greeks not conducting them to that entire righteousness to which it is ascertained to co-operate, as the first and second flight of steps help you in your ascent to the upper room, and the grammarian helps the philosopher. Not as if by its abstraction, the perfect Word would be rendered incomplete, or truth perish; since also sight, and hearing, and the voice contribute to truth, but it is the mind which is the appropriate faculty for knowing it. But of those things which co-operate, some contribute a greater amount of power; some, a less. Perspicuity accordingly aids in the communication of truth, and logic in preventing us from falling under the heresies by which we are assailed. But the teaching, which is according to the Saviour, is complete in itself and without defect, being 'the power and wisdom of God;' and the Hellenic philosophy does not, by its approach, make the truth more powerful; but rendering powerless the assault of sophistry against it, and frustrating the treacherous plots laid against the truth, is said to be the proper 'fence and wall of the vineyard.' And the truth which is according to faith is as necessary for life as bread; while the preparatory discipline is like sauce and sweetmeats. 'At the end of the dinner, the dessert is pleasant,' according to the Theban Pindar. And the Scripture has expressly said, 'The innocent will become wiser by understanding, and the wise will receive knowledge.' 'And he that speaketh of himself,' saith the Lord, 'seeketh his own glory; but He that seeketh His glory that sent Him is true, and there is no unrighteousness in Him.' On the other hand, therefore, he who appropriates what belongs to the barbarians, and vaunts it as his own, does wrong, increasing his own glory, and falsifying the truth. It is such an one that is by Scripture called a 'thief.' It is therefore said, 'Son, be not a liar; for falsehood leads to theft.' Nevertheless the thief possesses really, what he has possessed himself of dishonestly, whether it be gold, or silver, or speech, or dogma. The ideas, then, which they have stolen, and which are partially true, they know by conjecture and necessary logical deduction: on becoming disciples, therefore, they will know them with intelligent apprehension.

[*Stromata* i. 20 (in A. Roberts and J. Donaldson (eds.), *The Anti-Nicene Fathers*, ii, Peabody, Mass.: Hendrickson, 1995, 323–4).]

17   Christianity and Plato

We have also to consider who it is whom Celsus would have us *follow* so that we may not be at a loss to find ancient leaders and holy men. He refers us to *inspired poets*, as he calls them, and *wise men and philosophers* without giving their names; and although he promises to show us the *guides*, he points to the inspired poets and wise men and philosophers without stating precisely whom he means. If he had given the names of each one of them, it might have seemed reasonable for us to contend that he is giving us as guides men who are blinded about the truth, with the consequence that we shall fall into error, or who, if they are not entirely blind, yet at any rate are wrong about many doctrines of the truth. Whoever he means by an *inspired poet*, whether Orpheus, or Parmenides, or Empedocles, or even Homer himself, or Hesiod, let anyone who likes show how those who use such guides travel a better road, and receive more help for the problems of life than people who, through the teaching of Jesus Christ, have abandoned all images and statues and, what is more, all Jewish superstition, and through the Logos of God look up to God alone, the Father of the Logos. And who also are the *wise men and philosophers* from whom Celsus would have us *hear many divine truths*? For he would have us leave Moses, God's servant, and the prophets of the Creator of the universe, though they uttered countless prophecies by genuine inspiration, and him who enlightened mankind and proclaimed a way to worship God, and, as far as he was able, left no one without some experience of his mysteries. On the contrary, because of his exceeding love towards man he was able to give the educated a conception of God which could raise their soul from earthly things, and nevertheless came down to the level even of the more defective capacities of ordinary men and simple women and slaves, and, in general, of people who have been helped by none but by Jesus alone to live a better life, so far as they can, and to accept doctrines about God such as they had the capacity to receive.

Then after this he refers us to *Plato* as *a more effective teacher of the problems of theology*, quoting his words from the Timaeus as follows: '*Now to find the Maker and Father of this universe is difficult, and after finding him it is impossible to declare him to all men.*' Then he adds to this: *You see how the way of truth is sought by seers and philosophers, and how Plato knew that it is impossible for all men to travel it. Since this is the reason why wise men have discovered it, that we might get some conception of the nameless First Being which manifests him either by synthesis with other things, or by analytical distinction from them, or by analogy, I would like to teach about that which is otherwise indescribable. But I would be amazed if you were able to follow, as you are completely bound to the flesh and see nothing pure.*

I admit that Plato's statement which he quotes is noble and impressive. But consider whether there is not more regard for the needs of mankind when the divine word introduces the divine Logos, who was in the beginning with God, as becoming flesh, that the Logos, of whom Plato says that after finding him it is impossible to declare him to all men, might be able to reach anybody. Plato may say that it is difficult to find the maker and father of this universe, indicating that it is not impossible for human nature to find God in a degree worthy of Him, or, if not worthy of Him, yet at least in a degree higher than that of the multitude. If this were true, and God really had been found by Plato or one of the Greeks, they would not have reverenced anything else and called it God and worshipped it, either abandoning the true God or combining with the majesty of God things which ought not to be associated with Him. But we affirm that human nature is not sufficient in any way to seek for God and to find Him in His pure nature, unless it is helped by the God who is object of the search. And He is found by those who, after doing what they can, admit that they need Him, and shows Himself to those to whom He judges it right to appear, so far as it is possible for God to be known to man and for the human soul which is still in the body to know God.

Moreover, when Plato says that it is impossible for the man who has found the maker and father of the universe to declare him to all, he does not say that he is *indescribable* and *nameless*, but that although he can be described it is only possible to declare him to a few. It is as though Celsus had forgotten the words of Plato which he quoted when he says that God is nameless, as follows: *Since this is the reason why wise men have discovered it, that we might get some conception of the nameless First Being.* But we affirm that it is not only God who is nameless, but that there are also others among the beings inferior to Him. Paul is striving to indicate this when he says that he 'heard unspeakable words which it is not lawful for man to utter', where he is using the word 'heard' in the sense of 'understood' as in the phrase 'He that hath ears to hear let him hear.'

We certainly maintain that it is difficult to see the Maker and Father of the universe. But He is seen, not only in the way implied in the words, 'Blessed are the pure in heart, for they shall see God', but also in the way implied in the saying of the Image of the invisible God that 'He who has seen me has seen the Father who sent me'. In these words no one of any intelligence would say that Jesus was here referring to his sensible body which was visible to men, when he said, 'He who has seen me has seen the Father who sent me.' For in that event God the Father would have been seen even by all those who said, 'Crucify him, crucify him', and by Pilate who received power over his human nature, which is absurd. That the words, 'He who has seen me has seen the Father who sent me', refer not to the ordinary meaning is obvious from the words he said to Philip: 'Have I been such a long time with you without your having known me, Philip?' He said this to him when he asked: 'Show us the Father, and it is enough for us.' Anyone, therefore, who has understood how we must think of the only begotten God, the Son of God, the firstborn of all creation, and how that the Logos became flesh, will see that anyone will come to know the Father and Maker of this universe by looking at the image of the invisible God.

Celsus thinks that God is known *either by synthesis with other things*, similar to the method called synthesis by geometricians, *or by analytical distinction* from other things, *or* also *by analogy*, like the method of analogy used by the same students, as if one were able to come in this way, if at all, 'to the threshold of the Good'. But when the Logos of God says that 'No man has known the Father except the Son, and the man to whom the Son may reveal him', he indicates that God is known by a certain divine grace, which does not come about in the soul without God's action, but with a sort of inspiration. Moreover, it is probable that the knowledge of God is beyond the capacity of human nature (that is why there are such great errors about God among men), but that by God's kindness and love to man and by a miraculous divine grace the knowledge of God extends to those who by God's foreknowledge have been previously determined, because they would live lives worthy of Him after He was made known to them. Such people in no way *debase their religious piety* towards Him, neither if they are led away to death by people who have no notion what piety is, and make out that piety is anything other than that which it really is, nor if they are thought to be *a laughing-stock*.

I believe that because God saw the arrogance or the disdainful attitude towards others of people who pride themselves on having known God and learnt the divine truths from philosophy, and yet like the most vulgar keep on with the images and their temples and the mysteries which are a matter of common gossip, He chose the foolish things of the world, the simplest of the Christians, who live lives more moderate and pure than many philosophers, that He might put to shame the wise, who are not ashamed to talk to lifeless things as if they were gods or images of gods.

What intelligent person would not laugh at a man who, after studying in philosophy the profoundest doctrines about God or gods, turns his eyes to images and either prays to them or, by means of the sight of these images, offers his prayer, indeed, to the God who is known spiritually, imagining that he must ascend to Him from that which is visible and external? Even an uneducated Christian is convinced that every place in the world is a part of the whole, since the whole world is a temple of God; and he prays in any place, and by shutting the eyes of sense and raising those of the soul he ascends beyond the entire world. He does not stop even at the vault of heaven, but comes in mind to the super-celestial region, being guided by the Divine Spirit, and being as it were outside the world he sends up his prayer to God. His prayer is not concerned with any everyday matters; for he has learnt from Jesus to seek for nothing small, that is, sensible, but only for things that are great and truly divine which, as God's gifts, help in the journey to the blessedness with Him attained through the mediation of His Son who is the Logos of God.

[*Contra Celsum* vii. 41–4 (trans. H. Chadwick, Cambridge: Cambridge University Press, 1953, 428–33).]

5. Again, when he blames party strife and schism, which are unquestionably evils, he at once adds heresy. What he links with evils, he is of course proclaiming to be itself an evil. Indeed in saying that he had believed in their schisms and parties just because he knew that heresies must come, he makes heresy the greater evil, showing that it was in view of the greater evil that he readily believed in the lesser ones. He cannot have meant that he believed in the evil things because heresy is good. He was warning them not to be surprised at temptations of an even worse character, which were intended, he said, to 'make manifest those who are approved,' that is, those whom heresy failed to corrupt. In short, as the whole passage aims at the preservation of unity and the restraint of faction, while heresy is just as destructive of unity as schism and party strife, it must be that he is setting heresy in the same reprehensible category as schism and party. So he is not approving those who have turned aside to heresy. On the contrary, he urges us with strong words to turn aside from them, and teaches us all to speak and think alike. That is what heresy will not allow.

6. I need say no more on that point, for it is the same Paul who elsewhere, when writing to the Galatians, classes heresy among the sins of the flesh, and who counsels Titus to shun a heretic after the first reproof because such a man is perverted and sinful, standing self-condemned. Besides, he censures heresy in almost every letter when he presses the duty of avoiding false doctrine, which is in fact the product of heresy. This is a Greek word meaning choice, the choice which anyone exercises when he teaches heresy or adopts it. That is why he calls a heretic self-condemned; he chooses for himself the cause of his condemnation. We Christians are forbidden to introduce anything on our own authority or to choose what someone else introduces on his own authority. Our authorities are the Lord's apostles, and they in turn chose to introduce nothing on their own authority. They faithfully passed on to the nations the teaching which they had received from Christ. So we should anathematize even an angel from heaven if he were to preach a different gospel. The Holy Ghost had already at that time foreseen that an angel of deceit would come in a virgin called Philumene, transforming himself into an angel of light, by whose miracles and tricks Apelles was deceived into introducing a new heresy.

7. These are human and demonic doctrines, engendered for itching ears by the ingenuity of that worldly wisdom which the Lord called foolishness, choosing the foolish things of the world to put philosophy to shame. For worldly wisdom culminates in philosophy with its rash interpretation of God's nature and purpose. It is philosophy that supplies the heresies with their equipment. From philosophy come the aeons and those infinite forms—whatever

they are—and Valentinus's human trinity. He had been a Platonist. From philosophy came Marcion's God, the better for his inactivity. He had come from the Stoics. The idea of a mortal soul was picked up from the Epicureans, and the denial of the restitution of the flesh was taken over from the common tradition of the philosophical schools. Zeno taught them to equate God and matter, and Heracleitus comes on the scene when anything is being laid down about a god of fire. Heretics and philosophers perpend the same themes and are caught up in the same discussions. What is the origin of evil, and why? The origin of man, and how? And—Valentinus's latest subject—what is the origin of God? No doubt in Desire and Abortion! A plague on Aristotle, who taught them dialectic, the art which destroys as much as it builds, which changes its opinions like a coat, forces its conjectures, is stubborn in argument, works hard at being contentious and is a burden even to itself. For it reconsiders every point to make sure it never finishes a discussion.

From philosophy come those fables and endless genealogies and fruitless questionings, those 'words that creep like as doth a canker.' To hold us back from such things, the Apostle testifies expressly in his letter to the Colossians that we should beware of philosophy. 'Take heed lest any man circumvent you through philosophy or vain deceit, after the tradition of men,' against the providence of the Holy Ghost. He had been at Athens where he had come to grips with the human wisdom which attacks and perverts truth, being itself divided up into its own swarm of heresies by the variety of its mutually antagonistic sects. What has Jerusalem to do with Athens, the Church with the Academy, the Christian with the heretic? Our principles come from the Porch of Solomon, who had himself taught that the Lord is to be sought in simplicity of heart. I have no use for a Stoic or a Platonic or a dialectic Christianity. After Jesus Christ we have no need of speculation, after the Gospel no need of research. When we come to believe, we have no desire to believe anything else; for we begin by believing that there is nothing else which we have to believe.

8. I come then to the point which members of the Church adduce to justify speculation and which heretics press in order to import scruple and hesitation. It is written, they say: 'Seek, and ye shall find.' But we must not forget *when* the Lord said these words. It was surely at the very beginning of his teaching when everyone was still doubtful whether he was the Christ. Peter had not yet pronounced him to be the Son of God, and even John had lost his conviction about him. It was right to say: 'Seek, and ye shall find,' at the time when, being still unrecognized, he had still to be sought. Besides, it applied only to the Jews. Every word in that criticism was pointed at those who had the means of seeking Christ. 'They have Moses and Elijah,' it says; that is, the law and the prophets which preach Christ. Similarly he says elsewhere, and plainly: 'Search the Scriptures, in which ye hope for salvation, for they speak of me.' That will be what he meant by 'Seek, and ye shall find.'

The following words, 'Knock, and it shall be opened unto you,' obviously apply to the Jews. At one time inside the house of God, the Jews found themselves outside when they were thrown out because of their sins. The Gentiles, however, were never in God's house. They were but a drop from the bucket, dust from the threshing-floor, always outside. How can anyone who has always been outside knock where he has never been? How can he recognize the door if he has never been taken in or thrown out by it? Surely it is the man who knows that he was once inside and was turned out, who recognizes the door and knocks? Again, the words, 'Ask, and ye shall receive,' fit those who know whom to ask and by whom something has been promised, namely the God of Abraham, of Isaac, and of Jacob, of whose person and promises the Gentiles were equally ignorant. Accordingly he said to Israel: 'I am not sent but unto the lost sheep of the house of Israel.' He had not yet begun to cast the children's bread to the dogs nor yet told the apostles to go into the way of the Gentiles. If at the end he ordered them to go and teach and baptize the Gentiles, it was only because they were soon to receive the Holy Spirit, the Paraclete, who would guide them into all truth. This also supports our conclusion. If the apostles, the appointed teachers of the Gentiles, were themselves to receive the Paraclete as their teacher, then the words, 'Seek, and ye shall find,' were much less applicable to us than to the Jews. For we were to be taught by the apostles without any effort of our own, as they were taught by the Holy Spirit. All the Lord's sayings, I admit, were set down for all men. They have come through the ears of the Jews to us Christians. Still, many were aimed at particular people and constitute for us an example rather than a command immediately applicable to ourselves.

9. However, I shall now make you a present of that point. Suppose that 'Seek, and ye shall find' was said to us all. Even then it would be wrong to determine the sense without reference to the guiding principles of exegesis. No word of God is so unqualified or so unrestricted in application that the mere words can be pleaded without respect to their underlying meaning.

My first principle is this. Christ laid down one definite system of truth which the world must believe without qualification, and which we must seek precisely in order to believe it when we find it. Now you cannot search indefinitely for a single definite truth. You must seek until you find, and when you find, you must believe. Then you have simply to keep what you have come to believe, since you also believe that there is nothing else to believe, and therefore nothing else to seek, once you have found and believed what he taught who bids you seek nothing beyond what he taught. If you feel any doubt as to what this truth is, I undertake to establish that Christ's teaching is to be found with us. For the moment, my confidence in my proof allow me to anticipate it, and I warn certain people not to seek for anything beyond what they came to believe, for that was all they needed to seek for. They must not interpret, 'Seek, and ye shall find,' without regard to reasonable methods of exegesis.

10. The reasonable exegesis of this saying turns on three points: matter, time, and limitation. As to matter, you are to consider what is to be sought; as to time,

when; and as to limitation, how far. What you must seek is what Christ taught, and precisely as long as you are not finding it, precisely until you do find it. And you did find it when you came to believe. You would not have believed if you had not found, just as you would not have sought except in order to find. Since finding was the object of your search and belief of your finding, your acceptance of the faith debars any prolongation of seeking and finding. The very success of your seeking has set up this limitation for you. Your boundary has been marked out by him who would not have you believe, and so would not have you seek, outside the limits of his teaching.

But if we are bound to go on seeking as long as there is any possibility of finding, simply because so much has been taught by others as well, we shall be always seeking and never believing. What end will there be to seeking? What point of rest for belief? Where the fruition of finding? With Marcion? But Valentinus also propounds: 'Seek, and ye shall find.' With Valentinus? But Apelles also will knock at my door with the same pronouncement, and Ebion and Simon and the whole row of them can find no other way to ingratiate themselves with me and bring me over to their side. There will be no end, as long as I meet everywhere with, 'Seek and ye shall find,' and I shall wish I had never begun to seek, if I never grasp what Christ taught, what should be sought, what must be believed.

[*The Prescriptions against the Heretics* (in S. L. Greenslade (ed.), *Early Latin Theology*, Library of Christian Classics, London: SCM Press, 1956, 34–5).]

JOHN PHILOPONUS

19 Is the World Eternal?

So since past time will be actually infinite, if the *kosmos* is uncreated, the individuals which have come into being in that infinite time must also be actually infinite in number. Hence, if the *kosmos* is uncreated, the result will be that there exists and has occurred an actually infinite number. But it is in no way possible for the infinite to exist in actuality, neither by existing all at once, nor by coming into being part at a time, as we shall show more completely, God willing, in what follows. For after refuting all the puzzles designed to show that the *kosmos* is everlasting, we then establish for our part that the *kosmos* cannot be everlasting. And I shall add to the exposition Aristotle himself establishing this particular point. I say that the infinite cannot in any way exist in actuality, and I think this is clear from the following. Since the infinite cannot exist all together and at once, for the very same reason it cannot emerge into actuality by existing part at a time. For if it were at all possible for the infinite to exist part at a time, and so to emerge in actuality, what reason would there be to prevent it from existing in actuality all at once? For saying that it is brought to birth in actuality part at a time, and counted, so to speak, unit by unit, one after another, would appear much more impossible than saying that it exists all together and at once. For if it exists all at once perhaps it will not have to be traversed unit by unit and, so to speak, enumerated. But if it comes into being part at a time, one unit always existing after another, so that eventually an actual infinity of units will have come into being, then even if it does not exist all together at once (since some units will have ceased when others exist), none the less it will have come to be traversed. And that is impossible: traversing the infinite and, so to speak, counting it off unit by unit, even if the one who does the counting is everlasting. For by nature the infinite cannot be traversed, or it would not be infinite. Hence if the infinite cannot be traversed, but the succession of the race has proceeded one individual at a time, and come down through an infinity of individuals to those who exist now, then the infinite has come to be traversed, which is impossible. So the number of earlier individuals is not infinite. If it were, the succession of the race would not have come down as far as each of us, since it is impossible to traverse the infinite.

Moreover, suppose the *kosmos* had no beginning, then the number of individuals down, say, to Socrates will have been infinite. But there will have been added to it the individuals who came into existence between Socrates and the present, so that there will be something greater than infinity, which is impossible.

Again, the number of men who have come into existence will be infinite, but the number of horses which have come into existence will also be infinite. You will double the infinity; if you add the number of dogs, you will triple it, and the number will be multiplied as each of the other species is added. This is one of the most impossible things. For it is not possible to be larger than infinity, not to say many times larger. Thus if these strange consequences must occur, and more besides, as we shall show elsewhere, if the *kosmos* is uncreated, then it cannot be uncreated or lack a beginning.

[*De Aeternitate Mundi contra Proclum*, ed. H. Rabe, Leipzig, 1899 (trans. in Richard Sorabji, *Time, Creation and the Continuum*, London: Duckworth, 1983, 214–15).]

AUGUSTINE OF HIPPO

20 Faith and Reason

Augustine. See now whether reason also judges the inner sense. I am not asking whether you have any doubt that reason is better than the inner sense because I am sure that this is your judgment. Yet I feel that now we should not even have to ask whether reason passes judgment on the inner sense. For in the case of things inferior to it, namely, bodies, the bodily senses, and the inner sense, is it not, after all, reason itself that tells us how one is better than the other and how far superior reason itself is to all of them? This would not be possible at all unless reason were to judge them.

Evodius. Obviously.

Aug. Consequently, that nature which not only exists but also lives, though it does not understand, such as the soul of beasts, is superior to one that merely exists and neither lives nor understands, such as the inanimate body. Again, that nature which at once exists and lives and understands, such as the rational mind in man, is superior to the animal nature. Do you think that anything can be found in us, namely, something among those elements which complete our nature and make us men, that is more excellent than that very thing which we made the third in those three classes of things? It is clear that we have a body and a kind of living principle which quickens the body itself and makes it grow, and we recognize that these two are also found in beasts. And it is also clear that there is a third something, the apex, so to speak, or eye of the soul, or whatever more appropriate term may be employed to designate reason and under-standing, which the animal nature does not possess. So I ask you to consider whether there is anything in man's nature more excellent than reason.

Ev. I see nothing at all that is better.

Aug. But suppose we could find something which you are certain not only exists but is also superior to our reason, would you hesitate to call this reality, whatever it is, God?

Ev. If I were able to find something which is better than what is best in my nature, I would not immediately call it God. I do not like to call something God because my reason is inferior to it, but rather to call that reality God which has nothing superior to it.

Aug. That is perfectly true. For God Himself has given this reason of yours the power to think of Him with such reverence and truth. But I will ask you this: if you should find that there is nothing above our reason but an eternal and changeless reality, would you hesitate to say that this is God? You notice how bodies are subject to change, and it is clear that the living principle animating the body is not free from change but passes through various states. And reason itself is clearly shown to be changeable, seeing that at one time it endeavours to reach the truth, and at another time it does not, sometimes it arrives at the truth, sometimes it does not. If reason sees something eternal and changeless not by any bodily organ, neither by touch nor taste nor smell nor hearing nor sight, nor by any sense inferior to it, but sees this of itself, and sees at the same time its own inferiority, it will have to acknowledge that this being is its God.

Ev. I will openly acknowledge that to be God, if, as all agree, there is nothing higher existing.

Aug. Good! It will be enough for me to show that something of this kind exists. Either you will admit that *this* is God or, if there is something higher, you will admit that *it* is God. Accordingly, whether there exists something higher or not, it will become clear that God exists, when, with His assistance, I shall prove, as I promised, that there exists something above reason.

Ev. Prove then what you are promising. [...]

[*Aug.*] You would in no way deny, then, that there exists unchangeable truth that embraces all things that are immutably true. You cannot call this truth mine or yours, or anyone else's. Rather, it is there to manifest itself as something common to all who behold immutable truths, as a light that in wondrous ways is both hidden and public. But how could anyone say that anything which is present in common to all endowed with reason and understanding is something that belongs to the nature of any one of these in particular? You recall, I believe, the result of our discussion a short time ago concerning the bodily senses, namely, that the objects perceived by us in common by sight and hearing, such as colour and sound, which you and I see and hear together, are not identified with the nature of our eyes or ears, but are common objects of our perception. So too, you would never say that the things each one of us perceives in common with his own mind, belong to the nature of either of our minds. You cannot say that what two people perceive at the same time with their eyes is identified with the eyes of either one; it is a third something toward which the view of both is directed.

Ev. That is perfectly clear and true.

Aug. This truth, therefore, which we have discussed at length and in which, though it is one, we perceive so many things—do you think that compared to our minds it is more excellent, equally excellent, or inferior? Now if it were inferior, we would not be making judgments according to it, but about it. We do make judgments, for example, about bodies because they are lower, and we often state not only that they exist or do not exist this way, but also that they ought or ought not so to exist. So too with our souls; we not only know that our soul is in a certain state, but often know besides that this is the way it ought to be. We also make similar judgments about bodies, as when we say that a body is not so bright or so square as it ought to be, and so on, and also of souls, when we say the soul is not so well disposed as it ought to be, or that it is not so gentle or not so forceful, according to the dictates of our moral norms.

We make these judgments according to those rules of truth within us which we see in common, but no one ever passes judgment on the rules themselves. For whenever anyone affirms that the eternal ought to be valued above the things of time, or that seven and three are ten, no one judges that it ought to be so, but merely recognizes that it is so. He is not an examiner making corrections, but merely a discoverer, rejoicing over his discovery.

But if this truth were of equal standing with our minds, it would itself also be changeable. At times our minds see more of it, at other times less, thereby acknowledging that they are subject to change. But the truth which abides in itself, does not increase or decrease by our seeing more or less of it, but, remaining whole or inviolable, its light brings delight to those who have turned to it, and punishes with blindness those who have turned from it.

And what of the fact that we judge about our own minds in the light of this truth, though we are unable to judge at all about the truth itself? We say that our mind does not understand as well as it ought, or that it understands as much as it ought. But the mind's understanding should be in proportion to its ability to be drawn more closely and to cling to the unchangeable truth. Consequently, if truth is neither inferior nor equal to our minds, it has to be higher and more excellent.

I had promised to show you, if you recall, that there is something higher than our mind and reason. There you have it—truth itself! Embrace it, if you can, and enjoy it; 'find delight in the Lord and He will grant you the petitions of your heart.' For what more do you desire than to be happy? And who is happier than the man who finds joy in the firm, changeless, and most excellent truth?

Men proclaim they are happy when they embrace the beautiful bodies of their wives and even of harlots, which they desire so passionately, and shall we doubt that we are happy in the embrace of truth? Men proclaim they are happy when, suffering from parched throats, they come to a copious spring of healthful waters, or, when hungry, they come upon a big dinner or supper sumptuously prepared. Shall we deny we are happy when we are refreshed and nourished by truth? We often hear men proclaim they are happy if they recline amid roses and other flowers, or delight in the fragrance of ointments. But what is more fragrant, what more delightful, than the breath of truth? And shall we hesitate to say we are happy when we are filled with the breath of truth? Many decide that for them the happy life is found in vocal music and in the sounds of string instruments and flutes. Whenever these are absent, they account themselves unhappy, whereas when they are at hand, they are thrilled with joy. When truth steals into our minds with a kind of eloquent silence without, as it were, the noisy intrusion of words, shall we look for another happy life and not enjoy that which is so sure and intimately present to us? Men delight in the glitter of gold and silver, in the lustre of gems, and are delighted by the charm and splendour of light, whether it be the light in our own eyes, or that of fires on earth, or the light in the stars, the moon, or the sun. And they think themselves happy when they are not withdrawn from these enjoyments by some kind of trouble or penury, and they would like to go on living forever for the sake of those delights. And shall we be afraid to find our happiness in the light of truth?

Quite the contrary. Since it is in truth that we know and possess the highest good, and since that truth is wisdom, let us see in wisdom our highest good. Let us make it our aim to enjoy fully, for happy indeed is the man whose delight is in the highest good.

It is this truth which throws light on all things that are truly good and which men choose according to their mental capacity, either singly or severally, for their enjoyment. By the light of the sun men choose what they like to look at and find delight in it. If some of them are perchance endowed with a sound, healthy, and powerful vision, they will like nothing better than to gaze at the sun itself which also sheds its light on other things in which weaker eyes find delight. Similarly, when the sharp and strong vision of the mind beholds a number of immutable truths known with certainty, it directs its gaze to truth itself, which illumines all that is true. As if unmindful of all else, it clings to this truth and, in enjoying it, enjoys everything else at the same time. For whatever is delightful in other truths is made delightful by the truth itself.

Our freedom is found in submission to this truth. And it is our God Himself who frees us from death, namely, from our sinful condition. It is the Truth Himself, speaking also as a man with men, who says to those believing in him: 'If you remain in my word, you are indeed my disciples, and you shall know the truth and the truth shall make you free.' But the soul is not free in the enjoyment of anything unless it is secure in that enjoyment.

[*The Free Choice of the Will* ii. 6, 12–13 (trans. Robert P. Russell OSA, in *The Fathers of the Church: St Augustine; The Teacher, The Free Choice of the Will, Grace and Free Will,* Washington, DC: Catholic University of America Press, 1968, 123–4, 142–6).]

AUGUSTINE OF HIPPO
....
21 Plato and Christianity

THE PHILOSOPHY THAT APPROXIMATES MOST NEARLY TO CHRISTIANITY

Thus there are philosophers who have conceived of God, the supreme and true God, as the author of all created things, the light of knowledge, the Final Good of all activity, and who have recognized him as being for us the origin of existence, the truth of doctrine and the blessedness of life. They may be called, most suitably, Platonists; or they may give some other title to their school. It may be that it was only the leading members of the Ionian school who held the same opinions as Plato, and who understood him thoroughly; on the other hand, the same concepts may have been held also by Italian philosophers, because of Pythagoras and the Pythagoreans, and perhaps by some others of the same way of thinking and from the same part of the world. There may be others to be found who perceived and taught this truth among those who were esteemed as sages or philosophers in other nations: Libyans of Atlas, Egyptians, Indians, Persians, Chaldeans, Scythians, Gauls, Spaniards. Whoever they may have been, we rank such thinkers above all others and acknowledge them as representing the closest approximation to our Christian position.

CHRISTIANITY AND PHILOSOPHY

A Christian whose education has been confined to the study of the Church's literature may be quite unfamiliar with the name of Platonist, and may not know of the existence of two types of Greek-speaking philosophy, the Ionian and the Italian. For all that, he is not so out of touch with life in general as to be unaware that philosophers profess the pursuit of wisdom, or even the possession of it. But he is wary of those whose philosophy is 'based on the elements of this world', and not on God, the world's creator. That is because he is put on his guard by the Apostle's injunction, and gives an attentive hearing to those words: 'Take care that no one leads you astray by philosophy and useless misleading teaching, based on the elements of the world.' However, he is prevented from regarding all thinkers as belonging to this class, when he listens to the Apostle's remarks about some of them. 'What can be known of God has been revealed among them. God in fact has revealed it to them. For his invisible realities, from the foundation of the world, have been made visible to the intelligence through his created works, as well as his eternal power and divinity.' And in his speech to the Athenians, after uttering that great saying about God, a saying which only a few can understand, 'It is in him that we have our life, our movement, and our being,' Paul goes on to say, 'as some of your own writers have also said.' The Christian knows, to be sure, that he must be on his guard against their errors. For while the Apostle says that through his created works God has revealed to them his invisible qualities by making them visible to the intelligence, he says at the same time that they have not offered the right sort of worship to God himself, because they have transferred the divine honours, due to God alone, to other objects, which have no right to them.

Though having some acquaintance with God, they have not glorified him as God, nor have they given thanks to him; but they have dwindled into futility in their thinking and their stupid heart is shrouded in darkness. In claiming to be wise they have become fools and have exchanged the glory of the incorruptible God for images representing corruptible man, or birds, beasts or snakes.

In this passage Paul intends us to understand a reference to the Romans, the Greeks and the Egyptians, who were proud of their reputation for wisdom. We shall later on engage in argument with them on this subject. But they agree with us in the conception of one God, who is the author of this whole universe, who is not only above all material things, as immaterial, but also, as incorruptible, above all souls, who is, in fact, our source, our light, our good; and in respect of this we rank them above all the others.

A Christian may be unacquainted with the writings of the philosophers; he may not employ in debate words which he has never learnt; he may not apply the Latin term 'natural' or the Greek term 'physical' to the division of philosophy which deals with the study of nature, or the term 'rational', or 'logical', to the division which discusses how we can reach the truth; or 'moral' or 'ethical' to the part which treats of morality, of the good ends which are to be pursued and the evil ends to be avoided. It does not follow that he fails to realize that we derive from the one true God of all goodness the nature with which we were created in his image. It does not mean that he is ignorant of the teaching thanks to which we acquire knowledge of God and of ourselves, nor that he is ignorant of the grace through which we are united to him and thus attain our happiness.

This is why we rate the Platonists above the rest of the philosophers. The others have employed their talents and concentrated their interests on the investigation of the causes of things, of the method of acquiring knowledge, and the rules of the moral life, while the Platonists, coming to a knowledge of God, have found the cause of the organized universe, the light by which truth is perceived, and the spring which offers the drink of felicity. All philosophers who have this conception of God are in agreement with our idea of him, whether they are Platonists or philosophers of any other kind, of any nation. The reason why I have decided to concentrate on the Platonists is that their writings are more generally known. For one thing, the Greeks, whose language enjoys a pre-eminent position internationally, have given the Platonists the widest publicity; for another, the Latins, struck by their excellence, or by their renown, have studied their writings in preference to others, and by translating them into our language have made them better known and more highly regarded.

[*City of God* viii. 9–10 (trans. H. Bettenson, Harmondsworth: Penguin, 1972, 311–13).]

22   The Creation

These philosophers agree that the world was created by God, but they go on to ask us how we reply to questions about the date of creation. So let us now find out what they themselves would reply to questions about the position of the creation. For the question, 'Why at this time and not previously?' is on the same footing as, 'Why in this place rather than that?' For if they imagine that there were infinite stretches of time before the world existed, an infinity in which they cannot conceive of God's being inactive, they will, on the same showing, imagine infinite stretches of space; and if anyone says that the Omnipotent could have been inoperative anywhere in that infinity, it will follow that they are compelled to share the Epicurean fantasy of innumerable worlds. The only difference would be that while Epicurus asserts that these worlds come into being and then disintegrate through the fortuitous movements of atoms, the Platonists will say that they are created by the action of God. This infinite number of worlds must follow, if they refuse to allow God to be inactive throughout the boundless immensity of space which stretches everywhere around the world, and if they hold that nothing can cause the destruction of those worlds, which is what they believe about this world of ours.

For we are now disputing with those who agree with us in believing that God is an immaterial being, the creator of all things other than himself. It would not be worth while to admit other pagans to this discussion on matters of religion, for this reason in particular; that among those who consider that the honours of worship should be paid to many gods, those Platonist philosophers excel all others in reputation and authority, just because they are nearer to the truth than the rest, even though they are a long way from it.

Now those thinkers have a right conception of God in that they do not confine his being to any place, nor set bounds to it, nor extend it spatially: they acknowledge that God's being is everywhere entire, in his immaterial presence. Are they going to say that his being is absent from those immense tracts of space outside the world? That he is enclosed in this one space in which the world is situated, so tiny a space, compared with that infinity? I do not suppose that they will go in for such nonsense as this.

They say that this one world, for all its material vastness, is finite and bounded by its own space, and that it was created by the action of God. If they have an answer about the infinite spaces outside this world, if they can answer the question why God 'ceases from his work' in that infinity, then they can answer their own question about the infinity of time before the world, and why God was inactive then. It does not follow that it was by mere chance rather than by divine reason that God has established this world where it is and not else-where, since this space could be chosen among the infinite spaces available everywhere, with no differences of eligibility, even though the divine reason which determined the choice is beyond human comprehension. In the same way it does not follow that we conceive of anything fortuitous in God's action in creating the world at that particular time rather than earlier, since the previous ages had passed without any difference which might make one time preferable to another.

Now if they assert that it is idle for men's imagination to conceive of infinite tracts of space, since there is no space beyond this world, then the reply is: it is idle for men to imagine previous ages of God's inactivity, since there is no time before the world began.

THE BEGINNING OF THE WORLD AND THE BEGINNING OF TIME ARE THE SAME

If we are right in finding the distinction between eternity and time in the fact that without motion and change there is no time, while in eternity there is no change, who can fail to see that there would have been no time, if there had been no creation to bring in movement and change, and that time depends on this motion and change, and is measured by the longer or shorter intervals by which things that cannot happen simultaneously succeed one another? Since God, in whose eternity there is no change at all, is the creator and director of time, I cannot see how it can be said that he created the world after a lapse of ages, unless it is asserted that there was some creation before this world existed, whose movements would make possible the course of time.

The Bible says (and the Bible never lies): 'In the beginning God made heaven and earth.' It must be inferred that God had created nothing before that; 'in the beginning' must refer to whatever he made before all his other works. Thus there can be no doubt that the world was not created *in* time but *with* time. An event in time happens after one time and before another, after the past and before the future. But at the time of creation there could have been no past, because there was nothing created to provide the change and movement which is the condition of time.

The world was in fact made *with* time, if at the time of its creation change and motion came into existence. This is clearly the situation in the order of the first six or seven days, in which morning and evening are named, until God's creation was finished on the sixth day, and on the seventh day God's rest is emphasized as something conveying a mystic meaning. What kind of days these are is difficult or even impossible for us to imagine, to say nothing of describing them.

[*City of God* xi. 5–6 (trans. H. Bettenson, Harmondsworth: Penguin, 1972, 434–6).]

BOETHIUS

23 The Perfection of Happiness

'Now since you have seen what is the form both of the imperfect and of perfect good, I think we must now show where this perfection of happiness is set. And in this I think we first have to inquire whether any good of this kind, as you have just defined it, can exist in the world, lest we are deceived by an empty imagining going beyond the truth of the reality before us. But that there exists this thing, as it were a kind of fount of all goods, cannot be denied. For everything which is called imperfect is held to be imperfect because of some diminution of what is perfect. Hence it happens that if in any class something seems to be imperfect, there must also be something perfect of that class; for if we take away perfection altogether, it cannot even be imagined how that which is held to be imperfect can exist. For the universe did not take its origin from diminished and unfinished beginnings, but proceeding from beginnings whole and completely finished it lapses into this latest, exhausted state. But if, as we have just shown, there is a certain imperfect happiness in a good that perishes, it cannot be doubted that there is some enduring and perfect happiness.'

'The conclusion is most firmly and truly drawn,' I said.

'Now where that dwells,' she said, 'consider in this way. That God, the principle of all things, is good is proved by the common concept of all men's minds; for since nothing better than God can be conceived of, who can doubt that that, than which nothing is better, is good? But reason so much shows that God is good that it proves clearly that perfect good also is in him. For unless he were such, he could not be the principle of all things; for there would be something possessing perfect good more excellent than he, which in this would seem to be prior and more ancient. For it has become clear that all perfect things are prior to the less perfect. Therefore, so that our argument does not fall into an infinite regress, we must admit that the most high God is full of the most high and perfect good; but we have decided that the perfect good is true happiness; therefore true happiness must reside in the most high God.'

'I accept that,' I said, 'nor can it in any way be contradicted.'

'But now I ask you,' said she, 'see how solemnly and inviolably you approve what we said of the most high God being filled full of the highest good.'

'How?' I asked.

'So that you may not suppose that he, the Father of all things, has received that highest good, of which it is agreed he is filled, from outside, or in such a way naturally possesses it, as if you might think that the substance of the happiness possessed is different from that of God the possessor. For if you thought it was received from outside, you could think that which gave it more excellent than that which received it: but we most rightly confess that he is the most excellent of all things. But if it is by nature that it is in him, but it is essentially different, then since we are speaking of God the Author of all things, let him imagine who can who it was joined these two different natures. Finally, that which is different from something is not that from which it is understood to be different; therefore that which is different in its nature from the highest good is not itself the highest good, which it would be wicked to think of him than whom it is agreed there is nothing more excellent. For since there could exist no nature of anything at all better than its own principle, therefore I would conclude with the truest reasoning, that which is the principle of all things is also in its substance the highest good.'

'Most rightly,' I said.

'But we have granted that the highest good is happiness.'

'That is so,' I said.

'Therefore,' she said, 'it must be confessed that happiness is itself God.'

'I both am unable to refute your previous propositions,' I said, 'and see that this inference follows from them.'

'Consider,' she said, 'whether the same is not more firmly proved also from this, that two highest goods different from one another cannot exist. For it is clear that when two goods are different, the one is not the other; and therefore neither could be perfect, since the one is lacking from the other; but it is obvious that what is not perfect is not the highest; and therefore in no way can those highest goods be different from one another. But we have concluded that both God and happiness are the highest good, so that that must be the highest happiness which is the highest divinity.'

'No conclusion could be drawn,' I said, 'more genuinely true, more firmly based on argument, or more worthy of God.'

'Now in addition to these things,' she said, 'just as geometricians are used to draw from the theorems they have proved what they call *porismata* (corollaries), so I shall give you too a kind of corollary. For since men are made happy by the acquisition of happiness, but happiness is itself divinity, it is obvious that they are made happy by the acquisition of divinity. But as by the acquisition of justice they become just, or by the acquisition of wisdom, wise, so by the same argument they must, when they have acquired divinity, become gods. Therefore every happy man is a god, though by nature God is one only: but nothing prevents there being as many as you like by participation.'

'That is both a beautiful and a precious thing,' I said, 'whether you prefer it to be called a *porisma* or a corollary.'

'And yet there is nothing more beautiful than this, which reason persuades us should be added to what we have said.'

'What?' I asked.

'Since happiness,' she said, 'seems to include many things, do they all join, with a certain variability of parts, to make as it were one body of happiness or is there some one of them which completely makes up the substance of happiness, and to which all the rest are related?'

'I should like you to make this clear,' I said, 'by mentioning the things themselves.'

'Now we think happiness is good, do we not?'

'And indeed the highest good,' I agreed.

'You may add that to each of them,' she said, 'for happiness is also judged to be the highest sufficiency, the highest power, and the highest respect, fame and pleasure. What, then? Are all these—good, sufficiency, power and so on—as it were members of the body, happiness, or do they all stand in relation to the good as it were to their head?'

'I understand what you are proposing for our investigation,' I said, 'but I long to hear what your conclusion is.'

'Hear then how we distinguish in this matter. If all these things were parts of happiness, they would also differ from one another, for this is the nature of parts, that being different they make up one body; yet all these things have been shown to be one and the same; therefore they are not parts. Otherwise happiness will seem to be conjoined of one part, which cannot be done.'

'Well that, certainly, is beyond doubt,' I said, 'but I am waiting for the rest.'

'Clearly, then, the others are related to the good. This is why sufficiency is sought after, because it is adjudged to be good; this is why power is sought after, because it too is thought to be good; and the same may be inferred of respect, fame, and pleasure. The sum and cause of all things that are to be sought after is the good: for that which holds no good in itself either in reality or by some resemblance cannot by any means be sought after. And on the other hand, those things which are not good by nature, provided they seem so, are sought as though they were really good. That is why it is rightly held that the chief or cardinal cause of all things sought after is goodness. Now the cause for which a thing is sought is seen to be most greatly desired, as for example if a man wanted to ride for the sake of his health, he does not so much desire the motion of riding, but the effect, health. Therefore, since all things are sought after for the sake of good, they are not so much desired by all as the good itself. But we have granted that that for which the rest are desired is happiness; so in the same way, only happiness is sought after. From this it clearly appears that the substance of goodness and of happiness is one and the same.'

'I see no reason why anyone could disagree,' I said.

'But we have shown that God and true happiness are one and the same.'

'Yes,' I said.

'We may therefore safely conclude that the substance of God too is established in goodness itself and nowhere else.'

[*The Consolation of Philosophy* iii. 10 (trans. S. J. Tester, Loeb Classical Library, Cambridge, Mass.: Harvard University Press, 1973, 275–85).]

PSEUDO-DIONYSIUS

24 Knowing God

The divine Mind does not acquire the knowledge of things from things. Rather, of itself and in itself it precontains and comprehends the awareness and understanding and being of everything in terms of their cause. This is not a knowledge of each specific class. What is here is a single embracing causality which knows and contains all things. Take the example of light. In itself it has a prior and causal knowledge of darkness. What it knows about darkness it knows not from another, but from the fact of being light. So too the divine Wisdom knows all things by knowing itself. Uniquely it knows and produces all things by its oneness: material things immaterially, divisible things indivisibly, plurality in a single act. If with one causal gesture God bestows being on everything, in that one same act of causation he will know everything through derivation from him and through their preexistence in him, and, therefore, his knowledge of things will not be owed to the things themselves. He will be a leader, giving to each the knowledge it has of itself and of others. Consequently, God does not possess a private knowledge of himwself and a separate knowledge of all the creatures in common. The universal Cause, by knowing itself, can hardly be ignorant of the things which proceed from it and of which it is the source. This, then, is how God knows all things, not by understanding things, but by understanding himself.

Scripture also says that the angels know the things of earth not because these latter may be perceived by the senses but because of the proper capacity and nature inherent in a Godlike intelligence.

3. If God cannot be grasped by mind or sense-perception, if he is not a particular being, how do we know him? This is something we must inquire into.

It might be more accurate to say that we cannot know God in his nature, since this is unknowable and is beyond the reach of mind or of reason. But we know him from the arrangement of everything, because everything is, in a sense, projected out from him, and this order possesses certain images and semblances of his divine paradigms. We therefore approach that which is beyond all as far as our capacities allow us and we pass by way of the denial and the transcendence of all things and by way of the cause of all things. God is therefore known in all things and as distinct from all things. He is known through knowledge and through unknowing. Of him there is conception, reason, understanding, touch, perception, opinion, imagination, name, and many other things. On the other hand he cannot be understood, words cannot contain him, and no name can lay hold of him. He is not one of the things that are and he cannot be known in any of them. He is all things in all things and he is no thing among things. He is known to all from all things and he is known to no one from anything.

This is the sort of language we must use about God, for he is praised from all things according to their proportion to him as their Cause. But again, the most divine knowledge of God, that which comes through unknowing, is achieved in the union far beyond mind, when mind turns away from all things, even from itself, and when it is made one with the dazzling rays, being then and there enlightened by the inscrutable depth of Wisdom.

Still, as I have said already, we must learn about Wisdom from all things. As scripture says, Wisdom has made and continues always to adapt everything. It is the cause of the unbreakable accommodation and order of all things and it is forever linking the goals of one set of things with the sources of another and in this fashion it makes a thing of beauty of the unity and the harmony of the whole.

4. God is praised as 'Logos' [word] by the sacred scriptures not only as the leader of word, mind, and wisdom, but because he also initially carries within his own unity the causes of all things and because he penetrates all things, reaching, as scripture says, to the very end of all things. But the title is used especially because the divine Logos is simpler than any simplicity and, in its utter transcendence, is independent of everything. This Word is simple total truth. Divine faith revolves around it because it is pure and unwavering knowledge of all. It is the one sure foundation for those who believe, binding them to the

truth, building the truth in them as something unshakably firm so that they have an uncomplicated knowledge of the truth of what they believe. If knowledge unites knower and known, while ignorance is always the cause of change and of the inconsistency of the ignorant, then, as scripture tells us, nothing shall separate the one who believes in truth from the ground of true faith and it is there that he will come into the possession of enduring, unchanging identity. The man in union with truth knows clearly that all is well with him, even if everyone else thinks that he has gone out of his mind. What they fail to see, naturally, is that he has gone out of the path of error and has in his real faith arrived at truth. He knows that far from being mad, as they imagine him to be, he has been rescued from the instability and the constant changes which bore him along the variety of error and that he has been set free by simple and immutable stable truth. That is why the principal leaders of our divine wisdom die each day for the truth. They bear witness in every word and deed to the single knowledge of the truth possessed by Christians. They prove that truth to be more simple and more divine than every other. Or, rather, what they show is that here is the only true, single, and simple knowledge of God.

[*The Divine Names* (*The Complete Works*, trans. Colm Luibheid and Paul Rorem, London: SPCK, 1987, 108–10).]

SAADIA

25 Creation out of Nothing

I. THE NATURE OF THE PROBLEM

The problem dealt with in this chapter is one on which we have no data from actual observation or from sense perception, but conclusions which can be derived only from postulates of the pure Reason. We mean the problem of the origin of the world. The ultimate proposition which we seek to establish is of a very subtle nature. It cannot be grasped by the senses, and one can only endeavour to comprehend it by thought. This being the nature of the subject, one who inquires into it must necessarily expect to arrive at results of a corresponding nature, and one ought not to reject such results, or try to obtain results of a different character. It is quite certain that the origin of things is a matter concerning which no human being was ever able to give evidence as an eye-witness. But we all seek to probe this distant and profound matter which is beyond the grasp of our senses, and regarding which it has been said by the wise king, 'That which was is far off, and exceeding deep; who can find it out?' (Eccl. 7: 24). Should, therefore, our inquiry lead us to the conclusion that all things were created *ex nihilo*—a thing the like of which was never experienced by sense perception—we have no right to reject it out of hand on the ground that we never experience the like of it, so how can we believe it; for what we tried to find from the very outset of our inquiry was precisely something the like of which we never experienced. We must welcome this solution and rejoice in it, since it presents a success on our part in attaining the object of our inquiry.

I thought it necessary to make the above introductory remark in order to warn the reader of this book not to expect me to demonstrate the *creatio ex nihilo* by way of sense perception. I have made it clear in my Introduction that if this were possible there would be no need for argument or speculation or logical inferences. Furthermore, there would be agreement between us and all other people in regard to its truth, and opinions would not be divided on any point connected with this problem. But in fact we do depend on speculation to reveal to us the truth of the matter, and on arguments to clarify it, since it in no way comes within the domain of experience or sense perception.

We are, in fact, not the only ones who have agreed to accept a cosmological theory which has no basis in sense perception. All those who discuss this problem and seek a solution are agreed on this point. Those, for instance, who believe in the eternity of the world seek to prove the existence of something which has neither beginning nor end. Surely, they never came across a thing which they perceived with their senses to be without beginning or end, but they seek to establish their theory by means of postulates of Reason. Likewise, the Dualists exert themselves to prove the co-existence of two separate and opposing principles, the mixture of which caused the world to come into being. Surely they never witnessed two separate and opposing principles, nor the assumed process of mixture, but they try to produce arguments derived from the pure Reason in favour of their theory. In a similar way, those who believe in an eternal Matter regard it as a *Hyle*, i.e. something in which there is originally no quality of hot or cold, moist or dry, but which becomes transformed by a certain force and thus produces those four qualities. Surely their senses never perceived a thing which is lacking in all those four qualities, nor did they ever perceive a process of transformation and the generation of the four qualities such as is suggested. But they seek to prove their theory by means of arguments drawn from the pure Reason. And so it is with all other opinions, as I shall explain later. This being so, it is clear that all have agreed to accept some view concerning the origin of the world which has no basis in sense perception. If, therefore, our treatment of the subject produces something similar, namely, the doctrine of the *creatio ex nihilo*, let the reader of this book who inquires into this problem not be hasty in rejecting our theory, since from the very outset of his inquiry he was virtually asking for some result similar to this, and every student of this problem is asking for such a result. But the reader may be assured that our arguments are stronger than theirs, and that, moreover, we are in a position to disprove their arguments, whatever their school of thought. We have, too, the advantage of being supported in our doctrine by the signs and miracles of Scripture which were intended to confirm our belief. I would ask the reader to bear in mind these three facts which will meet him in every part of this book, namely, (1) that our arguments are stronger than theirs; (2) that we are able to disprove the arguments of our opponents; and (3) that we have in the bargain the testimony of the miracles narrated in Scripture.

2. FOUR ARGUMENTS FOR CREATION

From these introductory remarks I go on to affirm that our Lord (be He Exalted) has informed us that all things were created in time, and that He created them *ex nihilo*, as it is said, 'In the beginning God created the heaven and the earth' (Gen. 1: 1), and as it is further said, 'I am the Lord that maketh all things; that stretched forth the heavens alone; that spread abroad the earth by Myself' (Isa. 44: 24). He verified this truth for us by signs and miracles, and we have accepted it. I probed further into this matter with the object of finding out whether it could be verified by speculation as it had been verified by prophecy. I found that this was the case for a number of reasons, from which, for the sake of brevity, I select the following four.

(1) The first proof is based on the finite character of the universe. It is clear that heaven and earth are finite in magnitude, since the earth occupies the centre and the heaven revolves round it. From this it follows that the force residing in them is finite in magnitude. For it is impossible for an infinite force to reside in a body which is finite in magnitude. This would be contradictory to the dictates of Reason. Since, therefore, the force which preserves heaven and earth is finite, it necessarily follows that the world has a beginning and an end. Being struck by the force of this argument, I subjected it to a close examination, taking good care not to be hasty in drawing definite conclusions before having scrutinized it. I, therefore, asked myself: Perhaps the earth is infinite in length, breadth and depth? I answered: If this were the case, the sun could not encompass it and complete his revolution once every day and night, rising again in the place in which he rose the day before, and setting again in the place in which he set the day before; and so with the moon and the stars. Then I asked myself: Perhaps the heaven is infinite? To this I answered: How could this be the case seeing that all celestial bodies are moving and continually revolving round the earth? For it cannot be supposed that only the sphere that is next to us performs this rotation, whereas the others are too large to perform any movement. For by 'heaven' we understand the body which revolves, and we are not aware of anything else beyond it, far less do we believe it to be the heaven and not revolving. Then I explored further and asked: Perhaps there exists a plurality of earths and heavens, each heaven revolving round its earth. This would involve the assumption of the co-existence of an infinite number of worlds, a thing in its nature impossible. For it is inconceivable that, nature being what it is, some earth should exist above the fire, or that air should be found beneath the water. For both fire and air are light, and both earth and water are heavy. I cannot doubt

that if there were a clod of earth outside our earth, it would break through all air and fire until it reached the dust of our earth. The same would happen if there were a mass of water outside the waters of our oceans. It would cut through air and fire until it met our waters. It is, therefore, perfectly clear to me that there exists no heaven apart from our heaven, and no earth except our earth; moreover, that this heaven and this earth are finite, and that in the same way as their bodies are limited, their respective force, too, is limited and ceases to exist once it reaches its limit. It is impossible that heaven and earth should continue to exist after their force is spent, and that they should have existed before their force came into being. I found that Scripture testifies to the finite character of the world by saying, 'From the one end of the earth, even unto the other end of the earth' (Deut. 13: 8), and, 'From the one end of heaven unto the other' (Deut. 4: 32). It further testifies that the sun revolves round the earth and completes its circle every day by saying, 'The sun also ariseth, and the sun goeth down, and hasteneth to his place where he ariseth' (Eccl. 1: 5).

(2) The second proof is derived from the union of parts and the composition of segments. I saw that bodies consist of combined parts and segments fitted together. This clearly indicated to me that they are the skilful work of a skilful artisan and creator. Then I asked myself: Perhaps these unions and combinations are peculiar to the small bodies only, that is to say the bodies of the animals and plants. I, therefore, extended my observation to the earth, and found the same was true of her. For she is a union of soil and stone and sand, and the like. Then I turned my mental gaze to the heavens and found that in them there are many layers of spheres, one within another, and that there are in them also groups of luminaries called stars which are distinguished from one another by being great or small, and by being more luminous or less luminous, and these luminaries are set in those spheres. Having noted these clear signs of the union and composition which has been created in the body of the heaven and the other bodies, I believe also, on the strength of this proof, that the heaven and all it contains are created. I found that Scripture also declares that the separateness of the parts of parts of the organisms and their combination prove that they are created. In regard to man it is said, 'Thy hands have made me and fashioned me' (Ps. 119: 73); in regard to the earth it is said, 'He is God, that formed the earth and made it, He established it' (Isa. 45: 18); in regard to the heaven it is said, 'When I behold Thy heavens, the work of Thy fingers, the moon and the stars, which Thou hast established' (Ps. 8: 4).

(3) The third proof is based on the nature of the accidents. I found that no bodies are devoid of accidents which affect them either directly or indirectly. Animals, e.g. are generated, grow until they reach their maturity, then waste away and decompose. I then said to myself: Perhaps the earth as a whole is free from these accidents? On reflection, however, I found that the earth is inseparable from plants and animals which themselves are created, and it is well known that whatsoever is inseparable from things created must likewise be

created. Then I asked myself: Perhaps the heavens are free from such accidents? But, going into the matter, I found that this was not the case. The first and principal accident affecting them is their intrinsic movement which goes on without pause. There are, however, many different kinds of movement. If you compare them, you will find that some planets move slowly, others quickly. And another kind of accident is the transmission of light from one celestial body to another one, which becomes illumined by it, like the moon. The colours of the various stars also differ. Some are whitish, some reddish, others yellowish and greenish. Having thus established that these bodies are affected by accidents which are coeval with them, I firmly believe that everything which has accidents coeval with it must be created like the accident, since the accident enters into its definition. Scripture also uses the accidents of heaven and earth as argument for their beginning in time by saying, 'I, even I, have made the earth and created man upon it; I, even My hands, have stretched out the heavens, and all their hosts have I commanded' (Isa. 45: 12).

(4) The fourth proof is based on the nature of Time. I know that time is threefold: past, present and future. Although the present is smaller than any instant, I take the instant as one takes a point and say: If a man should try in his thought to ascend from that point in time to the uppermost point, it would be impossible for him to do so, inasmuch as time is now assumed to be infinite and it is impossible for thought to penetrate to the furthest point of that which is infinite. The same reason will also make it impossible that the process of generation should traverse an infinite period down to the lowest point so as ultimately to reach us. Yet if the process of generation did not reach us, we would not be generated, from which it necessarily follows that we, the multitude of generated beings, would not be generated and the beings now existent would not be existent. And since I find myself existent, I know that the process of generation has traversed time until it has reached us, and that if time were not finite, the process of generation would not have traversed it. I profess unhesitatingly the same belief with regard to future time as with regard to past time. I find that Scripture speaks in similar terms of the far distant time by saying, 'All men have looked thereon; man beholdeth it afar off' (Job 36: 25); and the faithful one says, 'I will fetch my knowledge from afar' (Job 36: 3).

It has come to my notice that a certain heretic in conversation with one of the Believers in the Unity (of God) objected to this proof. He said: 'It is possible for a man to traverse that which has an infinite number of parts by walking. For if we consider any distance which a man walks, be it a mile, or an ell, we shall find that it can be divided into an infinite number of parts.' To answer this argument some thinkers resorted to the doctrine of the indivisible atom. Others spoke of tafra (the leap). Others again asserted that all the parts (in space) are covered by corresponding parts (in time). Having carefully examined the objection raised I found it to be a sophism for this reason: the infinite divisibility of a thing is only a matter of imagination, but not a matter of reality. It is too subtle to be a matter of reality, and no such division occurs. Now if the process of generation had traversed the past in the imagination, and not in reality, then, by my life, the objection raised would be valid. But seeing that the process of generation has traversed the real time and reached us, the argument cannot invalidate our proof, because infinite divisibility exists only in the imagination.

[*Book of Doctrine and Beliefs* (trans. Alexander Altmann, in Arthur Hyman and James Walsh (eds.), *Philosophy in the Middle Ages*, Indianapolis: Hackett, 1977, 334–8).]

JOHN SCOTUS ERIUGENA
....
26 Philosophy, Scripture, and Reason

St Augustine says: 'A principal point about man's salvation is the belief and teaching that philosophy or the pursuit of wisdom is not something other than religion, for those whose teaching we disapprove of are precisely those who do not share our faith.' I say, What is the practice of philosophy but the explanation of the precepts of true religion in which the first and supreme cause of all that exists is worshipped with humility and investigated by reason? It ensues from this thought that true philosophy is true religion, and that true religion is true philosophy. Thus every type of perfect and holy teaching, wherein the rational grounds for anything is sought most earnestly and found most clearly, is that branch of learning the Greeks call 'philosophy'. [. . .]

'A Samaritan woman came to draw water' (John 4: 7). Samaria signifies the Gentiles. The woman who came out from the city is the Church, gathered from among the Gentiles, who, having accepted faith, now desire to drink of the fountain of truth itself, that is, Christ. The woman going out of the city also signifies human nature in its search for the fountain of reason to quench its thirst, that is, its innate desire for true knowledge. This desire could never be fully satisfied prior to the incarnation of Christ, who is the fount of life. By investigating the author of nature and the nature of all things by means of a study of their activities, man found that he could drink only with great effort from the natural spring of reason.

'Jesus said to her, "Give me a drink", for his disciples had gone to town in order to buy food' (John 4: 8–9). Sitting at the well, Jesus implores the infant Church, which he has chosen from among the Gentiles, to imbibe the drink of faith by which all men will believe in him. He also asks them to imbibe the drink of reason by which the Creator and Redeemer is made known through the study of nature. The disciples, searching for food in the city, represent the apostles sent into the world in order to purchase spiritual nourishment. Such nourishment, by which all the spiritual masters of the Church are satisfied, consists of faith, action, and knowledge. The first of these they request is faith, which enables them to preach; next are the actions that accord with such faith; and last, there is the rational search and understanding of the truth. This provides not only the reason why faith is preached, but also explains how action and knowledge are brought to perfection. [. . .]

The reward of those who wrestle with Sacred Scripture is pure and perfect understanding. O Lord Jesus, no other reward, no other felicity, no other joy do I request from you except to understand your words which were inspired by the Holy Spirit and were uttered without error and without recourse to falsity. This is my supreme happiness. It is the aim of perfect contemplation, because even the purest soul will not discover anything beyond this, for nothing lies beyond it. [. . .]

Properly speaking, wisdom (*sapientia*) is that capacity by which the contemplative mind, be it angelic or human, considers what is divine, eternal, and immutable; and whether this be the First Cause of all things or whether it is the First Cause of all things, which the Father has produced simultaneously and all at once in his Word. This part of reason wise men call *theology*. Understanding (*scientia*), on the other hand, is that capacity by which the theoretical mind, be it angelic or human, considers the natures of things which come forth from the first causes in the process of generation, and are subsequently divided into genera and species by means of differences and properties. . . . This part of reason is called *physics*; for physics is that natural science which considers natures that are perceptible to the senses or intellect.

[*On Predestination*, ch. 1 (from *Patrologia Latina*, ed. J. P. Migne, vol. 122, cols. 357–8); *A Commentary on St John's Gospel* (ibid. cols. 333–4); *On the Division of Nature* v. 38 (ibid. col. 1010) and iii. 3 (ibid. col. 629A); all trans. Martin Stone.]

Section III

The Medieval Period

INTRODUCTION

I t is of course ludicrous to suppose that one can provide a balanced summary of one thousand years of intense discussion of the relations between faith and reason in fifty pages of extracts, or even in 500 pages. What the reader has been presented with here is no more than a taster. The medieval era was an intensely philosophical and theological period, when reason was brought to further and further refinement in an effort to elucidate, speculate about, and defend the faith; or rather, the faiths. For Muslim and Jewish philosophers used similar means to elucidate their faiths, though often in areas of common concern. Indeed, one of the crucial developments in this period, which marked the beginnings of scholasticism, was that the Arabs transmitted the works of Aristotle to Christianity, a development which had a profound effect on the course of medieval philosophy and theology.

Until then, Augustine remained the dominant figure, both theologically and philosophically, at least in the Western half of Christendom, working out not only a positive relation between Platonism and Christianity (a relation which he gives graphic personal expression to in his *Confessions*), but also the limitations; where God's revelation speaks clearly, then non-Christian thought must yield. But Augustine frequently tempers this by affirming that anticipations of revealed truth can often be found in the best classical authors. As we noted, it is in Augustine that the programme of faith seeking understanding through philosophical reflection and argument achieves self-conscious expression, a programme which came to be the dominant motif of Anselm's work.

So if, in the Western Church at least, the towering figure of St Augustine remained the dominant theological influence, the resources of reason were augmented by the rediscovery of Aristotle by Christian thinkers. This marks one important difference between the early medieval period, represented by St Anselm, and what followed. But even by the time of Anselm there is a notable tightening up of philosophical style by comparison with the rather florid and rhetorical Augustine; one might even say that such a development was made in anticipation of the arrival of Aristotle on the scene.

The rediscovery of Aristotle found its culmination in the stupendous synthesis of Christian and Aristotelian thought by Aquinas in the *SummaTheologiae* and the *Summa contra Gentiles* and in numerous other writings. It was a synthesis, and not a take-over. One reason for this was the determination of such as Aquinas to remain faithful to Scripture and the teaching of the early church and of Augustine. So Aquinas, for example, does not hesitate to depart from the teaching of 'the philosopher' when he judges the need to; as over the eternity of matter (where the testimony of revelation has priority over Aristotle's arguments), over the nature of angels, and over much else besides. Nevertheless, the way in which Aquinas finds intellectual resources in Aristotle to develop article after article of the Christian faith is truly amazing. Another reason why Aristotle did not take over the Christian faith lies in the continuing influence of the negative theology of the Pseudo-Dionysius. Indeed the degree of such influence can often act as a litmus test heralding different theological and philosophical approaches, not only among Christians, but also among Arabs and Jews. This influence, when stressed at the expense of everything else, takes the writer out of the realm in which faith and reason interact, into mysticism. The three-way conversation between Jew, Christian, and Arab over matters of faith and reason provides one of the most notable and characteristic features of medieval intellectual life.

Anselm continues the Augustinian project of faith seeking understanding; he sees his ontological argument not as a free-standing proof of God's existence, but as a reflection on the inner nature of God, his perfection. Though he regards human reason as a powerful tool, he also recognizes the limits of human understanding; he is no rationalist. Another approach to the Augustinian project which also finds warrant in Augustine himself is to think of the understanding in question as a direct apprehension, as Bonaventure characteristically does.

The synthesis of Christian theology and Aristotle epitomized in Aquinas is reflected in selections of the proofs of God's existence, in which the influence of Aristotle's theology, and of God as the unmoved mover, is evident. Less clear is the exact position of the proofs in Aquinas's scheme of things. In what sense are the proofs necessary for making the faith reasonable? Are they endeavours of faith, or prerequisites? Perhaps it is necessary for some, but not for everyone, that there are convincing proofs of God's existence. Aquinas is also represented by extracts on the beginning of the world (in which he sharply departs from Aristotle in his appeal to revelation) and on the nature of faith itself, on the uneasy combination of the cognitive (for faith involves believing propositions) and the volitional (for faith is meritorious); and of its rational incompleteness and yet its certainty.

In stressing, as we are doing, the positive interactions between faith and reason, both in the development of natural theology and in the gaining of a greater understanding of the faith, it is easy to lose sight of the firmness with which all Christian thinkers in this era adhered to God's revelation in the Bible. So Alexander of Hales (1170–1245) could say 'What is known by divine inspiration is recognized as more true than what is known by human reason, inasmuch as it is impossible for falsehood to be in inspiration while reason is infected with many.'

The *Sentences* of Peter Lombard was a compendium of extracts from the Church Fathers and others, and became very influential, with many theologians cutting their teeth with commentaries on the sentences. The extract included here is typical in style and indicates a clear subordination of reason to matters of faith.

However, it would be wrong to think of the estimate of the ability of reason to aid faith as being uniform. The medieval period was not a dull monochrome. So while towards the end of this period natural theology is given renewed expression in the thinking of Duns Scotus, William of Ockham argues for a much more limited role for reason, and he may be said to foreshadow the renewed emphasis upon the supreme authority of the Bible that was characteristic of the Reformation. And the extract from Petrarcha is a herald of the Renaissance.

27 The Ontological Argument

O Lord, I acknowledge and give thanks that You created in me Your image so that I may remember, contemplate, and love You. But this image has been so effaced by the abrasion of transgressions, so hidden from sight by the dark billows of sin, that unless You renew and refashion it, it cannot do what it was created to do. Lord, I do not attempt to comprehend Your sublimity, because my intellect is not at all equal to such a task. But I yearn to understand some measure of Your truth, which my heart believes and loves. For I do not seek to understand in order to believe but I believe in order to understand. For I believe even this: that I shall not understand unless I believe.

CHAPTER TWO: GOD TRULY, [OR REALLY], EXISTS

Therefore, Lord, Giver of understanding to faith, grant me to understand—to the degree You deem best—that You exist, as we believe, and that You are what we believe You to be. Indeed, we believe You to be something than which nothing greater can be thought. Is there, then, no such nature as You, for the Fool has said in his heart that God does not exist? But surely when this very Fool hears the words 'something than which nothing greater can be thought,' he understands what he hears. And what he understands is in his understanding, even if he does not understand [judge] it to exist. Indeed, for a thing to be in the understanding is different from understanding [judging] that this thing exists. For when an artist envisions what he is about to paint, he has it in his understanding, but he does not yet understand [judge] that there exists what he has not yet painted. But after he has painted it, he has it in his understanding and he understands [judges] that what he has painted exists. So even the Fool is convinced that something than which nothing greater can be thought exists at least in his understanding; for when he hears of this being, he understands [what he hears], and whatever is understood is in the understanding. But surely that than which a greater cannot be thought cannot be only in the understanding. For if it were only in the understanding, it could be thought to exist also in reality—which is greater [than existing only in the understanding]. Therefore, if that than which a greater cannot be thought existed only in the understanding, then that which a greater *cannot* be thought would be that than which a greater *can* be thought! But surely this conclusion is impossible. Hence, without doubt, something than which a greater cannot be thought exists both in the understanding and in reality.

CHAPTER THREE: GOD CANNOT BE THOUGHT NOT TO EXIST

Assuredly, this being exists so truly [really] that it cannot even be thought not to exist. For there can be thought to exist something whose non-existence is inconceivable; and this thing is greater than anything whose non-existence is conceivable. Therefore, if that than which a greater cannot be thought could be thought not to exist, then that than which a greater cannot be thought would not be that than which a greater cannot be thought—a contradiction. Hence, something than which a greater cannot be thought exists so truly [really] that it cannot even be thought not to exist.

And You are this being, O Lord our God. Therefore, Lord my God, You exist so truly [really] that You cannot even be thought not to exist. And this is rightly the case. For if any mind could conceive of something better than You, the creature would rise above the Creator and would sit in judgment over the Creator—an utterly preposterous consequence. Indeed, except for You alone, whatever else exists can be conceived not to exist. Therefore, You alone exist most truly [really] of all and thus most greatly of all; for whatever else there is does not exist as truly [really] as You and thus does not exist as much as do You. Since, then, it is so readily clear to a rational mind that You exist most greatly of all, why did the Fool say in his heart that God does not exist? Why indeed except because he is foolish and simple!

CHAPTER FOUR: HOW THE FOOL SAID IN HIS HEART WHAT CANNOT BE THOUGHT

Yet, since to say something in one's heart is to think it, how did the Fool say in his heart what he was not able to think, or how was he unable to think what he did say in his heart? Now, if he really—rather, since he really—both thought [what he did] because he said it in his heart and did not say it in his heart because he was unable to think it, then there is not merely one sense in which something is said in one's heart, or is thought. For in one sense an object is thought when the word signifying it is thought, and in another when what the object is [i.e., its essence] is understood. Thus, in the first sense but not at all in the second, God can be thought not to exist. Indeed, no one who understands what God is can think that God does not exist, even though he says these words [viz. 'God does not exist'] in his heart either meaninglessly or else bizarrely. For God is that than which a greater cannot be thought. Anyone who comprehends (*bene intelligit*) this, surely understands (*intelligit*) that God so exists that He cannot even conceivably not exist. Therefore, anyone who understands that this is the manner in which God exists cannot think that He does not exist.

I thank You, good Lord, I thank You that what at first I believed through Your giving, now by Your enlightening I so understand that even if I did not want to believe that You exist, I could not fail to understand [that You exist].

[*Proslogion* (in *Anselm of Canterbury*, i, ed. and trans. Jasper Hopkins and Herbert W. Richardson, London: SCM Press, 1974, 93–5).]

But furthermore, just as the will of God is the cause that what has not yet been made should come to be in the first place, so too is it no less powerful a cause that things that have been lost should return to the rank [appropriate to] their station. 'For do I will the death of the impious?, says the Lord. Rather, I will that he be converted and live' (Ez. 18: 23).

So, to get back to the point, what prevents God from being able to raise up a virgin after falling? Is he unable to do it because he does not want to? And does he not want to because it is evil, just as it was said that God neither wants nor is able to lie, to commit perjury, or to do anything evil? But heaven forbid that it should be bad for a violated woman to turn into a virgin! Indeed, just as it is evil for a virgin to be violated, so there is no doubt it would be good for her, once violated, to revert to [being a] virgin [again], if the order of the divine plan granted it. . . .

To be sure, for a virgin to be 'raised up' after falling is understood in two ways, namely, either with respect to the fullness of merit or with respect to the integrity of the flesh. So let us see whether God is strong enough to do both.

Now with respect to merit, the Apostle calls the company of the faithful a 'virgin' when he says to the Corinthians, 'For I promised you to one man, a chaste virgin to show to Christ' (2 Cor. 11: 2). For in that people of God there were not only virgins, but also many women bound in marriage or living continently after losing their virginity.

And the Lord says through the prophet, 'If a man puts his wife aside, and she goes off and takes another man, will he ever go back to her? Will not the woman be called defiled and polluted? But you have fornicated with many lovers. Nevertheless, come back to me, says the Lord' (Jer. 3: 1).

This coming back to the Lord, as far as the quality of the merit is concerned, is plainly this, that a corrupted woman should become whole [again], that a virgin be retrieved from prostitution. . . .

Observe that it has been proved, in my opinion, that with respect to merit, God can 'raise up' a virgin after falling.

But with respect to the flesh, who can doubt even with an insane mind that he, who restores crushed [spirits], [who] releases those in chains, who cures every weakness and every infirmity, cannot restore the virginal barrier? Oh yes, he who put the body itself together out of the thinnest seminal fluid, who in the human form diversified the species through the various features of the limbs, who made what did not yet exist into the pinnacle of creation—once it existed, he could not get it back when it went bad?

I say it outright, I say without fear of contradiction by scoffing quibbles, I affirm that the omnipotent God is strong enough to make any woman, [even one who has been] married many times, a virgin again, and to restore in her flesh the seal of incorruption, just as she emerged from her mother's womb.

I have said these things, not to defame blessed Jerome, who spoke with pious zeal, but to disprove with the unconquerable reason of faith those who take the occasion from his words to assert that God is incapable.[. . .]

XVII

[. . .] we can say without absurdity that God, in that invariable and always most stable eternity of his, can make it so that what was made, with respect to our transcience, was not made. That is, so that we may say 'God is able to act so that Rome, which was founded in antiquity, was not founded'. The expression 'is able', in the present tense, is used appropriately here, as far as the immovable eternity of the omnipotent God is concerned. But with respect to us, for whom there is uninterrupted mobility and continuous movement, we would more properly say 'was able', as we usually do.

Hence we understand the above statement 'God is able [to act] so that Rome was not founded' from the point of view of him, namely, for whom 'there is no shifting, or shadow of alteration' (James 1: 17). Of course for us this means 'God was able'. For with respect to his eternity, whatever God was able [to do], he also is able [to do] it, because his present never turns into the past, his today does not change into tomorrow or into any alteration of time. Rather, just as he always is what he is, so [too] whatever is present before him is always present before him.

Thus, just as we can properly say 'God was able [to bring it about] that Rome, before it had been founded, was not founded', so can we no less appropriately say 'God is able [to bring it about] that Rome, even after it has been founded, was not founded'. He 'was able' with respect to us; he 'is able' with respect to himself. For the being able that God had before Rome came to be persists, always unchangeable and immovable, in God's eternity. Hence, whatever thing we can say God 'was able' [to do], so no less can we say that God 'is able' [to do] it. For his being able, which is of course coeternal with him, is always fixed and immobile. It is only with respect to us that there is a 'having been able' for God. With respect to himself, however, there is no having been able, but rather always an unmoved, fixed and invariable being able.

Whatever God was able [to do] no doubt he also is able to do. For him, certainly, just as there is no being and having been, but [only] everlasting being, so [too] as a consequence [there is] no having been able and being able, but [only] an always immobile and everlasting being able.

Just as he does not say 'I am who was and am' but rather 'I am who am' and 'He who is, sent me to you' (Exod. 3: 14), so there is no doubt that he says as a consequence not 'I am who was able and am able' but rather '[I am] who immovably and eternally am able'. For that being able that was with God before the ages [still] is today, and that being able that belongs to him today belonged [to him] no less before the ages, and will eternally persist, still fixed and immobile, for all the ages to come.

Therefore, just as God was able, before all things were made, [to bring it about] that they would not be made, so no less is he able even now [to bring it about] that the things that were made had not existed. For the being able that he had then is neither changed nor taken away. Rather, just as he always is what he is, so too God's being able cannot be changed. For it is he who says through the prophet, 'I am God, and I am not changed' (Mal. 2: 6), and in the Gospel, 'Before Abraham came to be, I am' (John 8: 58). He is not changed, after the fashion of our [own] condition, from being about to be to being, or from being to having been. Rather, he is always the same, and always is what he is.

Thus, just as one and the same God always is, so being able [to do] all things is present in him, imperishably and without failing. And just as we say truly and without any contradiction that what now and always is God was [also] before the ages, so no less truly do we say that what now and always God is able [to do] he was [also] able [to do] before the ages. Thus, if through all [ages] God is able [to do] whatever he was able [to do] at the beginning, but before the foundation of things he was able [to bring it about] that things that have now been made were not made in any way, therefore he is able [to bring it about] that the made [things] did not exist at all.

In fact, his being able is fixed and eternal, so that anything he was ever able [to do] he always is able [to do]. Neither does the difference of times make any room for change in eternity. Rather, just as he is the same now as he was in the beginning, so too he is able [to do] everything whatsoever that he was able [to do] before the ages.

We must, therefore, put an end to the dispute before us. Accordingly, if being able [to do] all things is coeternal with God, God was able [to bring it about] that things that have been made were not made. Therefore, it is to be asserted stead-fastly and faithfully that God, just as he is said [to be] omnipotent, so with absolutely no exception he is truly able [to do] all things, whether with respect to things that have been made or with respect to things that have not been made.

Thus, the passage of Esther may be placed as an inviolable seal at the end of our work: 'Lord, omnipotent king, all things are put in your power, and there is no one who can resist your will. For you made heaven and earth and whatever is contained in the circuit of the heaven. You are lord of all; neither is there anyone who resists your majesty' (Esther 13: 9–11).

[*Letter on Divine Omnipotence* iii–v, xvii (in Andrew B. Schoedinger (ed.), *Readings in Medieval Philosophy*, New York: Oxford University Press, 1996, 298–9, 301–2).]

MOSES MAIMONIDES

29   Language and Creation

It will now be clear to you, that every time you establish by proof the negation of a thing in reference to God, you become more perfect, while with every additional positive assertion you follow your imagination and recede from the true knowledge of God. Only by such ways must we approach the knowledge of God, and by such researches and studies as would show us the inapplicability of what is inadmissible as regards the Creator, not by such methods as would prove the necessity of ascribing to Him anything extraneous to His essence, or asserting that He has a certain perfection, when we find it to be a perfection in relation to us. The perfections are all to some extent acquired properties, and a property which must be acquired does not exist in everything capable of making such acquisition.

You must bear in mind, that by affirming anything of God, you are removed from Him in two respects; first, whatever you affirm, is only a perfection in relation to us; secondly, He does not possess anything superadded to this essence; His essence includes all His perfections, as we have shown. Since it is a well-known fact that even that knowledge of God which is accessible to man cannot be attained except by negations, and that negations do not convey a true idea of the being to which they refer, all people, both of past and present generations, declared that God cannot be the object of human comprehension, that none but Himself comprehends what He is, and that our knowledge consists in knowing that we are unable truly to comprehend Him. All philosophers say, 'He has overpowered us by His grace, and is invisible to us through the intensity of His light,' like the sun which cannot be perceived by eyes which are too weak to bear its rays. Much more has been said on this topic, but it is useless to repeat it here. The idea is best expressed in the book of Psalms, 'Silence is praise to Thee' (lxv. 2). It is a very expressive remark on this subject; for whatever we utter with the intention of extolling and of praising Him, contains something that cannot be applied to God, and includes derogatory expressions; it is therefore more becoming to be silent, and to be content with intellectual reflection, as has been recommended by men of the highest culture, in the words 'Commune with your own heart upon your bed, and be still' (Ps. iv. 4). You must surely know the following celebrated passage in the Talmud—would that all passages in the Talmud were like that!—although it is known to you, I quote it literally, as I wish to point out to you the ideas contained in it: 'A certain person, reading prayers in the presence of Rabbi Haninah, said, "God, the great, the valiant and the tremendous, the powerful, the strong, and the mighty."—The rabbi said to him, Have you finished all the praises of your Master? The three epithets, "God, the great, the valiant and the tremendous," we should not have applied to God, had Moses not mentioned them in the Law, and had not the men of the Great Synagogue come forward subsequently and established their use in the prayer; and you say all this! Let this be illustrated by a parable. There was once an earthly king, possessing millions of gold coin; he was praised for owning millions of silver coin; was this not really dispraise to him?' Thus far the opinion of the pious rabbi. Consider, first, how repulsive and annoying the accumulation of all these positive attributes was to him; next, how he showed that, if we had only to follow our reason, we should never have composed these prayers, and we should not have uttered any of them. It has, however, become necessary to address men in words that should leave some idea in their minds, and, in accordance with the saying of our Sages, 'The Torah speaks in the language of men,' the Creator has been described to us in terms of our own perfections; but we should not on that account have uttered any other than the three above-mentioned attributes, and we should not have used them as names of God except when meeting with them in reading the Law. Subsequently, the men of the Great Synagogue, who were prophets, introduced these expressions also into the prayer, but we should not on that account use [in our prayers] any other attributes of God. The principal lesson to be derived from this passage is that there are two reasons for our employing those phrases in our prayers: first, they occur in the Pentateuch; secondly, the Prophets introduced them into the prayer. Were it not for the first reason, we should never have uttered them; and were it not for the second reason, we should not have copied them from the Pentateuch to recite them in our prayers; how then could we approve of the use of those numerous attributes! You also learn from this that we ought not to mention and employ in our prayers all the attributes we find applied to God in the books of the Prophets; for he does not say, 'Were it not that Moses, our Teacher, said them, we should not have been able to use them'; but he adds another condition—'and had not the men of the Great Synagogue come forward and established their use in the prayer,' because only for that reason are we allowed to use them in our prayers. We cannot approve of what those foolish persons do who are extravagant in praise, fluent and prolix in the prayers they compose, and in the hymns they make in the desire to approach the Creator. They describe God in attributes which would be an offence if applied to a human being; for those persons have no knowledge of these great and important principles, which are not accessible to the ordinary intelligence of man. Treating the Creator as a familiar object, they describe Him and speak of Him in any expressions they think proper; they eloquently continue to praise Him in that manner, and believe that they can thereby influence Him and produce an effect on Him. If they find some phrase suited to their object in the words of the Prophets they are still more inclined to consider that they are free to make use of such texts—which should at least be explained—to employ them in their literal sense, to derive new expressions from them, to form from them numerous variations, and to found whole compositions on them. This license is frequently met with in the compositions of the singers, preachers, and others who imagine themselves to be able to compose a poem. Such authors write things which partly are real heresy, partly contain such folly and absurdity that they naturally cause those who hear them to laugh, but also to feel grieved at the thought that such things can be uttered in reference to God. Were it not that I pitied the authors for their defects, and did not wish to injure them, I should have cited some passages to show you their mistakes; besides, the fault of their compositions is obvious to all intelligent persons. You must consider it, and think thus: If slander and libel is a great sin, how much greater is the sin of those who speak with looseness of tongue in reference to God, and describe Him by attributes which are far below Him; and I declare that they not only commit an ordinary sin, but unconsciously at least incur the guilt of profanity and blasphemy. This applies both to the multitude that listens to such prayers, and to the foolish man that recites them. Men, however, who understand the fault of such compositions, and, nevertheless, recite them, may be classed, according to my opinion, among those to whom the following words are applied: 'And the children of Israel used words that were not right against the Lord their God' (2 Kings xvii. 9); and "utter error against the Lord" (Isa. xxxii. 6). If you are of those who regard the honour of their Creator, do not listen in any way to them, much less utter what they say, and still less compose such prayers, knowing how great is the offence of one who hurls aspersions against the Supreme Being. There is no necessity at all for you to use positive attributes of God with the view of magnifying Him in your thoughts, or to go beyond the limits which the men of the Great Synagogue have introduced in the prayers and in the blessings, for this is sufficient for all purposes, and even more than sufficient, as Rabbi Haninah said. Other attributes, such as occur in the books of the Prophets, may be uttered when we meet with them in reading those books; but we must bear in mind what has already been explained, that they are either attributes of God's actions, or expressions implying the negation of the opposite. This likewise should not be divulged to the multitude; but a reflection of this kind is fitted for the few only who believe that the glorification of God does not consist in *uttering* that which is not to be uttered, but in *reflecting* on that on which man should reflect.

We will now conclude our exposition of the wise words of R. Haninah. He does not employ any such simile as: 'A king who possesses millions of gold denarii, and is praised as having hundreds'; for this would imply that God's perfections, although more perfect than those ascribed to man are still of the same kind; but this is not the case, as has been proved. The excellence of the simile consists in the words: 'who possesses golden denarii, and is praised as having silver denarii'; this implies that these attributes, though perfections as regards ourselves, are not such as regards God; in reference to Him they would all be defects, as is distinctly suggested in the remark, 'Is this not an offence to Him?'

I have already told you that all these attributes, whatever perfection they may denote according to your idea, imply defects in reference to God, if applied to Him in the same sense as they are used in reference to ourselves. Solomon has already given us sufficient instruction on this subject by saying, 'For God is in heaven, and thou upon earth; therefore let thy words be few' (Eccles. v. 2).

I will give you in this chapter some illustrations, in order that you may better understand the propriety of forming as many negative attributes as possible, and the impropriety of ascribing to God any positive attributes. A person may know for certain that a 'ship' is in existence, but he may not know to what object that name is applied, whether to a substance or to an accident; a second person then learns that the ship is not an accident; a third, that it is not a mineral; a fourth, that it is not a plant growing in the earth; a fifth, that it is not a body whose parts are joined together by nature; a sixth, that it is not a flat object like boards or doors; a seventh, that it is not a sphere; an eighth, that it is not pointed; a ninth, that it is not round-shaped; nor equilateral; a tenth, that it is not solid. It is clear that this tenth person has almost arrived at the correct notion of a 'ship' by the foregoing negative attributes, as if he had exactly the same notion as those have who imagine it to be a wooden substance which is hollow, long, and composed of many pieces of wood, that is to say, who know it by positive attributes. Of the other persons in our illustration, each one is more remote from the correct notion of a ship than the next mentioned, so that the first knows nothing about it but the name. In the same manner you will come nearer to the knowledge and comprehension of God by the negative attributes. But you must be careful, in what you negative, to negative by proof, not by mere words, for each time you ascertain by proof that a certain thing, believed to exist in the Creator, must be negatived, you have undoubtedly come one step nearer to the knowledge of God.

It is in this sense that some men come very near to God, and others remain exceedingly remote from Him, not in the sense of those who are deprived of vision, and believe that God occupies a place, which man can physically approach or from which he can recede. Examine this well, know it, and be content with it. The way which will bring you nearer to God has been clearly shown to you; walk in it, if you have the desire. On the other hand, there is a great danger in applying positive attributes to God. For it has been shown that every perfection we could imagine, even if existing in God in accordance with the opinion of those who assert the existence of attributes, would in reality not be of the same kind as that imagined by us, but would only be called by the same name, according to our explanation; it would in fact amount to a negation. Suppose, e.g., you say He has knowledge, and that knowledge, which admits of no change and of no plurality, embraces many changeable things; His knowledge remains unaltered, while new things are constantly formed, and His knowledge of a thing before it exists, while it exists, and when it has ceased to exist, is the same without the least change: you would thereby declare that His knowledge is not like ours; and similarly that His existence is not like ours. You thus necessarily arrive at some negation, without obtaining a true conception of an essential attribute; on the contrary, you are led to assume that there is a plurality in God, and to believe that He, though one essence, has several unknown attributes. For if you intend to affirm them, you cannot compare them with those attributes known by us, and they are consequently not of the same kind. You are, as it were, brought by the belief in the reality of the attributes, to say that God is one subject of which several things are predicated; though the subject is not like ordinary subjects, and the predicates are not like ordinary predicates. This belief would ultimately lead us to associate other things with God, and not to believe that He is One. For of every subject certain things can undoubtedly be predicated, and although in reality subject and predicate are combined in one thing, by the actual definition they consist of two elements, the notion contained in the subject not being the same as that contained in the predicate. In the course of this treatise it will be proved to you that God cannot be a compound, and that He is simple in the strictest sense of the word.

I do not merely declare that he who affirms attributes of God has not sufficient knowledge concerning the Creator, admits some association with God, or conceives Him to be different from what He is; but I say that he unconsciously loses his belief in God. For he whose knowledge concerning a thing is insufficient, understands one part of it while he is ignorant of the other, as, e.g., a person who knows that man possesses life, but does not know that man possesses understanding; but in reference to God, in whose real existence there is no plurality, it is impossible that one thing should be known, and another unknown. Similarly he who associates an object with [the properties of] another object, conceives a true and correct notion of the one object, and applies that notion also to the other; while those who admit the attributes of God, do not consider them as identical with His essence, but as extraneous elements. Again, he who conceives an incorrect notion of an object, must necessarily have a correct idea of the object to some extent; he, however, who says that taste belongs to the category of quantity has not, according to my opinion, an incorrect notion of taste, but is entirely ignorant of its nature, for he does not know to what object the term 'taste' is to be applied.—This is a very difficult subject; consider it well.

According to this explanation you will understand, that those who do not recognize, in reference to God, the negation of things, which others negative by clear proof, are deficient in the knowledge of God, and are remote from comprehending Him. Consequently, the smaller the number of things is which a person can negative in relation to God, the less he knows of Him, as has been explained in the beginning of this chapter; but the man who affirms an attribute of God, knows nothing but the name; for the object to which, in his imagination, he applies that name, does not exist; it is a mere fiction and invention, as if he applied that name to a non-existing being, for there is, in reality, no such object. E.g., some one has heard of the elephant, and knows that it is an animal, and wishes to know its form and nature. A person, who is either misled or misleading, tells him it is an animal with one leg, three wings, lives in the depth of the sea, has a transparent body; its face is wide like that of a man, has the same form and shape, speaks like a man, flies sometimes in the air, and sometimes swims like a fish. I should not say that he described the elephant incorrectly, or that he has an insufficient knowledge of the elephant, but I would say that the thing thus described is an invention and fiction, and that in reality there exists nothing like it; it is a non-existing being, called by the name of a really existing being, and like the griffin, the centaur, and similar imaginary combinations for which simple and compound names have been borrowed from real things. The present case is analogous; namely, God, praised be His name, exists, and His existence has been proved to be absolute and perfectly simple, as I shall explain. If such a simple, absolutely existing essence were said to have attributes, as has been contended, and were combined with extraneous elements, it would in no way be an existing thing, as has been proved by us; and when we say that that essence, which is called 'God,' is a substance with many properties by which it can be described, we apply that name to an object which does not at all exist. Consider, therefore, what are the consequences of affirming attributes to God! As to those attributes of God which occur in the Pentateuch, or in the books of the Prophets, we must assume that they are exclusively employed, as has been stated by us, to convey to us some notion of the perfections of the Creator, or to express qualities of actions emanating from Him.

[*The Guide for the Perplexed*, chs. 59–60 (trans. M. Friedlander, London: Routledge and Kegan Paul, 1951, 84–9).]

PETER LOMBARD
....

30   How Creatures Manifest God

The Apostle says: 'Since the creation of the world his [God's] invisible attributes are clearly seen—his everlasting power also and divinity—being understood through the things that are made' [Rom. 1: 20]. [According to the *Ordinary Glosses*,] 'creation of the world' refers to man, either 'because he excels all other creatures by reason of his eminent position or else because he embodies something of the perfection of every other creature.' With his mind's eye, then, man has been able to grasp, or has seen, God's invisible attributes by means of the visible and invisible creation. That the truth might be made clear to him, man was given two things to help him: a nature that is rational and works fashioned by God. That is why the Apostle says: 'God manifested this to him,' namely when God created works that provide some evidence of who made them.

As [Pseudo-] Ambrose says: 'That God, who is invisible by nature, might also be known from what is visible, he fashioned a work which by its visibility made its maker manifest, so that the uncertain might be known from what is certain and that he who made what man cannot may be believed to be the God of all.' Therefore, they could have known, or did know, that he transcends every creature who produced what nothing created could either make or destroy. Let a creature possess such power and let it fashion such a heaven and such an earth and I shall admit that it is God. But because no creature can make such things, it is clear that he who did produce them surpasses every creature. By this was the human mind able to know that he is God.

Reason could have led, and did lead them to the truth about God in still another way. As Augustine says in *The City of God*: 'The most exalted philosophers recognized no body could be God and, therefore, in their quest for him they went beyond everything bodily. Convinced also that nothing mutable could be the most high God, the principle or source of all things, they looked beyond every soul or spirit subject to change. Then they saw that what is mutable can only exist in virtue of him who exists in an unqualified and incommunicable sense. They realized then that he had made all these things and was himself made by none of them.

'They considered also that whatever subsists is either a body or a spirit and that a spirit is better than a body. Better by far, however, is he who made both body and spirit.

'They also understood the beauty of a body to be sensible and the beauty of the soul to be intelligible, and they preferred intellectual to sensible beauty. We call "sensible" such things as can be seen or touched and "intelligible" such as can be perceived by mental vision. Once they perceived various degrees of beauty in mind and body, they realized if all form or beauty were lacking, things would cease to exist. They recognized there was something which produced these beautiful things, something in which beauty was ultimate and immutable, and therefore beyond compare. And they believed, with every right, that this was the source of all things, that source which itself was never made but is that by which all else was made.' See in how many ways, then, the truth of God could have been known. Though God is but one simple essence, which does not consist of different parts or accidents, the Apostle, nevertheless, speaks in the plural of the 'invisible attributes of God' because there are many ways in which the truth about God is gleaned from the things that he made. The perpetuity of creatures indicates their maker is eternal; the greatness of creatures argues to his omnipotence, from their order and arrangement he is known to be wise, from their governance he is recognized as good. All these attributes refer to divine nature as a unity.

What remains to be shown is whether the things that were made contain some trace or slight indication that God is a Trinity. On this point Augustine says: 'When we speak of the mind beholding the Creator in what he has made, we should understand this of the Trinity. For creatures do contain some trace or vestige of the Trinity. Everything produced by divine artistry manifests (a) unity, (b) form or beauty, and (c) order. Consider what creature you will and you find it to be one (e.g. bodies or souls), to have some form or beauty (e.g. bodily shapes or qualities, learning, and mental skills), and that it strives for or maintains some position or order (e.g. weights, bodily complexes, intellectual loves, or mental delights). Consequently some trace of the Trinity is to be found in creatures. For it is the Trinity that represents the ultimate origin, the most perfect beauty, and the ultimate delight of everything.' As Augustine shows in his work *Of True Religion*, the ultimate origin refers to God the Father, from whom are all things, from whom also are the Son and the Holy Spirit. 'The most perfect beauty' refers to the Son, who is the Truth of the Father in whom and with whom we venerate the Truth. 'He is in all respects like the Father and is the form of all things that have been made by the One and which strive for unity. But all things would not have been made by the Father through the Son, nor would they be preserved safe within their boundaries, if God were not supremely good. He begrudges no one anything, for to all he has given the possibility of being good. By "goodness" we understand the Holy Spirit, who is the Gift of God, whom we worship and hold to be equally unchangeable with Father and Son in a Trinity of one substance. From the consideration of creatures, then, we understand a Trinity of one substance, one God, namely, the Father from whom, the Son through whom, and the Holy Spirit in whom we have our being, i.e. a principle to which we have recourse, a form which we imitate, and the grace by which we are reconciled. In a word, there is one God by whom we were made, and his likeness by whom we are formed for unity, and his peace whereby we cleave to unity; God who spoke and it was done; and the Word by whom all was made that has substance and nature; and the Gift of his benignity by which he was pleased that nothing made through the Word and reconciled with its author, should perish.'

See that it has been shown here just how some likeness at least of the Trinity is found in creatures. Without interior revelation or a revelation of this doctrine, however, adequate knowledge of the Trinity neither was nor can be obtained from contemplation of creatures. That is why ancient philosophers could only see this trinitarian truth in a haze, as it were, and from afar. Like Pharaoh's magicians after the third plague [Exod. 8: 19], their recognition of God was defective. Nevertheless our belief in what we cannot see is helped by means of the things that were made.

[*The Sentences* i. 3. 1 (in John F. Wippel and Allan B. Wolter (eds.), *Mediaeval Philosophy*, New York: Free Press, 1969).]

ODO RIGAULD

31   Theology and Science

To the question 'Whether theology is a science?' I reply as follows. To understand the question we must note that there are two ways in which the term science can be spoken of: (i) specially and (ii) in a more general way. In the specific sense, science is the name of a disposition having certitude, which is within the scope of reason or the power of the intellect. As such, it is the name of an acquired disposition. In this sense, theology is not a science. Reason is not elevated and aided by the gift of faith since it is unable to provide us with knowledge which transcends that of all the arts and sciences both by virtue of its subject-matter (i.e. God, who transcends all things) and by reason of its technique. Theology does not advance through mere human arguments, but has reasons and principles of its own which are distinct from those of other sciences. While these principles are made evident by the grace of faith and are made manifest to a soul illumined by such grace, they are not evident to an unbeliever. Any infidel can know metaphysics because it unfolds by conceptual processes that fall within reason, but only a believer can know theology for the reasons cited above.

But if science is understood in a more general way as any kind of certain intellectual knowledge and not as a virtue (and here I say 'intellectual' to distinguish it from sensory knowledge; 'certain' to differentiate it from opinions; and 'not a virtue' to set it apart from faith) then I grant that theology is a science. Herein lies the basis for those arguments that purport to show that theology is a science. Understood in this fashion, science embraces both wisdom and knowledge.

[. . .] As for the objection that theology ought not to be called science but wisdom since science is concerned with the temporal and wisdom with the eternal, one must point out that theology is neither science nor wisdom in the sense that Augustine speaks of, for he has in mind the gifts of the Holy Spirit. If theological knowledge is accompanied by an experience of internal grace, however, we can grant that it would be proper to speak of it as wisdom rather than as science. A distinction of the following sort ought to be introduced. There is knowledge as science, of which the liberal arts provide us with the best example. Then there is wisdom as science, and this is metaphysics or first philosophy. Here, there is no internal pleasure as in our experience of the gifts of the Holy Spirit. Then there is science as wisdom; we find this in the Old Testament. Finally, there is wisdom as wisdom, which we find in the New Testament. That theology is wisdom, then, one can readily grant, but this does not prevent it from being called a science in the general sense of this term.

[*Theological Questions*, q. 1 (*Codex Vaticanus Latinus* 4263, fos. 44b–45c, trans. Martin Stone).]

THOMAS AQUINAS

32 **Whether there is a God**

Under the first of these questions there are three points of inquiry:

1. is it self-evident that there is a God?
2. can it be made evident?
3. is there a God?

ARTICLE I. IS IT SELF-EVIDENT THAT THERE IS A GOD?

The first point: 1. It seems self-evident that there is a God. For things are said to be self-evident to us when we are innately aware of them, as, for example, first principles. Now as Damascene says when beginning his book, *the awareness that God exists is implanted by nature in everybody*. That God exists is therefore self-evident.

2. Moreover, a proposition is self-evident if we perceive its truth immediately upon perceiving the meaning of its terms: a characteristic, according to Aristotle, of first principles of demonstration. For example, when we know what wholes and parts are, we know at once that wholes are always bigger than their parts. Now once we understand the meaning of the word 'God' it follows that God exists. For the word means 'that than which nothing greater can be meant'. Consequently, since existence in thought and fact is greater than existence in thought alone, and since, once we understand the word 'God', he exists in thought, he must also exist in fact. It is therefore self-evident that there is a God.

3. Moreover, it is self-evident that truth exists, for even denying it would admit it. Were there no such thing as truth, then it would be true that there is no truth; something then is true, and therefore there is truth. Now God is truth itself; *I am the way, the truth and the life*. That there is a God, then, is self-evident.

On the other hand, nobody can think the opposite of a self-evident proposition, as Aristotle's discussion of first principles makes clear. But the opposite of the proposition 'God exists' can be thought, for *the fool* in the psalms *said in his heart: There is no God*. That God exists is therefore not self-evident.

Reply: A self-evident proposition, though always self-evident in itself, is sometimes self-evident to us and sometimes not. For a proposition is self-evident when the predicate forms part of what the subject means; thus it is self-evident that man is an animal, since being an animal is part of the meaning of man. If therefore it is evident to everybody what it is to be this subject and what it is to have such a predicate, the proposition itself will be self-evident to everybody. This is clearly the case with first principles of demonstration, which employ common terms evident to all, such as 'be' and 'not be', 'whole' and 'part'. But if what it is to be this subject or have such a predicate is not evident to some people, then the proposition, though self-evident in itself, will not be so to those to whom its subject and predicate are not evident. And this is why Boethius can say that *certain notions are* self-evident and *commonplaces only to the learned, as, for example, that only bodies can occupy space*.

I maintain then that the proposition 'God exists' is self-evident in itself, for, as we shall see later, its subject and predicate are identical, since God is his own existence. But, because what it is to be God is not evident to us, the proposition is not self-evident to us, and needs to be made evident. This is done by means of things which, though less evident in themselves, are nevertheless more evident to us, by means, namely, of God's effects.

Hence: 1. The awareness that God exists is not implanted in us by nature in any clear or specific way. Admittedly, man is by nature aware of what by nature he desires, and he desires by nature a happiness which is to be found only in God. But this is not, simply speaking, awareness that there is a God, any more than to be aware of someone approaching is to be aware of Peter, even should it be Peter approaching: many, in fact, believe the ultimate good which will make us happy to be riches, or pleasure, or some such thing.

2. Someone hearing the word 'God' may very well not understand it to mean 'that than which nothing greater can be thought', indeed, some people have believed God to be a body. And even if the meaning of the word 'God' were generally recognized to be 'that than which nothing greater can be thought', nothing thus defined would thereby be granted existence in the world of fact, but merely as thought about. Unless one is given that something in fact exists than which nothing greater can be thought—and this nobody denying the existence of God would grant—the conclusion that God in fact exists does not follow.

3. It is self-evident that there exists truth in general, but it is not self-evident to us that there exists a First Truth.

ARTICLE 2. CAN IT BE MADE EVIDENT?

The second point: 1. That God exists cannot, it seems, be made evident. For that God exists is an article of faith, and since, as St Paul says, faith is concerned with *the unseen*, its propositions cannot be demonstrated, that is made evident. It is therefore impossible to demonstrate that God exists.

2. Moreover, the central link of demonstration is a definition. But Damascene tells us that we cannot define what God is, but only what he is not. Hence we cannot demonstrate that God exists.

3. Moreover, if demonstration of God's existence were possible, this could only be by arguing from his effects. Now God and his effects are incommensurable; for God is infinite and his effects finite, and the finite cannot measure the infinite. Consequently, since effects incommensurate with their cause cannot make it evident, it does not seem possible to demonstrate that God exists.

On the other hand, St Paul tells us that *the hidden things of God can be clearly understood from the things that he has made*. If so, one must be able to demonstrate that God exists from the things that he has made, for knowing whether a thing exists is the first step towards understanding it.

Reply: There are two types of demonstration. One, showing 'why', follows the natural order of things among themselves, arguing from cause to effect; the other, showing 'that', follows the order in which we know things, arguing from effect to cause (for when an effect is more apparent to us than its cause, we come to know the cause through the effect). Now any effect of a cause demonstrates that that cause exists, in cases where the effect is better known to us, since effects are dependent upon causes, and can only occur if the causes already exist. From effects evident to us, therefore, we can demonstrate what in itself is not evident to us, namely, that God exists.

Hence: 1. The truths about God which St Paul says we can know by our natural powers of reasoning—that God exists, for example—are not numbered among the articles of faith, but are presupposed to them. For faith presupposes natural knowledge, just as grace does nature and all perfections that which they perfect. However, there is nothing to stop a man accepting on faith some truth which he personally cannot demonstrate, even if that truth in itself is such that demonstration could make it evident.

2. When we argue from effect to cause, the effect will take the place of a definition of the cause in the proof that the cause exists; and this especially if the cause is God. For when proving anything to exist, the central link is not what that thing is (we cannot even ask what it is until we know that it exists), but rather what we are using the name of the thing to mean. Now when demonstrating from effects that God exists, we are able to start from what the word 'God' means, for, as we shall see, the names of God are derived from these effects.

3. Effects can give comprehensive knowledge of their cause only when commensurate with it: but, as we have said, any effect whatever can make it clear that a cause exists. God's effects, therefore, can serve to demonstrate that God exists, even though they cannot help us to know him comprehensively for what he is.

ARTICLE 3: IS THERE A GOD?

The third point: 1. It seems that there is no God. For if, of two mutually exclusive things, one were to exist without limit, the other would cease to exist. But by the word 'God' is implied some limitless good. If God then existed, nobody would ever encounter evil. But evil is encountered in the world. God therefore does not exist.

2. Moreover, if a few causes fully account for some effect, one does not seek more. Now it seems that everything we observe in this world can be fully accounted for by other causes, without assuming a God. Thus natural effects are explained by natural causes, and contrived effects by human reasoning and will. There is therefore no need to suppose that a God exists.

On the other hand, Scripture represents God as declaring, *I am who am.*

Reply: There are five ways in which one can prove that there is a God.

The first and most obvious way is based on change. Some things in the world are certainly in process of change: this we plainly see. Now anything in process of change is being changed by something else. This is so because it is character-istic of things in process of change that they do not yet have the perfection towards which they move, though able to have it; whereas it is characteristic of something causing change to have that perfection already. For to cause change is to bring into being what was previously only able to be, and this can only be done by something that already is: thus fire, which is actually hot, causes wood, which is able to be hot, to become actually hot, and in this way causes change in the wood. Now the same thing cannot at the same time be both actually x and potentially x, though it can be actually x and potentially y: the actually hot cannot at the same time be potentially hot, though it can be potentially cold. Consequently, a thing in process of change cannot itself cause that same change; it cannot change itself. Of necessity therefore anything in process of change is being changed by something else. Moreover, this something else, if in process of change, is itself being changed by yet another thing; and this last by another. Now we must stop somewhere, otherwise there will be no first cause of the change, and, as a result, no subsequent causes. For it is only when acted upon by the first cause that the intermediate causes will produce the change: if the hand does not move the stick, the stick will not move anything else. Hence one is bound to arrive at some first cause of change not itself being changed by anything, and this is what everybody understands by God.

The second way is based on the nature of causation. In the observable world causes are found to be ordered in series; we never observe, nor ever could, something causing itself, for this would mean it preceded itself, and this is not possible. Such a series of causes must however stop somewhere; for in it an earlier member causes an intermediate and the intermediate a last (whether the intermediate be one or many). Now if you eliminate a cause you also eliminate its effects, so that you cannot have a last cause, nor an intermediate one, unless you have a first. Given therefore no stop in the series of causes, and hence no first cause, there would be no intermediate causes either, and no last effect, and this would be an open mistake. One is therefore forced to suppose some first cause, to which everyone gives the name 'God'.

The third way is based on what need not be and on what must be, and runs as follows. Some of the things we come across can be but need not be, for we find them springing up and dying away, thus sometimes in being and sometimes not. Now everything cannot be like this, for a thing that need not be, once was not; and if everything need not be, once upon a time there was nothing. But if that were true there would be nothing even now, because something that does not exist can only be brought into being by something already existing. So that if nothing was in being nothing could be brought into being, and nothing would be in being now, which contradicts observation. Not everything therefore is the sort of thing that need not be; there has got to be something that must be. Now a thing that must be, may or may not owe this necessity to something else. But just as we must stop somewhere in a series of causes, so also in the series of things which must be and owe this to other things. One is forced therefore to suppose something which must be, and owes this to no other thing than itself; indeed it itself is the cause that other things must be.

The fourth way is based on the gradation observed in things. Some things are found to be more good, more true, more noble, and so on, and other things less. But such comparative terms describe varying degrees of approximation to a superlative; for example, things are hotter and hotter the nearer they approach what is hottest. Something, therefore, is the truest and best and most noble of things, and hence the most fully in being; for Aristotle says that the truest things are the things most fully in being. Now *when many things possess some property in common, the one most fully possessing it causes it in the others: fire,* to use Aristotle's example, *the hottest of all things, causes all other things to be hot.* There is something therefore which causes in all other things their being, their goodness, and whatever other perfection they have. And this we call 'God'.

The fifth way is based on the guidedness of nature. An orderedness of actions to an end is observed in all bodies obeying natural laws, even when they lack awareness. For their behaviour hardly ever varies, and will practically always turn out well; which shows that they truly tend to a goal, and do not merely hit it by accident. Nothing however that lacks awareness tends to a goal, except under the direction of someone with awareness and with understanding; the arrow, for example, requires an archer. Everything in nature, therefore, is directed to its goal by someone with intelligence, and this we call 'God'.

[*Summa Theologiae* 1a. 1. 2 (trans. T. McDermott OP, Garden City, NY: Image Books/Doubleday, 1969, 62–70).]

THOMAS AQUINAS

33   Faith and Reason

CHAPTER 4

THAT THE TRUTH ABOUT GOD TO WHICH THE NATURAL REASON REACHES IS FITTINGLY PROPOSED TO MEN FOR BELIEF

[1] Since, therefore, there exists a twofold truth concerning the divine being, one to which the inquiry of the reason can reach, the other which surpasses the whole ability of the human reason, it is fitting that both of these truths be proposed to man divinely for belief. This point must first be shown concerning the truth that is open to the inquiry of the reason; otherwise, it might perhaps seem to someone that, since such a truth can be known by the reason, it was uselessly given to men through a supernatural inspiration as an object of belief.

[2] Yet, if this truth were left solely as a matter of inquiry for the human reason, three awkward consequences would follow.

[3] The first is that few men would possess the knowledge of God. For there are three reasons why most men are cut off from the fruit of diligent inquiry which is the discovery of truth. Some do not have the physical disposition for such work. As a result, there are many who are naturally not fitted to pursue knowledge; and so, however much they tried, they would be unable to reach the highest level of human knowledge which consists in knowing God. Others are cut off from pursuing this truth by the necessities imposed upon them by their daily lives. For some men must devote themselves to taking care of temporal matters. Such men would not be able to give so much time to the leisure of contemplative inquiry as to reach the highest peak at which human investigation can arrive, namely, the knowledge of God. Finally, there are some who are cut off by indolence. In order to know the things that the reason can investigate concerning God, a knowledge of many things must already be possessed. For almost all of philosophy is directed towards the knowledge of God, and that is why metaphysics, which deals with divine things, is the last part of philosophy to be learned. This means that we are able to arrive at the inquiry concerning the aforementioned truth only on the basis of a great deal of labour spent in study. Now, those who wish to undergo such a labour for the mere love of knowledge are few, even though God has inserted into the minds of men a natural appetite for knowledge.

[4] The second awkward effect is that those who would come to discover the above-mentioned truth would barely reach it after a great deal of time. The reasons are several. There is the profundity of this truth, which the human intellect is made capable of grasping by natural inquiry only after a long training. Then, there are many things that must be presupposed, as we have said. There is also the fact that, in youth, when the soul is swayed by the various movements of the passions, it is not in a suitable state for the knowledge of such lofty truth. On the contrary, 'one becomes wise and knowing in repose,' as it is said in the *Physics*. The result is this. If the only way open to us for the knowledge of God were solely that of the reason, the human race would remain in the blackest shadows of ignorance. For then the knowledge of God, which especially renders men perfect and good, would come to be possessed only by a few, and these few would require a great deal of time in order to reach it.

[5] The third awkward effect is this. The investigation of the human reason for the most part has falsity present within it, and this is due partly to the weakness of our intellect in judgment, and partly to the admixture of images. The result is that many, remaining ignorant of the power of demonstration, would hold in doubt those things that have been most truly demonstrated. This would be particularly the case since they see that, among those who are reputed to be wise men, each one teaches his own brand of doctrine. Furthermore, with the many truths that are demonstrated, there sometimes is mingled something that is false, which is not demonstrated but rather asserted on the basis of some probable or sophistical argument, which yet has the credit of being a demonstration.

That is why it was necessary that the unshakeable certitude and pure truth concerning divine things should be presented to men by way of faith.

[6] Beneficially, therefore, did the divine Mercy provide that it should instruct us to hold by faith even those truths that the human reason is able to investigate. In this way, all men would easily be able to have a share in the knowledge of God, and this without uncertainty and error.

[7] Hence it is written: 'Henceforward you walk not as also the Gentiles walk in the vanity of their mind, having their understanding darkened' (Eph. 4: 17–18). And again: 'All thy children shall be taught of the Lord' (Isa. 54: 13).

CHAPTER 5
THAT THE TRUTHS THE HUMAN REASON IS NOT ABLE TO
INVESTIGATE ARE FITTINGLY PROPOSED TO MEN FOR BELIEF

[1] Now, perhaps some will think that men should not be asked to believe what the reason is not adequate to investigate, since the divine Wisdom provides in the case of each thing according to the mode of its nature. We must therefore prove that it is necessary for man to receive from God as objects of belief even those truths that are above the human reason.

[2] No one tends with desire and zeal towards something that is not already known to him. But, as we shall examine later on in this work, men are ordained by the divine Providence towards a higher good than human fragility can experience in the present life. That is why it was necessary for the human mind to be called to something higher than the human reason here and now can reach, so that it would thus learn to desire something and with zeal tend towards something that surpasses the whole state of the present life. This belongs especially to the Christian religion, which in a unique way promises spiritual and eternal goods. And so there are many things proposed to men in it that transcend human sense. The Old Law, on the other hand, whose promises were of a temporal character, contained very few proposals that transcended the inquiry of the human reason. Following this same direction, the philosophers themselves, in order that they might lead men from the pleasure of sensible things to virtue, were concerned to show that there were in existence other goods of a higher nature than these things of sense, and that those who gave themselves to the active or contemplative virtues would find much sweeter enjoyment in the taste of these higher goods.

[3] It is also necessary that such truth be proposed to men for belief so that they may have a truer knowledge of God. For then only do we know God truly when we believe Him to be above everything that it is possible for man to think about Him; for, as we have shown, the divine substance surpasses the natural knowledge of which man is capable. Hence, by the fact that some things about God are proposed to man that surpass his reason, there is strengthened in man the view that God is something above what he can think.

[4] Another benefit that comes from the revelation to men of truths that

exceed the reason is the curbing of presumption, which is the mother of error. For there are some who have such a presumptuous opinion of their own ability that they deem themselves able to measure the nature of everything; I mean to say that, in their estimation, everything is true that seems to them so, and everything is false that does not. So that the human mind, therefore, might be freed from this presumption and come to a humble inquiry after truth, it was necessary that some things should be proposed to man by God that would completely surpass his intellect.

[5] A still further benefit may also be seen in what Aristotle says in the *Ethics*. There was a certain Simonides who exhorted people to put aside the knowledge of divine things and to apply their talents to human occupations. He said that 'he who is a man should know human things, and he who is mortal, things that are mortal.' Against Simonides Aristotle says that 'man should draw himself towards what is immortal and divine as much as he can.' And so he says in the *De animalibus* that, although what we know of the higher substances is very little, yet that little is loved and desired more than all the knowledge that we have about less noble substances. He also says in the *De caelo et mundo* that when questions about the heavenly bodies can be given even a modest and merely plausible solution, he who hears this experiences intense joy. From all these considerations it is clear that even the most imperfect knowledge about the most noble realities brings the greatest perfection to the soul. Therefore, although the human reason cannot grasp fully the truths that are above it, yet, if it somehow holds these truths at least by faith, it acquires great perfection for itself.

[6] Therefore it is written: 'For many things are shown to thee above the understanding of men' (Ecclus. 3: 25). Again: 'So the things that are of God no man knoweth but the Spirit of God. But to us God hath revealed them by His Spirit' (1 Cor. 2: 11, 10).

CHAPTER 6
THAT TO GIVE ASSENT TO THE TRUTHS OF FAITH IS NOT FOOLISHNESS EVEN THOUGH THEY ARE ABOVE REASON

[1] Those who place their faith in this truth, however, 'for which the human reason offers no experimental evidence,' do not believe foolishly, as though 'following artificial fables' (2 Peter 1: 16). For these 'secrets of divine Wisdom' (Job 11: 6) the divine Wisdom itself, which knows all things to the full, has deigned to reveal to men. It reveals its own presence, as well as the truth of its teaching and inspiration, by fitting arguments; and in order to confirm those truths that exceed natural knowledge, it gives visible manifestation to works that surpass the ability of all nature. Thus, there are the wonderful cures of illnesses, there is the raising of the dead, and the wonderful immutation in the heavenly bodies; and what is more wonderful, there is the inspiration given to human minds, so that simple and untutored persons, filled with the gift of the

Holy Spirit, come to possess instantaneously the highest wisdom and the readiest eloquence. When these arguments were examined, through the efficacy of the above-mentioned proof, and not the violent assault of arms or the promise of pleasures, and (what is most wonderful of all) in the midst of the tyranny of the persecutors, an innumerable throng of people, both simple and most learned, flocked to the Christian faith. In this faith there are truths preached that surpass every human intellect; the pleasures of the flesh are curbed; it is taught that the things of the world should be spurned. Now, for the minds of mortal men to assent to these things is the greatest of miracles, just as it is a manifest work of divine inspiration that, spurning visible things, men should seek only what is invisible. Now, that this has happened neither without preparation nor by chance, but as a result of the disposition of God, is clear from the fact that through many pronouncements of the ancient prophets God had foretold that He would do this. The books of these prophets are held in veneration among us Christians, since they give witness to our faith.

[2] The manner of this confirmation is touched on by St Paul: 'Which,' that is, human salvation, 'having begun to be declared by the Lord, was confirmed unto us by them that hear Him: God also bearing them witness of signs, and wonders, and divers miracles, and distributions of the Holy Ghost' (Heb. 2: 3–4).

[3] This wonderful conversion of the world to the Christian faith is the clearest witness of the signs given in the past; so that it is not necessary that they should be further repeated, since they appear most clearly in their effect. For it would be truly more wonderful than all signs if the world had been led by simple and humble men to believe such lofty truths, to accomplish such difficult actions, and to have such high hopes. Yet it is also a fact that, even in our own time, God does not cease to work miracles through His saints for the confirmation of the faith.

[4] On the other hand, those who founded sects committed to erroneous doctrines proceeded in a way that is opposite to this. The point is clear in the case of Mohammed. He seduced the people by promises of carnal pleasure to which the concupiscence of the flesh goads us. His teaching also contained precepts that were in conformity with his promises, and he gave free rein to carnal pleasure. In all this, as is not unexpected, he was obeyed by carnal men. As for proofs of the truth of his doctrine, he brought forward only such as could be grasped by the natural ability of anyone with a very modest wisdom. Indeed, the truths that he taught he mingled with many fables and with doctrines of the greatest falsity. He did not bring forth any signs produced in a supernatural way, which alone fittingly gives witness to divine inspiration; for a visible action that can be only divine reveals an invisibly inspired teacher of truth. On the contrary, Mohammed said that he was sent in the power of his arms—which are signs not lacking even to robbers and tyrants. What is more, no wise men, men trained in things divine and human, believed in him from

the beginning. Those who believed in him were brutal men and desert wanderers, utterly ignorant of all divine teaching, through whose numbers Mohammed forced others to become his followers by the violence of his arms. Nor do divine pronouncements on the part of preceding prophets offer him any witness. On the contrary, he perverts almost all the testimonies of the Old and New Testaments by making them into fabrications of his own, as can be seen by anyone who examines his law. It was, therefore, a shrewd decision on his part to forbid his followers to read the Old and New Testaments, lest these books convict him of falsity. It is thus clear that those who place any faith in his words believe foolishly.

CHAPTER 7
THAT THE TRUTH OF REASON IS NOT OPPOSED TO THE TRUTH OF THE CHRISTIAN FAITH

[1] Now, although the truth of the Christian faith which we have discussed surpasses the capacity of the reason, nevertheless that truth that the human reason is naturally endowed to know cannot be opposed to the truth of the Christian faith. For that with which the human reason is naturally endowed is clearly most true; so much so, that it is impossible for us to think of such truths as false. Nor is it permissible to believe as false that which we hold by faith, since this is confirmed in a way that is so clearly divine. Since, therefore, only the false is opposed to the true, as is clearly evident from an examination of their definitions, it is impossible that the truth of faith should be opposed to those principles that the human reason knows naturally.

[2] Furthermore, that which is introduced into the soul of the student by the teacher is contained in the knowledge of the teacher—unless his teaching is fictitious, which it is improper to say of God. Now, the knowledge of the principles that are known to us naturally has been implanted in us by God; for God is the Author of our nature. These principles, therefore, are also contained by the divine Wisdom. Hence, whatever is opposed to them is opposed to the divine Wisdom, and, therefore, cannot come from God. That which we hold by faith as divinely revealed, therefore, cannot be contrary to our natural knowledge.

[3] Again. In the presence of contrary arguments our intellect is chained, so that it cannot proceed to the knowledge of the truth. If, therefore, contrary knowledges were implanted in us by God, our intellect would be hindered from knowing truth by this very fact. Now, such an effect cannot come from God.

[4] And again. What is natural cannot change as long as nature does not. Now, it is impossible that contrary opinions should exist in the same knowing subject at the same time. No opinion or belief, therefore, is implanted in man by God which is contrary to man's natural knowledge.

[5] Therefore, the Apostle says: 'The word is nigh thee, even in thy mouth and

in thy heart. This is the word of faith, which we preach' (Rom. 10: 8). But because it overcomes reason, there are some who think that it is opposed to it: which is impossible.

[6] The authority of St Augustine also agrees with this. He writes as follows: 'That which truth will reveal cannot in any way be opposed to the sacred books of the Old and the New Testament.'

[7] From this we evidently gather the following conclusion: whatever arguments are brought forward against the doctrines of faith are conclusions incorrectly derived from the first and self-evident principles imbedded in nature. Such conclusions do not have the force of demonstration; they are arguments that are either probable or sophistical. And so, there exists the possibility to answer them.

[*Summa contra Gentiles* 1. 4–7 (trans. Anton C. Pegis, Garden City, NY: Image
Books/Doubleday, 1955, 66–75).]

THOMAS AQUINAS

34   **The Inner Act of Faith**

ARTICLE 3. WHETHER BELIEF IN ANYTHING BEYOND HUMAN REASON IS NECESSARY FOR SALVATION

The third point: 1. To believe does not seem necessary for salvation. What seems to suffice for the well being and fulfilment of any reality is whatever belongs to it in keeping with its own nature. Since matters of faith are unseen, they are beyond the nature of man's reason. Thus believing seems not to be necessary for salvation.

2. Further, on the basis of Job, *Doth not the ear discern words?*, a person takes a risk in assenting to matters the truth or falsity of which escapes his power to judge. Now when it comes to matters of faith, we cannot judge the true and the false, because there is no possibility of tracing such matters back to the first principles whereby we judge everything. Consequently, it is risky to give credence to such matters, and faith is, therefore, not required for salvation.

3. Further, man's salvation lies in God; *But the salvation of the just is from the Lord.* Yet *the invisible things of God are clearly seen, being understood by the things that are made; his eternal power also and divinity.* Since we do not believe things that we see clearly, for our salvation we do not need to believe anything.

On the other hand, *Without faith it is impossible to please God.*

Reply: We discover everywhere that where there is an ordered pattern of natures two factors concur in the full development of those lower in the pattern: one on the basis of their own operation; the other, on the basis of the operation of a higher nature. An example: on the basis of its own operation water flows towards the centre, but in virtue of lunar influence it flows around the centre—the tides come in and go out. Another example: by the movement proper to them planetary bodies go from west to east; by the influence of the primary body, from east to west.

Only the rational creature has an immediate order to God. Other creatures do not reach anything universal, but only the particular, in so far as they share in the divine good either merely by existing, the case with inanimate beings, or also by living and by knowing particulars, the case with plants or animals. In that the intelligent creature understands the meaning of good as such and of being as such, it has an immediate order to the universal source of being. For this reason the full development of the rational creature consists not only in what is proper to it in keeping with its own nature, but also in what can be ascribed to it by reason of a certain supernatural share in the divine good. This is the basis for our earlier determination that man's ultimate beatitude consists in a certain vision of God that surpasses the natural.

No one can attain to this vision of God except by being a learner with God as his teacher; *Every one that hath heard of the Father and hath learned cometh to me.* Now a person becomes a sharer in this learning not all at once but step-by-step, in keeping with human nature. Even Aristotle says that *every learner must first be a believer* in order that he may come to full knowledge. Thus in order that a person come to the full, beatific vision, the first requisite is that he believe God, as a learner believing the master teaching him.

Hence: 1. The nature of man being dependent upon a higher nature, natural knowledge is not enough for his fulfilment; a certain supernatural knowledge is needed, as we have shown.

2. Just as a person assents to the first principles through the inborn light of reason, so also a virtuous person, through the disposition given by virtue, has a right judgment about what is in keeping with his virtue. This is the way that anyone, through the light of faith divinely infused, gives assent to what is of faith and not to the opposite. There is then nothing of danger nor of *condemnation for those who are in Christ Jesus,* i.e. those enlightened by him through faith.

3. With regard to the hidden things of God faith perceives them in a higher way on many points than does natural intelligence reasoning from creatures to God. Thus the text, *Many things are shown to thee above the understanding of man.*

ARTICLE 4. WHETHER IT IS NECESSARY TO BELIEVE WHAT IS PROVABLE BY REASON

The fourth point: 1. There seems to be no need to believe matters provable by reason. Superfluity is even less a mark of God's works than it is of the works of nature. Now when something can be accomplished by the one means, anything additional is superfluous. Thus to take on faith what can be known by reason would be superfluous.

2. Further, it is necessary to believe the things of faith. But faith and science, as we have shown, do not co-exist with regard to the same point. Since, then, science extends to all that is naturally knowable, it seems that there is no place for belief in the same things.

3. Further, all matters of science share a common intelligibility. Consequently, if any of them were proposed for belief, it would be necessary to have faith with regard to them all. This is obviously false. Therefore there is no reason for us to believe anything knowable by reason.

On the other hand, we must have faith that God is one and incorporeal, points proved through reason by the philosophers.

Reply: There is a necessity for some people to assent by an act of faith not only to what surpasses reason, but also to what is within its range. There are three reasons.

The first reason is that God's truth be known sooner. That science capable of proving God's existence and other such matters about him is the last to be studied, many other sciences being presupposed to it. Consequently, without faith a person would come to a knowledge about God only late in life.

The second reason is that more people may have knowledge of God. Many people are unable to make progress in the pursuit of learning, whether because of dullness of mind, the conflicting cares and needs of daily life, or their own apathy towards study. Such people would be entirely deprived of a knowledge of God were not divine things proposed to them by way of faith.

The third reason has to do with certitude. The mind of man falls far short when it comes to the things of God. Look at the philosophers; even in searching into questions about man they have erred in many points and held contradictory views. To the end, therefore, that a knowledge of God, undoubted and secure, might be present among men, it was necessary that divine things be taught by way of faith, spoken as it were by the word of God who cannot lie.

Hence: 1. The searching of natural reason does not fill mankind's need to know even those divine realities which reason could prove. Belief in them is not, therefore, superfluous.

2. Science and faith cannot co-exist in the one person with reference to the one point. But, as already shown, it is possible with regard to the one point that one person have science, another faith.

3. Even if all scientific matters were as one in their knowability, they are not as one in being equal guides to blessedness. They are not, therefore, all proposed for belief.

[*Summa Theologiae* 2a. 2ae. 2, 3–4 (trans. T. C. O'Brien, London: Eyre and Spottiswoode, 1974, 69–79).]

35 **The Beginning**

ARTICLE 2. IS IT AN ARTICLE OF FAITH THAT THE WORLD BEGAN?

The second point: 1. No, for it appears to be a demonstrable conclusion, not a matter of faith, that the world began. For everything that is made has a beginning to its duration. Now that God is the cause producing the world can be demonstrated; indeed the more approved philosophers draw this conclusion. Accordingly it is demonstrable that the world began.

2. Moreover, we cannot but admit that the world was made by God, and therefore either from nothing or from something. But not from something, for in that event its material would have preceded the world, and Aristotle's arguments are against this when maintaining that the heavens are not produced by generation. Hence we have to subscribe to the alternative, that the world was made from nothing. This implies that it had existence after non-existence. Which means that it began to exist.

3. Besides, anything at work through intelligence sets a start for its action, as is shown by the procedure of human art. God produces things through intelligence, and therefore marks a beginning for his action. The world is his work, and therefore was not always.

4. Besides, it would clearly appear that human cultures and their geographical settlement arise at definite periods of time. This would not have happened had the world always existed.

5. That nothing can be God's equal is certain. Yet an eternal world would be his equal in duration. Hence it is certainly not eternal.

6. Moreover, if the world had always existed an infinity of days would have preceded today. An infinity of points, however, cannot be traversed. And so we would never have arrived at today, which is patently untrue.

7. Further, were the world eternal so also would be the generation of things, and one man would be generated by another *ad infinitum*, for, according to the *Physics*, the parent is the efficient cause of the child. On this supposition you would have an infinite series of efficient causes, which is disproved in the *Metaphysics*.

8. Further, if the world and generation have been going on for ever then an infinite number of human beings have come before us. Now the human soul is immortal. Consequently an infinite number of human souls would now exist, which is impossible. Therefore we can cogently argue that the world began; and the conclusion is not held by faith alone.

On the other hand the article of faith cannot be demonstratively proved, for faith is about things *that appear not*. That God is the creator of a world that began to be is an article of faith; we profess it in the Creed. For his part Gregory teaches that Moses prophesied of the past when he declared that in the beginning God created heaven and earth, for his implication was that the world was new. This therefore is held through revelation alone, and cannot be demonstrated.

Reply: That the world has not always existed cannot be demonstratively proved but is held by faith alone. We make the same stand here as with regard to the mystery of the Trinity.

The reason is this: the world considered in itself offers no grounds for demonstrating that it was once all new. For the principle for demonstrating an object is its definition. Now the specific nature of each and every object abstracts from the here and now, which is why universals are described as being *everywhere and always*. Hence it cannot be demonstrated that man or the heavens or stone did not always exist.

Nor is demonstration open to us through the efficient cause. Here this is a voluntary agent. God's will is unsearchable, except as regards what he cannot but will, and his willing about creatures is not necessarily bound up with that, as we have seen.

His will, however, can be manifested to man through Revelation, the ground of faith. That the world had a beginning, therefore, is credible, but not scientifically demonstrable.

And it is well to take warning here, to forestall rash attempts at demonstration by arguments that are not cogent, and so provide unbelievers with the occasion for laughing at us and thinking that these are our reasons for believing the things of faith.

Hence: 1. According to St Augustine there were two opinions among philosophers who held the world was eternal. To some the world's substance did not come from God, an error not to be borne and to be convincingly refuted. To others, however, it existed from all ages yet all the same was produced by God. *For they hold that the world has a beginning, not of time, but of creation, which means that, in some scarcely intelligible fashion, it ever was made.* He tells us also that they try to explain themselves as follows. *Were a foot, they say, in the dust from eternity there would always be a footprint there and nobody could doubt that it had been imprinted by him who trod there, so likewise the world always was because he who made it always existed.*

For the explanation: we agree that an efficient cause which works through change must precede its effect in time, for the effect enters as the term of the action whereas the agent is its start. Yet in the event of the action being instantaneous and not successive, it is not required for the maker to be prior in duration to the thing made, as appears in the case of illumination. Hence they point out that because God is the active cause of the world it does not necessarily follow that he is prior to it in duration, for as we have seen, creation, whereby he produced the world, is not a successive change.

2. Those who hold the eternity of the world would agree that it was made by God from nothing, in the sense that it was not made from anything, not that it was made after nothing, which is what we understand. Accordingly some of them, Avicenna for instance, do not even reject the word 'creation'.

3. This is the argument of Anaxagoras reported in the *Physics*. Yet it is conclusive only with regard to a mind which deliberates according to a procedure like change. Such is the human mind, but not, as we have shown, the divine mind.

4. Those who teach that world is everlasting also think that a particular region has undergone an indefinite number of changes from being uninhabitable to being habitable, and vice versa, and also that the arts because of various decadences and events are endlessly being discovered and lost. On this matter we may quote Aristotle, it is absurd to base our opinion about the newness of the whole world on such provincial changes.

5. Even if it were everlasting the world would not be God's equal, as Boëthius points out towards the end of his *De consolatione*, for the divine being is existence whole and all at once without succession, while it is not so with the world's being.

6. The objection proceeds on the assumption that given two extremes there is an infinity of intermediate points between them. Now a passage is always from one term to another, and whichever day from the past we pick on, there is only a limited number between then and today, and this span can be traversed.

7. An infinite series of efficient causes essentially subordinate to one another is impossible, that is causes that are *per se* required for the effect, as when a stone is moved by a stick, a stick by a hand, and so forth: such a series cannot be prolonged indefinitely. All the same an infinite series of efficient causes incidentally subordinate to one another is not counted impossible, as when they are all ranged under causal heading and how many there are is quite incidental. For example, when a smith picks up many hammers because one after another has broken in his hand, it is accidental to one particular hammer that it is employed after another particular hammer. So is the fact that another has procreated him to the procreating act of a particular man, for he does this as a man, and not as the son of a father. For all men in begetting hold the same rank in the order of efficient causes, namely that of being a particular parent. Hence it is not out of the question for a man to be begotten by a man and so on endlessly. This would not be the case were this begetting to depend on another man or on material elements and solar energy and so on; such a series cannot be interminable.

8. The proponents of the world's eternity escape from this objection in various ways. Some reckon that an actual infinity of souls is not impossible; in his *Metaphysics* Algazel holds that this would amount to an accidental infinity. This position, however, we have already disproved. Others hold that the soul decays with the body. Others again that from many souls one alone survives. Yet others, as Augustine tells us, on this account assert the doctrine of transmigration, namely that disembodied souls return again to bodies after a determinate course of time. We shall deal with these matters later.

Observe, all the same, that the argument in the objection is limited to the particular; it could be answered by saying that the world was eternal, at least in some creatures, such as angels, though not men. Our inquiry, however, is couched in wider terms, and asks whether any creature at all existed from eternity.

[*Summa Theologiae* 1a. 46. 2 (trans. Thomas Gilby OP, London: Eyre and Spottiswoode, 1967, 77–85).]

AL-KINDI
....

36   A *Kalam* Cosmological Argument

The eternal is that which must never have been a non-existent being, the eternal having no existential 'before' to its being; the eternal's subsistence is not due to another; the eternal has no cause; the eternal has neither subject nor predicate, nor agent nor reason, i.e., that for the sake of which it is—for there are no causes other than the ones which have been previously stated. The eternal has no genus, for if it has a genus, then it is species, a species being composed of its genus, which is common to it and to others, and of a specific difference which does not exist in others. It (sc. species), moreover, has a subject, viz., the genus which receives its form and the form of others; and a predicate, viz., the form particular to it and not to others. It (sc. the eternal) therefore has a subject and predicate. It has, however, already been explained that the eternal has neither subject nor predicate, and this (contradiction) is an impossible absurdity; the eternal then, has no genus.

The eternal does not perish, perishing being but the changing of the predicate, not of the primary substratum; as for the primary substratum, which is being, it does not change, for the perishing of a perishable object does not involve the being of its being. Now every change is into its nearest contrary only, i.e., that which is with it in one genus, as heat which changes with cold—for we don't consider opposition like that of heat with aridity, or with sweetness or with length, or anything like that—and related contraries comprise one genus. A perishable object therefore has a genus, and if the eternal is corruptible, it has a genus. However, it has no genus, this is an impossible contradiction, and therefore it is impossible for the eternal to perish.

Motion is change, and the eternal does not move, for it neither changes nor removes from deficiency to perfection. Locomotion is a kind of motion, and the eternal does not remove to perfection, since it does not move. Now the perfect object is that which has a fixed state, whereby it excels; while the deficient object is that which has no fixed state, whereby it may excel. The eternal cannot be deficient, for it cannot remove to a state whereby it may excel, since it cannot ever move to (a state) more excellent, nor to (a state) more deficient, than it; the eternal is, therefore, of necessity perfect.

Now, inasmuch as a body has genus and species, while the eternal has no genus, a body is not eternal; and let us now say that it is not possible, either for an eternal body or for other objects which have quantity or quality, to be infinite in actuality, infinity being only in potentiality.

I say, moreover, that among the true first premises which are thought with no meditation are: all bodies of which one is not greater than the other are equal; equal bodies are those where the dimensions between their limits are equal in actuality and potentiality; that which is finite is not infinite; when a body is added to one of equal bodies it becomes the greatest of them, and greater than what it had been before that body was added to it; whenever two bodies of finite magnitude are joined, the body which comes to be from both of them is of finite magnitude, this being necessary in (the case of) every magnitude as well as in (the case of) every object which possesses magnitude; the smaller of every two generically related things is inferior to the larger, or inferior to a portion of it.

Now, if there is an infinite body, then whenever a body of finite magnitude is separated from it, that which remains of it will either be a finite magnitude or an infinite magnitude.

If that which remains of it is a finite magnitude, then whenever that finite magnitude which is separated from it is added to it, the body which comes to be from them both together is a finite magnitude; though that which comes to be from them both is that which was infinite before something was separated from it. It is thus finite and infinite, and this is an impossible contradiction.

If the remainder is an infinite magnitude, then whenever that which was taken from it is added to it, it will either be greater than or equal to what it was before the addition.

If it is greater than it was, then that which has infinity will be greater than that which has infinity, the smaller of two things being inferior to the greater, or inferior to a portion of it, and therefore the smaller of two bodies which have infinity being inferior to the greater of them or inferior to a portion of it—if the smaller body is inferior to the greater, then it most certainly is inferior to a portion of it—and thus the smaller of the two is equal to a portion of the greater. Now two equal things are those whose similarity is that the dimensions between their limits are the same, and therefore the two things possess limits— for 'equal' bodies which are not similar are those (in) which one part is numbered the same, though (as a whole) they differ in abundance or quality or both, they (too) being finite—and thus the smaller infinite object is finite, and this is an impossible contradiction, and one of them is not greater than the other.

If it is not greater than that which it was before it was added to, a body having been added to a body and not having increased anything, and the whole of this is equal to it alone—it alone being a part of it—and to its (own) part, which two (parts) join, then the part is like the all, (and) this is an impossible contradiction.

It has now been explained that it is impossible for a body to have infinity, and in this manner it has been explained that any quantitative thing cannot have infinity in actuality. Now time is quantitative, and it is impossible that time have infinity in actuality, time having a finite beginning.

Things predicated of a finite object are also, of necessity, finite. Every predicate of a body, whether quantity, place, motion or time—that which is segmented through motion—and the sum of everything which is predicated of a body in actuality, is also finite, since the body is finite. Therefore, the body of the universe is finite, and so is everything inferior predicated of it.

As it is possible through the imagination for something to be continually added to the body of the universe, if we imagine something greater than it, then continually something greater than that—there being no limit to addition as a possibility—the body of the universe is potentially infinite, since potentiality is nothing other than the possibility that the thing said to be in potentiality will occur. Everything, moreover, within that which has infinity in potentiality also potentially has infinity, including motion and time. That which has infinity exists only in potentiality, whereas in actuality it is impossible for something to have infinity, for (reasons) which we have given previously, and this is necessary.

It has thus been shown that it is impossible for time in actuality to have infinity. Time is the time, i.e., duration, of the body of the universe. If time is finite, then the being of (this) body is finite, since time is not an (independent) existent. Nor is there any body without time, as time is but the number of motion, i.e., it is a duration counted by motion. If there is motion, there is time; and if there were not motion, there would not be time.

Motion is the motion of a body only:

If there is a body, there is motion, and otherwise there would not be motion. Motion is some change: the change of place, (either) of the parts of a body and its centre, or of all the parts of the body only, is local motion; the change of place, to which the body is brought by its limits, either in nearness to or farness from its centre, is increase and decrease; the change only of its predicate qualities is alteration; and the change of its substance is generation and corruption. Every change is a counting of the number of the duration of the body, all change belonging to that which is temporal.

If, therefore, there is motion, there is of necessity a body, while if there is a body, then there must of necessity either be motion or not be motion.

If there is a body and there was no motion, then either there would be no motion at all, or it would not be, though it would be possible for it to be. If there were no motion at all, then motion would not be an existent. However, since body exists, motion is an existent, and this is an impossible contradiction and it is not possible for there to be no motion at all, if a body exists. If furthermore, when there is an existing body, it is possible that there is existing motion, then motion necessarily exists in some bodies, for that which is possible is that which exists in some possessors of its substance; as the (art of) writing which may be affirmed as a possibility for Muhammad, though it is not in him in actuality, since it does exist in some human substance, i.e., in another man. Motion, therefore, necessarily exists in some bodies, and exists in the simple body, existing necessarily in the simple body; accordingly body exists and motion exists.

Now it has been said that there may not be motion when a body exists. Accordingly, there will be motion when body exists, and there will not be motion when body exists, and this is an absurdity and an impossible contradiction, and it is not possible for there to be body and not motion; thus, when there is a body there is motion necessarily.

It is sometimes assumed that it is possible for the body of the universe to have been at rest originally, having the possibility to move, and then to have moved. This opinion, however, is false of necessity: for if the body of the universe was at rest originally and then moved, then (either) the body of the universe would have to be a generation from nothing or eternal.

If it is a generation from nothing, the coming to be of being from nothing being generation, then its becoming is motion in accordance with our previous classification of motion, (viz.) that generation is one of the species of motion. If, then, body is not prior (to motion, motion) is (of) its essence and therefore the generation of a body can never precede motion. It was said, however, to have been originally without motion: Thus it was, and no motion existed, and it was not, and no motion existed, and this is an impossible contradiction and it is impossible, if a body is a generation from nothing, for it to be prior to motion.

If, on the other hand, the body (of the universe) is eternal, having rested and then moved, it having had the possibility to move, then the body of the universe, which is eternal, will have moved from actual rest to actual movement, whereas that which is eternal does not move, as we have explained previously. The body of the universe is then moving and not moving, and this is an impossible contradiction and it is not possible for the body of the universe to be eternal, resting in actuality, and then to have moved into movement in actuality.

Motion, therefore, exists in the body of the universe, which, accordingly, is never prior to motion. Thus if there is motion there is, necessarily, a body, while if there is a body there is, necessarily, motion.

It has been explained previously that time is not prior to motion; nor, of necessity, is time prior to body, since there is no time other than through motion, and since there is no body unless there is motion and no motion unless there is body. Nor does body exist without duration, since duration is that in which its being is, i.e., that in which there is that which it is; and there is no duration of body unless there is motion, since body always occurs with motion, as has been explained. The duration of the body, which is always a concomitant of the body, is counted by the motion of the body, which is (also) always a concomitant of the body. Body, therefore, is never prior to time; and thus body, motion and time are never prior to one another.

It has, in accordance with this, already been explained that it is impossible for time to have infinity, since it is impossible for quantity or something which has quantity to have infinity in actuality. All time is therefore finite in actuality, and since body is not prior to time, it is not possible for the body of the universe, due to its being, to have infinity. The being of the body of the universe is thus necessarily finite, and it is impossible for the body of the universe to be eternal.

[*Al-Kindi's Metaphysics*, trans. Alfred L. Ivry (Albany, NY: SUNY Press, 1974), 67–73.]

BONAVENTURE

37   The Journey of the Mind to God

1. Accordingly, the mind has reached the end of the way of the six contemplations. They have been like the six steps by which one arrives at the throne of the true Solomon and at peace, where, as in an inner Jerusalem, the true man of peace rests with a tranquil soul. These six reflections are also like the six wings of the Cherubim, by which the mind of the true contemplative, flooded by the light of heavenly wisdom, is enabled to soar on high. They are also like the first six days during which the mind must be at work so that it may finally reach the Sabbath of rest.

After our mind has beheld God outside itself through and in vestiges of Him, and within itself through and in an image of Him, and above itself through the similitude of the divine Light shining above us and in the divine Light itself in so far as it is possible in our state as wayfarer and by the effort of our own mind, and when at last the mind has reached the sixth step, where it can behold in the first and highest Principle and in the Mediator of God and men, Jesus Christ, things the like of which cannot possibly be found among creatures, and which transcend all acuteness of the human intellect—when the mind has done all this, it must still, in beholding these things, transcend and pass over, not only this visible world, but even itself. In this passing over, Christ is the way and the door; Christ is the ladder and the vehicle, being, as it were, the Mercy-Seat above the Ark of God and *the mystery which has been hidden from eternity*.

2. He who turns his full countenance toward this Mercy-Seat and with faith, hope, and love, devotion, admiration, joy, appreciation, praise and rejoicing, beholds Christ hanging on the Cross, such a one celebrates the Pasch, that is, the Passover, with Him. Thus, using the rod of the Cross, he may pass over the Red Sea, going from Egypt into the desert, where it is given to him to taste the *hidden manna*; he may rest with Christ in the tomb, as one dead to the outer world, but experiencing, nevertheless, as far as is possible in this present state as wayfarer, what was said on the Cross to the thief who was hanging there with Christ: *This day you shall be with me in Paradise.*

3. This also was shown to the Blessed Francis, when, in a transport of contemplation on the mountain height—where I pondered over the matter that is here written—there appeared to him the six-winged Seraph fastened to a cross, as I and many others have heard from the companion who was then with him at that very place. Here he passed over into God in a transport of contemplation. He is set forth as an example of perfect contemplation, just as previously he had been of action, like a second Jacob-Israel. And thus, through him, more by example than by word, God would invite all truly spiritual men to this passing over and this transport of soul.

4. In this passing over, if it is to be perfect, all intellectual activities ought to be relinquished and the loftiest affection transported to God, and transformed into Him. This, however, is mystical and most secret, *which no one knows except him who receives it*, and no one receives it except him who desires it, and no one desires it except he who is penetrated to the marrow by the fire of the Holy Spirit, Whom Christ sent into the world. That is why the Apostle says that this mystical wisdom is revealed by the Holy Spirit.

5. And since, therefore, nature avails nothing and human endeavour but little, little should be attributed to inquiry, but much to unction; little to the tongue, but very much to interior joy; little to the spoken or written word, but everything to the Gift of God, that is, to the Holy Spirit. Little or nothing should be attributed to the creature, but everything to the Creative Essence—the Father, the Son, and the Holy Spirit. And thus, with Dionysius, we address the Triune God: 'O Trinity, Essence above all essence, and Deity above all deity, supremely best Guardian of the divine wisdom of Christians, direct us to the supremely unknown, superluminous, and most sublime height of mystical knowledge. There new mysteries—absolute and changeless mysteries of theology—are shrouded in the superluminous darkness of a silence that teaches secretly in a most dark manner that is above all manifestation and resplendent above all splendour, and in which everything shines forth—a darkness which fills invisible intellects by an abundance above all plenitude with the splendours of invisible good things that are above all good.' All this pertains to God.

To the friend, however, for whom these words were written, we can say with Dionysius: And you, my friend, in this matter of mystical visions, renew your journey, 'abandon the senses, intellectual activities, and all visible and invisible things—everything that is not and everything that is—and, oblivious of yourself, let yourself be brought back, in so far as it is possible, to union with Him Who is above all essence and all knowledge. And transcending yourself and all things, ascend to the superessential gleam of the divine darkness by an incommensurable and absolute transport of a pure mind.'

6. If you wish to know how these things may come about, ask grace, not learning; desire, not understanding; the groaning of prayer, not diligence in reading; the Bridegroom, not the teacher; God, not man; darkness, not clarity;

not light, but the fire that wholly inflames and carries one into God through transporting unctions and consuming affections. God Himself is this fire, and *His furnace is in Jerusalem*; and it is Christ who enkindles it in the white flame of His most burning Passion. This fire he alone truly perceives who says: *My soul chooses hanging, and my bones, death.* He who loves this death can see God, for it is absolutely true that *Man shall not see me and live.*

Let us, then, die and enter into this darkness. Let us silence all our cares, our desires, and our imaginings. With Christ crucified, let us pass *out of this world to the Father*, so that, when the Father is shown to us, we may say with Philip: *It is enough for us.* Let us hear with Paul: *My grace is sufficient for you*, and rejoice with David, saying: *My flesh and my heart have fainted away: You are the God of my heart, and the God that is my portion forever. Blessed be the Lord forever, and let all the people say: so be it, so be it.* Amen.

[*The Journey of the Mind to God* vii (trans. Philotheus Boehner, Indianapolis: Hackett, 1993, 37–9).]

DUNS SCOTUS

38 Proofs for God

Now there are two properties of God which have reference to creatures, one is eminence in goodness, the other is causality. Eminence is not subdivided further, but causality is. According to some, its divisions are: exemplar, efficient and final cause. Such say that the exemplar cause gives a thing its essential being. But I say here (and later on in more detail) that the exemplar cause is not to be numbered alongside of the efficient cause, for it is only as a concomitant factor of an efficient cause that the exemplar in the mind of the artisan gives any being to a thing. And if [the exemplar in view of its effect] can be considered as a formal cause, then it would pertain to eminence rather than to causality, for the more excellent being contains virtually the forms of other things and contains them unitively. Hence in God there are these three: eminence, efficiency, and finality.

I. THE ARGUMENT FROM EFFICIENCY

Now efficiency can be considered either as a metaphysical or as a physical property. The metaphysical property is more extensive than the physical for 'to give existence to another' is of broader scope than 'to give existence by way of movement or change.' And even if all existence were given in the latter fashion, the notion of the one is still not that of the other.

It is not efficiency as a physical attribute, however, but efficiency as the metaphysician considers it that provides a more effective way of proving God's existence, for there are more attributes in metaphysics than in physics whereby the existence of God can be established. It can be shown, for example, from 'composition and simplicity,' from 'act and potency,' from 'one and many,' from those features which are properties of being. Wherefore, if you find one extreme of the disjunction imperfectly realized in a creature, you conclude that the alternate, the perfect extreme exists in God.

Averroës, therefore, in attacking Avicenna at the end of Bk. I of the *Physics*, is incorrect when he claims that to prove that God exists is the job of the physicist alone, because this can be established only by way of motion, and in no other way—as if metaphysics began with a conclusion which was not evident in itself, but needed to be proved in physics (for Averroës asserts this falsehood at the end of the first book of the *Physics*). In point of fact, however, [God's existence] can be shown more truly and in a greater variety of ways by means of those metaphysical attributes which characterize being. The proof lies in this, that the first efficient cause imparts not merely this fluid existence [called motion] but existence in an unqualified sense, which is still more perfect and widespread. Now the existence of a primacy in the higher class does not follow logically from the existence of a primary in a lower [or more specific] class, unless that member is the most noble. For example, this does not follow: 'The most noble donkey exists, therefore the most noble animal exists.' Consequently, from the property of being the most noble being, one can argue better to a primacy among beings than from the primacy characteristic of a prime mover.

Hence, we omit the physical argument by which a prime mover is shown to exist and, using the efficiency characteristic of beings, we argue that among beings there is one which is a first efficient cause. And this is Richard's argument in Bk. I, chapter eight *On the Trinity*.

Some being is not eternal, and therefore it does not exist of itself, neither is it caused by nothing, because nothing produces itself. Hence, it is from some other being. The latter either gives existence in virtue of something other than itself or not. And its existence, too, it either gets from another or not. If neither be true—i.e., if it neither imparts existence in virtue of another nor receives its own existence from another—then this is the first efficient cause, for such is the meaning of the term. But if either of the above alternatives holds [viz. if it receives existence, or imparts it to others only in virtue of another], then I inquire about the latter as I did before. One cannot go on his way ad infinitum. Hence, we end up with some first efficient cause, which neither imparts existence in virtue of another nor receives its own existence from another.

Objections, however, are raised against this argument. To begin with, it seems to beg the question, for it assumes that there is an order and a first among causes. But if no efficient cause is first, then both the order and the terminus in such causes would have to be denied.

Furthermore, inasmuch as the argument begins with a contingent premise, it does not seem to be a demonstration. For a demonstration proceeds from necessary premises, and everything exists contingently which owes its existence to God. Consequently, with reference to God this statement is contingent: 'Some being is non-eternal,' because from it this statement follows: 'Some non-eternal being exists,' and this latter is contingent.

Furthermore, since there is no demonstration of the reasoned fact, neither does there seem to be any demonstration of the simple fact. For, whenever some conclusion is established by a demonstration of the latter type, one can always set up a converse demonstration of the reasoned fact (from cause to effect). But from the existence of the first cause, the existence of other things cannot be inferred by a demonstration of the reasoned fact; therefore, neither is the converse relation demonstrable as a simple fact.

To solve these objections, then, know this to begin with. Incidental [*per accidens*] causes are not the same as causes that are ordered to one another incidentally, just as essential [per se] causes are not the same as causes essentially ordered to one another. For when I speak of essential [i.e., per se] and incidental [i.e., *per accidens*] causes, I express a one to one relationship, viz. between a cause and its effect. But when causes are said to be incidentally or essentially ordered, two causes are being considered with reference to a single effect, so that we have a two to one relationship. Now causes are essentially ordered if one is ordered to the other so that [together] they cause a third thing, the effect. But causes are incidentally ordered if one is not ordered to the other in the very act of causing the effect. This would be the case with father and grandfather with regard to the son.

Secondly, it follows from this that essentially ordered causes differ from incidentally ordered causes in a threefold way:

The first difference is this: one cause depends essentially upon the other in order to produce an effect, which is not the case with causes that are ordered to a single effect only incidentally. Wherefore, the single causality of one of the incidentally ordered causes suffices to produce the single effect, whereas the causality of only one of the essentially ordered causes does not suffice.

From this, the second difference follows, viz. where essentially ordered causes are concerned, their causality differs in kind and they are not related to their effect in the same way. But the causality of all the incidentally ordered causes is of the same kind, since they can be referred immediately to the same effect.

From this, too, the third difference arises, viz. that the causalities of all of the essentially ordered causes concur simultaneously to produce the effect. For what is needed to cause an effect is that all its necessary causes concur. But all the essentially ordered causes are necessary causes. Therefore, all such must actually concur to bring about the effect. But this is not required where incidentally ordered causes are concerned, because each of itself possesses perfect causality as regards its effect, and they are of one kind so far as their immediate effect is concerned.

With these things presupposed, then, what remains to be shown is that the proof for a first cause does not involve a begging of the question. Therefore, I first prove that there is such a first where essentially ordered causes are concerned. I do this:

First, by the argument of the Philosopher, Bk. II of the *Metaphysics* (and that of Avicenna, too, Bk. VIII, chapter one) which seems to be this: All causes intermediate between the first and the last, cause by virtue of the first, so that their causality is derived from the first. As the Philosopher points out there, it is not derived from the last but from the first, for if 'to cause' pertains to any of them, a fortiori it will pertain to the first. Now the minor of his argument seems to be this: 'If the series of causes is infinite then all are intermediate causes.' Consequently they all cause in virtue of some first cause, so that it is necessary to assume a first among efficient causes.

But you may object: When you say in the minor, 'Every cause in an infinite series is an intermediate cause,' either you mean by intermediate such causes as lie between a first and a last in the series, and so assume that there is a first, or else you mean it in a purely negative sense [i.e., as being neither the first nor last], in which case there are four terms, and again the conclusion does not follow.

I say, therefore, that the statement first assumed by the Philosopher is not the major in the argument, but is antecedent thereto. The argument, consequently, goes in this way. Every intermediary cause having a first and a last, derives its causality from the first. Hence the causality of the intermediary causes comes from the first. But if there were an infinity of such causes, they would all be intermediary. Hence, their causality is derived from some first. But if they are infinite, then there is no first. Hence, there is and there is not a first cause!

Proof of the aforesaid consequence:

All causes in any way intermediate, be they positively or negatively so, are caused. Therefore, the whole concatenation of intermediary causes is caused. Hence, it is caused by something which is outside the concatenated series. Hence, there is a first.

What is more, the causalities of all the essential causes must concur simultaneously to produce their effect, as was pointed out above. But an infinity of things cannot so concur to produce one thing, hence there is not an infinity of such causes and therefore a first cause does exist.

Furthermore, a cause which is prior as regards the causation has a more perfect causality, and the more it is prior, the more perfect its causality. Hence, a cause with infinite priority would have an infinite causality. But if there were an infinite regress in essentially ordered causes, then there is a cause with infinite priority. To assume an infinite regress, then, is to grant a cause whose causality is infinite. But surely a cause which exercises infinite causality when it causes, does not depend upon anything else, and as such it would be the first. Therefore, etc.

Furthermore, to be able to produce something is not a property which of itself entails imperfection. But whatever is of such like is able to exist in something without imperfection. And thus there must be an efficient cause in which it can exist in this way, which is impossible if the cause does not produce its effect independently, and this means it is the first efficient cause. Therefore, etc.

Likewise, if one assumes an infinity of incidentally ordered causes, it still follows that there is a first in essentially ordered causes, for those causes which are incidentally ordered are in individuals of the same species. Then [one argues] as follows: No deformity is perpetual, unless it is brought about by a perpetual cause—outside this coordination—which perpetuates this deformity. Proof: Nothing that is part of this concatenation can be the cause of the whole of this perpetuated deformity, because in such incidentally ordered [causes], one is the cause of one only. Therefore, it is necessary to postulate—beyond this deformed concatenation—some first essential cause which perpetuates it. The deformation, then, is due to the deformed cause, but the continual uniformity of this deformity will be due to a cause outside this concatenation. And thus, if there is a process in incidentally ordered causes, there will still be a terminal point in some first essential cause upon which all the incidentally ordered causes depend.

In this way we avoid begging the question as regards a terminus and order of essential causes.

Now for the second objection raised against the aforesaid argument, viz. that it proceeds from something contingent, scil. 'Something other than God exists.' The philosophers would say that this is something necessary because of the essential order that holds between the cause and what it produces.

But I say, first, that even though it be contingent with reference to God, it is nevertheless most evident, so that anyone who would deny the existence of some being which is not eternal needs senses and punishment. And therefore, from what is contingent in this way we can establish something necessary, for from the contingent something necessary follows, but not vice versa.

Also, I say that although things other than God are actually contingent as regards their actual existence, this is not true with regard to potential existence. Wherefore, those things which are said to be contingent with reference to actual existence are necessary with respect to potential existence. Thus, though 'Man exists' is contingent, 'It is possible for man to exist' is necessary, because it does not include a contradiction as regards existence. For, for something other than God to be possible, then, is necessary. Being is divided into what must exist and what can but need not be. And just as necessity is of the very essence or constitution of what must be, so possibility is of the very essence of what can but need not be. Therefore, let the former argument be couched in terms of possible being and the proposition will become necessary. Thus: It is possible that something other than God exists which neither exists of itself (for then it would not be possible being) nor exists by reason of nothing. Therefore, it can exist by reason of another. Either this other can both exist and act in virtue of itself and not in virtue of another, or it cannot do so. If it can, then it can be the first cause, and if it can exist, it does exist—as was proved above. If it cannot [both be and act independently of every other thing] and there is no infinite regress, then at some point we end up [with a first cause].

To the other objection (viz. that whenever an argument proceeds by way of a demonstration of simple fact, a converse demonstration of the reasoned fact can be constructed), one must say that such is not always true, because when we argue from the effect to the existence of a cause our argument may merely prove that the latter is a necessary condition rather than a sufficient reason for the effect. But it is only when the argument from effect to cause establishes [in addition] that the latter is a sufficient reason that the above principle [of converse demonstration] holds good.

And so we show from efficiency, to begin with, that something which is first exists, for—as we have made clear—something exists which makes all possible things possible. But that which makes all possibles possible cannot fail to exist of itself, for otherwise it would be from nothing. Therefore, it must needs be actually self-existent. And so our thesis is proved.

2. THE ARGUMENT FROM FINALITY

That something first exists is established secondly from finality. Something is suited by its very nature to be an end. Hence it so functions either in virtue of itself or in virtue of another. If the first be the case, we have something which is first; if it functions as an end only in virtue of another then this other is suited by its very nature to be an end, and since there is no infinite regress, we arrive at some end which is first. This is the argument of the Philosopher in *Metaphysics*, Bk. II and Bk. XII about the most perfect good, and it is also the argument of Augustine in *On the Trinity*, Bk. VIII, chapter three: 'Consider this good and that good, abstract from the "this" and the "that," and consider, if you can, simply the good itself, and thus you will see God, who is not good by reason of some other good but is the goodness of all that is good.'

3. THE ARGUMENT FROM EMINENT PERFECTION

The third way is that of eminence. Some good is exceeded in perfection, or is able to be exceeded if you prefer to argue from possibility. Therefore, there is something which exceeds or is able to exceed something else in perfection. The latter either is or is not able to be exceeded or is actually exceeded in perfection by something else. If it is not, then it is first in the order of eminence, if it is not first and there is no regress ad infinitum, then we argue the same as before.

And so we show that something is first in three ways, first in the order of efficiency, first in the order of eminence and first in the order of ends.

And this triple 'first' is one and the same because the first efficient cause is fully actualized, while the most eminent is the best of things. But what is fully actualized is also the best, with no mixture of evil or potentiality. Then too, the first efficient cause does not act for the sake of anything other than itself, for if it did, this other would be better than it. Consequently, it is the ultimate end, and hence first in the order of ends. The same thing, then, enjoys [a triple primacy].

Before establishing that some being is infinite, we prove God is his own knowledge, for if his knowledge were not his nature but something accidental to it, then as the first efficient cause of everything, he would produce his knowledge. But God acts with knowledge; hence he would have to know about this knowledge beforehand. About this prior knowledge we inquire as before. Either there will be an infinite regress before something is known—and then nothing will be known—[or we admit finally that God is his own knowledge].

[*A Treatise on God as First Principle*, ed. and trans. Alan B. Wolter (Quincy, Ill.: Franciscan Press, 1965); in Andrew B. Schoedinger (ed.), *Readings in Medieval Philosophy* (New York: Oxford University Press, 1996), 74–8.]

WILLIAM OF OCKHAM

39   Can it be Proved that there is Only One God?

It can be proved: For one world has only one ruler, as is stated in the 12th book of the *Metaphysics*; but it can be proved by natural reason that there is only one world, according to Aristotle in the first book of the *De Caelo*; therefore by natural reason it can be proved that there is only one ruler; but this ruler of the world is God, therefore, etc.

To the contrary: An article of faith cannot be evidently proved; but that there is only one God is an article of faith; therefore, etc.

As regards this question, I shall first explain what is meant by the name 'God'; secondly I shall answer the question.

Concerning the first point I say that the name 'God' can have various descriptions. One of them is: 'God is some thing more noble and more perfect than anything else besides Him'. Another is: 'God is that than which nothing is more noble and more perfect'.

Concerning the second point, I maintain that if we understand 'God' according to the first description, then it cannot be demonstratively proved that there is only one God. The reason for this is that it cannot be evidently known that God, understood in this sense, exists. Therefore it cannot be evidently known that there is only one God. The inference is plain. The antecedent is proved in this way. The proposition 'God exists' is not known by itself, since many doubt it; nor can it be proved from propositions known by themselves, since in every argument something doubtful or derived from faith will be assumed; nor is it known by experience, as is manifest.

Secondly I maintain: If it could be evidently proved that God exists—'God' being understood in the present sense—then the unicity of God could be evidently proved. The reason for this is the following: If there were two Gods, let us call them A and B, then in virtue of our description God A would be more perfect than anything else, therefore God A would be more perfect than God B, and God B would be more imperfect than God A. But God B would also be more perfect than God A, because according to our assumption God B would be God. Consequently God B would be more perfect and more imperfect than God A, and God A than God B, which is a manifest contradiction. If, therefore, it could be evidently proved that God exists—'God' being understood in the present sense—then the unicity of God could be evidently proved.

Thirdly I maintain that the unicity of God cannot be evidently proved if we understand 'God' according to the second description. Yet this negative proposition, 'The unicity of God cannot be evidently proved', cannot be proved demonstratively either. For it cannot be demonstrated that the unicity of God cannot be evidently proved, except by rebutting the arguments to the contrary. For instance, it cannot be demonstratively proved that the stars make up an even number, nor can the Trinity of Persons be demonstrated. Nevertheless, these negative propositions, 'It cannot be demonstrated that the stars make up an even number', 'The Trinity of Persons cannot be demonstrated', cannot be evidently proved.

We must understand, however, that it can be proved that God exists, if we understand 'God' according to the second description. For otherwise we could go on *ad infinitum*, if there were not someone among beings to which nothing is prior or superior in perfection. But from this it does not follow that it can be demonstrated that there is only one such being. This we hold only by faith.

The answer to the main objection is clear from the aforesaid.

[*Quodlibeta* 1. q. 1 (*Philosophical Writings*, ed. and trans. P. Boehner, Indianapolis: Bobbs-Merrill, 1964, 139–40).]

40   On his own Ignorance

It may perhaps be daring to say so, but it is true, unless I am mistaken: It seems to me that he saw of happiness as much as the night owl does of the sun, namely, its light and rays and not the sun itself. For Aristotle did not establish happiness within its own boundaries and did not found it on solid ground, as a high building ought to be founded, but far away in foreign territory on a trembling site, and consequently did not comprehend two things, or, if he did, ignored them. These are the two things without which there can be absolutely no happiness: Faith and Immortality. I already regret saying that he did not comprehend them or ignored them. For I ought to have said only one of the two phrases. Faith and immortality were not yet comprehended: he did not know of them, nor could he know of them or hope for them. The true light had not yet begun to shine, which lights every man who comes into this world. He and all the others fancied what they wished and what by his very nature every man wishes and whose opposite no one can wish: a happiness of which they sang as one sings of the absent beloved, and which they adorned with words. They did not see it. Like people made happy by a dream, they rejoiced in an absolute nothing. In fact, they were miserable and to be roused to their misery by the thunder of approaching death, to see with open eyes what that happiness really is like, with which they had dealt in their dreams.

Some may believe that I have said all this out of my own imagination and therefore but too frivolously. Let them then read Augustine's thirteenth book on the Trinity. There they will find many weighty and acute discussions on this subject against those philosophers who—I use his words:—'shaped their happy lives for themselves, just as it pleased each of them.' This, I confess, I have said often before, and I will say it as long as I can speak, because I am confident that I have spoken the truth and shall speak it in the future, too. If they consider it a sacrilege, they may accuse me of violating religion, but then they must accuse Jerome too, 'who does not care what Aristotle but what Christ said.' I, on the contrary, should not doubt that it is they who are impious and sacrilegious if they have a different opinion. God may take my life and whatever I love most dearly before I change this pious, true, and saving conviction or disown Christ from love of Aristotle.

Let them certainly be philosophers and Aristotelians, though they are neither, but let them be both: I do not envy them these brilliant names of which they boast, and even that wrongly. In return they ought not to envy me the humble and true name of Christian and Catholic. But why do I ask for this? I know they are willing to comply with this demand quite spontaneously and will do what I ask. Such things they do not envy us; they spurn them as simple and contemptible, inadequate for their genius and unworthy of it. We accept in humble faith the secrets of nature and the mysteries of God, which are higher still; they attempt to seize them in haughty arrogance. They do not manage to reach them, not even to approach them; but in their insanity they believe that they have reached them and strike heaven with their fists. They feel just as if they had it in their grip, satisfied with their own opinion and rejoicing in their error. They are not held back from their insanity—I will not say by the impossibility of such an attempt, as is expressed in the words of the Apostle to the Romans: 'Who has known the mind of the Lord, or who has been His counsellor?' Not even by the ecclesiastical and heavenly counsel: 'Seek not what is above thee and search not out things above thy strength; the things that God hath commanded to thee, think thereupon always and be not inquisitive in His many works; for it is not necessary for thee to behold what is hidden.' Of all this I will not speak: indiscriminately they despise whatever they know has been said from Heaven—yea, let me say, what is actually true—whatever has been said from a Catholic point of view. However, there is at least a witty word not ineptly said by Democritus: 'No one looks at what is before his feet,' he said; 'it is the regions of the sky they scrutinize.' And there are very clever remarks Cicero made to ridicule frivolous disputants who are heedlessly arguing and arguing about nothing, 'as if they just came from the council of the gods' and had seen with their eyes what was going on there. And, finally, there are Homer's more ancient and sharper words, by which Jupiter deters in grave sentences not a mortal man, not any one of the common crowd of the gods, but Juno, his wife and sister, the queen of the gods, from daring to investigate his intimate secret or presumptuously believing it could be known to her at all.

But let us return to Aristotle. His brilliance has stunned many bleary and weak eyes and made many a man fall into the ditches of error. I know, Aristotle has declared himself for the rule of one, as Homer had done before him. For Homer says thus, as far as it has been translated for us into our prose: 'Multido-minion is not good; let one be the lord, one the supreme commander'; and Aristotle says: 'Plurality of rule is not good; let therefore one be the ruler.' Homer meant human rulership, Aristotle divine dominion; Homer was speaking of the principate of the Greeks, the other of that of all men; Homer made Agamemnon the Atride king and ruler, Aristotle God—so far had the dazzling brightness of truth brought light to his mind. He did not know who this king is, I believe, nor did he know how great He is. He discussed the most trifling things with so much curiosity and did not see this one and greatest of things, which many illiterate people have seen, not by another light, but because it shed a very different illumination. If these friends of mind do not see that this is the case, I see that they are altogether blind and bereft of eyesight; and I should not hesitate to believe that it must be visible to all who have sound eyes, just as it can be seen that the emerald is green, the snow white, and the raven black.

[*On his own Ignorance and that of Others*, trans. Hans Nachod (*The Renaissance Philosophy of Man*, ed. Ernst Cassirer, Paul Oskar Kristeller, and John Herman Randall, Jr., Chicago: University of Chicago Press, 1948, 74–8).]

Section IV

Renaissance and Reformation

INTRODUCTION

It is a commonplace that the Renaissance and the Reformation broke up the medieval synthesis of faith and reason, even though we have seen, in the previous section, that synthesis already coming under internal strain, particularly in the more voluntaristic and fideistic emphases of William of Ockham. But the breakup could not be, and was not thought to be, a complete rupture. Recent scholarship has done much to emphasize the elements of continuity between medieval scholasticism and the thinking of the leaders of the Renaissance as well as of the Protestant Reformers, despite the obvious ecclesiastical ruptures that the Reformation brought.

In this section we explore some of the elements in the plurality of approaches that developed during the sixteenth and seventeenth centuries. Generalizations are dangerous, but perhaps it is possible to discern at least three different significant approaches to the issues of faith and reason.

In this period 'reason' as a term comes to embrace the use of the intellect both in scientific discovery and the rediscovery of the ancient learning. Each of these developments had a strong anti-scholastic tendency, but in one respect they had the effect, at least in the minds of many, of reaffirming the claims of the faith. For among the ancient learning that was rediscovered was the text of the Bible, and the renewed use of the original languages in its study. In the Protestant Reformation, and particularly in its Reformed wing, the Bible came to have supreme authority in all matters of faith, particularly in those matters where it was believed that church tradition had distorted and eclipsed biblical teaching. So the relation between faith and reason, which now more commonly came to be seen as the controversy between revelation and reason, was renewed and in many ways sharpened as the Reformers stressed the evangelical imperatives of the Bible.

That is one important theme. But just as Protestants emphasized the need to return to Christian sources, so others, taking their cue from the rediscovery of Plato, stressed the need to renew the appeal to reason. And others, of course, emphasized the importance of returning to the ancient learning and of cultivating a recognition of the limitations both of reason and of revelation.

Erasmus is typical of those learned Renaissance scholars who while not anti-theological in their views were untheological in temper, seeing their faith mainly in terms of moral precepts which they were confident that men and women could fulfil.

Luther is scathing about the supposed ability of human beings to fulfil their duty, for the human will is in bondage to sin. But it is interesting to note that, even while attacking the claims of human ability unaided by special divine grace, Luther uses in defence of his Protestantism the terminology and some of the arguments that he had learned as an Augustinian monk. His idea of faith as trust comes over vividly in the extract on faith in the justice of God. Luther is often crude and outspoken, but the extracts provided here indicate that he was by no means the rednecked anti-intellectual that he has often been painted as. In the other Reformer used in this section, John Calvin, we see a more measured response. The recognition of natural theology, however minimalist, indicates unbroken (or re-established) lines of continuity with the medieval period. The point is, in the first Protestant Reformers one sees a change of interest rather than an overall repudiation of the medieval position. But in the face of the renewed controversy of the Counter-Reformation, and theological discord within the ranks of the Reformed Churches, Protestantism had need to develop its own scholasticism.

Proof that the intellectual lines of communication between the medieval period and later were never completely severed is seen in the fact that the intellectual sophistication characteristic of medieval scholasticism came to reassert itself (partly owing to pressure from the Counter-Reformation) in unexpected quarters; in the defence by the Puritan John Owen of the supreme authority of Holy Scripture, and in Jeremy Taylor's reassertion of an Anglicized version of the medieval synthesis of faith and reason.

The third emphasis, the appeal to divine incomprehensibility, and with it a recognition of the limitations of human reason, as seen in Luther and also in Calvin, together with the rediscovery of the writings of the ancient sceptics, gave rise to religious scepticism. Competition between increasingly diverse theological parties was tragically expressed in political division and war. With scepticism came fideism, the belief that matters of faith fell outside the province of reason. Bayle is an example of this; Bayle, as a Calvinist, emphasized both the incomprehensibility of God and the incapacity of human reason, while remaining confident of the reality of divine grace. In Montaigne one finds a more conservative position; at a time of unresolved intellectual conflict the prudent thing to do is to adhere to the old ways even if one can provide no rational justification for doing so. And as Richard Popkin has shown, such scepticism gave rise to fideism even in Counter-Reformation Catholicism.

Although the scientific achievements of the Middle Ages ought not to be forgotten, this period is characterized by the first great conflict between religion and science, the Galileo controversy, and the first steps towards developing a hermeneutic of the Bible that would allow for scientific discovery seemingly at odds with its teaching. 'Reason' here is scientific reason, and faith is faith in the letter of the Bible, and the attempt to resolve the ensuing tension invoked the idea of accommodation, the claim that the language of the Bible was not scientifically exact, but was accommodated to the needs and situations of its readers. The Bible is not a scientific textbook, and its language is popular and commonplace. It is therefore possible both to hold to the Bible and to science at the same time. Cardinal Bellarmine demurred.

But in the face of continuing religious conflict, intellectual and military, there were not lacking those who sought a more irenic path. In Herbert of Cherbury one finds an approach to religion which claims that through the diversity of theological approaches a common core of rational religion can be discerned by those who have eyes to see. The Cambridge Platonist Nathaniel Culverwel renews the claims of reason. The idiosyncratic Thomas Hobbes also may be said to foreshadow those who viewed the rationality of the entire enterprise of religion with suspicion, as being the product of fear, or greed, or priest-craft. Such thinkers heralded the Enlightenment.

41 The Freedom of the Will

Likewise, just as in those who lack grace (I speak now of peculiar grace) reason was obscured but not extinguished, so it is probable that in them, too, the power of the will was not completely extinguished, but that it was unable to perform the good. What the eye is to the body, reason is to the soul. This is partly enlightened by that native light which is implanted in all men, though not in equal measure, as the psalm reminds us: 'The light of thy countenance is impressed upon us, O Lord!' (Ps. 4: 6), and partly by divine precepts and Holy Scriptures, according as our psalmist says: 'Thy word is a lamp to my feet' (Ps. 119: 105). Thus there arises for us a threefold kind of law: law of nature, law of works, law of faith, to use Paul's words. The law of nature is thoroughly engraved in the minds of all men, among the Scythians as among the Greeks, and declares it to be a crime if any does to another what he would not wish done to himself. And the philosophers, without the light of faith, and without the assistance of Holy Scripture, drew from created things the knowledge of the everlasting power and divinity of God, and left many precepts concerning the good life, agreeing wholeheartedly with the teachings of the Gospels, and with many words exhorting to virtue and the detestation of wickedness. And in these things it is probable that there was a will in some way ready for the good but useless for eternal salvation without the addition of grace by faith. The law of works, on the other hand, commands and threatens punishment. It doubles sin and engenders death, not that it is evil, but because it commands actions which we cannot perform without grace. The law of faith commands more arduous things than the law of works, yet because grace is plentifully added to it, not only does it make things easy which of themselves are impossible, but it makes them agreeable also. Faith, therefore, cures reason, which has been wounded by sin, and charity bears onward the weak will. The law of works was like this: 'You may freely eat of every tree of the garden, but of the tree of the knowledge of good and evil you shall not eat, for in the day that you eat of it you shall die' (Gen. 2: 16–17). This law of works was further revealed by Moses: 'You shall not kill: if you have killed, you shall be killed'; 'You shall not commit adultery' (Exod. 20: 13–14). But what says the law of faith, which orders us to love our enemies, to carry our cross daily, to despise our life? 'Fear not, little flock, for yours is the kingdom of heaven' (Luke 12: 32). And 'Be of good cheer, I have overcome the world' (John 16: 33). And 'I am with you always, to the close of the age' (Matt. 28: 20). This law the apostles showed forth when, after being beaten with rods for the name of Jesus, they went away rejoicing from the presence of the Council. Thus Paul: 'I can do all things in him who strengthens me' (Phil. 4: 13). And no doubt this is what Ecclesiasticus had in mind in saying: 'He established with them an eternal covenant, and showed them his judgments' (Ecclus.

17: 12). For whom? In the first place, for those two founders of the human race in person, then the Jewish people by Moses and the prophets. The Law shows what God wills, sets out the penalty to him who disobeys and the reward to the obedient. For the rest it leaves the power of choice to the will that was created in them free and able rapidly to turn to one or the other. And, therefore, it says: 'If you will keep the commandments, they shall keep you' (Ecclus. 15: 15). And again: 'Stretch out your hand to whatever you wish' (v. 16). If the power to distinguish good and evil and the will of God had been hidden from men, it could not be imputed to them if they made the wrong choice. If the will had not been free, sin could not have been imputed, for sin would cease to be sin if it were not voluntary, save when error or the restriction of the will is itself the fruit of sin. Thus the responsibility for rape is not imputed to the one who has suffered violence.

Although this quotation from Ecclesiasticus seems peculiarly suited to our first parents, yet in a certain sense it is relevant to all the posterity of Adam, but it would be irrelevant if there were no strength of free choice at all in us. For although free choice is damaged by sin, it is nevertheless not extinguished by it. And although it has become so lame in the process that before we receive grace we are more readily inclined toward evil than good, yet it is not altogether cut out, except that the enormity of crimes which have become a kind of second nature so clouds the judgment and overwhelms the freedom of the will that the one seems to be destroyed and the other utterly lost.

[*Hyperaspistes* (*Luther and Erasmus: Free Will and Salvation*, ed. and trans. G. Rupp and Philip Watson, London: SCM Press, 1969, 49–51).]

MARTIN LUTHER

42   The Bondage of the Will

Now let us turn to the passage from Ecclesiasticus and compare with it, too, that first 'probable' opinion. The opinion says that free choice cannot will good, but the passage from Ecclesiasticus is cited to prove that free choice is something and can do something. The opinion that is to be confirmed by Ecclesiasticus, therefore, states one thing and Ecclesiasticus is cited in confirmation of another. It is as if someone set out to prove that Christ was the Messiah, and cited a passage which proved that Pilate was governor of Syria, or something else equally wide of the mark. That is just how free choice is proved here, not to mention what I pointed out above, that nothing is clearly and definitely said or proved as to what free choice is or can do. But it is worthwhile to examine this whole passage.

First it says, 'God made man from the beginning.' Here it speaks of the creation of man, and says nothing as yet either about free choice or about precepts. Then follows: 'And left him in the hand of his own counsel.' What have we here? Is free choice set up here? But not even here is there any mention of precepts, for which free choice is required, nor do we read anything on this subject in the account of the creation of man. If anything is meant, therefore, by 'the hand of his own counsel,' it is rather as we read in Gen. chs. 1 and 2, that man was appointed lord of things, so as to exercise dominion over them freely, as Moses says: 'Let us make man, and let them have dominion over the fish of the sea' (Gen. 1: 26). Nor can anything else be proved from those words. For in that state, man was able to deal with things according to his own choice, in that they were subject to him; and this is called man's counsel, as distinct from God's counsel. But then, after saying that man was thus made and left in the hand of his own counsel, it goes on: 'He added his commandments and precepts.' What did he add them to? Surely the counsel and choice of man, and over and above the establishing of man's dominion over the rest of the creatures. And by these precepts he took away from man the dominion over one part of the creatures (for instance, over the tree of the knowledge of good and evil) and willed rather that he should not be free.

Then, however, when the precepts have been added, he comes to man's choice in relation to God and the things of God: 'If thou wilt observe the commandments, they shall preserve thee,' etc. It is therefore at this point, 'If thou wilt,' that the question of free choice arises. We thus learn from Ecclesiasticus that man is divided between two kingdoms, in one of which he is directed by his own choice and counsel, apart from any precepts and commandments of God, namely, in his dealings with the lower creatures. Here he reigns and is lord, as having been left in the hand of his own counsel. Not that God so leaves him as not to cooperate with him in everything, but he has granted him the free use of things according to his own choice, and has not restricted him by any laws or injunctions. By way of comparison one might say that the gospel has left us in the hand of our own counsel, to have dominion over things and use them as we wish; but Moses and the pope have not left us to that counsel, but have coerced us with laws and have subjected us rather to their own choice.

In the other Kingdom, however, man is not left in the hand of his own counsel, but is directed and led by the choice and counsel of God, so that just as in his own kingdom he is directed by his own counsel, without regard to the precepts of another, so in the Kingdom of God he is directed by the precepts of another without regard to his own choice. And this is what Ecclesiasticus means by: 'He added his precepts and commandments. If thou wilt,' etc.

If, then, these things are sufficiently clear, we have gained our point that this passage of Ecclesiasticus is evidence, not for, but against free choice, since by it man is subjected to the precepts and choice of God, and withdrawn from his own choice. If they are not sufficiently clear, at least we have made the point that this passage cannot be evidence in favour of free choice, since it can be understood in a different sense from theirs, namely in ours, which has just been stated, and which is not absurd but entirely sound and in harmony with the whole tenor of Scripture, whereas theirs is at variance with Scripture as a whole and is derived from this one passage alone, in contradiction to it. We stand, therefore, quite confidently by the good sense that the negative of free choice makes here, until they confirm their strained and forced affirmative.

When, therefore, Ecclesiasticus says: 'If thou wilt observe the commandments and keep acceptable fidelity forever, they shall preserve thee,' I do not see how free choice is proved by these words. For the verb is in the subjunctive mood ('If thou wilt'), which asserts nothing. As the logicians say, a conditional asserts nothing indicatively: for example, 'If the devil is God, it is right to worship him; if an ass flies, an ass has wings; if free choice exists, grace is nothing.' Ecclesiasticus, however, should have spoken as follows, if he had wished to assert free choice: 'Man can keep the commandments of God,' or: 'Man has the power to keep the commandments.'

But here Diatribe will retort that by saying, 'If thou wilt keep,' Ecclesiasticus indicates that there is in man a will capable of keeping and not keeping commandments; otherwise, what point is there in saying to one who has no will, 'If thou wilt'? Would it not be ridiculous to say to a blind person, 'If you will look, you will find a treasure,' or to a deaf person, 'If you will listen, I will tell you a good story'? This would simply be laughing at their misfortune. I reply: These are the arguments of human Reason, which has a habit of producing such bits of wisdom. We now have to argue, therefore, not with Ecclesiasticus, but with human Reason about an inference; for Reason interprets the Scriptures of God by her own inferences and syllogisms, and turns them in any direction she pleases. We will do this gladly and with confidence, knowing that she talks nothing but follies and absurdities, especially when she starts displaying her wisdom on sacred subjects.

To begin with, if I ask how it is proved that the presence of a free will in man is signified or implied every time it is said, 'If thou wilt, if thou shalt do, if thou shalt hear.' Reason will say, 'Because the nature of words and the use of language among men seem to require it.' She thus measures divine things and words by the usage and concerns of men; and what can be more perverse than this, seeing that the former are heavenly and the latter earthly? So the stupid thing betrays herself, showing how she has nothing but human thoughts about God. But what if I prove that the nature of words and the use of language even among men is not always such as to make a laughing-stock of those who are impotent whenever they are told: 'If thou wilt, if thou shalt do, if thou shalt hear'? How often do parents have a game with their children by telling them to come to them, or to do this or that, simply for the sake of showing them how unable they are, and compelling them to call for the help of the parents' hand! How often does a good doctor order a self-confident patient to do or stop doing things that are either impossible or painful to him, so as to bring him through his own experience to an awareness of his illness or weakness, to which he could not lead him by any other means? And what is more frequent than words of insult and provocation when we want to show either friends or enemies what they can and cannot do?

I mention these things merely in order to show Reason how foolish she is in tacking her inferences onto the Scriptures, and how blind she is not to see that they are not always applicable even with regard to human speech and action, for if she sees a thing happen once or twice, she immediately jumps to the conclusion that it happens quite generally and with regard to all the words of God and men, making a universal out of a particular in the usual manner of her wisdom.

If now God deals with us as a father with his children, so as to show our ignorant selves our helplessness, or like a good doctor makes our disease known to us, or tramples on us as enemies of his who proudly resist his counsel, and in laws which he issues (the most effective method of all) says: 'Do, hear, keep,' or, 'If thou shalt hear, if thou wilt, if thou shalt do,' will the correct conclusion to be drawn from this be: 'Therefore we can act freely, or else God is mocking us'? Why does it not rather follow: 'Therefore, God is putting us to the test so as to lead us by means of the law to a knowledge of our impotence if we are his friends or truly and deservedly to trample on and mock us if we are his proud enemies'? That is the reason why God gives laws, as Paul teaches (Rom. 3: 20). For human nature is so blind that it does not know its own powers, or rather diseases, and so proud as to imagine that it knows and can do everything; and for this pride and blindness God has no readier remedy than the propounding of his law, a subject on which we shall have more to say in the proper place.

[*The Bondage of the Will* (*Luther and Erasmus: Free Will and Salvation*, ed. and trans. G. Rupp and Philip Watson, London: SCM Press, 1969, 182–5).]

MARTIN LUTHER

43   Faith in the Justice of God

You may be worried that it is hard to defend the mercy and equity of God in damning the undeserving, that is, ungodly persons, who, being born in ungodliness, can by no means avoid being ungodly, and staying so, and being damned, but are compelled by natural necessity to sin and perish; as Paul says: 'We were all the children of wrath, even as others' (Eph. 2: 3), created such by God Himself from a seed that had been corrupted by the sin of the one man, Adam. But here God must be reverenced and held in awe, as being most merciful to those whom He justifies and saves in their own utter unworthiness; and we must show some measure of deference to His Divine wisdom by believing Him just when to us He seems unjust. If His justice were such as could be adjudged just by human reckoning, it clearly would not be Divine; it would in no way differ from human justice. But inasmuch as He is the one true God, wholly incomprehensible and inaccessible to man's understanding, it is reasonable, indeed inevitable, that His justice also should be incomprehensible; as Paul cries, saying: 'O the depth of the riches both of the wisdom and knowledge of God! How unsearchable are His judgments, and His ways past finding out!' (Rom. 11: 33). They would not, however, be 'unsearchable' if we could at every point grasp the grounds on which they are just. What is man compared with God? How much can our power achieve compared with His power? What is our strength compared with His strength? What is our knowledge compared with His wisdom? What is our substance compared with His substance? In a word, what is all that we are compared with all that He is? If, now, even nature teaches us to acknowledge that human power, strength, wisdom, knowledge and substance, and all that is ours, is as nothing compared with the Divine power, strength, wisdom, knowledge and substance, what perversity is it on our part to worry at the justice and the judgment of the only God, and to arrogate so much to our own judgment as to presume to comprehend, judge and evaluate God's judgment! Why do we not in like manner say at this point: 'Our judgment is nothing compared with God's judgment'? Ask reason whether force of conviction does not compel her to acknowledge herself foolish and rash for not allowing God's judgment to be incomprehensible, when she confesses that all the other things of God are incomprehensible! In everything else, we allow God His Divine Majesty; in the single case of His judgment, we are ready to deny it! To think that we cannot for a little while *believe* that He is just, when He has actually promised us that when He reveals His glory we shall all clearly *see* that He both was and is just!

I will give a parallel case, in order to strengthen our faith in God's justice, and to reassure that 'evil eye' which holds Him under suspicion of injustice. Behold! God governs the external affairs of the world in such a way that, if you regard and follow the judgment of human reason, you are forced to say, either that there is no God, or that God is unjust; as the poet said: 'I am often tempted to think there are no gods.' See the great prosperity of the wicked, and by contrast the great adversity of the good. Proverbs, and experience, the parent of proverbs, bear record that the more abandoned men are, the more successful they are. 'The tabernacle of robbers prosper,' says Job (12: 6), and Ps. 72 complains that sinners in the world are full of riches (Ps. 73: 12). Is it not, pray, universally held to be most unjust that bad men should prosper, and good men be afflicted? Yet that is the way of the world. Hereupon some of the greatest minds have fallen into denying the existence of God, and imagining that Chance governs all things at random. Such were the Epicureans, and Pliny. And Aristotle, wishing to set his 'prime Being' free from misery, holds that he sees nothing but himself; for Aristotle supposes that it would be very irksome to such a Being to behold so many evils and injustices! And the Prophets, who believed in God's existence, were still more tempted concerning the injustice of God. Jeremiah, Job, David, Asaph and others are cases in point. What do you suppose Demosthenes and Cicero thought, when, having done all they could, they received as their reward an unhappy death? Yet all this, which looks so much like injustice in God, and is traduced as such by arguments which no reason or light of nature can resist, is most easily cleared up by the light of the gospel and the knowledge of grace, which teaches us that though the wicked flourish in their bodies, yet they perish in their souls. And a summary explanation of this whole inexplicable problem is found in a single little word: *There is a life after this life; and all that is not punished and repaid here will be punished and repaid there; for this life is nothing more than a precursor, or, rather, a beginning, of the life that is to come.*

If, now, this problem, which was debated in every age but never solved, is swept away and settled so easily by the light of the gospel, which shines only in the Word and to faith, how do you think it will be when the light of the Word and faith shall cease, and the real facts, and the Majesty of God, shall be revealed as they are? Do you not think that the light of glory will be able with the greatest ease to solve problems that are insoluble in the light of the word and grace, now that the light of grace has so easily solved this problem, which was insoluble by the light of nature?

Keep in view three lights: the light of nature, the light of grace, and the light of glory (this is a common and a good distinction). By the light of nature, it is inexplicable that it should be just for the good to be afflicted and the bad to prosper; but the light of grace explains it. By the light of grace, it is inexplicable how God can damn him who by his own strength can do nothing but sin and become guilty. Both the light of nature and the light of grace here insist that the fault lies not in the wretchedness of man, but in the injustice of God; nor can they judge otherwise of a God who crowns the ungodly freely, without merit, and does not crown, but damns another, who is perhaps less, and certainly not more, ungodly. But the light of glory insists otherwise, and will one day reveal God, to whom alone belongs a judgment whose justice is incomprehensible, as a God Whose justice is most righteous and evident—provided only that in the meanwhile we *believe* it, as we are instructed and encouraged to do by the example of the light of grace explaining what was a puzzle of the same order to the light of nature.

[*The Bondage of the Will*, trans J. I. Packer and O. R. Johnston (London: James Clarke, 1957), 314–17.]

44 The *Sensus Divinitatis*

There is within the human mind, and indeed by natural instinct, an awareness of divinity. This we take to be beyond controversy. To prevent anyone from taking refuge in the pretence of ignorance, God himself has implanted in all men a certain understanding of his divine majesty. Ever renewing its memory, he repeatedly sheds fresh drops. Since, therefore, men one and all perceive that there is a God and that he is their Maker, they are condemned by their own testimony because they have failed to honour him and to consecrate their lives to his will. If ignorance of God is to be looked for anywhere, surely one is most likely to find an example of it among the more backward folk and those more remote from civilization. Yet there is, as the eminent pagan says, no nation so barbarous, no people so savage, that they have not a deep-seated conviction that there is a God. And they who in other aspects of life seem least to differ from brutes still continue to retain some seed of religion. So deeply does the common conception occupy the minds of all, so tenaciously does it inhere in the hearts of all! Therefore, since from the beginning of the world there has been no region, no city, in short, no household, that could do without religion, there lies in this a tacit confession of a sense of deity inscribed in the hearts of all.

Indeed, even idolatry is ample proof of this conception. We know how man does not willingly humble himself so as to place other creatures over himself. Since, then, he prefers to worship wood and stone rather than to be thought of as having no God, clearly this is a most vivid impression of a divine being. So impossible is it to blot this from man's mind that natural disposition would be more easily altered, as altered indeed it is when man voluntarily sinks from his natural haughtiness to the very depths in order to honour God!

Therefore it is utterly vain for some men to say that religion was invented by the subtlety and craft of a few to hold the simple folk in thrall by this device and that those very persons who originated the worship of God for others did not in the least believe that any God existed. I confess, indeed, that in order to hold men's minds in greater subjection, clever men have devised very many things in religion by which to inspire the common folk with reverence and to strike them with terror. But they would never have achieved this if men's minds had not already been imbued with a firm conviction about God, from which the inclination toward religion springs as from a seed. And indeed it is not credible that those who craftily imposed upon the ruder folk under pretence of religion were entirely devoid of the knowledge of God. If, indeed, there were some in the past, and today not a few appear, who deny that God exists, yet willy-nilly they from time to time feel an inkling of what they desire not to believe. One reads of no one who burst forth into bolder or more unbridled contempt of deity than Gaius Caligula; yet no one trembled more miserably when any sign of God's wrath manifested itself; thus—albeit unwillingly—he shuddered at the God whom he professedly sought to despise. You may see now and again how this also happens to those like him; how he who is the boldest despiser of God is of all men the most startled at the rustle of a falling leaf [cf. Lev. 26: 36]. Whence does this arise but from the vengeance of divine majesty, which strikes their consciences all the more violently the more they try to flee from it? Indeed, they seek out every subterfuge to hide themselves from the Lord's presence, and to efface it again from their minds. But in spite of themselves they are always entrapped. Although it may sometimes seem to vanish for a moment, it returns at once and rushes in with new force. If for these there is any respite from anxiety of conscience, it is not much different from the sleep of drunken or frenzied persons, who do not rest peacefully even while sleeping because they are continually troubled with dire and dreadful dreams. The impious themselves therefore exemplify the fact that some conception of God is ever alive in all men's minds.

Men of sound judgment will always be sure that a sense of divinity which can never be effaced is engraved upon men's minds. Indeed, the perversity of the impious, who though they struggle furiously are unable to extricate themselves from the fear of God, is abundant testimony that this conviction, namely, that there is some God, is naturally inborn in all, and is fixed deep within, as it were in the very marrow. Although Diagoras and his like may jest at whatever has been believed in every age concerning religion, and Dionysius may mock the heavenly judgment, this is sardonic laughter, for the worm of conscience, sharper than any cauterizing iron, gnaws away within. I do not say, as Cicero did, that errors disappear with the lapse of time, and that religion grows and becomes better each day. For the world (something will have to be said of this a little later) tries as far as it is able to cast away all knowledge of God, and by every means to corrupt the worship of him. I only say that though the stupid hardness in their minds, which the impious eagerly conjure up to reject God, wastes away, yet the sense of divinity, which they greatly wished to have extinguished, thrives and presently burgeons. From this we conclude that it is not a doctrine that must first be learned in school, but one of which each of us is master from his mother's womb and which nature itself permits no one to forget, although many strive with every nerve to this end.

Besides, if all men are born and live to the end that they may know God, and yet if knowledge of God is unstable and fleeting unless it progresses to this degree, it is clear that all those who do not direct every thought and action in their lives to this goal degenerate from the law of their creation. This was not unknown to the philosophers. Plato meant nothing but this when he often taught that the highest good of the soul is likeness to God, where, when the soul has grasped the knowledge of God, it is wholly transformed into his likeness. In the same manner also Gryllus, in the writings of Plutarch, reasons very skillfully, affirming that, if once religion is absent from their life, men are in no wise superior to brute beasts, but are in many respects far more miserable. Subject, then, to so many forms of wickedness, they drag out their lives in ceaseless tumult and disquiet. Therefore, it is worship of God alone that renders men higher than the brutes, and through it alone they aspire to immortality.

[*Institutes of the Christian Religion*, I. iii. 1–3 (ed. John T. McNeill, trans. Ford Lewis Battles, London: SCM Press, 1960, 43–7).]

45 The Testimony of the Spirit

We ought to remember what I said a bit ago: credibility of doctrine is not established until we are persuaded beyond doubt that God is its Author. Thus, the highest proof of Scripture derives in general from the fact that God in person speaks in it. The prophets and apostles do not boast either of their keenness or of anything that obtains credit for them as they speak; nor do they dwell upon rational proofs. Rather, they bring forward God's holy name, that by it the whole world may be brought into obedience to him. Now we ought to see how apparent it is not only by plausible opinion but by clear truth that they do not call upon God's name heedlessly or falsely. If we desire to provide in the best way for our consciences—that they may not be perpetually beset by the instability of doubt or vacillation, and that they may not also boggle at the smallest quibbles—we ought to seek our conviction in a higher place than human reasons, judgments, or conjectures, that is, in the secret testimony of the Spirit. True, if we wished to proceed by arguments, we might advance many things that would easily prove—if there is any god in heaven—that the law, the prophets, and the gospel come from him. Indeed, ever so learned men, endowed with the highest judgment, rise up in opposition and bring to bear and display all their mental powers in this debate. Yet, unless they become hardened to the point of hopeless impudence, this confession will be wrested from them: that they see manifest signs of God speaking in Scripture. From this is it clear that the teaching of Scripture is from heaven. And a little later we shall see that all the books of Sacred Scripture far surpass all other writings. Yes, if we turn pure eyes and upright senses toward it, the majesty of God will immediately come to view, subdue our bold rejection, and compel us to obey.

Yet they who strive to build up firm faith in Scripture through disputation are doing things backwards. For my part, although I do not excel either in great dexterity or eloquence, if I were struggling against the most crafty sort of despisers of God, who seek to appear shrewd and witty in disparaging Scripture, I am confident it would not be difficult for me to silence their clamorous voices. And if it were a useful labour to refute their cavils, I would with no great trouble shatter the boasts they mutter in their lurking places. But even if anyone clears God's Sacred Word from man's evil speaking, he will not at once imprint upon their hearts that certainty which piety requires. Since for unbelieving men religion seems to stand by opinion alone, they, in order not to believe anything foolishly or lightly, both wish and demand rational proof that Moses and the prophets spoke divinely. But I reply: the testimony of the Spirit is more excellent than all reason. For as God alone is a fit witness of himself in his Word, so also the Word will not find acceptance in men's hearts before it is sealed by the inward testimony of the Spirit. The same Spirit, therefore, who has spoken through the mouths of the prophets must penetrate into our hearts to persuade us that they faithfully proclaimed what had been divinely commanded. Isaiah very aptly expresses this connection in these words: 'My Spirit which is in you, and the words that I have put in your mouth, and the mouths of your offspring, shall never fail' [Isa. 59: 21 p.]. Some good folk are annoyed that a clear proof is not ready at hand when the impious, unpunished, murmur against God's Word. As if the Spirit were not called both 'seal' and 'guarantee' [2 Cor. 1: 22] for confirming the faith of the godly; because until he illumines their minds, they ever waver among many doubts!

Let this point therefore stand: that those whom the Holy Spirit has inwardly taught truly rest upon Scripture and that Scripture indeed is self-authenticated; hence, it is not right to subject it to proof and reasoning. And the certainty it deserves with us, it attains by the testimony of the Spirit. For even if it wins reverence for itself by its own majesty, it seriously affects us only when it is sealed upon our hearts through the Spirit. Therefore, illumined by his power, we believe neither by our own nor by anyone else's judgment that Scripture is from God; but above human judgment we affirm with utter certainty (just as if we were gazing upon the majesty of God himself) that it has flowed to us from the very mouth of God by the ministry of men. We seek no proofs, no marks of genuineness upon which our judgment may lean; but we subject our judgment and wit to it as to a thing far beyond any guesswork! This we do, not as persons accustomed to seize upon some unknown thing, which, under closer scrutiny, displeases them, but fully conscious that we hold the unassailable truth! Nor do we do this as those miserable men who habitually bind over their minds to the thralldom of superstition; but we feel that the undoubted power of his divine majesty lives and breathes there. By this power we are drawn and inflamed, knowingly and willingly, to obey him, yet also more vitally and more effectively than by mere human willing or knowing!

God, therefore, very rightly proclaims through Isaiah that the prophets together with the whole people are witnesses to him; for they, instructed by prophecies, unhesitatingly held that God has spoken without deceit or ambiguity [Isa. 43: 10]. Such, then, is a conviction that requires no reasons; such, a knowledge with which the best reason agrees—in which the mind truly reposes more securely and constantly than in any reasons; such, finally, a feeling that can be born only of heavenly revelation. I speak of nothing other than what each believer experiences within himself—though my words fall far beneath a just explanation of the matter.

I now refrain from saying more, since I shall have opportunity to discuss this matter elsewhere. Let us, then, know that the only true faith is that which the Spirit of God seals in our hearts. Indeed, the modest and teachable reader will be content with this one reason: Isaiah promised all the children of the renewed church that 'they would be God's disciples' [Isa. 54: 13]. God deems worthy of singular privilege only his elect, whom he distinguishes from the human race as a whole. Indeed, what is the beginning of true doctrine but a prompt eagerness to hearken to God's voice? But God asks to be heard through the mouth of Moses, as it is written: 'Say not in your heart, who will ascend into heaven, or who will descend into the abyss: behold, the word is in your mouth' [conflation of Deut. 30: 12, 14 and Ps. 107: 26; 106: 26, Vg.]. If God has willed this treasure of understanding to be hidden from his children, it is no wonder or absurdity that the multitude of men are so ignorant and stupid! Among the 'multitude' I include even certain distinguished folk, until they become engrafted into the body of the church. Besides, Isaiah, warning that the prophetic teaching would be beyond belief, not only to foreigners but also to the Jews who wanted to be reckoned as members of the Lord's household, at the same time adds the reason: 'The arm of God will not be revealed' to all [Isa. 53: 1 p.]. Whenever, then, the fewness of believers disturbs us, let the converse come to mind, that only those to whom it is given can comprehend the mysteries of God [cf. Matt. 13: 11].

> [*Institutes of the Christian Religion*, i. 7 (ed. John T. McNeill, trans. Ford Lewis Battles, London: SCM Press, 1960, 78–81).]

HERBERT OF CHERBURY

46   True Religion

When for a long time I had employed my most serious thoughts in considering whether any common means for the obtaining eternal salvation were so proposed to all mankind, that from thence we might necessarily conclude and infer the certainty of a universal divine providence, I met with many doubts and difficulties, not easy to be solved. I found that very many fathers of the Church had not only a mean and contemptible opinion of the ancient divulged religion of the heathens; but also absolutely and entirely condemned it. The divines of this last age also pronounce as severe a sentence against all those that were without their pale; for that, according to their opinions, the far greatest part of mankind must be inevitably sentenced to eternal punishment.

This appearing to me too rigid and severe to be consistent with the attributes of the most great and good God, I began to consult the writings of the heathens themselves. But when, by their own histories, I found their gods were often not only mere men, but also some of the most vile; and when I had observed that their religious worship, rites and ceremonies, were ridiculous and extravagant, I was very much inclined to be of the common opinion against them. But then again, when I considered that this was altogether incompatible with the dignity of a *universal divine providence*, I began to make diligent enquiry, whether they meant the same by God as we now do.

Now by God we understand a perfect, immense, and eternal being; and I found, that with them it sometimes signified nature, or a certain imperfect, finite and transitory power; for that not only heaven, the planets, stars, ethereal and aerial spirits; but those men also who had deserved well of mankind in general, or their own country in particular, were unanimously translated into the number of their deities. Their emperors also (some of whom were the worst of men) were deified in their life time; and even the *fever, fear and paleness* were esteemed gods and goddesses by them; so that they ascribed divine honour to whatsoever was above the common rank of mankind, or exceeded the apprehension of the vulgar. But still it is very evident, that wherever we find the attributes of *summus, optimus, maximus*; most supreme, most good, and most great, they meant the same God and common Father with us. So that the homonymy of the word being explained, the doubts that arise by comparing our God with theirs, will soon be cleared.

But yet neither their religious worship or rites, could ever make me have an ill opinion of the common people, they being the invention of the priests only; wherefore this crime ought solely to be imputed to their great men, and not to the populace, who were only passive in the matter. I suppose none will deny but that priests have introduced superstition and idolatry, as well as sown quarrels and dissensions wherever they came: This inclined me not to make so rash and peremptory a determination, concerning the future state of the laity, as some divines have done; they being only culpable, for totally devoting and subjecting themselves to the authority of their priests. Their great defection from the pure worship of the *Supreme God* being justly to be attributed to the sacerdotal order, put me upon the enquiry, whether amongst those heaps of ethnical superstitions, a thread of truth might be found, by the assistance of which it was possible for them to extricate themselves out of that *labyrinth* of error, in which they were involved.

Upon this, five undeniable propositions presently occurred; which not only we, but all mankind in general, must needs acknowledge:

I   *That there is one supreme God.*
II   *That he ought to be worshipped.*
III *That virtue and piety are the chief parts of divine worship.*
IV   *That we ought to be sorry for our sins, and repent of them.*
V   *That divine goodness doth dispense rewards and punishments both in this life, and after it.*

All these I will explain at large, at the end of my book, after I have treated of the following parts of their religion; as also shown where that thread may be found, by the help whereof (as we conceive) the most perspicacious amongst the heathens got out of this *labyrinth*.

Let not my reader think I have made use of the word *labyrinth* here inconsiderately; for as there were formerly four *labyrinths*, very artificially contrived; *viz.*

the *Cretick, Egyptian, Lemnian* and *Italian*; so these places more especially have furnished the rest of the world with almost all their superstitious worship. I could heartily wish the modern divines were more considerate in their determinations concerning the souls of the heathens or pagans. The most rigid, such generally as are least acquainted with learning in general, but especially humane learning, express themselves much after this manner. 'After the Fall of *Adam*, all mankind was formed and produced out of a degenerate mass; some of them, out of the mere good pleasure of God and the intervention of the death of Christ, were elected to eternal glory; but the far greater part, nay even those that had never heard of the name of Christ, were reprobated and determined to eternal perdition; and that the most innocent and commendable lives the heathens could lead, would avail them nothing, in regard their works were merely moral; and upon that account altogether insignificant.'

Now when I perceived that they resolved the causes of eternal salvation or damnation only into the good pleasure of God, and the death of Christ; I found that their opinion was grounded not on reason, but some peremptory decrees, which nobody did pretend to know, and I could not think that they were so privy to the secret counsels of God, as to be able to establish anything for certain; wherefore I left them, as entertaining mean, base, and unworthy thoughts of the *most good and great God*, and mankind in general. How could I believe, that a just God could take pleasure in the eternal reprobation of those to whom he never afforded any means of salvation, or endued with souls made after his own image; and whom he foresaw must be damned of absolute necessity, without the least hopes or possibility of escaping it? I could not understand how they could call that God *most good and great*, who created men only to damn them, without their knowledge, and against their will.

Then I met with some other divines, who asserted, that Christ was revealed to such heathens as led pious and honest lives, at the very moment of their death, and so they were conveyed to Paradise. But their opinion being neither founded on history, tradition, or rational conjecture, it appeared to me very improbable; but I must needs confess, these divines show much more tenderness towards humankind, though they have nothing solid to support their assertion.

At last, I consulted those who are called the schoolmen, to see if their sentiments concerning the heathen were more just and regular; but they skipping from faith to reason, and then immediately again from reason to faith, with wonderful agility; and finding them so very nice and subtle in their distinctions as to split a hair, I could not receive the least satisfaction from them. Amongst other axioms, I found this an established one amongst them: *facientibus quod in se est, non deesse gratiam salutarem*: Saving grace is never wanting, to those that do all that is in their power.

Then I had recourse to other authors, but especially *Crellius*, a very learned man, who has written concerning the souls of the heathen; he quotes several very excellent passages upon this subject out of the most ancient fathers; by which I found they were of opinion, that some of the best amongst the heathen, through the infinite mercy of God, might be capable of eternal salvation. I soon embraced their opinion, not seeing how the doctrine of a *universal divine providence* could be solved otherwise, than that some means should be afforded unto all men, by which they might come to God. And seeing that nature or common providence, did supply us here with all things that were necessary and convenient for food and raiment; I could not conceive how the same God, either could or would, leave any man quite destitute (either by nature or grace) of the means of obtaining a more happy state; and though the heathen did not make so good use of them as they might have done, yet the most *good and great God*, was not in the least to be charged with their miscarriage.

I know it is a generally received opinion that common providence does not afford sufficient means, without the concurrence of grace and particular providence: But my design is to make it evident that a universal providence is extended to all mankind. Now forasmuch as the heathen (as the holy scriptures testify and learned divines acknowledge) worshipped the same God as we do; had the same abhorrence of sin; believed rewards and punishment after this life; I cannot but think that after they had led a good life they were made partakers of the fullness of that divine grace; especially in regard they knew the most rational and perspicuous parts of the true divine worship.

I pretend not to defend the gross of the heathen religion, which I always esteemed foolish, incongruous and absurd; but only propose those truths which shined in the midst of their greatest obscurity. Now when they mixed superstitions and fictions with them, and had polluted their souls with such crimes as no repentance could sufficiently purge and expiate; their destruction was justly owing to themselves; but let glory be to the great God for ever. Whether these means for attaining a better state are so sufficiently effectual that eternal happiness will be the necessary consequence, shall be discoursed of hereafter in its place.

[*De Religione Gentilium* (1663), trans. W. Lewis (London, 1705), 1–7.]

47 Science and the Interpretation of the Bible

So you see, if I am not mistaken, how disorderly is the procedure of those who in disputes about natural phenomena that do not directly involve the Faith give first place to scriptural passages, which they quite often misunderstand anyway. However, if these people really believe they have grasped the true meaning of a particular scriptural passage, and if they consequently feel sure of possessing the absolute truth on the question they intend to dispute about, then let them sincerely tell me whether they think that someone in a scientific dispute who happens to be right has a great advantage over another who happens to be wrong. I know they will answer Yes, and that the one who supports the true side will be able to provide a thousand experiments and a thousand necessary demonstrations for his side, whereas the other person can have nothing but sophisms, paralogisms, and fallacies. But if they know they have such an advantage over their opponents as long as the discussion is limited to physical questions and only philosophical weapons are used, why is it that when they come to the meeting they immediately introduce an irresistible and terrible weapon, the mere sight of which terrifies even the most skilful and expert champion? If I must tell the truth, I believe it is they who are the most terrified, and that they are trying to find a way of not letting the opponent approach because they feel unable to resist his assaults. However, consider that, as I just said, whoever has truth on his side has a great, indeed the greatest, advantage over the opponent, and that it is impossible for two truths to contradict each other; it follows therefore that we must not fear any assaults launched against us by anyone, as long as we are allowed to speak and to be heard by competent persons who are not excessively upset by their own emotions and interests.

To confirm this I now come to examining the specific passage of Joshua, concerning which you put forth three theses for their Most Serene Highnesses. I take the third one, which you advanced as mine (as indeed it is), but I add some other consideration that I do not believe I have ever told you.

Let us then assume and concede to the opponent that the words of the sacred text should be taken precisely in their literal meaning, namely that in answer to Joshua's prayers God made the sun stop and lengthened the day, so that as a result he achieved victory; but I request that the same rule should apply to both, so that the opponent should not pretend to tie me and to leave himself free to change or modify the meanings of the words. Given this, I say that this passage shows clearly the falsity and impossibility of the Aristotelian and Ptolemaic world system, and on the other hand agrees very well with the Copernican one.

I first ask the opponent whether he knows with how many motions the sun moves. If he knows, he must answer that it moves with two motions, namely with the annual motion from west to east and with the diurnal motion in the opposite direction from east to west.

Then, secondly, I ask him whether these two motions, so different and almost contrary to each other, belong to the sun and are its own to an equal extent. The answer must be No, but that only one is specifically its own, namely the annual motion, whereas the other is not but belongs to the highest heaven, I mean the Prime Mobile; the latter carries along with it the sun as well as the other planets and the stellar sphere, forcing them to make a revolution around the earth in twenty-four hours, with a motion, as I said, almost contrary to their own natural motion.

Coming to the third question, I ask him with which of these two motions the sun produces night and day, that is, whether with its own motion or else with that of the Prime Mobile. The answer must be that night and day are effects of the motion of the Prime Mobile, and that what depends on the sun's own motion is not night and day but the various seasons and the year itself.

Now, if the day derives not from the sun's motion but from that of the Prime Mobile, who does not see that to lengthen the day one must stop the Prime Mobile and not the sun? Indeed, is there anyone who understands these first elements of astronomy and does not know that, if God had stopped the sun's motion, He would have cut and shortened the day instead of lengthening it? For, the sun's motion being contrary to the diurnal turning, the more the sun moves toward the east the more its progression toward the west is slowed down, whereas by its motion being diminished or annihilated the sun would set that much sooner; this phenomenon is observed in the moon, whose diurnal revolutions are slower than those of the sun inasmuch as its own motion is faster than that of the sun. It follows that it is absolutely impossible to stop the sun and lengthen the day in the system of Ptolemy and Aristotle, and therefore either the motions must not be arranged as Ptolemy says or we must modify the meaning of the words of the Scripture; we would have to claim that, when it says that God stopped the sun, it meant to say that He stopped the Prime Mobile, and that it said the contrary of what it would have said if speaking to educated men in order to adapt itself to the capacity of those who are barely able to understand the rising and setting of the sun.

Add to this that it is not believable that God would stop only the sun, letting the other spheres proceed; for He would have unnecessarily altered and upset all the order, appearances, and arrangements of the other stars in relation to the sun, and would have greatly disturbed the whole system of nature. On the other hand, it is believable that He would stop the whole system of celestial spheres, which could then together return to their operations without any confusion or change after the period of intervening rest.

However, we have already agreed not to change the meaning of the words in the text; therefore it is necessary to resort to another arrangement of the parts of the world, and to see whether the literal meaning of the words flows directly and without obstacle from its point of view. This is in fact what we see happening.

For I have discovered and conclusively demonstrated that the solar globe turns on itself, completing an entire rotation in about one lunar month, in exactly the same direction as all the other heavenly revolutions; moreover, it is very probable and reasonable that, as the chief instrument and minister of nature and almost the heart of the world, the sun gives not only light (as it obviously does) but also motion to all the planets that revolve around it; hence, if in conformity with Copernicus's position the diurnal motion is attributed to the earth, anyone can see that it sufficed stopping the sun to stop the whole system, and thus to lengthen the period of the diurnal illumination without altering in any way the rest of the mutual relationships of the planets; and that is exactly how the words of the sacred text sound. Here then is the manner in which by stopping the sun one can lengthen the day on the earth, without introducing any confusion among the parts of the world and without altering the words of the Scripture.

I have written much more than is appropriate in view of my slight illness. So I end by reminding you that I am at your service, and I kiss your hands and pray the Lord to give you happy holidays and all you desire.

Florence, 21 December 1613.

To Your Very Reverend Paternity.

Your Most Affectionate Servant,
Galileo Galilei.

To the Very Reverend Father Paolo Antonio Foscarini, Provincial of the Carmelites in the Province of Calabria:

My Very Reverend Father,

I have read with interest the letter in Italian and the essay in Latin which Your Paternity sent me; I thank you for the one and for the other and confess that they are all full of intelligence and erudition. You ask for my opinion, and so I shall give it to you, but very briefly, since now you have little time for reading and I for writing.

First, I say that it seems to me that Your Paternity and Mr Galileo are proceeding prudently by limiting yourselves to speaking suppositionally and not absolutely, as I have always believed that Copernicus spoke. For there is no danger in saying that, by assuming the earth moves and the sun stands still, one saves all the appearances better than by postulating eccentrics and epicycles; and that is sufficient for the mathematician. However, it is different to want to affirm that in reality the sun is at the centre of the world and only turns on itself without moving from east to west, and the earth is in the third heaven and revolves with great speed around the sun; this is a very dangerous thing, likely not only to irritate all scholastic philosophers and theologians, but also to harm the Holy Faith by rendering Holy Scripture false. For Your Paternity has well shown many ways of interpreting Holy Scripture, but has not applied them to particular cases; without a doubt you would have encountered very great difficulties if you had wanted to interpret all those passages you yourself cited.

Second, I say that, as you know, the Council prohibits interpreting Scripture against the common consensus of the Holy Fathers; and if Your Paternity wants to read not only the Holy Fathers, but also the modern commentaries on Genesis, the Psalms, Ecclesiastes, and Joshua, you will find all agreeing in the literal interpretation that the sun is in heaven and turns around the earth with great speed, and that the earth is very far from heaven and sits motionless at the centre of the world. Consider now, with your sense of prudence, whether the

Church can tolerate giving Scripture a meaning contrary to the Holy Fathers and to all the Greek and Latin commentators. Nor can one answer that this is not a matter of faith, since if it is not a matter of faith 'as regards the topic,' it is a matter of faith 'as regards the speaker'; and so it would be heretical to say that Abraham did not have two children and Jacob twelve, as well as to say that Christ was not born of a virgin, because both are said by the Holy Spirit through the mouth of the prophets and the apostles.

Third, I say that if there were a true demonstration that the sun is at the centre of the world and the earth in the third heaven, and that the sun does not circle the earth but the earth circles the sun, then one would have to proceed with great care in explaining the Scriptures that appear contrary, and say rather that we do not understand them than that what is demonstrated is false. But I will not believe that there is such a demonstration, until it is shown me. Nor is it the same to demonstrate that by supposing the sun to be at the centre and the earth in heaven one can save the appearances, and to demonstrate that in truth the sun is at the centre and the earth in heaven; for I believe the first demonstration may be available, but I have very great doubts about the second, and in case of doubt one must not abandon the Holy Scripture as interpreted by the Holy Fathers. I add that the one who wrote, 'The sun also ariseth, and the sun goeth down, and hasteth to his place where he arose,' was Solomon, who not only spoke inspired by God, but was a man above all others wise and learned in the human sciences and in the knowledge of created things; he received all this wisdom from God; therefore it is not likely that he was affirming something that was contrary to truth already demonstrated or capable of being demonstrated. Now, suppose you say that Solomon speaks in accordance with appearances, since it seems to us that the sun moves (while the earth does not), just as to someone who moves away from the seashore on a ship it looks like the shore is moving. I shall answer that when someone moves away from the shore, although it appears to him that the shore is moving away from him, nevertheless he knows that this is an error and corrects it, seeing clearly that the ship moves and not the shore; but in regard to the sun and the earth, no scientist has any need to correct the error, since he clearly experiences that the earth stands still and that the eye is not in error when it judges that the sun moves, as it also is not in error when it judges that the moon and the stars move. And this is enough for now.

With this I greet dearly Your Paternity, and I pray to God to grant you all your wishes.

At home, 12 April 1615.

To Your Very Reverend Paternity.

As a Brother,
Cardinal Bellarmine.

[Galileo to Castelli and Bellarmine to Foscarini, in Maurice A. Finocchiaro (ed. and trans.), *The Galileo Affair: A Documentary History* (Berkeley, University of California Press, 1989), 52–4, 57–9.]

But, it will be said, was Tertullian grossly mistaken when he put the ordinary Christian above the philosophers? I answer that his assertion can be very well corrected. It only has to be said that the poorest Christian workman firmly believes more things about the nature of God than the greatest philosophers of paganism were able to know. It only has to be asserted that with his catechism alone he will give so much detail that, for each item that they only partly affirm, he will affirm forty without any hesitation. This is what Tertullian might have said without being at all mistaken. But these Christians who are so knowledge-able in comparison to Thales and all the other philosophers of ancient Greece would say as little and be as silent as Thales if they were to say nothing but what they clearly and distinctly comprehended. And they owe their great knowledge only to the luck of having been raised in a Church where they have acquired a historical faith, and sometimes even a justifying faith of revealed truths. This convinces them of several things that they do not comprehend at all. Our greatest theologians, if they acted like Simonides, that is, if they would not assert anything about the nature of God except that which would, to the light of reason, appear incontestible, evident, and safe from all objections, would perpetually demand new delays of all the Hieros in the world. Add also that Simonides, if he had consulted and examined Scripture without the influence of either education or grace, would not have extricated himself from his labyrinth or his silence. Reason would have prevented him from denying the facts contained in Scripture and from not seeing something supernatural in the chain of these facts, but this would not have been sufficient to enable him to have come to a decision about this. The powers of reason and philosophical exami-nation go no further than to keep us in suspense and in fear of error, whether we affirm, or whether we deny. It is necessary that either the grace of God or childhood education should come to their assistance. And observe that there is no hypothesis against which reason furnishes more objections than against that of the Gospel. The mystery of the Trinity, the Incarnation of the Word, his death for the expiation of our sins, the propagation of the sin of Adam, the eternal predestination of a small number of persons to the happiness of heaven, the eternal condemnation of almost all mankind to the endless torments of hell, the extinction of free will since the Fall of Adam, and the like, are matters that would have thrown Simonides into greater doubts than all that his imagi-nation suggested to him. Let us consider St Paul's words, not only that the Gospel was 'a stumbling block to the Jews, and to the Greeks foolishness, but also that God saved men by the foolishness of preaching' (1 Corinthians 1: 23 and 21).

Here is a thought which, perhaps, ought not to be rejected. Simonides apparently found himself in difficulties concerning the genus of his definition. He did not dare say that God was a body. A hundred objections kept him from this. He did not dare say that God was a pure spirit, for he only conceived of things in terms of the idea of extension. Until Descartes, all our learned men, whether theologians or philosophers, had ascribed extension to spirits—an infinite one to God, and a finite one to angels and rational souls. It is true that they maintained that this extension is not material nor composed of parts and that spirits are completely in every part of space that they occupy (*toti in toto et toti in singulis partibus*). From this it followed that there are three kinds of local presence: the limited presence of bodies, the definite presence of spirits, and the omnipresence of God. The Cartesians have overthrown all these doctrines. They say that spirits have no kind of extension, nor local presence. But their view is rejected as absurd. Let us say then that even today almost all our philosophers and all our theologians teach, in conformity with popular views, that God is diffused throughout infinite spaces. Now it is certain that this amounts to destroying with one hand what was built by the other. In effect, the materiality of God is restored after it had been removed. You say that he is a spirit. Well and good! This gives him a nature different from matter. But at the same time you say that his substance is diffused everywhere; you say, therefore, that it is extended. Now we do not have any idea of two kinds of extension. We conceive clearly that all extension whatsoever has parts that are distinct, impenetrable, and separable from one another. It is monstrous to contend that the soul is entirely in the brain and entirely in the heart. It is not conceivable that divine extension and material extension can be in the same place. This would constitute a real penetration of dimensions that our reason cannot conceive. Besides this, things that are penetrated by a third object are penetrated by one another; and thus the heavens and the sphere of the earth are penetrated by one another; for they would be penetrated by the divine substance, which according to you, has no parts. From this it follows that the sun is penetrated by the same being as the earth is. In a word, if matter is only matter because it is extended, it follows that all extension is matter. You are challenged to name any other attribute that makes matter matter. The impenetrability of bodies comes only from extension. We can conceive of no other basis for it. And thus you ought to say that if spirits were extended, they would be impenetrable. They would then not differ from bodies at all by penetrability. After all, according to the ordinary view, divine extension is neither more nor less penetrable or impenetrable than that of bodies. Its parts, call them virtual as much as you please, its parts I say, cannot be penetrated by one another; but they may so be by the parts of matter. Is this not what you say of the parts of matter; they cannot be penetrated by one another, but they can be penetrated by the virtual parts of divine extension? If you carefully consult common sense, you will see that when two extensions are penetratively in the same place, one is as penetrable as the other. It cannot therefore be said that the extension of matter differs from any other kind of extension by impenetrability. It is thus certain that all extension is matter, and consequently you take away from God only the name of body and leave all the reality of it in him when you say that he is extended. Since it is impossible for you to do otherwise, you should not find it strange that Simonides did not dare deny that God was a body; he did not dare affirm it either. He preferred to keep quiet. Let us remember that the most subtle Cartesians maintain that we have no idea at all of a spiritual substance. We know only by experience that it thinks, but we do not know what the nature of a being is whose modifications are thoughts. We do not know what is the subject, nor what is the substratum in which thoughts inhere. Simonides was perhaps led by this not to risk asserting that God was a spirit. He had no idea at all of what a spirit was.

For the rest, a Jesuit [Lescalopier], who has commented on Cicero's *De natura deorum*, does not condemn the caution of Simonides; and he wishes that the ancient philosophers and poets and the heretics had imitated it. What he says concerning the incomprehensibility of God deserves to be transcribed. 'What Tertullian imputes to ignorance, others ascribe to modesty. And I wish the ancient philosophers and poets, and the heretics who followed them, had been as modest in this point as Thales or Simonides. They certainly would not have falsely ascribed so many absurd, impious, and blasphemous things to the divine nature, nor even have fallen into the grossest errors, which we see with great regret that presumptuous men have run into. We are all possessed with a strong desire for knowledge, but with a much greater desire of knowing God; whence we may infer that God is willing to be known by us, but within certain prescribed limits, between pillars, upon which he inscribed with his own finger, *ne plus ultra*. For there are in divine things some secret recesses into which almighty God would not have us penetrate. But if any person influenced by rashness and pride proceeds farther and attempts to break into this sacred recess, the farther he advances, the thicker is the darkness he encounters, so that he may, if he be wise, confess the unfathomable majesty of God and the weakness of the human mind and be obliged to confess with Simonides, "The longer I consider this, the more obscure it appears to me." . . .' He then cites a fine passage from St Augustine on this. A French author [La Mothe le Vayer] has regarded the behavior of Simonides as an act of piety, and has used this as an occasion to condemn the confidence of the Eunomians. 'Remember the pious modesty of Simonides,' he says, 'who having asked King Hiero for only one day to prepare to discuss the divine essence before him, then asked two days, then three, protesting that the more he thought about it, the more difficulties he found in keeping his promise. For my part, I do not doubt that this humble profession of ignorance was more pleasing to the supreme being, pagan though Simonides was, than the insolence of a Eunomius and that sect of his Arian followers, who boasted of knowing God exactly as he is able to know himself.' Du Plessis Mornay in the chapter in which he proves both by authorities and arguments that it is impossible to know God does not forget the reply of Simonides. He remarks, without giving any citation, that this poet 'very justly taught that God is wisdom itself.' He also says that 'Aristotle in his *Metaphysics* cites and praises the common response of Simonides to Hiero, that this says in substance that it belongs only to God to be a metaphysician, that is, to speak of things that are beyond nature.'

['Simonides', in *Historical and Critical Dictionary: Selections*, trans. Richard H. Popkin (Indianapolis: Hackett, 1991), 279–83.]

THOMAS HOBBES

49 Of Religion

1. Seeing there are no signs, nor fruit of *religion*, but in man only; there is no cause to doubt, but that the seed of *religion*, is also only in man; and consisteth in some peculiar quality, or at least in some eminent degree thereof, not to be found in any other living creatures.

2. And first, it is peculiar to the nature of man, to be inquisitive into the causes of the events they see, some more, some less; but all men so much, as to be curious in the search of the causes of their own good and evil fortune.

3. Secondly, upon the sight of any thing that hath a beginning, to think also it had a cause, which determined the same to begin, then when it did, rather than sooner or later.

4. Thirdly, whereas there is no other felicity of beasts, but the enjoying of their quotidian [daily] food, ease, and lusts; as having little or no foresight of the time to come, for want of observation, and memory of the order, consequence, and dependence of the things they see; man observeth how one event hath been produced by another; and remembereth in them antecedence and consequence; and when he cannot assure himself of the true causes of things, (for the causes of good and evil fortune for the most part are invisible,) he supposes causes of them, either such as his own fancy suggesteth; or trusteth to the authority of other men, such as he thinks to be his friends, and wiser than himself.

5. The two first, make anxiety. For being assured that there be causes of all things that have arrived hitherto, or shall arrive hereafter; it is impossible for a man, who continually endeavoureth to secure himself against the evil he fears, and procure the good he desireth, not to be in a perpetual solicitude of the time to come; so that every man, especially those that are over provident, are in a state like to that of Prometheus. For as Prometheus, (which interpreted, is, *the prudent man,*) was bound to the hill Caucasus, a place of large prospect, where, an eagle feeding on his liver, devoured in the day, as much as was repaired in the night: so that man, which looks too far before him, in the care of future time,

hath his heart all the day long, gnawed on by fear of death, poverty, or other calamity; and has no repose, nor pause of his anxiety, but in sleep.

6. This perpetual fear, always accompanying mankind in the ignorance of causes, as it were in the dark, must needs have for object something. And therefore when there is nothing to be seen, there is nothing to accuse, either of their good, or evil fortune, but some *power*, or agent *invisible*: in which sense perhaps it was, that some of the old poets said, that the gods were at first created by human fear: which spoken of the gods, (that is to say, of the many gods of the Gentiles) is very true. But the acknowledging of one God, eternal, infinite, and omnipotent, may more easily be derived, from the desire men have to know the causes of natural bodies, and their several virtues, and operations; than from the fear of what was to befall them in time to come. For he that from any effect he seeth come to pass, should reason to the next and immediate cause thereof, and from thence to the cause of that cause, and plunge himself profoundly in the pursuit of causes; shall at last come to this, that there must be (as even the heathen philosophers confessed) one first mover; that is, a first, and an eternal cause of all things; which is that which men mean by the name of God: and all this without thought of their fortune; the solicitude whereof, both inclines to fear, and hinders them from the search of the causes of other things; and thereby gives occasion of feigning of as many gods, as there be men that feign them.

7. And for the matter, or substance of the invisible agents, so fancied; they could not by natural cogitation, fall upon any other conceit, but that it was the same with that of the soul of man; and that the soul of man, was of the same substance, with that which appeareth in a dream, to one that sleepeth; or in a looking-glass, to one that is awake; which, men not knowing that such apparitions are nothing else but creatures of the fancy, think to be real, and external substances; and therefore call them ghosts; as the Latins called them *imagines*, and *umbrae*; and thought them spirits, that is, thin aërial bodies; and those invisible agents, which they feared, to be like them; save that they appear, and vanish when they please. But the opinion that such spirits were incorporeal, or immaterial, could never enter into the mind of any man by nature; because, though men may put together words of contradictory signification, as *spirit*, and *incorporeal*; yet they can never have the imagination of any thing answering to them: and therefore, men that by their own meditation, arrive to the acknowledgement of one infinite, omnipotent, and eternal God, chose rather to confess he is incomprehensible, and above their understanding, than to define his nature by *spirit incorporeal*, and then confess their definition to be unintelligible: or if they give him such a title, it is not *dogmatically*, with intention to make the divine nature understood; but *piously*, to honour him with attributes, of significations, as remote as they can from the grossness of bodies visible.

8. Then, for the way by which they think these invisible agents wrought their effects; that is to say, what immediate causes they used, in bringing things to pass,

men that know not what it is that we call *causing*, (that is, almost all men) have no other rule to guess by, but by observing, and remembering what they have seen to precede the like effect at some other time, or times before, without seeing between the antecedent and subsequent event, any dependence or connexion at all: and therefore from the like things past, they expect the like things to come; and hope for good or evil luck, superstitiously, from things that have no part at all in the causing of it: as the Athenians did for their war at Lepanto, demand another Phormio; the Pompeian faction for their war in Africa, another Scipio; and others have done in divers other occasions since. In like manner they attribute their fortune to a stander by, to a lucky or unlucky place, to words spoken, especially if the name of God be amongst them; as charming and conjuring (the liturgy of witches;) insomuch as to believe, they have power to turn a stone into bread, bread into a man, or any thing, into any thing.

9. Thirdly, for the worship which naturally men exhibit to powers invisible, it can be no other, but such expressions of their reverence, as they would use towards men; gifts, petitions, thanks, submission of body, considerate addresses, sober behaviour, premeditated words, swearing (that is, assuring one another of their promises,) by invoking them. Beyond that reason suggesteth nothing; but leaves them either to rest there; or for further ceremonies, to rely on those they believe to be wiser than themselves.

10. Lastly, concerning how these invisible powers declare to men the things which shall hereafter come to pass, especially concerning their good or evil fortune in general, or good or ill success in any particular undertaking, men are naturally at a stand; save that using to conjecture of the time to come, by the time past, they are very apt, not only to take casual things, after one or two encounters, for prognostics of the like encounter ever after, but also to believe the like prognostics from other men, of whom they have once conceived a good opinion.

11. And in these four things, opinion of ghosts, ignorance of second causes, devotion towards what men fear, and taking of things casual for prognostics, consisteth the natural seed of *religion*; which by reason of the different fancies, judgments, and passions of several men, hath grown up into ceremonies so different, that those which are used by one man, are for the most part ridiculous to another.

[*Leviathan*, ch. 12 (ed. J. C. A. Gaskin, Oxford: Oxford University Press, 1996).]

MICHEL DE MONTAIGNE
....

50 **Christianity Conceived Only by Faith**

Now, a few days before his death, my father, having by chance found this book under a pile of other neglected papers, bade me put it into French for him. It is easy to translate authors like this one, in whom there is little save the matter to set forth; but those who have much ministered to grace of style and elegance of language are dangerous to undertake; especially to render in a weaker idiom. It was a very strange and novel occupation for me; but being, by chance, at leisure at the time, and being unable to refuse any thing to the bidding of the best father that ever was, I accomplished it as I could; in which he took a peculiar pleasure and ordered that it should be printed; this was done after his death.

I found this author's ideas excellent, the structure of the work well carried out, and his plan full of piety. Forasmuch as many persons take pleasure in reading it, and especially ladies, to whom we owe the most service, I have often found myself able to assist them by exonerating the book from two main objections that are made to it. Its purpose is bold and courageous, for it undertakes, by human and natural arguments, to establish and verify against atheists all the articles of the Christian religion; wherein, truly, I find it so solid and so successful that I do not think it possible to do better in that argument, and I believe that no one has equalled him. As this work seems to me too full of matter and too fine for an author whose name is so little known, and of whom all we know is that he was a Spaniard teaching medicine at Toulouse about two hundred years since, I enquired in other days of Adrian Turnebus, who knew every thing, what might be the nature of this book. He replied that he believed its essential part to be derived from Saint Thomas Aquinas; for in truth that mind, full of infinite erudition, and of a marvellous subtlety, was alone capable of such ideas. However that may be, and whoever is their author and inventor (and there is no justice in depriving Sebond of that title without some greater occasion), it was a very able man, possessing many noble qualities.

The first censure that is made regarding his work is that Christians wrong themselves in desiring to support their belief by human reasons, since it is conceived only by faith and by a special inspiration of divine favour. In this objection it seems that there may be some pious zeal, and therefore we must try with all the more gentleness and respect to satisfy those who put it forward. This would better be the office of a man versed in theology than for me, who therein know nothing. However, I thus conceive, that in a matter so divine and so lofty and so far surpassing human intelligence as is this truth with which it has pleased the goodness of God to enlighten us, there is great need that he still lend us his aid with extraordinary and peculiar favour, to enable us to conceive it and implant it in ourselves. And I do not believe that purely human agencies are in any wise capable thereof; for if they were, so many rare and superior souls in ancient times, so abundantly supplied with natural powers, would not have failed, by their reasoning, to attain this knowledge. It is faith alone which grasps vividly and certainly the high mysteries of our religion. But this is not to say that it is not a very fine and very praiseworthy undertaking to adapt also to the service of our faith the natural and human instruments which God has given us. It must not be doubted that it is the most honourable use to which we could apply them, and that there is no occupation and no purpose more worthy a

Christian man than to aim by all his studies and reflections to embellish, to extend, and to amplify the truth of his faith. We do not content ourselves by serving God in mind and soul: we owe him also, and render to him, a corporeal homage; we dispose even our limbs and our motions and external things to do him honour. We must needs do the like here and accompany our faith with all the reasoning power that is in us; but always with this understanding, that we do not think it is on us that it depends, or that our efforts and arguments can attain a knowledge so supernatural and divine. If it does not enter into us by an infusion of peculiar nature; if it enters, not only by way of the reason, but also by human influences, we have it not in its dignity or in its splendour.

And truly I fear, howsoever, that we possess it in that way only. If we held fast to God through the mediation of a lively faith; if we held fast to God through himself, not through ourselves; if we had a divine base and foundation, human chances would not have the power to stagger us as they do; our fortress would not then surrender to so feeble an assault; the love of novelty, the compulsion of princes, the good fortune of a faction, the reckless and haphazard changing of our opinions would not have the power to disturb and alter our belief; we should not let it be troubled at the will and pleasure of a new argument and by persuasion—no, not by that of all the rhetoric that ever was.

['An Apology for Raymond Sebond' (*The Essays of Montaigne*, trans. George B. Ives, Cambridge: Cambridge University Press, 1925, ii. 185–7).]

NATHANIEL CULVERWEL
....

51 **The Light of Nature**

But some are so strangely prejudiced against reason (and that upon sufficient reason too, as they think, which yet involves a flat contradiction) as that they look upon it not as 'the candle of the Lord,' but as on some blazing comet that portends ruin to the church and to the soul and carries a fatal and venomous influence along with it. And because the unruly head of Socinus and his followers, by their mere pretences to reason, have made shipwreck of faith and have been very injurious to the Gospel, therefore these weak and staggering apprehensions are afraid of understanding anything; and think that the very name of reason, especially in a pulpit, in matters of religion must needs have at least a thousand heresies couched in it. If you do but offer to make a syllogism, they'll straightway cry it down for carnal reasoning. What would these men have? Would they be banished from their own essences? Would they forfeit and renounce their understandings? Or have they any to forfeit or disclaim? Would they put out this 'candle of the Lord,' intellectuals of his lighting? Or have they any to put out? Would they creep into some lower species and go a-grazing with Nebuchadnezzar among the beasts of the field? [Dan. 4: 33] or are they not there already? Or, if they themselves can be willing to be so shamefully degraded, do they think that all others too are bound to follow their example? Oh, what hard thoughts have these of religion? Do they look upon it only as on a bird of prey, that comes to peck out the eyes of men? Is this all the nobility that it gives, that men by virtue of it must be beheaded presently? Does it chop off the intellectuals at one blow? Let's hear awhile what are the offences of reason. Are they so heinous and capital? What has it done? What laws has it violated? Whose commands has it broken? What did it ever do against the crown and dignity of Heaven, or against the peace and tranquillity of men? Why are a weak and perverse generation so angry and displeased with it? Is it because this 'daughter of the morning' is fallen from her primitive glory, from her original vigour and perfection? Far be it from me to extenuate that great and fatal overthrow which the sons of men had in their first and original apostasy from their God—that under which the whole creation sighs and groans [cf. Rom. 8: 22]. But of this we are sure, it did not annihilate the soul, it did not destroy the essence, the powers and faculties, nor the operations of the soul, though it did defile them and disorder them and every way indispose them.

Well, then, because the eye of reason is weakened and vitiated, will they therefore pluck it out immediately? And must Leah be hated upon no other account but because she is blear-eyed? The whole head is wounded and aches, and is there no other way but to cut it off? 'The candle of the Lord' does not shine so clearly as it was wont; must it therefore be extinguished presently? Is it not better to enjoy the faint and languishing light of this 'candle of the Lord' rather than to be in palpable and disconsolate darkness? There are indeed but a few seminal sparks left in the ashes, and must there be whole floods of water cast on them to quench them? 'Tis but an old imperfect manuscript, with some broken periods, some letters worn out; must they therefore with an unmerciful indignation rend it and tear it asunder? 'Tis granted that the picture has lost its gloss and beauty, the oriency of its colours, the elegancy of its lineaments, the comeliness of its proportion; must it therefore be totally defaced? Must it be made one great blot?—and must the very frame of it be broken in pieces? Would you persuade the lutenist to cut all his strings in sunder because they are out of tune? And will you break the bow upon no other account but because it is unbended? Because men have not so much reason as they should, will they therefore resolve to have none at all? Will you throw away your gold because it's mixed with dross? Thy very being, that's imperfect too; thy graces, they are imperfect; wilt thou refuse these also? And then consider that the very apprehending the weakness of reason, even this in some measure comes from reason. Reason, when awakened, it feels her own wounds, it hears her own jarrings, she sees the dimness of her own sight. 'Tis a glass that discovers its own spots; and must it therefore be broke in pieces? Reason herself has made many sad complaints unto you. She has told you often, and that with tears in her eyes, what a great shipwreck she has suffered, what goods she has lost, how hardly she escaped with a poor decayed being. She has shown you often some broken relics, as the sad remembrancers of her former ruins. She told you that when she swam for her life, she had nothing but two or three jewels about her, two or three common notions; and would you rob her of them also? Is this all your tenderness and compassion? Is this your kindness to your friend? Will you trample upon her now she is so low? Is this a sufficient cause to give her a Bill of Divorcement, because she has lost her former beauty and fruitfulness?

Or is reason thus offensive to them because she cannot grasp and comprehend the things of God? Vain men, will they pluck out their eyes because they cannot look upon the sun in his brightness and glory? What though reason cannot reach to the depths, to the bottoms of the ocean, may it not therefore swim and hold up the head as well as it can? What though it cannot enter into the *sanctum sanctorum* [holy of holies] and pierce within the veil, may it not, notwithstanding, lie in the porch, 'at the gate of the temple called Beautiful' and 'be a door-keeper in the house of its God' [Acts 3: 2; Ps. 84: 10]? Its wings are clipt indeed; it cannot fly so high as it might have done; it cannot fly so swiftly, so strongly, as once it could. Will they not therefore allow it to move, to stir, to flutter up and down, as well as it can? The turrets and pinnacles of the stately structure are fallen: will they therefore demolish the whole fabric, and shake the very foundations of it and down with it to the ground? Though it be not a Jacob's ladder to climb to heaven by [Gen. 28: 12], yet may they not use it as a staff to walk upon earth withal? And then reason itself knows this also and acknowledges that 'tis dazzled with the majesty and glory of God; that it cannot pierce into his mysterious and unsearchable ways; it never was so vain as to go about to measure immensity by its own infinite compass, or to span out absolute eternity by its own more imperfect duration. True reason did never go about to comprise the Bible in its own nutshell. And if reason be content with its own sphere, why should it not have the liberty of its proper motion?

Is it because it opposes the things of God and wrangles against the mysteries of salvation, is it therefore excluded? An heinous and frequent accusation indeed; but nothing more false and injurious. And if it had been an open enemy that had done her this wrong, why then she could have borne it. But it's thou, her friend and companion, ye have 'took sweet counsel together' [Ps. 55: 14], and have entered into the house of God as friends, 'tis you, that have your dependence upon her, that cannot speak one word of purpose against her without her help and assistance. What mean you thus to revile your most intimate and inseparable self? Why do you thus slander your own being? Would you have all this to be true, which you say? Name but the time, if you can, whenever right reason did oppose one jot or apex of the work of God. Certainly these men speak of distorted reason all this while. Surely they do not speak of the 'candle of the Lord,' but of some shadow and appearance of it. But if they tell us that all reason is distorted, whether then is theirs so in telling us so? If they say that they do not know this by reason, but by the Word of God, whether then is that their reason, when it acknowledges the Word of God? Whether is it then distorted, or no? Besides, if there were no right reason in the world, what difference between sobriety and madness, between these men and wiser ones? How then were the 'heathen left without excuse' [cf. Rom. 1: 20], who had nothing to see by but this 'candle of the Lord'? And how does this thrust men below sensitive creatures?—for better have no reason at all than such as does perpetually deceive them and delude them.

[*An Elegant and Learned Discourse of the Light of Nature* (1652), in G. R. Cragg (ed.), *The Cambridge Platonists* (New York: Oxford University Press, 1968), 55–8.]

JOHN OWEN

52 The Reason of Faith

(1) He makes himself known unto us by the *innate principles of our nature*, unto which he hath communicated, as a power of apprehending, so an indelible sense of his being, his authority, and his will, so far as our natural dependence on him and moral subjection unto him do require: for whereas there are two things in this natural light and these first dictates of reason; first, *a power of conceiving*, discerning, and assenting; and, secondly, a *power of judging* and determining upon the things so discerned and assented unto,—by the one God makes known his being and essential properties, and by the other his sovereign authority over all.

As to the first, the apostle affirms that τὸ γνωστὸν τοῦ Θεοῦ φανερόν ἐστιν ἐν αὐτοῖς, Rom. i. 19,—'that which may be known of God' (his essence, being, subsistence, his natural, necessary, essential properties) 'is manifest in them;' that is, it hath a self-evidencing power, acting itself in the minds of all men endued with natural light and reason. And as unto his *sovereign authority*, he doth evidence it in and by the *consciences of men*; which are the judgment that they make, and cannot but make, of themselves and their actions, with respect unto the authority and judgment of God, Rom. ii. 14, 15. And thus the mind doth assent unto the principles of God's being and authority, antecedently unto any actual exercise of the discursive faculty of reason, or other testimony whatever.

(2) He doth it unto our *reason in its exercise*, by proposing such things unto its consideration as from whence it may and cannot but conclude in an assent unto the truth of what God intends to reveal unto us that way. This he doth by the works of creation and providence, which present themselves unavoidably unto reason in its exercise, to instruct us in the nature, being, and properties of God. Thus 'the heavens declare the glory of God; and the firmament showeth his handywork. Day unto day uttereth speech, and night unto night

showeth knowledge. There is no speech nor language, where their voice is not heard,' Ps. xix. 1–3. But yet they do not thus declare, evidence, and reveal the glory of God unto the first principles and notions of natural light without the actual exercise of reason. They only do so 'when we consider his heavens, the work of his fingers, the moon and the stars, which he hath ordained,' as the same psalmist speaks, Ps. viii. 3. A rational consideration of them, their great-ness, order, beauty, and use, is required unto that testimony and evidence which God gives in them and by them unto himself, his glorious being and power. To this purpose the apostle discourseth at large concerning the works of creation, Rom. i. 20, 21, as also of those of providence, Acts xiv. 15–17, xvii, 24–28, and the rational use we are to make of them, verse 29. So God calls unto men for the exercise of their reason about these things, reproaching them with stupidity and brutishness where they are wanting therein, Isa. xlvi. 5–8, xliv. 18–20.

(3) God reveals himself unto *our faith*, or that power of our souls whereby we are able to assent unto the truth of what is proposed unto us upon testimony. And this he doth by his word, or the Scriptures, proposed unto us in the manner and way before expressed.

He doth not reveal himself by his word unto the principles of natural light, nor unto reason in its exercise; but yet these principles, and reason itself, with all the faculties of our minds, are consequently affected with that revelation, and are drawn forth into their proper exercise by it. But in the gospel the 'righteousness of God is revealed from faith to faith,' Rom. i. 17,—not to natural light, sense, or reason, in the first place; and it is faith that is 'the evidence of things not seen,' as revealed in the word, Heb. xi. 1. Unto this kind of revelation, 'Thus saith the Lord' is the only ground and reason of our assent; and that assent is the assent of faith, because it is resolved into testi-mony alone.

And concerning these several ways of the communication or revelation of the knowledge of God, it must be always observed that there is a *perfect conso-nancy in the things revealed by them all*. If any thing pretends from the one what is absolutely contradictory unto the other, or our senses as the means of them, it is not to be received.

The foundation of the whole, as of all the actings of our souls, is in the inbred principles of natural light, or first necessary dictates of our intellectual, rational nature. This, so far as it extends, is a *rule unto our apprehension* in all that follows. Wherefore, if any pretend, in the exercise of reason, to conclude unto any thing concerning the nature, being, or will of God, that is directly *contradictory* unto those principles and dictates, it is no divine revelation unto our reason, but a *paralogism* from the defect of reason in its exercise. This is that which the apostle chargeth on and vehemently urgeth against the *heathen philosophers*. Inbred notions they had in themselves of the being and eternal power of God; and these were so manifest in them thereby that they could not but own them. Hereon they set their rational, *discursive faculty* at work in the consideration of God and his being; but herein were they so vain and foolish as to draw conclusions *directly contrary* unto the first principles of natural light, and the unavoidable notions which they had of the eternal being of God, Rom. i. 21–5. And many, upon their pretended rational consideration of the *promiscuous event of things* in the world, have foolishly concluded that all things had a *fortuitous beginning*, and have *fortuitous events*, or such as, from a concatenation of antecedent causes, are *fatally necessary*, and are not disposed by an infinitely wise, unerring, holy providence. And this also is directly *contradictory* unto the first principles and notions of natural light; whereby it openly proclaims itself not to be an effect of reason in its due exercise, but a mere delusion.

So if any pretend unto *revelations by faith* which are contradictory unto the first principles of natural light or reason, in its proper exercise about its proper objects, it is a delusion. On this ground the Roman doctrine of transubstantiation is justly rejected; for it proposeth that as a revelation by faith which is expressly contradictory unto our sense and reason, in their proper exercise about their proper objects. And a supposition of the possibility of any such thing would make the ways whereby God reveals and makes known himself to cross and interfere one with another; which would leave us no certainty in any thing, divine or human.

But yet as these means of divine revelation do *harmonize* and perfectly agree one with the other, so they are not *objectively equal*, or equally extensive, nor are they co-ordinate, but subordinate unto one another. Wherefore, there are many things discernible by reason in its exercise which do not appear unto the first principles of natural light. So the sober philosophers of old attained unto many true and great conceptions of God and the excellencies of his nature, above what they arrived unto who either did not or could not cultivate and improve the principles of natural light in the same manner as they did. It is, therefore, folly to pretend that things so made known of God are not infallibly true and certain, because they are not obvious unto the first conceptions of natural light, without the due exercise of reason, provided they are not contradictory thereunto. And there are many things revealed unto faith that are above and beyond the comprehension of reason in the best and utmost of its most proper exercise: such are all the principal mysteries of Christian religion. And it is the height of folly to reject them, as some do, because they are not discernible and comprehensible by reason, seeing they are not contradictory thereunto. Wherefore, these ways of God's revelation of himself are not equally extensive or commensurate, but are so subordinate one unto another that what is wanting unto the one is supposed by the other, unto the accomplishment of the whole and entire end of divine revelation; and the truth of God is the same in them all.

[*The Reason of Faith* (*The Works of John Owen*, ed. W. H. Goold, Edinburgh: Johnstone and Hunter, 1850–3, iv. 84–6).]

§ 27. I. Right reason (meaning our right reason, or human reason) is not the affirmative or positive measure of things divine, or of articles and mysteries of faith; and the reasons are plain: because,

1) Many of them depend upon the free will of God, for which, till He gives us reasons, we are to be still and silent, admiring the secret, and adoring the wisdom, and expecting till the curtain be drawn, or till Elias come and tell us all things. But he that will enquire and pry into the reason of the mystery, and because he cannot perceive it, will disbelieve the thing, or undervalue it, and say it is not at all, because he does not understand the reason of it, and why it should be so, may as well say that his prince does not raise an army in time of peace, because he does not know a reason why he should; or that God never did suffer a brave prince to die ignobly, because it was a thousand pities he should. There is a *ragione di stato*, and a *ragione di regno*, and a *ragione di cielo*, after which none but fools will enquire, and none but the humble shall ever find.

§ 28. Who can tell why the devil, who is a wise and intelligent creature, should so spitefully, and for no end but for mischief, tempt so many souls to ruin, when he knows it can do him no good, no pleasure, but fantastic? or who can tell why he should be delighted in a pleasure that can be nothing but fantastic, when he knows things by intuition, not by fantasm, and hath no low conceit of things as we have? or why he should do so many things against God, whom he knows he cannot hurt, and against souls, whose ruin cannot add one moment of pleasure to him? and if it makes any change it is infinitely to the worse. That these things are so, our religion tells us; but our reason cannot reach it why it is so, or how. Whose reason can give an account why, or understand it to be reasonable, that God should permit evil for good ends, when He hates that evil, and can produce that good without that evil? and yet that He does so we are taught by our religion. Whose reason can make it intelligible, that God who delights not in the death of a sinner, but He and His Christ, and all their angels, rejoice infinitely in the salvation of a sinner, yet that He should not cause that every sinner should be saved; working in him a mighty and a prevailing grace, without which grace he shall not in the event of things be saved, and yet this grace is wholly His own production.

Why does not He work in us all to will and to do, not only that we can will, but that we shall will? for if the actual willing be any thing, it is His creation; we can create nothing, we cannot will unless He effect it in us, and why He does not do that which so well pleases Him, and for the want of the doing of which He is so displeased, and yet He alone is to do it some way or other; human reason cannot give a wise or a probable account.

Where is the wise discourser, that can tell how it can be, that God foreknows certainly what I shall do ten years hence, and yet it is free for me at that time, to will or not to will, to do or not to do that thing? Where is the discerning searcher of secrets, that can give the reason why God should determine for so many ages before, that Judas should betray Christ, and yet that God should kill him eternally for effecting the divine purpose, and fore-determined counsel? Well may we wonder that God should wash a soul with water, and with bread and wine nourish us up to immortality, and make real impresses upon our spirits by the blood of the vine, and the kidneys of wheat; but who can tell why He should choose such mean instruments to effect such glorious promises? since even the greatest things of this world had not been disproportionable instruments to such effects, nor yet too great for our understanding; and that we are fain to stoop to make these mean elements be even with our faith, and with our understanding. Who can divine, and give us the cause, or understand the reason, why God should give us so great rewards for such nothings, and yet damn men for such insignificant mischief, for thoughts, for words, for secret wishes, that effect no evil abroad, but only might have done, or it may be were resolved to be unactive? For if the goodness of God be so overflowing in some cases, we in our reason should not expect, that in such a great goodness, there should be so great an aptness to destroy men greatly for little things: and if all mankind should join in search, it could never be told, why God should adjudge the heathen or the Israelites to an eternal hell, of which He never gave them warning, nor created fears great enough to produce caution equal to their danger; and who can give a reason why for temporal and transient actions of sin, the world is to expect never-ceasing torments in hell to eternal ages? That these things are thus, we are taught in scripture, but here our reason is not instructed to tell why or how; and therefore our reason is not the positive measure of mysteries, and we must believe what we cannot understand.

§ 29. Thus are they to be blamed, who make intricacies and circles in mysterious articles, because they cannot wade through them; it is not to be understood why God should send His holy Son from His bosom to redeem us, to pay our price; nor to be told why God should exact a price of Himself for His own creature; nor to be made intelligible to us, why He who loved us so well, as to send His Son to save us, should at the same time so hate us, as to resolve to damn us, unless His Son should come and save us. But the Socinians who conclude that this was not thus, because they know not how it can be thus, are highly to be reproved for their excess in the enquiries of reason, not where she is not a competent judge, but where she is not competently instructed; and that is the second reason.

§ 30. 2) The reason of man is a right judge always when she is truly informed; but in many things she knows nothing but the face of the article: the mysteries of faith are oftentimes like cherubim's heads placed over the propitiatory, where you may see a clear and a bright face and golden wings, but there is no body to be handled; there is light and splendour upon the brow, but you may not grasp it; and though you see the revelation clear, and the article plain, yet the reason of it we cannot see at all; that is, the whole knowledge which we can have here is dark and obscure; 'We see as in a glass darkly,' saith St Paul, that is, we can see what, but not why, and what we do see is the least part of that which does not appear; but in these cases our understanding is to submit, and wholly to be obedient, but not to enquire further. *Delicata est illa obedientia quæ causas quærit.* If the understanding will not consent to a revelation, until it see a reason of the proposition, it does not obey at all, for it will not submit, till it cannot choose. In these cases, reason and religion are like Leah and Rachel: reason is fruitful indeed, and brings forth the first-born, but she is blear-eyed, and oftentimes knows not the secrets of her Lord; but Rachel produces two children, Faith and Piety, and Obedience is midwife to them both, and Modesty is the nurse.

§ 31. From hence it follows that we cannot safely conclude thus, This is agreeable to right reason, therefore this is so in scripture, or in the counsel of God; not that one reason can be against another, when all things are equal, but that the state of things, and of discourses is imperfect; and though it be right reason in such a constitution of affairs, yet it is not so in others; that a man may repel force by force is right reason, and a natural right, but yet it follows not that it can be lawful for a private Christian to do it, or that Christ hath not forbidden us to strike him that strikes us. The reason of the difference is this. In nature it is just that it be so, because we are permitted only to nature's provisions, and she hath made us equal, and the condition of all men indifferent; and therefore we have the same power over another that he hath over us; besides, we will do it naturally, and till a law forbad it, it could not be amiss, and there was no reason in nature to restrain it, but much to warrant it. But since the law of God hath forbidden it, He hath made other provisions for our indemnity, and where He permits us to be defenceless (as in cases of martyrdom and the like) He hath promised a reward to make infinite amends: so that 'we may repel force by force,' says nature, 'we may not,' says Christ, and yet they are not two contradictory propositions. For nature says we may, when otherwise we have no security, and no reward for suffering; but Christ hath given both the defence of laws and authority, and the reward of heaven, and therefore in this case it is reasonable. And thus we cannot conclude, This man is a wicked man because he is afflicted, or his cause is evil because it does not thrive; although it be right reason, that good men ought to be happy and prosperous; because although reason says right in it, yet no reason can wisely conclude, that therefore so it should be in this world, when faith and reason too tell us it may be better hereafter. The result is this; every thing that is above our understanding is not therefore to be suspected or disbelieved, neither is any thing to be admitted that is against scripture, though it be agreeable to right reason, until all information is brought in by which the sentence is to be made.

§ 32. For as it happens in dreams and madness, where the argument is good, and the discourse reasonable oftentimes; but because it is inferred from weak phantasms, and trifling and imperfect notices of things, and obscure apprehensions, therefore it is not only desultorious and light, but insignificant, and far from ministering to knowledge: so it is in our reason as to matters of religion, it argues well and wisely, but because it is from trifling, or false, or uncertain principles, and unsure information, it oftentimes is but a witty nothing: reason is an excellent limbeck, and will extract rare quintessences, but if you put in nothing but mushrooms, or egg-shells, or the juice of coloquintida, or the filthy gingran, you must expect productions accordingly, useless or unpleasant, dangerous or damnable.

§ 33. 2. Although right reason is not the positive and affirmative measure of any article, yet it is the negative measure of every one; so that, whatsoever is contradictory to right reason, is at no hand to be admitted as a mystery of faith, and this is certain upon an infinite account.

§ 34. 1) Because nothing can be true and false at the same time, otherwise it would follow that there could be two truths contrary to each other: for if the affirmative be true, and the negative true too, then the affirmative is true and is not true, which were a perfect contradiction, and we were bound to believe a lie, and hate a truth; and yet at the same time obey what we hate, and consent to what we disbelieve. No man can serve two such masters.

§ 35. 2) Out of truth nothing can follow but truth; whatsoever therefore is truth, this is therefore safe to be followed, because no error can be the product of it. It follows therefore, that by believing one truth, no man can be tied to disbelieve another. Whatsoever therefore is contrary to right reason, or to a certain truth in any faculty, cannot be a truth, for one truth is not contrary to another: if therefore any proposition be said to be the doctrine of scripture, and confessed to be against right reason, it is certainly not the doctrine of scripture, because it cannot be true, and yet be against what is true.

§ 36. 3) All truths are emanations and derivatives from God, and therefore whatsoever is contrary to any truth in any faculty whatsoever, is against the truth of God, and God cannot be contrary to Himself; for as God is one, so truth is one; for truth is God's eldest daughter, and so like Himself, that God may as well be multiplied, as abstracted truth.

[*Ductor Dubitanitium, or, The Rule of Conscience* (*Works*, ed. R. Heber, London, 1850–6, iv. 84–6).]

Section V

The Seventeenth and Eighteenth Centuries

INTRODUCTION

If the period of the Renaissance and Reformation is characterized by diversity, the seventeenth and eighteenth centuries, the period of the Enlightenment, is more so. As we have seen the Renaissance and Reformation were characterized by disputes about the nature of religious authority with the Church, the Bible, tradition, and reason vying with each other for supremacy. By contrast the Enlightenment is characterized by disputes about the nature of philosophy, prompted particularly over the quest for certainty, both to find a way out of the competing religious claims, and to combat scepticism. From these resources was mounted a much sharper critique of the theological claims of Christianity.

A key influence is Descartes, with his characteristic appeal to the clear and distinct ideas of reason. Such an appeal was foundationalistic in a stronger sense than, it is generally agreed, was evident in the medieval and Reformation periods. This appeal was not, in his case, an expression of an anti-religious temper. Nevertheless his procedure is revolutionary, for God plays a secondary epistemological rule to the ideas. The very attempt to start from scratch gave Descartes's rationalism, and the temper that it engendered, a modernist emphasis. For no tradition or previous way of doing things was sacrosanct. Descartes's appeal to reason was developed thoroughly by Leibniz, for whose entire metaphysics the principle of sufficient reason was a keystone. Spinoza severely curtailed the scope and claims of Scripture, leaving a free path for spec-ulation. All these thinkers developed theological and philosophical systems by a variety of a priori appeals to human reason. An appeal to revelation was unnecessary.

The other key figure is Locke, who developed an empiricist epistemology of an avowedly anti-scholastic kind and worked out a kind of philosophical *apologia* for Anglicanism; an appeal to revelation, but one that is immune to what he regarded as enthusiasm, the appeal to immediate inspiration charac-teristic of some of the more radical sects of the Commonwealth period. So faith and reason have, as Locke put it, 'distinct provinces', but faith must show itself to be in accord with reason.

From the fountainhead of Cartesian rationalism and of Lockian theologi-cally moderate empiricism at least three developments are discernible. First, a reaction against the claims of reason both in the direction of voluntarism, in the case of Pascal, as seen in his famous Wager Argument, and in the case of Hume the development of a more radical empiricism. This is seen not only in his critique of the appeal to miracles as the foundation of a religion, but also in his sharp critique of the argument from design, and of religious language. In many ways Hume has set the agenda for what, until recently, has formed the staple fare of the philosophy of religion, though the immediate influence of his ideas on the eighteenth century can be exaggerated.

Secondly, the 'reasonableness of Christianity' approach of Locke continued in less radical and more radical forms. Locke and Berkeley set the temper of much eighteenth-century religious apologetics, of which Butler, Berkeley, and Paley are notable proponents. They laid stress on the assembling of evidence for Christianity a posteriori, by inductive, cumulative methods. More radically, Locke's appeal to reasonableness, as well as the impact of Newtonian science, led in England to the deism of such as Matthew Tindal, and on the Continent to the *philosophes*. As we have noted earlier, eighteenth-century deism also had sources going back to the previous century, to Herbert of Cherbury, according to whom it was possible to discern a religion of reason which did not require an appeal to revelation or to supernatural claims of any kind. Paradoxically the New England philosopher and theologian Jonathan Edwards is notable for his use of Locke against the deists and in support of the Puritan theology of his forebears.

The third development is probably the most radical of all, and certainly the one with the most far-reaching consequences for religion and theology. The anthropocentric emphasis of Descartes, and the view of Spinoza that the scope of Scripture ought to be confined to ethical matters, has already been noted. In Kant these emphases received a definitive form. In his *Critique of Pure Reason* Kant argued against any form of cognitivism in theology; the traditional proofs were unpersuasive, and in any case invoking the God of metaphysics, the timeless and spaceless God of the Augustinian tradition (via an appeal to revelation, say) was an attempt by the human mind to go beyond the categories of space and time resulting not in an increase in knowledge, but in the generation of antinomies, paradoxes of thought. Nevertheless, though God's existence could not be proved by the theoretical reason, it was necessary, postulated by the practical reason, in accordance with the demands of morality.

Kant's God had a purely moral character, functioning as the provider of the *summum bonum*, the final end of the imperatives of morality. In the hands of Kant faith was no longer reliance upon the word of God, or the person of Christ, but the recognition of all duties as divine commands. The result was a purely moral religion, a religion requiring neither empirical nor metaphysical support; indeed a religion with which such support was quite at odds. A religion without revelation, a life of faith without any divinely appointed means of grace. Such religious immanentism became characteristic of Protestantism until the First World War: a moral immanentism in Kant's case; a romantic immanentism in Schleiermacher's case; a historical immanentism in Hegel's case.

Hence there remains only the idea of God, concerning which we must consider whether it is something which cannot have proceeded from me myself. By the name God I understand a substance that is infinite [eternal, immutable], independent, all-knowing, all-powerful, and by which I myself and everything else, if anything else does exist, have been created. Now all these characteristics are such that the more diligently I attend to them, the less do they appear capable of proceeding from me alone; hence, from what has been already said, we must conclude that God necessarily exists.

For although the idea of substance is within me owing to the fact that I am substance, nevertheless I should not have the idea of an infinite substance—since I am finite—if it had not proceeded from some substance which was veritably infinite.

Nor should I imagine that I do not perceive the infinite by a true idea, but only by the negation of the finite, just as I perceive repose and darkness by the negation of movement and of light; for, on the contrary, I see that there is manifestly more reality in infinite substance than in finite, and therefore that in some way I have in me the notion of the infinite earlier than the finite—to wit, the notion of God before that of myself. For how would it be possible that I should know that I doubt and desire, that is to say, that something is lacking to me, and that I am not quite perfect, unless I had within me some idea of a Being more perfect than myself, in comparison with which I should recognize the deficiencies of my nature?

And we cannot say that this idea of God is perhaps materially false and that consequently I can derive it from nought [i.e. that possibly it exists in me because I am imperfect], as I have just said is the case with ideas of heat, cold and other such things; for, on the contrary, as this idea is very clear and distinct and contains within it more objective reality than any other, there can be none which is of itself more true, nor any in which there can be less suspicion of falsehood. The idea, I say, of this Being who is absolutely perfect and infinite, is entirely true; for although, perhaps, we can imagine that such a Being does not exist, we cannot nevertheless imagine that His idea represents nothing real to me, as I have said of the idea of cold. This idea is also very clear and distinct; since all that I conceive clearly and distinctly of the real and the true, and of what conveys some perfection, is in its entirety contained in this idea. And this does not cease to be true although I do not comprehend the infinite, or though in God there is an infinitude of things which I cannot comprehend, nor possibly even reach in any way by thought; for it is of the nature of the infinite that my nature, which is finite and limited, should not comprehend it; and it is sufficient that I should understand this, and that I should judge that all things which I clearly perceive and in which I know that there is some perfection, and possibly likewise an infinitude of properties of which I am ignorant, are in God formally or eminently, so that the idea which I have of Him may become the most true, most clear, and most distinct of all the ideas that are in my mind.

But possibly I am something more than I suppose myself to be, and perhaps all those perfections which I attribute to God are in some way potentially in me, although they do not yet disclose themselves, or issue in action. As a matter of fact I am already sensible that my knowledge increases [and perfects itself] little by little, and I see nothing which can prevent it from increasing more and more into infinitude; nor do I see, after it has thus been increased [or perfected], anything to prevent my being able to acquire by its means all the other perfections of the Divine nature; nor finally why the power I have of acquiring these perfections, if it really exists in me, shall not suffice to produce the ideas of them.

At the same time I recognize that this cannot be. For, in the first place, although it were true that every day my knowledge acquired new degrees of perfection, and that there were in my nature many things potentially which are not yet there actually, nevertheless these excellences do not pertain to [or make the smallest approach to] the idea which I have of God in whom there is nothing merely potential [but in whom all is present really and actually]; for it is an infallible token of imperfection in my knowledge that it increases little by little. And further, although my knowledge grows more and more, nevertheless I do not for that reason believe that it can ever be actually infinite, since it can never reach a point so high that it will be unable to attain to any greater increase. But I understand God to be actually infinite, so that He can add nothing to His supreme perfection. And finally I perceive that the objective being of an idea cannot be produced by a being that exists potentially only, which properly speaking is nothing, but only by a being which is formal or actual.

To speak the truth, I see nothing in all that I have just said which by the light of nature is not manifest to anyone who desires to think attentively on the subject; but when I slightly relax my attention, my mind, finding its vision somewhat obscured and so to speak blinded by the images of sensible objects, I do not easily recollect the reason why the idea that I possess of a being more perfect than I, must necessarily have been placed in me by a being which is really more perfect; and this is why I wish here to go on to inquire whether I, who have this idea, can exist if no such being exists.

And I ask, from whom do I then derive my existence? Perhaps from myself or from my parents, or from some other source less perfect than God; for we can imagine nothing more perfect than God, or even as perfect as He is.

But [were I independent of every other and] were I myself the author of my being, I should doubt nothing and I should desire nothing, and finally no perfection would be lacking to me; for I should have bestowed on myself every perfection of which I possessed any idea and should thus be God. And it must not be imagined that those things that are lacking to me are perhaps more diffi-cult of attainment than those which I already possess; for, on the contrary, it is quite evident that it was a matter of much greater difficulty to bring to pass that I, that is to say, a thing or a substance that thinks, should emerge out of nothing, than it would be to attain to the knowledge of many things of which I am ignorant, and which are only the accidents of this thinking substance. But it is clear that if I had of myself possessed this greater perfection of which I have just spoken [that is to say, if I had been the author of my own existence], I should not at least have denied myself the things which are the more easy to acquire [to wit, many branches of knowledge of which my nature is destitute]; nor should I have deprived myself of any of the things contained in the idea which I form of God, because there are none of them which seem to me specially difficult to acquire: and if there were any that were more difficult to acquire, they would certainly appear to me to be such (supposing I myself were the origin of the other things which I possess) since I should discover in them that my powers were limited.

But though I assume that perhaps I have always existed just as I am at present, neither can I escape the force of this reasoning, and imagine that the conclusion to be drawn from this is, that I need not seek for any author of my existence. For all the course of my life may be divided into an infinite number of parts, none of which is in any way dependent on the other; and thus from the fact that I was in existence a short time ago it does not follow that I must be in existence now, unless some cause at this instant, so to speak, produces me anew, that is to say, conserves me. It is as a matter of fact perfectly clear and evident to all those who consider with attention the nature of time, that, in order to be conserved in each moment in which it endures, a substance has need of the same power and action as would be necessary to produce and create it anew, supposing it did not yet exist, so that the light of nature shows us clearly that the distinction between creation and conservation is solely a distinction of the reason.

All that I thus require here is that I should interrogate myself, if I wish to know whether I possess a power which is capable of bringing it to pass that I who now am shall still be in the future; for since I am nothing but a thinking thing, or at least since thus far it is only this portion of myself which is precisely in question at present, if such a power did reside in me, I should certainly be conscious of it. But I am conscious of nothing of the kind, and by this I know clearly that I depend on some being different from myself.

Possibly, however, this being on which I depend is not that which I call God, and I am created either by my parents or by some other cause less perfect than God. This cannot be, because, as I have just said, it is perfectly evident that there must be at least as much reality in the cause as in the effect; and thus since I am a thinking thing, and possess an idea of God within me, whatever in the end be the cause assigned to my existence, it must be allowed that it is likewise a thinking thing and that it possesses in itself the idea of all the perfections which I attribute to God. We may again inquire whether this cause derives its origin from itself or from some other thing. For if from itself, it follows by the reasons before brought forward, that this cause must itself be God; for since it possesses the virtue of self-existence, it must also without doubt have the power of actually possessing all the perfections of which it has the idea, that is, all those which I conceive as existing in God. But if it derives its existence from some other cause than itself, we shall again ask, for the same reason, whether this second cause exists by itself or through another, until from one step to another, we finally arrive at an ultimate cause, which will be God.

And it is perfectly manifest that in this there can be no regression into infinity, since what is in question is not so much the cause which formerly created me, as that which conserves me at the present time.

Nor can we suppose that several causes may have concurred in my production, and that from one I have received the idea of one of the perfections which I attribute to God, and from another the idea of some other, so that all these perfections indeed exist somewhere in the universe, but not as complete in one unity which is God. On the contrary, the unity, the simplicity or the inseparability of all things which are in God is one of the principal perfections which I conceive to be in Him. And certainly the idea of this unity of all Divine perfections cannot have been placed in me by any cause from which I have not likewise received the ideas of all the other perfections; for this cause could not make me able to comprehend them as joined together in an inseparable unity without having at the same time caused me in some measure to know what they are [and in some way to recognize each one of them].

Finally, so far as my parents [from whom it appears I have sprung] are concerned, although all that I have ever been able to believe of them were true, that does not make it follow that it is they who conserve me, nor are they even the authors of my being in any sense, in so far as I am a thinking being; since what they did was merely to implant certain dispositions in that matter in which the self—i.e. the mind, which alone I at present identify with myself—is by me deemed to exist. And thus there can be no difficulty in their regard, but we must of necessity conclude from the fact alone that I exist, or that the ideas of a Being supremely perfect—that is of God—is in me, that the proof of God's existence is grounded on the highest evidence.

It only remains to me to examine into the manner in which I have acquired this idea from God; for I have not received it through the senses, and it is never presented to me unexpectedly, as is usual with the ideas of sensible things when these things present themselves, or seem to present themselves, to the external organs of my senses; nor is it likewise a fiction of my mind, for it is not in my power to take from or to add anything to it; and consequently the only alternative is that it is innate in me, just as the idea of myself is innate in me.

And one certainly ought not to find it strange that God, in creating me, placed this idea within me to be like the mark of the workman imprinted on his work; and it is likewise not essential that the mark shall be something different from the work itself. For from the sole fact that God created me it is most probable that in some way he has placed his image and similitude upon me, and that I perceive this similitude (in which the idea of God is contained) by means of the same faculty by which I perceive myself—that is to say, when I reflect on myself I not only know that I am something [imperfect], incomplete and dependent on another, which incessantly aspires after something which is better and greater than myself, but I also know that He on whom I depend possesses in Himself all the great things towards which I aspire [and the ideas of which I find within myself], and that not indefinitely or potentially alone, but really, actually and infinitely; and that thus He is God. And the whole strength of the argument which I have here made use of to prove the existence of God consists in this, that I recognize that it is not possible that my nature should be what it is, and indeed that I should have in myself the idea of a God, if God did not veritably exist—a God, I say, whose idea is in me, i.e. who possesses all those supreme perfections of which our mind may indeed have some idea but without understanding them all, who is liable to no errors or defect [and who has none of all those marks which denote imperfection]. From this it is manifest that He cannot be a deceiver, since the light of nature teaches us that fraud and deception necessarily proceed from some defect.

[*Meditations* (*Works*, trans. E. S. Haldane and G. R. T. Ross, Cambridge: Cambridge University Press, 1931, i. 165–71).]

BENEDICT SPINOZA

55 Reason and Scripture

Now, seeing that we have the rare happiness of living in a republic, where everyone's judgment is free and unshackled, where each may worship God as his conscience dictates, and where freedom is esteemed before all things dear and precious, I have believed that I should be undertaking no ungrateful or unprofitable task, in demonstrating that not only can such freedom be granted without prejudice to the public peace, but also, that without such freedom, piety cannot flourish nor the public peace be secure.

Such is the chief conclusion I seek to establish in this treatise; but, in order to reach it, I must first point out the misconceptions which, like scars of our former bondage, still disfigure our notion of religion, and must expose the false views about the civil authority which many have most impudently advocated, endeavouring to turn the mind of the people, still prone to heathen superstition, away from its legitimate rulers, and so bring us again into slavery. As to the order of my treatise I will speak presently, but first I will recount the causes which led me to write.

I have often wondered, that persons who make a boast of professing the Christian religion, namely, love, joy, peace, temperance, and charity to all men, should quarrel with such rancorous animosity, and display daily towards one another such bitter hatred, that this, rather than the virtues they claim, is the readiest criterion of their faith. Matters have long since come to such a pass, that one can only pronounce a man Christian, Turk, Jew, or Heathen, by his general appearance and attire, by his frequenting this or that place of worship, or employing the phraseology of a particular sect—as for manner of life, it is in all cases the same. Inquiry into the cause of this anomaly leads me unhesitatingly to ascribe it to the fact, that the ministries of the Church are regarded by the masses merely as dignities, her offices as posts of emolument—in short, popular religion may be summed up as respect for ecclesiastics. The spread of this misconception inflamed every worthless fellow with an intense desire to enter holy orders, and thus the love of diffusing God's religion degenerated into sordid avarice and ambition. Every church became a theatre, where orators, instead of church teachers, harangued, caring not to instruct the people, but striving to attract admiration, to bring opponents to public scorn, and to preach only novelties and paradoxes, such as would tickle the ears of their congregation. This state of things necessarily stirred up an amount of controversy, envy, and hatred, which no lapse of time could appease; so that we can scarcely wonder that of the old religion nothing survives but its outward forms (even these, in the mouth of the multitude, seem rather adulation than adoration of the Deity), and that faith has become a mere compound of credulity and prejudices—aye, prejudices too, which degrade man from rational being to beast, which completely stifle the power of judgment between true and false, which seem, in fact, carefully fostered for the purpose of extinguishing the last spark of reason! Piety, great God! and religion are become a tissue of ridiculous mysteries; men, who flatly despise reason, who reject and turn away from understanding as naturally corrupt, these, I say, these of all men, are thought, O lie most horrible! to possess light from on High. Verily, if they had but one spark of light from on High, they would not insolently rave, but would learn to worship God more wisely, and would be as marked among their fellows for mercy as they now are for malice; if they were concerned for their opponents' souls, instead of for their own reputations, they would no longer fiercely persecute, but rather be filled with pity and compassion.

Furthermore, if any Divine light were in them, it would appear from their doctrine. I grant that they are never tired of professing their wonder at the profound mysteries of Holy Writ; still I cannot discover that they teach anything but speculations of Platonists and Aristotelians, to which (in order to save their credit for Christianity) they have made Holy Writ conform; not content to rave with the Greeks themselves, they want to make the prophets rave also; showing conclusively, that never even in sleep have they caught a glimpse of Scripture's Divine nature. The very vehemence of their admiration for the mysteries plainly attests, that their belief in the Bible is a formal assent rather than a living faith: and the fact is made still more apparent by their laying down beforehand, as a foundation for the study and true interpretation of Scripture, the principle that it is in every passage true and divine. Such a doctrine should be reached only after strict scrutiny and thorough comprehension of the Sacred Books (which would teach it much better, for they stand in need of no human fictions), and not be set up on the threshold, as it were, of inquiry.

As I pondered over the facts that the light of reason is not only despised, but by many even execrated as a source of impiety, that human commentaries are accepted as divine records, and that credulity is extolled as faith; as I marked the fierce controversies of philosophers raging in Church and State, the source of bitter hatred and dissension, the ready instruments of sedition and other ills innumerable, I determined to examine the Bible afresh in a careful, impartial, and unfettered spirit, making no assumptions concerning it, and attributing to it no doctrines, which I do not find clearly therein set down. With these precautions I constructed a method of Scriptural interpretation, and thus equipped proceeded to inquire—What is prophecy? in what sense did God reveal Himself to the prophets, and why were these particular men chosen by Him? Was it on account of the sublimity of their thoughts about the Deity and nature, or was it solely on account of their piety? These questions being answered, I was easily able to conclude, that the authority of the prophets has weight only in matters of morality, and that their speculative doctrines affect us little.

Next I inquired, why the Hebrews were called God's chosen people, and discovering that it was only because God had chosen for them a certain strip of territory, where they might live peaceably and at ease, I learnt that the Law revealed by God to Moses was merely the law of the individual Hebrew state, therefore that it was binding on none but Hebrews, and not even on Hebrews after the downfall of their nation. Further, in order to ascertain, whether it could be concluded from Scripture, that the human understanding is naturally corrupt, I inquired whether the Universal Religion, the Divine Law revealed through the Prophets and Apostles to the whole human race, differs from that which is taught by the light of natural reason, whether miracles can take place in violation of the laws of nature, and if so, whether they imply the existence of God more surely and clearly than events, which we understand plainly and distinctly through their immediate natural causes.

Now, as in the whole course of my investigation I found nothing taught expressly by Scripture, which does not agree with our understanding, or which is repugnant thereto, and as I saw that the prophets taught nothing, which is not very simple and easily to be grasped by all, and further, that they clothed their teaching in the style, and confirmed it with the reasons, which would most deeply move the mind of the masses to devotion towards God, I became thoroughly convinced, that the Bible leaves reason absolutely free, that it has nothing in common with philosophy, in fact, that Revelation and Philosophy stand on totally different footings. In order to set this forth categorically and exhaust the whole question, I point out the way in which the Bible should be interpreted, and show that all knowledge of spiritual questions should be sought from it alone, and not from the objects of ordinary knowledge. Thence I pass on to indicate the false notions, which have arisen from the fact that the multitude—ever prone to superstition, and caring more for the shreds of antiquity than for eternal truths—pays homage to the Books of the Bible, rather than to the Word of God. I show that the Word of God has not been revealed as a certain number of books, but was displayed to the prophets as a simple idea of the Divine mind, namely, obedience to God in singleness of heart, and in the practice of justice and charity; and I further point out, that this doctrine is set forth in Scripture in accordance with the opinions and understandings of those, among whom the Apostles and Prophets preached, to the end that men might receive it willingly, and with their whole heart.

Having thus laid bare the bases of belief, I draw the conclusion that Revelation has obedience for its sole object, and therefore, in purpose no less than in foundation and method, stands entirely aloof from ordinary knowledge; each has its separate province, neither can be called the handmaid of the other.

Furthermore, as men's habits of mind differ, so that some more readily embrace one form of faith, some another, for what moves one to pray may move another only to scoff, I conclude, in accordance with what has gone before, that everyone should be free to choose for himself the foundations of his creed, and that faith should be judged only by its fruits; each would then obey God freely with his whole heart, while nothing would be publicly honoured save justice and charity.

[*A Theological-Political Treatise* (*The Chief Works of Benedict de Spinoza*, trans. R. H. M.
Elwes, New York: Dover Publications, 1951,i. 6–10).]

BLAISE PASCAL

56   Faith beyond Reason

451 *Infinity—nothing*: Our soul is cast into the body, where it finds number, time and dimensions. On these it reasons, calling them natural and necessary, and it can believe in nothing else.

A unit joined to infinity adds nothing to it, any more than one foot added to infinite length. The finite is annihilated in the presence of infinity, and becomes a pure zero. So is our intellect before God, so is our justice before divine justice. But there is not so much disproportion between our justice and God's as there is between unity and infinity.

God's justice must be vast, like His compassion. Now justice towards the reprobate is less vast, and must be less amazing than mercy towards the elect.

We know that there is an infinite, and do not know its nature. As we know it to be untrue that numbers are finite, it is therefore true that there is a numerical infinity. But we do not know its nature; it cannot be even and it cannot be odd, for the addition of a unit cannot change it. Nevertheless it is a number, and all numbers are either even or odd (this is certainly true of every finite number). So, we may well know that there is a God without knowing what He is.

Is there no substantial truth, seeing that there are so many truths that are not the truth itself?

We know then the existence and nature of the finite, because we too are finite and have extension. We know the existence of the infinite, and do not know its nature, because it has extension like us, but unlike us no limits. But we know neither the existence nor the nature of God, because He has neither extension nor limits.

But by faith we know that He exists; in glory we shall know His nature. Now I have already shown that we can very well know a thing exists without knowing its nature.

Let us now speak according to the light of nature.

If there is a God, He is infinitely incomprehensible, since, being undivided and without limits, He bears no relation to us. We are, therefore, incapable of knowing either what He is, or whether He exists. This being so, who will be so rash as to decide the question? Not we who bear no relation to Him.

Who, then, will blame Christians for being unable to give a reason for their belief, since they profess a religion which they cannot explain by reason? In proclaiming it to the world, they declare that it is a foolishness, *stultitiam*,—and then you complain that they do not prove it. If they proved it, they would be denying their own statement; their lack of proof shows that they are not lacking in sense.

'Yes, but although this excuses those who present religion in that way, and we cannot, therefore, blame them for doing so without advancing reasons, it does not excuse those who accept it.'

Let us then examine this point, and say: 'Either God is, or He is not.' But which side shall we take? Reason can decide nothing here; there is an infinite chaos between us. A game is on, at the other side of this infinite distance, and the coin will fall heads or tails. Which will you gamble on? According to reason you cannot gamble on either; according to reason you cannot defend either choice.

But do not blame those who have decided for making a wrong choice; you know nothing about the matter.

'No, I shall not blame them for the choice they have made, but for making any choice at all. For the man who calls heads and the man who calls tails have made the same mistake. They are both wrong: the proper thing is not to bet at all.'

Yes, but you must bet. There is no option; you have embarked on the business. Which will you choose, then? Let us see. Since you must choose, let us see which will profit you less. You have two things to lose: truth and good, and two things to stake: your reason and your will, your knowledge and your happiness. And your nature has two things to avoid: error and misery. Since you must necessarily choose, it is no more unreasonable to make one choice than the other. That is one point cleared up. But your happiness? Let us weigh the gain and loss in calling heads, that God exists. Let us estimate the two chances; if you win, you win everything; if you lose, you lose nothing. Do not hesitate, then; gamble on His existence.

'This is splendid. Yes, I must make the bet; but perhaps I shall stake too much.'

Let us see. There being an equal chance of gain or loss, supposing you had two lives to gain for one, you might still gamble. But if you stood to gain three you would have to (being compelled to take part in the game). And since you have to play you would be foolish not to stake your one life for three in a game where the chances of gain and loss are equal. But here there is an eternity of life and happiness to be won. And this being so, even if there were an infinity of chances and only one in your favour, you would be right to stake one life against two; and it would be absurd, since you are compelled to play, to refuse to stake one life against three in a game in which one of an infinity of chances is in your favour, if what you stood to gain was an infinity of infinite happiness. But there *is* an infinity of infinite happiness to be gained, there is one chance of winning against a finite number of chances that you will lose, and what you are staking is finite. And so, since you are compelled to play, you would be mad to cling to your life instead of risking it for an infinite gain, which is as liable to turn up as a loss—of nothing.

For it is no use saying that our gain is uncertain, and that the infinite distance between the certainty of what we stake and the uncertainty of what we gain puts the finite good which we certainly risk on a level with the infinite, which is uncertain. This is not the case. Every gambler risks a certain sum to gain an uncertain one; and yet when he stakes a finite certainty to gain a finite uncertainty, he is not acting unreasonably. There is not an infinite difference between the certainty of the stake and the uncertainty of the gain; not at all. There is, indeed, an infinity between the certainty of gain and the certainty of loss. But the uncertainty of winning is proportionate to the certain amount of the stake, and the odds in favour of gain or loss. If therefore there are as many chances on one side as on the other, the odds are equal; and the fixed sum at stake is equal to the uncertain gain; there is no infinity of difference between them. And so our argument is infinitely strong when only the finite is at stake in a game in which the chances of gain and loss are equal, and infinity is to be won. This is demonstrable; and if men are susceptible to any truth, here is one.

'I confess and admit it. But yet, is there no way of seeing the face of the cards?' . . .

Yes, Holy Scripture and other writings, etc.

'Yes. But my hands are tied and my mouth is gagged. I am forced to play, and I am not free. Something holds me back, for I am so made that I cannot believe. What would you have me do?'

What you say is true. But at least be aware that your inability to believe arises from your passions. For your reason urges you to it, and yet you find it impossible. Endeavour, therefore, to gain conviction, not by an increase of divine proofs, but by the diminution of your passions. You wish to come to faith, but do not know the way. You wish to cure yourself of unbelief, and you ask for remedies. Learn from those who have been hampered like you, and who now stake all their possessions. These are the people who know the road that you wish to follow; they are cured of the disease of which you wish to be cured. Follow the way by which they began: by behaving as if they believed, by taking holy water, by having masses said, etc. This will bring you to belief in the natural way, and will soothe your mind.

'But that is just what I am afraid of.'

And why? What have you to lose?

But to show you that this will lead you there, it is this that will lessen your passions, which are your great obstacles. (*End of this discourse.*) Now what harm will come to you if you follow this course? You will be faithful, honest, humble, grateful, generous, sincere friend, and a truthful man. Certainly you will be without those poisonous pleasures, ambition and luxury. But will you not have others? I tell you that you will gain in this life, and that at every step you take on this road you will see such certainty of gain and such nothingness in your stake that you will finally realize you have gambled on something certain and infinite, and have risked nothing for it.

'Oh your words transport me, ravish me, etc.'

If this argument pleases you, and seems convincing, let me say that it is the utterance of a man who has knelt before and after, praying that infinite and undivided Being to whom he submits all he has that He may bring all your being likewise into submission, for your own good and His glory, and that thus strength may be brought into touch with weakness.

[*The Pensées*, trans. J. M. Cohen (Harmondsworth: Penguin, 1961), 155–9.]

JOHN LOCKE

57   **The Provinces of Faith and Reason**

2. I find every sect, as far as reason will help them, makes use of it gladly; and where it fails them, they cry out, *It is matter of faith, and above reason.* And I do not see how they can argue with anyone, or ever convince a gainsayer who makes use of the same plea, without setting down strict boundaries between *faith* and *reason*, which ought to be the first point established in all questions where *faith* has anything to do.

Reason, therefore, here, as contradistinguished to *faith*, I take to be the discovery of the certainty or probability of such propositions or truths, which the mind arrives at by deduction made from such *ideas* which it has got by the use of its natural faculties, viz. by sensation or reflection.

Faith, on the other side, is the assent to any proposition, not thus made out by the deductions of reason, but upon the credit of the proposer as coming from GOD, in some extraordinary way of communication. This way of discovering truths to men we call *revelation*.

3. First, then, I say that *no man inspired by* GOD *can by any revelation communicate to others any new simple ideas* which they had not before from sensation or reflection. For, whatsoever impressions he himself may have from the immediate hand of GOD, this revelation, if it be of new simple *ideas*, cannot be conveyed to another, either by words or any other signs. Because words, by their immediate operation on us, cause no other *ideas* but of their natural sounds; and it is by the custom of using them for signs that they excite and revive in our minds latent *ideas*, but yet only such *ideas* as were there before. For words seen or heard recall to our thoughts those *ideas* only which to us they have been wont to be signs of, but cannot introduce any perfectly new and formerly unknown simple *ideas*. The same holds in all other signs, which cannot signify to us things of which we have before never had any *idea* at all.

Thus whatever things were discovered to St *Paul*, when he was rapt up into the third heaven, whatever new *ideas* his mind there received, all the description he can make to others of that place is only this, that there are such things *as eye hath not seen, nor ear heard, nor hath it entered into the heart of man to conceive*. And supposing GOD should discover to anyone supernaturally, a species of creatures inhabiting, for example, *Jupiter* or *Saturn* (for that it is possible there may be such, nobody can deny) which had six senses, and imprint on his mind the *ideas* conveyed to theirs by that sixth sense: he could no more, by words, produce in the minds of other men those *ideas* imprinted by that sixth sense, than one of us could convey the *idea* of any colour, by the sounds of words, into a man who, having the other four senses perfect, had always totally wanted the fifth, of seeing. For our simple *ideas*, then, which are the foundation and sole matter of all our notions and knowledge, we must depend wholly on our reason, I mean, our natural faculties; and can by no means receive them, or any of them, from *traditional revelation*, I say *traditional revelation* in distinction to *original revelation*. By the one, I mean that first impression which is made immediately by GOD on the mind of any man, to which we cannot set any bounds; and by the other, those impressions delivered over to others in words and the ordinary ways of conveying our conceptions one to another.

4. *Secondly*, I say that *the same truths may be discovered and conveyed down from revelation, which are discoverable to us by reason*, and by those *ideas* we naturally may have. So GOD might, by revelation, discover the truth of any proposition in *Euclid*; as well as men, by the natural use of their faculties, come to make the

discovery themselves. In all things of this kind there is little need or use of *revelation*, GOD having furnished us with natural and surer means to arrive at the knowledge of them. For whatsoever truth we come to the clear discovery of, from the knowledge and contemplation of our own ideas, will always be certainer to us than those which are conveyed to us by *traditional revelation*. For the knowledge we have that this *revelation* came at first from GOD can never be so sure as the knowledge we have from the clear and distinct perception of the agreement or disagreement of our own *ideas*: v.g. if it were revealed, some ages since, that the three angles of a triangle were equal to two right ones, I might assent to the truth of that proposition upon the credit of the tradition that it was revealed; but that would never amount to so great a certainty as the knowledge of it upon the comparing and measuring my own *ideas* of two right angles and the three angles of a triangle. The like holds in matter of fact knowable by our senses: v.g. the history of the deluge is conveyed to us by writings which had their original from revelation; and yet nobody, I think, will say he has as certain and clear a knowledge of the flood as *Noah*, that saw it, or that he himself would have had, had he then been alive and seen it. For he has no greater an assurance than that of his senses, that it is writ in the book supposed writ by *Moses* inspired; but he has not so great an assurance that *Moses* wrote that book as if he had seen *Moses* write it. So that the assurance of its being a revelation is less still than the assurance of his senses.

5. In propositions, then, whose certainty is built upon the clear perception of the agreement or disagreement of our *ideas*, attained either by immediate intuition, as in self-evident propositions, or by evident deductions of reason in demonstrations, we need not the assistance of *revelation*, as necessary to gain our assent and introduce them into our minds. Because the natural ways of knowledge could settle them there, or had done it already; which is the greatest assurance we can possibly have of anything, unless where GOD immediately reveals it to us; and there too our assurance can be no greater than our knowledge is, that it is a *revelation* from GOD. But yet nothing, I think, can under that title shake or overrule plain knowledge, or rationally prevail with any man to admit it for true in a direct contradiction to the clear evidence of his own understanding. For since no evidence of our faculties, by which we receive such *revelations*, can exceed, if equal, the certainty of our intuitive knowledge, we can never receive for a truth anything that is directly contrary to our clear and distinct knowledge: v.g. the *ideas* of one body and one place do so clearly agree, and the mind has so evident a perception of their agreement, that we can never assent to a proposition that affirms the same body to be in two distant places at once, however it should pretend to the authority of a divine *revelation*: since the evidence, *first*, that we deceive not ourselves in ascribing it to GOD; *secondly*, that we understand it right, can never be so great as the evidence of our own intuitive knowledge whereby we discern it impossible for the same body to be in two places at once. And therefore *no proposition can be received for divine revelation*

or obtain the assent due to all such, *if it be contradictory to our clear intuitive knowledge*. Because this would be to subvert the principles and foundations of all knowledge, evidence, and assent whatsoever; and there would be left no difference between truth and falsehood, no measures of credible and incredible in the world, if doubtful propositions shall take place before self-evident, and what we certainly know give way to what we may possibly be mistaken in. In propositions therefore contrary to the clear perception of the agreement or disagreement of any of our *ideas*, it will be in vain to urge them as matters of *faith*. They cannot move our assent under that or any other title whatsoever. For *faith* can never convince us of anything that contradicts our knowledge. Because, though *faith* be founded on the testimony of GOD (who cannot lie) revealing any proposition to us: yet we cannot have an assurance of the truth of its being a divine revelation greater than our own knowledge: since the whole strength of the certainty depends upon our knowledge that GOD revealed it; which, in this case, where the proposition supposed revealed contradicts our knowledge or reason, will always have this objection hanging to it, (viz.) that we cannot tell how to conceive that to come from GOD, the bountiful Author of our being, which, if received for true, must overturn all the principles and foundations of knowledge he has given us; render all our faculties useless; wholly destroy the most excellent part of his workmanship, our understandings; and put a man in a condition wherein he will have less light, less conduct than the beast that perisheth. For if the mind of man can never have a clearer (and, perhaps, not so clear) evidence of anything to be a divine *revelation*, as it has of the principles of its own reason, it can never have a ground to quit the clear evidence of its reason, to give place to a proposition whose *revelation* has not a greater evidence than those principles have.

6. Thus far a man has use of reason and ought to hearken to it, even in immediate and original *revelation*, where it is supposed to be made to himself. But to all those who pretend not to immediate *revelation*, but are required to pay obedience and to receive the truths revealed to others which, by the tradition of writings or word of mouth, are conveyed down to them, reason has a great deal more to do, and is that only which can induce us to receive them. For matter of faith being only divine revelation and nothing else, *faith*, as we use the word (called commonly, *divine faith*) has to do with no propositions but those which are supposed to be divinely revealed. So that I do not see how those who make revelation alone the sole object of *faith* can say that it is a matter of *faith*, and not of *reason*, to believe that such or such a proposition, to be found in such or such a book, is of divine inspiration, unless it be revealed that that proposition, or all in that book, was communicated by divine inspiration. Without such a *revelation*, the believing or not believing that proposition or book to be of divine authority can never be matter of *faith*, but matter of reason, and such as I must come to an assent to only by the use of my reason, which can never require or enable me to believe that which is contrary to itself: it being impossible for

reason ever to procure any assent to that which to itself appears unreasonable.

In all things, therefore, where we have clear evidence from our *ideas* and those principles of knowledge I have above mentioned, *reason* is the proper judge; and *revelation*, though it may, in consenting with it, confirm its dictates, yet cannot in such cases invalidate its decrees; *nor can we be obliged, where we have the clear and evident sentence of reason, to quit it for the contrary opinion, under a pretence that it is matter of faith*, which can have no authority against the plain and clear dictates of *reason*.

[*An Essay Concerning Human Understanding*, ed. J. W. Yolton (London: Dent, 1964), ii. 281–5.]

WILLIAM PALEY
....
58 **The Argument from Design**

In crossing a heath, suppose I pitched my foot against a *stone*, and were asked how the stone came to be there; I might possibly answer, that, for any thing I knew to the contrary, it had lain there for ever; nor would it perhaps be very easy to shew the absurdity of this answer. But suppose I had found a *watch* upon the ground, and it should be enquired how the watch happened to be in that place; I should hardly think of the answer which I had before given, that, for anything I knew, the watch might have always been there. Yet why should not this answer serve for the watch as well as for the stone? why is it not as admissible in the second case, as in the first? For this reason, and for no other, viz. that, when we come to inspect the watch, we perceive (what we could not discover in the stone) that its several parts are framed and put together for a purpose, *e.g.* that they are so formed and adjusted as to produce motion, and that motion so regulated as to point out the hour of the day; that, if the several parts had been differently shaped from what they are, of a different size from what they are, or placed after any other manner, or in any other order, than that in which they are placed, either no motion at all would have been carried on in the machine, or none which would have answered the use that is now served by it. To reckon up a few of the plainest of these parts, and of their offices, all tending to one result:—We see a cylindrical box containing a coiled, elastic spring, which, by its endeavour to relax itself, turns round the box. We next observe a flexible chain (artificially wrought for the sake of flexure) communicating the action of the spring from the box to the fusee. We then find a series of wheels, the teeth of which catch in, and apply to, each other, conducting the motion from the fusee to the balance, and from the balance to the pointer; and at the same time, by the size and shape of those wheels, so regulating that motion, as to terminate in causing an index, by an equable and measured progression, to pass over a given space in a given time. We take notice, that the wheels are made of brass, in order to keep them from rust; the springs of steel, no other metal being so elastic; that over the face of the watch there is placed a glass, a material employed in no other part of the work, but in the room of which, if there had been any other than a transparent substance, the hour could not be seen without opening the case. This mechanism being observed, (it requires indeed an examination of the instrument, and perhaps some previous knowledge of the subject, to perceive and understand it; but being once, as we have said, observed and understood,) the inference, we think, is inevitable, that the watch must have had a maker: that there must have existed, at some time, and at some place or other, an artificer or artificers who formed it for the purpose which we find it actually to answer; who comprehended its construction, and designed its use.

I. Nor would it, I apprehend, weaken the conclusion, that we had never seen a watch made; that we had never known an artist capable of making one; that we were altogether incapable of executing such a piece of workmanship ourselves, or of understanding in what manner it was performed; all this being no more than what is true of some exquisite remains of ancient art, of some lost arts, and, to the generality of mankind, of the more curious productions of modern manufacture. Does one man in a million know how oval frames are turned? Ignorance of this kind exalts our opinion of the unseen and unknown artist's skill, if he be unseen and unknown, but raises no doubt in our minds of the existence and agency of such an artist, at some former time, and in some place or other. Nor can I perceive that it varies at all the inference, whether the question arise concerning a human agent, or concerning an agent of a different species, or an agent possessing, in some respects, a different nature.

II. Neither, secondly, would it invalidate our conclusion, that the watch sometimes went wrong, or that it seldom went exactly right. The purpose of the machinery, the design, and the designer, might be evident, and in the case supposed would be evident, in whatever way we accounted for the irregularity of the movement, or whether we could account for it or not. It is not necessary that a machine be perfect, in order to shew with what design it was made: still less necessary, where the only question is, whether it were made with any design at all.

III. Nor, thirdly, would it bring any uncertainty into the argument, if there were a few parts of the watch, concerning which we could not discover, or had not yet discovered, in what manner they conduced to the general effect; or even some parts, concerning which we could not ascertain, whether they conduced to that effect in any manner whatever. For, as to the first branch of the case; if by the loss, or disorder, or decay of the parts in question, the movement of the watch were found in fact to be stopped, or disturbed, or retarded, no doubt would remain in our minds as to the utility or intention of these parts, although we should be unable to investigate the manner according to which, or the connection by which, the ultimate effect depended upon their action or assistance; and the more complex is the machine, the more likely is this obscurity to arise. Then, as to the second thing supposed, namely, that there were parts which might be spared, without prejudice to the movement of the watch, and that we had proved this by experiment,—these superfluous parts, even if we were completely assured that they were such, would not vacate the reasoning which we had instituted concerning other parts. The indication of contrivance remained, with respect to them, nearly as it was before.

IV. Nor, fourthly, would any man in his senses think the existence of the watch, with its various machinery, accounted for, by being told that it was one out of possible combinations of material forms; that whatever he had found in the place where he found the watch, must have contained some internal configuration or other; and that this configuration might be the structure now exhibited, viz. of the works of a watch, as well as a different structure.

V. Nor, fifthly, would it yield his enquiry more satisfaction to be answered, that there existed in things a principle of order, which had disposed the parts of the watch into their present form and situation. He never knew a watch made by the principle of order; nor can he even form to himself an idea of what is meant by a principle of order, distinct from the intelligence of the watch-maker.

VI. Sixthly, he would be surprised to hear, that the mechanism of the watch was no proof of contrivance, only a motive to induce the mind to think so:

VII. And not less surprised to be informed, that the watch in his hand was nothing more than the result of the laws of *metallic* nature.—It is a perversion of language to assign any law, as the efficient, operative cause of any thing. A law presupposes an agent; for it is only the mode, according to which an agent proceeds: it implies a power; for it is the order, according to which that power acts. Without this agent, without this power, which are both distinct from itself, the *law* does nothing; is nothing. The expression, 'the law of metallic nature,' may sound strange and harsh to a philosophic ear; but it seems quite as justifiable as some others which are more familiar to him, such as 'the law of vegetable nature,'—'the law of animal nature,' or indeed as 'the law of nature' in general, when assigned as the cause of phænomena, in exclusion of agency and power; or when it is substituted into the place of these.

VIII. Neither, lastly, would our observer be driven out of his conclusion, or from his confidence in its truth, by being told that he knew nothing at all about the matter. He knows enough for his argument: he knows the utility of the end: he knows the subserviency and adaptation of the means to the end. These points being known, his ignorance of other points, his doubts concerning other points, affect not the certainty of his reasoning. The consciousness of knowing little, need not beget a distrust of that which he does know.

[*Natural Theology* (London, 1807), 1–8.]

59 **Analogies and Disanalogies**

The discoveries by microscopes, as they open a new universe in miniature, are still objections, according to you; arguments, according to me. The further we push our researches of this kind, we are still led to infer the universal cause of all to be vastly different from mankind, or from any object of human experience and observation.

And what say you to the discoveries in anatomy, chemistry, botany? . . . These surely are no objections, replied Cleanthes; they only discover new instances of art and contrivance. It is still the image of mind reflected on us from innumerable objects. Add a mind *like the human*, said Philo. I know of no other, replied Cleanthes. And the liker, the better, insisted Philo. To be sure, said Cleanthes.

Now, Cleanthes, said Philo, with an air of alacrity and triumph, mark the consequences. *First*, by this method of reasoning you renounce all claim to infinity in any of the attributes of the Deity. For, as the cause ought only to be proportioned to the effect, and the effect, so far as it falls under our cognizance, is not infinite, what pretensions have we, upon your suppositions, to ascribe that attribute to the divine Being? You will still insist that, by removing him so much from all similarity to human creatures, we give in to the most arbitrary hypothesis, and at the same time weaken all proofs of his existence.

Secondly, you have no reason, on your theory, for ascribing perfection to the Deity, even in his finite capacity; or for supposing him free from every error, mistake, or incoherence, in his undertakings. There are many inexplicable difficulties in the works of nature which, if we allow a perfect author to be proved *a priori*, are easily solved, and become only seeming difficulties from the narrow capacity of man, who cannot trace infinite relations. But according to your method of reasoning, these difficulties become all real; and, perhaps, will be insisted on as new instances of likeness to human art and contrivance. At least, you must acknowledge that it is impossible for us to tell, from our limited views, whether this system contains any great faults or deserves any considerable praise if compared to other possible and even real systems. Could a peasant, if the *Aeneid* were read to him, pronounce that poem to be absolutely faultless, or even assign to it its proper rank among the productions of human wit, he who had never seen any other production?

But were this world ever so perfect a production, it must still remain uncertain whether all the excellences of the work can justly be ascribed to the workman. If we survey a ship, what an exalted idea must we form of the ingenuity of the carpenter who framed so complicated, useful, and beautiful a machine? And what surprise must we feel when we find him a stupid mechanic who imitated others, and copied an art which, through a long succession of ages, after multiplied trials, mistakes, corrections, deliberations, and controversies, had been gradually improving? Many worlds might have been botched and bungled, throughout an eternity, ere this system was struck out; much labour lost; many fruitless trials made; and a slow but continued improvement carried on during infinite ages in the art of world-making. In such subjects, who can determine where the truth, nay, who can conjecture where the probability lies, amidst a great number of hypotheses which may be proposed, and a still greater which may be imagined?

And what shadow of an argument, continued Philo, can you produce from your hypothesis to prove the unity of the Deity? A great number of men join in building a house or ship, in rearing a city, in framing a commonwealth; why may not several deities combine in contriving and framing a world? This is only so much greater similarity to human affairs. By sharing the work among several, we may so much further limit the attributes of each, and get rid of that extensive power and knowledge which must be supposed in one deity, and which, according to you, can only serve to weaken the proof of his existence. And if such foolish, such vicious creatures as man can yet often unite in framing and executing one plan, how much more those deities or demons, whom we may suppose several degrees more perfect?

To multiply causes without necessity is indeed contrary to true philosophy, but this principle applies not to the present case. Were one deity antecedently proved by your theory who were possessed of every attribute requisite to the production of the universe, it would be needless, I own (though not absurd), to suppose any other deity existent. But while it is still a question whether all these attributes are united in one subject or dispersed among several independent beings; by what phenomena in nature can we pretend to decide the controversy? Where we see a body raised in a scale, we are sure that there is in the opposite scale, however concealed from sight, some counterpoising weight equal to it; but it is still allowed to doubt whether that weight be an aggregate of several distinct bodies or one uniform united mass. And if the weight requisite very much exceeds anything which we have ever seen conjoined in any single body, the former supposition becomes still more probable and natural. An intelligent being of such vast power and capacity as is necessary to produce the universe—or, to speak in the language of ancient philosophy, so prodigious an animal—exceeds all analogy and even comprehension.

But further, Cleanthes, men are mortal, and renew their species by generation; and this is common to all living creatures. The two great sexes of male and female, says Milton, animate the world. Why must this circumstance, so universal, so essential, be excluded from those numerous and limited deities? Behold, then, the theogeny of ancient times brought back upon us.

And why not become a perfect anthropomorphite? Why not assert the deity or deities to be corporeal, and to have eyes, a nose, mouth, ears, etc.? Epicurus maintained that no man had ever seen reason but in a human figure; therefore, the gods must have a human figure. And this argument, which is deservedly so much ridiculed by Cicero, becomes, according to you, solid and philosophical.

In a word, Cleanthes, a man who follows your hypothesis is able, perhaps, to assert or conjecture that the universe sometime arose from something like design; but beyond that position he cannot ascertain one single circumstance, and is left afterwards to fix every point of his theology by the utmost license of fancy and hypothesis. This world, for aught he knows, is very faulty and imperfect, compared to a superior standard; and was only the first rude essay of some infant deity who afterwards abandoned it, ashamed of his lame performance; it is the work only of some dependent, inferior deity, and is the object of derision to his superiors; it is the production of old age and dotage in some superannuated deity; and ever since his death has run on at adventures, from the first impulse and active force which it received from him. You justly give signs of horror, Demea, at these strange suppositions; but these, and a thousand more of the same kind, are Cleanthes' suppositions, not mine. From the moment the attributes of the Deity are supposed finite, all these have place. And I cannot, for my part, think that so wild and unsettled a system of theology is, in any respect, preferable to none at all.

These suppositions I absolutely disown, cried Cleanthes; they strike me, however, with no horror, especially when proposed in that rambling way in which they drop from you. On the contrary, they give me pleasure when I see that, by the utmost indulgence of your imagination, you never get rid of the hypothesis of design in the universe, but are obliged at every turn to have recourse to it. To this concession I adhere steadily; and this I regard as a sufficient foundation for religion.

[*Dialogues Concerning Natural Religion*, ed. with commentary by Nelson Pike (Indianapolis: Bobbs-Merrill, 1970), 50–3.]

JOSEPH BUTLER

60 Probability the Guide to Life

§7

It is not my design to inquire further into the nature, the foundation, and measure of probability; or whence it proceeds that *likeness* should beget that presumption, opinion, and full conviction, which the human mind is formed to receive from it, and which it does necessarily produce in every one; or to guard against the errors, to which reasoning from analogy is liable. This belongs to the subject of Logic; and is a part of that subject which has not yet been thoroughly considered. Indeed I shall not take upon me to say, how far the extent, compass, and force, of analogical reasoning, can be reduced to general heads and rules; and the whole be formed into a system. But though so little in this way has been attempted by those who have treated of our intellectual powers, and the exercise of them; this does not hinder but that we may be, as we unquestionably are, assured, that analogy is of weight, in various degrees, towards determining our judgment and our practice. Nor does it in any wise cease to be of weight in those cases, because persons, either given to dispute, or who require things to be stated with greater exactness than our faculties appear to admit of in practical matters, may find other cases in which it is not easy to say, whether it be, or be not, of any weight; or instances of seeming analogies, which are really of none. It is enough to the present purpose to observe, that this general way of arguing is evidently natural, just, and conclusive. For there is no man can make a question, but that the sun will rise to-morrow, and be seen, where it is seen at all, in the figure of a circle, and not in that of a square.

§8

Hence, namely from analogical reasoning, Origen has with singular sagacity observed, that *he who believes the scripture to have proceeded from him who is the Author of nature, may well expect to find the same sort of difficulties in it, as are found in the constitution of nature.* And in a like way of reflection it may be added, that he who denies the scripture to have been from God upon account of these difficulties, may, for the very same reason, deny the world to have been formed by him. On the other hand, if there be an analogy or likeness between that system of things and dispensation of Providence, which revelation informs us of, and that system of things and dispensation of Providence, which experience together with reason informs us of, i.e. the known course of nature; this is a presumption, that they have both the same author and cause; at least so far as to answer objections against the former's being from God, drawn from any thing which is analogical or similar to what is in the latter, which is acknowledged to be from him; for an Author of nature is here supposed.

§9

Forming our notions of the constitution and government of the world upon reasoning, without foundation for the principles which we assume, whether from the attributes of God, or any thing else, is building a world upon hypothesis, like Descartes. Forming our notions upon reasoning from principles which are certain, but applied to cases to which we have no ground to apply them, (like those who explain the structure of the human body, and the nature of diseases and medicines from mere mathematics without sufficient *data*,) is an error much akin to the former: since what is assumed in order to make the reasoning applicable, is hypothesis. But it must be allowed just, to join abstract reasonings with the observation of facts, and argue from such facts as are known, to others that are like them; from that part of the divine government over intelligent creatures which comes under our view, to that larger and more general government over them which is beyond it; and from what is present, to collect what is likely, credible, or not incredible, will be hereafter.

§10

This method then of concluding and determining being practical, and what, if we will act at all, we cannot but act upon in the common pursuits of life; being evidently conclusive, in various degrees, proportionable to the degree and exactness of the whole analogy or likeness; and having so great authority for its introduction into the subject of religion, even revealed religion; my design is to apply it to that subject in general, both natural and revealed: taking for proved, that there is an intelligent Author of nature, and natural Governor of the world. For as there is no presumption against this prior to the proof of it: so it has been often proved with accumulated evidence; from this argument of analogy and final causes; from abstract reasonings; from the most ancient tradition and testimony; and from the general consent of mankind. Nor does it appear, so far as I can find, to be denied by the generality of those who profess themselves dissatisfied with the evidence of religion.

§11

As there are some, who, instead of thus attending to what is in fact the constitution of nature, form their notions of God's government upon hypothesis: so there are others, who indulge themselves in vain and idle speculations, how the world might possibly have been framed otherwise than it is; and upon supposition that things might, in imagining that they should, have been disposed and carried on after a better model, than what appears in the present disposition and conduct of them. Suppose now a person of such a turn of mind, to go on with his reveries, till he had at length fixed upon some particular plan of nature, as appearing to him the best.—One shall scarce be thought guilty of detraction against human understanding, if one should say, even beforehand, that the plan which this speculative person would fix upon, though he were the wisest of the sons of men, probably would not be the very best, even according to his own notions of *best*; whether he thought that to be so, which afforded occasions and motives for the exercise of the greatest virtue, or which was productive of the greatest happiness, or that these two were necessarily connected, and run up into one and the same plan. However, it may not be amiss once for all to see, what would be the amount of these emendations and imaginary improvements upon the system of nature, or how far they would mislead us. And it seems there could be no stopping, till we came to some such conclusions as these: that all creatures should at first be made as perfect and as happy as they were capable of ever being: that nothing, to be sure, of hazard or danger should be put upon them to do; some indolent persons would perhaps think nothing at all: or certainly, that effectual care should be taken, that they should, whether necessarily or not, yet eventually and in fact, always do what was right and most conducive to happiness, which would be thought easy for infinite power to effect; either by not giving them any principles which would endanger their going wrong; or by laying the right motive of action in every instance before their minds continually in so strong a manner, as would never fail of inducing them to act conformably to it: and that the whole method of government by punishments should be rejected as absurd; as an awkward roundabout method of carrying things on; nay, as contrary to a principal purpose, for which it would be supposed creatures were made, namely, happiness.

§12

Now, without considering what is to be said in particular to the several parts of this train of folly and extravagance; what has been above intimated, is a full direct general answer to it, namely, that we may see beforehand that we have not faculties for this kind of speculation. For though it be admitted, that, from the first principles of our nature, we unavoidably judge or determine some ends to be absolutely in themselves preferable to others, and that the ends now mentioned, or if they run up into one, that this one is absolutely the best; and consequently that we must conclude the ultimate end designed, in the constitution of nature and conduct of Providence, is the most virtue and happiness possible: yet we are far from being able to judge what particular disposition of things would be most friendly and assistant to virtue; or what means might be absolutely necessary to produce the most happiness in a system of such extent as our own world may be, taking in all that is past and to come, though we should suppose it detached from the whole of things. Indeed we are so far from being able to judge of this, that we are not judges what may be the necessary means of raising and conducting one person to the highest perfection and happiness of his nature. Nay, even in the little affairs of the present life, we find men of different educations and ranks are not competent judges of the conduct of each other.

§13

Our whole nature leads us to ascribe all moral perfection to God, and to deny all imperfection of him. And this will for ever be a practical proof of his moral character, to such as will consider what a practical proof is; because it is the voice of God speaking in us. And from hence we conclude, that virtue must be the happiness, and vice the misery, of every creature; and that regularity and order and right cannot but prevail finally in a universe under his government. But we are in no sort judges, what are the necessary means of accomplishing this end.

[*The Analogy of Religion* (*The Works of Joseph Butler*, ed. W. E. Gladstone, Oxford: Clarendon Press, 1897, 7–13).]

GEORGE BERKELEY

61   Logic and Reason in Faith and Science

8. Shall we not admit the same method of arguing, the same rules of logic, reason, and good sense, to obtain in things spiritual and things corporeal, in faith and science? and shall we not use the same candour, and make the same

allowances, in examining the revelations of God and the inventions of men? For aught I see, that philosopher cannot be free from bias and prejudice, or be said to weigh things in an equal balance, who shall maintain the doctrine of force and reject that of grace, who shall admit the abstract idea of a triangle, and at the same time ridicule the Holy Trinity. But, however partial or prejudiced other minute philosophers might be, you have laid it down for a maxim, that the same logic which obtains in other matters must be admitted in religion.

Lysicles. I think, Alciphron, it would be more prudent to abide by the way of wit and humour than thus to try religion by the dry test of reason and logic.

Alciphron. Fear not: by all the rules of right reason, it is absolutely impossible that any mystery, and least of all the Trinity, should really be the object of man's faith.

Euphranor. I do not wonder you thought so, as long as you maintained that no man could assent to a proposition without perceiving or framing in his mind distinct ideas marked by the terms of it. But, although terms are signs, yet having granted that those signs may be significant, though they should not suggest ideas represented by them, provided they serve to regulate and influence our wills, passions, or conduct, you have consequently granted that the mind of man may assent to propositions containing such terms, when it is so directed or affected by them, notwithstanding it should not perceive distinct ideas marked by those terms. Whence it seems to follow that a man may believe the doctrine of the Trinity, if he finds it revealed in Holy Scripture that the Father, the Son, and the Holy Ghost, are God, and that there is but one God, although he doth not frame in his mind any abstract or distinct ideas of trinity, substance, or personality; provided that this doctrine of a Creator, Redeemer, and Sanctifier makes proper impressions on his mind, producing therein love, hope, gratitude, and obedience, and thereby becomes a lively operative principle, influencing his life and actions, agreeably to that notion of saving faith which is required in a Christian. This, I say, whether right or wrong, seems to follow from your own principles and concessions. But, for further satisfaction, it may not be amiss to inquire whether there be anything parallel to this Christian faith in the minute philosophy. Suppose a fine gentleman or lady of fashion, who are too much employed to think for themselves, and are only free-thinkers at second-hand, have the advantage of being betimes initiated in the principles of your sect, by conversing with men of depth and genius, who have often declared it to be their opinion, the world is governed either by fate or by chance, it matters not which; will you deny it possible for such persons to yield their assent to either of these propositions?

Alc. I will not.

Euph. And may not their assent be properly called *faith*?

Alc. It may.

Euph. And yet it is possible those disciples of the minute philosophy may not dive so deep as to be able to frame any abstract, or precise, or any determinate idea whatsoever, either of fate or of chance?

Alc. This too I grant.

Euph. So that, according to you, this same gentleman or lady may be said to believe or have faith where they have not ideas?

Alc. They may.

Euph. And may not this faith or persuasion produce real effects, and show itself in the conduct and tenor of their lives, freeing them from the fears of superstition, and giving them a true relish of the world, with a noble indolence or indifference about what comes after?

Alc. It may.

Euph. And may not Christians, with equal reason, be allowed to believe the Divinity of our Saviour, or that in Him God and man make one Person, and be verily persuaded thereof, so far as for such faith or belief to become a real principle of life and conduct? inasmuch as, by virtue of such persuasion, they submit to His government, believe His doctrine, and practise His precepts, although they frame no abstract idea of the union between the Divine and human nature; nor may be able to clear up the notion of person to the contentment of a minute philosopher? To me it seems evident that if none but those who had nicely examined, and could themselves explain, the principle of individuation in man, or untie the knots and answer the objections which may be raised even about human personal identity, would require of us to explain the Divine mysteries, we should not be often called upon for a clear and distinct idea of person in relation to the Trinity, nor would the difficulties on that head be often objected to our faith.

Alc. Methinks, there is no such mystery in personal identity.

Euph. Pray, in what do you take it to consist?

Alc. In consciousness.

Euph. Whatever is possible may be supposed?

Alc. It may.

Euph. We will suppose now (which is possible in the nature of things, and reported to be fact) that a person, through some violent accident or distemper, should fall into such a total oblivion as to lose all consciousness of his past life and former ideas. I ask, is he not still the same person?

Alc. He is the same man, but not the same person. Indeed you ought not to suppose that a person loseth its former consciousness; for this is impossible, though a man perhaps may; but then he becomes another person. In the same person, it must be owned, some old ideas may be lost, and some new ones got; but a total change is inconsistent with identity of person.

Euph. Let us then suppose that a person hath ideas and is conscious during a certain space of time, which we will divide into three equal parts, whereof the later terms are marked by the letters A, B, C. In the first part of time, the person gets a certain number of ideas, which are retained in A: during the second part of time, he retains one-half of his old ideas, and loseth the other half, in place of which he acquires as many new ones: so that in B his ideas are half old and half new. And in the third part, we suppose him to lose the remainder of the ideas acquired in the first, and to get new ones in their stead, which are retained in C, together with those acquired in the second part of time. Is this a possible fair supposition?

Alc. It is.

Euph. Upon these premises, I am tempted to think one may demonstrate that personal identity doth not consist in consciousness.

Alc. As how?

Euph. You shall judge: but thus it seems to me. The persons in A and B are the same, being conscious of common ideas by supposition. The person in B is (for the same reason) one and the same with the person in C. Therefore, the person in A is the same with the person in C, by that undoubted axiom, *Quæ conveniunt uni tertio conveniunt inter se.* But the person in C hath no idea in common with the person in A. Therefore personal identity doth not consist in consciousness. What do you think, Alciphron, is not this a plain inference?

Alc. I tell you what I think: you will never assist my faith, by puzzling my knowledge.

9. *Euph.* There is, if I mistake not, a practical faith, or assent, which showeth itself in the will and actions of a man, although his understanding may not be furnished with those abstract, precise, distinct ideas, which, whatever a philosopher may pretend, are acknowledged to be above the talents of common men; among whom, nevertheless, may be found, even according to your own concession, many instances of such practical faith, in other matters which do not concern religion. What should hinder, therefore, but that doctrines relating to heavenly mysteries might be taught, in this saving sense, to vulgar minds, which you may well think incapable of all teaching and faith, in the sense you suppose?

Which mistaken sense, said Crito, has given occasion to much profane and misapplied raillery. But all this may very justly be retorted on the minute philosophers themselves, who confound Scholasticism with Christianity, and impute to other men those perplexities, chimeras, and inconsistent ideas which are often the workmanship of their own brains, and proceed from their own wrong way of thinking. Who doth not see that such an ideal abstracted faith is never thought of by the bulk of Christians, husbandmen, for instance, artisans, or servants? Or what footsteps are there in the Holy Scripture to make us think that the wiredrawing of abstract ideas was a task enjoined either Jews or Christians? Is there anything in the law or the prophets, the evangelists or apostles, that looks like it? Everyone whose understanding is not perverted by science falsely so-called may see the saving faith of Christians is quite of another kind, a vital operative principle, productive of charity and obedience.

[*The Alciphron* (1732), ed. David Berman (London: Routledge, 1993), 129–33.]

This attempt to alter the procedure which has hitherto prevailed in meta-physics, by completely revolutionizing it in accordance with the example set by the geometers and physicists, forms indeed the main purpose of this critique of pure speculative reason. It is a treatise on the method, not a system of the science itself. But at the same time it marks out the whole plan of the science, both as regards its limits and as regards its entire internal structure. For pure speculative reason has this peculiarity, that it can measure its powers according to the different ways in which it chooses the objects of its thinking, and can also give an exhaustive enumeration of the various ways in which it propounds its problems, and so is able, nay bound, to trace the complete outline of a system of metaphysics. As regards the first point, nothing in *a priori* knowledge can be ascribed to objects save what the thinking subject derives from itself; as regards the second point, pure reason, so far as the principles of its knowledge are concerned, is a quite separate self-subsistent unity, in which, as in an organized body, every member exists for every other, and all for the sake of each, so that no principle can safely be taken in *any one* relation, unless it has been investigated in the *entirety* of its relations to the whole employment of pure reason. Consequently, metaphysics has also this singular advantage, such as falls to the lot of no other science which deals with objects (for *logic* is concerned only with the form of thought in general), that should it, through this critique, be set upon the secure path of a science, it is capable of acquiring exhaustive knowledge of its entire field. Metaphysics has to deal only with principles, and with the limits of their employment as determined by these principles themselves, and it can therefore finish its work and bequeath it to posterity as a capital to which no addition can be made. Since it is a fundamental science, it is under obligation to achieve this completeness. We must be able to say of it: *nil actum reputans, si quid superesset agendum.*

But, it will be asked, what sort of a treasure is this that we propose to bequeath to posterity? What is the value of the metaphysics that is alleged to be thus purified by criticism and established once for all? On a cursory view of the present work it may seem that its results are merely *negative*, warning us that we must never venture with speculative reason beyond the limits of experience. Such is in fact its primary use. But such teaching at once acquires a *positive* value when we recognize that the principles with which speculative reason ventures out beyond its proper limits do not in effect *extend* the employment of reason, but, as we find on closer scrutiny, inevitably *narrow* it. These principles properly belong [not to reason but] to sensibility, and when thus employed they threaten to make the bounds of sensibility coextensive with the real, and so to supplant reason in its pure (practical) employment. So far, therefore, as our Critique limits speculative reason, it is indeed *negative*; but since it thereby removes an obstacle which stands in the way of the employment of practical reason, nay threatens to destroy it, it has in reality a *positive* and very important use. At least this is so, immediately we are convinced that there is an absolutely necessary *practical* employment of pure reason—the *moral*—in which it inevitably goes beyond the limits of sensibility. Though [practical] reason, in thus proceeding, requires no assistance from speculative reason, it must yet be assured against its opposition, that reason may not be brought into conflict with itself. To deny that the service which the Critique renders is *positive* in character, would thus be like saying that the police are of no positive benefit, inasmuch as their main business is merely to prevent the violence of which citizens stand in mutual fear, in order that each may pursue his vocation in peace and security. That space and time are only forms of sensible intuition, and so only conditions of the existence of things as appearances; that, moreover, we have no concepts of understanding, and consequently no elements for the knowledge of things, save in so far as intuition can be given corresponding to these concepts; and that we can therefore have no knowledge of any object as thing in itself, but only in so far as it is an object of sensible intuition, that is, an appearance—all this is proved in the analytical part of the Critique. Thus it does indeed follow that all possible speculative knowledge of reason is limited to mere objects of *experience*. But our further contention must also be duly borne in mind, namely, that though we cannot *know* these objects as things in themselves, we must yet be in position at least to *think* them as things in themselves; otherwise we should be landed in the absurd conclusion that there can be appearance without anything that appears. Now let us suppose that the distinction, which our Critique has shown to be necessary, between things as objects of experience and those same things as things in themselves, had not been made. In that case all things in general, as far as they are efficient causes, would be determined by the principle of causality, and consequently by the mechanism of nature. I could not, therefore, without palpable contradiction, say of one and the same being, for instance the human soul, that its will is free and yet is subject to natural necessity, that is, is not free. For I have taken the soul in both propositions *in one and the same sense*, namely as a thing in general, that is, as a thing in itself; and save by means of a preceding critique, could not have done otherwise. But if our Critique is not in error in teaching that the object is to be taken *in a twofold sense*, namely as appearance and as thing in itself; if the deduction of the concepts of understanding is valid, and the principle of causality therefore applies only to things taken in the former sense, namely, in so far as they are objects of experience—these same objects, taken in the other sense, not being subject to the principle—then there is no contradiction in supposing that one and the same will is, in the appearance, that is, in its visible acts, necessarily subject to the law of nature, and so far *not free*, while yet, as belonging to a thing in itself, it is not subject to that law, and is therefore *free*. My soul, viewed from the latter standpoint, cannot indeed be known by means of speculative reason (and still less through empirical observation); and freedom as a property of a being to which I attribute effects in the sensible world, is therefore also not knowable in any such fashion. For I should then have to know such a being as determined in its existence, and yet as not determined in time—which is impossible, since I cannot support my concept by any intuition. But though I cannot *know*, I can yet *think* freedom; that is to say, the representation of it is at least not self-contradictory, provided due account be taken of our critical distinction between the two modes of representation, the sensible and the intellectual, and of the resulting limitation of the pure concepts of understanding and of the principles which flow from them.

If we grant that morality necessarily presupposes freedom (in the strictest sense) as a property of our will; if, that is to say, we grant that it yields practical principles—original principles, proper to our reason—as *a priori data* of reason, and that this would be absolutely impossible save on the assumption of freedom; and if at the same time we grant that speculative reason has proved that such freedom does not allow of being thought, then the former supposition—that made on behalf of morality—would have to give way to this other contention, the opposite of which involves a palpable contradiction. For since it is only on the assumption of freedom that the negation of morality contains any contradiction, freedom, and with it morality, would have to yield to the mechanism of nature.

Morality does not, indeed, require that freedom should be understood, but only that it should not contradict itself, and so should at least allow of being thought, and that as thus thought it should place no obstacle in the way of a free act (viewed in another relation) likewise conforming to the mechanism of nature. The doctrine of morality and the doctrine of nature may each, therefore, make good its position. This, however, is only possible in so far as criticism has previously established our unavoidable ignorance of things in themselves, and has limited all that we can theoretically know to mere appearances.

This discussion as to the positive advantage of critical principles of pure reason can be similarly developed in regard to the concept of *God* and of the *simple nature* of our *soul*; but for the sake of brevity such further discussion may be omitted. [From what has already been said, it is evident that] even the *assumption*—as made on behalf of the necessary practical employment of my reason—of *God*, *freedom*, and *immortality* is not permissible unless at the same time speculative reason be deprived of its pretensions to transcendent insight. For in order to arrive at such insight it must make use of principles which, in fact, extend only to objects of possible experience, and which, if also applied to what cannot be an object of experience, always really change this into an appearance, thus rendering all *practical extension* of pure reason impossible. I have therefore found it necessary to deny *knowledge*, in order to make room for *faith*.

[*Critique of Pure Reason*, 2nd edn., trans. N. K. Smith (London: Macmillan, 1933), 25–9.]

63 Faith as Feeling

I wish I could present religion to you in some well-known form so that you might immediately remember its features, its movements, and its manners and exclaim that you have here or there seen it just this way in real life. But I would deceive you. For it is not found among human beings as undisguised as it appears to the conjurer, and for some time has not let itself be viewed in the form peculiar to it. The particular disposition of various cultivated peoples no longer shows itself so purely and distinctly in individual actions, since their commerce has become more many-sided and what they have in common has increased through all sorts of connections. Only the imagination can grasp the entire idea behind these qualities, which are encountered only singly as dispersed and mixed with much that is foreign. This is also the case with spiritual things, and among them with religion. It is well known to you how everything is now full of harmonious development; and precisely this has caused such a completed and extended sociability and friendliness within the human soul that none of the soul's powers in fact now acts among us distinctly, as much as we like to think of them as distinct. In every accomplishment each is immediately precipitated by polite love and beneficial support of the other and is somewhat deflected from its path. One looks around vainly in this cultured world for an action that could furnish a true expression of some capacity of spirit, be it sensibility or understanding, ethical life or religion.

Do not, therefore, be indignant and explain it as disdain for the present if, for the sake of clarity, I frequently lead you back to those more childlike times where, in a less perfected state, everything was still, distinct and individual. If I begin at once with that theme, and in some way or other meticulously come back to it, this is to warn you emphatically about the confusion of religion with things that sometimes look similar to it and with which you will everywhere find it mixed.

If you put yourselves on the highest standpoint of metaphysics and morals, you will find that both have the same object as religion, namely, the universe and the relationship of humanity to it. This similarity has long since been a basis of manifold aberrations; metaphysics and morals have therefore invaded religion on many occasions, and much that belongs to religion has concealed itself in metaphysics or morals under an unseemly form. But shall you, for this reason, believe that it is identical with the one or the other? I know that your instinct tells you the contrary, and it also follows from your opinions; for you never admit that religion walks with the firm step of which metaphysics is capable, and you do not forget to observe diligently that there are quite a few ugly immoral blemishes on its history. If religion is thus to be differentiated, then it must be set off from those in some manner, regardless of the common subject-matter. Religion must treat this subject-matter completely differently, express or work out another relationship of humanity to it, have another mode of procedure or another goal; for only in this way can that which is similar in its subject-matter to something else achieve a determinate nature and a unique existence. I ask you, therefore, What does your metaphysics do—or, if you want to have nothing to do with the outmoded name that is too historical for you, your transcendental philosophy? It classifies the universe and divides it into this being and that, seeks out the reasons for what exists, and deduces the necessity of what is real while spinning the reality of the world and its laws out of itself. Into this realm, therefore, religion must not venture too far. It must not have the tendency to posit essences and to determine natures, to lose itself in an infinity of reasons and deductions, to seek out final causes, and to proclaim eternal truths.

And what does your morality do? It develops a system of duties out of human nature and our relationship to the universe; it commands and forbids actions with unlimited authority. Yet religion must not even presume to do that; it must not use the universe in order to derive duties and is not permitted to contain a code of laws. 'And yet what one calls religion seems to consist only of fragments of these various fields.' This is indeed the common concept. I have just imparted to you doubts about that; now it is time to annihilate it altogether. The theorists in religion, who aim at knowledge of the nature of the universe and a highest being whose work it is, are metaphysicians, but also discreet enough not to disdain some morality. The practical people, to whom the will of God is the primary thing, are moralists, but a little in the style of metaphysics. You take the idea of the good and carry it into metaphysics as the natural law of an unlimited and plenteous being, and you take the idea of a primal being from metaphysics and carry it into morality so that this great work should not remain anonymous, but so that the picture of the lawgiver might be engraved at the front of so splendid a code. But mix and stir as you will, these never go together; you play an empty game with materials that are not suited to each other. You always retain only metaphysics and morals. This mixture of opinions about the highest being or the world and of precepts for a human life (or even for two) you call religion! And the instinct, which seeks those opinions, together with the dim presentiments that are the actual final sanction of these precepts, you call religiousness! But how then do you come to regard a mere compilation, an anthology for beginners, as an integral work, as an individual with its own origin and power? How do you come to mention it, even if only to refute it? Why have you not long since analysed it into its parts and discovered the shameful plagiarism?

I would take pleasure in alarming you with some Socratic questions and bringing you to confess that, even in the most common things, you know the principles according to which like must be related to like and the particular

206 THE SEVENTEENTH AND EIGHTEENTH CENTURIES

subordinated to the universal, and that you only wish not to apply these principles here in order to be able to make fun of a serious subject in a worldly manner. Where, then, is the unity in this whole? Where does the unifying principle lie for this dissimilar material? If it is an attractive force of its own, then you must confess that religion is the highest in philosophy and that metaphysics and morals are only subordinate divisions of it; for that in which two varied but opposed concepts are one can only be the higher under which the other two belong. If this binding principle lies in metaphysics, you have recognized, for reasons that are related to metaphysics, a highest being as the moral lawgiver. Therefore annihilate practical philosophy, and admit that it, and with it religion, is only a small chapter of the theoretical. If you want to assert the converse, then metaphysics and religion must be swallowed up by morality, for which indeed, nothing may any longer be impossible after it has learned to believe and in its old age has acquiesced in preparing a quiet spot in its innermost sanctuary for the secret embraces of two self-loving worlds.

Or do you want to say that the metaphysical in religion does not depend on the moral, nor the latter on the former? Or that there is a remarkable parallelism between the theoretical and the practical, and that to perceive and represent this is religion? To be sure, the solution to this parallelism can lie neither in practical philosophy, which is not concerned about it, nor in theoretical philosophy, which, as part of its function, strives most zealously to pursue and annihilate the parallelism as far as possible. But I think that you, driven by this need, have already been seeking for some time a highest philosophy in which these two categories unite and are always on the verge of finding it; and religion would lie so close to this! Would philosophy really have to flee to religion as the opponents of philosophy like to maintain? Pay close heed to what you say there. With all this either you receive a religion that stands far above philosophy as it exists at present, or you must be honest enough to restore to both parts of philosophy what belongs to them and admit that you are still ignorant of what concerns religion. I do not wish to hold you to the former, for I want to take no position that I could not maintain, but you will very likely agree to the latter.

Let us deal honestly with one another. You do not like religion; we started from that assumption. But in conducting an honest battle against it, which is not completely without effort, you do not want to have fought against a shadow like the one with which we have struggled. Religion must indeed be something integral that could have arisen in the human heart, something thinkable from which a concept can be formulated about which one can speak and argue. I find it very unjust if you yourselves stitch together something untenable out of such disparate things, call it religion, and then make so much needless ado about it. [...]

In order to take possession of its own domain, religion renounces herewith all claims to whatever belongs to those others and gives back everything that has been forced upon it. It does not wish to determine and explain the universe according to its nature as does metaphysics; it does not desire to continue the universe's development and perfect it by the power of freedom and the divine free choice of a human being as does morals. Religion's essence is neither thinking nor acting, but intuition and feeling. It wishes to intuit the universe, wishes devoutly to overhear the universe's own manifestations and actions, longs to be grasped and filled by the universe's immediate influences in childlike passivity. Thus, religion is opposed to these two in everything that makes up its essence and in everything that characterizes its effects. Metaphysics and morals see in the whole universe only humanity as the centre of all relatedness, as the condition of all being and the cause of all becoming; religion wishes to see the infinite, its imprint and its manifestation, in humanity no less than in all other individual and finite forms. Metaphysics proceeds from finite human nature and wants to define consciously, from its simplest concept, the extent of its powers, and its receptivity, what the universe can be for us and how we necessarily must view it. Religion also lives its whole life in nature, but in the infinite nature of totality, the one and all; what holds in nature for everything individual also holds for the human being; and wherever everything, including man, may press on or tarry within this eternal ferment of individual forms and beings, religion wishes to intuit and to divine this in detail in quiet submissiveness. Morality proceeds from the consciousness of freedom; it wishes to extend freedom's realm to infinity and to make everything subservient to it. Religion breathes there where freedom itself has once more become nature; it apprehends man beyond the play of his particular powers and his personality, and views him from the vantage point where he must be what he is, whether he likes it or not.

Thus religion maintains its own sphere and its own character only by completely removing itself from the sphere and character of speculation as well as from that of praxis. Only when it places itself next to both of them is the common ground perfectly filled out and human nature completed from this dimension. Religion shows itself to you as the necessary and indispensable third next to those two, as their natural counterpart, not slighter in worth and splendour than what you wish of them.

[*On Religion: Speeches to its Cultured Despisers* (1799), trans. Richard Crouter (Cambridge: Cambridge University Press, 1988), 97–100, 101–2.]

GEORGE HEGEL

64   Faith is More than Feeling

Since, however, feeling in general is supposed to be the seat and source of what is authentic, the essential nature of feeling is overlooked, that it is of itself a *mere form*, of itself indeterminate, and can comprise any content. There is nothing that cannot be felt and is not felt. God, truth, and duty are felt, as are evil, false-hood, and wrong. All human states and relationships are felt; all representations of one's own relationship to spiritual and natural things become feelings. Who would endeavour to name and enumerate all feelings, from religious feeling, the feeling of duty, sympathizing, etc., down to envy, hatred, pride, vanity, joy, sorrow, sadness, and so forth? The very diversity, still more the opposing and contradictory nature of feelings, leads ordinary thinking to the correct conclu-sion that feeling is only something formal and cannot be a principle for a genuine determination. Moreover it is no less correct to conclude that if *feeling* is made the principle all that is needed is to leave it to the *subject* to decide *which* feelings it wants to have. It is the absolute indeterminacy feeling gives itself as standard and justification—i.e., arbitrary free will, the choice to be and do as it pleases and to make itself the oracle of what is deemed of value, what kinds of religion, duty, and right are deemed of high value.

Religion, like duty and right, will become and also ought to become an affair of feeling and enter into the heart, the same way that freedom in general descends into feeling and a feeling of freedom comes about in human being. But it is a completely different matter whether a content such as God, truth, or freedom is created out of feeling, whether these objects are to have feeling as their justification, or whether conversely such objective content is deemed valid in and for itself and first enters heart and feeling: it is only from this content that feelings derive not only their content but also their determination, their orien-tation and justification. On *this difference of attitude* everything depends. On it rests the divorce between on the one hand old-fashioned honesty and faith, genuine religious sentiment and ethical life, which makes God, truth, and duty *the prime element*, and on the other hand the perversity, the conceit, and the absolute selfishness that has arisen in our time and makes one's own will, opinion, and inclination the rule governing religious sentiment and right. Obedience, discipline, and faith in the old sense of the term are sentiments that cohere with and derive from the former attitude, while vanity, conceit, shal-lowness, and pride are the feelings that derive from the latter attitude, or rather it is these feelings of the solely natural human being from which this attitude originates.

What has been said above could have provided the material for a far-ranging exposition, such as I have already in part given elsewhere, covering several aspects of the material, while in part this is not the place for such an exposition. Let the foregoing remarks be no more than reminders of the viewpoints that have been highlighted in order to denote more precisely what constitutes the evil *of our day* and consequently *its need*. This *evil*, namely the *contingent* and *capricious* nature of *subjective* feeling and its opinions, combined with the *culture of reflection*, which claims that spirit is *incapable of knowing truth*, has from ancient times been called *sophistry*. This is what merits the nickname of *worldly wisdom*, which has recently been given fresh publicity by Herr Friedrich von

Schlegel; for it is a wisdom in and of what is usually called the *world*, of what is contingent, untrue, and temporal. It is the vanity that makes what is vain, the contingency of feeling and the whimsical nature of opinion, the absolute principle of what is right and duty, faith and truth. To be sure, we often have to hear these sophistical presentations termed philosophy. Yet this doctrine itself is at odds with the practice of applying the name of philosophy to it, for it can frequently be heard claiming *that it has nothing to do with philosophy*. It is right in wishing to know nothing of philosophy; in this way it expresses an awareness of what in fact it wants and is. Philosophy has ever been engaged in combating sophistry; all that sophistry can take from philosophy is the formal weapon, the culture of reflection, but it has nothing in common with it in regard to content, for its very being is to shun everything objective in respect of truth. Nor can it use to gain as a content the other source of truth—insofar as truth is an affair of religion—namely the holy scriptures of revelation; for this doctrine recognizes no other ground than the vanity of its own asserting and revealing.

As regards the *need* of our time, however, it emerges that the *common* need of *religion* and *philosophy* is directed to a *substantial, objective content of truth*. To the extent that religion for its part and in its manner regained respect, reverence, and authority vis-à-vis the arbitrary forming of opinion, and made itself a nexus of objective faith, doctrine, and also worship, this far-reaching self-examination would at the same time have to take the contemporary empirical condition in its multifarious tendencies into consideration, and thus it would be not only out of place here but also in general not merely philosophical in nature. In regard to one part of the business of satisfying this need, however, the two spheres of religion and philosophy come together. For this can at least be mentioned, that the development of the spirit of the times has resulted in *thinking* (and the way of viewing things connected with thinking) becoming for consciousness an *indispensable criterion of what consciousness is to accept and recognize as true*. It is here a matter of indifference to establish to what extent it would be only one part of the religious community that would be unable to continue living, i.e., existing spiritually, without the freedom of thinking spirit, or to what extent it is rather the whole of those communities in which this higher principle has reared itself for which the form of thinking, developed to whatever level, is henceforward an indispensable demand of their faith. Development and return to principles may occur at a multitude of levels; for in order to express itself in popular fashion, thinking may be placed in the position of reducing particular cases, propositions, etc., to one *immanent, universal proposition*, which is relatively speaking the *basic proposition* for the material that is made dependent on it in consciousness. What is thus at one level of the development of thought a basic principle, something irreducibly firm, at another level needs once more to be further reduced to yet more general, deeper basic propositions. But the basic propositions are a content held fast by consciousness in conviction, a content to which its spirit has witnessed, and which is now indistinguishable from thinking and one's own selfhood. If the basic propositions are surrendered to rationalizing, we have noted above the deviation by which they are replaced by subjective opinion and arbitrariness and culminate in sophistry.

But the mode and manner of conviction that occurs in religion can retain the shape of what is properly called *faith*, though it must be borne in mind that faith too must not be represented as something external to be offered mechanically; in order that it may be living and not a servitude, faith essentially needs the testimony of the indwelling spirit of truth and must have been implanted in one's own heart. If, however, religious need has been permeated with the element of the basic principles, then it is inseparable from the need and activity of thought, and in this respect religion requires a *science* of religion—a theology. Whatever in theology goes beyond (or only in theology deserves to go beyond) the general familiarity with religion that pertains to any member of each and every culture, that science has in common with philosophy. Thus it was that *scholastic theology* came into being in the Middle Ages—a science that developed religion in the direction of thinking and reason and endeavoured to grasp the most profound doctrines of revealed religion in thinking fashion. As compared with the lofty aim of such a science, that mode of theology is very backward which locates the scientific distinction between it and the general teaching of religion merely in the historical element that, in all its breadth and length and its boundless individual details, it adds to religion. The absolute content of religion is essentially something present, and it is therefore not in the external addition of previously taught historical material but only in rational cognition that spirit can find the further material, present to it and free, that can satisfy its external need to think and so add infinite form to the infinite content of religion.

Scholastic theology fortunately did not yet have to fight the prejudice with which philosophizing on the topic of religion currently has to fight, namely that the divine cannot be *conceived*, or rather that the very concept and the kind of cognition that conceives demotes God and the divine attributes to the domain of finitude and by so doing annihilates them. The honour and worth of thinking cognition had not been abased to that extent; on the contrary, it had been left unimpaired, still unaffected. It was only modern philosophy itself that so misunderstood its own element, the concept, and brought it into such discredit. It did not recognize the infinitude of the concept and confused it with finite reflection, the understanding—so much so that only the understanding is supposed to be able to think, while reason is supposed not to be able to think but only to know immediately, i.e., only feel and intuit and so only *know in sensuous fashion*.

The ancient Greek writers represented divine justice in terms of the gods opposing and abasing whatever raises itself up, whatever is happy and excellent. Purer thought of the divine banished this image: Plato and Aristotle teach that *God* is *not jealous* and does not withhold from human beings knowledge of godself and of the truth. What would it be but *jealousy* for God to deny to consciousness the knowledge of God? In so doing God would have denied to consciousness all truth, for God is alone what is true. Whatever else is true and may seem to have no divine content is only true to the extent that it is grounded in God and known from God; in other respects it is a temporal appearance. The cognition of God and of truth is the only thing that raises human beings above animals, that sets them apart and makes them happy, or rather, according to Plato and Aristotle as well as Christian doctrine, blessed.

It is the quite distinctive phenomenon of our time to have reverted at the pinnacle of its culture to the ancient notion that God is uncommunicative and does not reveal the divine nature to human spirit. Within the sphere of the Christian religion this assertion of the jealousy of God is all the more striking in that this religion is and seeks to be nothing other than the *revelation* of what God is, and the Christian community is supposed to be nothing other than the community into which the Spirit of God is sent and in which this spirit—for the very reason that it is spirit, not sensuousness and feeling, not a representing of what is sensuous, but thinking, knowing, cognizing, and because it is the divine Holy Spirit—is only the thinking, knowing, and cognizing of God, and leads its members into cognition of God. Without this cognition what would the Christian community still be? What is a theology without cognition of God? Just what a philosophy is without cognition of God, a noisy gong and a clanging cymbal! [1 Cor. 13: 1.]

[Foreword to Hinrich's *Religion* (1822), trans. J. M. Stewart, in *G. W. F. Hegel*, ed. Peter Hodgson (Minneapolis: Fortress Press, 1997), 166–70.]

GOTTFRIED LEIBNIZ
....
65 The Conformity of Faith and Reason

5. It seems, according to what I have just said, that there is often some confusion in the expressions of those who set at variance philosophy and theology, or faith and reason: they confuse the terms 'explain', 'comprehend', 'prove', 'uphold'. And I find that M. Bayle, shrewd as he is, is not always free from this confusion. Mysteries may be *explained* sufficiently to justify belief in them; but one cannot *comprehend* them, nor give understanding of how they come to pass. Thus even in natural philosophy we explain up to a certain point sundry perceptible qualities, but in an imperfect manner, for we do not comprehend them. Nor is it possible for us, either, to prove Mysteries by reason; for all that which can be proved *a priori*, or by pure reason, can be comprehended. All that remains for us then, after having believed in the Mysteries by reason of the proofs of the truth of religion (which are called 'motives of credibility') is to be able to *uphold* them against objections. Without that our belief in them would

have no firm foundation; for all that which can be refuted in a sound and conclusive manner cannot but be false. And such proofs of the truth of religion as can give only a *moral certainty* would be balanced and even outweighed by such objections as would give an *absolute certainty*, provided they were convincing and altogether conclusive. [. . .]

22. . . . In general, one must take care never to abandon the necessary and eternal truths for the sake of upholding Mysteries, lest the enemies of religion seize upon such an occasion for decrying both religion and Mysteries.

23. The distinction which is generally drawn between that which is *above* reason and that which is *against* reason is tolerably in accord with the distinction which has just been made between the two kinds of necessity. For what is contrary to reason is contrary to the absolutely certain and inevitable truths; and what is above reason is in opposition only to what one is wont to experience or to understand. That is why I am surprised that there are people of intelligence who dispute this distinction, and that M. Bayle should be of this number. The distinction is assuredly very well founded. A truth is above reason when our mind (or even every created mind) cannot comprehend it. Such is, as it seems to me, the Holy Trinity; such are the miracles reserved for God alone, as for instance Creation; such is the choice of the order of the universe, which depends upon universal harmony, and upon the clear knowledge of an infinity of things at once. But a truth can never be contrary to reason, and once a dogma has been disputed and refuted by reason, instead of its being incomprehensible, one may say that nothing is easier to understand, nor more obvious, than its absurdity. For I observed at the beginning that by REASON here I do not mean the opinions and discourses of men, nor even the habit they have formed of judging things according to the usual course of Nature, but rather the inviolable linking together of truths.

24. I must come now to the great question which M. Bayle brought up recently, to wit, whether a truth, and especially a truth of faith, can prove to be subject to irrefutable objections. This excellent author appears to answer with a bold affirmative: he quotes theologians of repute in his party, and even in the Church of Rome, who appear to say the same as he affirms; and he cites philosophers who have believed that there are even philosophical truths whose champions cannot answer the objections that are brought up against them. He believes that the theological doctrine of predestination is of this nature, and in philosophy that of the composition of the *Continuum*. These are, indeed, the two labyrinths which have ever exercised theologians and philosophers. Libertus Fromondus, a theologian of Louvain (a great friend of Jansenius, whose posthumous book entitled *Augustinus* he in fact published), who also wrote a book entitled explicitly *Labyrinthus de Compositione Continui*, experienced in full measure the difficulties inherent in both doctrines; and the renowned Ochino admirably presented what he calls 'the labyrinths of predestination'.

25. But these writers have not denied the possibility of finding a thread in the labyrinth; they have recognized the difficulty, but they have surely not turned difficulty into sheer impossibility. As for me, I confess that I cannot agree with those who maintain that a truth can admit of irrefutable objections: for is an *objection* anything but an argument whose conclusion contradicts our thesis? And is not an irrefutable argument a *demonstration*? And how can one know the certainty of demonstrations except by examining the argument in detail, the form and the matter, in order to see if the form is good, and then if each premiss is either admitted or proved by another argument of like force, until one is able to make do with admitted premisses alone? Now if there is such an objection against our thesis we must say that the falsity of this thesis is demonstrated, and that it is impossible for us to have reasons sufficient to prove it; otherwise two contradictories would be true at once. One must always yield to proofs, whether they be proposed in positive form or advanced in the shape of objections. And it is wrong and fruitless to try to weaken opponents' proofs, under the pretext that they are only objections, since the opponent can play the same game and can reverse the denominations, exalting his arguments by naming them 'proofs' and sinking ours under the blighting title of 'objections'.

26. It is another question whether we are always obliged to examine the objections we may have to face, and to retain some doubt in respect of our own opinion, or what is called *formido oppositi*, until this examination has been made. I would venture to say no, for otherwise one would never attain to certainty and our conclusion would be always provisional. I believe that able geometricians will scarce be troubled by the objections of Joseph Scaliger against Archimedes, or by those of Mr Hobbes against Euclid; but that is because they have fully understood and are sure of the proofs. Nevertheless it is sometimes well to show oneself ready to examine certain objections. On the one hand it may serve to rescue people from their error, while on the other we ourselves may profit by it; for specious fallacies often contain some useful solution and bring about the removal of considerable difficulties. That is why I have always liked ingenious objections made against my own opinions, and I have never examined them without profit: witness those which M. Bayle formerly made against my System of Pre-established Harmony, not to mention those which M. Arnauld, M. L'Abbé Foucher and Father Lami, O.S.B., made to me on the same subject. But to return to the principal question, I conclude from reasons I have just set forth that when an objection is put forward against some truth, it is always possible to answer it satisfactorily.

27. It may be also that M. Bayle does not mean 'insoluble objections' in the sense that I have just explained. I observe that he varies, at least in his expressions: for in his posthumous Reply to M. le Clerc he does not admit that one can bring demonstrations against the truths of faith. It appears therefore that he takes the objections to be insoluble only in respect of our present degree of enlightenment; and in this Reply, p. 35, he even does not despair of the possibility that one

day a solution hitherto unknown may be found by someone. Concerning that more will be said later. I hold an opinion, however, that will perchance cause surprise, namely that this solution has been discovered entire, and is not even particularly difficult. Indeed a mediocre intelligence capable of sufficient care, and using correctly the rules of common logic, is in a position to answer the most embarrassing objection made against truth, when the objection is only taken from reason, and when it is claimed to be a 'demonstration'. Whatever scorn the generality of moderns have to-day for the logic of Aristotle, one must acknowledge that it teaches infallible ways of resisting error in these conjunctures. For one has only to examine the argument according to the rules and it will always be possible to see whether it is lacking in form or whether there are premisses such as are not yet proved by a good argument.

28. It is quite another matter when there is only a question of *probabilities*, for the art of judging from probable reasons is not yet well established; so that our logic in this connexion is still very imperfect, and to this very day we have little beyond the art of judging from demonstrations. But this art is sufficient here: for when it is a question of opposing reason to an article of our faith, one is not disturbed by objections that only attain probability. Everyone agrees that appearances are against Mysteries, and that they are by no means probable when regarded only from the standpoint of reason; but it suffices that they have in them nothing of absurdity. Thus demonstrations are required if they are to be refuted.

29. And doubtless we are so to understand it when Holy Scripture warns us that the wisdom of God is foolishness before men, and when St Paul observed that the Gospel of Jesus Christ is foolishness unto the Greeks, as well as unto the Jews a stumbling-block. For, after all, one truth cannot contradict another, and the light of reason is no less a gift of God than that of revelation. Also it is a matter of no difficulty among theologians who are expert in their profession, that the motives of credibility justify, once for all, the authority of Holy Scripture before the tribunal of reason, so that reason in consequence gives way before it, as before a new light, and sacrifices thereto all its probabilities. It is more or less as if a new president sent by the prince must show his letters patent in the assembly where he is afterwards to preside. That is the tendency of sundry good books that we have on the truth of religion, such as those of Augustinus Steuchus, of Du Plessis-Mornay or of Grotius: for the true religion must needs have marks that the false religions have not, else would Zoroaster, Brahma, Somonacodom and Mahomet be as worthy of belief as Moses and Jesus Christ. Nevertheless divine faith itself, when it is kindled in the soul, is something more than an opinion, and depends not upon the occasion or the motives that have given it birth; it advances beyond the intellect, and takes possession of the will and of the heart, to make us act with zeal and joyfully as the law of God commands. Then we have no further need to think of reasons or to pause over the difficulties of argument which the mind may anticipate.

30. Thus what we have just said of human reason, which is extolled and decried by turns, and often without rule or measure, may show our lack of exactitude and how much we are accessory to our own errors. Nothing would be so easy to terminate as these disputes on the rights of faith and of reason if men would make use of the commonest rules of logic and reason with even a modicum of attention.

[*The Theodicy*, trans. E. M. Huggard, abridged and ed. Diogenes Allen, Library of Liberal Arts (Indianapolis: Bobbs-Merrill, 1966), 12–16.]

MATTHEW TINDAL

66 Reason, God, and Duty

B. That we may the better know whether the *Law*, or *Religion of Nature* is universal, and the Gospel a Republication of it, and not a new Religion; I desire you will give a Definition of the *Religion of Nature*.

A. By *Natural Religion*, I understand the Belief of the Existence of a God, and the Sense and Practice of those Duties which result from the Knowledge we, by our Reason, have of him and his Perfections; and of ourselves, and our own Imperfections; and of the relation we stand in to him and our Fellow-Creatures; so that the *Religion of Nature* takes in every thing that is founded on the Reason and Nature of things. . . .

I suppose you will allow, that 'tis evident by the *Light of Nature*, that there is a God; or in other words, a Being absolutely perfect, and infinitely happy in himself, who is the Source of all other Beings; and that what Perfections soever the Creatures have, they are wholly deriv'd from him.

B. This, no doubt, has been demonstrated over and over; and I must own, that I can't be more certain of my own Existence, than of the Existence of such a Being.

A. Since then it is demonstrable there is such a Being, it is equally demonstrable, that the Creatures can neither add to, or take from the Happiness of that Being; and that he could have no Motive in framing his Creatures, or in giving Laws to such of them as he made capable of knowing his Will, but their own Good.

To imagine he created them at first for his own sake, and has since required things of them for that Reason, is to suppose he was not perfectly happy in himself before the Creation; and that the Creatures, by either observing, or not observing the Rules prescrib'd them, cou'd add to, or take from his Happiness.

If then a Being infinitely happy in himself, cou'd not command his Creatures any thing for his own Good; nor an all-wise Being things to no end or purpose; nor an all-good Being any thing but for their good: It unavoidably follows, nothing can be a part of the divine Law, but what tends to promote the common

Interest, and mutual Happiness of his rational Creatures; and everything that does so, must be a part of it.

As God can require nothing of us, but what makes for our Happiness; so he, who can't envy us any Happiness our Nature is capable of, can forbid us those Things only, which tend to our Hurt; and this we are as certain of, as that there is a God infinitely happy in himself, infinitely good and wise; and as God can design nothing by his Laws but our Good, so by being infinitely powerful, he can bring every thing to pass which he designs for that End.

From the Consideration of these Perfections, we cannot but have the highest Veneration, nay, the greatest Adoration and Love for this supreme Being; who, that we may not fail to be as happy as possible for such Creatures to be, has made our acting for our *present*, to be the only Means of obtaining our *future* Happiness; so that we can't sin against him, but by acting against ourselves, *i.e.* our reasonable Natures: These Reflections, which occur to every one who in the least considers, must give us a wonderful and surprising Sense of the divine Goodness, fill us with Admiration, Transport and Extasy; (of which we daily see among contemplative Persons remarkable Instances): And no only force us to express a never-failing Gratitude in Raptures of the highest Praise and Thanksgiving; but make us strive to imitate him in our extensive Love to our Fellow-Creatures: And thus copying after the Divine Original, and taking God himself for our Precedent, must conform us to his Image, who is all Perfection and all Happiness; and who must have an inexhaustible Love for all, who thus endeavour to imitate him. . . .

The difference between the supreme Being, infinitely happy in himself, and the Creatures who are not so, is, That all his Actions, in relation to his Creatures, flow from a pure disinterested Love: whereas the Spring of all the Actions of the Creatures is their own Good: *We love God, because he first loved us* [1 John 4: 19]; and consequently, our Love to him will be in proportion to our Sense of his Goodness to us. Nor can we in the least vary from those Sentiments, which the Consideration of the divine Attributes implant in us, but we must in proportion take off from the Goodness of God, and from those Motives we have to love him as we ought.

Our Reason, which gives us a Demonstration of the divine Perfections, affords us the same concerning the Nature of those Duties God requires; not only with relation to himself, but to ourselves, and one another: These we can't but see, if we look into ourselves, consider our own Natures, and the Circumstances God has placed us in with relation to our Fellow-Creatures, and what conduces to our mutual Happiness: Our Senses, our Reason, the Experience of others as well as our own, can't fail to give us sufficient Information.

With relation to ourselves, we can't but know how we are to act; if we consider, that God has endow'd Man with such a Nature, as makes him necessarily desire his own Good; and, therefore, he may be sure, that God, who has bestow'd this Nature on him, could not require any thing of him in prejudice of it; but, on the contrary, that he should do every thing which tends to promote the Good of it. The Health of the Body, and the Vigour of the Mind, being highly conducing to our Good, we must be sensible we offend our Maker, if we indulge our Senses to the prejudice of these: And because not only all irregular Passions, all unfriendly Affections carry their own Torment with them, and endless Inconveniences attend the Excess of sensual Delights; and all immoderate Desires (human Nature being able to bear but a certain Proportion) disorder both Mind and Body; we can't but know we ought to use great Moderation with relation to our Passions, or in other Words, govern all our Actions by Reason; That, and our true Interest being inseparable. And, in a word, whoever so regulates his natural Appetites, as will conduce most to the Exercise of his Reason, the Health of his Body, and the Pleasure of his Senses, taken and consider'd together, (since herein his Happiness consists) may be certain he can never offend his Maker; who, as he governs all things according to their Natures, can't but expect his rational Creatures should act according to their Natures.

As to what God expects from Man with relation to each other; every one must know his Duty, who considers that the common Parent of Mankind has the whole Species alike under his Protection, and will equally punish him for injuring others, as he would others for injuring him; and consequently, that it is his Duty to deal with them, as he expects they should deal with him in the like Circumstances. How much this is his Duty, every one must perceive, who considers himself as a weak Creature, not able to subsist without the Assistance of others, who have it in their Power to retaliate the Usage he gives them: And that he may expect, if he breaks those Rules which are necessary for Men's mutual Happiness, to be treated like a common Enemy, not only by the Persons injur'd, but by all others; who, by the common Ties of Nature, are obliged to defend and assist each other. And not only a Man's own particular Interest, but that of his Children, his Family, and all that's dear to him, obliges him to promote the common Happiness, and to endeavour to convey the fame to Posterity. . . .

In short, considering the variety of Circumstances Men are under, and these continually changing, as well as being for the most part unforeseen; 'tis impossible to have Rules laid down by any *External* Revelation for every particular Case; and therefore, there must be some standing Rule, discoverable by the *Light of Nature*, to direct us in all such Cases. And we can't be more certain, that 'tis the Will of God, that those Effects which flow from natural Causes should so flow; than we are, that 'tis the Will of God, that Men should observe, whatever the Nature of Things, and the Relation they have to one another, make fit to be observ'd; or in other Words, we can't but know, if we in the least consider, that, whatever Circumstances Men are plac'd in, by the universal Cause of all things; that 'tis his eternal and immutable Will, by his placing them in these Circumstances, that they act as these require. 'Tis absurd to imagine we are oblig'd to act thus in some Cases, and not in others; when the reason for acting thus in all is the same. This Consideration alone will direct a Man how to act in all Conditions of Life, whether *Father, Son, Husband, Servant, Subject, Master, King,* &c. Thus we see how the reason of things, or the relation they have to each other, teaches us our Duty in all cases whatever. And I may add, that the better to cause Men to observe those Rules, which make for their mutual Benefit, infinite Goodness has sown in their Hearts Seeds of Pity, Humanity and Tenderness, which, without much difficulty, cannot be eradicated; but nothing operates more strongly than that Desire Men have of being in Esteem, Credit, and Reputation with their Fellow-Creatures, not to be obtain'd without acting on the Principles of natural Justice, Equity, Benevolence, &c.

In a word, as a most beneficent Disposition in the supreme Being is the Source of all his Actions in relation to his Creatures; so he has implanted in Man, whom he has made after his own Image, a Love for his Species; the gratifying of which, in doing Acts of Benevolence, Compassion, and Good Will, produces a Pleasure that never satiates; as on the contrary, Actions of Ill-Nature, Envy, Malice, &c. never fail to produce Shame, Confusion, and everlasting Self-reproach.

And now let any one say, how 'tis possible God could more fully make known his Will to all intelligent Creatures, than by making every thing within, and without them a Declaration of it, and an Argument for observing it.

Having thus discovered our Duty, we may be sure it will always be the same; since Inconstancy, as it argues a Defect either of Wisdom or Power, can't belong to a Being infinitely wise and powerful: What unerring Wisdom has once instituted, can have no Defects; and as God is entirely free from all Partiality, his Laws must alike extend to all Times and Places.

From these Premises, I think, we may boldly draw this Conclusion, That if Religion consists in the Practice of those Duties, that result from the Relation we stand in to God and Man, our Religion must always be the same. If God is unchangeable, our Duty to him must be so too; if Human Nature continues the same, and Men at all Times stand in the same Relation to one another, the Duties which result from thence too, must always be the same: And consequently our Duty both to God and Man must, from the Beginning of the World to the End, remain unalterable; be always alike plain and perspicous; neither chang'd in Whole, or Part: which demonstrates that no Person, if he comes from God, can teach us any other Religion, or give us any Precepts, but what are founded on those Relations. *Heaven and Earth shall sooner pass away,* than *one Tittle of this* Eternal *Law shall either be abrogated, or alter'd.*

[*Christianity as Old as Creation* (1732 edn.), in Peter Gay (ed.), *Deism: An Anthology* (Princeton: Van Nostrand, 1968), 102–7.]

§1. By reason, I mean that power or faculty an intelligent being has to judge of the truth of propositions; either immediately, by only looking on the propositions, which is judging by intuition and self-evidence; or by putting together several propositions, which are already evident by intuition, or at least whose evidence is originally derived from intuition.

Great part of Tindal's arguing, in his *Christianity as old as the Creation*, proceeds on this ground, That since reason is the judge whether there be any revelation, or whether any pretended revelation be really such; therefore reason, *without* revelation, or *undirected* by revelation, must be the judge concerning each doctrine and proposition contained in that pretended revelation. This is an unreasonable way of arguing. It is as much as to say, that seeing reason is to judge of the truth of any *general* proposition, therefore, in all cases, reason alone, without regard to that proposition, is to judge separately and independently of each particular proposition implied in, or depending and consequent upon, that general proposition. For, whether any supposed or pretended divine revelation be indeed such, is a general proposition: and the particular truths delivered in and by it, are particular propositions implied in, and consequent on, that general one. Tindal supposes each of these truths must be judged of by themselves, independently of our judging of that general truth, that the revelation that declares them is the word of God; evidently supposing, that if each of these propositions, thus judged of particularly, cannot be found to be agreeable to reason; or if reason alone will not show the truth of them, then, that general proposition on which they depend, *viz.* That the word which declares them is a divine revelation, is to be rejected: which is most unreasonable, and contrary to all the rules of common sense, and of the proceeding of all mankind, in their reasoning and judging of things in all affairs whatsoever.— For this is certain, that a proposition may be evidently true, or we may have good reason to receive it as true, though the particular propositions that depend upon it, and follow from it, may be such, that our reason, independent of it, cannot see the truth, or can see it to be true by no other means, than by first establishing that other truth on which it depends. For otherwise, there is an end of all use of our reasoning powers; an end of all arguing one proposition from another; and nothing is to be judged true, but what appears true by looking on it directly and immediately, without the help of another proposition first established, on which the evidence of it depends.—For therein consists all reasoning or argumentation whatsoever; *viz.* in discovering the truth of a proposition, whose truth does not appear to our reason immediately, or when we consider it alone, but by the help of some other proposition on which it depends.

§2. If this be not allowed, we must believe nothing at all, but self-evident propositions, and then we must have done with all such things as arguments; and all argumentation whatsoever, and all Tindal's argumentations in particular, are absurd. He himself, throughout his whole book, proceeds in that very method which this principle explodes. He argues, and attempts to make evident, one proposition, by another first established.—There are some general propositions, the truth of which can be known only by reason, from whence an infinite multitude of other propositions are inferred, and reasonably and justly determined to be true, and rested in as such, on the ground of the truth of that general proposition from which they are inferred by the common consent of all mankind, being led thereto by the common and universal sense of the human mind. And yet not one of those propositions can be known to be true by reason, if reason consider them by themselves, independently of that general proposition.

Thus, for instance, what numberless truths are known only by consequence from that general proposition, that the testimony of our senses may be depended on! The truth of numberless particular propositions, cannot be known by reason, considered independently of the testimony of our senses, and without an implicit faith in that testimony. That general truth, that the testimony of our memories is worthy of credit, can be proved only by reason; and yet, what numberless truths are there, which we know no other way, and cannot be known to be true by reason, considering the truths in themselves, or any otherwise than by testimony of our memory, and an implicit faith in this testimony! That the agreed testimony of all we see, and converse with continually, is to be credited, is a general proposition, the truth of which can be known only by reason. And yet, how infinitely numerous propositions do men receive as truth, that cannot be known to be true by reason, viewing them separately from such testimony; even all occurrences, and matters of fact, persons, things, actions, works, events, and circumstances, that we are told of in our neighbourhood, in our own country, or in any other part of the world that we have not seen ourselves! [. . .]

§12. In order to judge what sort of difficulties are to be expected in a revelation made to mankind by God, such as Christians suppose the Scriptures to be, we must remember that it is a revelation of what God knows to be the very truth concerning his own nature: of the acts and operations of his mind with respect to his creatures; of the grand scheme of infinite wisdom in his works, especially with respect to the intelligent and moral world: a revelation of the spiritual and invisible world; a revelation of that invisible world which men shall belong to after this life; a revelation of the greatest works of God, the manner of his creating the world, and of his governing of it, especially with regard to the higher and more important parts of it; a revelation delivered in ancient languages.

Difficulties and incomprehensible mysteries are reasonably to be expected in a declaration from God, of the precise truth as he knows it, in matters of a spiritual nature; as we see things that are invisible, and not the objects of any of the external senses, are very mysterious, involved much more in darkness, attended with more mystery and difficulty to the understanding, than others; as many things concerning even the nature of our own souls themselves, that are the nearest to us, and the most intimately present with us, and so most in our view of any spiritual things whatsoever.

The further things are from the nature of what language is chiefly formed to express, *viz.* things appertaining to the common business and vulgar affairs of life—things obvious to sense and men's direct view and most vulgar observation, without speculation, reflection, and abstraction, the more difficult it is clearly to express them in words. Our expressions concerning them will be attended with greater abstruseness, difficulty, and seeming inconsistence; language not being well fitted to express these things; words and phrases not being prepared for that end. Such a reference to sensible and vulgar things, is unavoidably introduced, that naturally confounds the mind, and involves it in darkness.

§13. If God gives a revelation of religious things, it must be mainly concerning the affairs of the moral and intelligent universe: which is the grand system of spirits: it must be chiefly about himself and intelligent creatures. It may well be supposed, that a revelation concerning another and an invisible world, a future state that we are to be in when separated from the body, should be attended with much mystery. It may well be supposed, that the things of such a world, are of an exceeding different nature from the things of this world, the things of sense, and all the objects and affairs which earthly language was made to express; and that they are not agreeable to such notions, imaginations, and ways of thinking that grow up with us, and are connatural to us, as we are from our infancy formed to an agreeableness to the things which we are conversant with in this world. We could not conceive of the things of *sense*, if we had never had these external senses. And if we had only some of these senses and not others; as, for instance, if we had only a sense of feeling, without the senses of seeing and hearing, how mysterious would a declaration of things of these last senses be! Or, if we had feeling and hearing, but had been born without eyes or optic nerves, the things of light, even when declared to us, would many of them be involved in mystery, and would appear exceedingly strange to us.

§14. Thus, persons without the sense of seeing, but who had the other senses, might be informed by all about them, that they can perceive things at a distance, and perceive as plainly, and in some respects more plainly, than by touching them; yea, that they could perceive things at so great a distance, that it would take up many ages to travel to them. They might be informed of many things concerning colours, that would all be perfectly incomprehensible, and yet might be believed; and it could not be said that nothing at all is proposed to their belief, because they have no idea of colour.

They might be told that they perceive an extension, a length and breadth of colour, and terminations and limits, and so a figure of this kind of extension; and yet, that it is nothing that can be felt. This would be perfectly mysterious to them, and would seem an inconsistence, as they have no ideas of any such things as length, breadth, and limits, and figure of extension, but only certain ideas they have by touch. They might be informed, that they could perceive *at once* the extent and shape of a thing so great and multiform as a tree, without touch: this would seem very strange and impossible.—They might be told that, to those who see, some things appear a thousand times as great as some others, which yet are made up of more visible parts than those others: which would be very mysterious, and seem quite inconsistent with reason.—These, and many other things, would be attended with unsearchable mystery to them, concerning objects of sight; and, concerning which, they could never fully see how they can be reconciled to reason; at least, not without very long, particular, gradual, and elaborate instruction; and which, after all, they would not fully comprehend, so as clearly to see how the ideas connected in these propositions do agree.—And yet I suppose, in such a case, the most rational persons would give full credit to things that they know not by reason, but only by the revelation of the word of those that see. I suppose, a person born blind in the manner described, would nevertheless give full credit to the united testimony of the seeing world, in things which they said about light and colours, and would entirely rest on their testimony.

['The Insufficiency of Reason as a Substitute for Revelation', in *Miscellaneous Observations*, ch. 5 (*Works*, ed. E. Hickman, London, 1834, ii. 479–80, 481–2).]

Section VI

The Nineteenth Century

INTRODUCTION

K ant argued that it was necessary to postulate God's existence in order to vindicate the imperatives of rational morality, for only by believing that God exists as the rewarder of virtue and the punisher of vice can the obligations of morality be supported. It is, however, a small step from *postulating* God's existence, which was for Kant an eminently rational activity, to *projecting* his existence for less than fully rational considerations. Why, given the confident Enlightenment critique of religion, does it nevertheless persist? One characteristic nineteenth-century theme is that religious belief has no rational ground but that it nevertheless persists because of the presence in mankind, or in all of mankind except for an enlightened élite, of irrational belief-producing mechanisms. Such a thought was not novel; it harks back at least to the Hobbesian view that religion is due to fear, superstition, and priestcraft. Nevertheless the theme was developed in a concerted way in the nineteenth century, and of course still persists.

There are a number of variations on this theme, of which four are represented in this section. Feuerbach claimed that endemic moral failure and oppression lead mankind to postulate one who, because of his sympathetic and benevolent character, will compensate for the suffering and moral failure of the present life in the world to come. (The contours of Kantianism are closely followed here, particularly Kant's critique of metaphysical theology and his subsequent religious immanentism, but of course with an entirely different temper.) Marx took up Feuerbach's theme and gave it a characteristic twist. It is because of the class system, economic exploitation by one class of another, that men seek compensation for existence in this vale of woe by inhaling the opium of religion.

In Freud the same explanatory mechanism was employed in speculations about sexuality; religion compensates for the need for a father figure. For all these thinkers religion is or is likely to be a pathological condition; the cure for the disease lies in the revolution in which classlessness will disappear and with it the need for the compensatory fantasies of religion; or in analysis. In Durkheim the same theme is given a social and anthropological dimension, though with a less obvious animus against religion.

At times it appears that such theories of the ineliminability of religious belief are being offered as empirical hypotheses. They are certainly causal claims, attempting to expose religion not because it is unreasonable but because of its allegedly disreputable parentage. Marx seems to specify conditions under which his hypothesis might be falsified. But at other times it would appear that any attempt to repudiate such a theory, whether based upon evidence or upon a priori reasoning, would simply count as further evidence for its truth in the eyes of its proponents. Just as, with fairies, you have to believe in them in order to see them, so with projectionist theories of religion, it seems you have to believe that the theory is true in order to see that it is.

There are two general characteristics of these positions which are worthy of note. First, essential to such views is a sharp distinction between the surface of human life and its depths. On the surface men and women have religious beliefs and may give a variety of reasons for holding them. But such beliefs and the reasons for them are only superficial; such reasoning is not a guide to what is really the case. For the reality is that deep down men and women have unconscious drives or needs the key to which only theorists of some kind or other possess. Reason in religion is thus sidelined in favour of the postulation of some mechanism or other which produces beliefs, sustains them, and gives people the further belief that they are reasonable. Secondly, it follows from this that all reasoning about religion is in fact unconsciously or subconsciously motivated rationalization; the provision of 'reasons' for that for which in fact there are no good reasons, and perhaps could not be.

It is interesting to note that the idea of religion in view here is largely Kant's: a religion that is incapable of having empirical or metaphysical support. Such a view continued to offer an ethical inspiration for religion and to discount its evidential aspects, as is seen most notably in Kierkegaard, but which is also present in hosts of minor figures in the period.

In Nietzsche one finds a critique of Christianity of a rather different kind, a moral critique. Christianity, and particularly its ethic, is an ethic of weakness and is therefore to be repudiated.

Others appeal to Kant in rather different ways; for example Mansel invokes Kant's agnosticism about the metaphysical character of God to reinstate a kind of negative theology. We cannot know the nature of God. However, such theology is sufficiently positive to have regulative force; the language of revelation provides the necessary degree of religious guidance. Mansel's position is criticized by John Stuart Mill, who represents the continuing influence of empiricism as does W. K. Clifford, whose rather strident and uncompromising empiricism met with resistance from William James. The reasonable, probabilistic apologetic approach developed by Paley and Butler in the eighteenth century can be said to be carried forward in the nineteenth century by Newman and by many others.

This section closes with a consideration of the impact of Charles Darwin. Darwin's theory of evolution by natural selection heralded a resurgence of the appeal to reason against the claims of faith, in this case the reason of an empirically confirmed scientific hypothesis, and in the eyes of many, including Darwin himself, the plausibility of that hypothesis spelt the end of the argument from design which since the eighteenth century had been the cornerstone of particularly Protestant natural theology, so overthrowing the reasonableness of belief in God. But it is sometimes forgotten that many quite conservative Christians were receptive to the idea of evolution by natural selection. The last extract is from one such conservative, B. B. Warfield, arguing that Darwin was muddled about the idea of design.

Religion is man's earliest and also indirect form of self-knowledge. Hence, religion everywhere precedes philosophy, as in the history of the race, so also in that of the individual. Man first of all sees his nature as if *out of* himself, before he finds it in himself. His own nature is in the first instance contemplated by him as that of another being. Religion is the childlike condition of humanity; but the child sees his nature—man—out of himself; in childhood a man is an object to himself, under the form of another man. Hence the historical progress of religion consists in this: that what by an earlier religion was regarded as objective, is now recognized as subjective; that is, what was formerly contemplated and worshipped as God is now perceived to be something *human*. What was at first religion becomes at a later period idolatry; man is seen to have adored his own nature. Man has given objectivity to himself, but has not recognized the object as his own nature: a later religion takes this forward step; every advance in religion is therefore a deeper self-knowledge. But every particular religion, while it pronounces its predecessors idolatrous, excepts itself—and necessarily so, otherwise it would no longer be religion—from the fate, the common nature of all religions: it imputes only to other religions what is the fault, if fault it be, of religion in general. Because it has a different object, a different tenor, because it has transcended the ideas of preceding religions, it erroneously supposes itself exalted above the necessary eternal laws which constitute the essence of religion—it fancies its object, its ideas, to be superhuman. But the essence of religion, thus hidden from the religious, is evident to the thinker, by whom religion is viewed objectively, which it cannot be by its votaries. And it is our task to show that the antithesis of divine and human is altogether illusory, that it is nothing else than the antithesis between the human nature in general and the human individual; that, consequently, the object and contents of the Christian religion are altogether human.

Religion, at least the Christian, is the relation of man to himself, or more correctly to his own nature (*i.e.*, his subjective nature); but a relation to it, viewed as a nature apart from his own. The divine being is nothing else than the human being, or, rather, the human nature purified, freed from the limits of the individual man, made objective—*i.e.*, contemplated and revered as another, a distinct being. All the attributes of the divine nature are, therefore, attributes of the human nature.

In relation to the attributes, the predicates, of the Divine Being, this is admitted without hesitation, but by no means in relation to the subject of these predicates. The negation of the subject is held to be irreligion, nay, atheism; though not so the negation of the predicates. But that which has no predicates or qualities, has no effect upon me; that which has no effect upon me has no existence for me. To deny all the qualities of a being is equivalent to denying the being himself. A being without qualities is one which cannot become an object to the mind, and such a being is virtually non-existent. Where man deprives God of all qualities, God is no longer anything more to him than a negative being. To the truly religious man, God is not a being without qualities, because to him he is a positive, real being. The theory that God cannot be defined, and consequently cannot be known by man, is therefore the offspring of recent times, a product of modern unbelief.

As reason is and can be pronounced finite only where man regards sensual enjoyment, or religious emotion, or æsthetic contemplation, or moral sentiment, as the absolute, the true; so the proposition that God is unknowable or undefinable, can only be enunciated and become fixed as a dogma, where this object has no longer any interest for the intellect; where the real, the positive, alone has any hold on man, where the real alone has for him the significance of the essential, of the absolute, divine object, but where at the same time, in contradiction with this purely worldly tendency, there yet exist some old remains of religiousness. On the ground that God is unknowable, man excuses himself to what is yet remaining of his religious conscience for his forgetfulness of God, his absorption in the world: he denies God practically by his conduct,—the world has possession of all his thoughts and inclinations,—but he does not deny him theoretically, he does not attack his existence; he lets that rest. But this existence does not affect or incommode him; it is a merely negative existence, an existence without existence, a self-contradictory existence,—a state of being which, as to its effects, is not distinguishable from non-being. The denial of determinate, positive predicates concerning the divine nature is nothing else than a denial of religion, with, however, an appearance of religion in its favour, so that it is not recognized as a denial; it is simply a subtle, disguised atheism. The alleged religious horror of limiting God by positive predicates is only the irreligious wish to know nothing more of God, to banish God from the mind. Dread of limitation is dread of existence. All real existence, *i.e.*, all existence which is truly such, is qualitative, determinative existence. He who earnestly believes in the Divine existence is not shocked at the attributing even of gross sensuous qualities to God. He who dreads an existence that may give offence, who shrinks from the grossness of a positive predicate, may as well renounce existence altogether. A God who is injured by determinate qualities has not the courage and the strength to exist. Qualities are the fire, the vital breath, the oxygen, the salt of existence. An existence in general, an existence without qualities, is an insipidity, an absurdity. But there can be no more in God than is supplied by religion. Only where man loses his taste for religion, and thus religion itself becomes insipid, does the existence of God become an insipid existence—an existence without qualities.

There is, however, a still milder way of denying the divine predicates than the direct one just described. It is admitted that the predicates of the divine nature are finite, and, more particularly, human qualities, but their rejection is rejected; they are even taken under protection, because it is necessary to man to have a definite conception of God, and since he is man he can form no other than a human conception of him. In relation to God, it is said, these predicates are certainly without any objective validity; but to me, if he is to exist for me, he cannot appear otherwise than as he does appear to me, namely, as a being with attributes analogous to the human. But this distinction between what God is in himself, and what he is for me destroys the peace of religion, and is besides in itself an unfounded and untenable distinction. I cannot know whether God is something else in himself or for himself than he is for me; what he is to me is to me all that he is. For me, there lies in these predicates under which he exists for me, what he is in himself, his very nature; he is for me what he can alone ever be for me. The religious man finds perfect satisfaction in that which God is in relation to himself; of any other relation he knows nothing, for God is to him what he can alone be to man. In the distinction above stated, man takes a point of view above himself, *i.e.*, above his nature, the absolute measure of his being; but this transcendentalism is only an illusion; for I can make the distinction between the object as it is in itself, and the object as it is for me, only where an object can really appear otherwise to me, not where it appears to me such as the absolute measure of my nature determines it to appear—such as it must appear to me. It is true that I may have a merely subjective conception, *i.e.*, one which does not arise out of the general constitution of my species; but if my conception is determined by the constitution of my species, the distinction between what an object is in itself, and what it is for me ceases; for this conception is itself an absolute one. The measure of the species is the absolute measure, law, and criterion of man. And, indeed, religion has the conviction that its conceptions, its predicates of God, are such as every man ought to have, and must have, if he would have the true ones—that they are the conceptions necessary to human nature; nay, further, that they are objectively true, representing God as he is. To every religion the gods of *other* religions are only notions concerning God, but its own conception of God is to it God himself, the true God—God such as he is in himself. Religion is satisfied only with a complete Deity, a God without reservation; it will not have a mere phantasm of God; it demands God himself. Religion gives up its own existence when it gives up the nature of God; it is no longer a truth when it renounces the possession of the true God. Scepticism is the arch-enemy of religion; but the distinction between object and conception—between God as he is in himself, and God as he is for me—is a sceptical distinction, and therefore an irreligious one.

[*The Essence of Christianity*, trans. Marian Evans (London: Kegan Paul, Trench, Trubner, 1893), 13–17.]

KARL MARX

For Germany the *criticism of religion* is in the main complete, and criticism of religion is the premise of all criticism.

The *profane* existence of error is discredited after its *heavenly oratio pro aris et focis* [Speech for the altars and hearths] has been rejected. Man, who looked for a superman in the fantastic reality of heaven and found nothing there but the *reflexion* of himself; will no longer be disposed to find but the *semblance* of himself, the non-human [*Unmensch*] where he seeks and must seek his true reality.

The basis of irreligious criticism is: *Man makes religion*, religion does not make man. In other words, religion is the self-consciousness and self-feeling of man who has either not yet found himself or has already lost himself again. But *man* is no abstract being squatting outside the world. Man is *the world of man*, the state, society. This state, this society, produce religion, *a reversed world-consciousness*, because they are a *reversed world*. Religion is the general theory of that world, its encyclopaedic compendium, its logic in a popular form, its spiritualistic *point d'honneur*, its enthusiasm, its moral sanction, its solemn completion, its universal ground for consolation and justification. It is *the fantastic realization* of the human essence because the *human essence* has no true reality. The struggle against religion is therefore mediately the fight against *the other world*, of which religion is the spiritual *aroma*.

Religious distress is at the same time the *expression* of real distress and the *protest* against real distress. Religion is the sigh of the oppressed creature, the heart of a heartless world, just as it is the spirit of a spiritless situation. It is the *opium* of the people.

The abolition of religion as the *illusory* happiness of the people is required for their *real* happiness. The demand to give up the illusions about its condition is the *demand to give up a condition which needs illusions*. The criticism of religion is therefore in embryo the criticism of the vale of woe, the halo of which is religion.

Criticism has plucked the imaginary flowers from the chain not so that man will wear the chain without any fantasy or consolation but so that he will shake off the chain and cull the living flower. The criticism of religion disillusions man to make him think and act and shape his reality like a man who has been disillusioned and has come to reason, so that he will revolve round himself and therefore round his true sun. Religion is only the illusory sun which revolves round man as long as he does not revolve round himself.

The task of history, therefore, once the *world beyond the truth* has disappeared, is to establish *the truth of this world*. The immediate *task of philosophy*, which is at the service of history, once the *saintly form* of human self-alienation has been unmasked, is to unmask self-alienation in its *unholy forms*.

Thus the criticism of heaven turns into the criticism of the earth, the *criticism of religion* into the *criticism of right* and the *criticism of theology* into the *criticism of politics*.

[*Contribution to the Critique of Hegel's Philosophy of Right*, in K. Marx and F. Engels, *On Religion* (Moscow: Foreign Languages Publishing House, 1955), 41–2.]

SØREN KIERKEGAARD

70 The Absolute Paradox

I always reason from existence, not toward existence, whether I move in the sphere of palpable sensible fact or in the realm of thought. I do not, for example, prove that a stone exists, but that some existing thing is a stone. The procedure in a court of justice does not prove that a criminal exists, but that the accused, whose existence is given, is a criminal. Whether we call existence an *accessorium* or the eternal *prius*, it is never subject to demonstration. Let us take ample time for consideration. We have no such reason for haste as have those who from concern for themselves or for the God or for some other thing, must make haste to get existence demonstrated. Under such circumstances there may indeed be need for haste, especially if the prover sincerely seeks to appreciate the danger that he himself, or the thing in question, may be non-existent unless the proof is finished and does not surreptitiously entertain the thought that it exists whether he succeeds in proving it or not.

If it were proposed to prove Napoleon's existence from Napoleon's deeds, would it not be a most curious proceeding? His existence does indeed explain his deeds, but the deeds do not prove *his* existence, unless I have already understood the word 'his' so as thereby to have assumed his existence. But Napoleon is only an individual, and in so far there exists no absolute relationship between him and his deeds; some other person might have performed the same deeds. Perhaps this is the reason why I cannot pass from the deeds to existence. If I call these deeds the deeds of Napoleon the proof becomes superfluous, since I have already named him; if I ignore this, I can never prove from the deeds that they are Napoleon's, but only in a purely ideal manner that such deeds are the deeds of a great general, and so forth. But between the God and his works there is an absolute relationship; the God is not a name but a concept. Is this perhaps the reason that his *essentia involvit existentiam*? The works of God are such that only the God can perform them. Just so, but where then are the works of the God? The works from which I would deduce his existence are not directly and immediately given. The wisdom in nature, the goodness, the wisdom in the governance of the world—are all these manifest, perhaps, upon the very face of things? Are we not here confronted with the most terrible temptations to doubt, and is it not impossible finally to dispose of all these doubts? But from such an order of things I will surely not attempt to prove God's existence; and even if I began I would never finish, and would in addition have to live constantly in suspense, lest something so terrible should suddenly happen that my bit of proof would be demolished. From what works then do I propose to derive the proof? From the works as apprehended through an ideal interpretation, i.e., such as they do not immediately reveal themselves. But in that case it is not from the works that I make the proof; I merely develop the ideality I have presupposed, and because of my confidence in *this* I make so bold as to defy all objections, even those that have not yet been made. In beginning my proof I presuppose the ideal interpretation, and also that I will be successful in carrying it through; but what else is this but to presuppose that the God exists, so that I really begin by virtue of confidence in him?

And how does the God's existence emerge from the proof? Does it follow straightway, without any breach of continuity? Or have we not here an analogy to the behaviour of the little Cartesian dolls? As soon as I let go of the doll it stands on its head. As soon as I let it go—I must therefore let it go. So also with the proof. As long as I keep my hold on the proof, i.e., continue to demonstrate, the existence does not come out, if for no other reason than that I am engaged in proving it; but when I let the proof go, the existence is there. But this act of letting go is surely also something; it is indeed a contribution of mine. Must not this also be taken into the account, this little moment, brief as it may be—it need not be long, for it is a *leap*. However brief this moment, if only an instantaneous now, this 'now' must be included in the reckoning. If anyone wishes to have it ignored, I will use it to tell a little anecdote, in order to show that it nevertheless does exist. Chrysippus was experimenting with a sorites to see if he could not bring about a break in its quality, either progressively or retrogressively. But Carneades could not get it in his head when the new quality actually emerged. Then Chrysippus told him to try making a little pause in the reckoning, and so—so it would be easier to understand. Carneades replied: With the greatest pleasure, please do not hesitate on my account; you may not only pause, but even lie down to sleep, and it will help you just as little; for when you awake we will begin again where you left off. Just so; it boots as little to try to get rid of something by sleeping as to try to come into the possession of something in the same manner.

Whoever therefore attempts to demonstrate the existence of God (except in the sense of clarifying the concept, and without the *reservatio finalis* noted above, that the existence emerges from the demonstration by a leap) proves in lieu thereof something else, something which at times perhaps does not need a proof, and in any case needs none better; for the fool says in his heart that there is no God, but whoever says in his heart or to men: Wait just a little and I will prove it—what a rare man of wisdom is he! If in the moment of beginning his proof it is not absolutely undetermined whether the God exists or not, he does not prove it; and if it is thus undetermined in the beginning he will never come to begin, partly from fear of failure, since the God perhaps does not exist, and partly because he has nothing with which to begin.—A project of this kind would scarcely have been undertaken by the ancients. Socrates at least, who is credited with having put forth the physico-teleological proof for God's existence, did not go about it in any such manner. He always presupposes the God's existence, and under this presupposition seeks to interpenetrate nature with the idea of purpose. Had he been asked why he pursued this method, he would doubtless have explained that he lacked the courage to venture out upon so perilous a voyage of discovery without having made sure of the God's existence behind him. At the word of the God he casts his net as if to catch the idea of purpose; for nature herself finds many means of frightening the inquirer, and distracts him by many a digression.

[*Philosophical Fragments*, trans. D.F. Swenson and Howard V. Hong (Princeton: Princeton University Press, 1962), 50–4.]

SIGMUND FREUD

71   Religion as Wish-Fulfilment

I think we have prepared the way sufficiently for an answer to both these questions. It will be found if we turn our attention to the psychical origin of religious ideas. These, which are given out as teachings, are not precipitates of experience or end-results of thinking: they are illusions, fulfilments of the oldest, strongest and most urgent wishes of mankind. The secret of their strength lies in the strength of those wishes. As we already know, the terrifying impression of helplessness in childhood aroused the need for protection—for protection through love—which was provided by the father; and the recognition that this helplessness lasts throughout life made it necessary to cling to the existence of a father, but this time a more powerful one. Thus the benevolent rule of a divine Providence allays our fear of the dangers of life; the establishment of a moral world-order ensures the fulfilment of the demands of justice, which have so often remained unfulfilled in human civilization; and the prolongation of earthly existence in a future life provides the local and temporal framework in which these wish-fulfilments shall take place. Answers to the riddles that tempt the curiosity of man, such as how the universe began or what the relation is between body and mind, are developed in conformity with the underlying assumptions of this system. It is an enormous relief to the individual psyche if the conflicts of its childhood arising from the father-complex—conflicts which it has never wholly overcome—are removed from it and brought to a solution which is universally accepted.

When I say that these things are all illusions, I must define the meaning of the word. An illusion is not the same thing as an error; nor is it necessarily an error. Aristotle's belief that vermin are developed out of dung (a belief to which ignorant people still cling) was an error; so was the belief of a former generation of doctors that *tabes dorsalis* is the result of sexual excess. It would be incorrect to call these errors illusions. On the other hand, it was an illusion of Columbus's that he had discovered a new sea-route to the Indies. The part played by his wish in this error is very clear. One may describe as an illusion the assertion made by certain nationalists that the Indo-Germanic race is the only one capable of civilization; or the belief, which was only destroyed by psycho-analysis, that children are creatures without sexuality. What is characteristic of illusions is that they are derived from human wishes. In this respect they come near to psychiatric delusions. But they differ from them, too, apart from the more complicated structure of delusions. In the case of delusions, we empha-size as essential their being in contradiction with reality. Illusions need not necessarily be false—that is to say, unrealizable or in contradiction to reality. For instance, a middle-class girl may have the illusion that a prince will come and marry her. This is possible; and a few such cases have occurred. That the Messiah will come and found a golden age is much less likely. Whether one classifies this belief as an illusion or as something analogous to a delusion will depend on one's personal attitude. Examples of illusions which have proved true are not easy to find, but the illusion of the alchemists that all metals can be turned into gold might be one of them. The wish to have a great deal of gold, as much gold as possible, has, it is true, been a good deal damped by our present-day knowledge to the determinants of wealth, but chemistry no longer regards the transmutation of metals into gold as impossible. Thus we call a belief an illusion when a wish-fulfilment is a prominent factor in its moti-vation, and in doing so we disregard its relations to reality, just as the illusion itself sets no store by verification.

Having thus taken our bearings, let us return once more to the question of religious doctrines. We can now repeat that all of them are illusions and insus-ceptible of proof. No one can be compelled to think them true, to believe in them. Some of them are so improbable, so incompatible with everything we have laboriously discovered about the reality of the world, that we may compare them—if we pay proper regard to the psychological differences—to delusions. Of the reality value of most of them we cannot judge; just as they cannot be proved, so they cannot be refuted. We still know too little to make a critical approach to them. The riddles of the universe reveal themselves only slowly to our investigation; there are many questions to which science to-day can give no answer. But scientific work is the only road which can lead us to a knowledge of reality outside ourselves. It is once again merely an illusion to expect anything from intuition and introspection; they can give us nothing but particulars about our own mental life, which are hard to interpret, never any information about the questions which religious doctrine finds it so easy to answer. It would be insolent to let one's own arbitrary will step into the breach and, according to one's personal estimate, declare this or that part of the religious system to be less or more acceptable. Such questions are too momentous for that; they might be called too sacred.

At this point one must expect to meet with an objection. 'Well then, if even obdurate sceptics admit that the assertions of religion cannot be refuted by reason, why should I not believe in them, since they have so much on their side—tradition, the agreement of mankind, and all the consolations they offer?' Why not, indeed? Just as no one can be forced to believe, so no one can be forced to disbelieve. But do not let us be satisfied with deceiving ourselves that arguments like these take us along the road of correct thinking. If ever there was a case of a lame excuse we have it here. Ignorance is ignorance; no right to believe anything can be derived from it. In other matters no sensible person will behave so irresponsibly or rest content with such feeble grounds for his opinions and for the line he takes. It is only in the highest and most sacred things that he allows himself to do so. In reality these are only attempts at pretending to oneself or to other people that one is still firmly attached to religion, when one has long since cut oneself loose from it. Where questions of religion are concerned, people are guilty of every possible sort of dishonesty and intellectual misdemeanour. Philosophers stretch the meaning of words until they retain scarcely anything of their original sense. They give the name of 'God' to some vague abstraction which they have created for themselves; having done so they can pose before all the world as deists, as believers in God, and they can even boast that they have recognized a higher, purer concept of God, notwithstanding that their God is now nothing more than an insubstantial shadow and no longer the mighty personality of religious doctrines. Critics persist in describing as 'deeply religious' anyone who admits to a sense of man's insignificance or impotence in the face of the universe, although what constitutes the essence of the religious attitude is not this feeling but only the next step after it, the reaction to it which seeks a remedy for it. The man who goes no further, but humbly acquiesces in the small part which human beings play in the great world—such a man is, on the contrary, irreligious in the truest sense of the word.

To assess the truth-value of religious doctrines does not lie within the scope of the present inquiry. It is enough for us that we have recognized them as being, in their psychological nature, illusions. But we do not have to conceal the fact that this discovery also strongly influences our attitude to the question which must appear to many to be the most important of all. We know approximately at what periods and by what kind of men religious doctrines were created. If in addition we discover the motives which led to this, our attitude to the problem of religion will undergo a marked displacement. We shall tell ourselves that it would be very nice if there were a God who created the world and was a benevolent Providence, and if there were a moral order in the universe and an afterlife; but it is a very striking fact that all this is exactly as we are bound to wish it to be. And it would be more remarkable still if our wretched, ignorant and downtrodden ancestors had succeeded in solving all these difficult riddles of the universe.

[*The Future of an Illusion* (1927), in *Civilisation, Society and Religion* (Harmondsworth: Penguin, 1985), 212–15.]

ÉMILE DURKHEIM

72 Religion as a Social Construction

More often than not, the theorists who have proceeded to explain religion in rational terms have seen it to be above all a system of ideas corresponding to a definite object. This object has been visualized in many ways: nature, the infinite, the unknowable, the ideal, etc., but the differences are not important. In all these cases it is the *représentations*, the beliefs, which are considered to be the essential element of religion. From this point of view, the rites appear as merely an external, contingent and material expression of those internal states which alone are considered to have an intrinsic value. This idea is so widespread that the arguments on the subject of religion mostly turn on the question of knowing whether or not religion can be reconciled with science, in other words, whether alongside scientific knowledge there is room for another form of thought which is specifically religious.

But the believers, those who live the religious life and who have the direct sensation of what it really is, object to this way of looking at it on the grounds that it does not bear out their day to day experiences. In fact they feel that the true function of religion is not to make us think, to enrich our own knowledge, to add to the *représentations* that we owe to science others of a different origin and character, but to urge us to action, to help us to live. The believer who has entered into communion with his god is not only a man who sees new truths which the unbeliever does not know, he is a man who is *capable* of doing more. He is given greater strength whether it be in enduring the difficulties of existence or in conquering them. It is as if he were raised above human misery because he is set above his condition as a man. He believes that he is delivered from evil in whatever form he visualizes it. The first article of every creed is the belief in salvation by faith. Now, it is difficult to see how a simple idea could be so effective. An idea is only a part of ourselves; how can it confer on us powers superior to those which are ours by nature? However rich it may be in affective virtues it cannot add to our natural vitality; it can only release the emotive forces which are within us, and neither create nor augment them. From the fact that we imagine an object worthy of being loved and sought after, it does not follow that we feel stronger. But it is necessary that the superior energies to those which we have at our command should emanate from this object and that, moreover, there should be some means of allowing these energies to penetrate within us and combine with our interior life. For that to be possible it is not enough to think about them. It is essential that we put ourselves within their sphere of influence and that we should turn to embrace their influence: in short, we must act and repeat the necessary action each time we need to renew their effects. It can be seen how from this point of view the regular repetition of the set of actions which make up the cult assumes its full importance. In fact, anyone who has really practised a religion well knows that it is the cult which gives rise to those impressions of joy, internal peace, serenity and enthusiasm which are for the believer a kind of experimental proof of his faith. The cult is not merely a system of symbols by which faith is expressed externally, it is the collection of the means by which it periodically creates and recreates itself. Whether it consists in material manoeuvres or mental operations, the cult is always that which is effective.

The whole of our study rests on the assumption that this unanimous sentiment of believers all through history cannot be purely illusory. Along with a recent apologist for the faith, we admit that religious beliefs are based on a specific experience whose demonstrative value is in a sense no way inferior to that of scientific experiments, whilst, at the same time being different. We also believe that 'by their fruits ye shall know them', and that its fruitfulness is the best proof of the health of its roots. From the fact that there exists, if you like, a 'religious experience' which can to some extent be justified—is there any case of an experience which cannot?—it does not follow that the reality justifying it conforms objectively to the believers' conception of it. The very fact that the way in which it has been conceived has varied infinitely according to time, is sufficient proof that none of these conceptions expresses it adequately. If the scientist takes it as axiomatic that the sensations of heat and light experienced by men correspond to some objective cause, he does not conclude that this is what it appears to be to the senses. Similarly, the impressions experienced by the faithful, although they are not imaginary, do not however constitute privileged intuitions. There is no reason to believe that they tell us more about the nature of their object than do ordinary sensations about the nature of bodies and their properties. In order to discover what constitutes this object, we must accordingly subject the impression to an examination analogous to that which substitutes for the tangible *représentation* of the world one that is scientific and conceptual.

Now this is precisely what we have attempted to do. We have seen that the reality is society, which mythologies have visualized in so many different forms and which is the objective, universal and eternal cause of those *sui generis* sensations which make up religious experience. We have shown what moral forces society develops and how it awakens the feeling of support, protection and tutelary dependence which links the believer to his cult. It is society which raises him above himself: we might even say that he is made by society, for the thing that makes man is that totality of intellectual assets which constitutes civilization, and civilization is the work of society. This explains the leading role of the cult in every kind of religion. It is because society can only make its influence felt if it is active, and it is only active if the individuals of which it is composed are assembled together and act in common. In common action it becomes aware of itself and establishes itself: it is above all an active co-operation. As we have shown, collective ideas and sentiments are only possible because of the external movements which symbolize them. Thus action dominates religious life simply because it is society which is its source.

To all the reasons which have been given to justify this conception, a final one may be added which emerges from our work seen as a whole. As we have proceeded, we have established that the fundamental categories of thought, and consequently of science, have religious origins. We have seen that the same is true of magic and as a result of the various techniques derived from it. On the other hand, it has been known for a long time that, until a relatively recent stage of evolution, the rules of morality and law were indistinguishable from ritual prescriptions. In short, we can say that almost all the great social institutions were born of religion. If the main aspects of collective life began as mere aspects of the religious life, it is obvious that the religious life must have been the eminent form of collective life and a shorthand expression of it viewed in its entirety. If religion has given birth to everything that is essential in society, the reason is that the idea of society is the soul of religion.

Religious forces are therefore human and moral forces. No doubt because collective sentiments cannot become conscious of themselves without being attached to external objects, these moral forces have assumed some of the characteristics of things in order to become established. In this way they have acquired a kind of physical nature which has enabled them to intermingle with the life of the material world and through them an explanation of what is happening in it has been thought possible. When, however, they are considered strictly from this angle and in this role, only the most superficial aspects of them are seen. In fact, it is from the *conscience* that the essential elements of which they are composed are borrowed. Normally it seems that they only have a human character when they are imagined in human form: but even the most impersonal and anonymous of them are nothing more than objectified sentiments.

[*The Elementary Forms of Religious Life*, trans. Jacqueline Redding and W. S. F. Pickering, in *Durkheim on Religion*, ed. W. S. F. Pickering (London: Routledge and Kegan Paul, 1975), 145–8.]

73 The Ethics of Belief

A shipowner was about to send to sea an emigrant-ship. He knew that she was old, and not over-well built at the first; that she had seen many seas and climes, and often had needed repairs. Doubts had been suggested to him that possibly she was not seaworthy. These doubts preyed upon his mind, and made him unhappy; he thought that perhaps he ought to have her thoroughly overhauled and refitted, even though this should put him to great expense. Before the ship sailed, however, he succeeded in overcoming these melancholy reflections. He said to himself that she had gone safely through so many voyages and weathered so many storms that it was idle to suppose she would not come safely home from this trip also. He would put his trust in Providence, which could hardly fail to protect all these unhappy families that were leaving their fatherland to seek for better times elsewhere. He would dismiss from his mind all ungenerous suspicions about the honesty of builders and contractors. In such ways he acquired a sincere and comfortable conviction that his vessel was thoroughly safe and seaworthy; he watched her departure with a light heart, and benevolent wishes for the success of the exiles in their strange new home that was to be; and he got his insurance-money when she went down in mid-ocean and told no tales.

What shall we say of him? Surely this, that he was verily guilty of the death of those men. It is admitted that he did sincerely believe in the soundness of his ship; but the sincerity of his conviction can in no wise help him, because *he had no right to believe on such evidence as was before him*. He had acquired his belief not by honestly earning it in patient investigation, but by stifling his doubts. And although in the end he may have felt so sure about it that he could not think otherwise, yet inasmuch as he had knowingly and willingly worked himself into that frame of mind, he must be held responsible for it.

Let us alter the case a little, and suppose that the ship was not unsound after all; that she made her voyage safely, and many others after it. Will that diminish the guilt of her owner? Not one jot. When an action is once done, it is right or wrong for ever; no accidental failure of its good or evil fruits can possibly alter that. The man would not have been innocent, he would only have been not found out. The question of right or wrong has to do with the origin of his belief, not the matter of it; not what it was, but how he got it; not whether it turned out to be true or false, but whether he had a right to believe on such evidence as was before him.

There was once an island in which some of the inhabitants professed a religion teaching neither the doctrine of original sin nor that of eternal punishment. A suspicion got abroad that the professors of this religion had made use of unfair means to get their doctrines taught to children. They were accused of wresting the laws of their country in such a way as to remove children from the care of their natural and legal guardians; and even of stealing them away and keeping them concealed from their friends and relations. A certain number of men formed themselves into a society for the purpose of agitating the public about this matter. They published grave accusations against individual citizens of the highest position and character, and did all in their power to injure these citizens in the exercise of their professions. So great was the noise they made, that a Commission was appointed to investigate the facts; but after the Commission had carefully inquired into all the evidence that could be got, it appeared that the accused were innocent. Not only had they been accused on insufficient evidence, but the evidence of their innocence was such as the agitators might easily have obtained, if they had attempted a fair inquiry. After these disclosures the inhabitants of that country looked upon the members of the agitating society, not only as persons whose judgment was to be distrusted, but also as no longer to be counted honourable men. For although they had sincerely and conscientiously believed in the charges they had made, yet *they had no right to believe on such evidence as was before them.* Their sincere convictions, instead of being honestly earned by patient inquiring, were stolen by listening to the voice of prejudice and passion.

Let us vary this case also, and suppose, other things remaining as before, that a still more accurate investigation proved the accused to have been really guilty. Would this make any difference in the guilt of the accusers? Clearly not; the question is not whether their belief was true or false, but whether they entertained it on wrong grounds. They would no doubt say, 'Now you see that we were right after all; next time perhaps you will believe us.' And they might be believed, but they would not thereby become honourable men. They would not be innocent, they would only be not found out. Every one of them, if he chose to examine himself *in foro conscientiæ*, would know that he had acquired and nourished a belief, when he had no right to believe on such evidence as was before him; and therein he would know that he had done a wrong thing.

It may be said, however, that in both of these supposed cases it is not the belief which is judged to be wrong, but the action following upon it. The shipowner might say, 'I am perfectly certain that my ship is sound, but still I feel it my duty to have her examined, before trusting the lives of so many people to her.' And it might be said to the agitator, 'However convinced you were of the justice of your cause and the truth of your convictions, you ought not to have made a public attack upon any man's character until you had examined the evidence on both sides with the utmost patience and care.'

In the first place, let us admit that, so far as it goes, this view of the case is right and necessary; right, because even when a man's belief is so fixed that he cannot think otherwise, he still has a choice in regard to the action suggested by it, and so cannot escape the duty of investigating on the ground of the strength of his convictions; and necessary, because those who are not yet capable of controlling their feelings and thoughts must have a plain rule dealing with overt acts.

But this being premised as necessary, it becomes clear that it is not sufficient, and that our previous judgment is required to supplement it. For it is not possible so to sever the belief from the action it suggests as to condemn the one without condemning the other. No man holding a strong belief on one side of a question, or even wishing to hold a belief on one side, can investigate it with such fairness and completeness as if he were really in doubt and unbiased; so that the existence of a belief not founded on fair inquiry unfits a man for the performance of this necessary duty.

Nor is that truly a belief at all which has not some influence upon the actions of him who holds it. He who truly believes that which prompts him to an action has looked upon the action to lust after it, he has committed it already in his heart. If a belief is not realized immediately in open deeds, it is stored up for the guidance of the future. It goes to make a part of that aggregate of beliefs which is the link between sensation and action at every moment of all our lives, and which is so organized and compacted together that no part of it can be isolated from the rest, but every new addition modifies the structure of the whole. No real belief, however trifling and fragmentary it may seem, is ever truly insignificant; it prepares us to receive more of its like, confirms those which resembled it before, and weakens others; and so gradually it lays a stealthy train in our inmost thoughts, which may some day explode into overt action, and leave its stamp upon our character for ever.

And no one man's belief is in any case a private matter which concerns himself alone. Our lives are guided by that general conception of the course of things which has been created by society for social purposes. Our words, our phrases, our forms and processes and modes of thought, are common property, fashioned and perfected from age to age; an heirloom which every succeeding generation inherits as a precious deposit and a sacred trust to be handed on to the next one, not unchanged but enlarged and purified, with some clear marks of its proper handiwork. Into this, for good or ill, is woven every belief of every man who has speech of his fellows. An awful privilege, and an awful responsibility, that we should help to create the world in which posterity will live.

[*Lectures and Essays* (London: Macmillan, 1879), ii. 177–82.]

WILLIAM JAMES

74   The Will to Believe

All this strikes one as healthy, even when expressed, as by Clifford, with somewhat too much of robustious pathos in the voice. Free-will and simple wishing do seem, in the matter of our credences, to be only fifth wheels to the coach. Yet if any one should thereupon assume that intellectual insight is what remains after wish and will and sentimental preference have taken wing, or that pure reason is what then settles our opinions, he would fly quite as directly in the teeth of the facts.

It is only our already dead hypotheses that our willing nature is unable to bring to life again. But what has made them dead for us is for the most part a previous action of our willing nature of an antagonistic kind. When I say 'willing nature,' I do not mean only such deliberate volitions as may have set up habits of belief that we cannot now escape from,—I mean all such factors of belief as fear and hope, prejudice and passion, imitation and partisanship, the circumpressure of our caste and set. As a matter of fact we find ourselves believing, we hardly know how or why. Mr Balfour gives the name of 'authority' to all those influences, born of the intellectual climate, that make hypotheses possible or impossible for us, alive or dead. Here in this room, we all of us believe in molecules and the conservation of energy, in democracy and necessary progress, in Protestant Christianity and the duty of fighting for 'the doctrine of the immortal Monroe,' all for no reasons worthy of the name. We see into these matters with no more inner clearness, and probably with much less, than any disbeliever in them might possess. His unconventionality would probably have some grounds to show for its conclusions; but for us, not insight, but the *prestige* of the opinions, is what makes the spark shoot from them and light up our sleeping magazines of faith. Our reason is quite satisfied, in nine hundred and ninety-nine cases out of every thousand of us, if it can find a few arguments that will do to recite in case our credulity is criticized by some one else. Our faith is faith in some one else's faith, and in the greatest matters this is most the case. Our belief in truth itself, for instance, that there is a truth, and that our minds and it are made for each other,—what is it but a passionate affirmation of desire, in which our social system backs us up? We want to have a truth; we want to believe that our experiments and studies and discussions must put us in a continually better and better position towards it; and on this line we agree to fight out our thinking lives. But if a pyrrhonistic sceptic asks us *how we know* all this, can our logic find a reply? No! certainly it cannot. It is just one volition against another,—we willing to go in for life upon a trust or assumption which he, for his part, does not care to make.

As a rule we disbelieve all facts and theories for which we have no use. Clifford's cosmic emotions find no use for Christian feelings. Huxley belabours the bishops because there is no use for sacerdotalism in his scheme of life. Newman, on the contrary, goes over to Romanism, and finds all sorts of reasons good for staying there, because a priestly system is for him an organic need and delight. Why do so few 'scientists' even look at the evidence for telepathy, so called? Because they think, as a leading biologist, now dead, once said to me, that even if such a thing were true, scientists ought to band together to keep it suppressed and concealed. It would undo the uniformity of Nature and all sorts of other things without which scientists cannot carry on their pursuits. But if this very man had been shown something which as a scientist he might *do* with telepathy, he might not only have examined the evidence, but even have found it good enough. This very law which the logicians would impose upon us—if I may give the name of logicians to those who would rule out our willing nature here—is based on nothing but their own natural wish to exclude all elements for which they, in their professional quality of logicians, can find no use.

Evidently, then, our non-intellectual nature does influence our convictions. There are passional tendencies and volitions which run before and others which come after belief, and it is only the latter that are too late for the fair; and they are not too late when the previous passional work has been already in their own direction. Pascal's argument, instead of being powerless, then seems a regular clincher, and is the last stroke needed to make our faith in masses and holy water complete. The state of things is evidently far from simple; and pure insight and logic, whatever they might do ideally, are not the only things that really do produce our creeds.

Our next duty, having recognized this mixed-up state of affairs, is to ask whether it be simply reprehensible and pathological, or whether, on the contrary, we must treat it a normal element in making up our minds. The thesis I defend is, briefly stated, this: *Our passional nature not only lawfully may, but must, decide an option between propositions, whenever it is a genuine option that cannot by its nature be decided on intellectual grounds; for to say, under such circumstances, 'Do not decide, but leave the question open,' is itself a passional decision,—just like deciding yes or no,—and is attended with the same risk of losing the truth.* [. . .]

Religions differ so much in their accidents that in discussing the religious question we must make it very generic and broad. What then do we now mean by the religious hypothesis? Science says things are; morality says some things are better than other things; and religion says essentially two things.

First, she says that the best things are the more eternal things, the overlapping things, the things in the universe that throw the last stone, so to speak, and say the final word. 'Perfection is eternal,'—this phrase of Charles Secrétan seems a good way of putting this first affirmation of religion, an affirmation which obviously cannot yet be verified scientifically at all.

The second affirmation of religion is that we are better off even now if we believe her first affirmation to be true.

Now, let us consider what the logical elements of this situation are *in case the religious hypothesis in both its branches be really true.* (Of course, we must admit that possibility at the outset. If we are to discuss the question at all, it must involve a living option. If for any of you religion be a hypothesis that cannot, by any living possibility be true, then you need go no farther. I speak to the 'saving remnant' alone.) So proceeding, we see, first, that religion offers itself as a *momentous* option. We are supposed to gain, even now, by our belief, and to lose by our non-belief, a certain vital good. Secondly, religion is a *forced* option, so far as that good goes. We cannot escape the issue by remaining sceptical and waiting for more light, because, although we do avoid error in that way *if reli-gion be untrue*, we lose the good, *if it be true*, just as certainly as if we positively chose to disbelieve. It is as if a man should hesitate indefinitely to ask a certain woman to marry him because he was not perfectly sure that she would prove an angel after he brought her home. Would he not cut himself off from that partic-ular angel-possibility as decisively as if he went and married some one else? Scepticism, then, is not avoidance of option; it is option of a certain particular kind of risk. *Better risk loss of truth than chance of error,*—that is your faith-vetoer's exact position. He is actively playing his stake as much as the believer is; he is backing the field against the religious hypothesis, just as the believer is backing the religious hypothesis against the field. To preach scepticism to us as a duty until 'sufficient evidence' for religion be found, is tantamount therefore to telling us, when in presence of the religious hypothesis, that to yield to our fear of its being error is wiser and better than to yield to our hope that it may be true. It is not intellect against all passions, then; it is only intellect with one passion laying down its law. And by what, forsooth, is the supreme wisdom of this passion warranted? Dupery for dupery, what proof is there that dupery through hope is so much worse than dupery through fear? I, for one, can see no proof; and I simply refuse obedience to the scientist's command to imitate his kind of option, in a case where my own stake is important enough to give me the right to choose my own form of risk. If religion be true and the evidence for it be still insufficient, I do not wish, by putting your extinguisher upon my nature (which feels to me as if it had after all some business in this matter), to forfeit my sole chance in life of getting upon the winning side,—that chance depending, of course, on my willingness to run the risk of acting as if my passional need of taking the world religiously might be prophetic and right.

All this is on the supposition that it really may be prophetic and right, and that, even to us who are discussing the matter, religion is a live hypothesis which may be true. Now, to most of us religion comes in a still further way that makes a veto on our active faith even more illogical. The more perfect and more eternal aspect of the universe is represented in our religions as having personal form. The universe is no longer a mere *It* to us, but a *Thou*, if we are religious; and any relation that may be possible from person to person might be possible here. For instance, although in one sense we are passive portions of the universe, in another we show a curious autonomy, as if we were small active centres on our own account. We feel, too, as if the appeal of religion to us were made to our own active good-will, as if evidence might be forever withheld from us unless we met the hypothesis half-way. To take a trivial illus-tration: just as a man who in a company of gentlemen made no advances, asked a warrant for every concession, and believed no one's word without proof, would cut himself off by such churlishness from all the social rewards that a more trusting spirit would earn,—so here, one who should shut himself up in snarling logicality and try to make the gods extort his recognition willy-nilly, or not get it at all, might cut himself off forever from his only opportunity of making the gods' acquaintance. This feeling, forced on us we know not whence, that by obstinately believing that there are gods (although not to do so would be so easy both for our logic and our life) we are doing the universe the deepest service we can, seems part of the living essence of the religious hypothesis. If the hypothesis *were* true in all its parts, including this one, then pure intellectualism, with its veto on our making willing advances, would be an absurdity; and some participation of our sympathetic nature would be logically required. I, therefore, for one, cannot see my way to accepting the agnostic rules for truth-seeking, or wilfully agree to keep my willing nature out of the game. I cannot do so for this plain reason, that *a rule of thinking which would absolutely prevent me from acknowledging certain kinds of truth if those kinds of truth were really there, would be an irrational rule.* That for me is the long and short of the formal logic of the situation, no matter what the kinds of truth might materially be.

[*The Will to Believe and Other Essays* (London: Longmans Green, 1917), 9–11, 25–9.]

FRIEDRICH NIETZSCHE

75   Reason, Conviction, Indifference

227

Reasons judged a posteriori on the basis of consequences.—All states and orderings within society—classes, marriage, education, law—all these derive their force and endurance solely from the faith the fettered spirits have in them: that is to say in the absence of reasons, or at least in the warding off of the demand for reasons. The fettered spirits are unwilling to admit this: they recognize that it constitutes a *pudendum* Christianity, which was very innocent in its intellectual notions, noticed nothing of this *pudendum*, demanded faith and nothing but faith and passionately repulsed the desire for reasons; it pointed to the success enjoyed by faith: you will soon see the advantage to be derived from faith, it intimated, it shall make you blessed. The state in fact does the same thing, and every father raises his son in the same fashion: only regard this as true, he says, and you will see how much good it will do you. What this means, however, is that the personal *utility* an opinion is supposed to demonstrate its *truth*, the advantageousness of a theory is supposed to guarantee its intellectual soundness and well-foundedness. It is as though a defendant said to the court: my counsel is telling the whole truth, for just see what follows from what he says: I shall be acquitted.—Because the fettered spirits harbour their principles on account of their utility, they suppose that the views of the free spirit are likewise held for utilitarian ends and that he regards as true only that which profits him. Since, however, this seems to be the opposite of that which is profitable to their country or class, they assume that the principles of the free spirit are dangerous to them; they say, or sense: he must not be right, for he is harmful to us. [. . .]

265

Reason in school.—The school has no more important task than to teach rigorous thinking, cautious judgement and consistent reasoning; therefore it has to avoid all those things that are of no use for these operations, for example religion. For it can be sure that, if the bow of thought has been stretched too tight, human unclarity, habit and need will afterwards relax it again. But so long as it exerts influence it ought to extort that which distinguishes and is the essence of man: 'reason and science, the *supremest* powers of man'—as Goethe at least judges.—The great naturalist von Baer sees the superiority of all Europeans when compared with Asiatics to lie in their inculcated ability to give reasons for what they believe, an ability the latter totally lack. Europe has attended the school of consistent and critical thinking, Asia still does not know how to distinguish between truth and fiction and is unaware whether its convictions stem from observation and correct thinking or from fantasies.—Reason in school has made Europe Europe: in the Middle Ages it was on the way to becoming again a piece and appendage of Asia—that is to say losing the scientific sense which it owed to the Greeks. [. . .]

630

Conviction is the belief that on some particular point of knowledge one is in possession of the unqualified truth. This belief thus presupposes that unqualified truths exist; likewise that perfect methods of attaining to them have been discovered; finally, that everyone who possesses convictions avails himself of these perfect methods. All three assertions demonstrate at once that the man of convictions is not the man of scientific thought; he stands before us in the age of theoretical innocence and is a child, however grown up he may be in other respects. But whole millennia have lived in these childish presuppositions and it is from them that mankind's mightiest sources of energy have flowed. Those countless numbers who have sacrificed themselves for their convictions thought they were doing so for unqualified truth. In this they were all wrong: probably a man has never yet sacrificed himself for truth; at least the dogmatic expression of his belief will have been unscientific or half-scientific. In reality one wanted to be in the right because one thought one *had* to be. To allow oneself to be deprived of one's belief perhaps meant calling one's eternal salvation into question. In a matter of such extreme importance as this the 'will' was only too audibly the prompter of the intellect. The presupposition of every believer of every kind was that he *could* not be refuted; if the counter-arguments proved very strong it was always left to him to defame reason itself and perhaps even to set up the *'credo quia absurdum est'* [I believe it because it is absurd] as the banner of the extremest fanaticism. It is not conflict of opinions that has made history so violent but conflict of belief in opinions, that is to say conflict of convictions. But if all those who have thought so highly of their convictions, brought to them sacrifices of every kind, and have not spared honour, body or life in their service, had devoted only half their energy to investigating with what right they adhered to this or that conviction, by what path they had arrived at it, how peaceable a picture the history of mankind would present! How much more knowledge there would be! We should have been spared all the cruel scenes attending the persecution of heretics of every kind, and for two reasons: firstly because the inquisitors would have conducted their inquisition above all within themselves and emerged out of the presumptuousness of being the defenders of unqualified truth; then because the heretics themselves would, after they had investigated them, have ceased to accord any further credence to such ill-founded propositions as the propositions of all religious sectarians and 'right believers' are.

[*Human, All Too Human*, trans. R. J. Hollingdale (Cambridge: Cambridge University Press, 1986), 109, 125–6, 199–200.]

HENRY MANSEL

76 The Limits of Religious Thought

What then is the practical lesson which these Lectures are designed to teach concerning the right use of reason in religious questions? and what are the just claims of a reasonable faith, as distinguished from a blind credulity? In the first place, it is obvious that, if there is any object whatever of which the human mind is unable to form a clear and distinct conception, the inability equally disqualifies us for proving or for disproving a given doctrine, in all cases in which such a conception is an indispensable condition of the argument. If, for example, we can form no positive notion of the Nature of God as an Infinite Being, we are not entitled either to demonstrate the mystery of the Trinity as a necessary property of that Nature, or to reject it as necessarily inconsistent therewith. Such mysteries clearly belong, not to Reason, but to Faith; and the preliminary inquiry which distinguishes a reasonable from an unreasonable belief, must be directed, not to the premises by which the doctrine can be proved or disproved as reasonable or unreasonable, but to the nature of the authority on which it rests, as revealed or unrevealed. The brief summary of Christian Evidences contained in my concluding Lecture, and others which might be added to them, are surely sufficient to form an ample field for the use of Reason, even in regard to those mysteries which it cannot directly examine. If to submit to an authority which can stand the test of such investigations, and to believe it when it tells us of things which we are unable to investigate,—if this be censured as a blind credulity, it is a blindness which in these things is a better guide than the opposite quality so justly described by the philosopher as 'the sharpsightedness of little souls.'

In the second place, a caution is needed concerning the kind of evidence which reason is competent to furnish within the legitimate sphere of its employment. If we have not such a conception of the Divine Nature as is suffi- cient for the à priori demonstration of religious truths, our rational conviction in any particular case must be regarded not as a *certainty*, but as a *probability*. We must remember the Aristotelian rule, to be content with such evidence as the nature of the object-matter allows. A single infallible criterion of all religious truth can be obtained only by the possession of a perfect Philosophy of the Infi- nite. If such a philosophy is unattainable; if the infinite can only be apprehended under finite symbols, and the authority of those symbols tested by finite evidences, there is always room for error, in consequence of the inadequacy of the conception to express completely the nature of the object. In other words, we must admit that human reason, though not *worthless*, is at least *fallible*, in dealing with religious questions; and that the probability of error is always increased in proportion to the partial nature of the evidence with which it deals. Those who set up some one supreme criterion of religious truth, their 'Chris- tian consciousness,' their 'religious intuitions,' their 'moral reason,' or any other of the favourite idols of the subjective school of theologians, and who treat with contempt every kind of evidence which does not harmonize with this, are especially liable to be led into error. They use the weight without the counterpoise, to the imminent peril of their mental equilibrium. This is the caution which it was the object of my concluding Lecture to enforce, princi- pally by means of two practical rules; namely, first, that the true evidence, for or against a religion, is not to be found in any single criterion, but in the result of many presumptions examined and compared together; and, secondly, that in proportion to the weight of the counter-evidence in favour of a religion, is the probability that we may be mistaken in supposing a particular class of objec- tions to have any real weight at all.

These considerations are no less applicable to moral than to speculative reasonings. The moral faculty, though furnishing undoubtedly some of the most important elements for the solution of the religious problem, is no more entitled than any other single principle of the human mind to be accepted as a sole and sufficient criterion. It is true that to our sense of moral obligation we owe our primary conception of God as a moral Governor: and it is also true that, were man left solely to à priori presumptions in forming his estimate of the nature and attributes of God, the moral sense, as being that one of all human faculties whose judgments are least dependent on experience, would furnish the principal, if not the only characteristics of his highest conception of God. But here, as elsewhere, the original presumption is modified and corrected by subsequent experience. It is a fact which experience forces upon us, and which it is useless, were it possible, to disguise, that the representation of God after the model of the highest human morality which we are capable of conceiving is not sufficient to account for all the phenomena exhibited by the course of His natural Providence. The infliction of physical suffering, the permission of moral evil, the adversity of the good, the prosperity of the wicked, the crimes of the guilty involving the misery of the innocent, the tardy appearance and partial distribution of moral and religious knowledge in the world,—these are facts which no doubt are reconcilable, we know not how, with the infinite Goodness of God; but which certainly are not to be explained on the supposition that its sole and sufficient type is to be found in the finite goodness of man. What right then has the philosopher to assume that a criterion which admits of so many exceptions in the facts of nature may be applied without qualification or exception to the statements of revelation?

The assertion that human morality contains in it a temporal and relative element, and cannot in its highest manifestation be regarded as a complete measure of the absolute Goodness of God, has been condemned by one critic as 'rank Occamism,' and contrasted with the teaching of 'that marvellously profound, cautious, and temperate thinker,' Bishop Butler: it has been denounced by another, of a very different school, as 'destructive of healthful moral perception.' That the doctrine in question, instead of being opposed to Butler, is directly taken from him, may be seen by any one who will take the trouble to read the extract from the *Analogy* quoted at p. 158. But it is of little importance by what authority an opinion is sanctioned, if it will not itself stand the test of sound criticism. The admission, that a divine command may under certain circumstances justify an act which would not be justifiable without it, is condemned by some critics as holding out an available excuse for any crime committed under any circumstances. If God can suspend, on any one occasion, the ordinary obligations of morality, how, it is asked, are we to know whether any criminal may not equally claim a divine sanction for his crimes? Now where, as in the present instance, the supposed exceptions are expressly stated as supernatural ones, analogous to the miraculous suspension of the ordinary laws of nature, this objection either proves too much, or proves nothing at all. If we believe in the possibility of a supernatural Providence at all, we may also believe that God is able to authenticate His own mission by proper evidences. The objection has no special relation to questions of moral duty. It may be asked, in like manner, how we are to distinguish a true from a false prophet, or a preacher sent by God from one acting on his own responsibility. The possibility of a special divine mission of any kind will of course be denied by those who reject the supernatural altogether; but this denial removes the question into an entirely different province of inquiry, where it has no relation to any peculiar infallibility supposed to attach to the moral reason above the other faculties of the human mind.

[*The Limits of Religious Thought*, 4th edn. (London: John Murray, 1859), pp. xi–xv.]

JOHN STUART MILL

77 The Infinite Goodness of God

Accordingly Mr Mansel combats, as a heresy of his opponents, the opinion that infinite goodness differs only in degree from finite goodness. The notion 'that the attributes of God differ from those of man in degree only, not in kind, and hence that certain mental and moral qualities of which we are immediately conscious in ourselves, furnish at the same time a true and adequate image of the infinite perfections of God,' (the word *adequate* must have slipped in by inadvertence, since otherwise it would be an inexcusable misrepresentation) he identifies with 'the vulgar Rationalism which regards the reason of man, in its ordinary and normal operation, as the supreme criterion of religious truth.' And in characterizing the mode of arguing of this vulgar Rationalism, he declares its principles to be, that 'all the excellences of which we are conscious in the creature, must necessarily exist in the same manner, though in a higher degree, in the Creator. God is indeed more wise, more just, more merciful, than man; but for that very reason, his wisdom and justice and mercy must contain nothing that is incompatible with the corresponding attributes in their human character.' It is against this doctrine that Mr Mansel feels called on to make an emphatic protest.

Here, then, I take my stand on the acknowledged principle of logic and of morality, that when we mean different things we have no right to call them by the same name, and to apply to them the same predicates, moral and intellectual. Language has no meaning for the words Just, Merciful, Benevolent, save that in which we predicate them of our fellow-creatures; and unless that is what we intend to express by them, we have no business to employ the words. If in affirming them of God we do not mean to affirm these very qualities, differing only as greater in degree, we are neither philosophically nor morally entitled to affirm them at all. If it be said that the qualities are the same, but that we cannot conceive them as they are when raised to the infinite, I grant that we cannot adequately conceive them in one of their elements, their infinity. But we can conceive them in their other elements, which are the very same in the infinite as in the finite development. Anything carried to the infinite must have all the properties of the same thing as finite, except those which depend upon the finiteness. Among the many who have said that we cannot conceive infinite space, did any one ever suppose that it is *not* space? that it does not possess all the properties by which space is characterized? Infinite Space cannot be cubical or spherical, because these are modes of being bounded: but does any one imagine that in ranging through it we might arrive at some region which was not extended; of which one part was not outside another; where, though no Body intervened, motion was impossible; or where the sum of two sides of a triangle was less than the third side? The parallel assertion may be made respecting infinite goodness. What belongs to it either as Infinite or as Absolute I do not pretend to know; but I know that infinite goodness must be goodness, and that what is not consistent with goodness, is not consistent with infinite goodness. If in ascribing goodness to God I do not mean what I mean by good-ness; if I do not mean the goodness of which I have some knowledge, but an incomprehensible attribute of an incomprehensible substance, which for aught I know may be a totally different quality from that which I love and venerate— and even must, if Mr Mansel is to be believed, be in some important particulars opposed to this—what do I mean by calling it goodness? and what reason have I for venerating it? If I know nothing about what the attribute is, I cannot tell that it is a proper object of veneration. To say that God's goodness may be different in kind from man's goodness, what is it but saying, with a slight change of phraseology, that God may possibly not be good? To assert in words what we do not think in meaning, is as suitable a definition as can be given of a moral false-hood. Besides, suppose that certain unknown attributes are ascribed to the Deity in a religion the external evidences of which are so conclusive to my mind, as effectually to convince me that it comes from God. Unless I believe God to possess the same moral attributes which I find, in however inferior a degree, in a good man, what ground of assurance have I of God's veracity? All trust in a Revelation presupposes a conviction that God's attributes are the same, in all but degree, with the best human attributes.

If, instead of the 'glad tidings' that there exists a Being in whom all the excel-lences which the highest human mind can conceive, exist in a degree inconceiv-able to us, I am informed that the world is ruled by a being whose attributes are infinite, but what they are we cannot learn, nor what are the principles of his government, except that 'the highest human morality which we are capable of conceiving' does not sanction them; convince me of it, and I will bear my fate as I may. But when I am told that I must believe this, and at the same time call this being by the names which express and affirm the highest human morality, I say in plain terms that I will not. Whatever power such a being may have over me, there is one thing which he shall not do: he shall not compel me to worship him. I will call no being good, who is not what I mean when I apply that epithet to my fellow-creatures; and if such a being can sentence me to hell for not so calling him, to hell I will go.

[*An Examination of Sir William Hamilton's Philosophy*, ed. J. M. Robson, in *The Collected Works of John Stuart Mill* (London: Routledge and Kegan Paul, 1979), ix. 101–3.]

In determining, as above, the main features of Natural Religion, and distinguishing it from the religion of philosophy or civilization, I may be accused of having taken a course of my own, for which I have no sufficient warrant. Such an accusation does not give me much concern. Every one who thinks on these subjects takes a course of his own, though it will also happen to be the course which others take besides himself. The minds of many separately bear them forward in the same direction, and they are confirmed in it by each other. This I consider to be my own case; if I have mis-stated or omitted notorious facts in my account of Natural Religion, if I have contradicted or disregarded anything which He who speaks through my conscience has told us all directly from Heaven, then indeed I have acted unjustifiably and have something to unsay; but, if I have done no more than view the notorious facts of the case in the medium of my primary mental experiences, under the aspects which they spontaneously present to me, and with the aid of my best illative sense, I only do on one side of the question what those who think differently do on the other. As they start with one set of first principles, I start with another. I gave notice just now that I should offer my own witness in the matter in question; though of course it would not be worth while my offering it, unless what I felt myself agreed with what is felt by hundreds and thousands besides me, as I am sure it does, whatever be the measure, more or less, of their explicit recognition of it.

In thus speaking of Natural Religion as in one sense a matter of private judgment, and that with a view of proceeding from it to the proof of Christianity, I seem to give up the intention of demonstrating either. Certainly I do; not that I deny that demonstration is possible. Truth certainly, as such, rests upon grounds intrinsically and objectively and abstractedly demonstrative, but it does not follow from this that the arguments producible in its favour are unanswerable and irresistible. These latter epithets are relative, and bear upon matters of fact; arguments in themselves ought to do, what perhaps in the particular case they cannot do. The fact of revelation is in itself demonstrably true, but it is not therefore true irresistibly; else, how comes it to be resisted? There is a vast distance between what it is in itself, and what it is to us. Light is a quality of matter, as truth is of Christianity; but light is not recognized by the blind, and there are those who do not recognize truth, from the fault, not of truth, but of themselves. I cannot convert men, when I ask for assumptions which they refuse to grant to me; and without assumptions no one can prove anything about anything.

I am suspicious then of scientific demonstrations in a question of concrete fact, in a discussion between fallible men. However, let those demonstrate who have the gift; 'unusquisque in suo sensu abundet.' For me, it is more congenial to my own judgment to attempt to prove Christianity in the same informal way in which I can prove for certain that I have been born into this world, and that I shall die out of it. It is pleasant to my own feelings to follow a theological writer, such as Amort, who has dedicated to the great Pope, Benedict XIV, what he calls 'a new, modest, and easy way of demonstrating the Catholic Religion'. In this work he adopts the argument merely of the *greater* probability; I prefer to rely on that of an *accumulation* of various probabilities; but we both hold (that is, I hold with him), that from probabilities we may construct legitimate proof, sufficient for certitude. I follow him in holding, that, since a Good Providence watches over us, He blesses such means of argument as it has pleased Him to give us, in the nature of man and of the world, if we use them duly for those ends for which He has given them; and that, as in mathematics we are justified by the dictate of nature in withholding our assent from a conclusion of which we have not yet a strict logical demonstration, so by a like dictate we are not justified, in the case of concrete reasoning and especially of religious inquiry, in waiting till such logical demonstration is ours, but on the contrary are bound in conscience to seek truth and to look for certainty by modes of proof, which, when reduced to the shape of formal propositions, fail to satisfy the severe requisitions of science.

Here then at once is one momentous doctrine or principle, which enters into my own reasoning, and which another ignores, viz. the providence and intention of God; and of course there are other principles, explicit or implicit, which are in like circumstances. It is not wonderful then, that, while I can prove Christianity divine to my own satisfaction, I shall not be able to force it upon any one else. Multitudes indeed I ought to succeed in persuading of its truth without any force at all, because they and I start from the same principles, and what is a proof to me is a proof to them; but if any one starts from any other principles but ours, I have not the power to change his principles, or the conclusion which he draws from them, any more than I can make a crooked man straight. Whether his mind will ever grow straight, whether I can do anything towards its becoming straight, whether he is not responsible, responsible to his Maker, for being mentally crooked, is another matter; still the fact remains, that, in any inquiry about things in the concrete, men differ from each other, not so much in the soundness of their reasoning as in the principles which govern its exercise, that those principles are of a personal character, that where there is no common measure of minds, there is no common measure of arguments, and that the validity of proof is determined, not by any scientific test, but by the illative sense.

Accordingly, instead of saying that the truths of Revelation depend on those of Natural Religion, it is more pertinent to say that belief in revealed truths depends on belief in natural. Belief is a state of mind; belief generates belief; states of mind correspond to each other; the habits of thought and the reasonings which lead us on to a higher state of belief than our present, are the very same which we already possess in connexion with the lower state. Those Jews became Christians in Apostolic times who were already what may be called crypto-Christians; and those Christians in this day remain Christian only in name, and (if it so happen) at length fall away, who are nothing deeper or better than men of the world, *savants*, literary men, or politicians.

That a special preparation of mind is required for each separate department of inquiry and discussion (excepting, of course, that of abstract science) is strongly insisted upon in well-known passages of the Nicomachean ethics. Speaking of the variations which are found in the logical perfection of proof in various subject-matters, Aristotle says, 'A well-educated man will expect exactness in every class of subject, according as the nature of the thing admits; for it is much the same mistake to put up with a mathematician using probabilities, and to require demonstration of an orator. Each man judges skilfully in those things about which he is well-informed; it is of these that he is a good judge; viz. he, in each subject-matter, is a judge, who is well-educated in that subject-matter, and he is in an absolute sense a judge, who is in all of them well-educated.' Again: 'Young men come to be mathematicians and the like, but they cannot possess practical judgment; for this talent is employed upon individual facts, and these are learned only by experience; and a youth has not experience, for experience is only gained by a course of years. And so, again, it would appear that a boy may be a mathematician, but not a philosopher, or learned in physics, and for this reason,—because the one study deals with abstractions, while the other studies gain their principles from experience, and in the latter subjects youths do not give assent, but make assertions, but in the former they know what it is that they are handling.'

These words of a heathen philosopher, laying down broad principles about all knowledge, express a general rule, which in Scripture is applied authoritatively to the case of revealed knowledge in particular;—and that not once or twice only, but continually, as is notorious. For instance:—'I have understood,' says the Psalmist, 'more than all my teachers, because Thy testimonies are my meditation.' And so our Lord: 'He that hath ears, let him hear.' 'If any man will do His will, he shall know of the doctrine.' And 'He that is of God, heareth the words of God.' Thus too the Angels at the Nativity announce 'Peace to men of good will.' And we read in the Acts of the Apostles of 'Lydia, whose heart the Lord opened to attend to those things which were said by Paul.' And we are told on another occasion, that 'as many as were ordained,' or disposed by God, 'to life everlasting, believed.' And St John tells us, 'He that knoweth God, heareth us; he that is not of God, heareth us not; by this we know the spirit of truth, and the spirit of error.'

[*An Essay in Aid of the Grammar of Assent* (1840), ed. Nicholas Lash (Notre Dame, Ind.: University of Notre Dame Press, 1979), 318–23.]

Although I did not think much about the existence of a personal God until a considerably later period of my life, I will here give the vague conclusions to which I have been driven. The old argument from design in Nature, as given by Paley, which formerly seemed to me so conclusive, fails, now that the law of natural selection has been discovered. We can no longer argue that, for instance, the beautiful hinge of a bivalve shell must have been made by an intelligent being, like the hinge of a door by man. There seems to be no more design in the variability of organic beings, and in the action of natural selection, than in the course which the wind blows. But I have discussed this subject at the end of my book on the 'Variation of Domesticated Animals and Plants', and the argument there given has never, as far as I can see, been answered.

But passing over the endless beautiful adaptations which we everywhere meet with, it may be asked how can the generally beneficent arrangement of the world be accounted for? Some writers indeed are so much impressed with the amount of suffering in the world, that they doubt, if we look to all sentient beings, whether there is more of misery or of happiness; whether the world as a whole is a good or bad one. According to my judgment happiness decidedly prevails, though this would be very difficult to prove. If the truth of this conclusion be granted, it harmonizes well with the effects which we might expect from natural selection. If all the individuals of any species were habitually to suffer to an extreme degree, they would neglect to propagate their kind; but we have no reason to believe that this has ever, or at least often occurred. Some other considerations, moreover, lead to the belief that all sentient beings have been formed so as to enjoy, as a general rule, happiness.

Every one who believes, as I do, that all the corporeal and mental organs (excepting those which are neither advantageous nor disadvantageous to the possessor) of all beings have been developed through natural selection, or the survival of the fittest, together with use or habit, will admit that these organs have been formed so that their possessors may compete successfully with other beings, and thus increase in number. Now an animal may be led to pursue that course of action which is most beneficial to the species by suffering, such as pain, hunger, thirst, and fear; or by pleasure, as in eating and drinking, and in the propagation of the species, &c.; or by both means combined, as in the search for food. But pain or suffering of any kind, if long continued, causes depression and lessens the power of action, yet is well adapted to make a creature guard itself against any great or sudden evil. Pleasurable sensations, on the other hand, may be long continued without any depressing effect; on the contrary, they stimulate the whole system to increased action. Hence it has come to pass that most or all sentient beings have been developed in such a manner, through natural selection, that pleasurable sensations serve as their habitual guides. We see this in the pleasure from exertion, even occasionally from great exertion of the body or mind,—in the pleasure of our daily meals, and especially in the pleasure derived from sociability, and from loving our families. The sum of such pleasures as these, which are habitual or frequently recurrent, give, as I can hardly doubt, to most sentient beings an excess of happiness over misery, although many occasionally suffer much. Such suffering is quite compatible with the belief in Natural Selection, which is not perfect in its action, but tends only to render each species as successful as possible in the battle for life with other species, in wonderfully complex and changing circumstances.

That there is much suffering in the world no one disputes. Some have attempted to explain this with reference to man by imagining that it serves for his moral improvement. But the number of men in the world is as nothing compared with that of all other sentient beings, and they often suffer greatly without any moral improvement. This very old argument from the existence of suffering against the existence of an intelligent First Cause seems to me a strong one; whereas, as just remarked, the presence of much suffering agrees well with the view that all organic beings have been developed through variation and natural selection.

At the present day the most usual argument for the existence of an intelligent God is drawn from the deep inward conviction and feelings which are experienced by most persons.

Formerly I was led by feelings such as those just referred to (although I do not think that the religious sentiment was ever strongly developed in me), to the firm conviction of the existence of God, and of the immortality of the soul. In my Journal I wrote that whilst standing in the midst of the grandeur of a Brazilian forest, 'it is not possible to give an adequate idea of the higher feelings of wonder, admiration, and devotion, which fill and elevate the mind.' I well remember my conviction that there is more in man than the mere breath of his body. But now the grandest scenes would not cause any such convictions and feelings to rise in my mind. It may be truly said that I am like a man who has become colour-blind, and the universal belief by men of the existence of redness makes my present loss of perception of not the least value as evidence. This argument would be a valid one if all men of all races had the same inward conviction of the existence of one God; but we know that this is very far from being the case. Therefore I cannot see that such inward convictions and feelings are of any weight as evidence of what really exists. The state of mind which grand scenes formerly excited in me, and which was intimately connected with a belief in God, did not essentially differ from that which is often called the sense of sublimity; and however difficult it may be to explain the genesis of this sense, it can hardly be advanced as an argument for the existence of God, any more than the powerful though vague and similar feelings excited by music.

With respect to immortality, nothing shows me [so clearly] how strong and almost instinctive a belief it is, as the consideration of the view now held by most physicists, namely, that the sun with all the planets will in time grow too cold for life, unless indeed some great body dashes into the sun, and thus gives it fresh life. Believing as I do that man in the distant future will be a far more perfect creature than he now is, it is an intolerable thought that he and all other sentient beings are doomed to complete annihilation after such long-continued slow progress. To those who fully admit the immortality of the human soul, the destruction of our world will not appear so dreadful.

Another source of conviction in the existence of God, connected with the reason, and not with the feelings, impresses me as having much more weight. This follows from the extreme difficulty or rather impossibility of conceiving this immense and wonderful universe, including man with his capacity of looking far backwards and far into futurity, as the result of blind chance or necessity. When thus reflecting I feel compelled to look to a First Cause having an intelligent mind in some degree analogous to that of man; and I deserve to be called a Theist. This conclusion was strong in my mind about the time, as far as I can remember, when I wrote the 'Origin of Species;' and it is since that time that it has very gradually, with many fluctuations, become weaker. But then arises the doubt, can the mind of man, which has, as I fully believe, been developed from a mind as low as that possessed by the lowest animals, be trusted when it draws such grand conclusions?

I cannot pretend to throw the least light on such abstruse problems. The mystery of the beginning of all things is insoluble by us; and I for one must be content to remain an Agnostic.

[*Life and Letters of Charles Darwin*, ed. F. Darwin (London: John Murray, 1888), i. 309–13.]

BENJAMIN WARFIELD

80   Darwin and Design

[Darwin's] settled conviction of the sufficiency of natural selection to account for all differentiations in organic forms deeply affected Mr Darwin's idea of God and of His relation to the world. His notion at this time (1859), while theistic, appears to have been somewhat crassly deistic. He seems never to have been able fully to grasp the conception of divine immanence; but from the opening of his first notebook on Species to the end of his days he gives ever repeated reason to the reader to fear that the sole conceptions of God in His relation to the universe which were possible to him were either that God should do all things without second causes, or, having ordained second causes, should sit outside and beyond them and leave them to do all things without Him. Beginning with this deistic conception, which pushed God out of His works, it is perhaps not strange that he could never be sure that he saw Him in His works; and when he could trace effects to a 'natural cause' or group a body of phenomena under a 'natural law,' this seemed to him equivalent to disproving the connection of God with them. The result was that the theistic proofs gradually grew more and more meaningless to him, until, at last, no one of them carried conviction to his mind.

Sir Charles Lyell was not left alone in his efforts to clarify Mr Darwin's thinking on such subjects; soon Dr Asa Gray took his place by his side and became at once the chief force in the endeavour. Nevertheless, Mr Darwin outlines already in a letter to Lyell in 1860 the arguments by which he stood unto the end. 'I must say one more word,' he writes, 'about our quasi-theological controversy about natural selection. . . . Do you consider that the successive variations in the size of the crop of the Pouter Pigeon, which man has accumulated to please his caprice, have been due to "the creative and sustaining powers of Brahma"? In the sense that an omnipotent and omniscient Deity must order and know everything, this must be admitted; yet, in honest truth, I can hardly admit it. It seems preposterous that a maker of a universe should care about the crop of a pigeon solely to please man's silly fancies. But if you agree with me in thinking such an interposition of the Deity uncalled for, I can see no reason whatever for believing in such interpositions in the case of natural beings, in which strange and admirable peculiarities have been naturally selected for the creature's own benefit. Imagine a Pouter in a state of nature wading into the water, and then, being buoyed up by its inflated crop, sailing about in search of food. What admiration this would have excited—adaptation to the laws of hydrostatic pressure, etc. For the life of me I cannot see any difficulty in natural selection producing the most exquisite structure, *if such structure can be arrived at by gradation*, and I know from experience how hard it is to name any structure towards which at least some gradations are not known. . . . P.S.—The conclusion at which I have come, as I have told Asa Gray, is that such a question, as is touched on in this note, is beyond the human intellect, like "predestination and free will," or the "origin of evil."' There is much confused thought in this letter; but it concerns us now only to note that Mr Darwin's difficulty arises on the one side from his inability to conceive of God as immanent in the universe and his consequent total misapprehension of the nature of divine providence, and on the other from a very crude notion of final cause which posits a single extrinsic end as the sole purpose of the Creator. No one would hold to a doctrine of divine 'interpositions' such as appears to him here as the only alternative to divine absence. And no one would hold to a teleology of the raw sort which he here has in mind—a teleology which finds the end for which a thing exists in the misuse or abuse of it by an outside selecting agent. Mr Darwin himself felt a natural mental inability for dealing with such themes, and accordingly wavered long as to the attitude he ought to assume toward the evidences of God's hand in nature. Thus he wrote in May, 1860, to Dr Gray: 'With respect to the theological view of the question. This is always painful to me. I am bewildered. I had no intention to write atheistically. But I own that I cannot see as plainly as others do, and as I should wish to do, evidence of design and beneficence on all sides of us. There seems to me too much misery in the world. I cannot persuade myself that a beneficent and omnipotent God would have designedly created the Ichneumonidæ with the express intention of their feeding within the living bodies of Caterpillars, or that a cat should play with mice. Not believing this, I see no necessity in the belief that the eye was expressly designed. On the other hand, I cannot anyhow be contented to view this wonderful universe, and especially the nature of man, and to conclude that everything is the result of brute force. I am inclined to look at everything as resulting from designed laws, with the details, whether good or bad, left to the working out of what we may call chance. Not that this notion *at all* satisfies me. I feel most deeply that the whole subject is too profound for the human intellect. A dog might as well speculate on the mind of Newton. Let each man hope and believe what he can. Certainly I agree with you that my views are not at all necessarily atheistical. The lightning kills a man, whether a good one or bad one, owing to the excessively complex action of natural laws. A child (who may turn out an idiot) is born by the action of even more complex laws, and I can see no reason why a man, or other animal, may not have been aboriginally produced by other laws, and that all these laws may have been expressly designed by an omniscient Creator, who foresaw every future event and consequence. But the more I think the more bewildered I become; as indeed I have probably shown by this letter.' The reasoning of this extract, which supposes that the fact that a result is secured by appropriate conditions furnishes ground for regarding it as undesigned, is less suitable to a grave thinker than to a redoubtable champion like Mr Allan Quartermain, who actually makes use of it. 'At last he was dragged forth uninjured, though in a very pious and prayerful frame of mind,' he is made to say of a negro whom he had saved by killing an attacking buffalo; 'his "spirit had certainly looked that way," he said, or he would now have been dead. As I never like to interfere with true piety, I did not venture to suggest that his spirit had deigned to make use of my eight-bore in his interest.' Dr Gray appears to have rallied his correspondent in his reply, on his notion of an omniscient and omnipotent Creator, foreseeing all future events and consequences, and yet not responsible for the results of the laws which He ordains. At all events, Mr Darwin writes him again in July of the same year: 'One word more on "designed laws" and "undesigned results." I see a bird which I want for food, take my gun and kill it—I do this *designedly*. An innocent and good man stands under a tree and is killed by a flash of lightning. Do you believe (and I really should like to hear) that God *designedly* killed this man? Many or most people do believe this; I can't and don't. If you believe so, do you believe that when a swallow snaps up a gnat that God designed that that particular swallow should snap up that particular gnat at that particular instant? I believe that the man and the gnat are in the same predicament. If the death of neither man nor gnat are designed, I see no good reason to believe that their *first* birth or production should be necessarily designed.' We read such words with almost as much bewilderment as Mr Darwin says he wrote them with. It is almost incredible that he should have so inextricably confused the two senses of the word 'design'—so as to confound the question of intentional action with that of the evidences of contrivance, the question of the existence of a general plan in God's mind, in accordance with which all things come to pass, with that of the existence of marks of His hand in creation arising from intelligent adaptation of means to ends. It is equally incredible that he should present the case of a partic-ular swallow snapping up a particular gnat at a particular time as (to use his own words) 'a poser,' when he could scarcely have already forgotten that all Chris-tians, at least, have long since learned to understand that the care of God extends as easily to the infinitely little as to the infinitely great; that the very hairs of our head are numbered, and not one sparrow falls to the ground unnoted by our Heavenly Father. Yet this seems to him so self-evidently unbe-lievable, that he rests his case against God's direction of the line of develop-ment—for this is really what he is arguing against here—on its obvious incredibility.

['Charles Darwin's Religious Life', in *Studies in Theology* (New York: Oxford University Press, 1932), 556–61.]

The Twentieth Century: I. Faith and Hard Science

INTRODUCTION

This is the first of three sections devoted to twentieth-century discussions of philosophical issues raised by the dialogue between faith and reason. The divisions between these sections are somewhat arbitrary, and the reader can expect to find considerable overlap between them. Because we are dealing with contemporary or near-contemporary authors, in many cases the issues are a matter of ongoing debate. I have tried to make selections and to group the material so as to give a sense of this continuing dialogue and to make an informed guess as to what is likely to be of abiding interest in the field. For this reason the character of the last three sections differs from the first six in which I was more concerned to give extracts characteristic and representative of particular eras or centuries. The twentieth century, and particularly the second half of it, has seen not only the continuing increase in the findings and prestige of natural science, but the rise of scientific speculation which claims, in effect, that in certain areas scientific findings can and have supplanted traditional metaphysical reasoning. This amounts to the claim that in the debate between faith and reason the role of reason is taken by science and faith, if it does not completely atrophy, is faith in science and not faith in God. Insofar as it is faith in God then, it is claimed, science has shown such faith to be misplaced and unnecessary.

In this section there are three kinds of extracts. In the first selection we take up where we left off in the previous section, the impact of Darwinism upon religion and particularly upon the metaphysics of theism. It is a characteristic of some proponents of Darwinian evolution, as of Darwin himself, to argue that the fact of random natural selection excludes the possibility of divine design, and also to claim that human rationality and sensibility are the products of the processes of random mutation in environments which are sufficiently favourable. The claims of evolutionists that the theory has usurped the idea of design have intensified in the twentieth century, and we look at one representative statement of this, from Richard Dawkins, and critical responses from Alvin Plantinga and Peter van Inwagen. John Leslie thinks that the anthropic principle might now play the role of what William Paley earlier referred to as the 'contrivances of nature'.

In the second selection we sample some of the claims of science to (in Stephen Hawking's phrase) know 'the mind of God' in the sense of providing a final explanation of the existence and nature of the universe. But what exactly does this mean? Does it mean that the universe, if it existed at all, had to exist in precisely the form that it does exist? Presumably it does not mean that the universe, this universe, could not have failed to have existed. Keith Ward raises doubts about Hawking's claim. If such a final explanation from within science were to be possible, then although God might exist he would have no role to perform, and it would be in principle impossible to prove his existence by an appeal to the contingency of the universe in the way in which cosmological arguments for his existence have attempted, since there is nothing left for God to explain. William Craig argues, by contrast, that science and metaphysics converge in stressing the contingency of the universe, that everything that begins to be, including the universe, must have a cause.

These debates between faith and scientific reason, often of an extremely speculative turn, can be said to have brought the debate between faith and reason full circle. For they are new phases to old debates about the perennial question, is the universe just there, or is there some explanation for its physical character, and for its very existence? Could there be a scientific answer to these questions, an explanation that is in some sense internal to the character of the universe, or must there be (or may there be) an explanation in terms of the existence of God?

The root philosophical issue in all of these debates is over naturalism, over whether everything that exists could be explained naturalistically. The section concludes with an exchange between Smart and Haldane on this basic question.

We have dealt with all the alleged alternatives to the theory of natural selection except the oldest one. This is the theory that life was created, or its evolution master-minded, by a conscious designer. It would obviously be unfairly easy to demolish some particular version of this theory such as the one (or it may be two) spelled out in Genesis. Nearly all peoples have developed their own creation myth, and the Genesis story is just the one that happened to have been adopted by one particular tribe of Middle Eastern herders. It has no more special status than the belief of a particular West African tribe that the world was created from the excrement of ants. All these myths have in common that they depend upon the deliberate intentions of some kind of supernatural being.

At first sight there is an important distinction to be made between what might be called 'instantaneous creation' and 'guided evolution'. Modern theologians of any sophistication have given up believing in instantaneous creation. The evidence for some sort of evolution has become too overwhelming. But many theologians who call themselves evolutionists, for instance the Bishop of Birmingham quoted in Chapter 2, smuggle God in by the back door: they allow him some sort of supervisory role over the course that evolution has taken, either influencing key moments in evolutionary history (especially, of course, *human* evolutionary history), or even meddling more comprehensively in the day-to-day events that add up to evolutionary change.

We cannot disprove beliefs like these, especially if it is assumed that God took care that his interventions always closely mimicked what would be expected from evolution by natural selection. All that we can say about such beliefs is, firstly, that they are superfluous and, secondly, that they *assume* the existence of the main thing we want to *explain*, namely organized complexity. The one thing that makes evolution such a neat theory is that it explains how organized complexity can arise out of primeval simplicity.

If we want to postulate a deity capable of engineering all the organized complexity in the world, either instantaneously or by guiding evolution, that deity must already have been vastly complex in the first place. The creationist, whether a naïve Bible-thumper or an educated bishop, simply *postulates* an already existing being of prodigious intelligence and complexity. If we are going to allow ourselves the luxury of postulating organized complexity without offering an explanation, we might as well make a job of it and simply postulate the existence of life as we know it! In short, divine creation, whether instantaneous or in the form of guided evolution, joins the list of other theories we have considered in this chapter. All give some superficial appearance of being alternatives to Darwinism, whose merits might be tested by an appeal to evidence.

All turn out, on closer inspection, not to be rivals of Darwinism at all. The theory of evolution by cumulative natural selection is the only theory we know of that is in principle *capable* of explaining the existence of organized complexity. Even if the evidence did not favour it, it would *still* be the best theory available! In fact the evidence does favour it. But that is another story.

Let us hear the conclusion of the whole matter. The essence of life is statistical improbability on a colossal scale. Whatever is the explanation for life, therefore, it cannot be chance. The true explanation for the existence of life must embody the very antithesis of chance. The antithesis of chance is nonrandom survival, properly understood. Nonrandom survival, improperly understood, is not the antithesis of chance, it is chance itself. There is a continuum connecting these two extremes, and it is the continuum from single-step selection to cumulative selection. Single-step selection is just another way of saying pure chance. This is what I mean by nonrandom survival improperly understood. *Cumulative selection*, by slow and gradual degrees, is the explanation, the only workable explanation that has ever been proposed, for the existence of life's complex design.

The whole book has been dominated by the idea of chance, by the astronomically long odds against the spontaneous arising of order, complexity and apparent design. We have sought a way of taming chance, of drawing its fangs. 'Untamed chance', pure, naked chance, means ordered design springing into existence from nothing, in a single leap. It would be untamed chance if once there was no eye, and then, suddenly, in the twinkling of a generation, an eye appeared, fully fashioned, perfect and whole. This is possible, but the odds against it will keep us busy writing noughts till the end of time. The same applies to the odds against the spontaneous existence of any fully fashioned, perfect and whole beings, including—I see no way of avoiding the conclusion—deities.

To 'tame' chance means to break down the very improbable into less improbable small components arranged in series. No matter how improbable it is that an X could have arisen from a Y in a single step, it is always possible to conceive of a series of infinitesimally graded intermediates between them. However improbable a large-scale change may be, smaller changes are less improbable. And provided we postulate a sufficiently large series of sufficiently finely graded intermediates, we shall be able to derive anything from anything else, without invoking astronomical improbabilities. We are allowed to do this only if there has been sufficient time to fit all the intermediates in. And also only if there is a mechanism for guiding each step in some particular direction, otherwise the sequence of steps will career off in an endless random walk.

It is the contention of the Darwinian world-view that both these provisos are met, and that slow, gradual, cumulative natural selection is the ultimate explanation for our existence. If there are versions of the evolution theory that deny slow gradualism, and deny the central role of natural selection, they may be true in particular cases. But they cannot be the whole truth, for they deny the very heart of the evolution theory, which gives it the power to dissolve astronomical improbabilities and explain prodigies of apparent miracle.

[*The Blind Watchmaker* (Harmondsworth: Penguin, 1988), 316–18.]

ALVIN PLANTINGA

82   Evolution and True Belief

Most of us think (or would think on reflection) that at least *a* function or purpose of our cognitive faculties is to provide us with true beliefs. Moreover, we go on to think that when they function properly, in accord with our design plan, then for the most part they do precisely that. Qualifications are necessary, of course. There are various exceptions and special cases: visual illusions, mechanisms like forgetting the pain of childbirth, optimism about recovery not warranted by the relevant statistics, unintended conceptual by-products, and so on. There are also those areas of cognitive endeavour marked by enormous disagreement, wildly varying opinion: philosophy and Scripture scholarship come to mind. Here the sheer volume of disagreement and the great variety and contrariety of options proposed suggest that either not all of us are such that our cognitive faculties *do* function according to the design plan, in these areas, or that it is not the case that the relevant modules of the design plan are aimed at truth, or that the design plan for those areas is defective.

Nevertheless over a vast area of cognitive terrain we take it both that the purpose (function) of our cognitive faculties is to provide us with true or verisimilitudinous beliefs, and that, for the most part, that is just what they do. We suppose, for example, that most of the deliverances of memory are at least approximately correct. True, if you ask five witnesses how the accident happened, you may get five different stories. Still, they will agree that there was indeed an *accident*, and that it was an *automobile* accident (as opposed, say, to a naval disaster or a volcanic eruption); there will usually be agreement as to the number of vehicles involved (particularly if it is a small number), as well as the rough location of the accident (Aberdeen, Scotland, as opposed to Aberdeen, South Dakota), and so on. And all this is against the background of massive and much deeper agreement: that there are automobiles; that they do not disappear when no one is looking; that if released from a helicopter they fall down rather than up, that they are driven by people who use them to go places, that they are seldom driven by three-year-olds, that their drivers have purposes, hold beliefs, and often act on those purposes and beliefs, that few of them (or their drivers) have been more than a few miles from the surface of the earth, that the world has existed for a good long time—much longer than ten minutes, say—and a million more such Moorean truisms. (Of course, there is the occasional dissenter—in the grip, perhaps, of cognitive malfunction or a cognitively crippling philosophical theory.)

We think our faculties much better adapted to reach the truth in some areas than others; we are good at elementary arithmetic and logic, and the perception of middle-sized objects under ordinary conditions. We are also good at remembering certain sorts of things: I can easily remember what I had for breakfast this morning, where my office was located yesterday, and whether there was a large explosion in my house last night. Things get more difficult, however, when it comes to an accurate reconstruction of what it was like to be, say, a fifth century B.C. Greek (not to mention a bat), or whether the axiom of choice or the continuum hypothesis is true; things are even more difficult, perhaps, when it comes to figuring out how quantum mechanics is to be understood, and what the subnuclear realm of quark and gluon is really like, if indeed there really is a subnuclear realm of quark and gluon. Still, there remains a vast portion of our cognitive terrain where we think that our cognitive faculties do furnish us with truth.

But isn't there a problem, here, for the naturalist? At any rate for the naturalist who thinks that we and our cognitive capacities arrived upon the scene after some billions of years of evolution (by way of natural selection, genetic drift, and other blind processes working on such sources of genetic variation as random genetic mutation)? Richard Dawkins (according to Peter Medawar, 'one of the most brilliant of the rising generation of biologists') once leaned over and remarked to A. J. Ayer at one of those elegant, candle-lit, bibulous Oxford college dinners that he couldn't imagine being an atheist before 1859 (the year Darwin's Origin of Species was published); 'although atheism might have been logically tenable before Darwin,' said he, 'Darwin made it possible to be an intellectually fulfilled atheist.'

Now Dawkins thinks Darwin made it possible to be an intellectually fulfilled atheist. But perhaps Dawkins is dead wrong here. Perhaps the truth lies in the opposite direction. If our cognitive faculties have originated as Dawkins thinks, then their ultimate purpose or function (if they *have* a purpose or function) will be something like *survival* (of individual, species, gene, or genotype); but then it seems initially doubtful that among their functions—ultimate, proximate, or otherwise—would be the production of true beliefs. Taking up this theme, Patricia Churchland declares that the most important thing about the human brain is that it has evolved; hence, she says, its principal function is to enable the organism to *move* appropriately:

Boiled down to essentials, a nervous system enables the organism to succeed in the four F's: feeding, fleeing, fighting and reproducing. The principal chore of nervous systems is to get the body parts where they should be in order that the organism may survive. . . . Improvements in sensorimotor control confer an evolutionary advantage: a fancier style of representing is advantageous *so long as it is geared to the organism's way of life and enhances the organism's chances of survival* [Churchland's emphasis]. Truth, whatever that is, definitely takes the hindmost.

Her point, I think, is that (from a naturalistic perspective) what evolution guarantees is (at most) that we *behave* in certain ways—in such ways as to promote survival, or survival through childbearing age. The principal function or purpose, then, (the 'chore' says Churchland) of our cognitive faculties is not that of producing true or verisimilitudinous beliefs, but instead that of contributing to survival by getting the body parts in the right place. What evolution underwrites is only (at most) that our *behaviour* be reasonably adaptive to the circumstances in which our ancestors found themselves; hence (so far forth) it does not guarantee mostly true or verisimilitudinous beliefs. Of course our beliefs might be mostly true or verisimilitudinous (hereafter I'll omit the 'verisimilitudinous'); but there is no particular reason to think they *would* be: natural selection is interested not in truth, but in appropriate behaviour. What Churchland says suggests, therefore, that naturalistic evolution—that is, the conjunction of metaphysical naturalism with the view that we and our cognitive faculties have arisen by way of the mechanisms and processes proposed by contemporary evolutionary theory—gives us reason to doubt two things: (a) that a *purpose* of our cognitive systems is that of serving us with true beliefs, and (b) that they *do*, in fact, furnish us with mostly true beliefs.

W. v. O. Quine and Karl Popper, however, apparently demur. Popper argues that since we have evolved and survived, we may be pretty sure that our hypotheses and guesses as to what the world is like are mostly correct. And Quine says he finds encouragement in Darwin:

What does make clear sense is this other part of the problem of induction: why does our innate subjective spacing of qualities accord so well with the functionally relevant groupings in nature as to make our inductions tend to come out right? Why should our subjective spacing of qualities have a special purchase on nature and a lien on the future?

There is some encouragement in Darwin. If people's innate spacing of qualities is a gene-linked trait, then the spacing that has made for the most successful inductions will have tended to predominate through natural selection. Creatures inveterately wrong in their inductions have a pathetic but praiseworthy tendency to die before reproducing their kind.

Indeed, Quine finds a great deal more encouragement in Darwin than Darwin did. 'With me,' says Darwin,

the horrid doubt always arises whether the convictions of man's mind, which has been developed from the mind of the lower animals, are of any value or at all trustworthy. Would anyone trust in the convictions of a monkey's mind, if there are any convictions in such a mind?

So here we appear to have Quine and Popper on one side and Darwin and Churchland on the other. Who is right? But a prior question: what, precisely, is the issue? Darwin and Churchland seem to believe that (naturalistic) evolution gives one a reason to doubt that human cognitive faculties produce for the most part true beliefs: call this 'Darwin's Doubt'. Quine and Popper, on the other hand, apparently hold that evolution gives us reason to believe the opposite: that human cognitive faculties *do* produce for the most part true beliefs. How shall we understand this opposition?

[Warrant and Proper Function (Oxford: Oxford University Press, 1993), 216–19.]

PETER VAN INWAGEN

83 Genesis and Evolution

Let us now turn to the evolution of humanity, or, more exactly, to the evolution of those cognitive capacities that make humanity so strikingly different from all other species: I mean the capacities that allow us to do fantastic things like theoretical physics or evolutionary biology or drawing in perspective or, for that matter, making a promise or deciding not to plant wheat if there's a dry winter—things absolutely without analogues in any other species. The evolution of these capacities, unique in the history of life, is a phenomenon of microevolution, and, therefore, even if macroevolution involves other mechanisms than natural selection, it may be that our special cognitive capacities are entirely a product of natural selection. It must be understood that by 'cognitive capacities' I mean capacities determined by the physiology of the brain: not capacities that are conferred on one by one's culture and education, but capacities that are written on one's chromosomes. I think that no one doubts that our paleolithic ancestors—our ancestors of, say, thirty thousand years ago—had more or less the same cognitive capacities as we. A paleolithic infant, transported to our era by a time machine and raised in our culture, would be as likely to grow into a normal and useful member of our culture as an infant brought here by airplane from Tibet. Moreover, an immigrant paleolithic baby would be as likely to become a brilliant high-energy physicist or evolutionary biologist as an immigrant Tibetan baby. If this is true, then the cognitive capacities needed to master—and to excel at—any modern scientific discipline were already present, in more or less their present statistical distribution, among our paleolithic ancestors. (A race of mute, inglorious Miltons indeed!) And this means, according to the saganists, that these capacities evolved by the operation of natural selection among the ancestors of our paleolithic ancestors. And this, in its turn, implies that there was some character, or set of characters, such that (a) possession of those characters by some of its members conferred a reproductive advantage upon some population composed of our remote ancestors and (b) the presence of those characters within the present human population constitutes the biological basis of the human capacity for theoretical physics and evolutionary biology.

Have we any reason to think that there exists any set of characters having both these features? (Let us arbitrarily call a set of characters having both features *special*; I choose an arbitrary designation because an arbitrary designation is at least not tendentious.) If we have indeed evolved by natural selection from ancestors lacking the biological capacity to do physics and biology, then the answer to this question must be Yes; after all, we're here, and we are as we are. But if we set aside any conviction we may have that our cognitive capacities were produced by natural selection, can we discover any reason to believe that there exists—even as an abstract possibility—a 'special' set of characters? It might be said that we know that a special set exists because we can point to it: our collective name for it is 'intelligence.' Now 'intelligence' is a pretty vague concept, but not so vague that we can't see that this suggestion is wrong. I expect that no one would care to maintain that if (say) Albert Einstein and Thomas Mann had been switched in their cradles, Mann would have made fundamental contributions to physics—or even that he would have become a physicist. It is very doubtful whether Mann possessed (in however latent a form) the quality that Einstein's biographers call 'physical intuition,' a quality which Einstein possessed in an extraordinary degree and which even a run-of-the-mill physicist must possess in some degree. And yet it would be simply silly to say that Einstein was more *intelligent* than his fellow Nobel Prize winner. Einstein did not discover the general theory of relativity because he was so very bright—though doubtless high intelligence was a necessary condition for his achievement—but, insofar as a 'cause' can be named at all, because of his superb faculty of physical intuition. Couldn't we easily imagine a population whose members were as *intelligent* as we—if they were dispersed among us, we should hear them commended for their 'intelligence' with about the same frequency as we should hear the members of any randomly chosen group of our fellows commended—but who were as lacking in 'physical intuition' as the average accountant or philosopher or pure mathematician? (I mean, of course, to imagine a population that is *biologically* incapable of displaying any appreciable degree of physical intuition. No doubt certain genes must be present in an individual who possesses that enviable quality; what I want to imagine is a population of human beings within which some of these genes are so rare that the chance of the requisite combination of genes occurring in any of its members is negligible.) Couldn't such a population develop quite an impressive civilization—as impressive, say, as classical Chinese civilization or the civilization of ancient Egypt? The point raised by this question would seem to apply a fortiori to the reproductive success of such a population in a 'state of nature.' Why should a population with the gene frequencies I have imagined fare any worse in the forests or on the savannas than a population in which the genes that, in the right combination, yield the capacity for physical intuition are relatively numerous?

The saganists' answer to this question will, I think, go more or less as follows. 'You are making mysteries where none exist. You might as well make a mystery of my contention—and I do contend it—that the ability to play the cello is a product of natural selection. Isn't that mysterious, the mystery-monger asks, when there were no cellos, not even primitive cellos, on the primeval savannas? But the capacity to play the cello—that is, the biological capacity to be taught to play the cello in the right cultural circumstances, a biological capacity that was presumably about as frequent among our paleolithic ancestors as it is among us—is an aggregate of a lot of generally useful capacities. Two obvious ones are manual dexterity and the ability to discriminate pitches. Each was advantageous to our primitive ancestors, since they needed to chip flints and to interpret subtle changes in the chorus of insect noises in the forest night. We should also not neglect the fact that most, if not all, genes have many different effects on the constitution of the whole organism. It may therefore be that some of the genes whose co-presence in Einstein was responsible for his remarkable physical intuition were selected for in the remote past because of advantageous effects functionally unrelated to physical intuition. In sum, while we perhaps don't understand physical intuition all that well, there is no reason to doubt that its presence in a given present-day individual is due to a combination of genes that were, individually if not collectively, advantageous to our primitive ancestors.'

Well, if there is no reason to doubt this, is there any reason to believe it? If I wanted to pick someone to learn to chip flints or to interpret insect noises, I should certainly pick a cello player over someone who was all thumbs or someone who was tone-deaf. But if you know nothing about a certain person except that he or she is a first-rate theoretical physicist, what can you predict that that person will be good at—other than theoretical physics? You know that the physicist will be of high general intelligence, but you don't need to look for a physicist if you want intelligence. You know that the physicist will have a certain flair for thinking in terms of differential equations, though not necessarily a degree of mathematical ability that would excite the admiration of a mathematician. And that's about it. I don't suppose that you can predict that the physicist will have much in the way of spatial intuition (in the sense in which spatial intuition is required by an architectural draftsman). Nor is the physicist particularly likely to be a good mechanic or an accomplished inventor of mechanical devices or especially good at balancing a checkbook or counting cattle.

Quite possibly the first person to have the idea of the bow and arrow or to conceive the idea of making fire from the heat produced by friction would have to have had the qualities that would make a good physicist. Nevertheless, the intellectual conception of the great prehistoric inventions must have been a pretty rare occurrence; I can't see the great, but very rarely operative, advantages to a population of having in its gene pool the capacities for making such inventions as exerting much selection pressure on the population's gene pool. But let us concede that a population of modern human beings transported to some vastly ancient time (and divested of modern knowledge) would have had a distinct reproductive edge on otherwise similar populations that lacked the biological basis of physical intuition, owing to its capacity to invent the bow and arrow and fire-by-friction. This concession simply raises a further question: How did the gene frequencies that ground this capacity get established before—it must have been *before*—there was a relatively advanced technology to confer on them the opportunity to be advantageous? I find this question puzzling, but it may well have a plausible answer, and I don't want to let my case rest very heavily on the assumption that it has no plausible answer. I rest my case primarily on two further points.

First, *is* it all that clear that the idea of making fire by friction and the idea of understanding gravitation as a function of the curvature of space-time were arrived at by the exercise of the same cognitive capacity? 'This causes heat; greater heat than this causes fire; therefore doing this longer and harder may produce enough heat to cause fire' is a splendid piece of abstract reasoning. But is there any reason to believe that a population a few of whose members are capable of such reasoning must also contain a few people who are, genetically speaking, Newtons and Einsteins? I can see no reason to be confident about the answer to this question, one way or the other.

Secondly, the 'cello' analogy is deeply flawed. Cellos are human artifacts and are constructed to be playable by organisms that have such abilities as human beings happen to have. The structure of the science of physics is certainly not arbitrary in the way that the structure of a cello is. A race of intelligent beings descended from pigs rather than from primates might have invented stringed instruments radically different in structure from cellos and quite unplayable by human beings. And music itself is rather an arbitrary thing compared with science. If there are intelligent extraterrestrials who, like us, derive pleasure from listening to rhythmic sequences of sounds among which there are certain definite relations of pitch, it does not seem to be very reasonable to expect that we could make much of their sounds. To adapt an aphorism of Wittgenstein's, if a lion could sing, we shouldn't want to listen. But if extraterrestrials have invented physics, their physics will have to be a lot like ours. Extraterrestrial physics must resemble terrestrial physics because physical theories are about the real world, and the same real world confronts pig, primate, and extraterrestrial. And yet (to take one example of the sort of thing physicists look into) the structures of the various families of elementary particles, and the forces by which they interact, can hardly have had any sort of effect on the evolution of the cognitive capacities of our remote ancestors. There is no reason for the paleoanthropologist to learn about the decay modes of the $Z°$ boson in order to learn about how the brains of our ancestors evolved toward the possession of a capacity that is (among other things) a capacity to theorize about the decay modes of the $Z°$ boson. Our ability to do elementary-particle physics seems to me, therefore, to be as puzzling as our ability to play the cello would be if cellos were not artifacts but naturally occurring objects, objects whose occurrence in nature was wholly independent of the economy of *Homo habilis*. Suppose, for example, that cellos grew on trees and only in a part of the world never inhabited by our evolving ancestors. Wouldn't it be a striking coincidence that some of us could learn to play them so well? Isn't it a striking coincidence that we can theorize about elementary particles so well?

I once heard Noam Chomsky say that our ability to do physical science depends on a very specific set of cognitive capacities, and that, quite possibly, the reason that there are no real social sciences may be that we just happen to lack a certain equally specific set of cognitive capacities. He went on to speculate that we might one day discover among the stars a species as good at social science as we are at physical science and as bad at physical science as we are at social science. He did not raise the question why natural selection would bother to confer either of these highly specific sets of capacities on a species. (Presumably the answer would have to be that the right gene combinations for success in physical science were just part of the luck of our remote ancestors' draw and that, having arisen by chance, these gene combinations endured because they were in some way advantageous to our ancestors. But we have already been over this ground.) Einstein once remarked that the only thing that was unintelligible about the world was that it was intelligible. He was calling attention to the (or so it seemed to him) unreasonable simplicity of the laws of nature, and he supposed, I think, that the world was intelligible because it was simple. That does not seem to me to be quite right. The ultimate laws of nature may be simple, but that does not make them intelligible to highly intelligent people—Thomas Mann, say, or Virgil, or J. S. Mill, or Nietzsche—who lack the very specific set of cognitive capacities that enables physicists to pick their way through the flux of the phenomena to the deep simplicities. What is 'unintelligible' if anything in this area is, is that some of us should possess those capacities.

Saganists, therefore, owing to their adherence to natural selection as the sole engine of evolution, believe in what I have dubbed a 'special' set of characters—a set of characters that *both* conferred a reproduction advantage on some population of our remote ancestors *and* underlies our ability to do science. I, for reasons that I have tried to explain, am a skeptic about this. It seems to me that there is no very convincing argument a priori for the existence of a special set of characters and that the only argument a posteriori for its existence is that our scientific abilities could not be a consequence of natural selection unless such a set existed. For my part, however, I am going to suspend judgment about whether our scientific abilities are a consequence of natural selection till I see some reason to believe that there exists a special set of characters. Belief in a special set of characters, indeed, seems to me to be, in its epistemic features, very strongly analogous to belief in a Creator. More exactly, it is analogous to the type of belief in a Creator that is held by its adherents to rest on rational argument and public evidence—as opposed to private religious experience and historical revelation. There are, in my view, no *compelling* arguments for the existence or for the nonexistence of a Creator, no arguments that would force any-one who understood their premises to assent to their conclusion or else be ir-rational or perverse. There are compelling arguments for *some* conclusions: that the world is more than six thousand years old, for example, or that astrology is nonsense, but there are no compelling arguments for any conclusion of philo-sophical interest, whether its subject-matter be God or free will or universals or the nature of morality or anything else that philosophers have argued about. Nevertheless, there are some very *good* philosophical arguments: serious argu-ments which are worth the attention of serious thinkers and which lend a cer-tain amount of support to their conclusions. Among these, there are certain arguments having to do with God. The cosmological argument and the design argument, for example, appear to me to be arguments that are as good as any philosophical argument that has ever been adduced in support of any conclu-sion whatever. And yet the conclusions of these arguments (they are not quite the same) can be rejected by a perfectly rational person who understands per-fectly all the issues involved in evaluating them.

I very much doubt whether there is any argument for the existence of a spe-cial set of characters that is any better in this respect than the design argument or the cosmological argument. It may nevertheless be that certain people—pa-leoanthropologists, perhaps—know that a special set of characters exists. It may be that they know this because of their mastery of a vast range of data too complex to be summarized in anything so simple as a single argument. By the same token, however, it may be that there are certain people who know that a Creator exists and know this because of their mastery of a vast range of data too complex to be summarized in anything so simple as a single argument.

My own guess is that neither sort of knowledge exists. If there are people who *know* that there is a Creator, this must be due to factors other than (or, per-haps, in addition to) the inferences they have drawn from their observations of the natural world; and no one knows whether there is a special set of characters. Belief in a special set of characters is based on nothing more than a conviction that natural selection must be the ultimate basis of all evolutionary episodes (except those so minor that, if no explanation in terms of natural selection is ap-parent, they may plausibly be assigned to genetic drift). And that conviction, like the nineteenth-century conviction that the universe has always been much as it is at present, is one that is held mainly because of its supposed antitheistic implications. (Actually, it has no antitheistic implications, but it is widely be-lieved that it does.) Atheists often preach on the emotional attractiveness of the-ism. It needs to be pointed out that atheism is also a very attractive thesis. Very few people are atheists against their will. Atheism is attractive for at least two reasons. First, it is an attractive idea to suppose that one may well be one of the higher links in the Great Chain of Being—perhaps even the highest. (This idea is attractive for several reasons, not the least of which is that most people can-not quite rid themselves of the very well justified conviction that a being who knew all their motives and inmost thoughts might not entirely approve of them.) Secondly, there are very few atheists who do not admire themselves for possessing that combination of mental acuity and intellectual honesty that is, by their own grudging admission, the hallmark of atheists everywhere. The theist, however, is in a position to be an agnostic about the existence of a special set of characters, just as someone who accepts the saganists' science is in a position to be an agnostic about the existence of a Creator. Each is in a position to say, 'Well, I don't know. There may be such a thing. What are the arguments?'

[*God, Knowledge and Mystery* (Ithaca, NY: Cornell University Press, 1995), 152–9.]

JOHN LESLIE

84   Fine Tuning

9.1 If Chapter 2 was on anything like the right lines then the evidence of fine tuning is impressively strong. True, quite a few of the items listed may easily have been mistakes. Others of them, though, appear fairly well established. Even being wrong by factors of a thousand or a million would scarcely reduce the interest of many items when what is being claimed is a tuning accurate to one part in many billions of billions. Again, the sheer number of the claims is quite a strong insurance that not all of them are faulty. They were culled from the writings of experts. Physicists and cosmologists of today are little inclined to treat our universe's early conditions, and the physically and cosmologically important constants, as brute, inexplicable facts which are to be treated as 'natural' just because they characterize Nature as we find her. And they do not assume automatically that the same facts would be found in all physically possible universes. Instead they puzzle over such things as the early cosmic expansion speed, the cosmic smoothness, the excess of matter over antimatter, and so on.

Admittedly, many physicists and cosmologists are eager to show that this or that is dictated by physical principles so elegant that they just have to be right. There, after all, is the stuff of Nobel prizes. Yet it has come to look quaintly old-fashioned to take it for granted that absolutely all the main cosmic parameters will lend themselves to such treatment. For, first, we have long had indications that physics is probabilistic at a very basic level; second, we now have theories of symmetry breaking which show how force strengths and particle masses might vary probabilistically (2.52–.53; 4.19–.25), the Inflationary Cosmos supplying us with a mechanism which would allow even probabilistic affairs to be settled in the same way for as far out as our telescopes can probe; third, we also have fairly well-developed theories—that of Inflation is only one among many—which indicate that the region visible to us could very well be supplemented by vastly many other huge regions, 'universes' of the small-u kind; and fourth, fine tuning to Life's requirements would be easy to understand in the cases of *observable* universes if there were indeed vastly many universes and if their characteristics were very varied.

Surely no Principle of Pure Reason tells us that what we see *is not* subject to Observational Selection effects set up by Life's prerequisites: by the need, for example, for life-containing universes to be unturbulent or for their early expansion speeds to fall inside a narrow range, or for their force strengths and particle masses to be appropriately distributed. And evidence of fine tuning is plentiful enough to suggest that such observational selection effects are extremely important. (Remember, the words 'fine-tuning' are not being used in a way that begs the question of whether there is a divine Fine Tuner. *Evidence of fine tuning* just means (1.4) *evidence that living beings would not have evolved had fundamental conditions been slightly different.*)

At the very least, the apparent fine tuning would seem to reveal that if any theory dictates the values of absolutely all physical constants and other cosmologically important numbers then that theory is not 'so much simpler than its competitors that it just has to be right'. So far as concerns physics, this could be the book's most significant claim. One needs some kind of selection from a wider field: some selection *either* of life-encouraging numbers from among those allowed by a theory which is not all-dictating but leaves these numbers open to variation, most plausibly through random symmetry breaking, *or else* of a life-encouraging all-dictating theory taken from a field of more or less equally simple theories.

9.2 Now, one thing which the above paragraphs illustrate is that scientists try to build up world-pictures which are simple and consistent. Tidy hypotheses present themselves to their minds, together with ideas of what things they might well expect to discover were those hypotheses right. When they do then seem to discover such things, they look on the hypotheses as strengthened.

Still, other hypotheses might explain the same discoveries just as tidily. And in the case of the fine tuning, an account in terms of Multiple Worlds/universes plus Observational Selection may not be the sole one that deserves to be taken seriously. Much of the book has been concerned with two possible competitors. One of them is the God hypothesis: divine selection could replace Observational Selection. The other—it could be thought to have received oddly little attention in these pages when so many people would so much prefer it—is that any fine tuning is just an illusion of us Earthlings. Intelligent living organisms might often be very unlike those on Earth, and much less fussy in their requirements. They might stand in no need of chemistry, for example, or of planetary surfaces to inhabit.

9.3 It was argued (Chapter 8) that the God hypothesis is a strong one. God need not be viewed as a person whose existence and whose powers are utterly reasonless. One possibility is to treat the word 'God' in Neoplatonist fashion. God would then not be a person at all. God would be a creatively effective ethical requirement for the existence of a (good) universe or universes.

Again, even God-as-a-person would not have to exist reasonlessly. His existence, his benevolence, his knowledge, the creative efficacy of his acts of will, might all be accounted for in terms of their ethical requiredness.

There is nothing logically absurd in either of these positions. Just examining the concept of *an ethical requirement for the existence of something* cannot teach us that such a requirement will be creatively effective, yet neither does it reveal its ineffectiveness. *Requirements for the existence of things* could seem to be realities of the right general kind for creative tasks. And if ethical requirements were all of them creatively ineffective then, I reasoned, their *in*effectiveness would involve just as much ontological drama—just as many 'synthetic necessities' (8.6; 8.11[c])—as would their effectiveness.

True, the Problem of Evil presents a severe challenge to any belief in God. But instead of claiming that evils are unreal the theist can attribute them to conflicts between ethical requirements. (Some of the conflicts would be produced by our misuse of the good of free choice.) Moreover, the teachings of Experience are powerless to refute even Spinoza's theory that all experiences are those of a divine mind (8.18–.20). Knowing everything, such a mind would of course know just how it felt to be *you* and ignorant of many facts, including the fact that your thinkings were only elements in divine thinkings.

I have always felt very uncomfortable when suggesting that the Problem of Evil 'can be solved', i.e. that it fails to be decisive. One's gut feeling is that anyone who suggests this must be defending all manner of horrors. But although (as Hume so convincingly demonstrated) gut feelings have their place in philosophy, they oughtn't to be permitted to triumph immediately over even very strong counter-arguments. Now, the arguments against calling the Problem of Evil decisive do seem very strong.

The God hypothesis, besides being compatible with the hypothesis of multiple universes (for why should God be supposed to have created just a single universe?), can offer to explain affairs which that other hypothesis would appear to leave unexplained. It can offer to explain why natural laws are life-permitting, provided that such things as force strengths and particle masses take appropriate values (Chapter 3). Again, it can offer to explain why there is ever anything worth calling a natural law. *And* why there are things worth the name of *existing objects* (as distinct from mere possibilities and truths about them, e.g. the unconditionally true truth that it would be better that various unalleviatedly evil universes remained in the realm of mere possibility instead of taking on actual existence). Now, its potential ability to explain these affairs might encourage us to accept it despite the qualms that the Problem of Evil arouses.

This is in no way a denial that it ought to arouse them. The Problem of Evil is certainly strong enough to make theism an uncomfortable position. [. . .]

9.16 Associated with many philosophical demands for 'actual evidence' is grave head-shaking over 'mere Arguments from Analogy'. Even a defender of God and of Design will be struck, for instance, by how he can hit on 'nothing better than' the kind of analogical reasoning one might use in connection with Other Minds; now, of course nothing as weak as *that* could be useful for knocking sceptics down! So he will feel forced to adopt a tactic popular among modern defenders of religion, of saying that a way of looking on things, while of no earthly use for persuading any who are reluctant to share it, can still be 'not irrational', intellectually viable. New events experienced in accordance with this 'way of looking on things' can even strengthen it much as my initially disapproving attitude towards massacres may excite me to ever greater indignation as I watch them. Well, this book has certainly used analogies: firing squads and fishing and shooting at flies and being hit by arrows, buying a silk robe with a hole which the merchant's thumb is covering, seeing a sonnet which a monkey has typed, finding words in granite, and so forth. But that does not mean that it has been intended as just another addition to the literature of viable beliefs and attitudes.

'Argument from Analogy' tends to be used like 'Classical Physics'. If we still approve of a nineteenth-century way of doing physics then we call it 'modern physics' instead, and when we think an analogy strong then we talk of 'valid inductive generalization' or 'adopting a simple and consistent world-picture' rather than of 'reasoning analogically'. When analogical arguments are developed sensibly, the only thing wrong about them is their name. A great many of them are just means of reminding us about principles of everyday reasoning which we have managed to forget (7.9), but even those which are more nearly of the form, 'Thing number 1 has properties A, B, C, D, E; thing number 2 has properties A, B, C, D; and therefore thing number 2 quite probably has property E also', are not without their uses in a world in which no two apples, babies, or cats are ever precisely alike. Recognizing their uses is not equivalent to underwriting the move from 'My love is like a red, red rose' to 'My love will probably soon wither and die, as the rose will', neither need it lead straight to the conclusion that the world was designed by a blundering committee of demigods complete with the ulcers that torment human designers. Arguments from analogy only become disgracefully weak when they are handled in disgraceful ways. And there are sensible ways of handling the Design Argument while still leaving it as something perhaps worth classifying as an argument from analogy—although (7.8) that may well not be the most helpful way of classifying it.

9.17 It is high time we philosophers took the Design Argument seriously. Whether the evidence of fine tuning points to multiple universes or to God, it does do some exciting pointing; and it does it through being just the sort of evidence which too many of us have tended to dismiss as uninteresting. Too many philosophers construct such arguments as that if the universe were hostile to

Life then we shouldn't be here to see it, and that therefore there is nothing in fine tuning for anyone to get excited about; or that obviously there could be only the one universe and that therefore, because probability and improbability can be present only where repetitions are possible, its basic laws and conditions cannot be in any way 'improbable'. Again, too many have confused being rigorous with rejecting everything not directly observable.

My argument has been that the fine tuning is evidence, genuine evidence, of the following fact: *that God is real, and/or there are many and varied universes.* And it could be tempting to call the fact an observed one. Observed indirectly, but observed none the less.

[*Universes* (London: Routledge, 1989), 184–8.]

STEPHEN HAWKING

85   A Self-Contained Universe

We find ourselves in a bewildering world. We want to make sense of what we see around us and to ask: what is the nature of the universe? What is our place in it and where did it and we come from? Why is it the way it is?

To try to answer these questions we adopt some 'world picture'. Just as an infinite tower of tortoises supporting the flat earth is such a picture, so is the theory of superstrings. Both are theories of the universe, though the latter is much more mathematical and precise than the former. Both theories lack observational evidence: no-one has ever seen a giant tortoise with the earth on its back, but then, no-one has seen a superstring either. However, the tortoise theory fails to be a good scientific theory because it predicts that people should be able to fall off the edge of the world. This has not been found to agree with experience, unless that turns out to be the explanation for the people who are supposed to have disappeared in the Bermuda Triangle!

The earliest theoretical attempts to describe and explain the universe involved the idea that events and natural phenomena were controlled by spirits with human emotions who acted in a very humanlike and unpredictable manner. These spirits inhabited natural objects like rivers and mountains, including celestial bodies like the sun and moon. They had to be placated and their favours sought in order to ensure the fertility of the soil and the rotation of the seasons. Gradually, however, it must have been noticed that there were certain regularities: the sun always rose in the east and set in the west, whether or not a sacrifice had been made to the sun god. Further, the sun, the moon and the planets followed precise paths across the sky that could be predicted in advance with considerable accuracy. The sun and the moon might still be gods, but they were gods who obeyed strict laws, apparently without any exceptions, if one discounts stories like that of the sun stopping for Joshua.

At first, these regularities and laws were obvious only in astronomy and a few other situations. However, as civilization developed, and particularly in the last 300 years, more and more regularities and laws were discovered. The success of these laws led Laplace at the beginning of the nineteenth century to postulate scientific determinism, that is, he suggested that there would be a set of laws that would determine the evolution of the universe precisely, given its configuration at one time.

Laplace's determinism was incomplete in two ways. It did not say how the laws should be chosen and it did not specify the initial configuration of the universe. These were left to God. God would choose how the universe began and what laws it obeyed, but he would not intervene in the universe once it had started. In effect, God was confined to the areas that nineteenth-century science did not understand.

We now know that Laplace's hopes of determinism cannot be realized, at least in the terms he had in mind. The uncertainty principle of quantum mechanics implies that certain pairs of quantities, such as the position and velocity of a particle, cannot both be predicted with complete accuracy.

Quantum mechanics deals with this situation via a class of quantum theories in which particles don't have well-defined positions and velocities but are represented by a wave. These quantum theories are deterministic in the sense that they give laws for the evolution of the wave with time. Thus if one knows the wave at one time, one can calculate it at any other time. The unpredictable, random element comes in only when we try to interpret the wave in terms of the positions and velocities of particles. But maybe that is our mistake: maybe there are no particle positions and velocities, but only waves. It is just that we try to fit the waves to our preconceived ideas of positions and velocities. The resulting mismatch is the cause of the apparent unpredictability.

In effect, we have redefined the task of science to be the discovery of laws that will enable us to predict events up to the limits set by the uncertainty principle. The question remains, however: how or why were the laws and the initial state of the universe chosen?

In this book I have given special prominence to the laws that govern gravity, because it is gravity that shapes the large-scale structure of the universe, even though it is the weakest of the four categories of forces. The laws of gravity were incompatible with the view held until quite recently that the universe is unchanging in time: the fact that gravity is always attractive implies that the universe must be either expanding or contracting. According to the general theory of relativity, there must have been a state of infinite density in the past, the big bang, which would have been an effective beginning of time. Similarly, if the whole universe recollapsed, there must be another state of infinite density in the future, the big crunch, which would be an end of time. Even if the whole universe did not recollapse, there would be singularities in any localized regions that collapsed to form black holes. These singularities would be an end of time for anyone who fell into the black hole. At the big bang and other singularities, all the laws would have broken down, so God would still have had complete freedom to choose what happened and how the universe began.

When we combine quantum mechanics with general relativity, there seems to be a new possibility that did not arise before: that space and time together might form a finite, four-dimensional space without singularities or boundaries, like the surface of the earth but with more dimensions. It seems that this idea could explain many of the observed features of the universe, such as its large-scale uniformity and also the smaller-scale departures from homogeneity, like galaxies, stars, and even human beings. It could even account for the arrow of time that we observe. But if the universe is completely self-contained, with no singularities or boundaries, and completely described by a unified theory, that has profound implications for the role of God as Creator.

Einstein once asked the question: 'How much choice did God have in constructing the universe?' If the no boundary proposal is correct, he had no freedom at all to choose initial conditions. He would, of course, still have had the freedom to choose the laws that the universe obeyed. This, however, may not really have been all that much of a choice; there may well be only one, or a small number, of complete unified theories, such as the heterotic string theory, that are self-consistent and allow the existence of structures as complicated as human beings who can investigate the laws of the universe and ask about the nature of God.

Even if there is only one possible unified theory, it is just a set of rules and equations. What is it that breathes fire into the equations and makes a universe for them to describe? The usual approach of science of constructing a mathematical model cannot answer the questions of why there should be a universe for the model to describe. Why does the universe go to all the bother of existing? Is the unified theory so compelling that it brings about its own existence? Or does it need a creator, and, if so, does he have any other effect on the universe? And who created him?

Up to now, most scientists have been too occupied with the development of new theories that describe *what* the universe is to ask the question *why*. On the other hand, the people whose business it is to ask *why*, the philosophers, have not been able to keep up with the advance of scientific theories. In the eighteenth century, philosophers considered the whole of human knowledge, including science, to be their field and discussed questions such as: did the universe have a beginning? However, in the nineteenth and twentieth centuries, science became too technical and mathematical for the philosophers, or anyone else except a few specialists. Philosophers reduced the scope of their enquiries so much that Wittgenstein, the most famous philosopher of this century, said, 'The sole remaining task for philosophy is the analysis of language.' What a comedown from the great tradition of philosophy from Aristotle to Kant!

However, if we do discover a complete theory, it should in time be understandable in broad principle by everyone, not just a few scientists. Then we shall all, philosophers, scientists and just ordinary people, be able to take part in the discussion of the question of why it is that we and the universe exist. If we find the answer to that, it would be the ultimate triumph of human reason—for then we would know the mind of God.

[*A Brief History of Time* (London: Bantam Books, 1995), 189–93.]

WILLIAM LANE CRAIG

86   The Beginning of the Universe

Premiss (1) ['Whatever begins to exist has a cause of its existence'] strikes me as relatively non-controversial. It is based on the metaphysical intuition that something cannot come out of nothing. Hence, any argument for the principle is apt to be less obvious than the principle itself. Even the great skeptic David Hume admitted that he never asserted so absurd a proposition as that something might come into existence without a cause; he only denied that one could *prove* the obviously true causal principle. With regard to the universe, if originally there were absolutely *nothing*—no God, no space, no time—, then how could the universe possibly come to exist? The truth of the principle *ex nihilo, nihil fit* is so obvious that I think we are justified in foregoing an elaborate defense of the argument's first premiss.

Nevertheless, some thinkers, exercised to avoid the theism implicit in this premiss within the present context, have felt driven to deny its truth. In order to avoid its theistic implications, [Paul] Davies presents a scenario which, he confesses, 'should not be taken too seriously,' but which seems to have a powerful attraction for Davies. He has reference to a quantum theory of gravity according to which space-time itself could spring uncaused into being out of absolutely nothing. While admitting that there is 'still no satisfactory theory of quantum gravity,' such a theory 'would allow spacetime to be created and destroyed spontaneously and uncaused in the same way that particles are created and destroyed spontaneously and uncaused. The theory would entail a certain mathematically determined probability that, for instance, a blob of space would appear where none existed before. Thus, spacetime could pop out of nothingness as the result of a causeless quantum transition.'

Now in fact particle pair production furnishes no analogy for this radical *ex nihilo* becoming, as Davies seems to imply. This quantum phenomenon, even if an exception to the principle that every event has a cause, provides no analogy to something's coming into being out of nothing. Though physicists speak of this as particle pair creation and annihilation, such terms are philosophically misleading, for all that actually occurs is conversion of energy into matter or vice versa. As Davies admits, 'The processes described here do not represent the creation of matter out of nothing, but the conversion of pre-existing energy into material form.' Hence, Davies greatly misleads his reader when he claims that 'Particles . . . can appear out of nowhere without specific causation' and again, 'Yet the world of quantum physics routinely produces something for nothing.' On the contrary, the world of quantum physics *never* produces something for nothing.

But to consider the case on its own merits: quantum gravity is so poorly understood that the period prior to 10^{-43} sec, which this theory hopes to describe, has been compared by one wag to the regions on the maps of the ancient cartographers marked 'Here there be dragons': it can easily be filled with all sorts of fantasies. In fact, there seems to be no good reason to think that such a theory would involve the sort of spontaneous becoming *ex nihilo* which Davies suggests. A quantum theory of gravity has the goal of providing a theory of gravitation based on the exchange of particles (gravitons) rather than the geometry of space, which can then be brought into a Grand Unification Theory that unites all the forces of nature into a supersymmetrical state in which one fundamental force and a single kind of particle exist. But there seems to be nothing in this which suggests the possibility of spontaneous becoming *ex nihilo*.

Indeed, it is not at all clear that Davies's account is even intelligible. What can be meant, for example, by the claim that there is a mathematical probability that nothingness should spawn a region of spacetime 'where none existed before?' It cannot mean that given enough time a region of spacetime would pop into existence at a certain place, since neither place nor time exist apart from spacetime. The notion of some probability of something's coming out of nothing thus seems incoherent.

I am reminded in this connection of some remarks made by A. N. Prior concerning an argument put forward by Jonathan Edwards against something's coming into existence uncaused. This would be impossible, said Edwards, because it would then be inexplicable why just any and everything cannot or does not come to exist uncaused. One cannot respond that only things of a certain nature come into existence uncaused, since prior to their existence they have no nature which could control their coming to be. Prior made a cosmological application of Edwards's reasoning by commenting on the steady state model's postulating the continuous creation of hydrogen atoms *ex nihilo*:

It is no part of Hoyle's theory that this process is causeless, but I want to be more definite about this, and to say that if it is causeless, then what is alleged to happen is fantastic and incredible. If it is possible for objects—objects, now, which really are objects, 'substances endowed with capacities'—to start existing without a cause, then it is incredible that they should all turn out to be objects of the same sort, namely, hydrogen atoms. The peculiar nature of hydrogen atoms cannot possibly be what makes such starting-to-exist possible for them but not for objects of any other sort; for hydrogen atoms do not have this nature until they are there to have it, i.e. until their starting-to-exist has already occurred. That is Edwards's argument, in fact; and here it does seem entirely cogent.

Now in the case at hand, if originally absolutely nothing existed, then why should it be spacetime that springs spontaneously out of the void, rather than, say, hydrogen atoms or even rabbits? How can one talk about the probability of any particular thing's popping into being out of nothing?

Davies on one occasion seems to answer as if the laws of physics are the controlling factor which determines what may leap uncaused into being: 'But what of the laws? They have to be "there" to start with so that the universe can come into being. Quantum physics has to exist (in some sense) so that a quantum transition can generate the cosmos in the first place.' Now this seems exceedingly peculiar. Davies seems to attribute to the laws of nature themselves a sort of ontological and causal status such that they constrain spontaneous becoming. But this seems clearly wrong-headed: the laws of physics do not themselves cause or constrain anything; they are simply propositional descriptions of a certain form and generality of what does happen in the universe. And the issue Edwards raises is why, if there were absolutely nothing, it would be true that any one thing rather than another should pop into being uncaused? It is futile to say it somehow belongs to the nature of spacetime to do so, for if there were absolutely nothing then there would have been no nature to determine that spacetime should spring into being.

Even more fundamentally, however, what Davies envisions is surely metaphysical nonsense. Though his scenario is cast as a scientific theory, someone ought to be bold enough to say that the Emperor is wearing no clothes. Either the necessary and sufficient conditions for the appearance of space-time existed or not; if so, then it is not true that nothing existed; if not, then it would seem ontologically impossible that being should arise out of absolute non-being. To call such spontaneous springing into being out of non-being a 'quantum transition' or to attribute it to 'quantum gravity' explains nothing; indeed, on this account, there is no explanation. It just happens.

It seems to me, therefore, that Davies has not provided any plausible basis for denying the truth of the cosmological argument's first premiss. That whatever begins to exist has a cause would seem to be an ontologically necessary truth, one which is constantly confirmed in our experience.

[*Truth*, 3 (1991), 92–4.]

The question of whether or not this universe had a first moment of time is still not directly relevant to the question of whether it is created.

This may be clearer if one considers attempts to remove the initial singularity from cosmology by including it as a factor in a wider quantum-gravitational theory. In recent physics, this has been done in two main ways, by a quantum fluctuation theory and by the Hartle-Hawking model. On the quantum fluctuation view, matter originates by spontaneous quantum fluctuations in a vacuum (i.e. in the quiescent state of the background quantum fields). On this view, however, it is only matter that originates. What is presupposed as already existent is a background space-time, with quantum fields and laws of nature in operation. It is not, as is sometimes suggested, origination 'out of nothing', for space-time, quantum fields, and basic laws of nature remain as very definitely something, even if not material in the ordinary sense.

The Hartle-Hawking model goes further, in seeking to eliminate the background space-time, and generates the temporal process of this universe out of a wider timeless domain of three-spaces linked in 'fuzzy' ways. The model aims to resolve time, as we experience it, into a wider mathematically statable reality. This theory eliminates a 'beginning', and it led Hawking to say, 'So long as the universe had a beginning, we could suppose it had a creator. But if the universe is really completely self-contained, having no boundary or edge, it would have neither beginning nor end: it would simply be. What place, then, for a creator?' It is very odd to suppose that, if the universe had such properties as those of having four basic forces, acting according to invariable laws, being mathematically structured, and having a first temporal moment, then God might explain its existence, whereas if it had all those properties except for having a first temporal moment, God would be superfluous. What is so special about temporal origin that a God might explain it, and what is so satisfying about being a highly ordered domain that a God would be quite unnecessary? The fundamental question remains exactly the same in both cases, namely, what causes these properties to be as they are? I would think it was even odder, if anything, to say that a highly ordered mathematical domain exists on its own than to say that a material universe just comes into being on its own. For the postulation of such a 'thing' as a four-(or more-) dimensional superspace, containing, among other components, imaginary time and probabilistic 'non-reduced' quantum fields (i.e. fields not reduced to actuality by some observation), seems remarkably like positing a purely conceptual reality as the ontological basis of material and ordinarily temporal reality. The theistic hypothesis is, in part, precisely that the material world originates from a more stable and enduring conceptual (or spiritual) realm. Hawking has not made God superfluous; he has perhaps shown how the material cosmos can be understood as arising from a deeper, intelligible, beautiful, and non-material reality. This paves the way for a better understanding of God as a self-existent reality which generates the whole material universe. While the quasi-Platonic ontology of some mathematical physics does not *require* the postulation of a God, the natural place for conceptual realities to exist is in some supracosmic mind. From Philo onwards, Platonists have tended to locate the Forms in a divine mind. And it is not wholly without significance that Hawking speaks, however ironically, of knowing the ultimate laws of nature as 'knowing the mind of God'.

The theological import of the Hawking cosmology, as he seems to see it, is to eliminate the need for God as the initiator of the temporal process, leaving God with no explanatory role, a wholly superfluous hypothesis. The fundamental structures of the universe still need explaining, however. And those structures can no longer be seen as lying solely in some set of initial conditions and inflexible laws, from which every subsequent state of the universe will flow quasi-deductively. 'There is . . . an intrinsic openness to the future built somewhere into the structure of quantum theory.' What quantum cosmology asserts, on the standard Copenhagen interpretation, is the non-deterministic nature of the micro-processes which underlie the fundamental laws of nature. God can no longer be banished to the beginning of the universe, as in eighteenth-century deism. If there is an explanation of events in the temporal flow, that explanation must be such that it governs emergent and non-determined processes at every point in time. Sensing this point, Hawking writes, 'If one likes, one could ascribe (quantum) randomness to the intervention of God, but it would be a very strange kind of intervention: there is no evidence that it is directed toward any purpose.' He assumes here a picture and an evaluation of the universe which are both highly contentious.

The picture is that the universe is completely self-contained, so that God would have to intervene in it from outside to play any real part in its nature. But if 'the pleromatic four-sphere' (to use a phrase of Prof. Isham) is itself a reality in the mind of God, then God is not a separate reality 'outside' the universe. The physical universe is a state-reduction selected from a number of probabilistically quantified options. Both the selection of the original boundary conditions, which govern the emergence of a unique universe, and the reduction from probability to actuality suggest something analogous to an 'act of will' in the constituting of the universe itself. As Thomas Torrance puts it, 'There is no intrinsic reason in the universe why it should exist at all, or why it should be what it actually is: hence we deceive ourselves if in our natural science we think we can establish that the universe could only be what it is.' In other words, the universe is not 'self-contained', but is in fact contained in a mindlike reality whose creative act is not at some temporal beginning point, but coexistent with each temporal instant.

The evaluation Hawking makes is that there is no evidence of purpose in the cosmic process. Even on strictly physical grounds, one may question whether that is really true. However questionable some formulations of the anthropic principle may be, the features of the cosmos to which it draws attention do demonstrate a precise correlation of fundamental cosmic forces and their temporal development which is within the extremely narrow parameters required for the emergence of rational consciousnesses within the universe. Again, that does not compel one to postulate a designing mind, since such a vastly improbable universe is perhaps no more improbable, a priori, than any other. Nevertheless, the postulate of a God who willed to relate to created conscious beings would render the existence of such a universe vastly more probable than it would otherwise be. The demonstration of the amazing degree of elegant integration of the basic physical constants which is needed to produce exactly this result is very good evidence for purposiveness in the universe.

[*Religion and Creation* (Oxford: Clarendon Press, 1996), 294–8.]

J. J. C. SMART

88 Theism, Spirituality, and Science

SPIRITUALITY

The orthodox conception of God is that of a spiritual being. Though the concept of the spiritual pre-dates Descartes, the usual notion of the spirit is close to that of a Cartesian soul: something immaterial, not even physical. There is, however, an emasculated notion of spirituality that can cloud the issue. One might talk of the spirituality of some of Haydn's music, meaning no more than that it was uplifting or that Haydn was influenced in his writing of it by adventitious connections with his religious beliefs. A materialist about the mind could consistently use the word 'spiritual' in this emasculated way. Again even a materialist and an atheist could agree in describing Mary who is happy in an enclosed convent as a 'spiritual' person, meaning simply that she is a person who has a strong urge to engage in prayer and worship, notwithstanding the fact that the atheist will disagree about whether there is such to and fro communication with a divine being.

Prayer, and other cognate activities, at least as they are understood by orthodox believers, as opposed to sophisticated theologians who themselves verge on deism or atheism, do not seem to be explicable on normal physical principles. We communicate with one another by sound-waves and light rays. Such communication fits in with neurophysiology, optics, theory of sound and so on. What about prayer? Are there spiritual photons that are exchanged between

God and a soul? Perhaps the theist could say that God is able to influence the human brain directly by miraculous means and that he can know directly without physical intermediaries the worshipful thoughts in Mary's mind or brain. This story will just seem far-fetched to the deist or atheist.

MATERIALISM AND THE 'NEW PHYSICS'

Materialism has of course been thought to be inimical to theism and some theistic writers have incautiously rejoiced at the demise of nineteenth-century physics with its ontology of minute elastic particles, elastic jellies, and the like. That great man, Lord Kelvin, spent some of his exceptional talents and energies in trying to devise mechanical models to explain Maxwell's equations for electromagnetism. The idea is now bruited about that since modern physics rejects this sort of materialism the omens are better for a more spiritual account of the universe.

A good recent example of this can be found in the very title, *The Matter Myth*, of a popular book by Paul Davies and John Gribbin. Matter is not mythical: a stone is a piece of matter and it is trivial that stones exist. Looked at quantum mechanically (e.g. in terms of an extraordinarily complex wave function whose description we could never hope to write down) the stone indeed has properties that may look queer to common sense. Thus its constituents would not have simultaneous definite position and velocity, there would be phenomena of non-locality and descriptions would be more holistic than their rough equivalents in classical physics. Indeed even the stone, supposing it to be on the top of a cairn, would be only approximately there and it would to a tiny extent be everywhere else, though the extent would be so small that we can totally ignore it. Not so with small constituents of the stone, such as electrons, which cannot even approximately be treated classically. Still, being constituents of the stone they surely deserve the appellation 'matter'. Even so the domain of the physical is wider than that of the material. Thus I am inclined to believe in absolute space–time (though not absolute space and time taken separately) and to believe that space–time is made up of sets of points. Points and sets of them are hardly 'material', but if physics needs to postulate them we must regard them as physical. Similarly Quine has held that we should believe in mathematical objects, for example, numbers and sets of them, because mathematics is part of physical theory as a whole, and the theories are tested holistically by observation and experiment. If Quine is right we must regard the mathematical objects as physical, and yet they are not material. Thus I prefer to describe myself as a physicalist rather than as a materialist, except in the context of the philosophy of mind where I hold that the distinction is not important. A neuron or even a protein molecule is a macroscopic object by quantum mechanical standards. The theory of electrochemical nerve conduction, the operation of neurons, nerve nets, and so on, is hardly likely to be affected by quantum field theory and the like. I concede that quantum mechanical effects can occur in the neuro-physiological domain: thus the retina is sensitive to the absorption of a single photon. This need not be of any significant importance for understanding the general working of the brain.

As a corrective to the presently canvassed idea that the so-called 'New Physics' is more compatible with religious views than was the deterministic nineteenth-century physics of Newtonian particles and gravitational attractions, together with some ideas about electromagnetism and thermodynamics, let us compare the present situation with that of the middle and late nineteenth century when William Thomson (Lord Kelvin) questioned the estimates that geologists had made of the antiquity of the earth. Kelvin had several arguments, of which the most persuasive were (1) the rate of cooling of the sun, assuming that the only source of its radiant energy was due to the loss of potential energy in its gravitational collapse, and (2) calculations based on the rate of cooling of the earth and plausible assumptions about the initial temperatures inside the earth. Geology and evolutionary biology seemed incompatible with physical laws, since Kelvin's calculations allowed only an age of 50 or 100 million years at most. The situation was saved in Kelvin's old age by the discovery of radioactivity. This suggested that there were other possible sources of energy, even though the theory of nuclear fusion and of the reactions that keep the sun going still lay in the future. In any case Kelvin thought that it was unbelievable that the emergence of life could be accounted for on the basics of physical law. Though he was not a vitalist in the crude sense, since he denied the existence of a specific vital energy, he seems to have thought that though living beings obeyed the principle of conservation of energy, a vital principle enabled them to get round the second law of thermodynamics which had been propounded years before by Kelvin himself.

Contrast modern biology, with its strong biophysical and biochemical core, its neo-Mendelian and neo-Darwinian theory of evolution, and molecular biology in genetics. It is true that it is not known how life arose naturally from inorganic matter, but there are hints that the problem at least is not as hopeless as Kelvin thought.

IS THERE A CONFLICT BETWEEN SCIENCE AND RELIGION?

Why then is it commonly said that conflict between science and religion is a thing of the past? At least the outlook is bleak for those who see a 'God of the gaps'. Certainly the 'New Physics' makes us see the universe as very different from what untutored common sense tells us. Moreover the more physicists discover and the more they are able to unify their theories (e.g. of the four fundamental forces) the more wonderful the universe seems to be, and a religious type of emotion is liable to be aroused. On the other hand developments in biology can go the other way. As I suggested earlier, biology has become increasingly mechanistic. It is true that a sort of wonder is also appropriate, since it is hard imaginatively to grasp the amazing adaptations that have occurred by means of natural selection. Consider the complexity of the human immune system, or the extraordinarily subtle and complex sonar system of the bat. However I think that this wonder is different from that to which physics has led us. We have difficulty in grasping the biological complexity mainly because we fail imaginatively to grasp the vast periods of time in which this complexity developed as a result of mutation, recombination and natural selection. We can also forget the highly opportunistic ways in which earlier structures have been adapted to different functions, as in the evolution of the mammalian eye and ear. Sometimes also the theory of evolution can explain maladaptation. Consider the human sinuses, in which the 'sump hole' is at the top, thus predisposing us to infections, inflammation, catarrh and pain. This is because we evolved from four-legged mammals, whose heads were held downwards, and in their case the 'sump holes' were well positioned. It should be observed that if we have a plausible general idea of how something could have occurred in accordance with known scientific principles, then it is reasonable to hold that it did occur in this natural way or in some other such way, and to reject supernatural explanations. It is interesting that (so my observation in talking to them goes) biologists are more frequently hard boiled in metaphysics. They are forced to look at human beings mechanistically and have it deeply impressed on their minds that we are mammals—'poor forked creatures'—rather than partly spiritual beings, little lower than the angels. Moreover the medical and agricultural applications of theories of immunology, genetics, and so on, make it hard to take seriously the view fashionable among many literary and sociological academics that scientific theories are merely useful myths, and are destined to be overturned and replaced by others.

As I suggested at the beginning of this essay it is a mistake to think of theories, even in theoretical physics, merely as useful myths. A vulgarization of Thomas Kuhn's ideas has in some quarters led to much relativism about truth and reality. As a corrective to this I have frequently in the past had occasion to refer to an interesting article by Gerald Feinberg in which he claims that 'Thales' Problem', the problem of explaining the properties of 'ordinary matter', has been solved. The properties of the water of the sea, the earth and rocks of the land, the light and heat of the sun, the transparency of glass, and things of that sort, can be explained definitely using only the theory of the electron, proton, neutron, neutrino and photon and their antiparticles if any. This theory is ordinary quantum mechanics supplemented by the inverse square law of gravitation. (Deeper theories, such as quantum field theory, are needed to explain the fundamental properties of the electron, proton, neutron, neutrino and photon, requiring discussion of the more recondite and very transient particles produced at high energies, but that is another matter.) This part of physics, Feinberg argues, is complete. It is not likely to be relegated to the scrap heap, as was phlogiston theory. We must remember that even revolutions allow for approximate truth in the proper domain of application of the earlier theories. Newtonian mechanics gives predictions that are correct within observational error for objects whose velocities are not too high or which are not too near very massive bodies. Sometimes indeed there can be a change in ontology. General relativity shows how to replace the notion of gravitational force in favour of the geometrical notion of a geodesic, but much of classical mechanics has no need of this ontology and can be stated in terms of masses and their mutual accelerations.

[J. J. C. Smart and J. J. Haldane, *Atheism and Theism* (Oxford: Blackwell Publishers, 1996), 8–13.]

J. J. HALDANE

89   Theism and Science

An important tradition within Western philosophy believes in the primacy of natural science as a guide to truth. This is sometimes met with the charge that such an allegiance amounts to 'scientism'—the view that the only things that 'really' exist are those recognized by fundamental physical theory; and that the only forms of genuine knowledge are scientific ones. I shall try to show that a commitment to fundamental science as the *sole* arbiter of the real is indeed a form of unwarranted reductionism. But such a case has to be made. Name-calling is not a method of argument, and it is no less unsatisfactory to deride atheist materialism as 'scientistic' than it is to abuse theist anti-materialism by calling it 'superstitious'. If important questions are not to be begged one has to *show* that a rejection of all else other than scientific ontology and epistemology is unreasonable.

It might be so for a variety of reasons. First, it may be that the materialists's arguments against other ways of thinking are fallacious; second, it may be that while they avoid fallacies they are inconclusive and that this leaves other possibilities as rational options; and third, it may be that the materialist runs into difficulties in stating and arguing for his or her own position. It may even turn out that part of what he or she wants to say only or best makes sense given certain non-materialist, non-reductionist and perhaps even theistic assumptions. I shall be returning to these several ideas at various points but at this stage let me offer a brief illustration.

Smart's belief in science involves the kind of realism mentioned above. That is to say he assumes that the best explanation of our having certain ideas about the structure of the world, such as that it is constituted by material elements located in space-time, is that these ideas are the products of a history of interactions between elements in such a world and subjects who are themselves parts of it. This view rests on a number of further assumptions. First there is the

claim that the constituents of the world are possessed of more or less determinate natures and that these are intelligible to human beings. For that to be so
many things have to be true of them and of us. On the side of the objects, for
example, it is necessary that their intrinsic natures be relatively stable and that
they be describable in qualitative and quantitative terms. Assuming that the
world is dynamic, the patterns of interaction also need to exhibit a fairly high
degree of regularity. Unless these various conditions obtained no sense could be
made of biological, genetic, cosmological, chemical and physical theories, or of
the forms of observation and experimentation out of which they have developed. Regular orbits of planets around stars and of electrons around nuclei involve stable energy levels and angles of momentum; and considerable
intellectual powers of conception, discernment and inference have been exercised in socially shared and continuous histories of scientific enquiry in order to
get us to the stage we are at today.

Stability, regularity and intelligibility in world and mind are underlying assumptions of even the most limited claims of scientific realism. But suppose we
ask what reason we have for making these assumptions. The general answer
cannot be that they are *conclusions* of scientific enquiry, since they are part of
what makes it possible. Rather we should say that assumptions concerning the
intelligibility of objects and the intelligence of subjects are preconditions of
empirical enquiry revealed by reflection on thought and practice. This recognition raises a number of issues including that of whether such preconditions
serve to establish the existence of a God. I shall examine this in due course; but
for now I only want to observe that science involves an absolutely fundamental
and extensive commitment to the nature of reality; one that is presupposed
rather than derived from it; and one that makes ineliminable reference to the
idea that what there is is intelligible.

So viewed, it should now seem odd to *oppose* scientific and religious ways of
thinking about the nature of reality. On the contrary, it is plausible to regard
them as similar; for a central idea of theism is that we and the world we inhabit
constitute an objective order that exhibits intrinsic intelligibility. What is added
is the claim that both the existence and the intelligibility of this order call for an
explanation and that this is given by reference to a mindful creator. Thus science
is faith-like in resting upon 'credal' presuppositions, and inasmuch as these relate to the order and intelligibility of the universe they also resemble the content of a theistic conception of the world as an ordered creation. Furthermore
it seems that the theist carries the scientific impulse further by pressing on with
the question of how perceived order is possible, seeking the most fundamental
descriptions-cum-explanations of the existence and nature of the universe.

It will not do to respond that this further search is unscientific, for that is simply to beg the question against the theist. Assuming that by 'science' we understand investigation of and theorizing about the empirical order then properly
scientific attitudes and interests are certainly compatible with theism. Indeed the

Judaeo-Christian-Islamic doctrine of creation serves to underwrite science by assuring us that its operative assumptions of order and intelligibility are correct and by providing a motivation for pure science, namely understanding the composition and modes of operation of a vastly complex mind-reflecting artefact.

Let us pursue this approach a bit further. Smart's version of scientific realism is *reductionist*. He dismisses a familiar version of the design argument on the grounds that the apparent teleology of living systems is explicable by reference to the blind and purposeless operations of evolution—random mutation plus 'selection' of features having adaptive utility. This is something to which I shall return in the next section, but as above my concern at this stage is to query whether Smart's conception of science is not ideologically driven. Consider, then, the insistence upon reductionism. Like so many other expressions used by philosophers this is a term of art in need of definition. To begin with let me distinguish between ontological and conceptual-cum-explanatory reductions. These can go together but they need not.

An ontological reduction maintains that one purported category or class of entities is a construct and that the things belonging to it are derived from some more basic category. So, for example, the *average weight* of members of a population is an artefact derived from a series of *actual weights* upon which a mathematical operation has been performed: average weight W = the sum of real weights $(w^1, w^2, w^3, \ldots w^n)$ divided by the total number n in the population. Therefore, we might say there are no such things as average weights over and above real weights. Certainly some individual's weight may in fact be equal to the average; nevertheless his weight is real in a way that the average is not. This comes out in the fact that there need not be anyone whose weight equals the average; the latter is not an actual scale-impacting weight but rather an intellectual construct abstracted from such. At this point, however, the ontological reduction might be pressed further, since it may be claimed that actual weight is not a fundamental category either, but is itself an artefact reducible to 'real' features such as mass and gravitational acceleration. At some stage, however, the reductions will have to come to an end and this amounts to an identification of the class of basic entities.

In order to appreciate the difference between ontological and explanatory reductionism it is useful to distinguish between, on the one hand, things or natures and, on the other, concepts or terms. Ontological reductionism holds that what are identified as Xs are really Ys; explanatory reductionism maintains that talk of 'Xs' can be replaced without loss of content by talk of 'Ys'. In the philosophy of mind, for example, there are at least two kinds of behaviourism both of which involve reductionism. Some behaviourists argue that mentalistic concepts such as 'belief' and 'desire' classify patterns of actual and potential behaviour, and moreover that these concepts can be replaced by overtly behavioural ones without loss of meaning. In short, to say that A 'believes' something is not to describe or attribute a state additional to his or her behaviour. It is precisely to refer to that behaviour, and the same reference could be made using undisguisedly behavioural terms. This claim combines ontological and explanatory reductions by insisting both that there are no mental attributes over and above patterns of behaviour, and that mental concepts can be translated into or replaced by behavioural notions. However, while having reason to suppose that there are no relevant facts additional to behavioural ones someone might hold that mental concepts have a content that cannot be reduced to that of behavioural terms. In this event one might advance ontological but not conceptual or explanatory behaviourism. Every fact about 'minds' is a fact about behaviour but not every (or any?) mentalistic description is equivalent in content to a behavioural one.

The philosopher-theologian Bishop Butler (1692–1752) coined the maxim 'Everything is what it is and not another thing' and thereby pointed to a general difficulty for reductionism. If some class of entities does not really exist why are there terms purportedly referring to them? This question becomes the more pressing in a context in which someone insists upon ontological reduction but concedes that conceptual or explanatory reductions are unavailable. In the case of average weights the question is easily answered by indicating the convenience of averages so far as certain of our interests are concerned. But here the insistence upon ontological reduction is accompanied by an adequate explanatory reduction. Consider instead the philosophical example mentioned above, namely that of behaviourism. If, as is now generally accepted, mentalistic vocabulary *cannot* be reduced to behaviouristic terms, what can motivate and sustain the insistence that this fact notwithstanding there is really only behaviour, with apparent reference to mental states being an artefact of a way of speaking? One response would be to show that, appearances to the contrary, there are no irreducibly mental states because there could be none. The very idea, let us say, is contradictory.

In Smart's essay we find him arguing that a properly scientific view has no place for teleologies, not because he has an argument to show that there could be no such things as purposes but because he believes that such teleological talk can be shown to be like the case of average weights, a convenient *façon de parler*. However, from the terms in which he invokes neo-Darwinian theories of natural selection to set aside 'old'-style teleological arguments, it also seems that he accepts that were there irreducible purposes in nature that fact would support a case for theism. For my part I contest the claim that purposive descriptions and explanations are out of place in science. Not only do I believe that many teleological concepts are irreducible, I think that a commitment to the reality of objective natures, functions and associated values is presupposed by scientific enquiry and speculation. In effect, therefore, I am suggesting that Smart's approach is unwarrantedly 'scientistic' inasmuch as it is motivated by a prior concern to avoid non-natural explanations and its concept of nature is an austerely physicalist one.

[J. J. C. Smart and J. J. Haldane, *Atheism and Theism* (Oxford: Blackwell Publishers, 1996), 90–4.]

Section VIII

The Twentieth Century: II. Faith, Realism, and Pluralism

INTRODUCTION

We have seen earlier that philosophers have paid particular attention to issues of language when attempting to speak and write about God. We have noted the influence of the negative theology of Pseudo-Dionysius and the general importance of analogy and metaphor. Sometimes stress on the non-literalness of theological language, or on the idea of divine transcendence, has led to a form of theological agnosticism. And since language is crucial to thought and speech, some understanding of the powers and limits of language is crucial to assessing what results we can expect from our reason.

In the twentieth century this concern with language took a sharper turn with the claim made by the Logical Positivists in the 1930s and 1940s that all metaphysical language, including the metaphysical language of religion and value, was cognitively meaningless. The claims that God exists, or that he is good (or that he does not exist, or is not good) are neither true nor false; they say nothing that could be true or false, because all such utterances are unverifiable by sense experience. So such language, despite its appearance, cannot be used to express truths or possible truths about the world. Because such language is uncheckable in principle, it asserts nothing. And because it asserts nothing, there is nothing for reason to assess or faith to believe.

The extracts from Ayer and Flew provide classic statements of this position. In his response Heimbeck argues both that some theological claims can be verified or falsified in principle, and also that in any case such claims need not be verifiable or falsifiable in principle in order to be cognitively meaningful.

Besides this measured response of Heimbeck, the verificationist episode generated two different developments. One of these, associated with Don Cupitt, stressed the cultural relativism, and especially the linguistic relativism, of all our thought forms, including religion and theology, but nevertheless advocated the continued use of theological language for non-cognitive purposes. On this view the fact that religious language is not cognitively meaningful is no great loss, for its value does not lie in its claim to be true but, like parables or other fictions, it provides a focus for our religious attention, moral motivation, or self-understanding. This, a radical form of anti-realism in theology, is represented by an extract from Cupitt, and is challenged by

Davis. LePoidevin arrives at a similar conclusion to Cupitt, but for different reasons, the general failure of reason to provide support for religion.

The second development arising out of logical positivism is built on certain ideas of Wittgenstein, particularly his account of the meaning of language in terms of language-games or forms of life. Philosophers such as Winch and Phillips developed what might be called an internalist account of meaning and justification. It is mistaken in principle, they argue, to attempt to understand religion, for example, in terms of concepts brought to religion from outside itself. Religion has its own criteria of meaning and truth, and these must be respected. Such a claim obviously raises the question of the extent to which religious claims are objectively true. If, say, the claim 'God created the heavens and the earth' can only be understood from within religion, it presumably does not state anything that is objectively true since it has no meaning, and therefore cannot be true, outside religion. So it is hard to see how such an approach can have any room for the idea of objective truth. MacIntyre offers a response to this idea of understanding, and Alston critically assesses the use of the idea of a language game to justify this relativism.

The twentieth century has also been marked by a renewed interest in the idea of divine revelation. In the early part of the century, this was associated with Barth and Brunner, the 'theologians of the Word', who asserted the primacy of divine revelation, and the duty of reason to submit to God's revelation. In the extract from Karl Barth he argues that revelation has this primacy and is a person-inclusive idea; that is, a revelation occurs only if some person is revealed to in the sense that he or she actually receives the revelation. This seems to prevent anyone from understanding a revelation but failing to believe it, and thus seems to insulate such a revelation from any critical scrutiny. Keith Ward responds. Other philosophers have approached the idea of revelation from what might be called a Lockian perspective, arguing that, given certain theological conclusions arrived at independently of revelation, it may be reasonable to think that God has revealed himself. The extract from Richard Swinburne is one example of this.

Problems of realism and objectivism have also arisen in another context in the twentieth century, over the impact of the awareness of religious pluralism on the debate between faith and reason. The novelty of such awareness of religious pluralism can, of course, be exaggerated. But exaggerated or not, a plurality of religions raises an epistemological issue. It is the issue of how believers can be entitled to make claims for the objective truth of their religion and therefore for the objective reality of the God of that religion, given the many religions of the world. The question might be posed thus: given that we know that there are numerous competing and incompatible religions, how can anyone be confident that his or her own religion is the true one since, no matter what reasons we might give for the truth of our own religion, practitioners of other religions can do exactly the same? Hick argues that one cannot reasonably be confident of one's own religion to the exclusion of all others, claiming that the great religions are equally valid, though perhaps not equally valuable, ways of approaching the ultimate divine reality which lies beyond all knowledge. Plantinga argues for the reasonableness of exclusivism.

This mention of God brings us to the question of the possibility of religious knowledge. We shall see that this possibility has already been ruled out by our treatment of metaphysics. But, as this is a point of considerable interest, we may be permitted to discuss it at some length.

It is now generally admitted, at any rate by philosophers, that the existence of a being having the attributes which define the god of any non-animistic religion cannot be demonstratively proved. To see that this is so, we have only to ask ourselves what are the premises from which the existence of such a god could be deduced. If the conclusion that a god exists is to be demonstratively certain, then these premises must be certain; for, as the conclusion of a deductive argument is already contained in the premises, any uncertainty there may be about the truth of the premises is necessarily shared by it. But we know that no empirical proposition can ever be anything more than probable. It is only *a priori* propositions that are logically certain. But we cannot deduce the existence of a god from an *a priori* proposition. For we know that the reason why *a priori* propositions are certain is that they are tautologies. And from a set of tautologies nothing but a further tautology can be validly deduced. It follows that there is no possibility of demonstrating the existence of a god.

What is not so generally recognized is that there can be no way of proving that the existence of a god, such as the God of Christianity, is even probable. Yet this also is easily shown. For if the existence of such a god were probable, then the proposition that he existed would be an empirical hypothesis. And in that case it would be possible to deduce from it, and other empirical hypotheses, certain experiential propositions which were not deducible from those other hypotheses alone. But in fact this is not possible. It is sometimes claimed, indeed, that the existence of a certain sort of regularity in nature constitutes sufficient evidence for the existence of a god. But if the sentence 'God exists' entails no more than that certain types of phenomena occur in certain sequences, then to assert the existence of a god will be simply equivalent to asserting that there is the requisite regularity in nature; and no religious man would admit that this was all he intended to assert in asserting the existence of a god. He would say that in talking about God he was talking about a transcendent being who might be known through certain empirical manifestations, but certainly could not be defined in terms of those manifestations. But in that case the term 'god' is a metaphysical term. And if 'god' is a metaphysical term, then it cannot be even probable that a god exists. For to say that 'God exists' is to make a metaphysical utterance which cannot be either true or false. And by the same criterion, no sentence which purports to describe the nature of a transcendent god can possess any literal significance.

It is important not to confuse this view of religious assertions with the view that is adopted by atheists, or agnostics. For it is characteristic of an agnostic to hold that the existence of a god is a possibility in which there is no good reason either to believe or disbelieve; and it is characteristic of an atheist to hold that it is at least probable that no god exists. And our view that all utterances about the nature of God are nonsensical, so far from being identical with, or even lending any support to, either of these familiar contentions, is actually incompatible with them. For if the assertion that there is a god is nonsensical, then the atheist's assertion that there is no god is equally nonsensical, since it is only a significant proposition that can be significantly contradicted. As for the agnostic, although he refrains from saying either that there is or that there is not a god, he does not deny that the question whether a transcendent god exists is a genuine question. He does not deny that the two sentences 'There is a transcendent god' and 'There is no transcendent god' express propositions one of which is actually true and the other false. All he says is that we have no means of telling which of them is true, and therefore ought not to commit ourselves to either. But we have seen that the sentences in question do not express propositions at all. And this means that agnosticism also is ruled out.

Thus we offer the theist the same comfort as we gave to the moralist. His assertions cannot possibly be valid, but they cannot be invalid either. As he says nothing at all about the world, he cannot justly be accused of saying anything false, or anything for which he has insufficient grounds. It is only when the theist claims that in asserting the existence of a transcendent god he is expressing a genuine proposition that we are entitled to disagree with him.

[*Language, Truth and Logic* (Harmondsworth: Penguin, 1990), 119–21.]

ANTONY FLEW

91 Theology and Falsification

Let us begin with a parable. It is a parable developed from a tale told by John Wisdom in his haunting and revelatory article 'Gods'. Once upon a time two explorers came upon a clearing in the jungle. In the clearing were growing many flowers and many weeds. One explorer says, 'Some gardener must tend this plot.' The other disagrees, 'There is no gardener.' So they pitch their tents and set a watch. No gardener is ever seen. 'But perhaps he is an invisible gardener.' So they set up a barbed-wire fence. They electrify it. They patrol with bloodhounds. (For they remember how H. G. Wells's 'Invisible Man' could be both smelt and touched though he could not be seen.) But no shrieks ever suggested that some intruder has received a shock. No movements of the wire ever betray an invisible climber. The bloodhounds never give cry. Yet still the Believer is not convinced. 'But there is a gardener, invisible, intangible, insensible to electric shocks, a gardener who has no scent and makes no sound, a gardener who comes secretly to look after the garden which he loves.' At last the Sceptic despairs, 'But what remains of your original assertion? Just how does what you call an invisible, intangible, eternally elusive gardener differ from an imaginary gardener or even from no gardener at all?'

In this parable we can see how what starts as an assertion, that something exists or that there is some analogy between certain complexes of phenomena, may be reduced step by step to an altogether different status, to an expression perhaps of a 'picture preference'. The Sceptic says there is no gardener. The Believer says there is a gardener (but invisible, etc.). One man talks about sexual behaviour. Another man prefers to talk of Aphrodite (but knows that there is not really a superhuman person additional to, and somehow responsible for, all sexual phenomena). The process of qualification may be checked at any point before the original assertion is completely withdrawn and something of that first assertion will remain . . . . Mr Wells's invisible man could not, admittedly, be seen, but in all other respects he was a man like the rest of us. But though the process of qualification may be, and of course usually is, checked in time, it is not always judiciously so halted. Someone may dissipate his assertion completely without noticing that he has done so. A fine brash hypothesis may thus be killed by inches, the death by a thousand qualifications.

And in this, it seems to be, lies the peculiar danger, the endemic evil of theological utterance. Take such utterances as 'God has a plan', 'God created the world', 'God loves us as a father loves his children.' They look at first sight very much like assertions, vast cosmological assertions. Of course, this is no sure sign that they either are, or are intended to be, assertions. But let us confine ourselves to the cases where those who utter such sentences intend them to express assertions. (Merely remarking parenthetically that those who intend or interpret such utterances as crypto-commands, expressions of wishes, disguised ejaculations, concealed ethics, or as anything else but assertions, are unlikely to succeed in making them either properly orthodox or practically effective.)

Now to assert that such and such is the case is necessarily equivalent to denying that such and such is not the case. Suppose, then, that we are in doubt as to what someone who gives vent to an utterance is asserting, or suppose that, more radically, we are sceptical as to whether he is really asserting anything at all, one way of trying to understand (or perhaps it will be to expose) his utterance is to attempt to find what he would regard as counting against, or as being incompatible with, its truth. For if the utterance is indeed an assertion, it will necessarily be equivalent to a denial of the negation of that assertion. And anything which would count against the assertion, or which would induce the speaker to withdraw it and to admit that it had been mistaken, must be part of (or the whole of) the meaning of the negation of that assertion. And to know the meaning of the negation of an assertion, is as near as makes no matter, to know the meaning of that assertion. And if there is nothing which a putative assertion denies then there is nothing which it asserts either: and so it is not really an assertion. When the Sceptic in the parable asked the Believer, 'Just how does what you call an invisible, intangible, eternally elusive gardener differ from an imaginary gardener at all?' he was suggesting that the Believer's earlier statement had been so eroded by qualification that it was no longer an assertion at all.

Now it often seems to people who are not religious as if there was no conceivable event or series of events the occurrence of which would be admitted by sophisticated religious people to be a sufficient reason for conceding 'There wasn't a God after all' or 'God does not really love us then.' Someone tells us that God loves us as a father loves his children. We are reassured. But then we see a child dying of inoperable cancer of the throat. His earthly father is driven frantic in his efforts to help, but his Heavenly Father reveals no obvious sign of concern. Some qualification is made—God's love is 'not a merely human love' or it is 'an inscrutable love', perhaps—and we realize that such sufferings are quite compatible with the truth of the assertion that 'God loves us as a father (but, of course, ...).' We are reassured again. But then perhaps we ask: what is this assurance of God's (appropriately qualified) love worth, what is this apparent guarantee really a guarantee against? Just what would have to happen not merely (morally and wrongly) to tempt but also (logically and rightly) to entitle us to say 'God does not love us' or even 'God does not exist'? I therefore put to the succeeding symposiasts the simple central questions, 'What would have to occur or to have occurred to constitute for you a disproof of the love of, or of the existence of, God?'

['Theology and Falsification: A Symposium', in Antony Flew and Alasdair MacIntyre (eds.), *New Essays in Philosophical Theology* (London: SCM Press, 1955), 13–15.]

RAEBURNE S. HEIMBECK

92   The Meaningfulness of Theological Language

Flew also asks what in principle would have to occur or to have occurred to constitute a disproof of the existence of God. It is relatively simple to outline what would have to happen or to have happened in order to constitute a proof, rather than a disproof, of the existence of God. We shall start with the proof of the existence of God and take up the disproof afterwards.

In establishing a checking procedure for the statement made by 'God

exists', the first step that must be accomplished is the rejection of any unto-
ward strictures on 'exists'. Keeping the full range of actual applications of
'exists' in mind, we must oppose the demand that 'exists' be limited in application to what is empirical or to logical constructions out of empiricals. For it
surely makes sense to assert that there exists a prime number between 1 and
5. Yet the prime number 3 is not empirical, nor is talk about it reducible to talk
about numerals, which are empirical. And, again, it surely makes sense to say
that the state exists for the benefit of its citizens. The state, however, is not
empirical, and talk about the state is not logically equivalent to talk about the
citizens who comprise the state. Within their proper universes of discourse,
we may meaningfully speak of Huckleberry Finn existing (in the world of
fiction), of fairies and elves existing (in the world of make-believe, which is
like the world of fiction in some respects but different in other respects), of
motives and wishes and even suppressed or unconscious desires existing (in
the world of the mind), of tautologies and hence also of self-contradictions
existing (in the world of statements, not to be confused with the world of
sentences), and even of nothingness existing (cf. a void in memory, a vacuum
in space, a silence that deafens, the null class, oblivion that the mystic experiences, anti-matter—all these negatives are subjects of true and hence genuine
assertions and therefore must exist).

What is there then to prevent our speaking meaningfully of the existence
of God? 'God', in the numinous but not in the incarnation strand, does not
name anything empirical or any logical construction out of empiricals. But all
that follows from this observation is that the numinous strand of 'God'-talk is
not part of the empirical universe of discourse, that God has an existence-
status quite different from that of empirical objects, and that if we are to think
and speak properly of God we must disobjectify our thought and speech
about God, i.e. free them from the forms, associations, and demands which
control thought and speech about empirical or physical objects. It does not
follow from the above observation that 'God'-talk is ruled out as meaningless
discourse or that the assertion of God's existence understood disobjectifyingly is some sort of logical monstrosity. Granted, if God is meaningfully to
be said to exist disobjectifyingly (with an existence-status other than that of
empirical objects), then it must be possible to say clearly what this disobjecti-
fied existence-status is like and in what sense of 'exists' God exists. But this is
merely an invitation to characterize the universe of discourse to which the
numinous strand of 'God'-talk belongs by stating what sort of existent God is,
what the key properties are which single out, distinguish, and identify God
uniquely in thought.

The metatheological problem of identification is bound to arise—so
dominated are we by empirical forms of thinking and speaking—wherever it
is acknowledged (as it certainly is in classical Christian theism) that God is
not empirically indictable and talk about God not reducible to expressions

denoting only empiricals. That certain metatheological sceptics find the problem intractable derives partially from general empiricist predilections and partially from a confusion—the confusion of the problem of identifying God *in experience* with the problem of identifying God *in thought*. It is the former problem which they end up discussing, whereas it is the latter alone which has pertinence to the investigation of the cognitive significance of 'G'-sentences.

The confusion manifests itself in the attempt to assimilate the problem of identification to the problem of checkability by implying that an absence of checking procedures for the assertion that God exists would be tantamount to an absence of directions for identifying God in thought. But the two are quite different indeed. To attempt to assimilate them is another instance of the evidence-criteria conflation, a root mistake in much metatheological scepticism. One could without contradiction insist that God is identifiable in thought but not in experience, though the converse would not hold (if God is identifiable in experience he must be identifiable in thought, for being able to identify God in thought is a precondition for being able to identify any experience as an experience of God). And one could maintain without contradiction that there are truth-conditions (criteria) but no checking procedures (evidence) for the statement that God exists. In short, because of the clear difference between criteria and evidence, between truth-conditions and checking procedures, and between identification in thought and identification in experience, failure to be able to identify God in experience would not be equivalent to and would not entail failure to be able to identify God in thought.

[*Theology and Meaning* (London: George Allen and Unwin, 1969), 106–8.]

DON CUPITT

93   Anti-Realist Faith

The point here is hard to express without paradox, but let's try: our modern experience is that there isn't any objective, fixed, intelligible reality out there, such as may be replicated in our language and invoked to check our theories. We now live wholly *inside* our own history, our language and the flux of cultural change. We find that our world isn't made of Being any more, but of symbols and of conflicting arguments. The long-term effect of the critical revolution in our thinking has been to make us so much aware of our own theories, viewpoints and ways of thinking that objective reality has melted away. We haven't got a proper cosmos any longer, only a bunch of chronic disagreements.

Let us now by contrast briefly evoke the traditional religious and philosophical outlook of medieval Christianity. It was Platonic, making a sharp contrast between this changing and corruptible material world below and the eternal controlling intelligible world above. It was pre-critical, so that people made no very clear distinction between culture and nature. They blithely supposed that their own cultural conceptions were part of the natural order of things. It was pre-scientific, and many events were ascribed to supernatural causes. It was also pre-historical, and people's vision of the past was short and very hazy. Life was governed by tradition, a fixed body of knowledge that had come down from the Fathers and from above. Faith was therefore dogmatic, binding you to a body of truths and a form of life that would remain immutable from the primitive era until the end of historical time.

In such a context both philosophy and theology were oriented towards necessity, changelessness and ideal perfection. For both traditions the goal of human life was to attain absolute knowledge of absolute reality. In that timeless contemplation of absolute necessity and perfection, which religion called the Vision of God, you would find perfect fulfilment and happiness. Thus the old Christian culture was highly realistic in being centred around objective, eternal, necessary, intelligible and perfect Being. Faith was dogma-guided longing for Heaven, and the monk whose way of life anticipated Heaven was the highest human type. The body, time, culture, language, disagreement, history and biological life were all relatively neglected or disparaged.

Now consider how completely we have reversed the traditional outlook of Christian Platonism. The world above and all the absolutes are gone. The whole of our life and all our standards are now inside language and culture. For good or ill *we* make our own history, *we* have shaped our own world, *we* have together evolved all norms to which our life is subject. Religion for us must inevitably be something very different from what it was in the heyday of Platonic realism. Indeed, it is plain that if I am right, then Christianity must be revolutionized to survive.

There are people who still hope that the old order can be restored. For them, there is no intermediate position; the end of dogmatism is the beginning of nihilism. They are terrified by the thought of a world without certainties. They yearn for a society constrained by one absolute truth determined by one absolute power. But anti-realists like me reject their view, and claim that Christianity can and should be modernized. We invoke the symbol of the Day of Pentecost, when God scattered Himself and was distributed as spirit to each individual believer. Just as Truth has come down from heaven and is now immanent within the movement of our various human conversations; just as political sovereignty is no longer wholly vested in a superperson above society but is dispersed throughout the body politic; just as, indeed, the whole of the former world above is now resolved down into the life of this world— so God also is now in each of us.

This discussion has I hope made a little clearer what we mean by a non-realist philosophy of religion. Realists think our religious language tells of beings, events and forces that belong to a higher world, an invisible second world beyond this world of ours. But I believe that there is only one world and it is this world, the world we made, the human life-world, the world of language. To think of language as replicating the structure of some extra-linguistic reality, some world beyond the world of our language, is I believe a mistaken way of thinking of language *anyway*. Every word is more like a tool for doing a job than like a xerox copy of something that is not a word. The only language we can know is wholly human, completely adapted to its job of being the medium in which human life is lived in the only world we have. So we should see religious language in terms of the part it can play in our lives, rather than see it in a mythological way as conjuring up a picture of a second world. For us, there is only *one* world, and it is *this* world, the manifest world, the world of language, the world of everyday life, of politics and economics. And this world has no outside. It doesn't depend in any way on anything higher, and there is no meaning in the suggestion that our cultural beliefs and practices need to be set on any external foundation.

[in Joseph Runzo (ed.), *Is God Real?* (London: Macmillan, 1993), 48–50.]

STEPHEN DAVIS

94 Against Anti-Realist Faith

Most of us who believe in the existence of God made our peace long ago with the fact that there are intelligent and moral people who do not believe in God. We also know that some of these same people wish to retain certain aspects of the religious life. If Cupitt belongs in this last category (and I believe he does), there is nothing here so far that is particularly threatening to believers in God. But what does seem grotesque is Cupitt's implicit suggestion that his views are superior to belief in God for purely religious reasons.

The stakes here are high. Cupitt's thesis is not a matter of abstruse techni-calities at the theological margins. This is an issue about which Christians—scholars and laypersons alike—will care deeply.

Let me offer three criticisms of Cupitt's paper. The first concerns what we might call rhetorical method. Cupitt has an objectionable tendency to offer what I can only call absurd parodies of positions he opposes. It is almost as if being an orthodox Christian, or even a religious realist, is an exercise in sheer buffoonery. Now I take the term 'realism *vis-à-vis x*' to be the view that *x* exists (or does not exist) independently of beliefs about *x*. 'Realism *vis-à-vis* God', then, is the view that God either exists or does not exist quite independently of what anyone believes about God. But as Cupitt depicts realism, it entails all sorts of bizarre intellectual baggage—much of which would only startle most realists.

For example, according to Cupitt, realism entails: (a) that there are unchanging and invisible essences; (b) that there is an invisible higher world beyond this world which our language describes; (c) that meaning is a spirit-being that inhabits a word; (d) that mind is a spirit-being that inhabits a body; (e) that a law of nature is a spirit-principle that controls events by pulling them with invisible wires; and (f) that there are three (rather than the standard two) modalities of truth—'true', 'necessarily true', and 'absolutely true'.

Now perhaps there are realists who hold these views, but not all realists do or logically must. (a) Some realists believe in invisible essences and some do not (not all realists are Platonists). (b) Some realists posit an invisible higher world, and some do not. (c) I cannot think of anyone—realist or non-realist—who reifies meaning ('a spirit-being that inhabits a word') in the way Cupitt describes. (d) Some realists are Cartesian dualists, but some tend toward physicalism. (e) Most philosophically inclined folk these days realize that natural laws are descriptive rather than coercive. The law of gravity, for example, does not pull apples toward the centre of the earth—it describes the fact that in our experience apples (when left unsupported near the earth) always fall toward the centre of the earth. (f) I do not know what the term *absolutely true* means. I think I have a fairly good grip on what it is for a statement to be true; I also think I know what it is for a statement to be 'necessarily true'; but the modality Cupitt repeatedly criticizes throughout his paper ('absolutely true') is mysterious to me. At the very least, Cupitt needs to define what he means.

Religious realism, Cupitt says, includes or entails: (a) that Christianity is a timeless, coherent, and pragmatically immutable system of thought; (b) that the oldest version of the faith is the purest; (c) that biblical and Christian language has timeless, transcultural meaning; and (d) that God's language isn't real human language. As a result of religious realism, Cupitt says, Christianity has become barbarous ('locked into truly frightful excesses of power and guilt, cruelty and sentimentality').

But it surely seems possible to produce coherent versions of religious realism that contain *none* of these items. Aquinas, Schleiermacher, Barth and Tillich all seem to me to be religious realists who would embrace few or none of them. I count myself a religious realist, and I would embrace precisely none of them.

The point is that religious realism is not nearly so ridiculous a specimen as Cupitt implies. In order to demonstrate its implausibility, one must refute realism's most plausible versions, not just the absurd ones. A person can be a Christian realist without being committed to any of the picturesque caricatures that Cupitt dismisses.

My second criticism is that I believe Cupitt's position is self-stultifying, i.e. it refutes itself. If I were to make the statement, *I am unable to produce a sentence of English*, that statement would be self-stultifying. So would be the position of someone who claims to know that *Nothing whatever can be known*.

Cupitt describes sympathetically a position he calls perspectivism, the theory that we cannot know how things are but only how they seem to us. But does he think perspectivism is *true*? If it is true, then in one important respect, we *can* say how things are, namely that we cannot know how things are but only how they seem to us. Thus, perspectivism is self-stultifying. But if perspectivism is not supposed to be true but rather is itself only one among the available perspectives—t is merely somebody's point of view—then why should non-perspectivists take perspectivism seriously? What Cupitt must do is provide a reason why they should do so, an argument that involves no truth claims about perspectivism.

Similarly, Cupitt says, 'There is no single grand overarching dogmatic truth any longer.' I do not know exactly what this statement means, but I do wonder whether Cupitt considers it true. Does he think this very statement is itself the grand overarching truth that we must now respect? His paper certainly gives that impression. 'There cannot be any absolute descriptions of what is going on,' Cupitt also says. Again, I am not sure what the term *absolute* means here—perhaps it just means *true*. But the position that there cannot be any true description of anything (involving, as it does, a purported true description of something) refutes itself.

Later in the paper Cupitt allows that anti-realism is not 'the metaphysical truth of the human condition'. 'No one vision of things', he admits, 'can any longer be compulsory.' But then we wonder what epistemological status anti-realism is supposed to have. If it is just one among many perspectives, why should realists take it seriously? In another place, however, Cupitt seems to argue that religious realism is not only false but necessarily false. 'Religion', he says, 'is historical and cultural all the way through.' And then he adds, 'it could not have been otherwise.'

The point is that Cupitt's position is either self-stultifying, i.e. cannot consistently be held, or else is open to objections along these same lines to which he owes readers an answer.

My third criticism concerns the question of the essence of religion. One of the most intriguing aspects of Cupitt's position (and one that I suspect puzzles many laypersons) is that despite his views he goes right on practising religion. The answer, I think, is to be found in that line of Cupitt's paper where he says, '. . . the goal of the religious life is a spiritual state that is beyond all the symbols.' If spirituality (understood as a certain sort of psychological state) is the goal and heart of religion, then, obviously, one can be a non-realist or even an atheist and still be religious. Indeed, one of my friends—a practising Zen Buddhist—is an atheist, and his level of spirituality is, I believe, higher than mine.

I cannot disprove Cupitt's contention that spirituality precedes doctrine and is what really matters in religion. I can, however, lay on the table my own view. The essence of Christian faith is not a kind of spirituality to which God is logically and causally and (so to speak) teleologically dispensable. It rather concerns a call from God that we respond appropriately to the love of God as it is revealed pre-eminently in Christ. 'Man's chief end', as the Westminster Shorter Catechism of 1643 beautifully says, 'is to glorify God, and to enjoy him forever.' So God (by which I mean a being whose existence is independent of anybody's views about God) is essential to Christian faith.

The point is that the basic issue turns out to be belief in God. So anyone who wants to evaluate the turn Cupitt's theology has taken in recent years must begin by asking: Did God create us or did we create God? Those who believe that we created God and that accordingly there is little point in being religious will be atheists. Those who believe that we created God but that there is still value in being religious will follow a path like the one Cupitt has laid down. Those who believe that God created us and that our highest duty as human beings is to glorify God will be religious realists who will strive to live lives of worship and service.

[in Joseph Runzo (ed.), *Is God Real?* (London: Macmillan, 1993), 56–9.]

ROBIN LE POIDEVIN

95   Atheism and Religious Practice

In *A Path from Rome*, Anthony Kenny describes the doubts and conflicts which eventually led to his leaving the Catholic priesthood. He also tells us that, in spite of his agnosticism, he continued to attend church regularly, though never receiving Communion or reciting the Creed. He did this, not to pretend to a faith which he no longer had, but because of the important role that certain religious practices, including prayer, can continue to have even in the life of someone who has given up firm belief in theism. In an earlier book, *The God of the Philosophers*, he compares the agnostic at prayer to someone 'adrift in the ocean, trapped in a cave, or stranded on a mountainside, who cries for help though he may never be heard or fires a signal which may never be seen'. Just as there is nothing unreasonable in this latter activity, the implication is, so there is nothing unreasonable in the former: the agnostic does not know whether there is anyone listening to his prayer, but there is a chance that there is, and that the prayer will be answered.

What, for Kenny, justifies prayer does not extend to saying the Creed. Kenny's position is clearly a realist one, which implies that when one says 'I believe in God, the father Almighty, maker of heaven and earth . . .' one is stating what one intends to be the literal truth. An agnostic cannot utter these words without either hypocrisy or self-deception. This defence of a rather limited range of religious practices—just those which do not definitely commit one to any theistic doctrine—would not be accepted by the theological instrumentalist. If religion has a point, it is not, for the instrumentalist, because it *might*, for all we know, be true. It is neither true nor false. What is needed, for instrumentalism to be a viable theological position, is a defence of religious practice which allows an atheist, someone who believes that, realistically construed, theism is false, to engage in worship and prayer. I suggest that such a defence can be found in comparing the effects of religion to the beneficial effects of fiction. Of the four accounts of our emotional response to fiction that we considered in the previous section, the most plausible, I suggest, is Walton's. So let us apply Walton's account to religious practice.

To engage in religious practice, on this account, is to engage in a game of make-believe. We make-believe that there is a God, by reciting, in the context of the game, a statement of belief. We listen to what make-believedly are accounts of the activities of God and his people, and we pretend to worship and address prayers to that God. In Walton's terms, we locate ourselves in that fictional world, and in so doing we allow ourselves to become emotionally involved, to the extent that a religious service is capable of being an intense experience. The immediate object of our emotions is the fictional God, but there is a wider object, and that is the collection of real individuals in our lives. In the game of make-believe (for example, the Christian one), we are presented with a series of dramatic images: an all-powerful creator, who is able to judge our moral worth, to forgive us or to condemn, who appears on Earth in human form and who willingly allows himself to be put to death. What remains, when the game of make-believe is over, is an awareness of our responsibilities for ourselves and others, of the need to pursue spiritual goals, and so on.

How adequate is this account? A number of difficulties present themselves:

1 This justification of religious practice seems far less powerful than the one which is available to the realist, for whom prayer and worship really is God-directed, and for whom the emotions thus evoked are real, capable of having a direct effect on one's life. The instrumentalist, in contrast, has to make do with Walton's quasi-emotions: a make-believe imitation of the real thing. Is such a watered-down version of religious practice worth preserving?

2 In reading fiction as fiction, one is simply following the designs of the author, who is inviting one to participate in a game of make-believe. The authors of religious documents and rituals were not, surely, invariably issuing such an invitation (though some religious writing is explicitly fictional). To treat all religion as make-believe is arguably a perversion of its original purpose.

3 Any given fiction is a relatively fleeting thing: it is not possible to sustain a game of make-believe indefinitely. Yet religion is not merely something to

dip into. To lead a religious life is to have certain images almost constantly in front of one, informing one's activities. How could the religious picture be sustained, if it were not taken to be a reflection of reality?

Let us take these points in order.

The instrumentalist can answer the first point by pointing out that the realist justification of religious practice is an option that has already been rejected, on the grounds that theological realism is untenable. If theological realism is itself a highly problematic position, it can hardly provide an adequate justification of any practice based on it. The instrumentalist justification of religious practice is superior, simply because it is not based on dubious metaphysical assumptions. But there is still the point about emotions. Against the instrumentalist is the consideration that someone who believes in the literal truth of what is said in a religious ritual will, surely, experience genuine emotions which, because they are genuine, are far more likely to have an impact on their life than the quasi-emotions generated in a game of religious make-believe. What can be said about this? The true (i.e. in this context, the realist) believer will be motivated not just by the emotions caused by religious ritual but also by his beliefs. Now, if the instrumentalist is right, some of those beliefs, namely those concerning the literal truth of religious doctrines, are false, and therefore give rise to a degenerate kind of spiritual life. The effect of a literal faith on one's life may actually be (in part) a negative one. For example, recall the argument of Chapter 6: if we perform an act because we believe God wills it, then we are not genuinely autonomous agents: we abdicate the responsibility of deciding for ourselves what is right.

The second point draws attention to historical issues. What were the intentions of those responsible for religious writings and observances? Were they concerned to report, in unambiguous terms, a generally agreed set of truths? Or were they attempting to convey, in allegorical terms, ideas whose content was quite nebulous? Did they devise rituals whose purpose was to provide an appropriate setting for the promulgation of true propositions and for direct communion with God? Or was the purpose rather to exploit the aesthetic and dramatic impact of a communal activity, perhaps accompanied by music, and perhaps also in a place of size and beauty? Was it a combination of these, not necessarily conflicting, purposes? When we consider that the authors concerned were not a small group of contemporaries, but a large group scattered over the centuries and from a variety of cultures, the difficulty of giving a single clear answer to these questions becomes obvious. But this much is true: it is inconceivable that religious writings and rituals are not, to some extent, works of the imagination. This is so even if we accept the realist approach to theism. If there is a creator of the universe, then our ways of conceiving him still require imaginative effort. Even the realist, in explaining the impact of religion, must exploit the effect exerted on us by fiction and make-believe.

Let us now turn to the third point, on the transience of fiction and the permanence of religion. The contrast is, in fact, an entirely specious one. It is true that engagement with fiction is occasional. We read a book, become involved in it, finish it, continue to reflect on it for a time, but then become immersed in other activities, perhaps returning to the book after a few years. But then religion, too, is an occasional thing. Formal religious observance may take place once a day, but it is more likely to be once a week, once a year, or even less frequently than that. Of course, religious reflection can take place outside of a formal setting, but even then, other activities and concerns intervene. Still, it might be urged, although it is occasional, religious involvement can be a life-long thing. But then we do not have to look far to find a fictional parallel. Televised soap operas may only last half an hour and are broadcast one, two or three times a week, but they go on apparently indefinitely. As viewers of these programmes, we may continue to engage with a single fiction for years on end. It may, in fact, come to occupy a considerable portion of our thoughts, and the moral status of the various fictional goings-on may become a topic of animated discussion week after week. And if we eventually tire of these fictions, it is only because they lack the richness and complexity of religion, not because they are merely fictional. The constancy of religion is a testament to its dramatic power, not to its veracity.

Finally, I want to consider the objection that theological instrumentalism does not, after all, avoid the pitfalls it was intended to avoid. The general idea here is that, if a certain proposition is incoherent, then treating it as fictional will not make it coherent. To be more specific, let us think again about two moral arguments for atheism introduced in Part II. One was the problem of evil: how could a loving God permit suffering when he is in a position to prevent it? The other was the problem of moral autonomy: if I act simply because I believe that God wills me to act, then I am not truly autonomous, and am not acting for moral reasons. Do these problems not arise even if we treat religion as a game of make-believe? Let us look at them in turn.

Even if it is only fictionally the case that God is perfectly loving and all-powerful, then it is still *fictionally* the case that he permits suffering which he could have prevented. There is thus an apparent tension within the fiction itself. However, since we not only participate in, but also to some extent create, the game of make-believe, we can choose what to include in it. We may well include the idea of suffering. Indeed, for most theistic outlooks, suffering plays an important role in spiritual development. But we do not need to include the idea that the world contains an appalling amount of apparently pointless suffering. We will, in fact, simply avoid introducing anything which would result in tensions within the fiction. The counterpart of this manoeuvre within the realist scheme of things would be to shut our eyes to the state of things, so that it does not disturb our faith. That manoeuvre, however, looks far less acceptable.

What of the issue of autonomy? If I imagine God's requiring me to act in a particular way, and act because of that imagined requirement, then I am no more acting for truly moral reasons than if I act because I think God really is requiring me to do so. Although the requirement is only fictional, I am acting, it seems, as if I were not an autonomous agent. But this objection, too, is misplaced. The make-believe game in which I pretend that God is requiring me to do certain things does not affect my actions directly. Rather, in engaging with the game, I am led to certain true (not fictional) beliefs about what I ought to do. It is these beliefs on which I act, and I do so as a fully autonomous agent. When I decide what to do, I no longer do it on the basis of some make-believe requirement, but on a requirement I come to recognize when I play the game of make-believe. In general, fiction may influence the way we act, but our reasons for so acting need not involve any fictional beliefs.

Our account of religion as fiction, then, need not generate the problems which beset realism.

[*Arguing for Atheism* (London: Routledge, 1996), 118–22.]

DEWI PHILLIPS

96 Faith, Scepticism, and Religious Understanding

The relation between religion and philosophical reflection needs to be reconsidered. For the most part, in recent philosophy of religion, philosophers, believers, and non-believers alike, have been concerned with discovering *the grounds* of religious belief. Philosophy, they claim, is concerned with reasons; it considers what is to count as good evidence for a belief. In the case of religious beliefs, the philosopher ought to enquire into the reasons anyone could have for believing in the existence of God, for believing that life is a gift from God, or for believing that an action is the will of God. Where can such reasons be found? One class of reasons comes readily to mind. Religious believers, when asked why they believe in God, may reply in a variety of ways. They may say, 'I have had an experience of the living God', 'I believe on the Lord Jesus Christ', 'God saved me while I was a sinner', or, 'I just can't help believing'. Philosophers have not given such reasons very much attention. The so-called trouble is not so much with the content of the replies as with the fact that the replies are made by believers. The answers come from *within* religion, they presuppose the framework of Faith, and therefore cannot be treated as *evidence* for religious belief. Many philosophers who argue in this way seem to be searching for evidence or reasons for religious beliefs *external* to belief itself. It is assumed that such evidence and reasons would, if found, constitute the grounds of religious belief.

The philosophical assumption behind the ignoring of religious testimony as begging the question, and the search for external reasons for believing in God, is that one could settle the question of whether there is a God or not without referring to the form of life of which belief in God is a fundamental part. What would it be like for a philosopher to settle the question of the existence of God? Could a philosopher say that he believed that God exists and yet never pray to Him, rebel against Him, lament the fact that he could no longer pray, aspire to deepen his devotion, seek His will, try to hide from Him, or fear and tremble before Him? In short, could a man believe that God exists without his life being touched *at all* by the belief? Norman Malcolm asks with good reason, 'Would a belief that he exists, if it were completely non-affective, really be a belief that he exists? Would it be anything at all? What is "the form of life" into which it would enter? What difference would it make whether anyone did or did not have this belief?'

Yet many philosophers who search for the grounds of religious belief, claim, to their own satisfaction at least, to understand what a purely theoretical belief in the existence of God would be. But the accounts these philosophers give of what religious believers seem to be saying are often at variance with what many believers say, at least, when *they* are not philosophizing. Every student of the philosophy of religion will have been struck by the amount of talking at cross purposes within the subject. A philosopher may say that there is no God, but a believer may reply, 'You are creating and then attacking a fiction. The god whose existence you deny is not the God I believe in.' Another philosopher may say that religion is meaningless, but another believer may reply, 'You say that when applied to God, words such as "exists", "love", "will", etc., do not mean what they signify in certain non-religious contexts. I agree. You conclude from this that religion is meaningless, whereas the truth is that you are failing to grasp the meaning religion has.' Why is there this lack of contact between many philosophers and religious believers? One reason is that many philosophers who do not believe that God exists assume that they know what it means to say that there is a God. Norman Kemp Smith made a penetrating analysis of this fact when commenting on the widespread belief among American philosophers in his day of the uselessness of philosophy of religion.

... those who are of this way of thinking, however they may have thrown over the religious beliefs of the communities in which they have been nurtured, still continue to be influenced by the phraseology of religious devotion—a phraseology which, in its endeavour to be concrete and universally intelligible, is at little pains to guard against the misunderstandings to which it may so easily give rise. As they insist upon, and even exaggerate, the merely literal meaning of this phraseology, the God in whom they have ceased to believe is a Being whom they picture in an utterly anthropomorphic fashion.

...

The distinction between religious believers and atheistical philosophers is not, of course, as clear-cut as I have suggested. It is all too evident in contemporary philosophy of religion that many philosophers who *do* believe in God philosophize about religion in the way which Kemp Smith found to be true of philosophical non-believers. Here, one can say either that their philosophy reflects their belief, in which case they believe in superstition but not in God, or, taking the more charitable view, that they are failing to give a good philosophical account of what they really believe.

Insufficient attention has been paid to the question of what kind of philosophical enquiry the concept of divine reality calls for. Many philosophers assume that everyone knows *what* it means to say that there is a God, and that the only outstanding question is *whether* there is a God. Similarly, it might be thought, everyone knows what it means to say that there are unicorns, although people may disagree over whether in fact there are any unicorns. If there were an analogy between the existence of God and the existence of unicorns, then coming to see that there is a God would be like coming to see that an additional being exists. 'I know what people are doing when they worship,' a philosopher might say. 'They praise, they confess, they thank, and they ask for things. The only difference between myself and religious believers is that I do not believe that there is a being who receives their worship.' The assumption, here, is that the meaning of worship is contingently related to the question whether there is a God or not. The assumption might be justified by saying that there need be no consequences of existential beliefs. Just as one can say, 'There is a planet Mars, but I couldn't care less,' so one can say, 'There is a God, but I couldn't care less.' But what is one *saying* here when one says that there is a God? Despite the fact that one need take no interest in the existence of a planet, an account could be given of the kind of difference the existence of the planet makes, and of how one could find out whether the planet exists or not. But all this is foreign to the question whether there is a God. That is not something anyone could *find out*. It has been far too readily assumed that the dispute between the believer and the unbeliever is over a *matter of fact*. Philosophical reflection on the reality of God then becomes the philosophical reflection appropriate to an assertion of a matter of fact. I have tried to show that this is a misrepresentation of the religious concept, and that philosophy can claim justifiably to show what is meaningful in religion only if it is prepared to examine religious concepts in the contexts from which they derive their meaning.

A failure to take account of the above context has led some philosophers to ask religious language to satisfy criteria of meaningfulness alien to it. They say that religion must be rational if it is to be intelligible. Certainly, the distinction between the rational and the irrational must be central in any account one gives of meaning. But this is not to say that there is a paradigm of rationality to which all modes of discourse conform. A necessary prolegomenon to the philosophy of religion, then, is to show the diversity of criteria of rationality; to show that the distinction between the real and the unreal does not come to the same thing in every context. If this were observed, one would no longer wish to construe God's reality as being that of an existent among existents, an object among objects.

Coming to see that there is a God is not like coming to see that an additional being exists. If it were, there would be an extension of one's knowledge of facts, but no extension of one's understanding. Coming to see that there is a God involves seeing a new meaning in one's life, and being given a new understanding. The Hebrew-Christian conception of God is not a conception of a being among beings. Kierkegaard emphasized the point when he said bluntly, 'God does not exist. He is eternal.'

[*Faith and Philosophical Enquiry* (London: Routledge and Kegan Paul, 1970), 13–18.]

WILLIAM ALSTON

97   Taking the Curse off Language-Games

If 'God talk' is simply a way of articulating a set of attitudes towards human life in the natural world, then the arguments of natural theology for or against theism can have no bearing on its acceptability. Indeed, the question of acceptability never comes up in the way it does for statements that are made with a truth claim. To be sure, one may feel that my attitude is misguided, foolish, naïve or unrealistic; and, no doubt, the assertion that such an attitude is well taken is one that can be assessed in the light of a variety of considerations. But on the present interpretation of Phillips, the religious utterance is not identified with an assertion about an attitude, but with the expression of the attitude; and that cannot be confirmed or disconfirmed, shown to be true or false . . . by anything outside the language-game, for the simple reason that it is not subject to those modes of assessment at all. If that is how the religious language-game is being conducted, its players stand in no danger of any interference from without. Since in our religious talk we are not claiming to tell the truth about an objective supernatural reality, reasons for or against such truth claims have no bearing on the matter. We needn't worry about a 'stopping place'; in a sense we never get started.

This, then, is a way in which Phillips can purchase absolute epistemic autonomy for a religious language-game that does not make provision for the kinds of pro and con considerations he wishes to exclude. But has he bought this result at too dear a price? Many, I would think virtually all, religious believers would think so. In restricting religious belief and discourse to the reflection of attitudes and sentiments concerning human life and the natural world, one has emptied theistic religion, at any rate, of its life blood. If we are not in vital contact with a supreme being Who has the kind of reality that makes Him the arbiter of the truth of our beliefs, as well as of the language-game-standards that play that role according to Phillips, then we are of all men the most miserable. I have not conducted a systematic survey of believers' construals of the contents of their beliefs, any more than (I assume) Phillips has. It would be very difficult to design and carry out such a survey. I can just report that my sense of the matter is that I and most of the believers I know definitely do not regard their affirmations of religious belief to consist solely, or even most basically, in expressions of attitudes and sentiments toward the natural world and human life. [. . .] Philips seems to me to be recommending revisions in the usual way of taking religious beliefs, rather than just reading off the character of one or another religious form of life as it actually exists. I suspect that the form(s) of religiosity he is recommending are live options only for a handful of sophisticated, 'liberated' individuals, and, so far from being the normal religious actuality, are not even possibilities for most of our fellows.

Moreover, though the expressivist understanding of religious discourse provides an argument for Phillips's chosen stopping place, that argument would seem to be circular, in much the same way as the argument from the language-game relativity of truth. Phillips's main reasons for adopting his expressivist interpretation, and for rejecting more objectivist, 'referential' interpretations, are epistemic in character. They go something like this. There is no such thing as 'finding out' that God exists or is present, this by way of contrast with the way in which we can find out whether a cow exists or is present. But since the content of a belief or statement is given by what would count for or against it, it follows that what we are saying when we talk 'about God' is a radically different sort of thing from what we are saying when we talk about cows. (This is only one example of the pattern of argument, but it will suffice to make my point.) And therefore natural theology, historical research, etc. are irrelevant to the assessment of what we are saying in religion. But it is easy to see that this argument presupposes its conclusion. For if the considerations being excluded (including 'religious experience' of the sort that could be a perceptual awareness of God as an objective reality) were relevant, then the first premise that is supposed to lead, via a verificationist account of meaning, to the expressivist interpretation would be unacceptable. The first premise (that, for example, there is no way of finding out that God exists) presupposes that the considerations excluded in the conclusion have already been excluded. This indicates that the expressivist interpretation and the location of the stopping place are intimately connected, so intimately that it is impossible to use one to argue for the other.

[in T. Tessin and M. von der Ruhr (eds.), *Philosophy and the Grammar of Religious Belief* (London: Macmillan, 1995), 31–2.]

Winch argues that 'intelligibility takes many and varied forms'; that there is no 'norm for intelligibility in general.' He argues that 'criteria of logic are not a direct gift of God, but arise out of, and are only intelligible in the context of, ways of living or modes of social life as such. For instance, science is one such mode and religion is another; and each has criteria of intelligibility peculiar to itself. So within science or religion actions can be logical or illogical; in science, for example, it would be illogical to refuse to be bound by the results of a properly carried out experiment; in religion it would be illogical to suppose that one could pit one's own strength against God's; and so on. But we cannot sensibly say that either the practice of science itself or that of religion is either illogical or logical; both are non-logical.' It follows from this that anything that counts as a 'way of living' or a 'mode of social life' can only be understood and criticized in its own terms. Winch indeed argues that so far as religion is concerned, a sociologist can only identify religious actions under their religious descriptions and if he answers any questions about them of the form 'Do these two acts belong to the same kind of activity?' the answer will have to be 'given according to criteria which are not taken from sociology, but from religion itself. But if the judgements of identity—and hence the generalizations—of the sociologist of religion rest on criteria taken from religion, then his relation to the performers of religious activity cannot be just that of observer to observed. It must rather be analogous to the participation of the natural scientist with fellow-workers in the activities of scientific investigation.' That is, you can only understand it from the inside.

Winch therefore points to a theoretical justification for Evans-Pritchard's practice, and in so doing exposes its weakness. For there are not two alternatives: *either* embracing the metaphysical fiction of one over-all 'norm for intelligibility in general' *or* flying to total relativism. We can elicit the weakness of this position by considering the conceptual self-sufficiency claimed for 'ways of living' and 'modes of social life'. The examples given are 'religion' and 'science'. But at any given date in any given society the criteria in current use by religious believers or by scientists will differ from what they are at other times and places. Criteria have a history. This emerges strikingly if we ask how we are to think of magic on Winch's view. Is magic a 'mode of social life'? Or is it primitive religion? Or perhaps primitive science? For we do want to reject magic, and we want to reject it—in the terms which Winch has taken over for polemical purposes from Pareto—as illogical because it fails to come up to our criteria of rationality. An excellent case here is that of the witchcraft practised by the Azande. The Azande believe that the performance of certain rites in due form affects their common welfare; this belief cannot in fact be refuted. For they also believe that if the rites are ineffective it is because someone present at them had evil thoughts. Since this is always possible, there is never a year when it is unavoidable for them to admit that the rites were duly performed, but that they did not thrive. Now the belief of the Azande is not unfalsifiable in principle (we know perfectly well what would falsify it—the conjunction of the rite, no evil thoughts and disasters). But in fact it cannot be falsified. Does this belief stand in need of rational criticism? And if so by what standards? It seems to me that one could only hold the belief of the Azande rationally *in the absence of* any practice of science and technology in which criteria of effectiveness, ineffectiveness and kindred notions had been built up. But to say this is to recognize the appropriateness of scientific criteria of judgement from our standpoint. The Azande do not intend their belief either as a piece of science or as a piece of non-science. They do not possess these categories. It is only *post eventum*, in the light of later and more sophisticated understanding that their belief and concepts can be classified and evaluated at all.

This suggests strongly that beliefs and concepts are not merely to be evaluated by the criteria implicit in the practice of those who hold and use them. This conviction is reinforced by other considerations. The criteria implicit in the practice of a society or of a mode of social life are not necessarily coherent; their application to problems set within that social mode does not always yield *one* clear and unambiguous answer. When this is the case people start questioning their own criteria. They try to criticize the standards of intelligibility and rationality which they have held hitherto. On Winch's view it is difficult to see what this could mean. This is to return to the point that criteria and concepts have a history; it is not just activities which have a history while the criteria which govern action are timeless.

What I am quarrelling with ultimately is the suggestion that agreement in following a rule is sufficient to guarantee making sense. We can discriminate different types of example here. There are the cases where the anthropologist, in order to interpret what people say, has to reconstruct imaginatively a possible past situation where expressions had a sense which they no longer bear. Consider theories about what taboo is. To call something taboo is to prohibit it, but it is not to say that it is prohibited. To say that something is taboo is to distinguish it from actions which are prohibited but are not taboo. We could say that it is to give a reason for a prohibition, except that it is unintelligible what reason can be intended. So some theorists have constructed from the uses of taboo a sense which it might once have had and a possible history of how this sense was lost. One cannot take the sense from the use, for the use affords no sense, although the temptation to tell anthropologists that taboo is the name of a non-natural quality would be very strong for any Polynesian who had read G. E. Moore.

[in John Hick (ed.), *Faith and the Philosophers* (London: Macmillan, 1964), 119–22.]

There are similar confusions in MacIntyre's other paper: *Is Understanding Religion Compatible with Believing?* There he argues that when we detect an internal incoherence in the standards of intelligibility current in an alien society and try to show why this does not appear, or is made tolerable to that society's members, 'we have already invoked our standards'. In what sense is this true? Insofar as *we* 'detect' and 'show' something, obviously we do so in a sense intelligible to us; so we are limited by what *counts* (for us) as 'detecting', 'showing' something. Further, it may well be that the interest in showing and detecting such things is peculiar to our society—that we are doing something in which members of the studied society exhibit no interest, because the institutions in which such an interest could develop are lacking. Perhaps too the pursuit of that interest in our society has led to the development of techniques of inquiry and modes of argument which again are not to be found in the life of the studied society. But it cannot be guaranteed in advance that the methods and techniques we have used in the past—e.g., in elucidating the logical structure of arguments in our own language and culture—are going to be equally fruitful in this new context. They will perhaps need to be extended and modified. No doubt, if they are to have a logical relation to our previous forms of investigation, the new techniques will have to be recognizably continuous with previously used ones. But they must also so extend our conception of intelligibility as to make it possible for us to see what intelligibility amounts to in the life of the society we are investigating.

The task MacIntyre says we must undertake is to make intelligible (*a*) (to us) why it is that members of *S* think that certain of their practices are intelligible (*b*) (to them), when in fact they are not. I have introduced differentiating letters into my two uses of 'intelligible', to mark the complexity that MacIntyre's way of stating the position does not bring out: the fact that we are dealing with two different senses of the word 'intelligible'. The relation between these is precisely the question at issue. MacIntyre's task is not like that of making intelligible a natural phenomenon, where we are limited only by what counts as intelligibility for us. We must somehow bring *S*'s conception of intelligibility (*b*) into (intelligible!) relation with our own conception of intelligibility (*a*). That is, we have to create a new unity for the concept of intelligibility, having a certain relation to our old one and perhaps requiring a considerable realignment of our categories. We are not seeking a state in which things will appear to us just as they do to members of *S*, and perhaps such a state is unattainable anyway. But we *are* seeking a way of looking at things which goes beyond our previous way in that it has in some way taken

account of and incorporated the other way that members of S have of looking at things. Seriously to study another way of life is necessarily to seek to
extend our own—not simply to bring the other way within the already existing boundaries of our own, because the point about the latter in their present
form, is that they *ex hypothesi* exclude that other.

There is a dimension to the notions of rationality and intelligibility which
may make it easier to grasp the possibility of such an extension. I do not
think that MacIntyre takes sufficient account of this dimension and, indeed,
the way he talks about 'norms of rationality' obscures it. Rationality is not
just a concept *in* a language like any other; it is this too, for, like any other
concept it must be circumscribed by an established use: a use, that is, established in the language. But I think it is not a concept which a language may,
as a matter of fact, have and equally well may not have, as is, for instance,
the concept of politeness. It is a concept necessary to the existence of any
language: to say of a society that it has a language is also to say that it has a
concept of rationality. There need not perhaps be any *word* functioning in its
language as 'rational' does in ours, but at least there must be features of its
members' use of language analogous to those features of *our* use of
language which are connected with our use of the word 'rational'. Where
there is language it must make a difference what is said and this is only
possible where the saying of one thing rules out, on pain of failure to
communicate, the saying of something else. So in one sense MacIntyre is
right in saying that we have already invoked our concept of rationality in
saying of a collection of people that they constitute a society with a
language: in the sense, namely, that we imply formal analogies between
their behaviour and that behaviour in our society which we refer to in distinguishing between rationality and irrationality. This, however, is so far to say
nothing about what in particular constitutes rational behaviour in that society; that would require more particular knowledge about the norms they
appeal to in living their lives. In other words, it is not so much a matter of
invoking 'our own norms of rationality' as of invoking our notion of rationality in speaking of their behaviour in terms of 'conformity to norms'. But
how precisely this notion is to be applied to them will depend on our reading of their conformity to norms—what counts for them as conformity and
what does not.

Earlier I criticized MacIntyre's conception of a 'stock of available descriptions'. Similar criticisms apply to his talk about 'our norms of rationality', if
these norms are taken as forming some finite set. Certainly we learn to think,
speak, and act rationally *through* being trained to adhere to particular norms.
But having learned to speak, etc., rationally does not *consist* in having been
trained to follow those norms; to suppose that would be to overlook the
importance of the phrase 'and so on' in any description of what someone
who follows norms does. We must, if you like, be open to new possibilities of

what could be invoked and accepted under the rubric of 'rationality'—possibilities which are perhaps suggested and limited by what we have hitherto so accepted, but not uniquely determined thereby.

This point can be applied to the possibilities of our grasping forms of rationality different from ours in an alien culture. First, as I have indicated, these possibilities are limited by certain formal requirements centering round the demand for consistency. But these formal requirements tell us nothing about what in particular is to *count* as consistency, just as the rules of the propositional calculus limit, but do not themselves determine what are to be proper values of p, q, etc. We can only determine this by investigating the wider context of the life in which the activities in question are carried on. This investigation will take us beyond merely specifying the rules governing the carrying out of those activities. For, as MacIntyre quite rightly says, to note that certain rules are followed is so far to say nothing about the *point* of the rules; it is not even to decide whether or not they have a point at all.

MacIntyre's recipe for deciding this is that 'in bringing out this feature of the case one shows also whether the use of this concept is or is not a possible one for people who have the standards of intelligibility in speech and action which we have'. It is important to notice that his argument, contrary to what he supposes, does not in fact show that our *own* standards of rationality occupy a peculiarly central position. The appearance to the contrary is an optical illusion engendered by the fact that MacIntyre's case has been advanced in the English language and in the context of twentieth-century European culture. But a formally similar argument could be advanced in *any* language containing concepts playing a similar role in that language to those of 'intelligibility' and 'rationality' in ours. This shows that, so far from overcoming relativism, as he claims, MacIntyre himself falls into an extreme form of it. He disguises this from himself by committing the very error of which, wrongly as I have tried to show, he accuses me: the error of overlooking the fact that 'criteria and concepts have a history'. While he emphasizes this point when he is dealing with the concepts and criteria governing action in particular social contexts, he forgets it when he comes to talk of the *criticism* of such criteria. Do not the criteria appealed to in the criticism of existing institutions equally have a history? And in whose society do they have that history? MacIntyre's implicit answer is that it is in ours; but if we are to speak of difficulties and incoherencies appearing and being detected in the way certain practices have hitherto been carried on in a society, surely this can only be understood in connection with problems arising *in* the carrying on of the activity. Outside that context we could not begin to grasp what was problematical.

[in D. Z. Phillips (ed.), *Religion and Understanding* (Oxford: Basil Blackwell, 1967), 28–32.]

In practice the nature of the biblical answer to the question: Who is God in His revelation? is such as to answer at once the two other questions: What is He doing? and: What does He effect? and to answer them, not just incidentally, not just in such sort that what we hear can be erased the next time these other questions are put, but in such a way that in receiving the answer to the first question we are bound to hear the answer to the others too, so that the first answer is properly heard only when it is heard as given in the other answers. Is this true in regard to other records of revelation too? Possibly so, possibly not; that is not our concern here. It is certainly true in the Holy Scriptures of the Christian Church. The first question that must be answered is: Who is it that reveals Himself here? Who is God here? and then we must ask what He does and thirdly what He effects, accomplishes, creates and gives in His revelation. But if the first question is intelligently put, when it is answered the second and third questions will be answered as well, and only when answers to the second and third questions are received is an answer to the first question really received.

1. The Bible certainly tells us who the God is whom it attests as self-revealing. [. . .]

2. But does anyone really hear and understand here without also hearing and understanding what is said further about the That and the How of the revelation of this God? That this revelation happened and how it happened is no accident in face of the fact that we are referring specifically to the revelation of this God. In the That and the How of this revelation He also and specifically shows Himself to be this God. Indeed, this God will and can make Himself manifest in no other way than in the That and the How of this revelation. He is completely Himself in this That and How. [. . .]

3. But according to the direction of the whole Bible the question who God is in His revelation is to be answered thirdly with a reference to the men who receive the revelation, with a reference to what the Revealer wills and does with them, to what His revelation achieves in them, to what His being revealed thus signifies for them. [. . .]

All this, this revealedness of God attested in Scripture, is not just the effect of the Revealer and His revelation, an effect which is simply to be differentiated from these, as indeed it is. It is also the answer to the question: Who reveals Himself? and to the second question: How does He reveal Himself? Thus the man who asks about the God who reveals Himself according to the witness of the Bible must also pay heed to the self-revealing as such and to the men to whom this self-revealing applies.

The fact that in putting the first question we are led on at once to a second and a third is what first brings us close to the problem of the doctrine of the Trinity. Close, for we could not say that these considerations summon us to develop the doctrine of the Trinity. The one thing we now know is that the God who reveals Himself in the Bible must also be known in His revealing and His being revealed if He is to be known. These considerations become significant and indeed decisive in this context only when we go on to make the two statements that follow.

4. The question: Who is the self-revealing God? always receives a full and unrestricted answer also in what we learn about God's self-revealing as such and about His being revealed among men. God Himself is not just Himself. He is also His self-revealing. [. . .]

Again He Himself is not just Himself but also what He creates and achieves in men. [. . .]

Thus it is God Himself, it is the same God in unimpaired unity, who according to the biblical understanding of revelation is the revealing God and the event of revelation and its effect on man.

5. It does not seem possible, nor is any attempt made in the Bible, to dissolve the unity of the self-revealing God, His revelation and His being revealed into a union in which the barriers that separate the above three forms of His divine being in revelation are removed and they are reduced to a synthetic fourth and true reality. [. . .]

Thus to the same God who in unimpaired unity is the Revealer, the revelation and the revealedness, there is also ascribed in unimpaired differentiation within Himself this threefold mode of being.

It is only—but very truly—by observing the unity and the differentiation of God in His biblically attested revelation that we are set before the problem of the doctrine of the Trinity. [. . .]

2

Thus far we have merely established the fact that in enquiring into what Holy Scripture attests as revelation we come up against the doctrine of the Trinity and thus have good reason to turn our attention to this first. We need to examine it at this stage in order to make it clear that the Christian concept of revelation already includes within it the problem of the doctrine of the Trinity, that we cannot analyse the concept without attempting as our first step to bring the doctrine of the Trinity to expression.

According to Scripture God's revelation is God's own direct speech which is not to be distinguished from the act of speaking and therefore is not to be distinguished from God Himself, from the divine I which confronts man in this act in which it says Thou to him. Revelation is *Dei loquentis persona*.

From the standpoint of the comprehensive concept of God's Word it must be said that here in God's revelation God's Word is identical with God

Himself. Among the three forms of the Word of God this can be said unconditionally and with strictest propriety only of revelation. It can be said of Holy
Scripture and Church proclamation as well, but not so unconditionally and
directly. For if the same can and must be said of them too, we must certainly
add that their identity with God is an indirect one. Without wanting to deny
or even limit their character as God's Word we must bear in mind that the
Word of God is mediated here, first through the human persons of the
prophets and apostles who receive it and pass it on, and then through the
human persons of its expositors and preachers, so that Holy Scripture and
proclamation must always become God's Word in order to be it. If the Word
of God is God Himself even in Holy Scripture and Church proclamation, it is
because this is so in the revelation to which they bear witness. In understanding God's Word as the Word preached and written, we certainly do not understand it as God's Word to a lesser degree. But we understand the same Word
of God in its relation to revelation. On the other hand, when we understand
it as revealed, we understand it apart from such relations, or rather as the basis
of the relations in which it is also the Word of God. We thus understand it as
indistinguishable from the event in virtue of which it is the one Word of God
in those relations, and therefore as indistinguishable from God's direct speech
and hence from God Himself. It is this that—we do not say distinguishes,
since there is no question of higher rank or value—but rather characterizes
revelation in comparison with Holy Scripture and Church proclamation (cf.
on this § 4, 3 and 4).

According to Holy Scripture God's revelation is a ground which has no
higher or deeper ground above or below it but is an absolute ground in itself,
and therefore for man a court from which there can be no possible appeal to
a higher court. Its reality and its truth do not rest on a superior reality and
truth. They do not have to be actualized or validated as reality from this or
any other point. They are not measured by the reality and truth found at this
other point. They are not to be compared with any such nor judged and
understood as reality and truth by reference to such. On the contrary, God's
revelation has its reality and truth wholly and in every respect—both ontically
and noetically—within itself. Only if one denies it can one ascribe to it
another higher or deeper ground or try to understand and accept or reject it
from the standpoint of this higher or deeper ground. Obviously even the
acceptance of revelation from the standpoint of this different and supposedly
higher ground, e.g., an acceptance of revelation in which man first sets his
own conscience over it as judge, can only entail the denial of revelation.
Revelation is not made real and true by anything else, whether in itself or for
us. Both in itself and for us it is real and true through itself. This differentiates
it even from the witness which the prophets and apostles and the witness
which the expositors and preachers of Scripture bear to it, at any rate to the
extent that this witness is considered *per se*. If we can also say that the witness

both in itself and for us is grounded through itself, this is in virtue of the fact that this witness does not merely seek to relate itself to revelation but does actually relate itself to it, because revelation has become an event in it. This can happen. And it must happen if Scripture and proclamation are to be God's Word. They must become it. Revelation does not have to become it. The fullness of the original self-existent being of God's Word reposes and lives in it.

[*Church Dogmatics*, ii. 1, ed. G. W. Bromiley and T. F. Torrance (Edinburgh: T. and T. Clark, 1975), 297–305.]

KEITH WARD

101 Reason and Revelation

It is tempting for the Christian theologian simply to assert that God has spoken in the Bible, and nowhere else, and that is that. A standard exposition of such a view can be found in H. Kraemer, *The Christian Message in a Non-Christian World*, and also in the work of Emil Brunner and Karl Barth. Barth's view, in the *Church Dogmatics*, is particularly blunt. 'Religion', he says, 'is unbelief'. 'Man's attempts to know God from his own standpoint are wholly and entirely futile . . . in religion, man bolts and bars himself against revelation by providing a substitute.' Barth sees religion as a human enterprise which is really an attempt at human self-justification in the face of a God who is pictured in a capricious and arbitrary way. 'Religion is idolatry and self-righteousness . . . thoroughly self-centred.' It is idolatry because it creates a God in man's own image; human reason is not capable of attaining a true idea of God. And it is self-righteousness because it is an attempt at self-justification, at achieving a sense of righteousness by human effort.

Such statements are not based on exhaustive research into forms of religion; they are rather an a priori consequence of Barth's general view that 'man's I-ness . . . is in contradiction to the divine nature'. Thus any religion, as a human construct, including Christianity itself, in its institutional forms and speculative explorations, can be no more than a barrier against God; and the more it thinks it attains to God, the less it is capable of doing so. The difficulty for this view is that once one has characterized all religions, including one's own, as products of pride and stupidity, how is one ever to attain to truth about God? Barth's answer is hardly satisfactory. He simply asserts that 'Scripture is the only valid testimony to revelation'. But how can anyone know this, if every human judgement is sinful, *including this one*? Indeed, one can very easily turn the tables on Barth and insist (as it seems very plausible to do) that the belief that everyone else's revelation is incorrect and only one's own is true, is a particularly clear example of human pride and self-interest. Of course one has an interest in thinking one's own religion is the only true one;

it enables one to dismiss the others as of no account and so bask in the superiority of one's own possession of truth. One may claim that this possession is by the grace of God alone—but this only makes the element of human pride more pronounced, since one is now asserting that grace is only truly possessed by oneself. One can hardly get more proud, more self-righteous, and more short-sighted than that.

Emil Brunner falls into exactly the same trap. 'How do you know . . . the Word . . . is really God's Word?' he asks. For a moment one is perhaps hopeful of a serious attempt to answer the question; but it is not forthcoming. All Brunner says is, 'From God himself'. Naturally, all Muslims would say that of the Koran, all Mormons of the Book of Mormon, and all Sikhs of the Guru Granth Sahib. Brunner makes things even worse when he says, 'That which can be based on rational grounds is . . . not revelation.' He is not here simply objecting to attempts to prove doctrines like the Incarnation and the Trinity by reason. He is objecting to the process of giving any reasons for accepting something as revelation. 'Doubt is a form of sin,' he says; it 'springs from intellectual arrogance'. 'A theology that allows itself to be drawn into producing proofs for its claim to revelation has already thrown up the sponge.' The position he is maintaining is that no reasons can or should be given for accepting Christian revelation. Using the same reasoning, no reasons can be given for accepting Muslim revelation. So what is one to do when faced with a choice between them, a choice which many people in our world actually do face?

What may be confusing the issue is the thought that a good reason would have to persuade everyone. Now in religion there are few good reasons in this very strong sense. Reasons are person-relative. What seems an overwhelming reason to one person may not weigh very strongly with another, because there exists some other factor which weighs more strongly with that person. A reason is a factor rationally inclining choice. One need not be able to articulate all one's reasons for belief; it would be very rare to have that ability. But there must be reasons, factors which make it reasonable to believe as one does. That is what the theologian needs to spell out—the factors which make it seem reasonable to accept something as a Divine revelation. Barth and Brunner may be right in holding that there are no neutral reasons, which all rational persons can agree upon, for assenting to Christian (or any other) revelation. But they are wrong to draw the further conclusion that there are no factors which make it reasonable to accept something as a revelation at all. They may think that thereby they are freeing God's word from the tyranny of human pride; but in fact they are making it impossible to discover where God's word is to be found, amongst the many claimants to that status.

[*Religion and Revelation* (Oxford: Clarendon Press, 1994), 16–18.]

Divine Revelation may be either of God, or by God of propositional truth. Traditionally the Christian revelation has involved both; God became incarnate and was in some degree made manifest on Earth, and through that incarnate life various propositional truths were announced. My concern in this paper is only with revelation in the secondary sense of revelation of propositional truth. I am not concerned with all knowledge which God makes available to us, nor with all knowledge about himself, but with that knowledge which he communicates directly only to certain individuals, and they communicate to the rest of the world—where the grounds for the belief in these items of knowledge available to the first recipients are not available to the rest of the world, but the latter have to accept them, in the traditional phrase, 'upon the credit of the proposer, as coming from God in some extraordinary way of communication'. Religions often claim to have minor as well as major revelations. The former are purported particular messages to individuals about matters of more immediate concern; the latter are big messages of world-shaking significance for the practice of religion. My concern will be only with the latter. I wish to examine whether we have reason to expect a Revelation of this kind, what it will be like, and what kind of historical evidence would show that we had got it.

As with all claims about particular occurrences which are to be expected on one world-view but not on another, it is crucial to take into account the other evidence for that world view. Reports of observations are rightly viewed very sceptically when the phenomena purportedly observed are ruled out by a well-established scientific theory, but believed when they are to be expected in the light of such a theory. If you have a well-established theory which says that change does not occur in the heavenly regions (regions of the sky more distant from Earth than the Moon), you will rightly discount reports of observers who claim to have observed a new star appear where there was no star before, or to have observed comets pass through those regions (as opposed to being mere sublunary phenomena). When that theory has been abandoned, you require a lot less in the way of evidence to show the flare-up of new stars or the routes of comets through the heavens. So if there is other evidence which makes it quite likely that there is a God, all powerful and all good, who made the Earth and its inhabitants, then it becomes to some extent likely that he would intervene in human history to reveal things to them; and claims that he has done so require a lot less in the way of historical evidence than they would do otherwise. I have argued in *The Existence of God* that there is much evidence from other sources that there is an all-powerful and all-good God. If so, does that give us reason to suppose that he would intervene in human history to reveal things to us? I believe that it does.

A God who made men with capacities to make themselves saints would think it good that they should do so, and might well help them to do so. If they do become saints, he would think that that was such a good thing that it was worth preserving them after this life to pursue the supremely worth-while life of Heaven, centred on the worship of God. Although God could from the start have made men fitted for Heaven, it is obviously a good thing that men should have the opportunity to choose for themselves what kind of persons they are to be, and through deliberate exercise of that choice over a period of time to form their characters, preferably so as to be suited to live the life of Heaven. The only workable solution to the problem of evil is to my mind that centred in the free will defence, which has as an essential plank that God has made men who are not saints at the start but are capable, partly through their own choice, of making themselves saints. If there is a God, that is the kind of world he has made. If men are to have this choice, they need information as to what kind of life is a saintly life, is supremely worth living, and how to take steps to live that life. The information which they need is of four kinds. First, they need to know such general moral truths as that benefactors deserve gratitude, wrongdoers need to make atonement (by way of repentance, apology, reparation and penance) to those whom they have wronged, holy beings deserve worship; and so on. Secondly, they need factual information which will enable them to apply those moral truths, in seeing which particular actions are good or bad, obligatory or wrong. If there is a God, the crucial factual information will be that there is a God. From that it will follow that he is to be worshipped, and thanked, and that men must make atonement to him for wrongs against him (that is, sins). But it will also follow, as I have argued elsewhere, that it is very difficult for man to make atonement for his sins and to help his fellows to make their atonement, as he should. God could deal with this difficulty by himself becoming man and offering on man's behalf a perfect human life culminating in a death arising from its perfection; and, in order to allow the men whom he has created access to himself, he has reason to do so. If he has done so, it must be among the items of information which men need to have—that and how he has done so. For an atonement which another makes on our behalf can only be something through which we secure forgiveness and reconciliation if we offer it on our own behalf to him whom we have wronged. So men need, thirdly, the information of how, if at all, God became incarnate and made atonement for their sins; and the information of how to plead that atonement. God needs to have revealed himself in the primary sense, and to have made available information as to how in detail he has done this. And, finally, it provides a valuable encouragement (as well as important information about the good-ness of God) to know that there is a goal of Heaven to be had after this life for those who have obtained forgiveness for their sins and made themselves saints and so fitted for Heaven; and (if that is how it is) that there is a Hell, for those who ignore God, to be avoided.

If there is a God who wills men to do good and to be good he needs to ensure that men have the information of the kinds which I have set out. Cannot man's natural reason find out some, at least, of these things, without God needing to intervene in history to provide information in propositional form? Certainly natural reason can discover unaided the general moral truths, and there is perhaps enough evidence that there is a God without God needing to tell us so by a verbal communication. But even in these cases revelation helps—if an apparently knowledgeable person tells you that what you have concluded tentatively from your private investigation is true, that rightly gives you much more confidence in its truth. If God tells us basic moral truths, and assures us verbally that he is there, and makes it fairly clear to us that he is telling us these things, our confidence in their truth justifiably increases. I have claimed that we have some *a priori* reason to suppose that God will become incarnate and make atonement for us. But it is by no means certain that, if there is a God, he will do this. (Maybe, despite the difficulty of man making his own atonement, God judges it no better to make atonement for him than to leave him to try to make his own atonement.) And, anyway, mere *a priori* reasoning cannot tell us how and where the atonement will be made. We need historical information to show us this, and it is hard to see how it would do this without God, either himself or through another, telling us what was happening. And the goal of Heaven and the danger of Hell are things at which we can only guess without God telling us more. To strengthen some of these beliefs needed for our salvation, and to provide others of them, we need propositional revelation.

So there is some *a priori* reason to suppose that God will reveal to us those things needed for our salvation.

[in Kelly James Clark (ed.), *Our Knowledge of God: Essays on Natural and Philosophical Theology* (Dordrecht: Kluwer, 1992), 115–17.]

JOHN HICK

103 The Pluralistic Hypothesis

According to [Aquinas] we can say that God is, for example, good—not in the sense in which we say of a human being that he or she is good, nor on the other hand in a totally unrelated sense, but in the sense that there is in the divine nature a quality that is limitlessly superior and yet at the same time analogous to human goodness. But Aquinas was emphatic that we cannot know what the divine super-analogue of goodness is like: 'we cannot grasp what God is, but only what He is not and how other things are related to Him'. Further, the divine attributes which are distinguished in human thought and given such names as love, justice, knowledge, power, are identical in God. For 'God . . . as considered in Himself, is altogether one and simple, yet our intellect knows Him according to diverse conceptions because it cannot see Him as He is in Himself.' When we take these two doctrines together and apply them to the Real we see that, whilst there is a noumenal ground for the phenomenal divine attributes, this does not enable us to trace each attribute separately upwards into the Godhead or the Real. They represent the Real as both reflected and refracted within human thought and experience. But nevertheless the Real is the ultimate ground or source of those qualities which characterize each divine *persona* and *impersona* insofar as these are authentic phenomenal manifestations of the Real.

This relationship between the ultimate noumenon and its multiple phenomenal appearances, or between the limitless transcendent reality and our many partial human images of it, makes possible mythological speech about the Real. I define a myth as a story or statement which is not literally true but which tends to evoke an appropriate dispositional attitude to its subject-matter. Thus the truth of a myth is a practical truthfulness: a true myth is one which rightly relates us to a reality about which we cannot speak in non-mythological terms. For we exist inescapably in relation to the Real, and in all that we do and undergo we are inevitably having to do with it in and through our neighbours and our world. Our attitudes and actions are accordingly appropriate or inappropriate not only in relation to our physical and social environments but also in relation to our ultimate environment. And true religious myths are accordingly those that evoke in us attitudes and modes of behaviour which are appropriate to our situation in relation to the Real.

But what is it for human attitudes, behaviours, patterns of life to be appropriate or inappropriate within this ultimate situation? It is for the *persona* or *impersona* in relation to which we live to be an authentic manifestation of the Real and for our practical response to be appropriate to that manifestation. To the extent that a *persona* or *impersona* is in soteriological alignment with the Real, an appropriate response to that deity or absolute is an appropriate response to the Real. It need not however be the only such response: for other phenomenal manifestations of the Real within other human traditions evoke other responses which may be equally appropriate.

Why however use the term 'Real' in the singular? Why should there not be a number of ultimate realities? There is of course no reason, *a priori*, why the closest approximation that there is to a truly ultimate reality may not consist in either an orderly federation or a feuding multitude or an unrelated plurality. But if from a religious point of view we are trying to think, not merely of what is logically possible (namely, anything that is conceivable), but of the simplest hypothesis to account for the plurality of forms of religious experience and

thought, we are, I believe, led to postulate 'the Real'. For each of the great traditions is oriented to what it regards as the Ultimate as the sole creator or source
of the universe, or as that than which no greater can be conceived, or as the final
ground or nature of everything. Further, the 'truthfulness' of each tradition is
shown by its soteriological effectiveness. But what the traditions severally
regard as ultimates are different and therefore cannot all be truly ultimate. They
can however be different manifestations of the truly Ultimate within different
streams of human thought-and-experience—hence the postulation of the Real
an sich as the simplest way of accounting for the data. But we then find that if
we are going to speak of the Real at all, the exigencies of our language compel
us to refer to it in either the singular or the plural. Since there cannot be a plurality of ultimates, we affirm the true ultimacy of the Real by referring to it in the
singular. Indian thought meets this problem with the phrase 'The One without
a second'. The Real, then, is the ultimate Reality, not one among others; and yet
it cannot literally be numbered: it is the unique One without a second.

But if the Real in itself is not and cannot be humanly experienced, why
postulate such an unknown and unknowable *Ding an sich*? The answer is that
the divine noumenon is a necessary postulate of the pluralistic religious life of
humanity. For within each tradition we regard as real the object of our
worship or contemplation. If, as I have already argued, it is also proper to
regard as real the objects of worship or contemplation within the other traditions, we are led to postulate the Real *an sich* as the presupposition of the
veridical character of this range of forms of religious experience. Without
this postulate we should be left with a plurality of *personae* and *impersonae*
each of which is claimed to be the Ultimate, but no one of which alone can
be. We should have either to regard all the reported experiences as illusory or
else return to the confessional position in which we affirm the authenticity of
our own stream of religious experience whilst dismissing as illusory those
occurring within other traditions. But for those to whom neither of these
options seems realistic the pluralistic affirmation becomes inevitable, and
with it the postulation of the Real *an sich*, which is variously experienced and
thought as the range of divine phenomena described by the history of religion. This is accordingly the hypothesis that is now to be developed.

[*An Interpretation of Religion* (London: Macmillan, 1989), 247–9.]

ALVIN PLANTINGA

104   Epistemic Objections to Exclusivism

The pluralist objector sometimes claims that to hold exclusivist views, in
condition C, is *unjustified—epistemically* unjustified. Is this true? And what
does he mean when he makes this claim? As even a brief glance at the

contemporary epistemological literature shows, justification is a protean and multifarious notion. There are, I think, substantially two possibilities as to what he means. The central core of the notion, its beating heart, the paradigmatic centre to which most of the myriad contemporary variations are related by way of analogical extension and family resemblance, is the notion of *being within one's intellectual rights*, having violated no intellectual or cognitive duties or obligations in the formation and sustenance of the belief in question. This is the palimpsest, going back to Descartes and especially Locke, that underlies the multitudinous battery of contemporary inscriptions. There is no space to argue that point here; but chances are when the pluralist objector to exclusivism claims that the latter is unjustified, it is some notion lying in this neighbourhood that he has in mind. (And, here we should note the very close connection between the moral objections to exclusivism and the objection that exclusivism is epistemically unjustified.)

The duties involved, naturally enough, would be specifically *epistemic* duties: perhaps a duty to proportion degree of belief to (propositional) evidence from what is *certain*, that is, self-evident or incorrigible, as with Locke, or perhaps to try one's best to get into and stay in the right relation to the truth, as with Roderick Chisholm, the leading contemporary champion of the justificationist tradition with respect to knowledge. But at present there is widespread (and, as I see it, correct) agreement that there is no duty of the Lockean kind. Perhaps there is one of the Chisholmian kind; but isn't the exclusivist conforming to that duty if, after the sort of careful, indeed prayerful, consideration I mentioned in the response to the moral objection, it still seems to him strongly that (1), say, is true and he accordingly still believes it? It is therefore hard to see that the exclusivist is necessarily unjustified in this way.

The second possibility for understanding the charge—the charge that exclusivism is epistemically unjustified—has to do with the oft-repeated claim that exclusivism is intellectually *arbitrary*. Perhaps the idea is that there is an intellectual duty to treat similar cases similarly; the exclusivist violates this duty by arbitrarily choosing to believe (for the moment going along with the fiction that we *choose* beliefs of this sort) (1) and (2) in the face of the plurality of conflicting religious beliefs the world presents. But suppose there is such a duty. Clearly, you do not violate it if you nonculpably think the beliefs in question are *not* on a par. And, as an exclusivist, I *do* think (nonculpably, I hope) that they are not on a par: I think (1) and (2) *true* and those incompatible with either of them *false*.

The rejoinder, of course, will be that it is not *alethic* parity (their having the same truth value) that is at issue: it is *epistemic* parity that counts. What kind of epistemic parity? What would be relevant here, I should think, would be *internal* or internalist epistemic parity: parity with respect to what is internally available to the believer. What is internally available to the believer includes, for example, detectable relationships between the belief in question and other beliefs you hold; so internal parity would include parity of propositional evidence. What is internally available to the believer also includes the *phenomenology* that goes with the beliefs in question: the *sensuous* phenomenology, but also the nonsensuous phenomenology involved, for example, in the belief's just having the feel of being *right*. But once more, then, (1) and (2) are not on an internal par, for the exclusivist, with beliefs that are incompatible with them. (1) and (2), after all, seem to me to be true; they have for me the phenomenology that accompanies that seeming. The same cannot be said for propositions incompatible with them. If, furthermore, John Calvin is right in thinking that there is such a thing as the Sensus Divinitatis and the Internal Testimony of the Holy Spirit, then perhaps (1) and (2) are produced in me by those belief-producing processes, and have for me the phenomenology that goes with them; the same is not true for propositions incompatible with them.

But then the next rejoinder: isn't it probably true that those who reject (1) and (2) in favour of other beliefs have propositional evidence for their beliefs that is on a par with mine for my beliefs; and isn't it also probably true that the same or similar phenomenology accompanies their beliefs as accompanies mine? So that those beliefs really are epistemically and internally on a par with (1) and (2), and the exclusivist is still treating like cases differently? I don't think so: I think there really are arguments available for (1), at least, that are not available for its competitors. And as for similar phenomenology, this is not easy to say; it is not easy to look into the breast of another; the secrets of the human heart are hard to fathom; it is hard indeed to discover this sort of thing even with respect to someone you know really well. But I am prepared to stipulate both sorts of parity. Let's agree for purposes of argument that these beliefs are on an epistemic par in the sense that those of a different religious tradition have the same sort of internally available markers—evidence, phenomenology, and the like—for their beliefs as I have for (1) and (2). What follows?

Return to the case of moral belief. King David took Bathsheba, made her pregnant, and then, after the failure of various stratagems to get her husband Uriah to think the baby was his, arranged for Uriah to be killed. The prophet Nathan came to David and told him a story about a rich man and a poor man. The rich man had many flocks and herds; the poor man had only a single ewe lamb, which grew up with his children, 'ate at his table, drank from his cup, lay in his bosom, and was like a daughter to him.' The rich man had unexpected guests. Instead of slaughtering one of his own sheep, he took the poor man's single ewe lamb, slaughtered it, and served it to his guests. David exploded in anger: 'The man who did this deserves to die!' Then, in one of the most riveting passages in all the Bible, Nathan turns to David, stretches out his arm and points to him, and declares, *'You are that man!'* And David sees what he has done.

My interest here is in David's reaction to the story. I agree with David: such injustice is utterly and despicably wrong; there are really no words for it. I believe that such an action is wrong, and I believe that the proposition that it *isn't* wrong—either because really *nothing* is wrong, or because even if *some* things are wrong, *this* isn't—is false. As a matter of fact, there isn't a lot I believe more strongly. I recognize, however, that there are those who disagree with me; and once more, I doubt that I could find an argument to show them that I am right and they wrong. Further, for all I know, their conflicting beliefs have for them the same internally available epistemic markers, the same phenomenology, as mine have for me. Am I then being arbitrary, treating similar cases differently in continuing to hold, as I do, that in fact that kind of behaviour *is* dreadfully wrong? I don't think so. Am I wrong in thinking racial bigotry despicable, even though I know there are others who disagree, and even if I think they have the same internal markers for their beliefs as I have for mine? I don't think so. I believe in Serious Actualism, the view that no objects have properties in worlds in which they do not exist, not even nonexistence. Others do not believe this, and perhaps the internal markers of their dissenting views have for them the same quality as my views have for me. Am I being arbitrary in continuing to think as I do? I can't see how.

And the reason here is this: in each of these cases, the believer in question doesn't really think the beliefs in question *are* on a relevant epistemic par. She may agree that she and those who dissent are equally convinced of the truth of their belief, and even that they are internally on a par, that the internally available markers are similar, or relevantly similar. But she must still think that there is an important epistemic difference: she thinks that somehow the other person has *made a mistake*, or *has a blind spot*, or hasn't been wholly attentive, or hasn't received some grace she has, or is in some way epistemically less fortunate. And, of course, the pluralist critic is in no better case. He thinks the thing to do when there is internal epistemic parity is to withhold judgment; he knows there are others who don't think so, and for all he knows, that belief has internal parity with his; if he continues in that belief, therefore, he will be in the same condition as the exclusivist; and if he doesn't continue in this belief, he no longer has an objection to the exclusivist.

But couldn't I be wrong? Of course I could! But I don't avoid that risk by withholding all religious (or philosophical or moral) beliefs; I can go wrong that way as well as any other, treating all religions, or all philosophical thoughts, or all moral views, as on a par. Again, there is no safe haven here, no way to avoid risk. In particular, you won't reach safe haven by trying to take the same attitude toward all the historically available patterns of belief and withholding: for in so doing, you adopt a particular pattern of belief and withholding, one incompatible with some adopted by others. You pays your money and you takes your choice, realizing that you, like anyone else, can be desperately wrong. But what else can you do? You don't really have an alternative. And how can you do better than believe and withhold according to what, after serious and responsible consideration, seems to you to be the right pattern of belief and withholding?

['A Defence of Religious Exclusivism', in Thomas D. Senor (ed.), *The Rationality of Belief and the Plurality of Faith* (Ithaca, NY: Cornell University Press, 1995), 201–5.]

Section IX

The Twentieth Century: III. Reason and Belief in God

INTRODUCTION

In earlier sections we have seen that one important strand running through issues of faith and reason, some would say the most important strand, concerns the issue of natural theology, of whether the existence of God can be proved from premisses acceptable to any rational person. Some have argued that positive natural theology is indispensably necessary in order for faith to be reasonable, and also that the development of such a natural theology is possible; others have argued that natural theology is possible for reasonableness but not necessary; some have argued that it is neither possible nor necessary; and finally some have argued that it is necessary but not possible.

These debates about the possibility and the necessity of natural theology have continued vigorously in the twentieth century, and representatives of each approach are collected in this section, though it is important to note that not all representatives of each approach would agree among themselves. So the groupings are not meant to represent clearly defined schools of thought, but rather a series of very general common approaches.

This section begins with extracts from this last group. Flew claims that all rational argument about theism must start from the presumption of atheism. Hanson raises a problem for agnosticism. A prominent instance of those who argue that natural theology is both necessary and possible is Swinburne, who has revived and developed a form of the argument from design.

Alvin Plantinga has become an influential figure in arguing that natural theology is not necessary to establish the rationality of religious belief, claiming that a person is within his intellectual rights to have the proposition that God exists among the set of foundational beliefs that he possesses. Plantinga appeals to certain insights of the Reformer John Calvin, particularly his idea of the *sensus divinitatis*. Westphal argues that Plantinga has not taken the idea of the noetic effects of sin with sufficient seriousness; had he done so, he would have had a greater degree of suspicion about any form of foundationalism. Like Plantinga, but for rather different reasons, Cahn argues that it is not necessary for religion to prove the existence of God. Van Inwagen approaches foundationalism from a different direction, raising general questions about the nature of the appeal to evidence that has been characteristic of the strong foundationalism of the Enlightenment period and subsequently.

Both Swinburne and Plantinga are foundationalists. That is, they claim that rational belief in God may either be a basic belief for a person (Plantinga), or that it can be derived by reasonable steps from basic beliefs which everyone shares (Swinburne). But there are other patterns of rational belief formation besides foundationalism, whether strong or weak; for example, a pattern that stresses the accumulation of pieces of evidence, as occurs in the solving of a crime or a crossword puzzle. Basil Mitchell defends such a view. So Mitchell may be said to offer a natural theology of a weaker kind, appealing to the accumulation of various types of evidence to justify and make religious belief reasonable, but not such as is intended to convince the sceptic. Alston defends the rationality of appealing to religious experience.

The various positions that it is possible to take on the place and importance of natural theology have implication for the nature of faith. The extracts on faith provided here, from Swinburne, Helm, and Adams, think of faith as having some positive relation to well-grounded belief, though it is important to remember that many thinkers, taking their cue from Kierkegaard, if not from Kant, continue to think of faith as a leap that is not grounded in evidence. These ideas of faith, though they are of theological and religious importance, do not raise any questions about the relation between faith and reason, since they remove faith from the realm of rational appraisal. Swinburne, who lays stress on the cognitive character of religious belief, also stresses the voluntariness of faith, while Helm identifies a potential conflict between these views. Adams looks at one aspect of responsibility for faith, or for unbelief.

What does show the presumption of atheism to be the right one is what we have now to investigate.

(i) An obvious first move is to appeal to the old legal axiom: 'Ei incumbit probatio qui dicit, non qui negat.' Literally and unsympathetically translated this becomes: 'The onus of proof lies on the man who affirms, not on the man who denies.' To this the objection is almost equally obvious. Given just a very little verbal ingenuity, the content of any motion can be rendered alternatively in either a negative or a positive form: either, 'That this house affirms the existence of God'; or, 'That this house takes its stand for positive atheism'. So interpreted, therefore, our axiom provides no determinate guidance.

Suppose, however, that we take the hint already offered in the previous paragraph. A less literal but more sympathetic translation would be: 'The onus of proof lies on the proposition, not on the opposition.' The point of the change is to bring out that this maxim was offered in a legal context, and that our courts are institutions of debate. An axiom providing no determinate guidance outside that framework may nevertheless be fundamental for the effective conduct of orderly and decisive debate. Here the outcome is supposed to be decided on the merits of what is said within the debate itself, and of that alone. So no opposition can set about demolishing the proposition case until and unless that proposition has first provided them with a case for demolition: 'You've got to get something on your plate before you can start messing it around' (J. L. Austin).

Of course our maxim even when thus sympathetically interpreted still offers no direction on which contending parties ought to be made to undertake which roles. Granting that courts are to operate as debating institutions, and granting that this maxim is fundamental to debate, we have to appeal to some further premise principle before we become licensed to infer that the prosecution must propose and the defence oppose. This further principle is, once again, the familiar presumption of innocence. Were we, while retaining the conception of a court as an institution for reaching decisions by way of formalised debate, to embrace the opposite presumption, the presumption of guilt, we should need to adopt the opposite arrangements. In these the defence would first propose that the accused is after all innocent, and the prosecution would then respond by struggling to disintegrate the case proposed.

(ii) The first move examined cannot, therefore, be by itself sufficient. To have considered it does nevertheless help to show that to accept such a presumption is to adopt a policy. And policies have to be assessed by reference to the aims of those for whom they are suggested. If for you it is more important that no guilty person should ever be acquitted than that no innocent person should ever be convicted, then for you a presumption of guilt must be the rational policy. For you, with your preference structure, a presumption of innocence becomes simply irrational. To adopt this policy would be to adopt means calculated to frustrate your own chosen ends; which is, surely, paradigmatically irrational. Take, as an actual illustration, the controlling elite of a ruling Leninist party, which must as such refuse to recognize any individual rights if these conflict with the claims of the party, and which in fact treats all those suspected of actual or potential opposition much as if they were already known 'counter-revolutionaries', 'enemies of socialism', 'friends of the United States', 'advocates of free elections', and all other like things bad. I can, and do, fault this policy and its agents on many counts. Yet I cannot say that for them, once granted their scale of values, it is irrational.

What then are the aims by reference to which an atheist presumption might be justified? One key word in the answer, if not the key word, must be 'knowledge'. The context for which such a policy is proposed is that of inquiry about the existence of God; and the object of the exercise is, presumably, to discover whether it is possible to establish that the word 'God' does in fact have application. Now to establish must here be either to show that you know or to come to know. But knowledge is crucially different from mere true belief. All knowledge involves true belief; not all true belief constitutes knowledge. To have a true belief is simply and solely to believe that something is so, and to be in fact right. But someone may believe that this or that is so, and his belief may in fact be true, without its thereby and necessarily constituting knowledge. If a true belief is to achieve this more elevated status, then the believer has to be properly warranted so to believe. He must, that is, be in a position to know.

Obviously there is enormous scope for disagreement in particular cases: both about what is required in order to be in a position to know; and about whether these requirements have actually been satisfied. But the crucial distinction between believing truly and knowing is recognized as universally as the prior and equally vital distinction between believing and believing what is in fact true. If, for instance, there is a question whether a colleague performed some discreditable action, then all of us, though we have perhaps to admit that we cannot help believing that he did, are rightly scrupulous not to assert that this is known unless we have grounds sufficient to warrant the bolder claim. It is, therefore, not only incongruous but also scandalous in matters of life and death, and even of eternal life and death, to maintain that you know either on no grounds at all, or on grounds of a kind which on other and comparatively minor issues you yourself would insist to be inadequate.

It is by reference to this inescapable demand for grounds that the presumption of atheism is justified. If it is to be established that there is a God, then we have to have good grounds for believing that this is indeed so. Until and unless some such grounds are produced we have literally no reason at all for believing;

and in that situation the only reasonable posture must be that of either the negative atheist or the agnostic. So the onus of proof has to rest on the proposition. It must be up to them: first, to give whatever sense they choose to the word 'God', meeting any objection that so defined it would relate only to an incoherent pseudo-concept; and, second, to bring forward sufficient reasons to warrant their claim that, in their present sense of the word 'God', there is a God. The same applies, with appropriate alterations, if what is to be made out is, not that theism is known to be true, but only—more modestly—that it can be seen to be at least more or less probable.

[*The Presumption of Atheism* (London: Elek/Pemberton, 1976), 20–3.]

NORWOOD RUSSELL HANSON

106   The Agnostic's Dilemma

Many theologians hold the claim 'God exists' not to be central to the core of religious belief at all. In different ways, Niebuhr, Tillich, and Braithwaite have argued that the role of belief within human life remains fundamental whatever our decisions about the logical or factual status of the claim 'God exists'. Apparently it matters little to the reasonableness of one's religious beliefs whether or not he believes in God: indeed, it might remain reasonable for one to persist as a believer even after further thought has led him to deny God's existence.

This apologia has gained in popularity what it has lost in rationality. Clearly, a rational man will not continue to believe in what he has grounds for supposing does not exist. Nor will he maintain belief in that chain of claims which hang on a proposition he no longer thinks is true.

Hence, in this paper, 'God exists' is a synthetic claim; it could be false. Moreover, the claim could be contingently confirmed, as some theists say it already is. What have theists, atheists, and agnostics been arguing about, if not whether this existence claim is, or can be, factually established? Logically, the claim belongs in the centre of our discussion. Historically, that is where it always has been. Despite the hocus-pocus of theologians, the claim is also central within the lives of genuinely religious people. Surely most streetlevel believers would be affected in their religion by the disclosure that the New Testament was a forgery, or by a demonstration that God could not exist—assuming such a disclosure or demonstration to be possible.

Many theists will not be moved by these considerations. They will insist that 'God exists' is not the sort of claim that could be amenable to scientific observation, or even to logical scrutiny. Both reason and the senses fail when issues which turn on faith arise. This, of course, is a flight from reason. If neither logic nor experience can be allowed to affect our attitudes towards God's existence, then no argument and no ordinary experience can affect the theist's belief.

However, it then becomes a university's function to stress that religious belief, so construed, is not reasonable. Nor is it connected with ordinary experience—since, if the latter cannot count against such belief, then neither can it count for it. A university must help young adults to distinguish positions for which there are good grounds from other positions for which the grounds are not so good. When the theist lets his appeal collapse into faith alone, he concedes that his position rests on no rational grounds at all.

The agnostic, however, cannot adopt any such theistic device. He must grant, without qualification, that 'God exists' is contingent. He feels, nonetheless, that there are no compelling factual grounds for deciding the issue one way or the other. After the atheist has exposed as inadequate all known arguments for God's existence, someone will ask, 'But can you prove God does not exist?' Instead of realizing he has already done this, the atheist often hedges. This the agnostic mistakenly makes the basis for his universal dubiety.

If the argument between theists and atheists could have been settled by reflection, this would long since have been done. The theist's appeal to faith cannot settle any argument. So the agnostic adopts the only alternative, viz., that the argument concerns a matter of fact—whether or not God does in fact exist. But he remains in an equipoise of noncommitment by proclaiming that neither theist nor atheist has factual grounds for supposing the other's position to be refuted. How in detail does the agnostic argue this point?

Consider some logical preliminaries: entertain the claim 'All A's are B's'. If this ranges over a potential infinitude, then it can never be completely established by any finite number of observations of A's being B's. 'All bats are viviparous' receives each day a higher probability—but it is always less than 1, since the claim ranges over all past, present, and future bats, anywhere and everywhere.

This claim is easily disconfirmed, however. Discovering one oviparous bat would do it. Consider now the different claim: 'There exists an A which is a B'. This can never be disconfirmed. Being told that some bat is oviparous cannot be disconfirmed by appealing to everything now known about bats, as well as to all extant bats. The 'anywhere–everywhere' and 'past–present–future' conditions operate here too. However, we can confirm this claim by discovering one oviparous bat.

So, 'All A's are B's' can be disconfirmed, but never completely established. 'There exists an A which is B' can be established, but never disestablished.

'There is a God' has never been factually established. Any account of phenomena which at first seems to require God's existence is always explicable *via* some alternative account requiring no supernatural reference. Since appealing to God constitutes an end to further inquiry, the alternative accounts have been the more attractive; indeed, the history of science is a history of finding accounts of phenomena alternative to just appealing to God's existence.

Thus there is not one clearcut natural happening, nor any constellation of such happenings, which establishes God's existence—not as witnessing a bat laying an egg would establish 'There is an oviparous bat'.

In principle, God's existence could be established with the same clarity and directness one would expect in a verification of the claim 'some bats are oviparous'. Suppose that tomorrow morning, after breakfast, all of us are knocked to our knees by an ear-shattering thunderclap. Trees drop their leaves. The earth heaves. The sky blazes with light, and the clouds pull apart, revealing an immense and radiant Zeus-like figure. He frowns. He points at me and exclaims, for all to hear.

'Enough of your logic-chopping and word-watching matters of theology. Be assured henceforth that I most assuredly exist'. Nor is this a private transaction between the heavens and myself. Everyone in the world experienced this, and heard what was said to me.

Do not dismiss this example as a playful contrivance. The conceptual point is that were this to happen, I should be entirely convinced that God exists. The subtleties with which the learned devout discuss this existence claim would seem, after such an experience, like a discussion of colour in a home for the blind. That God exists would have been confirmed for me, and everyone else, in a manner as direct as that involved in any noncontroversial factual claim. Only, there is no good reason for supposing anything remotely like this ever to have happened, biblical mythology notwithstanding.

In short, not only is 'God exists' a factual claim—one can even specify what it would be like to confirm it. If the hypothetical description offered above is not rich or subtle enough, the reader can make the appropriate adjustments. But if no description, however rich and subtle, could be relevant to confirming the claim, then it could never be reasonable to believe in God's existence. Nor would it then be reasonable to base one's life on such a claim.

What about disconfirming 'God exists'? Here the agnostic should face the logical music—but he doesn't. What he does do, and as an agnostic must do, is as follows:

The agnostic treats 'God exists' as he should, as a factual claim the supporting evidence for which is insufficient for verification. However, he treats the denial of that claim quite differently. Now the agnostic chooses the logical point we sharpened above. No finite set of experiences which fail to support claims like 'Oviparous bats exist' and 'God exists' can by itself conclusively disconfirm such claims. Perhaps we have not been looking in the right places, or at the right things. We do not even know what it would be like to disconfirm such claims, since we cannot have all the possibly relevant experiences. But we do know what it would be like to establish that 'God exists'. Variations of the alarming encounter with the thundering God described above would confirm this claim.

The logical criterion invoked when the agnostic argues that 'there is a God' cannot be falsified applies to all existence claims. Hence, he has no grounds for denying that there is a Loch Ness Monster, or a five-headed Welshman, or a unicorn in New College garden. But there are excellent grounds for denying such claims. They consist in there being no reason whatever for supposing that these claims are true. And there being no reason for thinking a claim true is itself good reason for thinking it false. We know what it would be like to fish up the Loch Ness monster, or to encounter a five-headed Welshman, or to trap the New College unicorn. It just happens that there are no such things. We have the best factual grounds for saying this. Believers will feel that 'God exists' is better off than these other claims. They might even think it confirmed. But if they think this they must also grant that the evidence could go in the opposite direction. For if certain evidence can confirm a claim, other possible evidence must be such that, had it obtained, it would have disconfirmed that claim.

Precisely here the agnostic slips. While he grants that some possible evidence could confirm that God exists, but that it hasn't yet, he insists that no possible evidence could disconfirm this claim. The agnostic shifts logical ground when he supposes that evidence against the 'God exists' claim never could be good enough. Yet he must do this to remain agnostic. Otherwise, he could never achieve his 'perfect indecision' concerning whether God exists. For usually, when evidence is not good enough for us to conclude that X exists, we infer directly that X does not exist. Thus, the evidence fails to convince us that there is a Loch Ness monster, or a five-headed Welshman, or a New College unicorn; and since this is so, we conclude directly that such beings do not exist. These are the grounds usually offered for saying of something that it does not exist, namely, the evidence does not establish that it does.

The agnostic dons the mantle of rationality in the theist vs. atheist dispute. He seeks to appear as one whose reasonableness lifts him above the battle. But he can maintain this attitude only by being unreasonable, i.e., by shifting ground in his argument. if the agnostic insists that we could never disconfirm God's existence, then he must grant that we could never confirm the claim either. But if he feels we could confirm the claim, then he must grant that we could disconfirm it, too. To play the logician's game when saying that 'there are no oviparous bats' cannot be established, one must play the same game with 'there is an oviparous bat'. Even were a bat to lay an egg before such a person's very eyes, he would have to grant that, in strict logic, 'there exists an oviparous bat' was no more confirmed that its denial. But this is absurd. To see such a thing is to have been made able to claim that there is an oviparous bat. By this same criterion we assert today that 'there are no oviparous bats'. We take this to be confirmed in just that sense appropriate within any factual context.

The agnostic's position is therefore impossible. He begins by assessing 'God exists' as a fact-gatherer. He ends by appraising the claim's denial not as a fact-gatherer but as a logician. But consistency demands he either be a fact-gatherer on both counts or play logician on both counts. If the former, he must grant that there is ample factual reason for denying that God exists, namely, that the evidence in favour of his existence is just not good enough. If the latter, however—if he could make logical mileage out of 'it is not the case that God exists' by arguing that it can never be established—then he must treat 'God exists' the same way. He must say not only that the present evidence is not good enough, but that it never could be good enough.

In either case, the conclusion goes against the claim that God exists. The moment the agnostic chooses consistency he becomes an atheist. For, as either fact-gatherer or logician, he will discover that there are no good grounds for claiming that God exists. The alternative is for him to give up trying to be consistent and reasonable, and assert that God exists in faith. But then he will have to doff the mantle of rationality which so attracted him when he adopted his original position.

The drift of this argument is not new: it is not reasonable to believe in the existence of God. Reflective people may have other grounds for believing in God's existence, but these hinge not on any conception of 'having good reasons' familiar in science, logic, or philosophy. The point is that the agnostic, despite his pretensions, is not more reasonable than the atheist or the theist. The next step for him is easy: if he chooses to use his head, he will become an atheist. If he chooses to react to his glands, he will become a theist. Either he will grant that there is no good reason for believing in the existence of God, or he will choose to believe in the existence of God on the basis of no good reason.

[in Stephen Toulmin and Harry Woolf (eds.), *What I do not Believe and Other Essays*
(Dordrecht: Reidel, 1971), 303–8.]

RICHARD SWINBURNE

107 The World and its Order

The simple hypothesis of theism leads us to expect all the phenomena which I have been describing with some reasonable degree of probability. God being omnipotent is able to produce a world orderly in these respects. And he has good reason to choose to do so: a world containing human persons is a good thing. Persons have experiences, and thoughts, and can make choices, and their choices can make big differences to themselves, to others, and to the inanimate world. God, being perfectly good, is generous. He wants to share. And there is a particular kind of goodness in human persons with bodies in a law-governed universe. With a body we have a limited chunk of matter under our control, and, if we so choose, we can choose to learn how the world works and so learn which bodily actions will have more remote effects. We can learn quickly when rocks are likely to fall, predators to pounce, and plants to grow. Thereby God allows us to share in his creative activity of choosing. We can make choices crucial for ourselves—whether to avoid falling rocks, to escape from predators, to plant crops in order to get enough to eat, or not to bother; whether to build houses and live comfortably or to be content with a more primitive life-style.

And we can make choices crucial for others—whether to give them food or let them starve.

But, because the approximate observable regularities in the behaviour of medium-sized objects are due to more precise regularities in the behaviour of their small-scale components, we can, if we so choose, try to find out what are these latter components. With this knowledge we can build instruments which extend further our knowledge and control of the world. Humans can discover the laws of dynamics and chemistry and so make cars and aeroplanes, or—alternatively—bombs and guns; and so extend the range of our power from control merely of our bodies and their local environment to a much wider control of the world. Embodiment in an orderly world gives the possibility not merely of quick learning of regularities utilizable for survival, but of science and technology—of discovering by co-operative effort over the years deep laws which can be utilized to rebuild our world in the ways we choose. It is up to us whether we choose to learn and extend control, and up to us how we extend control. Like a good parent, a generous God has reason for not foisting on us a certain fixed measure of knowledge and control, but rather for giving us a choice of whether to grow in knowledge and control.

It is because it provides these opportunities for humans that God has a reason to create a world governed by natural laws of the kind we find. Of course God has reason to make many other things, and I would hesitate to say that one could be certain that he would make such a world. But clearly it is the sort of thing that there is some significant probability that he will make.

The suitability of the world as a theatre for humans is not the only reason for God to make an orderly world. The higher animals too are conscious, learn, and plan—and the predictability of things in their most easily detectable aspects enables them to do so. But beyond that an orderly world is a beautiful world. Beauty consists in patterns of order. Total chaos is ugly. The movements of the stars in accord with regular laws is a beautiful dance. The medievals thought of the planets as carried by spheres through the sky, and their regular movements producing the 'music of the spheres' whose beauty humans casually ignored, although it was one of the most beautiful things there is. God has reason to make an orderly world, because beauty is a good thing—in my view whether or not anyone ever observes it, but certainly if only one person ever observes it.

The argument to God from the world and its regularity is, I believe, a codification by philosophers of a natural and rational reaction to an orderly world deeply embedded in the human consciousness. Humans see the comprehensibility of the world as evidence of a comprehending creator. The prophet Jeremiah lived in an age in which the existence of a creator-god of some sort was taken for granted. What was at stake was the extent of his goodness, knowledge, and power. Jeremiah argued from the order of the world that he was a powerful and reliable god, that god was the sort of God that I described in Chapter 1. Jeremiah argued to the power of the creator from the extent of the creation—'The host of heaven cannot be numbered, neither the sand of the sea measured' (Jer. 33: 22); and he argued that its regular behaviour showed the reliability of the creator, and he spoke of the 'covenant of the day and night' whereby they follow each other regularly, and 'the ordinances of heaven and earth' (Jer. 33: 20–1 and 25–6). [. . .]

Of course, the universe may not have had a beginning with a Big Bang, but may have lasted forever. Even so, its matter must have had certain general features if at any time there was to be a state of the universe suited to produce animals and humans. There would need, for example, to be enough matter but not too much of it for chemical substances to be built up at some time or other—a lot of fundamental particles are needed but with large spaces between them. And only a certain range of laws would allow there to be animals and humans at any time ever. The recent scientific work on the fine-tuning of the universe has drawn attention to the fact that, whether or not the universe had a beginning, if it had laws of anything like the same kind as our actual ones (e.g. a law of gravitational attraction and the laws of the three other forces which physicists have analysed—electromagnetism, the strong nuclear force, and the weak nuclear force), the constants of those laws would need to lie within narrow bands if there was ever to be life anywhere in the universe. Again the materialist will have to leave it as an ultimate brute fact that an everlasting universe and its laws had those characteristics, whereas the theist has a simple ultimate explanation of why things are thus, following from his basic hypothesis which also leads him to expect the other phenomena we have been describing.

True, God could have created humans without doing so by the long process of evolution. But that is only an objection to the theistic hypothesis if you suppose that God's only reason for creating anything is for the sake of human beings. To repeat my earlier point—God also has reason to bring about animals. Animals are conscious beings who enjoy much life and perform intentional actions, even if they do not choose freely which ones to do. Of course God has a reason for giving life to elephants and giraffes, tigers and snails. And anyway the beauty of the evolution of the inanimate world from the Big Bang (or from eternity) would be quite enough of a reason for producing it, even if God were the only person to have observed it. But he is not; we ourselves can now admire earlier and earlier stages of cosmic evolution through our telescopes. God paints with a big brush from a large paintbox and he has no need to be stingy with the paint he uses to paint a beautiful universe.

Darwin showed that the universe is a machine for making animals and humans. But it is misleading to gloss that correct point in the way that Richard Dawkins does: 'our own existence once presented the greatest of all mysteries, but . . . it is a mystery no longer . . . Darwin and Wallace solved it' (The Blind Watchmaker, p. xiii). It is misleading because it ignores the interesting question of whether the existence and operation of that machine, the factors which

Darwin (and Wallace) cited to explain 'our own existence', themselves have a further explanation. I have argued that the principles of rational enquiry suggest that they do. Darwin gave a correct explanation of the existence of animals and humans; but not, I think, an ultimate one. The watch may have been made with the aid of some blind screwdrivers (or even a blind watch-making machine), but they were guided by a watchmaker with some very clear sight.

Stephen Hawking has suggested that the universe is not infinitely old, but that nevertheless it did not have a beginning, and so there was no need for it to begin in a particular initial state if animals and humans were to emerge. He suggests, as Einstein did, that space is closed—finite but without a boundary. Three-dimensional space, that is, is like the two-dimensional surface of a sphere. If you travel in any direction along the surface of a sphere, you will come back to your starting-point from the opposite side. It is indeed possible that three-dimensional space is also like this, though that remains a matter on which there is no scientific consensus. But Hawking also makes the paradoxical 'proposal' that the same is true with respect to time (see *A Brief History of Time* (1985), 136): time is closed because it is cyclical—if you live long enough after 1995 into the future, you would find yourself coming from 1994 into 1995 (looking and feeling just like you do now). Hawking claims that the 'real' test of his proposal is whether his theory which embodies it 'makes predictions that agree with observation'. But that is not the only test which his proposal must pass. As I noted in Chapter 2, a theory which entails a contradiction cannot be true, however successful it is in making predictions. And the 'proposal' that time is cyclical to my mind does entail a contradiction. It entails that tomorrow is both after and before today (because if you live long enough after tomorrow, you will find yourself back to today). That in turn entails that I today cause events tomorrow which in turn by a long causal chain cause my own existence today. But it is at any rate logically possible (whether or not possible in practice) that I should freely make different choices from the ones which I do make today; and in that case I could choose so to act today as to ensure that my parents were never born and so I never existed—which is a contradiction. Cyclical time allows the possibility of my acting so as to cause my not acting. And, since that is not possible, cyclical time is not possible. In saying this, I have no wish to challenge the correctness of Hawking's equations as parts of a theory which predicts observations. But I do wish to challenge the interpretation in words which Hawking gives of those equations.

The use to which Hawking puts his 'proposal' is contained in this paragraph:

The idea that space and time may form a closed surface without boundary also has profound implications for the role of God in the affairs of the universe. With the success of scientific theories in describing events, most people have come to believe that God allows the universe to evolve according to a set of laws and does not intervene in the universe to break these laws. However, the laws do not tell us what the universe should have looked like when it started—it would still be up to God to wind up the clockwork and choose how to start it off. So long as the universe had a beginning, we could suppose it had a creator. But if the universe is really completely self-contained, having no boundary or edge, it would have neither beginning nor end: it would simply be. What place, then, for a creator?

(*A Brief History of Time*, 140–1)

The theist's answer to this paragraph is twofold. First, whether or not God ever intervenes in the universe to break his laws, according to theism, he certainly can do so; and the continued operation of these laws is due to his constant conserving of them, his choosing not to break them. And, secondly, if the universe had a beginning, God made it begin one way rather than another. If the universe did not have a beginning, the only alternative is that it is everlasting. In that case, God may be held to keep it in being at each moment with the laws of nature as they are. It is through his choice at each moment that it exists at that moment and the laws of nature are as they are then.

[*Is There a God?* (Oxford: Oxford University Press, 1996), 52–4, 62–5.]

ALVIN PLANTINGA

108   Is Belief in God Properly Basic?

Many philosophers have urged the *evidentialist* objection to theistic belief; they have argued that belief in God is irrational or unreasonable or not rationally acceptable or intellectually irresponsible or noetically substandard, because, as they say, there is insufficient evidence for it. Many other philosophers and theologians—in particular, those in the great tradition of natural theology—have claimed that belief in God is intellectually acceptable, but only because the fact is there is sufficient evidence for it. These two groups unite in holding that theistic belief is rationally acceptable only if there is sufficient evidence for it. More exactly, they hold that a person is rational or reasonable in accepting theistic belief only if she has sufficient evidence for it—only if, that is, she knows or rationally believes some *other* propositions which support the one in question, and believes the latter on the basis of the former. In 'Is Belief in God Rational?' I argued that the evidentialist objection is rooted in *classical foundationalism*, an enormously popular picture or total way of looking at faith, knowledge, justified belief, rationality, and allied topics. This picture has been widely accepted ever since the days of Plato and Aristotle; its near relatives, perhaps, remain the dominant ways of thinking about these topics. We may think of the classical foundationalist as beginning with the observation that some of one's beliefs may be *based upon* others; it may be that there are a pair of propositions *A* and *B* such that I believe *A on the basis of B*. Although this relation isn't easy to characterize in a revealing and nontrivial fashion, it is nonetheless familiar. I believe that the word 'umbrageous' is spelled u-m-b-r-a-g-e-o-u-s; this belief is based on another belief of mine: the belief that that's how the dictionary says it's spelled. I believe that $72 \times 71 = 5112$. This belief is based upon several other beliefs I hold: that $1 \times 72 = 72$; $7 \times 2 = 14$; $7 \times 7 = 49$; $49 + 1 = 50$; and others. Some of my beliefs, however, I accept but don't accept on the basis of any other beliefs. Call these beliefs *basic*. I believe that $2 + 1 = 3$, for example, and don't believe it on the basis of other propositions. I also believe that I am seated at my desk, and that there is a mild pain in my right knee. These too are basic to me; I don't believe them on the basis of any other propositions. According to the classical foundationalist, some propositions are *properly* or *rightly* basic for a person and some are not. Those that are not, are rationally accepted only on the basis of *evidence*, where the evidence must trace back, ultimately, to what is properly basic. The existence of God, furthermore, is not among the propositions that are properly basic; hence a person is rational in accepting theistic belief only if he has evidence for it.

Now many Reformed thinkers and theologians have rejected *natural theology* (thought of as the attempt to provide proofs or arguments for the existence of God). They have held not merely that the proffered arguments are unsuccessful, but that the whole enterprise is in some way radically misguided. In 'The Reformed Objection to Natural Theology,' I argue that the reformed rejection of natural theology is best construed as an inchoate and unfocused rejection of classical foundationalism. What these Reformed thinkers really mean to hold, I think, is that belief in God need not be based on argument or evidence from other propositions at all. They mean to hold that the believer is entirely within his intellectual rights in believing as he does even if he doesn't know of any good theistic argument (deductive or inductive), even if he doesn't believe that there is any such argument, and even if in fact no such argument exists. They hold that it is perfectly rational to accept belief in God without accepting it on the basis of any other beliefs or propositions at all. In a word, they hold that *belief in God is properly basic*. In this paper I shall try to develop and defend this position.

But first we must achieve a deeper understanding of the evidentialist objection. It is important to see that this contention is a *normative* contention. The evidentialist objector holds that one who accepts theistic belief is in some way irrational or noetically substandard. Here 'rational' and 'irrational' are to be taken as normative or evaluative terms; according to the objector, the theist fails to measure up to a standard he ought to conform to. There is a right way and a wrong way with respect to belief as with respect to actions; we have duties, responsibilities, obligations with respect to the former just as with respect to the latter. So Professor Blanshard:

... everywhere and always belief has an ethical aspect. There is such a thing as a general ethics of the intellect. The main principle of that ethic I hold to be the same inside and outside religion. This principle is simple and sweeping: Equate your assent to the evidence.

This 'ethics of the intellect' can be construed variously; many fascinating issues—issues we must here forebear to enter—arise when we try to state more exactly the various options the evidentialist may mean to adopt. Initially it looks as if he holds that there is a duty or obligation of some sort not to accept without evidence such propositions as that God exists—a duty flouted by the theist who has no evidence. If he has no evidence, then it is his duty to cease believing. But there is an oft-remarked difficulty: one's beliefs, for the most part, are not directly under one's control. Most of those who believe in God could not divest themselves of that belief just by trying to do so, just as they could not in that way rid themselves of the belief that the world has existed for a very long time. So perhaps the relevant obligation is not that of divesting myself of theistic belief if I have no evidence (that is beyond my power), but to try to cultivate the sorts of intellectual habits that will tend (we hope) to issue in my accepting as basic only propositions that are properly basic.

Perhaps this obligation is to be thought of *teleologically*: it is a moral obligation arising out of a connection between certain intrinsic goods and evils and the way in which our beliefs are formed and held. (This seems to be W. K. Clifford's way of construing the matter.) Perhaps it is to be thought of *aretetically*: there are valuable noetic or intellectual states (whether intrinsically or extrinsically valuable); there are also corresponding intellectual virtues, habits of acting so as to promote and enhance those valuable states. Among one's obligations, then, is the duty to try to foster and cultivate these virtues in oneself or others. Or perhaps it is to be thought of *deontologically*: this obligation attaches to us just by virtue of our having the sort of noetic equipment human beings do in fact display; it does not arise out of a connection with valuable states of affairs. Such an obligation, furthermore, could be a special sort of moral obligation; on the other hand, perhaps it is a sui generis non-moral obligation.

Still further, perhaps the evidentialist need not speak of duty or obligation here at all. Consider someone who believes that Venus is smaller than Mercury, not because he has evidence of any sort, but because he finds it amusing to hold a belief no one else does—or consider someone who holds this belief on the basis of some outrageously bad argument. Perhaps there isn't any obligation he has failed to meet. Nevertheless his intellectual condition is deficient in some way; or perhaps alternatively there is a commonly achieved excellence he fails to display. And the evidentialist objection to theistic belief, then, might be understood as the claim, not that the theist without evidence has failed to meet an obligation, but that he suffers from a certain sort of intellectual deficiency (so that the proper attitude toward him would be sympathy rather than censure).

These are some of the ways, then, in which the evidentialist objection could be developed; and of course there are still other possibilities. For ease of exposition, let us take the claim deontologically; what I shall say will apply mutatis mutandis if we take it one of the other ways. The evidentialist objection, therefore, presupposes some view as to what sorts of propositions are correctly, or rightly, or justifiably taken as basic; it presupposes a view as to what is *properly* basic. And the minimally relevant claim for the evidentialist objector is that belief in God is *not* properly basic. Typically this objection has been rooted in some form of *classical foundationalism*, according to which a proposition *p* is properly basic for a person *S* if and only if *p* is either self-evident or incorrigible for *S* (modern foundationalism) or either self-evident or 'evident to the senses' for *S* (ancient and medieval foundationalism). In 'Is Belief in God Rational?,' I argued that both forms of foundationalism are self-referentially incoherent and must therefore be rejected.

Insofar as the evidentialist objection is rooted in classical foundationalism, it is poorly rooted indeed: and so far as I know, no one has developed and articulated any other reason for supposing that belief in God is not properly basic. Of course it doesn't follow that it is properly basic; perhaps the class of properly basic propositions is broader than classical foundationalists think, but still not broad enough to admit belief in God. But why think so? What might be the objections to the Reformed view that belief in God is properly basic?

I've heard it argued that if I have no evidence for the existence of God, then if I accept that proposition, my belief will be groundless, or gratuitous, or arbitrary. I think this is an error; let me explain.

Suppose we consider perceptual beliefs, memory beliefs, and beliefs which ascribe mental states to other persons: such beliefs as

    1. I see a tree,
    2. I had breakfast this morning,

and

    3. That person is angry.

Although beliefs of this sort are typically and properly taken as basic, it would be a mistake to describe them as *groundless*. Upon having experience of a certain sort, I believe that I am perceiving a tree. In the typical case I do not hold this belief on the basis of other beliefs; it is nonetheless not groundless. My having that characteristic sort of experience—to use Professor Chisholm's language, my being appeared treely to—plays a crucial role in the formation and justification of that belief. We might say this experience, together, perhaps, with other circumstances, is what *justifies* me in holding it; this is the *ground* of my justification, and, by extension, the ground of the belief itself.

If I see someone displaying typical pain behaviour, I take it that he or she is in pain. Again, I don't take the displayed behaviour as *evidence* for that belief; I don't infer that belief from others I hold; I don't accept it on the basis of other beliefs. Still, my perceiving the pain behaviour plays a unique role in the formation and justification of that belief; as in the previous case, it forms the ground of my justification for the belief in question. The same holds for memory beliefs. I seem to remember having breakfast this morning; that is, I have an inclination to believe the proposition that I had breakfast, along with a certain past-tinged experience that is familiar to all but hard to describe. Perhaps we should say that I am appeared to pastly; but perhaps this insufficiently distinguishes the experience in question from that accompanying beliefs about the past not grounded in my own memory. The phenomenology of memory is a rich and unexplored realm; her I have no time to explore it. In this case as in the others, however, there is a justifying circumstance present, a condition that forms the ground of my justification for accepting the memory belief in question.

In each of these cases, a belief is taken as basic, and in each case properly taken as basic. In each case there is some circumstance or condition that confers justification; there is a circumstance that serves as the *ground* of justification. So in each case there will be some true proposition of the sort

4. In condition C, S is justified in taking p as basic.

Of course C will vary with p. For a perceptual judgment such as

5. I see a rose-coloured wall before me,

C will include my being appeared to in a certain fashion. No doubt C will include more. If I'm appeared to in the familiar fashion but know that I'm wearing rose-coloured glasses, or that I am suffering from a disease that causes me to be thus appeared to, no matter what the colour of the nearby objects, then I'm not justified in taking (5) as basic. Similarly for memory. Suppose I know that my memory is unreliable; it often plays me tricks. In particular, when I seem to remember having breakfast, then, more often than not, I *haven't* had breakfast. Under these conditions I am not justified in taking it as basic that I had breakfast, even though I seem to remember that I did.

So being appropriately appeared to, in the perceptual case, is not sufficient for justification; some further condition—a condition hard to state in detail—is clearly necessary. The central point here, however, is that a belief is properly basic only in certain conditions; these conditions are, we might say, the ground of its justification and, by extension, the ground of the belief itself. In this sense, basic beliefs are not, or are not necessarily, *groundless* beliefs.

Now similar things may be said about belief in God. When the Reformers claim that this belief is properly basic, they do not mean to say, of course, that there are no justifying circumstances for it, or that it is in that sense groundless or gratuitous. Quite the contrary. Calvin holds that God 'reveals and daily discloses himself to the whole workmanship of the universe,' and the divine art 'reveals itself in the innumerable and yet distinct and well-ordered variety of the heavenly host.' God has so created us that we have a tendency or disposition to see his hand in the world about us. More precisely, there is in us a disposition to believe propositions of the sort *this flower was created by God* or *this vast and intricate universe was created by God* when we contemplate the flower or behold the starry heavens or think about the vast reaches of the universe.

Calvin recognizes, at least implicitly, that other sorts of conditions may trigger this disposition. Upon reading the Bible, one may be impressed with a deep sense that God is speaking to him. Upon having done what I know is cheap, or wrong, or wicked I may feel guilty in God's sight and form the belief *God disapproves of what I've done.* Upon confession and repentance, I may feel forgiven, forming the belief *God forgives me for what I've done.* A person in grave danger may turn to God, asking for his protection and help; and of course he or she then forms the belief that God is indeed able to hear and help if he sees fit. When life is sweet and satisfying, a spontaneous sense of gratitude may well up within the soul; someone in this condition may thank and praise the Lord for his goodness, and will of course form the accompanying belief that indeed the Lord is to be thanked and praised.

There are therefore many conditions and circumstances that call forth belief in God: guilt, gratitude, danger, a sense of God's presence, a sense that he speaks, perception of various parts of the universe. A complete job would explore the phenomenology of all these conditions and of more besides. This is a large and important topic; but here I can only point to the existence of these conditions.

Of course none of the beliefs I mentioned a moment ago is the simple belief that God exists. What we have instead are such beliefs as

      6. God is speaking to me,
      7. God has created all this,
      8. God disapproves of what I have done,
      9. God forgives me,

and

      10. God is to be thanked and praised.

These propositions are properly basic in the right circumstances. But it is quite consistent with this to suppose that the proposition *there is such a person as God* is neither properly basic nor taken as basic by those who believe in God. Perhaps what they take as basic are such propositions as (6)–(10), believing in the existence of God on the basis of propositions such as those. From this point of view, it isn't exactly right to say that it is belief in God that is properly basic; more exactly, what are properly basic are such propositions as (6)–(10), each of which self-evidently entails that God exists. It isn't the relatively high level and general proposition *God exists* that is properly basic, but instead propositions detailing some of his attributes or actions.

Suppose we return to the analogy between belief in God and belief in the existence of perceptual objects, other persons, and the past. Here too it is relatively specific and concrete propositions rather than their more general and abstract colleagues that are properly basic. Perhaps such items as

      11. There are trees,
      12. There are other persons,

and

13. The world has existed for more than five minutes,

are not in fact properly basic; it is instead such propositions as

14. I see a tree,
15. That person is pleased,

and

16. I had breakfast more than an hour ago,

that deserve that accolade. Of course propositions of the latter sort immediately and self-evidently entail propositions of the former sort; and perhaps there is thus no harm in speaking of the former as properly basic, even though so to speak is to speak a bit loosely.

The same must be said about belief in God. We may say, speaking loosely, that belief in God is properly basic; strictly speaking, however, it is probably not that proposition but such propositions as (6)–(10) that enjoy that status. But the main point, here, is that belief in God, or (6)–(10), are properly basic; to say so, however, is not to deny that there are justifying conditions for these beliefs, or conditions that confer justification on one who accepts them as basic. They are therefore not groundless or gratuitous.

A second objection I've often heard: if belief in God is properly basic, why can't *just any* belief be properly basic? Couldn't we say the same for any bizarre abberation we can think of? What about voodoo or astrology? What about the belief that the Great Pumpkin returns every Halloween? Could I properly take *that* as basic? And if I can't, why can I properly take belief in God as basic? Suppose I believe that if I flap my arms with sufficient vigour, I can take off and fly about the room; could I defend myself against the charge of irrationality by claiming this belief is basic? If we say that belief in God is properly basic, won't we be committed to holding that just anything, or nearly anything, can properly be taken as basic, thus throwing wide the gates to irrationalism and superstition?

Certainly not. What might lead one to think the Reformed epistemologist is in this kind of trouble? The fact that he rejects the criteria for proper basicality purveyed by classical foundationalism? But why should *that* be thought to commit him to such tolerance of irrationality? Consider an analogy. In the palmy days of positivism, the positivists went about confidently wielding their verifiability criterion and declaring meaningless much that was obviously meaningful. Now suppose someone rejected a formulation of that criterion—the one to be found in the second edition of A. J. Ayer's *Language, Truth and Logic*, for example. Would that mean she was committed to holding that

17. Twas brillig; and the slithy toves did gyre and gymble in the wabe,

contrary to appearances, makes good sense? Of course not. But then the same goes for the Reformed epistemologist; the fact that he rejects the classical foundationalist's criterion of proper basicality does not mean that he is committed to supposing just anything is properly basic.

But what then is the problem? Is it that the Reformed epistemologist not only rejects those criteria for proper basicality, but seems in no hurry to produce what he takes to be a better substitute? If he has no such criterion, how can he fairly reject belief in the Great Pumpkin as properly basic?

This objection betrays an important misconception. How do we rightly arrive at or develop criteria for meaningfulness, or justified belief, or proper basicality? Where do they come from? Must one have such a criterion before one can sensibly make any judgments—positive or negative—about proper basicality? Surely not. Suppose I don't know of a satisfactory substitute for the criteria proposed by classical foundationalism; I am nevertheless entirely within my rights in holding that certain propositions are not properly basic in certain conditions. Some propositions seem self-evident when in fact they are not; that is the lesson of some of the Russell paradoxes. Nevertheless it would be irrational to take as basic the denial of a proposition that seems self-evident to you. Similarly, suppose it seems to you that you see a tree; you would then be irrational in taking as basic the proposition that you don't see a tree, or that there aren't any trees. In the same way, even if I don't know of some illuminating criterion of meaning, I can quite properly declare (17) meaningless.

And this raises an important question—one Roderick Chisholm has taught us to ask. What is the status of criteria for knowledge, or proper basicality, or justified belief? Typically, these are universal statements. The modern foundationalist's criterion for proper basicality, for example, is doubly universal:

18. For any proposition A and person S, A is properly basic for S if and only if A is incorrigible for S or self-evident to S.

But how could one know a thing like that? What are its credentials? Clearly enough, (18) isn't self-evident or just obviously true. But if it isn't, how does one arrive at it? What sorts of arguments would be appropriate? Of course a foundationalist might find (18) so appealing, he simply takes it to be true, neither offering argument for it nor accepting it on the basis of other things he believes. If he does so, however, his noetic structure will be self-referentially incoherent. (18) itself is neither self-evident nor incorrigible; hence in accepting (18) as basic, the modern foundationalist violates the condition of proper basicality he himself lays down in accepting it. On the other hand, perhaps the foundationalist will try to produce some argument for it from premises that are self-evident or incorrigible: it is exceedingly hard to see, however, what such an argument might be like. And until he has produced such arguments, what shall the rest of us do—we who do not find (18) at all obvious or compelling? How could he use

(18) to show us that belief in God, for example, is not properly basic? Why should we believe (18), or pay it any attention?

The fact is, I think, that neither (18) nor any other revealing necessary and sufficient condition for proper basicality follows from clearly self-evident premises by clearly acceptable arguments. And hence the proper way to arrive at such a criterion is, broadly speaking, *inductive*. We must assemble examples of beliefs and conditions such that the former are obviously properly basic in the latter, and examples of beliefs and conditions such that the former are obviously *not* properly basic in the latter. We must then frame hypotheses as to the necessary and sufficient conditions of proper basicality and test these hypotheses by reference to those examples. Under the right conditions, for example, it is clearly rational to believe that you see a human person before you: a being who has thoughts and feelings, who knows and believes things, who makes decisions and acts. It is clear, furthermore, that you are under no obligation to reason to this belief from others you hold; under those conditions that belief is properly basic for you. But then (18) must be mistaken; the belief in question, under those circumstances, is properly basic, though neither self-evident nor incorrigible for you. Similarly, you may seem to remember that you had breakfast this morning, and perhaps you know of no reason to suppose your memory is playing you tricks. If so, you are entirely justified in taking that belief as basic. Of course it isn't properly basic on the criteria offered by classical foundationalists; but that fact counts not against you but against those criteria.

Accordingly, criteria for proper basicality must be reached from below rather than above; they should not be presented as ex cathedra, but argued to and tested by a relevant set of examples. But there is no reason to assume, in advance, that everyone will agree on the examples. The Christian will of course suppose that belief in God is entirely proper and rational; if he doesn't accept this belief on the basis of other propositions, he will conclude that it is basic for him, and quite properly so. Followers of Bertrand Russell and Madelyn Murray O'Hare may disagree, but how is that relevant? Must my criteria, or those of the Christian community, conform to their examples? Surely not. The Christian community is responsible to *its* set of examples, not to theirs.

Accordingly, the Reformed epistemologist can properly hold that belief in the Great Pumpkin is not properly basic, even though he holds that belief in God is properly basic and even if he has no full-fledged criterion of proper basicality. Of course he is committed to supposing that there is a relevant *difference* between belief in God and belief in the Great Pumpkin, if he holds that the former but not the latter is properly basic. But this should prove no great embarrassment; there are plenty of candidates. These candidates are to be found in the neighbourhood of the conditions I mentioned in the last section that justify and ground belief in God. Thus, for example, the Reformed epistemologist may concur with Calvin in holding that God has implanted in us a natural tendency to see his hand in the world around us; the same cannot be said for the Great Pumpkin, there being no Great Pumpkin and no natural tendency to accept beliefs about the Great Pumpkin.

By way of conclusion then: being self-evident, or incorrigible, or evident to the senses is not a necessary condition of proper basicality. Furthermore, one who holds that belief in God *is* properly basic is not thereby committed to the idea that belief in God is groundless or gratuitous or without justifying circumstances. And even if he lacks a general criterion of proper basicality, he is not obliged to suppose that just any or nearly any belief—belief in the Great Pumpkin, for example—is properly basic. Like everyone should, he begins with examples; and he may take belief in the Great Pumpkin as a paradigm of irrational basic belief.

[*Nous*, 15 (1981), 41–51.]

MEROLD WESTPHAL

109   Sin and Reason

As long as we operate in some foundationalist framework sin does not need to be an epistemological category. Or, to be more precise, sin appears and disappears from the epistemological scene at the same moment. For the foundationalist project is simultaneously the (more or less conscious) recognition of the problem of judgment distorted by devious desire and the solution to that problem. In that project method becomes the means, not of grace, but of our own self-purification. But from the moment we recognize the contingent particularity of our *a prioris* and the consequent ineluctability of the hermeneutical circle, this escape from the human condition becomes unavailable. The inescapable subjectivity of understanding leaves knowledge permanently vulnerable to distorted desire. Of course, it does not follow that we will begin to take Paul seriously. The door has been opened, but we need not go through it. The collapse of foundationalism offers new opportunity for making sin a significant epistemological variable. But this is no more inevitable for post-foundational reflection than it was for foundationalism. For it is entirely possible to find in the ashes of foundationalism only finitude and not sinfulness, to discover preunderstandings that are perspectival but not perverse. This is just what has happened for many, if not most, of those who have played major roles in the undermining of foundationalism.

(c) My third suggestion is that 'Reformed' or 'Calvinist' epistemology belongs in this camp, that while it shows the failure of foundationalism with exceptional clarity, the alternative it proposes does not take advantage of the new opportunity to make sin an essential epistemological category. If this is true it is, of course, ironical. For Calvin is in the front rank of those who take Paul seriously, and it would be strange if epistemological reflection that associates itself with his name should fail to do so. But that is what I shall try to show to be the case.

In addition to the specific invocation of Calvin, there are other features of 'Reformed' epistemology that seem to prepare the way for taking Paul seriously. First, its primary focus is religious knowledge, the primary locus of the noetic effects of sin for Calvin as for Paul (in keeping with the Law of Inverse Rationality). Second, it gives to epistemology the ethical framework mentioned at the beginning of this essay. It speaks freely of epistemic rights and duties. Third, in opposition to foundationalism it recognizes the pervasiveness of prejudice (in Gadamer's sense), the 'historical singularity' (Foucault) of the criteria (a prioris, control beliefs) at work in shaping the beliefs of various communities. Finally, it is explicitly aware that belief is not always innocent.

Yet for all this it seems that the issue is mentioned only to be, if not entirely repressed, at least restricted to a mere cameo role. In Plantinga's account, for example, the familiar Reformed suspicion of natural theology is an attempt to express the claim that we do not need arguments for the existence of God because belief in God is properly basic. Without fully realizing it, Calvin (along with Bavinck, Kuyper, and Barth) has anticipated the foundationalist-evidentialist objection to theistic belief and given the outlines of an alternative account of religious knowledge. I want to suggest that this is right as far as it goes, but that it falls short of capturing what Calvin is driving at.

Plantinga quotes Calvin's claim that 'there is within the human mind, and indeed by natural instinct, an awareness of divinity,' that 'God himself has implanted in all men a certain understanding of his divine majesty.' While citing other passages in which Calvin makes creation an epistemological category, but not those in which he does the same with the fall, Plantinga writes

Calvin's claim, then, is that God has created us in such a way that we have a strong tendency or inclination toward belief in him. This tendency has been in part overlaid or suppressed by sin. Were it not for the existence of sin in the world, human beings would believe in God to the same degree and with the same natural spontaneity that we believe in the existence of other persons, an external world, or the past. This is the natural human condition; it is because of our presently unnatural sinful condition that many of us find belief in God difficult or absurd. The fact is, Calvin thinks, one who does not believe in God is in an epistemically substandard position. . . . Although this disposition to believe in God is partially suppressed, it is nonetheless universally present.

Calvin would have put that last part rather differently, I suspect. In order to remind us that none of us come *naturally* to a proper knowledge of God, he would have said that while the tendency to believe is present, it is nevertheless suppressed, reversing Plantinga's order and emphasis. And in order to remind us that *none* of us comes naturally to a proper knowledge of God, he would have said that while the tendency to believe is universally present, it is *universally*, and not just partially, suppressed. Both terms are ambiguous and might miss his meaning. Universal suppression might be construed as degree rather than extension, suggesting that creation is entirely obliterated rather than that none of us is exempt from the distorting effects of sin. Partial suppression might be construed as extension rather than degree, suggesting that some of us are exempt rather than that our natural tendency to believe in God has been distorted but not obliterated. I do not doubt that Calvin would rather risk over-stating the damage by speaking of universal suppression than risk suggesting that some are exempt from the noetic effects of sin by speaking of a partial suppression.

But the latter implication is just what we find in Plantinga. The most natural reading of the passage quoted above is that sin is at work in the beliefs of unbe-lievers but not in those of believers. This is the same exemption for oneself and one's belief community which we found in Kant and Fichte. If this is Calvin's proper meaning, then we shall have to ask how seriously he himself takes Paul. But since he joins Paul in such a strong emphasis on the universality of sin, and since he sees the noetic effects of sin not so much in atheism and agnosticism as in idolatrous distortion of the divine nature, it is unlikely that this is his deepest intention. In any case, for believers to draw a line between themselves and unbe-lievers and to find the noetic effects of sin only on the other side of that line is closer to epistemological Phariseeism than it is to taking Paul seriously. For unbelief is not the only way of suppressing the truth about God. It is only the most honest.

['On Taking St Paul Seriously: Sin as an Epistemological Category', in T. Flint (ed.), *Christian Philosophy* (Notre Dame, Ind.: University of Notre Dame Press, 1990), 211–14.]

STEVEN CAHN

110 The Irrelevance of Proof to Religion

Philosophic proofs for the existence of God have a long and distinguished history. Almost every major Western philosopher has been seriously concerned with defending or refuting such proofs. Furthermore, many contemporary philosophers have exhibited keen interest in such proofs. A survey of the philo-sophical literature of the past decade reveals quite a concentration of work in this area.

One might expect that religious believers would be vitally interested in discussions of this subject. One might suppose that when a proof of God's exis-tence is presented and eloquently defended, believers would be most enthusi-astic, and that when a proof is attacked and persuasively refuted, believers would be seriously disappointed. But this is not at all the case. Religious believers seem remarkably uninterested in philosophic proofs for the existence of God. They seem to consider discussion of such proofs as a sort of intellectual game which has no relevance to religious belief or activity. And this view is shared by proponents of both supernaturalist and naturalist varieties of religion. For example, Søren Kierkegaard, a foremost proponent of supernaturalist religion, remarked: 'Whoever therefore attempts to demonstrate the existence of God . . . [is] an excellent subject for a comedy of the higher lunacy!' The same essential point is made in a somewhat less flamboyant manner by Mordecai M. Kaplan, a foremost proponent of naturalist religion, who remarks that the 'immense amount of mental effort to prove the existence of God . . . was in vain, since unbelievers seldom become believers as a result of logical arguments.'

In what follows, I wish to explain just why religious believers have so little interest in philosophic proofs for the existence of God. I wish to show that their lack of interest is entirely reasonable, and that whatever the philosophic relevance of such proofs, they have little or no relevance to religion.

The three classic proofs for the existence of God are the ontological, the cosmological, and the teleological. Each of these proofs is intended to prove something different. The ontological argument is intended to prove the existence (or necessary existence) of the most perfect conceivable Being. The cosmological argument is intended to prove the existence of a necessary Being who is the Prime Mover or First Cause of the universe. The teleological argument is intended to prove the existence of an all-good designer and creator of the universe.

Suppose we assume, contrary to what most philosophers, I among them, believe, that all of these proofs are valid. Let us grant the necessary existence (whatever that might mean) of the most perfect conceivable Being, a Being who is all-good and is the designer and creator of the universe. What implications can be drawn from this fact which would be of relevance to human life? In other words, what difference would it make in men's lives if God existed?

Perhaps some men would feel more secure in the knowledge that the universe had been planned by an all-good Being. Others, perhaps, would feel insecure, realizing the extent to which their very existence depended upon the will of this Being. In any case, most men, either out of fear or respect, would wish to act in accordance with the moral code advocated by this Being.

Note, however, that the proofs for the existence of God provide us with no hint whatever as to which actions God wishes us to perform, or what we ought to do so as to please or obey Him. We may affirm that God is all-good and yet have no way of knowing what the highest moral standards are. All we may be sure of is that whatever these standards may be, God always acts in accordance with them. One might assume that God would have implanted the correct moral standards in men's minds, but this seems doubtful in view of the wide variance in men's moral standards. Which of these numerous standards, if any, is the correct one is not known, and no appeal to a proof for the existence of God will cast the least light upon the matter.

For example, assuming that it can be proven that God exists, is murder immoral? One might argue that since God created man, it is immoral to murder, since it is immoral to destroy what God in His infinite wisdom and goodness has created. This argument, however, fails on several grounds. First, if God created man, He also created germs, viruses, disease-carrying rats, and man-eating sharks. Does it follow from the fact that God created these things that they ought not to be eliminated? Secondly, if God arranged for men to live, He also arranged for men to die. Does it follow from this that by committing murder we are assisting the work of God? Thirdly, if God created man, He provided him with the mental and physical capacity to commit murder. Does it follow from this that God wishes men to commit murder? Clearly, the attempt to deduce moral precepts from the fact of God's existence is but another case of trying to do what Hume long ago pointed out to be logically impossible, viz., the deduction of normative judgments from factual premisses. No such deduction is valid, and, thus, any moral principle is consistent with the existence of God.

The fact that the proofs of God's existence afford no means of distinguishing good from evil has the consequence that no man can be sure of how to obey God and do what is best in His eyes. One may hope that his actions are in accord with God's standards, but no test is available to check on this. Some seemingly good men suffer great ills, and some seemingly evil men achieve great happiness. Perhaps in a future life these things are rectified, but we have no way of ascertaining which men are ultimately rewarded and which are ultimately punished.

One can imagine that if a group of men believed in God's existence, they would be most anxious to learn His will, and consequently, they would tend to rely upon those individuals who claimed to know the will of God. Diviners, seers, and priests would be in a position of great influence. No doubt competition between them would be severe, for no man could be sure which of these oracles to believe. Assuming that God made no effort to reveal His will by granting one of these oracles truly superhuman powers (though, naturally, each oracle would claim that he possessed such powers), no man could distinguish the genuine prophet from the fraud.

It is clear that the situation I have described is paralleled by a stage in the actual development of religion. What men wanted at this stage was some way to find out the will of God. Individual prophets might gain a substantial following, but prophets died and their vital powers died with them. What was needed on practical grounds was a permanent record of God's will as revealed to His special prophet. And this need was eventually met by the writing of holy books, books in which God's will was revealed in a permanent fashion.

But there was more than one such book. Indeed, there were many such books. Which was to be believed? Which moral code was to be followed? Which prayers were to be recited? Which rituals were to be performed? Proofs for the existence of God are silent upon these crucial matters.

There is only one possible avenue to God's will. One must undergo a personal experience in which one senses the presence of God and apprehends which of the putative holy books is the genuine one. But it is most important not to be deceived in this experience. One must be absolutely certain that it is God whose presence one is experiencing and whose will one is apprehending. In other words, one must undergo a self-validating experience, one which carries its own guarantee of infallibility.

If one undergoes what he believes to be such an experience, he then is certain which holy book is the genuine one, and consequently he knows which actions, prayers, and rituals God wishes him to engage in. But notice that if he knows this, he has necessarily validated the existence of God, for unless he is absolutely certain that he has experienced God's presence, he cannot be sure that the message he has received is true. Thus, he has no further need for a proof of God's existence.

For one who does not undergo what he believes to be such a self-validating experience, several possibilities remain open. He may accept the validity of another person's self-validating experience. He thereby accepts the holy book which has been revealed as genuine, and he thereby also accepts the existence of God, since unless he believed that this other person had experienced the presence of God, he would not accept this person's opinion as to which is the genuine book.

It is possible, however, that one does not accept the validity of another person's supposedly self-validating experience. This may be due either to philosophical doubts concerning the logical possibility of such an experience or simply to practical doubts that anyone has, in fact, ever undergone such an experience. In either case, adherence to a particular supernatural religion is unreasonable.

But having no adherence to a supernatural religion does not imply that one does not still face the serious moral dilemmas which are inherent in life. How are these dilemmas to be solved? To believe that God exists is of no avail, for one cannot learn His will. Therefore, one must use one's own judgment. But this need not be solely an individual effort. One may join others in a communal effort to propound and promulgate a moral code. Such a group may have its own distinctive prayers and rituals which emphasize various aspects of the group's beliefs. Such a naturalistic religious organization does not depend upon its members' belief in the existence of God, for such a belief is irrelevant to the religious aims and activities of the group.

Is it surprising then that proponents of both supernaturalist and naturalist religion are uninterested in philosophic proofs for the existence of God? Not at all. A supernaturalist believes in God because of a personal self-validating experience which has shown him (or someone he trusts) not only that God exists, but also what His will is. A philosophic proof of the existence of God is thus of no use to the supernaturalist. If the proof is shown to be valid, it merely confirms what he already knows on the much stronger evidence of personal experience. If the proof is shown to be invalid, it casts no doubt on a self-validating experience.

On the other hand, a naturalist believes either that no one has learned or that no one can learn the will of God. If, therefore, a proof for the existence of God is shown to be valid, this has no implications for the naturalist, for such a proof does not provide him with any information which he can utilize in his religious practice. If, on the contrary, a proof for the existence of God is shown to be invalid, this casts no doubt on the naturalist's religious views, since these views have been formulated independently of a belief in the existence of God.

Who, then, is concerned with philosophic proofs for the existence of God? First, there are those who believe that if such proofs are invalid, religion is thereby undermined. This is, as I have shown, a wholly erroneous view. Neither supernaturalist nor naturalist religion depends at all upon philosophic proofs for the existence of God. To attack religion on the grounds that it cannot provide a philosophic proof for the existence of God is an instance of *ignoratio elenchi*.

Secondly, there are those who believe that if the philosophic proofs for the existence of God are invalid, our moral commitments are necessarily undermined. This is also, as I have shown, a wholly erroneous view. It is, however, a common view, and one which underlies the so-called moral argument for the existence of God. According to this argument, it is only if one believes in the existence of God that one can reasonably commit oneself to respect the importance of moral values. This argument is invalid, however, for, as I have shown, belief in the existence of God is compatible with any and all positions on moral issues. It is only if one can learn the will of God that one can derive any moral implications from His existence.

Thirdly, there are philosophers who discuss proofs for the existence of God because of the important philosophical issues which are brought to light and clarified in such discussions. So long as philosophers are aware of the purpose which their discussions serve, all is well and good. It is when philosophers and others use discussions of this sort as arguments for and against religion that they overstep their bounds. Religion may be rationally attacked or defended, but to refute philosophic proofs for the existence of God is not to attack religion, and to support philosophic proofs for the existence of God is not to defend religion.

['The Irrelevance to Religion of Philosophic Proofs for the Existence of God', *American Philosophical Quarterly*, 6 (1969), 170–2.]

The conception of reason presupposed by the familiar contrast between reason and faith is made explicit in the well-known statement by W. K. Clifford: 'It is wrong, always, everywhere and for everyone to believe anything upon insufficient evidence.' It follows that, in order to be rational, one must:

— have sufficient evidence for what one believes
— be prepared to produce the evidence on demand
— proportion one's confidence in the truth of the belief to the evidence as it stands at the time of speaking.

In all matters of any importance, in relation to one's moral, political or religious convictions, for example, the evidence is inevitably subtle, complex, and variable over time. Hence, it will not normally be possible, if one sticks to Clifford's dictum, to hold such beliefs in other than a tentative and provisional manner. Frequently, the only proper thing to do will be to suspend judgement. The paradigm case of the unprejudiced thinker is the scientist, who is entirely open-minded and accepts or rejects a hypothesis on the basis of the experimental evidence alone.

We are so used to this conception of reason that we often fail to notice how remote it is from the way people actually think. No-one was more aware of this or criticized it more effectively than John Henry Newman. Newman had encountered it in Locke and commented: 'He (Locke) consults his own ideal of how the mind ought to act, instead of investigating human nature as an existing thing, or as it is found in the world.' When he examined the way we actually think, Newman noticed a number of things:

(a) Much of our reasoning is tacit and informal. It cannot be neatly displayed as a set of conclusions derived by a straightforward process of inference from clear-cut premisses. Rather: 'It is the cumulation of probabilities, independent of each other, arising out of the nature and circumstances of the particular case which is under review; probabilities too fine to avail separately, too subtle and circuitous to be convertible into syllogisms, too numerous and various for such conversion, even were they convertible.'

(b) Thus, most arguments are cumulative in form. A wide range of considerations of very varied character is involved. No one of them suffices to generate the required conclusion, but, taken together, they may converge irresistibly upon it. Newman illustrates his contention with examples taken from everyday life:

Let a person only call to mind the clear impression he has about matters of every day's occurrence, that this man is bent on a certain object, or that that man was displeased, or another suspicious; or that that one is happy, and another unhappy; and how much depends in such impressions on manner, voice, accent, words offered, silence instead of words, and all the many symptoms which are felt by the mind, but cannot be contemplated; and let him consider how very poor account he is able to give of his impression, if he avows it and is called upon to justify it. This, indeed, is meant by what is called moral proof, in opposition to legal.

Some of the best examples are to be found in novels. One of my favourites is the passage in Jane Austen's *Emma* in which Emma discusses with Mr John Knightley, her brother-in-law, the attitude to her of the clergyman Mr Elton, and dismisses with indignation the suggestion that he is in love with her. Emma remarks:

'There is such perfect good temper and good will in Mr Elton as one cannot but value.'

'Yes', said Mr John Knightley presently, with some slyness, 'he seems to have a great deal of good-will towards *you*.'

'Me', she replied with a smile of astonishment, 'are you imagining me to be Mr Elton's object?'

'Such an imagination has crossed me, I own, Emma; and if it never occurred to you before, you may as well take it into consideration now.'

'Mr Elton in love with me!—What an idea!'

'I do not say it is so, but you will do well to consider whether it is so, or not, and to regulate your behaviour accordingly. I think your manner to him encouraging. I speak as a friend, Emma. You had better look about you, and ascertain what you do, and what you mean to do.'

'I thank you, but I assure you you are quite mistaken. Mr Elton and I are very good friends, and nothing more;' and she walked on, amusing herself in the consideration of the blunders which often arise from the partial knowledge of circumstance, of the mistakes which people of high pretension to judgement are for ever falling into; and not very well pleased with her brother for imagining her blind and ignorant, and in want of counsel.

There is a delightful irony in this. Emma wilfully misreads all the signs which seem so clear to Mr John Knightley who, as the reader knows, is in the right. Yet there is quite obviously no satisfactory way of formalizing the argument on either side.

(c) In estimating the force of the evidence and in deciding what is to be believed on the strength of it we are rightly influenced by considerations other than those provided by the evidence itself. We bring to the evidence antecedent assumptions which inevitably, and Newman thinks rightly, affect our interpretation of it. It is simply not the case that we approach the evidence, whatever it may be, with a totally open mind. At the very least we bring to bear upon it the concepts embedded in the language we use, but also a host of beliefs about things and people, about associations and institutions which we may not be fully aware of and, even if we were, could not clearly and fully articulate. This accounts for the enormous difficulty we sometimes experience in debating contentious issues with people who differ in principle from ourselves. It is not that they are, in any obvious way, less rational or less observant than we are, but, as we often say, they 'see things differently'. This often becomes particularly apparent in televised debates. People are at cross-purposes with one another, and if there is a presenter, he or she generally makes things worse. Instead of helping to trace the different assumptions of the disputants, and teasing out the variations in vocabulary, the presenter tries to reduce it all to some common formula which, it is supposed, we simple viewers will understand, and which inevitably misrepresents the positions of both the contending parties.

The expression 'antecedent assumptions' covers a range of things. Most straightforwardly, it includes theories or whole systems of thought which a particular individual takes for granted. It was interesting to observe the very different judgements upon the causes and development of the French Revolution, evoked by the bicentenary celebrations in France. The events look very different to liberal and to Marxist historians; different again to conservative anti-Jacobins. There is, of course, a sense in which they agree as to the evidence—that a mob stormed the Bastille, for example, on 14 July 1789 and found seven prisoners there, and innumerable comparable facts—but they differ profoundly as to what it is reasonable to believe on the basis of these facts. Moreover, as Newman uses the expression 'antecedent assumptions', it also includes the personality and even the moral character of the individual who makes the judgement. As Newman puts it: 'though a given evidence does not vary in force, the antecedent probability attending it does vary without limit, according to the temper of the mind surveying it.' That this is so is, perhaps, most evident in the case of those persons whose primary duty it is to free their minds from every kind of bias, namely judges. Two judges may be faced by the same evidence and be guided by the same precedents and statutes or—in the case of justices of the US Supreme Court—the same provisions of the Constitution, and yet come to different conclusions without there necessarily being any suggestion of bias or other impropriety.

(d) What we have said so far, following Newman, about the ways in which people actually think, about what constitutes 'rationality' in ordinary life, leads naturally to a fourth consideration which bears more closely on the relevance of faith. If our appreciation of evidence and our assessment of the conclusions that follow from it is generally tacit and implicit, and if the process of reasoning is conducted within a framework of assumptions which are to some extent influenced by the individual's entire character and personality, a certain stability over time in these assumptions is necessary. Clifford's dictum would require that any change in the weight of evidence for a system of belief should immediately be reflected in some modification of the system or some variation in the confidence reposed in it. But this manifestly does not happen. People hold on to their beliefs when things get difficult and must do so if they are to be properly developed and tested.

This feature of our large-scale beliefs is so important that it needs to be explored in greater depth. We must notice, first of all, that it applies even in the case of scientific systems which are thought to provide the very paradigm of open-mindedness. Clifford's dictum is appropriate only to what T. S. Kuhn calls 'normal science', in which the researcher is trying to test a hypothesis within the framework of a well-developed branch of the subject. In such a case the fundamental laws and central concepts of that branch of science are not in dispute or at all at risk from the outcome of the experiment. The researcher is entirely open-minded as to the truth of the hypothesis and will accept or reject it according as the experiment falls out. If the results of the experiment are inconclusive the researcher will have only such confidence in the hypothesis as the evidence warrants; if they are equivocal he or she will suspend judgement. This is because the antecedent assumptions are held steady throughout the proceedings and are not themselves called in question. The situation is quite different when more fundamental scientific laws or concepts are at issue. It was Kuhn's peculiar contribution to the history and philosophy of science to recognize that 'scientific revolutions' occur in the course of which the issue at stake is precisely what organizing concepts should be employed and what basic laws acknowledged. Kuhn has been criticized, rightly so far as I can judge, for exaggerating the difference between normal and revolutionary science, but his significance for our purposes is not affected by this. What we learn from him is that, in so far as fresh discoveries threaten the received scientific picture, it is simply not the case that the essential features of the system are at once abandoned or confidence in them allowed to fluctuate from day to day. A variety of devices is resorted to in order to avoid such a consequence. Comparatively low-level theories are jettisoned or modified in order to accommodate the new observations; sometimes the observations themselves are questioned; or the episode is placed in parenthesis, as it were, as an as yet unsolved problem. As Kuhn puts it epigrammatically: 'If any and every failure to fit were ground for theory rejection, all theories ought to be rejected at all times.' The 'puzzles' that 'normal science' attempts to solve are set precisely by the occurrence of observations that are incompatible with the findings of science as they now stand.

Meanwhile the existing overall structure is retained until there is available an alternative system which is better able to account for all the evidence and which, in turn, is able to generate programmes of research which will, of course, then be confronted by their own puzzles.

Hence, scientists operate what has been called a 'principle of tenacity', in virtue of which they do not let go of their fundamental beliefs when things get difficult, but rather persevere in the hope, or—shall we say?—the faith, that the problem will eventually be resolved. Their characteristic attitude is well expressed by Darwin in the concluding sentences of *The Origin of Species*: 'A crowd of difficulties will have occurred to the reader. Some of them are so grave that to this day I can never reflect on them without being staggered; but, to the best of my judgement, the greater number are only apparent; and those that are real are not, I think, fatal to my theory.' Two things are to be noticed here. One is that Darwin does not at all minimize the difficulties. He is, in that sense, open-minded and impartial. The other is that, in spite of fully acknowledging them, he continues to trust his theory. And it is apparent, I think, that both these attitudes are essential to scientific progress. Without an honest appreciation of the difficulties, the theory would never get tested and developed. Without the determination to soldier on in the face of difficulties the process of testing and development would never have time to operate effectively.

In the light of this discussion it becomes apparent that the contrast which is often drawn, not least by theologians, between the entirely open-minded approach of the scientist and the committed nature of religious faith is, at the very least, overdrawn. Nevertheless, it would be a mistake to pretend that there are no differences at all. The chief differences are, I suggest:

(a) that, in the natural sciences, at any rate, at any given time, the preponderance of evidence in favour of a particular complex of theories is likely to be so marked as to make it plainly sensible to persevere with it in the face of temporary difficulties;

(b) that, even when this is not so, the pragmatic advantages of a degree of tenacity are fairly obvious. Where scientists differ, and both cannot be right, the truth is more likely to emerge if both parties adhere pretty stubbornly to their own hypotheses, so that they can be fully tested against one another. In other words, 'faith' (if this is the right word to use) is such an obvious requirement of scientific procedures that, in this connection, there is no place for a 'problem of faith and reason'. Nevertheless we need to realize that such disagreements can be very persistent. Since the 1930s there has been a deep division among physicists about how to interpret the fundamental concepts of quantum mechanics. Each side in the dispute holds to its opinion, though well aware of the criticisms offered by the other.

[*Faith and Criticism* (Oxford: Clarendon Press, 1994), 10–19.]

WILLIAM ALSTON

112 Experience in Religious Belief

Apart from the purely a priori, then, the grounds of Christian belief can be reduced to forms of the perception of God and explanatory claims. How do these relate to each other in the total case for Christian belief?

The most obvious relation is an additive one. Such grounds as have some individual merit can be combined so that the total basis will be greater than any of its individual parts; just as the various bits of evidence that support a scientific or diagnostic hypothesis add up to a support that is greater than that contributed by any one piece of evidence alone. Thus the belief that God is supremely loving will be supported by the many perceptions of God as loving, by God's self-revelation in the New Testament, and, perhaps, by natural theology. But there is more than one reason why this simple additive relationship is not the whole story. For example, in this book we have run into more than one way in which CMP ['Christian Mystical Perception'] is dependent for its operation on a background system of belief that is based, at least in part, on grounds of other sorts. Hence we can't suppose that CMP simply adds a completely independent quantum of justification to that provided by the other grounds. The situation is more complicated than that. The ensuing discussion will bring out some dimensions of this complexity.

Perhaps the simplest of these further modes of interaction involves the way in which different grounds will support different propositions, will shore up different parts of the structure. Speaking most generally, mediate and immediate justification have complementary strengths and weaknesses. There is something of a 'percepts without concepts are blind, concepts without percepts are empty' situation here. Perception generates beliefs full of force and conviction. 'Seeing is believing.' 'There's no substitute for being there.' But often the content is very limited, and it doesn't give us by itself a full theoretical characterization. We have repeatedly pointed out the limits of what God experientially presents Himself to us *as*. With rare exceptions one doesn't suppose that God presents Himself as creator, three Persons in one Substance, the actor in salvation history, or even omnipotent, omniscient, and a se. To get all that we have to go to revelation and natural theology. To be sure, I have already claimed that the *message* form of revelation involves perceiving God as 'saying' something; and no limit can be put on what God could *tell* a human being, other than limits set by our capacities for understanding. But for present purposes let's set the content of divine messages to one side and confine mystical perception to what God presents Himself as being and doing. Here we have an area in which revelation and natural theology can give us what perception cannot.

On the other side, we have to recognize that perception has its own contribution to make by way of propositional content as well as by way of force and vividness. In mystical perception one can learn what God is doing vis-à-vis oneself at the moment, reproving, forgiving, instructing, guiding, comforting, just being present; and one can learn what God's will is for oneself in particular. We can't get any of this out of natural theology and general revelation. Thus each type of source has its own distinctive propositional contribution to make to the total system of belief. A given part of the structure will depend on some grounds and not on others—even though some parts will gain support from more than one source, as when the doctrine of creation is supported by divine messages, by other modes of revelation, and by natural theology.

Nor is this differential support a matter of mere aggregation. The relationship is often more intimate than that. The doxastic output from one source can fill out what is gleaned from another. Here I think particularly of the point, discussed in some detail in Chapter 2, that frequently what is explicitly presented in putative experience of God fails to uniquely identify the object as God. One is aware of God's being *very* loving and powerful but not infinitely loving and powerful. One is aware of something sustaining one in being, but not aware of it as the creator of all. Christians regularly fill out these fragmentary epiphanies with what they have garnered from their tradition, taking what they perceive to go beyond what is revealed in experience in ways spelled out in the Christian tradition. This is often made a reproach to mystical perception; since the perceiver is reading his tradition into what he perceives, the perception has no epistemic significance. But the alleged weakness is really a strength. It is precisely what happens in sense perception where we construe what we are seeing, feeling, or hearing in terms of what we take ourselves to know about the object from elsewhere. If we weren't able to do that we would learn much less from perception. To be sure, the value of this procedure depends on the credentials of this independent information. But given such credentials, it is of the first importance to be able to fill out the perceived situation in this way.

The filling out can go in the other direction as well; perception can fill out what we get from public revelation and natural theology. The latter may tell us what God is like and the broad outlines of what He has done, is doing, and will do in the world to carry out His plans, but they will not tell me what God has to say to me at this moment or what God's will for me is at this stage of my life, or how God is interacting with me at this moment. These details can be filled in by mystical perception. The other sources can give us the master plan; perception provides the application of that plan to the immediate situation.

Thus far the discussion in this section has concerned purely *additive* relationships in the sense of relations between contributions that are made by each source independently of any dependence on the others. We now move to more intimate relationships in which a given source is involved in the *operation* of another source, so that the support lent to religious belief by the latter is not wholly independent of the former.

To begin, let's remind ourselves of the ways in which we have already seen mystical perception to be beholden to other grounds. In justifiably forming beliefs about God on the basis of mystical perception we depend on a background system of belief at more than one point. First, we use that system to determine whether what we are aware of is God. As just noted, God does not uniquely identify Himself just by the way He appears to us. Even if He says that He is God, there is the problem of distinguishing the real thing from imposters. And apart from self-identification, though God may appear to one as good, powerful, and loving, He typically does not appear as *infinitely* good, powerful, or loving, or as possessing any other characteristics that are peculiar to God Himself. Hence we depend on the background theology and other aspects of the tradition for principles that lay down conditions under which what we are aware of is God.

It may also be that MP is dependent on other grounds for the principles linking phenomenal content with objective properties, for example, a principle that when one has an experience of such-and-such a phenomenal sort one is justified in taking what is appearing to one to be God pouring out His spirit. Such principles have to be true if objective attributions are to be justified by being based on appearances; and the subject must be justified in accepting such principles if he is to use them in reflective criticism of perceptual beliefs. Do we need some input from other sources of information about God to determine what appearances reliably indicate what features of what objects? I don't feel confident about any answer to this question. On the one hand, it is plausible to accept a blanket principle that licenses going from how something seems experientially to what it is, in the absence of sufficient reasons against this in a specific case. That would make mystical perception independent of other sources on this point. On the other hand what we are justified in believing about God and our relations to Him from other sources may well be required for justifiably accepting such principles. I won't try to decide this issue here.

Finally, putative perceptions of God are not 'self-authenticating', but instead are in principle subject to being shown to be incorrect, or inadequately based, by relevant considerations, that is, 'overridden'. But this is possible only if we have a stock of knowledge or justified belief concerning the matters in question, in this case concerning God, His nature, purposes, and activities. Thus mystical perception can function as a source of justification for M-beliefs only against the background of a system of epistemically justified beliefs concerning the matters just mentioned. Such a system is built up at least partly on the basis of mystical perception itself. But apart from worries as to how we could ever get started building up the system on the basis of MP if each utilization of MP (including the earliest ones) required that we already have such a system, we have seen that MP is limited in the range of beliefs that it can effectively support. Except for the matters on which God has communicated messages in a direct perceptual manner, MP will not by itself give us the word on the essential nature of God, His purposes, and the course of salvation history. Even where God has putatively conveyed messages on such matters, we need to distinguish genuine divine communications from counterfeits, and it is dubious that we could do that without relying on what we have learned about God from other sources. The upshot is that we can't have the kind of background system we need for overriding without relying on other sources of information. Hence MP depends on other grounds of religious belief for its viability as a source of epistemic justification.

What about the other grounds? Does each of them depend on other sources for its epistemic credentials? Well, consider the proposition that no one ground suffices by itself for building up the background system for overriders for beliefs based on that ground. And though I won't produce a full dress argument for that proposition, it seems very plausible on the basis of considerations we have already adduced. We have seen that each of the grounds in question is fitted to provide some parts of the total background system and not others. Hence, at least as far as the overrider system is concerned, each of the other grounds is also dependent on others for its effective operation.

Another way in which one ground depends on others has to do with the resolution of doubts. Doubts can be raised about the genuineness or the strength of any one of these grounds. These doubts can be, to some extent, assuaged by appeal to other grounds or their output. Although none of the grounds is immune from such worries, the fact that the output of each supports the claims made for the others rightfully increases our confidence in all of them, and thus increases the total support given to Christian belief by their combination.

[*Perceiving God* (Ithaca, NY: Cornell University Press, 1991), 292–6.]

PETER VAN INWAGEN

113 **Clifford's Principle**

Now let us turn to questions of religion. Is religion different from philosophy and politics in the respects we have been discussing? It is an extremely popular position that religion is different. Or, at least, it must be that many antireligious philosophers and other writers hostile to religious belief hold this position, for it seems to be presupposed by almost every aspect of their approach to the subject of religious belief. And yet, this position seems never to have been explicitly stated, much less argued for. Let us call it the Difference Thesis. A good example of the Difference Thesis at work is provided by W. K. Clifford's famous essay 'The Ethics of Belief.' One of the most interesting facts about 'The Ethics of Belief' is that nowhere in it is religious belief explicitly mentioned. It would, however, be disingenuous in the extreme to say that this essay is simply about the ethics of belief in general and is no more directed at religious belief than at any other kind of belief. 'Everyone knows,' as the phrase goes, that Clifford's target is religious belief. (Certainly the editors of anthologies know this. 'The Ethics of Belief' appears in just about every anthology devoted to the philosophy of religion. It has never appeared in an anthology devoted to epistemology.) The real thesis of Clifford's essay is that religious beliefs—belief in God; belief in an afterlife; belief in the central historical claims of Judaism or Christianity or Islam—are always or almost always held in ways that violate the famous ethico-epistemic principle: It is wrong always, everywhere, and for anyone, to believe anything upon insufficient evidence. If, moreover, he is of the opinion that beliefs in any other general category are always or almost always (or typically or rather often) held in ways that violate his principle, this is certainly not apparent.

Let us call this principle—'It is wrong always, everywhere, and for anyone . . .'

—Clifford's Principle. It is interesting to note that Clifford's Principle is almost never mentioned except in hostile examinations of religious belief, and that the antireligious writers who mention it never apply it to anything but religious beliefs. (With the exception of illustrative examples—like Clifford's example of the irresponsible shipowner—that are introduced in the course of explaining its content.) It is this that provides the primary evidence for my contention that many antireligious philosophers and other writers against religion tacitly accept the Difference Thesis. The fact that they apply Clifford's Principle only to religious beliefs is best explained by the assumption that they accept the Difference Thesis. The cases of Marxism and Freudianism are instructive examples of what I am talking about. It is easy to point to philosophers who believe that Marxism and Freudianism are nonsense: absurd parodies of scientific theories that get the real world wildly wrong. Presumably these philosophers do not believe that Marxism and Freudianism were adequately supported by the evidence that was available to Marx and Freud—or that they are adequately supported by the evidence that is available to any of the latter-day adherents of Marxism and Freudianism. But never once has any writer charged that Marx or Freud blotted his epistemic escutcheon by failing to apportion belief to evidence. I challenged anyone to find me a passage (other than an illustrative passage of the type I have mentioned) in which any devotee of Clifford's Principle has applied it to anything but religious belief. And yet, practically all philosophers—the literature will immediately demonstrate this to the most casual inquirer—subscribe to theses an obvious logical consequence of which is that the world abounds in gross violations of Clifford's Principle that have nothing to do with religion.

An explanation of the widespread tacit acceptance of the Difference Thesis is not far to seek. If Clifford's Principle were generally applied in philosophy (or in politics or historiography or even in many parts of the natural sciences), it would have to be applied practically everywhere. If its use became general, we'd all be constantly shoving it in one another's faces. And there would be no comfortable reply open to most of the recipients of a charge of violating Clifford's Principle. If I am an archaeologist who believes that an artifact found in a Neolithic tomb was a religious object used in a fertility rite, and if my rival, Professor Graves, believes that it was used to wind flax, how can I suppose that my belief is supported by the evidence? If my evidence really supports my belief, why doesn't it convert Professor Graves, who is as aware of it as I am, to my position? If we generally applied Clifford's Principle, we'd all have to become agnostics as regards most philosophical and political questions, or we'd have to find some reasonable answer to the challenge: 'In what sense can the evidence you have adduced support or justify your belief when there are many authorities as competent as you who regard it as unconvincing?' But no answer to this challenge is evident, and religion seems to be the only area of human life in which very many people are willing to be agnostics about the answers to very many questions.

It might, however, be objected that what I have been representing as obvious considerations are obvious only on a certain conception of the nature of evidence. Perhaps the Difference Thesis is defensible because the evidence that some people have for their philosophical and political (and archaeological and historiographical . . .) beliefs consists partly of the deliverances of that incommunicable 'insight' that I speculated about earlier. This objection would seem to be consistent with everything said in 'The Ethics of Belief,' for Clifford nowhere tells his readers what evidence is. If 'evidence' is evidence in the courtroom or laboratory sense (photographs, transcripts of sworn statements, the pronouncements of expert witnesses, tables of figures), then 'the evidence' pretty clearly does not support our philosophical and political beliefs. Let such evidence be eked out with logical inference and private sense experience and the memory of sense experience (my private experience and my memories, as opposed to my testimony about my experience and memories, cannot be entered as evidence in a court of law or published in *Physical Review Letters*, but they can be part of my evidence for my beliefs—or so the epistemologists tell us), and it still seems to be true that 'the evidence' does not support our philosophical and political beliefs. It is not that such evidence is impotent: It can support—I hope—many life-and-death courtroom judgments and such scientific theses as that the continents are in motion. But it does not seem to be sufficient to justify most of our philosophical and political beliefs, or our philosophical and political beliefs, surely, would be far more uniform than they are. If 'evidence' must be of the courtroom-and-laboratory sort, how can the Difference Thesis be defended?

If, however, 'evidence' can include 'insight' or some other incommunicable element—my private experience and my memories are not necessarily incommunicable—it may be that some of the philosophical and political beliefs of certain people are justified by the evidence available to them. But if evidence is understood in this way, how can anyone be confident that some of the religious beliefs of some people are not justified by the evidence available to them? If evidence can include incommunicable elements, how can anyone be confident that all religious believers are in violation of Clifford's Principle? If 'evidence' can include the incommunicable, how can the Difference Thesis be defended?

All that I have said so far in this section amounts to a polemic against what I perceive as a widespread double standard in writings about the relation of religious belief to evidence and argument. This double standard consists in setting religious belief a test it could not possibly pass, and in studiously ignoring the fact that almost none of our beliefs on any subject could possibly pass this test.

[in T. V. Morris (ed.), *God and the Philosophers* (New York: Oxford University Press, 1994), 44–6.]

While Lutheran faith involves both belief-that (however interpreted) and trust, Luther stresses that the trust is the important thing. Is a third form of faith possible where one can have the trust without the belief-that? I think that it is and that many recent writers who stress the irrelevance to faith of 'belief-that' have been feeling their way towards such a form of faith. I shall call such faith Pragmatist faith. As we have seen, one can act on assumptions which one does not believe. To do this is to do those actions which you would do if you did believe. In particular, you can act on the assumption not merely that God, whom you believe to exist, will do for you what you need or want, but also on the assumption that there is such a God (and that he has the properties which Christians have ascribed to him). One can do this by doing those actions which one would do if one believed these things. In Chapter 1 I quoted Pascal who replied to a man who said 'But I can't believe' with a recipe of how to acquire belief. The recipe was that the man should act as if he believed, do the actions which believers do, 'taking holy water, having masses said', etc. and that would produce belief. Although Pascal did not hold that acting-as-if it was the essence of faith, he saw it as a step on the road. But it is natural enough to develop this third view of faith according to which the belief-that is irrelevant, the acting-as-if is what matters. After all belief is a passive state; merit belongs only to actions. Surely if a man does those actions which a believer would do and for which he is to be esteemed, then the man should be esteemed whether or not he has the belief.

As we have seen, trusting God may be not just acting on assumptions; but doing so where one has good purposes. Those who have wanted to define faith in terms of trust alone would, I think, wish such a restriction to be included in the understanding of trust. So, on the Pragmatist view, a man S has faith if he acts on the assumptions that there is a God who has the properties which Christians ascribe to him and has provided for men the means of salvation and the prospect of glory, and that he will do for S what he knows that S needs or wants—so long also as S has good purposes. He will thus seek not his own fame, but long-term and deep well-being for himself and others. Seeking these things, he may believe that they are only to be had if there is a God who provides such well-being in this world and in the world to come. Hence he may act on the assumption that there is a God—for unless there is, that which is most worthwhile cannot be had. He will do the same things as the man with Lutheran faith will do. He will, for example, worship and pray and live a good life partly in the hope to find a better life in the world to come. He prays for his brethren, not necessarily because he believes that there is a God who hears his prayers, but because only if there is can the world be set to right. He lives the good life, not necessarily because he believes that God will reward him, but because only if there is a God who will reward him can he find the deep long-term well-being for which he seeks. He worships, not necessarily because he believes that there is a God who deserves worship, but because it is very important to express gratitude for existence if there is a God to whom to be grateful and there is some chance that there is.

THE COMMON STRUCTURE IN THE THREE VIEWS

Pragmatist faith is not, however, that far distant from Lutheran faith. The man of Pragmatist faith need not believe that there is a God, but he must have certain other beliefs. He has to have moral beliefs, e.g. that any God ought to be worshipped and that he ought to help others to happiness; beliefs about his long-term well-being, e.g. that it would consist in having the Beatific Vision of God rather than living a Lotus-eater life on Earth; and beliefs about the best route to attain that well-being, e.g. by seeking a life after death or a life of service in the African jungle (though he may believe that it is improbable that even the best route leads to that well-being). And he needs the belief that there is some (maybe small) finite probability that there is a God. It is no accident that Pragmatist faith as I have described it does involve such beliefs. These could not be detached from it and anything both rational and faith-like be left. For any advocate of a way of life, such as the Christian way, which prescribes for man certain conduct and has any pretence to rational justifiability, must have a belief as to why this conduct is to be pursued (e.g. because there is some chance that it is a duty, or because there is some chance that it will lead to happiness for oneself or others here or hereafter); and a belief as to why the goal cannot be attained more easily in some other way. The difference lies not in a fact that Pragmatist faith lacks belief-that, but simply that it involves less in the way of belief-that than does Lutheran faith. You need not believe that there is a God and that in consequence you will obtain deep and long-term well-being if you do certain actions (which will bring you deep and long-term well-being if there is a God); only that there may be a God and so that you are more likely to obtain happiness by doing these actions than you are if you assume that there is no God. Some sort of creed is difficult to avoid.

Also, as we have seen, Lutheran faith is not very different from Thomist 'meritorious faith' (i.e. faith 'formed' by a voluntary process and combined with a readiness to do works of love), although it is different from Thomist faith by itself. Also, as we have seen, in so far as belief (rather than assumption) is involved in faith, the faith will vary according to the beliefs with which credal propositions are being contrasted. It is by now, I hope, beginning to become clear that, on all three views of faith, the sort of faith which is meritorious involves belief of some sort and a good character, normally shown in good actions. On all these views of faith the actions which a man is ready to do include those which involve achieving good purposes, relying on the belief, or at any rate assumption, that God will do for us what we want or need. Given that the claims about God's nature and existence are not absolutely certain, there is some danger that he may not. If God does not do for us what we want or need, then, unless there is no God but is some other way to attain the goals of religion (to be discussed in the next chapter), such as salvation, there will be the bad consequence of our not obtaining those goals. Hence men's actions in relying on the cited belief can be described as putting trust in God. Hence faith involves trust on all three views. The real difference between kinds of faith (one which cuts across the Thomist/Lutheran division) seems to lie in just how strong the credal beliefs which faith contains have to be. This is a matter partly of whether the propositions of the Creed are believed (e.g. the belief is that God is the Father Almighty, Maker of Heaven and Earth); or whether they are simply assumptions which guide action, and so the belief is simply that our goals are most likely to be attained if we do act on the assumption that the Creed is true. The strength of belief that a proposition is true is also a matter of the alternatives with which the proposition is contrasted.

[*Faith and Reason* (Oxford: Clarendon Press, 1981), 115–18.]

PAUL HELM

115 Faith and Merit

Perhaps there are cases of trust which occur in the absence of evidence, but to de-couple trust and belief in the systematic way that Swinburne does leads to the following paradoxical situation. Suppose two people A and B and a proposition *p*, and suppose that A has evidence for *p* which renders *p* slightly more probable than not-*p* for him, while B has evidence that strongly probabilifies *p* for him. Each may behave in a similar way with respect to the truth expressed by *p*, but on Professor Swinburne's account one of these may be a man of considerable faith, acting on an assumption with a good purpose, the other will have a strong belief, acting as a consequence of good evidence, but may have only little faith. As Swinburne puts it, to trust is to 'do those actions which you would do if you believed the stated assumption strongly'. So someone who believes the assumption strongly, and rationally, that is, has good evidence for it, is badly placed to exercise trust, and so to possess and exercise faith. So it appears that the better grounded the belief, or for that matter the better grounded the unbelief, the less scope there is for faith. Strong belief or unbelief expel faith.

One might suppose that, whatever its difficulties, such a view is at least theologically sound; for does not St Paul imply that, while faith and hope are temporary, love is eternal? Perhaps he does. But it does not necessarily follow from this that there is no trust in a situation where faith is turned to sight. Perhaps the saints made perfect, who know and love God completely, also for that very reason trust him completely. What may be temporary is not trust but belief, which is replaced by knowledge in the life to come.

However this might be, it is here, at the point where faith is decoupled from belief, that what appears to be an interesting conflict of aims in Professor Swinburne's work as a philosopher of religion comes into view. For on the one hand he wishes, in many of his writings, vigorously to prosecute the question of whether or not there is good evidence that God exists, and to go to considerable pains to assemble that evidence. As is well known, Professor Swinburne takes the view that for belief in God's existence to be reasonable there must be more evidence for that proposition than for its opposite. And the more evidence that can be assembled for the truth of the proposition, the better. This is the burden of his book *The Existence of God*, for example.

So in order to be reasonable in his believing a person must strive to ensure that there is more evidence for the truth of the proposition that he believes than for some alternative proposition. He must have as one of his intellectual aims the grounding of belief in evidence as firmly as he can. According to Swinburne such belief is not free, for belief is not voluntary. He is a good Humean at this point; belief is that state of mind which is constrained by what that mind takes to be good evidence. Choosing to believe is incoherent. And the intellectually responsible person must tie his belief as firmly as he can to the evidence.

But such a view of belief has interesting and perhaps disturbing consequences for faith. According to Swinburne the better grounded a belief, the less free is that belief. Such belief is not so much an action as an effect, it is the mind being involuntarily impressed by what it takes to be evidence. So believing is not an action, and *a fortiori* it cannot be morally assessed as an action. It makes no sense to ask whether belief is meritorious or not, for example. A person can be neither praised or blamed for believing, nor blamed for not believing, though she may be praised or blamed for the way in which she approaches matters which are necessary conditions for believing, for example, the correct assessment of evidence. So, in the case of someone who has good evidence for p, and who accordingly believes strongly that p, there is less scope for free trust in what p expresses than where belief is less strongly grounded. And, because Swinburne links trust and human merit, there is less scope for merit. To the extent that the existence of God is evidentially established, it is more reasonable to believe that he exists than not, but for that very reason there is less opportunity for faith in him, for trust. Merit comes only from trust, but trust can only occur when there is evidential deficiency. On Professor Swinburne's view it would seem that as the God of the philosophers enters by the front door, the God of Abraham, Isaac, and Jacob is forced to leave by the rear exit!

So if you want to exercise trust in God, and to gain merit by its exercise, you had better not read Swinburne's *The Existence of God* and you most certainly ought not to let yourself be persuaded by strong grounds to believe in God's existence. For if you do you at the same time reduce the opportunities for trusting, for acting on an assumption while having a good purpose, and so you reduce the opportunities for faith, and so lessen your chances of gaining merit by exercising faith. But—it may perhaps be replied—the certain merit to be gained from an investigation into God's existence which includes reading *The Existence of God* has to be weighed against the prospect of being convinced by its arguments and so of reducing the opportunities for the exercise of meritorious faith in the future. So perhaps one has to balance the merit of reading *The Existence of God* against the merit of not reading it.

One might argue that one could be certain that God exists and be quite uncertain of some of God's properties and that trusting in God was in respect of those matters that one was uncertain of. This is certainly a possibility, though certainty of God's existence cannot be coupled with agnosticism about all his properties, presumably. But I do not think that Professor Swinburne has such a possibility in mind.

Perhaps indeed one has an *obligation* to investigate as thoroughly as one can the question of whether God exists. If one does so, one fulfils an obligation, and so (presumably) gains merit. But in fulfilling this obligation, and so gaining merit, one lessens the chances of living a life of faith, and so of gaining merit by such a life. So perhaps one has to balance the merit arising from responsibly investigating the grounds of one's faith against the merit to be gained from exercising that faith in an unreflective way. Such are the problems of meritology.

We have already noted that Swinburne tends to de-couple trust and belief, and to favour the view that trust is inversely proportional to belief. So strongly and clearly does Swinburne hold to the idea that trusting is an action, a case of acting on the assumption that he is able to contemplate with surprising equanimity the idea that there is a form of faith, Pragmatist faith, according to which the acting as if exists without any, or with very little belief-that about God. If he is consistent then he must also hold that such a view holds out the prospect of the greatest scope for trust, and of the greatest degree of merit in trusting. On such a view faith has an intentional object, but that object need not be God in order for the faith to be genuine. ('The difference lies not in a fact that Pragmatist faith lacks belief-that, but simply that it involves less in the way of belief-that than does Lutheran faith'.) If I believe that there is a God, then the intentional object of my belief is 'that there is a God', whereas if I believe that it is possible that there is a God, the intentional object of my belief is 'that it is possible there is a God'. Pragmatic faith is compatible with the belief that there just possibly may be a God. Such faith can hardly be said to be faith in God. On such a view God's existence is not impossible, but neither is it more probable than not. Indeed, for the Pragmatic view of faith it is more probable than not that God does not exist. To have faith in such circumstances is to act on the assumption that there is such a God, rather like the would-be believer in Pascal's Wager. As Swinburne puts it, 'It is natural enough to develop this third view of faith (i.e. the Pragmatist view) according to which the belief-that is irrelevant, the acting-as-if is what matters. After all belief is a passive state; merit belongs only to actions.'

Pragmatist faith emphasizes, perhaps places exclusive emphasis upon, trust, and trusting is acting on the assumption that p with a good purpose, when there is some reason, but not good reason, for thinking that p is true. So if, after having read and pondered Swinburne's *The Existence of God*, you still have doubts about whether God exists, you ought not to despair of faith; you may have faith, Pragmatist faith, provided that God's existence remains a possibility for you. To ensure that you have such faith you need to be able to act with a good purpose, to resolve not to be a scoundrel and to act accordingly. Indeed, in these circumstances you may have the greatest scope for faith. And so those who, epistemologically speaking, are first shall, fiducially speaking, be the last; and the last shall be first. The evidentially hungry shall be filled, while the evidentially rich shall be sent empty away.

[Not previously published.]

ROBERT M. ADAMS

116   The Sin of Unbelief

Thus far I have said relatively little about specifically religious faith and unbelief. It is time to turn our attention to them, and particularly to the sin of unbelief, as it occurs in the experience of Christians. We might think of unbelief as occurring in two forms: (1) not believing God when he speaks to us (that is, not believing what he says); and (2) not believing in God (that is, not trusting him, or not believing that he exists at all, or not believing important truths about him). In fact, however, these forms of unbelief cannot be sharply separated. If we do not believe God when he speaks to us, it is probably because we do not trust him; and if we sin by not believing in God, it is what he says to us about himself that we do not believe.

Let us dwell a bit on this last point. I think the sin of unbelief always involves rejection of something God has said to the sinner. Simply not believing that God exists is not the sin of unbelief, if God has never spoken to you. Butterflies presumably do not believe in God, but they are not therefore guilty of the sin of unbelief. If we, unlike butterflies, are guilty of the sin of unbelief, it is not because we are supposed to be able to *figure out* divine truth for ourselves, but because God has spoken to us. For this reason it behoves us to be particularly reluctant to accuse others of the sin of unbelief. How do we know what God has said to them? For it is the *internal* testimony of the Holy Spirit that most concerns us here.

You may expect me to say something here about atheism. But I will not, because I have never been an atheist and I think it is not my business here to anatomize the sins that atheists may be committing. No, I will take a concrete example of unbelief as it is found in the Christian life.

It is suggested to me that I ought to follow a certain course of action. Perhaps my wife suggests it, or perhaps the thought arises in me spontaneously, or is prompted by something I hear in a sermon. Initially the thought comes to me with the force of a minor revelation. But the more I think about it, the more I think of good reasons for not acting on the idea. I come to the conclusion that it would be a mistake; yet I remain disturbed about it.

What is going on? Maybe God was telling me to follow that course of action, and I am not believing him. God's speech is not ineffectual; so we should expect that if we do not believe something he has said to us, his word will leave at least a trace of uneasiness in us. In the state that I described I may no longer be in a good position to tell whether it was God or a foolish impulse of my own that pressed me at first to do the action. What is clear is that if it was God, I do not want to hear him. And that is sin.

Why don't I want to hear God if he is telling me to follow that course of action? Quite possibly because I am *afraid*. Perhaps the course of action is one that would risk offending people whom I fear to offend. And in this fear we find a deeper level of the sin of unbelief. For why am I afraid? Don't I believe that God will bless my obedience if I sincerely try to do his will? Don't I believe that he can bring greater good out of any disasters that may befall me? Don't I believe that there is greater happiness to be found in venturing for God than in playing it safe for myself? Yes, I believe all those things. That is, I would sincerely assert them. I might even preach them in a sermon, or exert myself to defend them against philosophical attack. But obviously I do not believe them with all my heart.

This is, I think, the central form of the sin of unbelief in the Christian life. It is not a refusal to assent intellectually to theological truths, but a failure to trust in truths to which we do assent. Of course an attempt to resolve the conflict could lead, unhappily, to withdrawal of assent from the truths, rather than to trust in God; but more than intellectual assent is involved here.

The relationship between unbelief and fear is important. Trust can be understood in part as a sort of freedom from fear. It is a conceptual truth that if I fear that God will let me down, I do not entirely trust him. Conversely, perfect trust in God would free us from that fear, and from many others.

The emotional ingredient in faith, and in unbelief, is significant for their relation to the intellectual life. There ought to be room in our conception of faith for honest investigation of all questions, and for feeling the force of objections to our faith, even while we are sustained in that faith. Three things should be distinguished. (1) To recognize that God's goodness is in some sense less than 100 per cent probable, that it is less certainly established, more open to doubt, than one's own existence, or that '2 + 2 = 4', is to see the element of venture in our faith. It is not necessarily to fall into the sin of unbelief. The sin is something else in our response to these objective facts about our epistemic situation. (2) We may *fear* that God will let us down. The fear adds something emotional, felt or unfelt, which pervasively poisons our attitudes and which normally does constitute some failure of trust in God. The certitude of faith has much more to do with confidence, or freedom from fear, which is partly an emotional state, than it has to do with judgments of certainty or great probability in any evidential sense. (3) To be complete, let us note that we might let the indecisiveness of the evidence affect our *action*. We might try to factor all the arguments, pro and con, into our decisions about what to do. In other words, we might hedge our bet on God's goodness. That would surely be a sin of unbelief.

There are, of course, cases in which evidence against beliefs that we hold ought to be factored into our decisions. If a hunter believes that the animal behind the bush is a deer, but recognizes that there is some reason to think it might be another hunter, the evidence against his belief ought certainly to influence his conduct. Some philosophers may hold that rationality, or even morality, requires us to factor into our decisions any uncertainty we recognize in the objective case for *any* belief we hold. But I think that is wrong. Our bet on God's love should not be hedged. Reasons to doubt other people's trustworthiness should sometimes be totally ignored. And our commitment to many ethical principles ought to be similarly unqualified. Suppose I see reason to doubt that there is any validity or binding force to morality at all; ought that uncertainty to be factored into my decision-making process? Surely not. So long as I do believe in morality, I must think that I ought absolutely to repudiate any hesitation to act on it, no matter what theoretical basis the hesitation may claim.

I have noted in section I that cognitive failures often owe their moral offensiveness at least in part to bad desires that are manifested in them. We may wonder whether a failure of trust in God is sinful on account of sinful desires that are manifested in it. This is a difficult question. The web of sin is a tangled mess of fears and desires which we cannot completely unravel. The fears that are obstacles to my believing what God says to me are not only fears of being let down by God; there are also fears of the frustration of my sinful desires. Perhaps to some extent I do not want to trust God because I sense that that threatens some idolatry that I have been cherishing. On the other hand, I wonder whether my sinful desires do not all *presuppose* a lack or weakness of trust in God's love. Could they stand in the face of a perfectly confident and vivid assurance of the riches of his goodness?

One motive that I think is particularly important in this context is lust for *control* of my own life and its circumstances. I would like to be able to plan my life and have it go according to plan. Or if I want to have some room in my life for the unplanned, the spontaneous and surprising, I would like the spontaneity to be my own caprice, and the surprises to be of certain sorts that please me.

(Santa Claus is welcome anytime he cares to call.) This sort of control depends heavily on my having a stable and reliable view of myself and my world. It depends also on my having a trustworthy method of modifying and extending my picture of reality as new events occur. I suspect that much of our emotional attachment to *rationality* has to do with our counting on it as a crucial part of our intellectual equipment for controlling our lives. We rely on rationality for at least three functions: (1) to enable us to know where we are going as we plan, scheme, contrive, or indulge a whim; (2) to tell us how to manipulate situations and people to achieve our goals; and (3) to give us judgments of probabilities so that we can limit our risks and place our emotional investments in the safest and most promising areas.

The control of which I am speaking is obviously related to freedom and the satisfaction of desire, but must not be identified with them. The power of the lust for control shows itself, indeed, in the extent to which we may be willing to sacrifice freedom and desire in order to stay in control. We will adjust our desires to 'reality,' and restrict our projects to those that are favoured by other people and our circumstances—all in order to avoid unpleasant surprises and the feeling that our life is out of our control.

The same motive may lead us to curtail our hopes. We adjust our plans easily to pleasant surprises, but unpleasant surprises threaten our control. From the standpoint of control, therefore, pessimism seems a stronger position than optimism. I think this fact is the main source of the intellectual machismo that prides itself on a sort of 'tough-mindedness' that refuses to hope for very much. The desire for control tempts us to believe that if we hope for too much we will make fools of ourselves, whereas if we turn out to have hoped for too little we will only have proved to be 'stronger' than we needed to be. This machismo is no more rational than the wishful thinking of which the hopeful are often accused. And when there is talk of 'wishful thinking,' we would do well to realize that if we have a nonrational motive for believing the best, most of us also have a nonrational motive for believing the worst. Pessimism is not happier than optimism; hope is happier than despair. But it is quite possible to prefer control to happiness.

What Christianity promises may seem 'too good to be true'; the emotional meaning of this is that Christianity promises more than we can hope for without giving up control. The supreme threat to our control, however, is God himself. In Christian faith we are invited to trust a person so much greater than ourselves that we cannot understand him very fully. We have to trust his power and goodness in general, without having a blueprint of what he is going to do in detail. This is very disturbing because it entails a loss of our control of our own lives.

God promises life; and the life that he promises is encounter with the alien and new. It is grace and good surprises. In this context the continued lust for control of one's life, in preference to opening oneself to grace, is sin. But what is its relation to the sin of unbelief? Is the desire for control something that inhibits me from trusting God? I must say that in my experience it seems to be so. The feeling that it is stronger, more controlling, to expect evil than to expect good is a powerful enemy of faith. On the other hand, when I consider the question whether I would have this passion for controlling my life if I were not afraid to begin with, I am inclined to think that the lust for control *presupposes* a lack of trust in God. Perhaps the two sins support each other and neither is absolutely prior to the other.

[*The Virtue of Faith and Other Essays in Philosophical Theology* (New York: Oxford University Press, 1987), 16–20.]

Select Bibliography

GENERAL

ABRAHAM, W. J., and HOLTZER, STEVEN W. (eds.) (1987), *The Rationality of Religious Belief: Essays in Honour of Basil Mitchell* (Oxford: Clarendon Press).

ALSTON, W. P. (1989), *Divine Nature and Human Language* (Ithaca, NY: Cornell University Press).

AUDI, ROBERT (1991), 'Faith, Belief and Rationality', in James E. Tomberlin (ed.), *Philosophy of Religion 1991,* Philosophical Perspectives, 5 (Atascadero, Calif.: Ridgeview).

—— and WAINWRIGHT, W. J. (1986), *Rationality, Religious Belief and Moral Commitment* (Ithaca, NY: Cornell University Press).

BARTLEY, W. W. (1984), *The Retreat to Commitment* (LaSalle, Ill.: Open Court).

BRODY, BARUCH A. (1974), *Readings in the Philosophy of Religion: An Analytic Approach* (Englewood Cliffs, NJ: Prentice-Hall).

BROWN, STUART C. (ed.) (1977), *Reason and Revelation* (Ithaca, NY: Cornell University Press).

CLARK, K. J. (1990), *Return to Reason* (Grand Rapids, Mich.: Eerdmans).

CRAIG, W. (1980), *The Cosmological Argument from Plato to Leibniz* (London: St Martin's Press).

DAVIS, S. (1997), *God, Reason and Theistic Proofs* (Edinburgh: Edinburgh University Press).

DELANEY, C. F. (ed.) (1979), *Rationality and Religious Belief* (Notre Dame, Ind.: University of Notre Dame Press).

EVANS, C. S. (1978), *Subjectivity and Religious Belief: An Historical, Critical Study* (Grand Rapids, Mich.: Eerdmans).

—— (1998), *Faith Beyond Reason* (Edinburgh: Edinburgh University Press).

GALE, R. (1991), *On the Nature and Existence of God* (Cambridge: Cambridge University Press).

GASKIN, J. C. A. (1989), *Varieties of Unbelief* (London: Macmillan).

GEACH, P. T. (1969), *God and the Soul* (London: Routledge).

GEIVETT, R. DOUGLAS, and SWEETMAN, BRENDAN (eds.) (1992), *Contemporary Perspectives on Religious Epistemology* (New York: Oxford University Press).

GREEN, RONALD M. (1978), *Religious Reason: The Rational and Moral Basis of Religious Belief* (New York: Oxford University Press).

GUTTING, GARY (1982), *Religious Belief and Religious Skepticism* (Notre Dame, Ind.: University of Notre Dame Press).

HELM, PAUL (1973), *The Varieties of Belief* (London: George Allen and Unwin).

HICK, JOHN (1957), *Faith and Knowledge* (Ithaca, NY: Cornell University Press).

HOUSTON, J. (1994), *Reported Miracles* (Cambridge: Cambridge University Press).

HOITENGA, D. (1991), *Faith and Reason from Plato to Plantinga* (Albany, NY: SUNY Press).

JORDAN, J. (1994), *Gambling on God: Essays on Pascal's Wager* (Lanham, Md.: Rowman and Littlefield).

KENNY, A. (1983), *Faith and Reason* (New York: Columbia University Press).

—— (1992) *What is Faith?* (Oxford: Oxford University Press).

MACKIE, J. L. (1982), *The Miracle of Theism* (Oxford: Clarendon Press).

MCTAGGART, J. M. E. (1906), *Some Dogmas of Religion* (London: Edward Arnold).

MARTIN, M. (1990), *Atheism: A Philosophical Justification* (Philadelphia: Temple University Press).

MAVRODES, GEORGE (1970), *Belief in God* (New York: Random House).

MESSER, R. (1993), *Does God's Existence Need Proof?* (Oxford: Clarendon Press).

MITCHELL, BASIL (ed.) (1971), *The Philosophy of Religion* (Oxford: Oxford University Press).

—— (1973), *The Justification of Religious Belief* (London: Macmillan).

NIELSEN, KAI (1971), *Contemporary Critiques of Religion* (London: Macmillan).

O'HEAR, A. (1984), *Experience, Explanation and Faith* (London: Routledge and Kegan Paul).

PADGETT, ALAN G. (ed.) (1994), *Reason and the Christian Religion* (Oxford: Clarendon Press).

PENELHUM, T. (1971), *Problems of Religious Knowledge* (London: Macmillan).

—— (1983), *God and Skepticism* (Dordrecht: Reidel).

—— (1989), *Faith* (London: Macmillan).

PLANTINGA, ALVIN, and WOLTERSTORFF, NICHOLAS (1983), *Faith and Rationality: Reason and Belief in God* (Notre Dame, Ind.: University of Notre Dame Press).

RESCHER, N. (1985), *Pascal's Wager* (Notre Dame, Ind.: University of Notre Dame Press).

ROSS, J. F. (1981), *Portraying Analogy* (Cambridge: Cambridge University Press).

QUINN, P. L., and TALIAFERRO, C. (1997), *A Companion to the Philosophy of Religion* (Oxford: Blackwell Publishers).

SESSIONS, WILLIAM LAD (1994), *The Concept of Faith* (Ithaca, NY: Cornell University Press).

STEIN, G. (ed.) (1980), *An Anthology of Atheism and Rationalism* (Buffalo, Prometheus Press).

SWINBURNE, R. (1970), *The Concept of Miracle* (London: Macmillan).

TRIGG, R. (1998), *Rationality and Religion* (Oxford: Blackwell Publishers).

WOLTERSTORFF, NICHOLAS (1976), *Reason within the Bounds of Religion* (Grand Rapids, Mich.: Eerdmans).

ZAGZEBSKI, L. (ed.) (1993), *Rational Faith* (Notre Dame, Ind.: University of Notre Dame Press).

GRAECO-ROMAN BACKGROUND

GERSON, L. P. (1990), *God and Greek Philosophy* (London: Routledge).

—— (ed.) (1996), *The Cambridge Companion to Plotinus* (Cambridge: Cambridge University Press).

JAEGER, W. (1947), *The Theology of the Early Greek Philosophers* (Oxford: Clarendon Press).

LONG, A. A., and SEDLEY, D. (1987), *The Hellenistic Philosophers* (2 vols.; Cambridge: Cambridge University Press).

VLASTOS, G. (1975), *Plato's Universe* (Seattle: University of Washington Press).

THE INTERACTION OF JUDAEO-CHRISTIANITY AND THE GRAECO-ROMAN WORLD

ARMSTRONG, A. H. (ed.) (1967), *The Cambridge History of Later Greek and Early Medieval Philosophy* (Cambridge: Cambridge University Press).

CHADWICK, H. (1966), *Early Christian Thought and the Classical Tradition* (Oxford: Clarendon Press).

—— (1981), *Boethius: The Consolation of Music, Logic, Theology and Philosophy* (Oxford: Clarendon Press).

—— (1986), *Augustine* (Oxford: Oxford University Press).

COCHRANE, C. N. (1944), *Christianity and Classical Culture* (London: Oxford University Press).

KRETZMANN, N. (1990), 'Faith Seeks, Understanding Finds: Augustine's Charter for Christian Philosophy', in T. P. Flint (ed.), *Christian Philosophy* (Notre Dame, Ind.: University of Notre Dame Press).

O'MEARA, D. (1982), *Neoplatonism and Christian Thought* (Albany, NY: SUNY Press).

OSBORN, E. (1981), *The Beginning of Christian Philosophy* (Cambridge: Cambridge University Press).

—— (1993), *The Emergence of Christian Theology* (Cambridge: Cambridge University Press).

—— (1997), *Tertullian: First Theologian of the West* (Cambridge: Cambridge University Press).

PELIKAN, J. (1993), *Christianity and Classical Culture* (New Haven: Yale University Press).

RIST, J. (1994), *Augustine: Ancient Thought Baptized* (Cambridge: Cambridge University Press).

SORABJI, R. (1983), *Time, Creation and the Continuum* (London: Duckworth).

—— (ed.) (1987), *Philoponus and the Rejection of Aristotelian Science* (London: Duckworth).

STEAD, C. (1977), *Divine Substance* (Oxford: Clarendon Press).

—— (1994), *Philosophy in Christian Antiquity* (Cambridge: Cambridge University Press).

WATSON, G. (1994), *Greek Philosophy and the Christian Notion of God* (Blackrock, Eire: Columba Press).

THE MEDIEVAL PERIOD

ADAMS, M. M. (1987), *William Ockham* (Notre Dame, Ind.: University of Notre Dame Press).

BURRELL, D. (1986), *Knowing the Unknowable God: Ibn Sina, Maimonides, Aquinas* (Notre Dame, Ind.: University of Notre Dame Press).

COPLESTON, F. (1972), *A History of Medieval Philosophy* (New York: Harper and Row).

CRAIG, W. L. (1979), *The Kalam Cosmological Argument* (London: Macmillan).

DAVIDSON, H. (1987), *Proofs of the Eternity, Creation and the Existence of God in Medieval, Islamic, and Jewish Philosophy* (Oxford: Clarendon Press).

DAVIES, B., OP (1992), *The Thought of Thomas Aquinas* (Oxford: Clarendon Press).

DRONKE, P. (ed.) (1988), *A History of Twelfth-Century Western Philosophy* (Cambridge: Cambridge University Press).

EVANS, G. R. (1993), *Philosophy and Theology in the Middle Ages* (London: Routledge).

GILSON, E. (1938), *Reason and Revelation in the Middle Ages* (New York: Charles Scribner's Sons).

HELM, P. (1997), *Faith and Understanding* (Edinburgh: Edinburgh University Press).

HOLOPAINEN, T. J. (1996), *Dialectic and Theology in the 1th Century* (Leiden: Brill).

HOPKINS, J. (1972), *A Companion to The Study of St. Anselm* (Minneapolis: University of Minnesota Press).

JENKINS, J. (1997), *Knowledge and Faith in Thomas Aquinas* (Cambridge: Cambridge University Press).

KENNY, A. J. P. (1980), *Aquinas* (Oxford: Oxford University Press).

KRETZMANN, N., KENNY, A. J. P., and PINBORG, J. (eds.) (1982), *The Cambridge Companion to Aquinas* (Cambridge: Cambridge University Press).

LEAMAN, O. (1985), *An Introduction to Medieval Islamic Philosophy* (Cambridge: Cambridge University Press).

LIVESEY, S. (1989), *Theology and Science in the Fourteenth Century* (Leiden: Brill).

NASR, S. H., and LEAMAN, O. (eds.) (1996), *History of Islamic Philosophy* (London: Routledge).

NOONAN, L. (1994), *Divine Power* (Oxford: Clarendon Press).

OBERMAN, H., and JONES, F. (1991), *Via Augustin: Augustine in the Later Middle Ages, Renaissance and Reformation* (Leiden: Brill).

O'MEARA, T. F. (1997), *Thomas Aquinas: Theologian* (Notre Dame, Ind.: University of Notre Dame Press).

PLANTINGA, A. (ed.) (1965), *The Ontological Argument from St. Anselm to Contemporary Philosophers* (London: Macmillan).

SIRAT, C. (1985), *A History of Jewish Philosophy in the Middle Ages* (Cambridge: Cambridge University Press).

VOS, ARVIN (1985), *Aquinas, Calvin and Contemporary Protestant Thought* (Grand Rapids, Mich.: Christian University Press).

WALZER, R. (1962), *Greek into Arabic: Essays in Islamic Philosophy* (Columbia, SC: University of South Carolina Press).

WOLTER, A. (1990), *The Philosophical Theology of John Duns Scotus* (Ithaca, NY: Cornell University Press).

RENAISSANCE AND REFORMATION

FUNKENSTEIN, A. (1986), *Theology and the Scientific Imagination* (Princeton: Princeton University Press).

GERRISH, B. (1962), *Grace and Reason* (Oxford: Clarendon Press).

McCONICA, J. *et al.* (eds.) (1993), *Renaissance Thinkers: Bacon, More, Montaigne, Erasmus* (Oxford: Oxford University Press).

McGRATH, A. (1987), *The Intellectual Origins of the European Reformation* (Oxford: Basil Blackwell).

OBERMANN, H. (1962), *The Harvest of Medieval Theology* (Cambridge, Mass.: Harvard University Press).

PARKER, T. H. L. (1969), *Calvin's Doctrine of the Knowledge of God* (Edinburgh: Oliver and Boyd).

POPKIN, R. H. (1957), *The History of Scepticism from Erasmus to Spinoza* (Los Angeles: UCLA Press).

SCHMITT, C. B. (1981), *Studies in Renaissance Philosophy and Science* (London: Variorum).

SKINNER, Q., and SCHMITT, C. B. (eds.) (1988), *The Cambridge History of Renaissance Philosophy* (Cambridge: Cambridge University Press).

SEVENTEENTH AND EIGHTEENTH CENTURIES

ADAMS, R. M. (1994), *Leibniz: Determinist, Theist, Idealist* (New York: Oxford University Press).

AYERS, M., and GARBER, D. (eds.) (1998), *The Cambridge History of Seventeenth-Century Philosophy* (Cambridge: Cambridge University Press).

BYRNE, P. (1989), *Natural Religion and the Nature of Religion* (London: Routledge).

CHAPPELL, V. (ed.) (1994), *The Cambridge Companion to Locke* (Cambridge: Cambridge University Press).

COLLINS, J. (1967), *The Emergence of the Philosophy of Religion* (New Haven: Yale University Press).

COTTINGHAM, J. (ed.) (1992), *The Cambridge Companion to Descartes* (Cambridge: Cambridge University Press).

FATE NORTON, D. (ed.) (1993), *The Cambridge Companion to Hume* (Cambridge: Cambridge University Press).

GARRETT, D. (ed.) (1996), *The Cambridge Companion to Spinoza* (Cambridge: Cambridge University Press).

GASKIN, J. C. A. (1978), *Hume's Philosophy of Religion* (London: Macmillan).

GUYER, P. (ed.) (1992), *The Cambridge Companion to Kant* (Cambridge: Cambridge University Press).

HARRISON, P. (1990), *Religion and the Religions in the English Enlightenment* (Cambridge: Cambridge University Press).

JOLLEY, N. (ed.) (1995), *The Cambridge Companion to Leibniz* (Cambridge: Cambridge University Press).

KANT, I. (1934), *Religion within the Limits of Reason Alone*, trans. T. M. Greene and H. H. Hudson (New York: Harper and Row).

WOLTERSTORFF, N. (1996), *John Locke and the Ethics of Belief* (Cambridge: Cambridge University Press).

WOOD, A. (1971), *Kant's Moral Religion* (Ithaca, NY: Cornell University Press).

—— (1978), *Kant's Philosophical Theology* (Ithaca, NY: Cornell University Press).

MASON, R. (1997), *The God of Spinoza* (Cambridge: Cambridge University Press).

THE NINETEENTH CENTURY

ADDICOTT, P. (1991), *Philosophy and Biblical Interpretation: A Study in Nineteenth-Century Conflict* (Cambridge: Cambridge University Press).

DANTO, A. C. (1968), *Nietzsche as Philosopher* (London: Macmillan).

HANNAY, A., and MARINO, G. (eds.) (1998), *The Cambridge Companion to Kierkegaard* (Cambridge: Cambridge University Press).

HARVEY, VAN A. (1995), *Feuerbach and the Interpretation of Religion* (Cambridge: Cambridge University Press).

HOLLINGDALE, R. J. (1973), *Nietzsche* (London: Routledge).

McKOWN, D. B. (1975), *The Classical Marxist Critiques of Religion* (The Hague: Nijhoff).

MILL, J. S. (1874), *Three Essays on Religion* (3rd edn., London: Longmans Green, 1885).

NEWMAN, J. H. (1955), *An Essay in Aid of a Grammar of Assent* (New York: Doubleday Image).

NIELSEN, K. (1996), *Naturalism without Foundations* (Buffalo: Prometheus Press).

SKORUPSKI, J. (ed.) (1998), *The Cambridge Companion to Mill* (Cambridge: Cambridge University Press).

WESTPHAL, M. (1993), *Suspicion and Faith: The Religious Uses of Modern Atheism* (Grand Rapids, Mich.: Eerdmans).

TWENTIETH CENTURY

1 *Hard Science*

BANNER, MICHAEL C. (1990), *The Justification of Science and the Rationality of Religious Belief* (Oxford: Clarendon Press).

BARLOW, C. (ed.) (1994), *Evolution Extended: Biological Debates on the Meaning of Life* (Cambridge, Mass.: MIT Press).

BARROW, J. and TIPLER, F. (1986), *The Anthropic Cosmological Principle* (Oxford: Clarendon Press).

EARMAN, J. (1987), 'The SAP also Rises: A Critical Examination of the Anthropic Principle', *American Philosophical Quarterly*, 24.

FORREST, P. (1996), *God without the Supernatural: A Defense of Scientific Theism* (Ithaca, NY: Cornell University Press).

LESLIE, J. (1989), *Universes* (London: Routledge).

McMULLIN, E. (ed.) (1985), *Evolution and Creation* (Notre Dame, Ind.: University of Notre Dame Press).

MURPHY, NANCY (1990), *Theology in the Age of Scientific Reasoning* (Ithaca, NY: Cornell University Press).

O'HEAR, A. (1998), *Beyond Evolution* (Oxford: Clarendon Press).

ROLSTON, H., III (1987), *Science and Religion: A Critical Survey* (New York: Random House).

RUSE, M. (1989), *The Darwinian Paradigm: Essays on its History, Philosophy and Religious Implications* (London: Routledge).

SMITH, Q., and CRAIG, W. L. (1993), *Theism, Atheism and Big Bang Cosmology* (Oxford: Clarendon Press).

2 *Faith, Objectivity, Pluralism*

BOUWSMA, O. K. (1984), *Without Proof or Evidence* (Lincoln: University of Nebraska Press).

BRAITHWAITE, R. B. (1955), *An Empiricist's View of the Nature of Religious Belief* (Cambridge: Cambridge University Press).

CUPITT, D. (1991), *What is a Story?* (London: SCM Press).

D'COSTA, G. [c.1990], *Christian Uniqueness Reconsidered* (Maryknoll, NY: Orbis Books).

FRANKENBERRY, N. (1987), *Religion and Radical Empiricism* (Albany, NY: SUNY Press).

GOWER, B. (ed.) (1987), *Logical Positivism in Perspective* (Totowa, NJ: Barnes and Noble).

HICK, J. (1973), *God and the Universe of Faiths* (London: Macmillan).

—— (1982), *God has Many Names* (Philadelphia: Westminster Press).

—— (1985), *Problems of Religious Pluralism* (London: Macmillan).

—— (1989), *An Interpretation of Religion* (London: Macmillan).

MacLEOD, M. (1993), *Rationality and Theistic Belief: An Essay on Reformed Epistemology* (Ithaca, NY: Cornell University Press).

NIELSEN, K. (1967), 'Wittgensteinian Fideism', *Philosophy*, 42.

PHILLIPS, D. Z. (1988), *Faith after Foundationalism* (London: Routledge).

PLANTINGA, A. (1983), 'How to be an anti-realist', *Proceedings and Addresses of the American Philosophical Association*, 47–70.

RUNZO, J. (1993), *Is God Real?* (London: Macmillan).

SOSKICE, J. M. (1984), *Metaphor and Religious Language* (Oxford: Clarendon Press).

TRIGG, R. (1973), *Reason and Commitment* (Cambridge: Cambridge University Press).

—— (1993), *Rationality and Science* (Oxford: Basil Blackwell).

VROOM, H. (ed.) (1989), *Religions and the Truth: Philosophical Reflections and Perspectives* (Grand Rapids, Mich.: Eerdmans).

WARD, K. (1994), *Religion and Revelation* (Oxford: Clarendon Press).

WINCH, P. (1987), 'Meaning and Religious Language' in *Trying to Make Sense* (Oxford: Basil Blackwell).

3 *Faith and Reason*

ABRAHAM, W. J. (1982), *Divine Revelation and the Limits of Historical Criticism* (Oxford: Oxford University Press).

BAILLIE, J. (1956), *The Idea of Revelation in Recent Thought* (New York: Columbia University Press).

BARTHOLEMEW, D. J. (1996), *Uncertain Belief* (Oxford: Clarendon Press).

CODE, L. (1991), *What Can She Know?* (Ithaca, NY: Cornell University Press).

HELM, P. (1982), *Revelation* (London: Marshall).

SWINBURNE, R. (1979), *The Existence of God* (Oxford: Clarendon Press, rev. 1991).

—— (1992), *Revelation: From Metaphor to Analogy* (Oxford: Clarendon Press).

WARD, K. (1994), *Religion and Revelation* (Oxford: Clarendon Press).

WOLTERSTORFF, N. (1995), *Divine Discourse: Philosophical Reflections on the Claim that God Speaks* (Cambridge: Cambridge University Press).

Biographical Notes

ADAMS, R. M. Professor of Philosophy at the University of Yale. He has published extensively on philosophy of religion, ethics, metaphysics, and the history of philosophy. Many important papers are brought together in his *The Virtue of Faith* (1987).

AL-KINDI (d. 866) The father of Islamic philosophy. By integrating strands of Greek philosophy with Islamic doctrine, he enlarged the Arabic philosophical terminology of his day. Twenty-four of his main works have been collected and edited by Abu Ridah into *Philosophical Treatises of Al-Kindi* (1950–3).

ALSTON, W. P. Professor of Philosophy Emeritus at Syracuse University. Important publications are *Epistemic Justification: Essays in the Theory of Knowledge* (1989); *Divine Nature and Human Language: Essays in Philosophical Theology* (1989); and *Perceiving God: The Epistemology of Religious Experience* (1991).

AYER, A. J. (1910–89) Grote Professor of the Philosophy of Mind and Logic at the University of London (1946–59), becoming Wykeham Professor of Logic in the University of Oxford (1959–78). Among his key publications are *Language, Truth and Logic* (1936); *Philosophical Essays* (1954); *The Problem of Knowledge* (1956); and *The Central Questions of Philosophy* (1973).

ANSELM (1033–1109) Philosopher, theologian, monk, and later Archbishop of Canterbury (1078). Anselm was a pioneer in using conceptual analysis to solve philosophical problems raised by Christian faith. He is perhaps most famous for his ontological proofs for the existence of God. His arguments are contained in *Monologion* (1078) and *Proslogion* (1079). Anselm's other great book *Cur Deus Homo?*, on the atonement, was written during exile in Rome.

AQUINAS, THOMAS (1225–74) Philosopher, theologian, and Dominican. Aquinas made Aristotle known and acceptable to the Christian West. His best-known works are his two massive syntheses, the *Summa contra Gentiles*, and the *Summa Theologiae*. They contain much material that is philosophical in method and content, as well as theological in intent and subject-matter. Perhaps his most famous contribution to the philosophy of religion is his 'Five Ways', proofs of the existence of God.

ARISTOTLE (384–322 BC) Aristotle founded the Lyceum in Athens, where he taught until he was forced out. We owe to Aristotle the major divisions of science and philosophy (physics, psychology, logic, ethics, metaphysics, etc.). His writings consist of concise treatises, the most famous including *De Anima*, *Politics*, and *Prior Analytics*.

AUGUSTINE (354–430) Christian theologian and philosopher, best-known for his autobiography, the *Confessions*, and *The City of God*, prompted by the sack of Rome in 410. His influence dominated medieval Western Christendom and later provided a powerful stimulus to the Reformation. He remains a resource for scholars second to none, and is immensely influential in his views on the relationship between faith and reason, grace and free will, and the corruption of human nature.

BARTH, K. (1886–1968) Taught at Gottingen, Münster, and Bonn, where he was dismissed in 1934 for opposing Hitler. He then held a professorship at his native Basle for the rest of his career. His major work is the multi-volume *Church Dogmatics* (1936–61).

BAYLE, P. (1647–1706) French philosopher who became a Catholic and later reconverted to Calvinism. His main work, *Dictionnaire historique et critique* (1695), argued sceptically against philosophical and theological theories, insisting that faith, not reason, must justify religious beliefs.

BELLARMINE, R. (1542–1621) The author of *Disputationes de Controversiis Christianae Fidei* (1586–93), a foremost defence of Roman Catholic theology at the time of the Counter-Reformation. In 1597 he became theologian to Pope Clement VIII and was involved in various important diplomatic missions on behalf of the Pope.

BERKELEY, G. (1685–1753) Irish philosopher, bishop, and apologist. Well-known for his immaterialism, which he developed in his *Principles of Human Knowledge* (1710) and *Three Dialogues between Hylas and Philonous* (1713). This view, which in some ways foreshadowed phenomenalism, he thought provided support for Christian theism.

BOETHIUS (*c*.480–524) Roman statesman and Christian philosopher. Accused of treason, he was imprisoned in Italy where he wrote his most famous book, *The Consolation of Philosophy*, to show how philosophy can contribute to an understanding of God. He was eventually executed. Boethius is a key transitional figure between the ancient and modern world and laid the foundations for the later study of theology and philosophy, and for the acceptance of a marriage between the best of the two disciplines.

BONAVENTURE (1221–74) Born in Tuscany, he was a scholastic theologian and Franciscan bishop. With his emphasis on individual devotion and Augustinianism, he helped pave the way for the Protestant Reformation. He also influenced and foreshadowed the great period of mysticism that followed in the fourteenth and fifteenth centuries. He is the author of *The Seven Journeys of Eternity* and *The Journey of the Mind to God*.

BUTLER, J. (1692–1752) Anglican bishop, religious apologist, and moral philosopher. His moral philosophy was mainly contained in his *Fifteen Sermons* (1726), and his *Analogy of Religion* (1736) was a refutation of deism. His appeal to probability in defence of the reasonableness of the Christian religion had considerable influence in the nineteenth century.

CAHN, S. M. Provost of the Graduate School of the City University of New York. Among his books are *Fate, Logic, and Time* (1967); *Education and the Democratic Ideal* (1979); and *Contemporary Philosophy of Religion*, edited with David Shatz (1982).

CALVIN, J. (1509–1564) Protestant Reformation theologian. He believed that there is a basic unity in the teaching of Scripture and it was his lifetime work to maintain a theology that is essentially a theology of the word of God. He was the first theologian to interpret the work of Christ systematically in terms of the threefold office of prophet, priest, and king. He wrote commentaries on nearly all the books in the Bible. In 1536 he published the first edition of his main work, the *Institutes of the Christian Religion* (final edition, 1559).

CICERO (106–43 BC) Roman politician, orator, and writer on rhetorical and philosophical questions. Although Cicero had studied philosophy as a young man, his eclectic writings were largely produced in his retirement from public life. He had a great influence on the development of Latin as a philosophical language.

CLEMENT OF ALEXANDRIA (*c.*150–215?) Christian scholar, and a rather enigmatic figure; little is known of his life. He was the first to embrace Greek philosophy as an ally of Christianity. He became head of the Alexandrian school but was forced to leave under the persecution of Septimius Severus. His chief work is a trilogy, *Stromateis, Protrepticus, Paedagogus* which attempted to win over the educated people of his day for the Christian faith.

CLIFFORD, W. K. (1845–79) Mathematician and philosopher, a Fellow of Trinity College, Cambridge, and later Professor of Applied Mathematics at University College London. He was at first sympathetic to Catholicism but later became an agnostic, attempting to construct a philosophy heavily influenced by science. Beside his collected *Lectures and Essays* (1879) and *Mathematical Papers* (1882) he published *The Commonsense of the Exact Sciences* (1885).

CRAIG, W. L. Visiting Professor at Talbot School of Theology, California. Key publications are *The Kalam Cosmological Argument* (1979); *The Cosmological Argument from Plato to Leibniz* (1980); *The Problem of Divine Foreknowledge and Future Contingents from Aristotle to Suarez* (1988); and *Theism, Atheism and Big Bang Cosmology*, with Quentin Smith (1993).

CULVERWEL, N. (1618?–1651?) A Cambridge Platonist who, unlike most of this general outlook, was a Puritan and a Calvinist. With the revival of the study of Plato at the end of the seventeenth century, the Cambridge Platonists gave renewed prominence to natural theology and the rational foundation of religion.

CUPITT, D. For many years Dean of Emmanuel College, Cambridge, and an outspoken advocate of theological non-realism. The imprisonment of thought, including philosophical and theological thought, in language, has anti-metaphysical and therefore anti-theological implications. Nevertheless, the traditional language of liturgy and theology still has value. Cupitt is the author of many books, including *Christ and the Hiddenness of God* (1971), *The Leap of Reason* (1976), and *The Sea of Faith* (1984).

DAMIAN, PETER (1007–72) Both a theologian and a church reformer (and an innovator in penitential flagellation). He became Cardinal Bishop of Ostia, though he later fled back to his hermitage.

DARWIN, C. (1809–82) His expedition to study flora and fauna led him to develop his theory of evolution which is expounded in *The Origin of Species* (1859) and *The Descent of Man* (1871). It claims that all living things have developed by a process of natural selection of random mutations.

DAVIS, S. T. Professor of Philosophy and Religion at Claremont McKenna College, California. Among his publications are *Faith, Skepticism, and Evidence* (1978); *Logic and the Nature of God* (1983); *Death and Afterlife* (1989); and *God, Reason and Theistic Proofs* (1997).

DAWKINS, R. M. Professor in the Public Understanding of Science at Oxford University. He studied at Oxford, and taught zoology at the University of California at Berkeley and at Oxford University. He has won several awards for literature and the furtherance of the public understanding of science. His most important works are *The Selfish Gene*

(1976); *The Extended Phenotype* (1982); *The Blind Watchmaker* (1986); *River Out of Eden* (1995) and *Climbing Mount Improbable* (1996).

DESCARTES, R. (1596–1650) A scientist and mathematician, he is widely regarded as the founding father of modern philosophy. In his search for certainty, he worked back to indisputable first principles of reason—formulating the well-known principle: 'I think therefore I am' (*cogito, ergo sum*). His method, with his emphasis on the primacy of epistemology, has influenced and shaped three hundred years of philosophical reflection. His philosophical publications include his *Discourse on Method* (1637), *Meditations* (1641), and *Principles* (1644).

DUNS SCOTUS (1255/6–1308) Scottish theologian and Franciscan. Critical of Aquinas's attempts to bring together Aristotle and Christianity, he argued that faith cannot be established by any rational process. He was a highly complex writer. Among his most important works is the *Tractate on the First Principle*.

DURKHEIM, E. (1858–1917) French sociologist and positivist who, with Max Weber, is regarded as a founder of modern sociological theory. In the sphere of religion he wrote a pioneering work, *The Elementary Forms of the Religious Life* (1912), in which he viewed religion and ritual as a symbolic representation of a social bond, classifying religion into two categories, the sacred and profane.

EDWARDS, J. (1703–58) American Calvinist theologian and philosopher. He was widely influential, not least for the way in which he brought English empiricist philosophy to bear on a personal knowledge of God, and in defence of Calvinistic orthodoxy against deist arguments. He also rejected the idea of indeterministic freedom in *The Freedom of the Will* (1754).

EPICURUS (341–270 BC) He founded his school in Athens around 307 BC. He taught that there was no form of human life after death. Although he wrote voluminously, his works are all lost apart from fragments. Of those that remain, *To Herodotus* describes his theory of nature and *To Menoeceus* outlines his moral position.

ERIUGENA, JOHN SCOTUS (*c*.810–*c*.877) An Irish Christian thinker notable for not making a sharp distinction between philosophy and theology. He was involved in controversies over predestination and the eucharist. Influenced by Neoplatonism, his thought forms an important bridge between Augustine and Anselm. His chief work is *De Divisione Naturae*.

ERASMUS, DESIDERIUS (1469–1536) Christian Humanist, he is regarded as the precursor of critical Christian scholarship. His anti-scholastic treatment of the scriptures led to the first publication of the Greek New Testament. He also brought out new editions of the Greek and Latin Fathers. At first he supported Luther in his attack on the abuses of the Church, but as Luther's radicalism became more apparent he distanced himself, defending the unity of the Church against Luther in *On the Freedom of the Will* (1524) and again in *Hyperapistes* (1526).

FEUERBACH, L. (1804–72) German philosopher, proponent of the view that religion is a projection of human aspirations on to a fictional God-figure. His most celebrated work is *The Essence of Christianity* (1841), which was extremely influential, not least on Marx.

FLEW, A. Professor Emeritus of Philosophy at the University of Reading. He was previously Professor of Philosophy at the University of Keele. Among the best-known of his many books are *God and Philosophy* (1966); *The Presumption of Atheism* (1984); and *David Hume: Philosopher of Moral Science* (1986).

FREUD, S. (1856–1939) The founder of psychoanalysis. His study of abnormal behaviour in adults, the early results of which were published in *The Interpretation of Dreams* (1899), led him to find its point in the unconscious, and to propound psychoanalysis (in *Introductory Lectures on Psychoanalysis* (1916)) as a therapy.

GALILEO GALILEI (1564–1642) Astronomer, mathematician, and physicist, founder of modern mechanics and inventor of the telescope. He supported Copernicus's theories of a universe centred on the sun. Over his *Dialogue on the Two Great World Systems*, he fell into conflict with the Inquisition, which led to his condemnation, and recantation in 1616. In his *Letter to Christina of Lorraine* (1615, but published only in 1636) he made a plea for the autonomy of science, arguing for the separation of theological and scientific issues. His final work, *Discourses Concerning Two New Sciences*, was published in 1638.

HALDANE, J. J. Professor of Philosophy at the University of St Andrews and Director of the Centre for Philosophy and Public Affairs there. He has published widely in metaphysics, philosophy of mind, and social philosophy, and is co-editor, with Crispin Wright, of *Reality, Representation and Projection*. He also co-edited, *Ian McFetridge, Logical Necessity and Other Essays*, with Roger Scruton (1990).

HANSON, N. R. (1924–67) Professor of Philosophy at Yale University (1963–7), and prior to that at the University of Indiana. Important works include *Patterns of Discovery* (1958); *A History of Science* (1965); *Perception and Discovery: An Introduction to Scientific Inquiry* (1969); *Observation and Explanation: A Guide to the Philosophy of Science* (1971); *Why I do not Believe and Other Essays*, edited by S. Toulmin and H. Woolf (1973); *Constellations and Conjectures*, edited by W. C. Humphrey (1973).

HAWKING, S. W. A leader in cosmological theory, Hawking is Lucasian Professor of Mathematics at Cambridge University and Fellow of Gonville and Caius College. Among his publications are *The Large Scale Structure of Space-Time*, with G. F. R. Ellis (1973); the best-selling *A Brief History of Time* (1987); and *The Nature of Space and Time*, with Roger Penrose (1996).

HEIMBECK, R. S. Professor of Philosophy, Central Washington University, specializing in the philosophy of religion, oriental philosophy, and the philosophy of the self.

HEGEL, G. W. F. (1770–1831) A German idealist philosopher, perhaps best known for his view of God as process and historical development as a threefold process of thesis, antithesis, and synthesis. Many of his best-known books arose out of his Berlin lectures and include *Philosophy of History* (1837), *Philosophy of Religion* (1832), and *Aesthetics* (1835–8).

HELM, PAUL Professor of the History and Philosophy of Religion at King's College, London. He is the author of *Eternal God* (1988), *The Providence of God* (1993), *Belief Policies* (1994), and *Faith and Understanding* (1997).

HERBERT OF CHERBURY (c.1583–1648) Philosopher, historian, and diplomat. Dubbed a deist—although not in the direct line with later deist thought—he brought religious epistemology under the umbrella of general epistemology. He held a theory of God-given innate ideas which was attacked by John Locke. His main works include *On the Truth* (1624), *De Causis Errorum* (1663), and *De Religione Gentilium* (1663).

HICK, J. Until his retirement was Danforth Professor of the Philosophy of Religion at Claremont Graduate School, California. Prior to that he was H. G. Wood Professor of Theology at the University of Birmingham. Important works include *Evil and the God of Love* (1966); *Faith and Knowledge* (1966); *An Interpretation of Religion* (1989); and *Philosophy of Religion* (1990).

HOBBES, T. (1588–1679) English political philosopher. Unpopular with both sides during the Civil War for his political views, he went into exile. He returned to England in 1651 and his magnum opus, *Leviathan*, a defence of political absolutism, appeared the same year. He was also the founding father of modern metaphysical 'materialism'.

HUME, D. (1711–76) Scottish philosopher, historian, and man of letters. A leading figure of the Scottish Enlightenment, he developed Locke's emphasis on the authority of sense-experience in knowledge in a sceptical direction. His cool, sceptical assessment of religion set the agenda for subsequent philosophy of religion. He published numerous philosophical works which include *A Treatise of Human Nature* (1739–40), *An Inquiry Concerning Human Understanding* (1748), and *Dialogues Concerning Natural Religion* (posthumously published in 1779).

JAMES, W. (1842–1910) An American psychologist and pragmatist philosopher who taught at Harvard. His philosophy, in such works as *Pragmatism* (1907) and *A Pluralistic Universe* (1909), was mostly written for a wide public and has an accessible, attractive style. He is probably best known for *The Varieties of Religious Experience* (1902).

JUSTIN MARTYR (c.100–165) An early Gentile convert to Christianity (c.130), he is considered the most important apologist to focus on the nature and meaning of Christ. In Rome he wrote his best-known works: the *First Apology*, addressed to the Emperor Antoninus Pius around 151, and the later *Second Apology*. In his *Dialogue with Trypho*, he seeks to persuade a Jew of the truth of Christianity. He was denounced and executed as a Christian along with some of his disciples.

KANT, I. (1724–1804) A seminal figure of the Enlightenment period whose 'Copernican Revolution' placed the autonomous human mind at the centre of metaphysics and ethics. Kant's ideas were the development of two philosophical traditions: British empiricism with its stress on experience, and Continental rationalism with its emphasis on innate ideas. Kant produced his most influential works late in life and the most important include the three Critiques: *Critique of Pure Reason* (1781), *Critique of Practical Reason* (1788), and *Critique of Judgement* (1790). His *Religion within the Limits of Reason Alone* (1793) is an influential reconstruction of Christian theology.

KIERKEGAARD, S. (1813–55) Danish philosopher critical of formal easy-going Christianity. He rejected an intellectualist notion of faith in favour of ethical decision in favour of Christ. A major figure of the nineteenth century, he was a great influence on subsequent philosophy and particularly theology, especially existentialism and the dialectical theology of Emil Brunner and Karl Barth.

LEIBNIZ, G. W. F. (1646–1716) German rationalist philosopher who defended the proofs for the existence of God and was the first to use the term theodicy (the justification of God's ways to man). In his *Theodicy* (1710) he produced an optimistic account of the world and his conclusion that the world was 'the best of all possible worlds' was satirized by Voltaire in his *Candide*. his other main works include the *New Essays on the Human Understanding (c.*1705).

LE POIDEVIN, R. Senior Lecturer in Philosophy at the University of Leeds. He is the author of *Change, Cause and Contradiction: A Defence of the Tenseless Theory of Time* (1991); and *Arguing for Atheism* (1996).

LESLIE, J. Professor of Philosophy at the University of Guelph, Canada. Publications include *Value and Existence* (1979); the edited collection *Physical Cosmology and Philosophy* (1989); and *Universes* (1989).

LOCKE, J. (1632–1704) The first of the great British empiricist philosophers, he stressed reasonableness in religion (unwittingly encouraging deism) but not at the expense of revelation. In his *Essay Concerning Human Understanding* (1690) he argued for religious knowledge through both reason and revelation. But in *The Reasonableness of Christianity* (1695), he defended revelation. The *Two Treatises of Government* (1690) was his other major work.

LOMBARD, P. (1100–59) He rose to become bishop of Paris just before his death in 1159. Whilst his intention was not to break new ground but to decide the truth on the basis of the established authorities, his theology of the sacraments was novel. His concept of seven sacraments became orthodoxy at the Council of Florence in 1439. He is remembered primarily, however, for his *Four Books of Sentences*, a text to which many subsequent theologians, such as Aquinas, devoted commentaries.

LUTHER, M. (1483–1546) German Protestant Reformer. Luther lived and wrote intensely, developing an evangelical theology which played a significant part in the Reformation. His declaration of Ninety-five Theses in October 1517, attacking the sale of indulgences in the Church, is legendary. His prolific writings include his lectures on Scripture, hymns, catechisms, and a significant number of treatises including: *To the Christian Nobility of the German Nation*; *On the Babylonish Captivity of the Church*; *Of the Liberty of a Christian Man*; and *The Bondage of the Will*.

MACINTYRE, A. C. He has held a number of academic posts in the United Kingdom, but has taught in the United States since 1970, and is currently Professor of Philosophy at Duke University. Important works include *A Short History of Ethics* (1966); *After Virtue* (1981); *Whose Justice? Which Rationality?* (1988); and his Gifford Lectures given at the University of Edinburgh, *Three Rival Versions of Moral Enquiry* (1990).

MAIMONIDES, M. (1135–1204) Jewish jurist, court physician, and philosopher. His medical writings were widely read, especially in Muslim circles, and translated from Arabic into Hebrew and Latin. His philosophical works were influential on Christian scholastics and were cited by Aquinas, Meister Eckhardt, and Duns Scotus. His writings include a commentary on the Mishnah tractate, *Avot* ('The Sayings of the Fathers'), which became a classic of Jewish ethics; and his *Moreh Nevukhim* (*Guide for the Perplexed*, written in Arabic) an influential work in medieval Jewish philosophy.

MANSEL, H. L. (1820–71) British theologian who became both professor of philosophy and Dean of St Paul's. He argued that philosophical theology is an impossibility; God cannot be known through reason alone, but by revelation which is beyond criticism. This view is best expressed in his 1858 lectures entitled *The Limits of Religious Thought Examined*.

MARX, K. (1818–83) Marx was first and foremost a German economist, born into a family of Jewish rabbis. He wrote his *Communist Manifesto* in 1847 and his magnum opus, *Das Kapital*, in 1867. Whilst he was scathing of the established church, he recognized the solace religion could provide and his early works are especially important for theology, containing many critical discussions of religion which he understood to be the pathological by-product of the class system.

MILL, J. S. (1806–73) English economist and philosopher, who spent the bulk of his working life with the East India Company. He made his name in philosophy with his *System of Logic* in 1843 and in political economy with an *Essay on Liberty* (1859). He argued in *Utilitarianism* (1863) that religion could be morally useful, but could also be dispensed with. In the *Three Essays on Religion* (1874) he defended an attenuated form of theism.

MITCHELL, B. Nolloth Professor Emeritus of the Philosophy of the Christian Religion at Oxford University. He has published *Faith and Logic* (ed.; 1957); *The Justification of Religious Belief* (1973); *Morality, Religious and Secular* (1980); and *Faith and Criticism* (1994).

MONTAIGNE, M. DE (1533–92) French humanist. He helped to revive and popularize interest in Greek sceptical theories during the Renaissance. His influence can be seen in writers such as Descartes and Pascal. He set out his own sceptical philosophy in the work *Apologie de Raymond Sebond* (1580).

NEWMAN, J. H. (1801–90) English theologian and philosopher. He converted to Roman Catholicism in mid-life, a move which he defended in his *Essay on the Development of Christian Doctrine* (1845). Although he became a cardinal in 1879, his relations with the Roman Catholic Church were never easy. The influence of his views on doctrinal development, on faith and reason, and his spiritual and moral insights, have been very great.

NIETZSCHE, F. (1844–1900) German philosopher and philologist, who taught at the University of Basle, retiring in 1879. He was a fierce critic of Christianity and regarded metaphysics as life-denying, a sign of weakness. Among his chief works are *The Birth of Tragedy* (1872) and *Thus Spake Zarathustra* (1883–92). His writings have an aphoristic, poetic quality, and this, coupled with his use of irony, makes them hard to interpret.

OCKHAM, W. (1280/5–1349) English philosopher, Franciscan and founder of nominalist philosophy. For Ockham, religious belief was primarily based on revelation. Therefore, unlike the Scholastics who sought the unification of philosophy with theology, Ockham separated them. His teaching thus displaced the medieval synthesis of faith and reason, but not before charges of heresy were brought against him. The *Commentary on the Sentences* offers the most complete account of Ockham's thought and the *Summa Logica* is a mature expression of his logic.

ORIGEN (*c*.185–254) Greek theologian and scholar. Deeply influenced by Platonism, his studies in contemporary philosophy and Hebrew became the basis of his theology. Because much of his teaching was later condemned, little survives in the original. His greatest work was perhaps *De Principiis*, the first attempt in history to give Christianity a philosophical framework, and a work of apologetics, *Contra Celsum*.

OWEN, J. (1616–83) A powerful expositor of Puritan theology and Vice-Chancellor of Oxford University during Oliver Cromwell's Protectorate. Together with theologians and preachers such as Richard Sibbes (1577–1635) and Thomas Goodwin (1600–80), he helped to make Puritan theology both accessible and scholarly. *A Display of Arminianism* (1643) was a vigorous exposition of classical Calvinism. In *Christ's Kingdom and Magistrates Power* (1652) he sought to show the differences between civil and religious authority.

PALEY, W. (1743–1805) English clergyman and scholar. He wrote a standard textbook on ethics, *The Principles of Moral and Political Philosophy* (1785). He is best known for his two books *A View of the Evidences of Christianity* (1794) and *Natural Theology* (1802), in which he saw creation in teleological terms and argued for the existence of God in terms of design.

PASCAL, B. (1623–62) French mathematician, physicist, and theologian. His chief legacy is an apologetic work on the Christian religion which was aimed at the educated unbelievers of his day. His striking insights concerning the human condition were compiled and published by the Jansenists as the *Pensées* in 1670.

PETRARCHA, FRANCESCO (1304–74) An early Renaissance scholar, 'the Father of humanism'. He devoted himself to the recovery of classical learning and the preservation and editing of Latin and Greek manuscripts. His view of scholasticism can be inferred from the fact that he was the first to call the medieval period 'the Dark Ages'.

PHILLIPS, D. Z. Danforth Professor of Philosophy of Religion at Claremont Graduate School. He taught for many years at the University College of Swansea, where he was Vice-Principal and Professor of Philosophy. Key works include *The Concept of Prayer* (1965); *Death and Immortality* (1970); *Faith and Philosophical Enquiry* (1970); *Religion without Explanation* (1976); and *Faith after Foundationalism* (1988).

PHILO (*c.*20 BC–AD 50) An Alexandrian Jew. Philo's great achievement was to synthesize Greek and Jewish ideas, most famously through his concept of the *logos*. He had a direct influence on Greek Christian thinkers such as Clement of Alexandria, Origen, and Ambrose (*c.*339–97). He laid the foundations for allegorical exegesis of Scripture as well as medieval Islamic, Jewish, and Latin Christian philosophy. His prolific writings remain an important historical source and the most complete guide to Hellenistic Jewish thought.

PHILOPONUS (*c.*490–*c.*570) Philosopher chiefly noted now for his rational defence of the creation of the universe *ex nihilo* in critical discussions of Aristotle's views. He also wrote on Christological issues, and was a Monophysite. Although he was a prolific author, many of his writings now exist only in fragmentary form.

PLANTINGA, A. C. John A. O'Brien Professor of Philosophy at the University of Notre Dame. He has also taught at Wayne State University and Calvin College. His most important books are *God and Other Minds* (1967); *The Nature of Necessity* (1974); *God, Freedom and Evil* (1974); *Faith and Rationality* (ed. with Nicholas Wolterstorff; 1983); *Warrant: The Current Debate* (1993); and *Warrant and Proper Function* (1993).

PLATO (427–347 BC) Plato, with the mathematician Theaetetus, founded the Academy. His philosophical influence has been lasting and profound. Plato produced around twenty-five works, nearly all in dialogue form, which include the *Phaedo*, the *Republic*, *Timaeus*, and *Laws*.

PLOTINUS (*c*.205–70) Plotinus studied at Alexandria and taught in Rome. He was a leading Neoplatonist whose philosophy approaches mysticism, but is systematic in its thoroughness, and covers every major branch of philosophy except politics. His pupil Porphyry (*c*.232–303) posthumously edited his writings and arranged them into six groups of nine, the *Enneads*.

PSEUDO-DIONYSIUS (*c*.500) Also known as Dionysius the Areopagite. Mystical theologian, probably Syrian, not to be confused with the Athenian converted by St Paul in Acts 17. His extant works, a synthesis of Christian thought and Neoplatonism, include *Mystical Theology*, *Celestial Hierarchy*, *Ecclesiastical Hierarchy*, and *Divine Names*. Among those he influenced was Thomas Aquinas.

RIGAULD, O. (*c*.1202–75) Influenced by Alexander of Hales, and writing fairly independently of the Aristotelianism of Thomas Aquinas, Rigauld's Commentaries on the *Sentences* of Peter Lombard were probably the first such by a Franciscan. He was Archbishop of Rouen from 1248 until his death.

SAADIA BEN JOSEPH (882–942) Jewish scholar and the first major Jewish philosopher of the Middle Ages. A historically influential figure, he made important contributions to all branches of Jewish study. He laid the foundations of Hebrew philology, was a liturgical poet and biblical exegete, and translated the Bible into Arabic. He was also a legal writer and Talmudic expert. His main philosophical work, *Book of Doctrines and Beliefs*, set out to provide, through Judaism, rational proofs for religious doctrines.

SCHLEIERMACHER, F. D. E. (1768–1834) Founder of liberal Protestantism, and deeply influenced by Kant. He advocated a form of theology which is the expression of religious life, and particularly of religious feeling. His theology is thus church theology, with no place for natural theology as traditionally understood. Besides *On Religion*, his best-known work is *The Christian Faith*.

SEXTUS EMPIRICUS (fl. *c*.AD 200) Sceptical philosopher and physician. The works of Sextus that survive include *Outlines of Pyrrhonism* and *Adversus Mathematicos*, a refutation of dogmatism. These are the fullest sources for ancient Scepticism and had a great influence on European philosophy following their 1569 reprinting.

SMART, J. J. C. Emeritus Professor at the Australian National University, where he was Professor of Philosophy in the Research School of Social Sciences from 1976 to 1985. He previously taught at the University of Adelaide and La Trobe University. He is the author of many books, including *Philosophy and Scientific Realism*; *Ethics*; *Persuasion and Truth*; and *Utilitarianism: For and Against*, with Bernard Williams.

SPINOZA, B. (1632–77) Jewish rationalist philosopher. An original thinker and public figure, he was expelled from the Synagogue in 1656 for his unorthodox pantheistic views. His *Treatise on Theology and Politics* (*Tractatus Theologico-Politicus*) was published in 1670 and banned in 1674 because of its radical views about the Bible. Because of this opposition, his major work, the *Ethics*, did not appear until after his death in 1677.

SWINBURNE, R. Nolloth Professor of the Philosophy of the Christian Religion at the University of Oxford since 1985. Key publications are *The Coherence of Theism* (1977); *The Existence of God* (1979); *Faith and Reason* (1981); *The Evolution of the Soul* (1986); and *The Christian God* (1994).

TAYLOR, J. (1613–67) Anglican controversial and devotional writer who was influential on the early thought of John Wesley. His best-known books are *Holy Living* (1650) and *Holy Dying* (1651), which have become devotional classics.

TERTULLIAN (*c.*160–220) A lawyer from Carthage who converted first to Christianity and later to Montanism, an ascetic sect. Tertullian was the first Christian theologian to write in Latin. His writings are largely polemical and include *Against Marcion*, an attack on dualism in the Church, and his treatise refuting Modalism (as a defence of the relations within the Godhead) entitled *Against Praxeas*.

TINDAL, M. (*c.*1656–1733) A Fellow of All Souls College, Oxford, from 1678 until his death, he is chiefly known for his *Christianity as Old as the Creation* (1730), one of the most important deist writings.

VAN INWAGEN, P. John Cardinal O'Hara Professor of Philosophy at the University of Notre Dame, having previously been at Syracuse University. Publications include *An Essay on Free Will* (1986); *Material Beings* (1990); *Metaphysics* (1993); and *God, Knowledge and Mystery: Essays in Philosophical Theology* (1995).

WARD, K. Regius Professor of Divinity at the University of Oxford, and formerly Professor of the History and Philosophy of Religion at King's College, London. His publications include *The Concept of God* (1974); *Holding Fast to God* (1982); *Divine Action* (1990); *Defending the Soul* (1992); *Religion and Creation* (1996); and *God, Chance and Necessity* (1996).

WARFIELD, B. B. (1851–1921) Warfield taught for many years at Princeton Theological Seminary, where he was Professor of Didactic and Polemical Theology. As a defender of historic Calvinism, he wrote a number of theological books, but his chief literary output was in journal articles, of which ten volumes were posthumously published by the Oxford University Press in the 1930s.

WESTPHAL, MEROLD Professor of Philosophy at Fordham University. He is the author of *Suspicion and Faith: The Religious Uses of Modern Atheism* (1993), and of numerous articles.

WINCH, P. G. (1926–97)He taught at King's College, London, and latterly at the University of Illinois. Important works include: *The Idea of a Social Science and its Relation to Philosophy* (1958); *Ethics and Action* (1972); and *Trying to Make Sense* (1987).

Acknowledgements

Robert M. Adams, 'The Virtue of Faith', from *Faith and Philosophy* 1: 1 (Jan. 1984), reprinted in *The Virtue of Faith and other Essays in Philosophical Theology* (Oxford: Oxford University Press, 1987), pp. 16–20. Reprinted by permission of *Faith and Philosophy*.

Al-Kindi, *Al-Kindi's Metaphysics*, trans. Alfred L. Ivry (Albany, NY: SUNY Press, 1974), © 1971 State University of New York, reprinted by permission of the State University of New York Press. All rights reserved.

William Alston, *Perceiving God* (Ithaca, NY: Cornell University Press, 1991), copyright 1991 by Cornell University, used by permission of the publisher, Cornell University Press.

William Alston, 'Taking the Curse off Language-Games', in T. Tessin and M. Von der Ruhr (eds.), *Philosophy and the Grammar of Religious Belief* (London: Macmillan, 1995), copyright © Timothy Tessin and Mario von der Ruhr 1995, reprinted by permission of Macmillan Press Ltd.

Anselm, *Proslogion*, in Jasper Hopkins and Herbert W. Richardson (eds.), *Anselm of Canterbury*, vol. i, trans. Jasper Hopkins and Herbert W. Mitchell (London: SCM Press Ltd., 1974), reprinted by permission of SCM Press Ltd.

Thomas Aquinas, *Summa Contra Gentiles* I 4, trans. Anton C. Pegis (Garden City, NY: Image Books, Doubleday, 1955), copyright © 1955 by Doubleday, a division of Bantam Doubleday Dell Publishing Group, Inc., reprinted by permission of Doubleday, a division of Bantam Doubleday Dell Publishing Group, Inc.

Thomas Aquinas, *Summa Theologiae* Ia 1.2, trans. T. McDermott OP (Garden City, NY: Image Books, Doubleday, 1969).

Thomas Aquinas, *Summa Theologiae* Ia 46.2, IIa IIae 2.3–4, trans. T. C. O'Brien (London: Eyre and Spottiswoode, 1967 and 1974).

Aristotle, *Physics* VIII 1, 5, *Metaphysics* XII 5, XII 9, in Richard McKeon (ed.), *The Basic Works of Aristotle* (Random House, 1941), reprinted by permission of Oxford University Press.

Augustine of Hippo, *The Free Choice of the Will*, Bk. II, chs. 6, 12–13, in the *Fathers of the Church: St. Augustine*, vol. 59, trans. Robert P. Russell, OSA (Washington: The Catholic University of America Press, 1968), reprinted by permission of the Catholic University of America Press.

Augustine of Hippo, *City of God* VIII 9–10, XI 5–6, trans. H. Bettenson (Penguin Classics, 1972), copyright © Henry Bettenson, 1972, reprinted by permission of Penguin Books Ltd.

A. J. Ayer, *Language, Truth and Logic* (Gollancz, 1946), reprinted by permission of Victor Gollancz Limited.

Karl Barth, *Church Dogmatics*, vol. ii, pt. 1, trans. G. W. Bromiley and T. F. Torrance (Edinburgh: T. & T. Clark, 1975), reprinted by permission of T. and T. Clark Ltd.

Pierre Bayle, 'Simonides', in *Historical and Critical Dictionary—Selections*, trans. Richard H. Popkin (Indianapolis: Hackett, 1994), reprinted by permission of Hackett Publishing Co., Indianapolis and Cambridge. All rights reserved.

George Berkeley, *The Alciphron*, ed. David Berman (London: Routledge, 1993), reprinted by permission of Routledge.

Boethius, *The Theological Tractates* 3.10, trans. E. K. Rand and H. F. Stewart (Cambridge, Mass.: Harvard University Press, Loeb Classical Library, 1973), © The President and Fellows of Harvard College, 1973, reprinted by permission of the publishers and the Loeb Classical Library.

Bonaventure, *The Journey of the Mind to God*, 7, trans. Philotheus Boehner (Indianapolis: Hackett, 1993), reprinted by permission of Hackett Publishing Co., Indianapolis and Cambridge. All rights reserved.

Joseph Butler, *The Analogy of Religion*, in W. E. Gladstone (ed.) *The Works of Joseph Butler* (Oxford, Clarendon Press, 1897), reprinted by permission of Oxford University Press.

Steven Cahn, 'The Irrelevance to Religion of Philosophic Proofs for the Existence of God' (*American Philosophical Quarterly*, 1969), reprinted by permission of *American Philosophical Quarterly*.

John Calvin, *Institutes of the Christian Religion*, 1.4 and 1.7, ed. John T. McNeil, trans. Ford Lewis Battles (London: SCM Press, Library of Christian Classics, 1960), reprinted by permission of SCM Press Ltd. and Westminster John Knox Press.

Cicero, *The Nature of the Gods* I 17–24, 43–9, II 42, trans. Horace C. P. McGregor (Penguin Classics, 1972) copyright © C. P. McGregor 1972, reprinted by permission of Penguin Books Limited.

W. K. Clifford, *Lectures and Essays*, vol. ii (London: Macmillan, 1879).

William Lane Craig, 'The Existence of God and the Beginning of the Universe', *Truth*, 3 (1991).

Nathaniel Culverwel, *An Elegant and Learned Discourse of the Light of Nature* (1652), in G. R. Cragg (ed.) *The Cambridge Platonists* (New York: Oxford University Press, 1968), reprinted by permission of Oxford University Press, Inc.

Don Cupitt, 'Anti-Realist Faith', in Joseph Runzo (ed.), *Is God Real?* (London: Macmillan, 1993), copyright © Claremont Graduate School, 1993, reprinted by permission of Macmillan Press Ltd. and St Martin's Press, Inc.

Peter Damian, *Letter on Divine Omnipotence*, from 'Peter Damian: Lettre sur la toute-puissance divine', in Andre Cantin (ed.), *Sources Chretiennes*, vol. 191 (Paris: Les Editions du Cerf, 1972), translated by Paul Vincent Spade, © 1989, reprinted in Andrew B. Shoedinger (ed.), *Readings in Medieval Philosophy* (New York: Oxford University Press, 1996), reprinted by permission of Les Editions du Cerf.

Stephen Davis, 'Against Anti-Realist Faith', in Joseph Runzo (ed.), *Is God Real?* (London: Macmillan, 1993), copyright © Claremont Graduate School, 1993, reprinted by permission of Macmillan Press Ltd. and St Martin's Press, Inc.

Richard Dawkins, *The Blind Watchmaker* (Penguin, 1988), reprinted by permission of the author.

René Descartes, *Meditations*, in *Philosophical Works*, vol. i, trans. E. S. Haldane and G. R. T. Ross (Cambridge: Cambridge University Press, 1931), reprinted by permission of Cambridge University Press.

Emil Durkheim, *The Elementary Forms of Religious Life*, trans. Jacqueline Redding and W. S. F. Pickering, in W. S. F. Pickering (ed.), *Durkheim on Religion* (London: Routledge and Kegan Paul, 1975), reprinted by permission of W. S. F. Pickering.

Epicurus, *Letter to Menoecus*, in Brad Inwood and L. P. Gerson (eds.), *The Epicurean Reader*, trans. Brad Inwood and L. P. Gerson (Indianapolis: Hackett, 1994), reprinted by permission of Hackett Publishing Co., Indianapolis and Cambridge. All rights reserved.

Desiderius Erasmus, *Hyperapistes*, in G. Rupp and Philip Watson (eds.), *Luther and Erasmus, Free Will and Salvation*, trans. G. Rupp and Philip Watson (London: SCM Press, Library of Christian Classics, 1970), reprinted by permission of SCM Press Ltd. and Westminster John Knox Press.

Duns Scotus, *A Treatise on God as First Principle*, trans. Alan B. Walter (Quincy, Ill.: Franciscan Press, 1965), in Andrew B. Schoedinger (ed.), *Readings in Medieval Philosophy* (New York: Oxford University Press, 1996), reprinted by permission of the Franciscan Press.

John Scotus Eriugena, from *On Predestination*, ch. 1: *A Commentary on St. John's Gospel*, and *On the Division of Nature*, vol. 38 and 3.3, in J. P. Migne (ed.), *Patrologia Latina*, vol. 122, trans. Martin Stone, by permission of Dr Martin Stone.

Antony Flew, 'Theology and Falsification: A Symposium', in Antony Flew and Alasdair MacIntyre (eds.), *New Essays in Philosophical Theology* (London: SCM Press, 1955), copyright © 1955 by Anthony Flew and Alasdair MacIntyre, renewed 1983, reprinted by permission of SCM Press Ltd. and Simon & Schuster.

Antony Flew, *The Presumption of Atheism* (London: Elek/Pemberton, 1976), reprinted by permission of the author.

Sigmund Freud, *The Future of an Illusion*, in James Strachey (ed.), *The Standard Edition of the Complete Psychological Works of Sigmund Freud*, trans. James Strachey (London: Hogarth Press, 1975), reprinted by permission of Sigmund Freud Copyrights, The Institute of Psycho-Analysis, and The Hogarth Press. Translation copyright © 1961 by James Strachey, renewed 1989 by Alix Strachey, reprinted by permission of W. W. Norton & Company Inc.

Galileo Galilei and Robert Bellarmine, 'Galileo to Castelli and Bellarmine to Foscarini', in Maurice A. Finocchiaro (ed.), *The Galileo Affair: A Documentary History*, trans. Maurice A. Finocchiaro (Berkeley: University of California Press, 1989), copyright © 1989 The Regents of the University of California, reprinted by permission of the University of California Press.

Genesis 1, 1–5; John 1, 1–13; Acts 17, 16–34; Corinthians 1, 18–29; Hebrews 11, 1–3, from The New Revised Standard Version Bible, copyright 1989, Division of Christian Education of the National Council of the Churches of Christ in the United States of America. Used by permission. All rights reserved.

J. J. Haldane, 'Theism and Science', in J. J. C. Smart and J. J. Haldane, *Atheism and Theism* (Oxford: Blackwell, 1996), copyright © J. J. C. Smart and J. Haldane, 1996, reprinted by permission of Blackwell Publishers.

Norwood Russell Hanson, in Stephen Toulmin and Harry Woolf (eds.), *What I do not Believe and Other Essays* (Dordrecht: D. Reidel Publishing Co., 1971), copyright © 1971 by D. Reidel Publishing Company, Dordrecht Holland, with kind permission from Kluwer Academic Publishers.

Stephen Hawking, *A Brief History of Time* (London: Bantam, 1995), copyright 1988 by Stephen W. Hawking, reprinted by arrangement with Writers House LLC as agent for the proprietor.

George Hegel, 'Foreword to Hinrich's *Religion* (1822)', in Peter C. Hodgson (ed.),*G. W. F. Hegel: Theologian of the Spirit*, trans. J. M. Stewart (Minneapolis: Fortress Press, 1997), copyright © 1997 Augsburg Fortress, reprinted by permission of Augsburg Fortress Publishers and T. and T. Clark Ltd., Edinburgh.

Raeburne S. Heimbeck, *Theology and Meaning* (London: George Allen & Unwin, 1969), reprinted by permission of Routledge.

404 ACKNOWLEDGEMENTS

John Hick, *An Interpretation of Religion* (London: Macmillan, 1989, New Haven: Yale University Press, 1989), © John Hick 1989, reprinted by permission of Macmillan Press Ltd. and Yale University Press.

Thomas Hobbes, *Leviathan*, ch XII, ed. J. L. A. Gaskin (Oxford: Oxford University Press, 1996), reprinted by permission of Oxford University Press.

David Hume, *Dialogues Concerning Natural Religion*, © 1989 Norman Kemp Smith, reprinted by permission of Prentice-Hall Inc., Upper Saddle River, NJ.

Justin Martyr, *The Dialogue with Trypho*, 3.5–7, trans. A. Lukyn Williams (London, SPCK, 1930), reprinted by permission of The Society for Promoting Christian Knowledge.

Immanuel Kant, *Critique of Pure Reason*, second edition, trans. N. Kemp-Smith (London: Macmillan, 1933), by permission of Macmillan Press Ltd. and St Martin's Press, Inc.

Søren Kierkegaard, *Philosophical Fragments*, trans. D. F. Swenson and Howard V. Hong (Princeton: Princeton University Press, 1985), copyright © 1985 by Princeton University Press, reprinted by permission of Princeton University Press.

Gottfried Leibniz, Diogenes Allan (ed.), *The Theodicy* (Indianapolis, Indiana: Bobbs-Merrill, 1966).

Robin Le Poidevin, *Arguing for Atheism* (London, Routledge, 1996), reprinted by permission of Routledge.

John Leslie, *Universes* (London: Routledge, 1989), reprinted by permission of Routledge.

Peter Lombard, *The Sentences*, 1.3.1, in John F. Wippel and Allan B. Wolter (eds.), *Medieval Philosophy: From St. Augustine to Nicolas of Cusa* (New York: Free Press, 1969), copyright © 1969 The Free Press, reprinted by permission of The Free Press, a Division of Simon & Schuster.

Martin Luther, *The Bondage of the Will*, in G. Rupp and Philip Watson (eds.), *Luther and Erasmus, Free Will and Salvation*, trans. G. Rupp and Philip Watson (London: SCM Press, Library of Christian Classics, 1970), reprinted by permission of SCM Press Ltd. and Westminster John Knox Press.

Martin Luther, *The Bondage of the Will*, trans. J. I. Packer and O. R. Johnston (London: James Clarke, 1957), reprinted by permission of James Clarke & Co., Ltd.

Alasdair MacIntyre, in John Hick (ed.), *Faith and the Philosophers* (London: Macmillan 1964), reprinted by permission of Macmillan Press Ltd.

Moses Maimonides, *The Guide for the Perplexed*, chs. 59–60, trans. M. Friedlander (London: Routledge and Kegan Paul Ltd., 1951).

John Stuart Mill, *An Examination of Sir William Hamilton's Philosophy*, in J. M. Robson (ed.), *The Collected Works of John Stuart Mill*, vol. ix (London: Routledge and Kegan Paul, 1979), reprinted by permission of University of Toronto Press.

Basil Mitchell, *Faith and Criticism* (Oxford: Oxford University Press, 1994), reprinted by permission of Oxford University Press.

Michel de Montaigne, 'An Apology for Raymond Sebond', in *The Essays of Montaigne*, vol. ii, trans. George B. Ives (Cambridge: Cambridge University Press, 1925), reprinted by permission of Cambridge University Press.

John Henry Newman, *An Essay in Aid of the Grammar of Assent* (Notre Dame, Ind.: University of Notre Dame Press, 1979), © 1979 by University of Notre Dame Press, used by permission.

Friedrich Nietzsche, *Human, All Too Human*, trans. R. J. Hollingdale (Cambridge: Cambridge University Press, 1986), reprinted by permission of Cambridge University Press.

William of Ockham, *Quodlibeta* I Q 1, in *Ockham: Philosophical Writings*, trans. and ed. Philotheus Boehner and revised by Stephen F. Brown, reprinted by permission of Hackett Publishing Company. All rights reserved.

Origen, *Contra Celsum*, 7.41–4, trans. H. Chadwick (Cambridge: Cambridge University Press, 1953), reprinted by permission of Cambridge University Press.

Blaise Pascal, *The Pensées*, trans. J. M. Cohen (Penguin, 1961), copyright © J. M. Cohen, 1961, reprinted by permission of Penguin Books Ltd.

Francesco Petrarca, 'On His Own Ignorance and that of others', trans. Hans Nachod, in Ernst Cassirer, Paul Oskar Kristellar, and John Herman Randall jun. (eds.), *The Renaissance Philosophy of Man* (Chicago: University of Chicago Press, 1948), reprinted by permission of the University of Chicago Press.

Dewi Phillips, *Faith and Philosophical Enquiry* (London: Routledge and Kegan Paul, 1970), reprinted by permission of Routledge.

John Philoponus, *De Aeternitate Mundi Contra Proclum*, ed. H. Rabe (Leipzig, 1899), trans. Richard Sorabji, in *Time, Creation and the Continuum* (London: Duckworth, 1983), reprinted by permission of Gerald Duckworth and Co. Ltd.

Alvin Plantinga, 'A Defence of Religious Exclusivism', in Thomas D. Senior (ed.), *The Rationality of Belief and the Plurality of Faith* (London and Ithaca, NY: Cornell University Press, 1995), copyright 1995 by Cornell University, used by permission of the publisher, Cornell University Press.

Alvin Plantinga, 'Is Belief in God Properly Basic?', *Nous*, 15 (1981), reprinted by permission of Blackwell Publishers.

Alvin Plantinga, *Warrant and Proper Function* (Oxford: Oxford University Press, 1993), reprinted by permission of Oxford University Press, Inc.

Plato, *The Republic*, IV, trans. B. Jowett (Random House, 1892), I, reprinted by permission of Oxford University Press.

Plato, *Timaeus*, trans B. Jowett (Random House, 1892) II, reprinted by permission of Oxford University Press.

Plato, *Laws* X, trans. B. Jowett (Random House, 1982) II, reprinted by permission of Oxford University Press.

Plotinus, *Enneads*, 6.9, in *The Essential Plotinus*, trans. Elmer O'Brien, SJ (Indianapolis: Hackett, 1975), reprinted by permission of Hackett Publishing Co., Indianapolis and Cambridge. All rights reserved.

Pseudo-Dionysius, *The Divine Names*, in *The Complete Works*, trans. Colm Luibheid and Paul Rorem (London: SPCK, 1987), copyright © 1987 by Colm Luibheid, reprinted by permission of Paulist Press.

Odo Rigauld, *Theological Questions*, q.1, in *Codex Vatinicus Latinus*, trans. Martin Stone, by permission of Dr Martin Stone.

Saadia, *Book of Doctrines and Beliefs*, trans. Alexander Altmann, in Arthur Hyman and James Walsh (eds.), *Philosophy in the Middle Ages* (Indianapolis: Hackett, 1977), reprinted from *Book of Doctrines and Beliefs* (London: East and West Library, 1946).

Friedrich Schleiermacher, *On Religion, Speeches to its Cultured Despisers* (1799), trans. Richard Crouter (Cambridge: Cambridge University Press, 1988), reprinted by permission of Cambridge University Press.

Sextus Empiricus, *Outlines of Pyrrhonism*, 3.3, trans. R. G. Bury (Cambridge, Mass.: Harvard University Press, 1936, Loeb Classical Library), © The President and Fellows of

406   ACKNOWLEDGEMENTS

Harvard College, 1936, reprinted by permission of the publishers and the Loeb Classical Library.

J. J. C. Smart, 'Theism, Spirituality and Science', in J. J. C. Smart and J. J. Haldane, *Atheism and Theism* (Oxford: Blackwell, 1996), copyright © J. J. C. Smart and J. J. Haldane, 1996 reprinted by permission of Blackwell Publishers.

Benedict Spinoza, *A Theological-Political Treatise*, in *The Chief Works of Benedict de Spinoza*, vol. i, trans. R. H. M. Elwes (New York: Dover Publications).

Richard Swinburne, in Kelly James Clark (ed.), *Our Knowledge of God: Essays on Natural and Philosophical Theology* (Dordrecht: Kluwer, 1992), © 1992 by Kluwer Academic Publishers, with kind permission of Kluwer Academic Publishers.

Richard Swinburne, *Is there a God?* (Oxford: Oxford University Press, 1996), reprinted by permission of Oxford University Press.

Richard Swinburne, *Faith and Reason* (Oxford: Clarendon Press, 1981), reprinted by permission of Oxford University Press.

Tertullian, *The Prescriptions Against the Heretics*, in S. L. Greenslade (ed.), *Early Latin Theology* (London: SCM Press, Library of Christian Classics, 1956), reprinted by permission of SCM Press Ltd. and Westminster John Knox Press.

Matthew Tindal, *Christianity as Old as Creation* (1732 edn.) in Peter Gay (ed.) *Deism: An Anthology* (Princeton: Van Nostrand, 1968).

Peter van Inwagen, 'Genesis and Evolution', in Eleonore Stump (ed.), *Reasoned Faith* (Cornell University Press, 1993), copyright 1993 by Cornell University, used by permission of the publisher, Cornell University Press.

Peter van Inwagen, in T. V. Morris (ed.), *God and the Philosophers* (New York: Oxford University Press, 1994), reprinted by permission of Oxford University Press, Inc.

Keith Ward, *Religion and Creation* (Oxford: Clarendon Press, 1996), reprinted by permission of Oxford University Press.

Keith Ward, *Religion and Revelation* (Oxford: Clarendon Press, 1994), reprinted by permission of Oxford University Press.

Benjamin Warfield, 'Charles Darwin's Religious Life', in *Studies in Theology* (New York: Oxford University Press, 1932), reprinted by permission of Oxford University Press, Inc.

Merold Westphal, 'On Taking St. Paul Seriously: Sin as an Epistemological Category', in T. Flint (ed.), *Christian Philosophy* (Notre Dame, Ind.: University of Notre Dame Press, 1990), © 1990 by University of Notre Dame Press. Used by permission.

Peter Winch, 'Understanding a Primitive Society' (*American Philosophical Quarterly*, 1 (1964)), reprinted in D. Z. Phillips (ed.), *Religion and Understanding* (Oxford: Blackwell, 1967), reprinted by permission of *American Philosophical Quarterly*.

Index